INSURANCE LAW
AND THE
FINANCIAL
OMBUDSMAN
SERVICE

INSURANCE LAW AND THE FINANCIAL OMBUDSMAN SERVICE

BY

DR JUDITH P SUMMER

Lloyd's List

LONDON
2010

Lloyd's List Law
Mortimer House
37–41 Mortimer Street
W1W 7RE
law.enquiries@informa.com
an Informa business

British Library Cataloguing in Publication Data
A catalogue record for this book is
available from the British Library

ISBN: 978–1–84311–902–9

Whilst every effort has been made to ensure that the
information contained in this book is correct, neither the
authors nor Lloyd's List Law can accept any responsibility for
any errors or omissions or for any consequences resulting therefrom.

[Lloyd's is the registered trade mark of the Society incorporated by the
Lloyd's Act 1871 by the name of Lloyd's]

Set in 10/12pt Times by
Interactive Sciences Ltd, Gloucester
Printed in Great Britain by
MPG Books, Bodmin, Cornwall
Printed on paper from sustainable sources

FOREWORD

This pioneering book breaks new ground. It represents the first serious attempt to analyse the work of the Financial Ombudsman Service, and it does so by putting it in the context of insurance law. Given that the private ombudsman model originated with the establishment of the Insurance Ombudsman Bureau in 1981, it is entirely appropriate that insurance law should be its focus. The history and background of the Service as an alternative dispute resolution mechanism is traced as well as its development over the past ten years. The body of case examples published by the Service over this period is extensively and carefully analysed to draw out the approaches that the ombudsmen have adopted towards both some of the familiar insurance principles – non disclosure, breach of warranty, fraudulent claims, measurement of loss; and also the main personal lines products: travel, household, motor (with a separate section on the contentious "keys in car" cases), life and personal accident, medical and legal expenses.

The Ombudsman Service has become, by virtue of the cost-free consumer access, *de facto* almost the exclusive forum for the adjudication of insurance disputes. The courts rarely if ever see such cases. This can be said to have the disadvantage that authoritative case law precedents are no longer set by the judiciary. The alternative view is that the benefits outweigh the disadvantages. As Rix LJ observed,

"For some years the insurance ombudsman (now within the FOS scheme) has been developing a new common law of insurance for consumer contracts, without which the courts would have been constrained to find, or alternatively to reject, solutions to problems from which they have been in the main shielded." R (on the application of Heather Moor & Edgecomb) v *Financial Ombudsman Service* [2008] EWCA Civ 642.

It is therefore all the more important that legal researchers and commentators take serious note of the ombudsman jurisdiction. While some have criticised ombudsman decision-making as inherently unpredictable and lacking in transparency, this book demonstrates clearly that the ombudsmen have succeeded in developing broadly consistent approaches to commonly seen issues (mostly applying insurance law principles) and that these are not difficult to observe from the material published by the Service. The author not only brings these to life in an organised framework and in a thematic manner, but also adds a scholarly critique and commentary, pointing the way to possible future policy and legal developments. Of particular interest, against the background of the work of the Law Commissions on consumer insurance law reform, is the treatment of non-disclosure where the Commissions have adopted some of the approach developed by the ombudsman.

One of the objectives of the Ombudsman Service has always been to feed back to its stakeholders in the industry and the consumer world the results of its work, from which insurers can learn better how to evaluate claims, and consumers can be advised how to avoid common pitfalls. It can be argued that although the Service's regular newsletters and topical website material can perform some of this function, the lack of a consolidated and easily referenced sourcebook has left this objective well short of achievement. In many ways this book will help to fill the gap, and for the public it has the advantage that it is written by an independent scholar and rather than by the Service itself.

This will not only be an extremely useful work of reference for legal and industry insurance practitioners, law students and other commentators, it will also be valuable for the Financial Ombudsman Service itself. I hope that it will challenge and inspire others to study the work of the Service in the fields of banking, credit and investment, thus providing a comprehensive documentation and analysis of what may be the "new common law of financial services consumer contracts".

WALTER MERRICKS
Chief Ombudsman, Financial Ombudsman Service 1999–2009

PREFACE

This book was inspired through frustrating years as a solicitor advising clients about insurance claims going before the Financial Ombudsman Service without any text book guidance or discussion being available. It has taken shape after three and a half years studying the Financial Ombudsman Service for a PhD and comparing its approach in insurance cases to that of the courts. The essential point is that the Financial Ombudsman Service does not have to follow the law, so its decisions and considerations may be different to those of a court. This book is aimed at solicitors, insurance claims handlers and consumer advisers who need to know how the two tend to differ.

I have analysed every available piece of information issued by the Financial Ombudsman Service, along with material from the Financial Services Authority and other sources, to try to portray an accurate picture of current Financial Ombudsman Service approaches. One major caveat is that the Ombudsman's approach to any particular matter can change without warning either in general, or simply in light of the circumstances of an individual case, so that what is written below in relation to the Ombudsman's approaches cannot be treated as a court precedent would be. The Financial Ombudsman Service's near monthly publication, *Ombudsman News* gives its own caveat to the information that it publishes there, saying that it gives general information on the position at the date of publication, that it is not a definitive statement of the law, the Ombudsman's approach or procedure and that the illustrative case studies are based broadly on real-life cases, but are not precedents and that individual cases are decided on their own facts.

Nevertheless, this book provides much-awaited guidance as to the likely Ombudsman approach, as it collates all the Ombudsman information publicly available. For ease of reference, all the insurance case studies published in *Ombudsman News* have been collated into the appendices to this book, along with other useful and relevant material. The book is up to date to 1 June 2010.

Throughout the book, in the interest of economy of paper and ink, the Financial Ombudsman Service will be referred to as the FOS, although it does not like the acronym and would prefer its name to be referred to in full.

I must acknowledge the support, encouragement and inspiration that Professor Robert Merkin has provided both as my former PhD supervisor, and as my current friend. Thanks must go to Walter Merricks CBE, the FOS's founding Chief Ombudsman, who has taken time to write the foreword to this book in the middle of a busy schedule as chair of the Office of the Health Professions Adjudicator, to Chris Betney, Liz Lewis and the team at Lloyd's List Law for their editorial input and to the FSA for giving copyright permissions. Warm appreciation needs to go to my husband and family who have given further encouragement and helped with childcare whilst I have written this book and who are so very proud of whatever I do. Finally, I dedicate my efforts to my gorgeous sons who have been so understanding of the need to lock myself away to write this book and who have provided just the right amount of cuddles whilst I work.

June 2010   DR JUDITH P SUMMER
                                                                              London

CONTENTS

APPENDICES

TABLE OF CASES

TABLE OF STATUTES

TABLE OF STATUTORY INSTRUMENTS AND EUROPEAN LEGISLATION

TABLE OF DISP (UPDATED), ICOB AND ICOBS

DEFINITIONS/ABBREVIATIONS

ABI	Association of British Insurers
CPR	Civil Procedure Rules
FSCS	Financial Services Compensation Scheme
FOS	Financial Ombudsman Service
FSA	Financial Services Authority
FSMA	Financial Services and Markets Act 2000
GISC	General Insurance Standards Council
IOB	Insurance Ombudsman Bureau
MIA	Marine Insurance Act 1906
OFT	Office of Fair Trading
PPI	Payment Protection Insurance
UCTA	Unfair Terms Act 1977
UTCCR	Unfair Terms in Consumer Contracts Regulations 1999 (SI 1999/2083)

CHAPTER 1

BACKGROUND

HISTORY AND FORMATION OF THE FOS

1.1 The Insurance Ombudsman Bureau ("IOB") was founded in 1981 by three leading insurance companies as a type of alternative dispute resolution service outside of the court system, to resolve complaints by customers against insurers who were members of the scheme. Complaints were to be dealt with independently, privately and without charge to the complainant. It was a voluntary, industry, non-governmental initiative, backed by the National Consumer Council, at a time when there was no regulator for the conduct of investment or insurance business. Most insurers opted to join the scheme. The law did not have to be applied strictly in the interests of resolving the disputes fairly. If this resulted in any occasional rough justice for insurers, it was outweighed by the cheap and effective alternative dispute resolution service which the IOB offered, particularly for small insurance disputes which were uneconomic to run in the court's litigation system, especially in a time before the Woolf reforms of court procedures.

1.2 The IOB was followed by the foundation of other ombudsman schemes for complaints against other types of institution, based on the IOB model. In 2000 the Financial Services Authority ("FSA") was established as a single financial regulator for most types of large financial businesses, and various separate ombudsman schemes merged to become the Financial Ombudsman Service ("FOS"). The FOS thereafter replaced the IOB, the Office of the Banking Ombudsman, the Office of the Building Societies Ombudsman, the Office of the Investment Ombudsman, the Personal Investment Authority Ombudsman Bureau, the Personal Insurance Arbitration Service and the Securities and Futures Authority Complaints Bureau.

1.3 The aims of the FOS are like its predecessor: to provide a private and confidential, independent dispute resolution scheme, paid for by firms and free for consumers, where decisions are made based on what is fair and reasonable in all the circumstances of the case rather than on a strict interpretation of the law. As an independent organisation, the FOS is not a regulator, trade body, watchdog or consumer champion. However, unlike the IOB, the jurisdiction of the FOS is compulsory for insurance companies, and is wider, as it can consider business interruption policies[1] and complaints from small businesses, charities, trustees and residents' associations.

1.4 Adjudicators and ombudsmen have a range of backgrounds and specialities and tend to have financial services, complaints-handling, compliance or legal experience or qualifications. Legal qualifications are not required. Indeed, although the FOS's first Chief Ombudsman, Walter Merricks CBE did have a legal background, his successor, Natalie Ceeney CBE,

---

1. E.g. Case Study 74/8 Dec 2008/Jan 2009.

who took up the post on 22 March 2010 does not. Her background is one of management consultancy and information management. The FOS staffing levels show its size; it employed about 1,000 people in 2006[2] and 1,500 in 2010.[3] It is one of the oldest, biggest and busiest ombudsman systems in the world.[4] It deals with thousands of disputes every week.[5]

THE RULES OF THE SCHEME: ESTABLISHMENT OF DISP AND ICOB/S

1.5 Until 1 December 2001, the FOS had to apply the rules of the scheme to which the complaint would have related before the FOS existed. Then on 1 December 2001, when the majority of the Financial Services and Markets Act 2000 ("FSMA") came into force, the FOS began dealing with all new complaints under one set of new rules, the Dispute Resolution: Complaints ("DISP") section of the FSA Handbook of Rules and Guidance.[6] DISP 1 provides rules and guidance for firms' internal handling of complaints and is not covered in detail in this book. DISP 2 deals with the jurisdiction of the FOS and DISP 3 sets out FOS procedures.

1.6 This means that a number of the earlier case studies about complaints dating from before 1 December 2001 and referred to throughout this book are technically actually comment on IOB rather than FOS approaches under DISP. However, they are included in this work because they seem to reflect the current FOS approach.

1.7 The industry codes for the conduct of business, against which the FOS could measure a firm's performance were overhauled by the FSA's introduction of its Insurance: Conduct of Business rules ("ICOB") on 14 January 2005, superseded by its Insurance: New Conduct of Business sourcebook ("ICOBS") on 6 January 2008. These can be found in the FSA Handbook[7] and contain the requirements for marketing, sales, product literature and claims handling of non-investment insurance. They apply to general insurance contracts such as motor or household insurance, and pure protection contracts such as critical illness and income protection, but not to long-term care insurance which is subject to the FSA's investment business rules. Reinsurance contracts are exempt from ICOB/S. However, apart from the limited circumstances when the FOS will treat a small business as a consumer in some breach of warranty situations, ICOB/S only apply to consumers.

AIMS AND VALUES

1.8 The aim of the FOS is to help resolve individual disputes between customers and financial firms, "quickly and with minimum formality by an independent person".[8] The

2. FOS Corporate Plan and 2006/7 Budget and FOS Annual Reviews 2005/6 and 2006/7.

3. *Ombudsman News* Apr/May 2010. FOS Annual Review 2009/10 gives an average figure of 1,015 with the rest made up of outsourced staff employed to deal with a sudden, huge increase in complaint numbers.

4. *Cf* FIN-NET organisations (para. 2.15, below), and ombudsmen systems in Australia, New Zealand and Hong Kong.

5. According to FOS Annual Review 2009/10, there were 925,095 front-line enquiries and complaints in that year, which turned into 163,012 cases referred to an adjudicator, and 166,321 complaints were resolved in that year. When the scheme was first established, it was only set up to resolve about 25,000 complaints a year.

6. Accessed via the FSA's website at www.fsa.gov.uk. Updated DISP 1 came into force on 1/11/07 (with minor amendments on 6/07/08). Updated DISP 2 (FOS jurisdiction) and DISP 3 (FOS procedures) came into force on 6/04/08. Under DISP TP1-1, the version of DISP to apply is that which applied at the date on which the firm received the complaint.

7. Accessed via the FSA's website at www.fsa.gov.uk.

8. S.225(1) FSMA.

ombudsman must make decisions which are "fair and reasonable in all the circumstances of the case".[9] This requirement is pivotal to every FOS decision. It overrides the duty to decide matters in accordance with the law.

1.9 Being fair and reasonable includes the FOS aiming to be accessible[10] to everyone, whatever their ethnic origin, age, disability, language or socio-economic situation etc. It will try to communicate in the format[11] or language required.[12] To aid accessibility, there is a free-phone telephone number available for complainants ringing from a landline, and a different free-phone number available from certain mobile telephones, and the FOS policy is to telephone someone back if they are concerned about the cost of the call. The FOS aims to approach complaints in a practical and business-like manner, looking at the evidence to determine facts, rather than how the case is presented, and giving clear reasons for its decisions. It considers that no-one should therefore need legal or other professional help to bring a complaint or understand a decision, so an order for reimbursement of any costs incurred in obtaining such advice will be unusual.

1.10 Another FOS aim is equality between complainants, so no-one should get priority within the FOS system based on who they are or on any press involvement. The FOS will only consider prioritising a complaint where a consumer might be disadvantaged by having to wait, perhaps financially or medically.[13]

1.11 To further the aim of providing an informal, private and relatively quick[14] and flexible alternative to the courts, the FOS does not have the courts' formal procedures, hearings or cross-examinations. The FOS system is geared to the requirements of ordinary people who have disputes with seemingly unassailable, well-resourced, powerful organisations which they might otherwise fear. Individual complaints are handled in confidence and not discussed in public, other than in a summarised and anonymised form in FOS publications such as the FOS near monthly journal, *Ombudsman News*. The evidence before the FOS is predominantly paper-based, although the process is informal enough for FOS staff to telephone the parties with queries or to speak informally and suggest a way forward. Adjudicators may attempt an informal mediation or conciliation, but if this is unsuccessful and the parties do not accept their views and conclusions, then the papers will be considered further and a formal ombudsman decision will be taken.

LAW REFORM

1.12 One justification that the FOS gives for adopting its own approaches instead of following the law is that it considers that the law is outdated and unfair to the consumer, in

9. S. 228(2) FSMA and DISP 3.6.1R and 3.6.2G.

10. *Cf* The Hunt Review 9/4/08 "Opening Up, Reaching Out and Aiming High", an independent review of FOS accessibility and transparency. Although it praises the FOS's work, management and development over the years, it suggests wide-ranging and radical reforms to further FOS accessibility and transparency. These include a far-reaching advertising campaign, publication of complaints data relating to firms and publication of what Lord Hunt calls FOSBOOK—a handbook setting out current FOS thinking on all scenarios and issues on which it bases its decisions. The FOS response and plan to implement some of the suggestions are on its website.

11. Including braille, large print, audio tape and calls using Text Relay.

12. The FOS provided information and handled enquiries in 20 languages over 2005/6 (FOS Annual Review 2005/6). The FOS Annual Review 2009/10 noted that information had been provided in that year in 46 languages other than English and Welsh.

13. *Cf* FOS website "Our service standards—How we allocate and prioritise cases".

14. 74% of all complaints excluding mortgage endowment complaints were resolved within six months, and 89% within one year, with a total of nearly 120,000 resolved during 2005/6 (FOS Annual Review 2005/6). In 2008/9, 113,949 complaints were resolved, 56% of them within six months, and 88% within one year (FOS Annual Review

particular in relation to the draconian avoidance consequences for non-disclosure and breach of warranty. There is a history of criticism of the law of non-disclosure and warranties, with several prominent calls for reform of insurance law, all slightly different from the proposals from the current Law Commissions of England and Wales and Scotland, none of which have been implemented, including:

(1) The Law Reform Committee of 1957[15];
(2) The Law Commission Report 1980[16];
(3) The National Consumer Council Report 1997;
(4) The Pat Saxton Memorial Lecture 2001 given by Lord Justice Longmore; and
(5) The British Insurance Association Report 2002.

SELF-REGULATION BY THE INSURANCE INDUSTRY

1.13 The insurance industry has historically successfully resisted law reform through promises of self-regulation for consumer insurance.

1.14 In 1977, as part of the deal to exempt insurance contracts from the Unfair Contract Terms Act 1977 ("UCTA"), the British Insurance Association (the predecessor to the Association of British Insurers) and Lloyd's issued a Statement of General Insurance Practice ("SGIP") and a Statement of Long-Term Insurance Practice ("SLIP"). The Statements purported to represent current industry practice, but provided no sanctions for non-compliance. They required insurers to ask clear questions about material matters and put warnings in proposal forms of the duty of disclosure and the consequences of non-disclosure. SGIP required actual inducement before avoiding as a result of an innocent misrepresentation or non-disclosure. SLIP required the insurer not unreasonably to reject a claim. Brokers were regulated through the Insurance Brokers (Registration) Act 1977.[17] Until May 2001, when the General Insurance Standards Council ("GISC") took over, brokers had to be registered under that Act (repealed by FSMA) so as to be able legally to call themselves brokers, and thereby were subject to codes of practice and conduct administered by the Insurance Brokers Registration Council.

1.15 On condition that the Statements of Practice were strengthened, the Government agreed not to implement the Law Commission's 1980 report, which had strongly criticised the use of voluntary self-regulation rather than statutory reform. However, unless a complaint reached the IOB/FOS, there was still no sanction for non-compliance. The 1986 version of SGIP remained in force until the FSA introduced ICOB on 14 January 2005, itself replaced by ICOBS on 6 January 2008.

1.16 Meanwhile, in 1981 the IOB was established to decide complaints in a "fair and reasonable" way. It might never have been born if the Law Commission's 1980 recommendations had been implemented.

1.17 The General Insurance Standards Council ("GISC") was established in July 2000 as a voluntary regulator for brokers instead of the Insurance Brokers Registration Council. It had one code for consumer insurance and one for business insurance. From May 2001 until 13 January 2005, intermediaries were expected to comply with its codes of conduct (which

2008/9). In 2009/10, 166,321 complaints were resolved, 67% within six months and 89% within one year (FOS Annual Review 2009/10).

15. Cmnd 62, Fifth report.
16. Insurance Law Non-Disclosure and Breach of Warranty 1980 Law Com No 104.
17. See below under "Jurisdiction—Intermediaries" at paras. 2.9 *et seq.*

built on the ABI codes which went before it) and dealt with issues like the obligation to explain details of the policy to a potential customer before inception. Until and including 13 January 2005, the GISC disputes resolution service dealt with complaints about intermediaries' non-compliance with its codes. These codes also had limited sanctions and were replaced by ICOB[18] when the FSA took over regulation of intermediaries and the FOS took over dealing with complaints against intermediaries on 14 January 2005.[19]

1.18 In February 2006, the ABI issued guidance on the design and wording of proposal forms for life and health insurance ("AFD"), and SLIP became its addendum. However, AFD is not binding in law on insurers.

1.19 In January 2008, the ABI issued guidance for life protection insurance,[20] which it upgraded to a Code of Practice in January 2009.[21] Compliance with its Codes is compulsory for ABI members. The FOS reported a significant fall in 2008/9 in these types of complaints since the ABI guidance was issued.[22]

IS SELF-REGULATION SUFFICIENT?

1.20 It is generally acknowledged that more needs to be done than this self-regulation, as there is limited redress for an insured unless it chooses to and can bring a complaint before the FOS. In particular:

(1) medium to large businesses cannot bring a complaint to the FOS even though they may have no more insurance knowledge or negotiation power than a consumer or a small business which can;

(2) those with claims worth over £100,000 are not fully catered for, because that part of a FOS award over £100,000 is non-binding and insurers do not always accept the FOS's recommendation to pay the additional amount;

(3) vulnerable consumers do not bring their complaint to the FOS,[23] because they do not understand the system or their rights, they believe that it would be pointless, they find it too stressful to fight, or they are too ill.[24] Without the law to protect them, they are especially vulnerable to financial businesses who do not follow the FOS approach, either unknowingly, or, more worryingly, deliberately, hoping not to get caught, or not to get caught too often;

(4) even non-vulnerable consumers may not realise that they have a right to complain to the FOS[25];

18. Later replaced by ICOBS.
19. See further below in section on FOS jurisdiction over intermediaries at paras. 2.9 *et seq.*
20. ABI Guidance, "Non-Disclosure and Treating Customers Fairly in Claims for Long-Term Protection Insurance Products" (January 2008).
21. ABI Code of Practice, "Managing Claims for Individual and Group Life, Critical Illness and Income Protection Insurance Products" (January 2009).
22. In 2006/7 the FOS closed 376 complaints where non-disclosure was the dominant issue in critical illness and income protection disputes, and in 2008/9 it closed 130 such cases.
23. The Hunt Review, 9 April 2008 suggests how to encourage more vulnerable people to complain.
24. Of the 190 FOS consumer cases about non-disclosure and misrepresentation which the current Law Commissions read, one-quarter of complainants were suffering from cancer, and two-thirds had some sort of physical or mental disability—Law Commissions Consultation Paper, Appendix C, 17 July 2007.
25. The FOS 2008/9 Annual Review, p. 75, states that "our research with consumers who do *not* use our service shows consistently that around 12% say they have recently complained to a financial services business. Of those who say they remained unhappy after their complaint, usually over half take no further action". The Legal Services Commission provided the following information to the Law Commissions (*cf* Law Commissions Final Report 15/12/09): In 2004 the Legal Services Commission interviewed over 5,000 people, of whom 45 said they had an

(5) the FOS cannot deal with disputed claims where witnesses need to be cross-examined[26];

(6) neither the FSA nor the FOS can tell the courts how to resolve a dispute. Self-regulatory codes can only attempt to prevent insurers from relying on their rights in law or aid the FOS in deciding what is fair and reasonable;

(7) the FOS becomes forced to take on the inappropriate role of policy-maker, as opposed to adjudicator, and the courts continue to be forced to reach unfair decisions based on the now outdated Marine Insurance Act 1906.

THE FOS SYSTEM AS A SUBSTITUTE FOR LAW REFORM

1.21 Without central reform of insurance contract law, and with self-regulation without teeth, the FOS has done an admirable job of trying to sort out the problems on a case-by-case basis, and hoping that insurers will generally follow its approach, even where the law does not have the same requirements. The FOS has only been able to stab haphazardly, unofficially and unmonitored at the basic problems. Unfortunately, this is not a substitute for law reform.

1.22 It cannot be right that a consumer has to rely in the first instance on the forbearance of an insurer in not applying the law, and then on a patchwork of confusing and sometimes conflicting self-regulation, which has muddled even insurers, and is only enforced if a complaint is brought before the FOS, and even then only if the FOS thinks it fair. The FOS has developed its own guidance overlaying the Statements/Codes which may differ from them, e.g. in allowing avoidance of only the most serious negligent misrepresentations (rather than all of them). It says that it continues the tradition of the IOB in applying the spirit of UCTA.[27] Presumably this is so when it applies its discretion in deciding what is fair and reasonable in all the circumstances, although there is limited or no reference to the Act in its various reported case studies.

1.23 It also cannot be right that whilst small businesses can complain to the FOS, and may in reality be similar to consumers, they cannot rely on the Codes/Statements or ICOBS which only protect consumers, other than in the limited circumstances when the FOS deems them as consumers in a breach of warranty situation. If there are to be differences in the treatment of consumers and businesses, surely this should be the result of much debated and considered law reform, rather than as a consequence of the jurisdictional limits of the FOS and FSA.

1.24 The law attempts to achieve justice in the majority of cases. If it is consistently not doing so, then the remedy is law reform, not the FOS trying to deal with the problem by itself, on a piecemeal basis, as it receives complaints. The creation of the FOS and other industry initiatives, like statements of practice, have arguably delayed the implementation of statutory amendments to the law which would have addressed many of its shortcomings. For if the perception is that the FOS is protecting the most vulnerable, what incentive is there for law reform?

---

insurance claim rejected unfairly. Out of these, only three people had contacted the ombudsman. The rest had either done nothing or attempted to handle the issue on their own.

26. DISP 3.3.4 R (10).

27. Law Commissions Issues Paper 2 (28/11/06).

CRITICISM OF THE FOS SYSTEM

Certainty and consistency

1.25 By not following the law strictly, even with the best intentions and safeguards in place, consistency in FOS decisions and certainty of outcome is less possible than through the precedent system of the courts. However, the FOS does have well-established internal systems in place to monitor and achieve consistency, and it may be said that its strength is its ability to be flexible in its approach to the particular circumstances of a case.

Reliance on policy wording

1.26 It may not be possible for a party to rely on clear policy wording that a court might uphold, as the FOS may interpret or ignore it if the policy has not been sold in accordance with the applicable sale codes, or simply if it would render a result which it considers unfair in the circumstances. Although this is a problem for contract certainty, it encourages firms to deal more fairly with its consumer customers.

Law has been developed over many years

1.27 Insurance law has been developed over hundreds of years of careful analysis. How can an ombudsman simply choose not to apply it in the particular circumstances of a case? The FOS response is that the law is outdated and unduly harsh to policyholders because it has not been reformed to keep up with a changing society with different insurance needs; it is no longer something arranged in coffee houses for merchant shippers.

Accountability of the FOS

1.28 The FOS has a wide discretion, but limited accountability for its decisions. It sets its own policies towards complaints. It is not accountable to the courts for its decisions other than through judicial review. But judicial review of a decision is rare and is unlikely to succeed because, as long as the FOS has considered the law and its decision is not irrational, a court will not interfere in the decision.

Limited availability of FOS material

1.29 FOS decisions are not public, and the reported case studies sometimes are only roughly based on real complaints, although there are plans for many more case reports to be written and published. Unless the FOS chooses to report on a point, its approach may not be clear and no comment or feedback can be made by the industry or academics. Although its award-winning website uses clear, simple language, users have to trawl through a lot of data to get the exact information they want, and it is not easy to search and find similar case studies to the one in question. Users will also have to plough through the whole of the website to find out if anything has changed since the last time they looked, unless they have set up some sort of alert system on their own computers, as the *Ombudsman News* journals do not highlight all changes since the last month's journal; for instance if a new FOS Technical Note has been produced or if the DISP rules have been amended. There is no other public alert system in place. For instance, there was a change of approach, without advertisement, noted by the Law

Commissions[28] in the way that the FOS viewed recklessness between its survey of FOS non-disclosure cases dated 2003 to 2005 and the Consultation Paper in 2007. With anonymity in the reports, there is less incentive for firms to follow the FOS approach, although this may change with the publication since September 2009 of general complaints data against named institutions.[29]

The Financial Services Authority ("FSA")

1.30 The FSA is the insurance regulator, so it should be enforcing its own codes of sale and complaint handling, and disciplining firms who are not complying under section 66 FSMA. However, the FOS is effectively policing the codes. In practice, the FSA refers an individual's complaint to the FOS without taking further action. It might be better if the FOS referred every case where there had been a breach of code to the FSA, as then the FSA could monitor and deal early with a problem that probably exists generally within the firm, without the scale of a problem escalating as it has with payment protection insurance, discussed below (at paragraphs 5.33 *et seq*). This would also protect those customers who do not or cannot complain to the FOS. The FOS is a dispute resolution service, not an industry regulator and Parliament has chosen to keep the two functions distinct.

THE CONTRIBUTION OF THE IOB AND FOS TO LAW REFORM

1.31 Notwithstanding the criticisms above, an ombudsman service offering quick, cheap and informal dispute resolution is extremely valuable. The IOB/FOS experience has highlighted where the law needs to be amended. The FOS policies have had a huge influence on the thinking of the current Law Commissions which propose to incorporate "the best elements of ombudsman practice". However, previous Law Commissions have come to similar conclusions as the current one without the benefit of FOS input. There is a continuing role for the FOS to decide approaches on issues with which the law has not yet had to deal. It is to be hoped that the courts would follow the FOS in these, although knowledge of and respect for FOS approaches amongst practising lawyers is currently limited.

THE CURRENT LAW COMMISSIONS

1.32 A sweeping reform of insurance contract law is proposed by the current Law Commission for England and Wales and the Scottish Law Commission, which have been consulting on this project since before their first scoping paper on the subject dated 18 January 2006. The FOS has been heavily involved in the consultation process and has provided the Law Commissions with access to its files to assist research. Many of the Law Commissions' proposals are based on the FOS approach, and will be referred to below at the relevant sections.

1.33 The main areas of perceived injustice in insurance law relate to disclosure and warranties for consumers. Much of the current law is based on the Marine Insurance Act

---

28. Consultation Paper 17/07/07.

29. Complaints data was published in September 2009 and February 2010 about the 150 or so firms which make up 90% of the complaints workload. Data will continue to be published every six months, with the FOS reviewing the arrangements in 2011.

1906, which is now perceived to be antiquated and out of date. The Law Commissions published a draft Consumer Insurance (Disclosure and Representations) Bill on 15 December 2009,[30] which, as its title suggests, does not tackle warranties (except in abolishing basis of contract clauses for consumers[31]) or business insurance. More bills on other areas of insurance law are expected to follow. The initial response of the Labour government to this bill in a House of Commons debate on 13 January 2010, was encouraging. As reported by the Law Commissions, Sarah McCarthy-Fry, at the time, the Exchequer Secretary to the Treasury, said:

" . . . the original 1906 statute has merely been over-layered to reduce its otherwise harsh effect. Further, the existence of the current patchwork of rules and codes makes the position confusing for consumers seeking to understand their rights and obligations. We support the Law Commission and the FOS view that in the long term such a disjoint between consumer interest and, indeed, industry best practice and the law is not sustainable . . . . We fully support the aims of the Law Commission in reviewing pre-contract disclosure and misrepresentation in consumer insurance law."

1.34 However, it remains unclear whether any parliamentary time will be made for the bill and what will be the effect of the new government from May 2010. It is of note that the Law Commissions' bill to amend the Third Parties (Rights against Insurers) Act 1930 was published in 2001 and approved by the Government in 2002 and although unopposed by any party, waited until 23 November 2009 for its first reading in the House of Lords. It was finally given Royal Assent on 25 March 2010 as part of a trial procedure for two bills[32] aimed at speeding up the parliamentary process for unopposed Law Commission bills, by allowing certain stages to be carried out in Committee, rather than on the floor of the House. It is to be hoped that this procedure will be available for the Consumer Insurance (Disclosure and Representations) Bill and that it does not have to wait as many years as the Third Parties (Rights against Insurers) Bill did.

1.35 Even if the bill reaches Parliament and gets through, the bill itself envisages further delay. Clause 12(2) provides that the Act would not come into force until one year after it was passed, so that the insurance industry would have time to prepare for the new regime, and clause 12(3) only applies the Act to consumer insurance contracts entered into or varied after the Act comes into force.

---

30. Reproduced in Appendix H, below.
31. See the section on "Warranties" below at paras. 14.4, 14.25 and 14.28.
32. The other bill which went through this process was the Perpetuities and Accumulations Bill, which received Royal Assent on 12 November 2009.

CHAPTER 2

THE WORKINGS OF THE FOS

JURISDICTION OF THE FOS[1]

Compulsory, voluntary and consumer credit jurisdictions

2.1 The FOS now has three jurisdictions: (1) compulsory; (2) voluntary; and (3) consumer credit. It gained its powers and began operating under the first two types of jurisdiction on 1 December 2001. It acquired the third from 6 April 2007, under the Consumer Credit Act 2006, whereby businesses with consumer credit licences issued (and regulated) by the Office of Fair Trading are also covered by the FOS even if they are not also regulated by the FSA.

2.2 The compulsory jurisdiction covers complaints relating to regulated activities. Included are firms that were covered by one of the predecessor ombudsman schemes for complaints about events before 1 December 2001 and are regulated by the FSA for complaints about events from 1 December 2001. So consumer complaints about UK insurance firms will fall within the FOS compulsory jurisdiction. From 6 April 2007, three additional activities became regulated by the FSA and were put within the remit of the FOS: advice on self-invested personal pensions; the sale and administration of home-reversion plans; and the sale and administration of Islamic home-purchase products. From 1 July 2009 "sale and rent-back" by home-owners, who can no longer afford their mortgages but wish to stay on as tenants, became regulated by the FSA and therefore come under the compulsory remit of the FOS. From 6 August 2009, activities of "reclaim funds" to which dormant bank and building society accounts are transferred fell under the FOS compulsory jurisdiction. From 1 November 2009, the FOS also covered money transfer operators.[2]

2.3 Some firms can choose to join the FOS scheme under its voluntary jurisdiction even though they do not fall under the compulsory jurisdiction. By joining, they formally agree to deal with complaints and submit to the authority of the FOS as if they did fall under the compulsory jurisdiction.[3] These voluntary jurisdiction (VJ) participants include:

   (i) Since March 2002, general insurance companies based in Europe and not regulated by the FSA that deal predominantly with customers in the UK.
  (ii) Since April 2003, certain firms regulated by the FSA from 1 December 2001 that wanted to be covered for complaints about events which occurred before that date.
 (iii) Since September 2005, National Savings and Investments, which are not regulated by the FSA.

---

1. *Cf* DISP 2 for fuller details.
2. *Cf* FSA Implementation of the Payment Services Directive Consultation Paper 08/14.
3. DISP 4.

(iv) Since 6 April 2009, freight-forwarders joined the voluntary jurisdiction for insurance-related complaints.

Relevant complaints

2.4 The FOS will be able to consider a complaint if all of the following criteria are met[4]:

(1) The complaint should relate to an action by the insurer which was taken after 1 December 2001 when the FOS came into being, rather than the insured event. So in Case Study 32/9,[5] the relevant date of the complaint was not the fire but the date of the matter complained about, which in this case was the date the claim was turned down.

Transitional arrangements were put in place for complaints already referred to an Ombudsman Scheme, but not resolved before 1 December 2001. Complaints referred to the FOS after 1 December 2001, but relating to an event when the firm was subject to a former scheme, i.e. a so-called "relevant new complaint", come within the FOS procedures under the Ombudsman Transitional Order, with only a few exceptions. However, under DISP 2.7.10G, a relevant new complaint must be made by an individual, and must not relate to a business or trade carried on by him, presumably because only individuals could have brought complaints under a former scheme.

(2) The firm in question and the activity to which the complaint relates must be subject to one of the three FOS jurisdictions.[6]

(3) The activity to which the complaint relates must have been carried on from an establishment in the UK[7] (not the Channel Islands). The exception to this rule is in the limited circumstances where the activities are carried out from another country within the EEA by a firm which falls under the FOS voluntary jurisdiction.[8] In either case, the complainant's residence or nationality is not important. This is illustrated by Case Study 32/11,[9] where the complaint was outside the jurisdiction because the firm's activities had been in the Channel Islands, and the complainant's Jersey nationality was not important

(4) The complaint must be brought by or on behalf of an "eligible complainant".[10]

Eligible complainants

2.5 Eligible complainants now include individuals, small businesses, charities and trusts. In this sense, the jurisdiction of the FOS is wider than that of its predecessor, the IOB, which could only consider complaints by individuals. However, small businesses only account for about 2%–3% of all complaints referred.[11]

---

4. *Cf* DISP 2.2.1G.
5. *Ombudsman News* Oct 2003.
6. *Cf* DISP 2.2.1G, DISP 2.3, DISP 2.4 and DISP 2.5.
7. DISP 2.6.1R, 2.6.3R.
8. DISP 2.6.4R.
9. *Ombudsman News* Oct 2003.
10. DISP 2.7.3R.
11. *Ombudsman News* Dec 2008/Jan 2009 said 2%; FOS Annual Review 2009/10 said 3%, which represented an increase to 4,758; *Ombudsman News* Apr/May 2010 commented that there were probably more complaints brought by small businesses than this, because sometimes sole-traders and micro-businesses register their complaints as individuals rather than businesses.

2.6 Until 30 October 2009, an "eligible complainant" was defined by DISP 2.7.3R as a private individual, a business with a group annual turnover of less than £1 million, a charity with an annual income of less than £1 million or a trustee of a trust with net assets worth less than £1 million at the time the complainant referred the complaint to the firm or VJ participant.

2.7 When the Payment Services Directive[12] came into effect on 1 November 2009, the definition of "business" was changed throughout the FOS jurisdiction to match that of micro-enterprise in the EU legislation.[13] So a business which can now be an eligible complainant will have to have a turnover of less than 2 million Euro with fewer than 10 staff. The ombudsman will determine the eligibility of a commercial complaint by reference to appropriate evidence such as audited accounts or VAT returns.[14]

2.8 To be eligible, the complainant must also have been a customer or a potential customer of the firm or VJ participant and the complaint must arise out of a matter relevant to that.[15]

Intermediaries

2.9 Before 14 January 2005, insurance intermediaries were not subject to FOS jurisdiction, and, until May 2001, were regulated and had complaints against them decided by the Insurance Brokers Registration Council and then by the General Insurance Standards Council ("GISC") as discussed at paragraphs 1.14 *et seq* above. The FOS only had jurisdiction if it determined that the intermediary was acting as agent of the insurer, in which case it could deal with the complaint as if it was brought against the insurer. Unfortunately, there is limited evidence in *Ombudsman News* of the FOS carefully analysing the broker relationship in terms of agency, and the FOS might consider a broker an agent of the insurer where the law does not. Now that it has this extended jurisdiction, it has addressed the question of agency in its Consumer Factsheet on Medical Non-Disclosure.[16]

2.10 For events which occurred on or after 14 January 2005, the FSA became the regulator, so the FOS gained jurisdiction of the following activities:

(1) dealing in insurance contracts as agent;
(2) arranging deals in insurance contracts;
(3) advising on insurance contracts; and
(4) assisting in the administration and performance of insurance contracts.

2.11 Exceptions to this extension of the FOS jurisdiction were:

(1) travel agents when the insurance is sold as part of a package holiday[17] (although this category was added to the FSA regulation and FOS jurisdiction from 1 January 2009[18]);
(2) retailers when selling extended warranties on goods;

---

12. 2007/64/EC.
13. As defined by Commission Recommendation 2003/361/EC 6 May 2003.
14. DISP 2.7.5G.
15. DISP 2.7.6R.
16. To be found on the FOS website; see "Non-disclosure by an Intermediary" below at paras. 13.58 *et seq* for more detail on the question of whose agent the FOS considers the broker to be.
17. According to the Annual Review 2006/7, 1 in 5 travel insurance complaints are from sales by travel agents.
18. *Cf* FOS website at the dedicated information resource for businesses.

(3) loss adjusters—but not loss assessors who act for customers in relation to insurance claims;

(4) the handling of insurance claims on behalf of insurers under a delegated authority.

2.12 The GISC retained jurisdiction only of complaints it was already handling before 14 January 2005. However, the jurisdiction of a "relevant transitional complaint" passed to the FOS and for these the FOS has to take account of what the GISC might have decided. A "relevant transitional complaint" is a complaint about events which occurred before 14 January 2005 but were complained about afterwards and where:

(1) the firm was a member of the GISC at the time of the event complained about;

(2) the complaint would previously have been covered by the GISC Dispute Resolution Facility;

(3) the complainant is an individual who is acting otherwise than solely for the purposes of his business; and

(4) the firm became regulated by the FSA on or after 14 January 2005.

Group schemes

2.13 Under the IOB rules, group scheme beneficiaries could only bring a complaint with the policyholder's permission or if the policyholder brought the claim on their behalf.[19] However, under the FOS rules, a member of a group scheme can bring a complaint directly to the FOS without needing the policyholder's permission. The FOS treats complaints by tenants whose interest is noted on a block building policy as if the tenant had arranged the insurance directly.[20] And employees can bring a claim about the benefit of an employer's group health scheme, as illustrated by Case Study 32/10,[21] as long as the policy is for the employee's benefit, even if it also benefits other employees.

2.14 However, there is still no FOS jurisdiction if a group policy is for the benefit of the company rather than for the beneficiary. An example, in the context of an employer's health insurance policy, is if it is a "key man" policy for the benefit of the company (as was the position in Case Study 32/8[22]), or if the employer is effectively reinsuring its own contractual liability to pay sickness benefits. In such a scenario, the employer can only bring the complaint if it is a small enough business to be an eligible complainant under DISP 2.7.3R. In determining whether a scheme benefits the company or the complainant, the FOS will look at the policy wording and employment contract. It is likely to be for the benefit of the employee if the benefits are paid or provided direct to him without the employer exercising any practical discretion over them, if the employee is involved in the claims process, and if the employer is only contractually obliged to pay benefits to the employee if the insurer accepts the claim.

---

19. *Cf* Case Study 32/7 (*Ombudsman News* Oct 2003) where the employee under a group personal health insurance policy complained about a matter which occurred before 1 December 2001, and the FOS had to rule in accordance with the IOB terms of reference which did not allow him to bring the complaint.
20. As reported in the Law Commissions' Summary of Responses—consumer issues 28/05/08.
21. *Ombudsman News* Oct 2003.
22. *Ombudsman News* Oct 2003.

Foreign firms

2.15 If the FOS has no jurisdiction under its voluntary jurisdiction over a foreign firm, the complainant may still be able to find an ombudsman scheme in the appropriate country through the International Network of Financial Services Ombudsman Schemes[23] or for EEA companies, FIN-NET.[24] FIN-NET is a network, to which the FOS belongs, of financial ombudsmen and consumer complaints organisations covering countries of the EEA. Any financial dispute resolution body within the EEA can join if it meets the standards set by the European Commission.[25] Members remain autonomous, agree to direct a complainant to the appropriate organisation in the firm's country, cooperate with each other and exchange practical information such as questions of law in the different countries. A similar system operates under the International Network of Financial Services Ombudsman Schemes for the appropriate member schemes. However, the systems in other countries are not simply foreign equivalents to the FOS, as they are structured differently, with a different ambit of cover and the European schemes have a generally more legalistic approach. Some have no organisation that will deal with insurance disputes,[26] some have different ones according to which type of insurance is involved.[27] None seem to be dealing with anything like as many complaints. By comparison, the FOS is ahead in its development.

Claims management services

2.16 The FOS does not have jurisdiction over claims management providers: the Ministry of Justice is the regulator.[28] Claims management providers charge the consumer either a fee or a share of the compensation in return for their services. The Compensation Act 2006 provides rules and a code of conduct for the provision of certain claims management services and from 6 April 2007, it became an offence to provide such services without specific authorisation or exemption.

Legal proceedings and commercial judgement

2.17 The IOB could not consider complaints about underwriting matters or where legal proceedings had been issued. The FOS has discretion to consider such complaints if it feels that the insurer has breached race, disability or sexual discrimination legislation or an industry code or agreement. So, for instance, the FOS might interfere with an insurer's decision not to maintain flood cover in breach of the ABI Statement of Principles on the Provision of Flooding Insurance. The FOS considers that non-compliance with a code indicates that the firm is unlikely to be making an appropriate use of its commercial judgement. However, the FOS will dismiss without consideration of merits a question that it considers involves a firm's legitimate exercise of commercial judgement, for instance in relation to refusing to insure a complainant, increasing the premium or applying special conditions to the policy. So in Case Study 23/13,[29] the FOS determined that the insurer was

---

23. *Cf* www.networkfso.org.
24. *Cf* www.fin-net.eu.
25. Commission Recommendation 98/257/EC of 30 March 1998.
26. Czech Republic, Austria, Spain and Liechtenstein.
27. Germany, France, Portugal and Finland.
28. *Cf Ombudsman News* Jan/February 2007; www.claimsregulation.gov.uk.
29. *Ombudsman News* Dec 2002.

entitled to change its own underwriting guidelines and decide not to offer renewal of car insurance to the complainant.

FUNDING: LEVIES AND CASE FEES

2.18 The FOS is funded entirely by the financial services industry, through a levy (raising 20% of the FOS funding) and case fees (raising the remaining 80% of the FOS funding). The levy is taken from every firm covered by the FSA and is calculated each year according to a firm's volume of business.[30] Individual case fees are billed at the end of the month in which the complaint is closed.[31] From 1 April 2004 to 31 March 2008, firms paying an annual levy were not charged for the first two complaints the FOS received about them in any one year, but thereafter a case fee was charged for each complaint against them, whatever the outcome. As from 1 April 2008, firms that pay the annual levy were not charged for the first three complaints. It is assumed that the legal and/or management costs to the firm of a policyholder taking the matter to court instead of to the FOS must be more than the case fee, so that the scheme in general still makes economic sense to insurers now that it is compulsory for them. In any event, the majority of firms have too few complaints against them every year to have to pay any case fees at all.[32]

2.19 The FOS will not charge a case fee where it is readily apparent that:

(1) the firm has not yet had a chance to deal with the complaint;
(2) the complainant is not an "eligible complainant" under DISP 2.7.3R;
(3) the complaint is out of its jurisdiction; or
(4) the complaint should be dismissed without consideration of its merits under DISP 3.3.4R.

2.20 However, if one of the above factors is not readily apparent and the FOS has to investigate matters before it can establish the point, a fee will be charged. This practice was supported by the Court of Appeal in *FOS v Heather Moor & Edgecomb Ltd*,[33] which held it not to be unreasonable or unlawful. A complaint via the FOS service review team to the FOS independent assessor (see below at paragraphs 2.50 *et seq*) that a case fee has been charged in these circumstances will not usually succeed.

2.21 Complainants may not pay a fee or costs either to the FOS or to a firm.[34] If a firm threatens to penalise a customer for bringing a complaint to the FOS, puts pressure on him not to complain or tries to persuade him that the process will cost him money, then the FOS

30. In 2003/4, the levy ranged from less than £100 for a small financial adviser to £300,000 for a large insurance company.

31. The rate of the case fee was £360 in 2006/7 for a standard case fee, or £475 for a special case fee. (The distinction depended on how much levy the firm in question paid, and was removed from 1 April 2008 when the rates became £450 for both standard and special case fees. They were increased to £500 from 1 April 2009 and are due to remain at this level over 2010/11 (FOS Corporate Plan and Budget 2010/11)).

32. FOS Annual Review 05/06 notes that 81.5% of all firms covered by the FOS had no complaint referred to the FOS during the year, 8% had one complaint and 3% had two complaints, so only 7% of firms covered by the FOS actually paid a case fee (compared to 5.5% in the previous year). Also 15 firms alone accounted for half all the case fees in 2003/4 (Walter Merricks' speech 12 and 28 October 2004) and only 12 firms accounted for half of all the case fees in 2005/6 (FOS Annual Review 2005/6). In 2008/9, more than 95% of all firms covered by the FOS had no complaint referred to the FOS, 1.25% paid a case fee and six financial services groups accounted for just over half the total number of cases referred. (FOS Annual Review 2008/9). In 2009/10, the figures were similar (FOS Annual Review 2009/10).

33. [2008] EWCA Civ 643.

34. S. 230(3) FSMA.

may report it to the FSA and the FSA will be entitled to take disciplinary action against it for having failed to meet the FSA's "Principles for Businesses".[35] The FOS may also award compensation for distress and inconvenience for such behaviour.[36] It is arguable that payment of fees or costs to the FOS would be a deterrent for persistent or obsessive complainants, although the contrary view was expressed by former Chief Ombudsman Walter Merricks. He has commented that he thinks that they would be happy to pay and would demand commensurate service.[37] In some other jurisdictions, a nominal case fee of the equivalent of £20–£40 is charged to the complainant which is recoverable if the complaint is upheld in full or part.[38] It is unclear whether such charges are meant to be a deterrent for the persistent complainant, or to cover some or all of the ombudsman's running costs, and whether there is an overall profit for the complaints service in question bearing in mind the administration involved. But this shows that a fee system for complainants is workable.

2.22 Unfortunately, financial risk is one of the unavoidable flaws of the judicial system, so perhaps it is right that it is not a factor for the complainant in a system set up as an effective, accessible alternative. However, it means that a minority of vexatious complainants can time and again pursue unreasonable complaints costing them nothing, but costing insurers in terms of management time and possible solicitors' fees. At least, however, the FOS has said[39] that it does not charge a case fee if it finds a complaint to be frivolous and vexatious, and that the number of such cases is small.[40] Even if a claimant is not frivolous and vexatious, if the value of the claim is less than the cost of the FOS referral, it will be economic for insurers to pay even unmeritorious claims.

2.23 Perhaps at the very least, the FOS should be able to make some sort of award payable to the FOS against vexatious complainants, or those who do not cooperate with the FOS and/ or insurers and those who have committed a fraud. Although not utilised, the power to make such rules exists under section 230(4) FSMA which allows the scheme operator to provide costs rules with the approval of the FSA for "the making of an award against the complainant in favour of the scheme operator . . . if in the opinion of the ombudsman—(a) the complainant's conduct was improper or unreasonable or (b) the complainant was responsible for an unreasonable delay".

INSURERS' COMPLAINTS HANDLING OBLIGATIONS

Obligations pre-complaint

2.24 DISP 1 of the FSA's Handbook sets out certain obligations with which firms should generally comply. The FOS cannot interpret or issue guidance in relation to these rules, which include the following: a firm may display a notice in branches or sales offices showing that it is covered by the FOS, although under the updated DISP of November 2007, this is

---

35. These are Principle 6 (A firm must pay due regard to the interests of its customers and treat them fairly) and Principle 8 (A firm must manage conflicts of interest fairly, both between itself and its customers and between a customer and another client).

36. *Cf Ombudsman News* Apr 2004.

37. Speech 12 and 28 October 2004.

38. E.g. in 2009, complaints to the Danish Insurance Complaints Board (DKK150), the Netherlands Financial Services Ombudsman (EUR50) and the Icelandic Insurance Complaints Committee (ISK6000).

39. FOS Annual Review 2009/10.

40. FOS Annual Review 2009/10 reported that it found in that year 702 out of 166,321 settled cases to be frivolous and vexatious, of which 677 were complaints mostly brought by case management companies about payment protection insurance policies which had never been taken out.

no longer a requirement[41]; firms may also use the FOS logo or put a statement on any relevant marketing material or correspondence[42] to show that they are covered by the FOS.[43]

Obligations post-complaint: the eight-week rule

2.25 Once a firm has received a complaint anywhere within its organisation, it has eight weeks in which to exhaust its own internal complaints procedure and send the complainant a final response letter or an explanation as to why it cannot make a final response yet. The FOS will not consider a complaint until either there is a final response letter or the eight weeks has expired,[44] and will usually forward to the firm any complaint it receives which has not been through this process. Firms resolve most complaints themselves, generally all but approximately 2–5% of non-mortgage endowment complaints.[45] DISP 1.6 sets out a more detailed timetable of what should be done, and by when, within this eight weeks.

2.26 The final response letter should include[46]:

    (1) a summary of the complaint;

    (2) a summary of the outcome of the firm's investigation;

    (3) whether the firm acknowledges any fault on its part;

    (4) details of any offer the firm has made to settle the complaint;

    (5) how long any offer to settle the complaint will remain open;

    (6) why (if) it thinks the complaint may be outside the FOS jurisdiction. But the firm should explain that jurisdiction is a matter for the FOS, not the firm to decide; and

    (7) express mention of the complainant's right to refer the complaint to the FOS within six months of the firm's final response, (otherwise the FOS will accept cases for consideration outside of the six months, as under DISP 2.8.3G, the time will not have started to run).

2.27 Firms must also send to customers the FOS contact details and a copy of the FOS standard explanatory leaflet[47] either with the final response letter or with the explanation of why it is not yet in a position to send its final response. Special rules apply to internet-based firms[48] about how they should provide this information.

2.28 The FOS publishes various guides for firms about complaint handling. The FOS treats an apology or expression of regret as recognition of the firm having an unhappy customer rather than an admission of liability,[49] although a court might regard it differently. The FOS does not like insurers to cite different reasons for rejecting a claim at different times, rather than all together. The FOS may penalise non-compliance with all of the above with an award to the complainant for maladministration.

---

41. DISP 1.2.5G.
42. DISP 1.2.5G.
43. *Cf, Ombudsman News* Apr 2004 and FOS Briefing Note—"Telling your customers about the FOS."
44. DISP 2.8.1R.
45. Figures from speech by Walter Merricks 12 and 28 October 2004.
46. *Cf* DISP 1.6.2R, the most up-to-date FOS guides for firms on the FOS's website and the FSA Handbook of Rules and Guidance at the glossary/definitions section of "final response".
47. DISP 1.6.2R.
48. *Ombudsman News* Aug 2008.
49. *Ombudsman News* Nov 2003.

TIME-LIMITS FOR BRINGING A COMPLAINT TO THE FOS

The six-month rule

2.29 The complainant has six months in which to bring a complaint to the FOS after receiving the firm's final response letter.[50] If the firm has not told the complainant about his right to complain to the FOS and about the six-month time-limit, then whatever letter has been sent, it will not constitute a final response letter, and the start of the six-month period will not have been triggered.[51] The FOS can consider extending this six-month period where:

(1) it considers that there have been exceptional circumstances,[52] such as the complainant's incapacity[53];

(2) it is required to do so by the Ombudsman Transitional Order[54]; or

(3) the firm has not objected to the FOS considering the complaint on the grounds of time limits.[55]

2.30 On 28 May 2010 the FSA announced a temporary rule[56] to suspend the six-month time limit for payment protection insurance complainants who were sent a final response from a firm between 28 November 2009 and 28 April 2010 inclusive. The suspension of the rule started from, and including, 28 May 2010 until 27 October 2010. This move was made to ensure that recent payment protection insurance complainants are not disadvantaged by running out of time to refer their complaint to the FOS while the FSA works to resolve a long-term solution to ensure customers are treated consistently and fairly when complaining about the sale of a payment protection insurance ("PPI") policy, or when buying a new one.

Legal limitation periods

2.31 The FOS cannot consider a complaint referred to it more than six years after the event complained of or (if later) more than three years from the date on which the complainant became aware (or ought reasonably to have become aware) that he had cause for complaint, unless[57]:

(1) he has referred the complaint to the firm or the FOS within that period and has a written acknowledgement or some other record of the complaint having been received;

(2) in the view of the FOS, the failure to comply with the time limits was as a result of exceptional circumstances;

(3) the Ombudsman Transitional Order requires the FOS to review the complaint; or

(4) the firm has not objected to the FOS considering the complaint on the grounds of time limits.[58]

---

50. DISP 2.8.2R.
51. DISP 2.8.3G.
52. DISP 2.8.2R(3).
53. DISP 2.8.4G.
54. DISP 2.8.2R(4).
55. DISP 2.8.2R(5).
56. FSA/PN/087/2010.
57. Also see DISP 2.8.5R, 2.8.6G and 2.8.7R regarding exceptions for reviews of past business and exceptions for certain mortgage endowment complaints.
58. DISP 2.8.2R(2) to (5).

2.32 The FOS will expect a firm which wishes to rely on these limitation periods or the six-month limit above, to do so as early as possible in the process, and will give a reminder of the requirement in its initial letter to the firm relating to the complaint. Where a firm regards a case as time-barred, it may reject the complaint without considering the merits, but must explain this to the complainant in the final response and indicate that the FOS may waive the time limits in exceptional circumstances.[59] The FOS has a discretion not even to apply the 15-year long stop in the Limitation Act 1980 for tortious claims, for instance in relation to advice from a broker or financial adviser. There is no 15-year long stop in the complaints-handling rules made under the FSMA and the Consumer Credit Act.[60] The FSA has reviewed the position and confirmed that it does not think there should be. It says that any such limitation clause adopted in firms' terms of business will be in breach of its regulations and, for consumers, also a breach of the Unfair Terms in Consumer Contracts Regulations, and would not be binding on the FOS which would still have to consider complaints presented to it within the time limits indicated in DISP.[61]

2.33 It should be noted that legal limitation periods for instigating and serving court proceedings will not be stayed automatically by bringing a matter to the FOS.

HOW COMPLAINTS ARE DEALT WITH

Overview

2.34 The FOS is a sophisticated body dealing primarily with paper claims. It has proved itself over the years to be able to adapt and deal with a huge increase in the number of complaints, including various sporadic surges in certain types of complaints, like those relating to endowment mortgages and payment protection insurance. It sets up specialist teams as they become necessary. There are appropriate support teams (including a "quality, information and knowledge" department[62]) and there are systems for applying and sharing knowledge, maintaining quality and achieving consistency. The FOS regularly surveys both firms and complainants for feedback. An independent six-month study[63] commissioned by the FOS Board, gave the FOS a glowing report and concluded that it was "doing a good job under difficult circumstances" and that the case-handling process was efficient and offered good value for money, especially compared with other dispute resolution methods. However, Lord Hunt in his later independent report of 9 April 2008[64] criticised it for not being accessible and transparent enough. The FOS has taken on board his criticisms and its continuing efforts to remedy them are set out on its website.

2.35 Bearing in mind that the majority of adults have some form of house, car, travel or health insurance,[65] the FOS does not receive that many insurance complaints proportionally, although the actual numbers that they have to deal with are quite high, especially if the

---

59. DISP 1.8.1R.
60. *Cf* FOS website "Time Bars".
61. *Cf* FSA Feedback Statement FS08/6 and update of 18 November 2009 on the FSA website.
62. *Cf, Ombudsman News* Aug 2006 for details of quality checking of live and closed cases and also FOS Annual Review 2009/10.
63. "Fair and reasonable—An assessment of the FOS" by Kempson, Collard and Moore, Personal Finance Research Centre, University of Bristol, July 2004.
64. *Supra* at para. 1.9.
65. Of all households, 76% take out contents insurance, 74% take out vehicle insurance, and 36% have life assurance: see Office for National Statistics, Family Spending: A Report on the 2007 Expenditure and Food Survey, table A1.

number of general enquiries is considered as well as the number that turn into actual complaints.[66]

2.36 Here follows an outline of the complaints process.

Technical advice desk

2.37 The Technical advice desk answers queries from firms and consumer advisers[67] about the complaints procedure and likely outcomes if the complaint were formally brought to the FOS.[68] Its suggestions are not binding and the firm must not refer to them when it writes or speaks to consumers. Customers' general queries are answered via the Customer Contact Division.

Customer Contact Division

2.38 Customers can telephone the FOS Customer Contact Division both for help and information before the FOS gets formally involved or to commence the complaints process. Whilst it may retain some of the details to avoid duplication later, the FOS will only begin its procedures to deal with complaints unresolved by the firm after the final response letter has been sent, or after eight weeks from the date of the complaint to the firm if sooner (see above at paragraphs 2.25 *et seq*).

2.39 The customer contact staff will help the complainant to complete over the telephone a complaint form, which he/she will be asked to check, sign and return complete with any supporting documents. The form is concise and well-designed with clear, sensible questions, including a request for a chronology of all relevant telephone conversations, meetings and/or correspondence, and for copies of any relevant documents. There is a separate box for the complainant to set out what he wants. The answers to some of the questions will enable the customer contact staff to tell the complainant immediately if there is anything obvious which would prevent the FOS from considering the matter at that time or at all. They will also look for opportunities to deal immediately with a straightforward problem, such as an administrative misunderstanding or error. They may step in to talk to both sides with practical suggestions, explain why it might be unhelpful or unproductive for the matter to be pursued further, or give an early steer on the likely FOS outcome. They will provide the firm complained about with additional information if it is unfamiliar with the process.

2.40 If the complaint survives this process, it will be passed on to one of the adjudicators, the firm will be notified and asked for its comments and evidence, and the case will become "chargeable".[69]

66. *Cf* Appendix B. In 2005/6, the customer contact division dealt with 672,973 front-line enquiries and complaints, representing more than 2,500 telephone and written enquiries a day (FOS Annual Review 2005/6). In 2008/9 the total was 789,877 and in 2009/10 the total was 925,095 (representing more than 3,500 each working day) about half of which for both years were made by phone and half written (including email) (FOS Annual Reviews 2008/9 and 2009/10).

67. Such as Trading Standards officers and Citizens' Advice Bureaux.

68. In 2005/6, the technical advice desk dealt with 20,595 enquiries (FOS Annual Review 2005/6). In 2009/10 the figure was 16,319 (FOS Annual Review 2009/10).

69. The Customer Contact Division referred 112,923 or 1 in 6 new cases to adjudicators in 2005/6, representing a 1.8% increase from 2004/5 (FOS Annual Review 2005/6). Mortgage endowment complaints accounted for about 61% of these referrals, but dropped steadily. 14,270 or 13% accounted for insurance related complaints which represents a 24% increase on 2004/5. The FOS Annual Review 2008/9 says that the customer contact division referred 127,471 new cases to adjudicators in that year, of which 50,168 were insurance claims, of which 31,066 related to payment protection insurance. The FOS Annual Review 2009/10 reported 163,012 cases referred to adjudicators, of which 69,034 were insurance related, of which 49,196 related to payment protection insurance.

Adjudicators

2.41 A named adjudicator will then be assigned to the case and keep the parties informed of progress. He will try to find a solution through informal mediation or conciliation, perhaps telephoning the parties. Adjudicators may ask for more documents and information, and may also contact third parties for this directly either by telephone or in writing. If the matter cannot be resolved by telephone, or if it is complex, the adjudicator may issue both parties with a formal adjudication report, detailing the dispute, his findings and any suggested redress. Either party can respond to the adjudicator, setting out if and why they do not agree with him or asking for clarification and the adjudicator may modify his view thereafter. Usually, both sides accept the adjudicator's findings and the complaint is settled. Otherwise, the firm or the complainant may ask for a review and final decision by an ombudsman.[70] A new design for the format of the decisions of adjudicators and ombudsman is being instigated,[71] rather than a letter, so that it is clear at a glance on one page what are the key conclusions, whether the firm needs to pay redress and what should be done next.

Oral hearings

2.42 When a party asks for an ombudsman to make a final decision, this is when any request for a hearing would be considered or when an ombudsman might invite the parties to take part in a hearing.[72] The request must be written, setting out which issues should be heard and whether the hearing should be private.[73] The Ombudsman will decide whether the issues are material, whether a hearing should take place, where[74] and whether it should be held in public or in private,[75] and he will have regard to the provisions of the European Convention on Human Rights.[76] However, he will not be in breach of the Convention if permission is not granted, as the right to a public hearing is satisfied by the possibility of judicial review proceedings and the FOS is an independent and impartial tribunal.[77] Under the updated DISP rules, hearings may be held by telephone.[78] No hearing can be held after the Ombudsman's final determination.[79] Although legal representation at a hearing is discouraged, if a firm wants legal representation at a hearing, the FOS may ask it also to pay for the consumer complainant to be legally represented. If cross-examination of witnesses is necessary, then the court is the correct forum.

2.43 Usually there is enough evidence for the case to be decided on paper, especially as the parties are always given ample opportunity to make their views known during the FOS

---

70. About 92% of cases in 2005/6 were resolved informally through mediation, recommended settlements and adjudication (FOS Annual Review 2005/6). The remaining 8% (or 9,203 cases) were resolved by a review and final determination by an ombudsman. The average figure is about 10% (FOS "A Guide for Complaints Handlers" 31.03.05 edition). According to the FOS Annual Review 2008/9, in that year, about one in eight cases, or 7.5% progressed from adjudicators to ombudsmen. The FOS Annual Review 2009/10 reported one in six as the economic crisis helped to entrench people's positions. In 2009/10 a record number of complaints up to that point were resolved, 166,321 in total, of which adjudicators resolved 155,591 and ombudsmen resolved 10,730.
71. *Cf, Ombudsman News* Apr/May 2010.
72. DISP 3.5.5R.
73. DISP 3.5.6R.
74. It would usually be at the FOS offices in London.
75. DISP 3.5.6R (3) to (5).
76. DISP 3.5.7G.
77. *R (on the application of Heather Moor & Edgecomb Ltd) v FOS & Simon Lodge* [2008] EWCA Civ 642 and *R (on the application of Heather Moor & Edgecomb Ltd) v FOS & Ross* [2009] EWHC 2701 (Admin).
78. DISP 3.5.5R.
79. DISP 3.5.5R.

process and in view of the inquisitorial role of the FOS. Very few hearings therefore take place.[80] Since the FOS was born, there has only been one insurance hearing reported in *Ombudsman News*, Case Study 18/2,[81] to help the Ombudsman determine whether the insurer had said at inception that the complainant's husband's angina would be covered. A hearing might be suitable if documentary evidence was inconclusive, or credibility was in issue, or the documents were finely balanced and the facts were in issue, and the ombudsman considered that a hearing would help him get to the bottom of the case.[82] The FOS Annual Review 2009/10 reports that only 20 oral hearings were held in that year.

Dismissal or termination without considering the merits

2.44 DISP 3.3.4R sets out 18 circumstances in which an ombudsman may dismiss a complaint without considering its merits. These are if the ombudsman is satisfied, after giving the complainant an opportunity to make representations,[83] that:

(1)   the complainant has not suffered, or is unlikely to suffer, financial loss, material distress or material inconvenience;

(2)   the complaint is frivolous or vexatious[84];

(3)   the complaint clearly does not have any reasonable prospect of success;

(4)   the firm has already made an offer of compensation (or a goodwill payment) which is: (a) fair and reasonable in relation to the circumstances alleged; and (b) still open for acceptance;

(5)   the firm has reviewed the subject matter of the complaint in accordance with: (a) the regulatory standards for the review of such transactions prevailing at the time of the review; or (b) the terms of a scheme order under section 404 FSMA 2000 (schemes for reviewing past business); or (c) any formal regulatory requirement, standard or guidance published by the FSA or other regulator in respect of that type of complaint (including, if appropriate, making an offer of redress to the complainant), unless the firm considers that they did not address the particular circumstances of the case;

(6)   the subject matter of the complaint has previously been considered or excluded under the FOS, or a former scheme (unless material new evidence which the Ombudsman considers likely to affect the outcome has subsequently become available to the complainant[85]);

(7)   the subject matter of the complaint has been dealt with, or is being dealt with, by a comparable independent complaints scheme or dispute resolution process;

(8)   the subject matter of the complaint has been the subject of court proceedings where there has been a decision on the merits;

80. See below, "Written versus oral evidence" at para. 4.16.

81. *Ombudsman News* July 2002.

82. *Cf* also the discussion in *R (on the application of Heather Moor & Edgecomb Ltd)* v *FOS & Simon Lodge* [2008] EWCA Civ 642 and *R (on the application of Heather Moor & Edgecomb Ltd)* v *FOS & Ross* [2009] EWHC 2701 (Admin), which cases envisaged that a hearing might also be suitable where the ombudsman wanted to establish what someone would have done if particular advice had been given.

83. DISP 3.3.1R.

84. See also above under "Funding: levies and case fees" at paras. 2.19 and 2.22.

85. *Cf, R (on the application of Cook)* v *FOS* [2009] EWHC 426 (Admin)—the FOS had not erred in declining to review a new expert report and could conclude that it was not material new evidence unavailable at the time of the investigation, because the report could with reasonable diligence have been obtained and submitted in response to the Ombudsman's provisional decision and before the final determination, which had been accepted in writing by the complainants.

(9) the subject matter of the complaint is the subject of current court proceedings unless proceedings are stayed or sisted (by agreement of all parties, or order of the court) in order that the matter may be considered under the FOS;

(10) it would be more suitable for the subject matter of the complaint to be dealt with by a court, arbitration or another complaints scheme;

(11) the complaint is about the legitimate exercise of a firm's commercial judgement;

(12) the complaint is about employment matters from an employee or employees of a firm;

(13) the complaint is about investment performance;

(14) the complaint is about a firm's decision when exercising a discretion under a will or private trust;

(15) the complaint is about a firm's failure to consult beneficiaries before exercising a discretion under a will or private trust, where there is no legal obligation to consult;

(16) it is a complaint which: (a) involves (or might involve) more than one eligible complainant; and (b) has been referred without the consent of the other complainant or complainants; and the Ombudsman considers that it would be inappropriate to deal with the complaint without that consent;

(16A) it is a complaint about a pure landlord and tenant issue arising out of a regulated sale and rent back agreement; or

(17) there are other compelling reasons why it is inappropriate for the complaint to be dealt with under the FOS.

2.45 The ombudsman may also dismiss a complaint without considering its merits under DISP 3.3.5R so that a court may consider it as a test case, if:

(1) before he has made a determination, he has received in writing from the firm:

    (a) a detailed statement of how and why, in the firm's opinion, the complaint raises an important or novel point of law with significant consequences; and

    (b) an undertaking in favour of the complainant that, if the complainant or the firm commences court proceedings against the other in respect of the complaint in any court in the United Kingdom within six months of the complaint being dismissed, the firm will: pay the complainant's reasonable costs and disbursements (to be assessed if not agreed on an indemnity basis) in connection with the proceedings at first instance and any subsequent appeal proceedings brought by the firm; and make interim payments on account of such costs if and to the extent that it appears reasonable to do so; and

(2) the Ombudsman considers that the complaint:

    (a) raises an important or novel point of law, which has important consequences; and

    (b) would more suitably be dealt with by a court as a test case.

2.46 DISP 3.3.6G sets out a non-exclusive list of factors which the ombudsman may take into account in considering whether to dismiss a complaint under DISP 3.3.5R. It is envisaged that test cases under DISP 3.3.5R will be rare.

Ombudsman's determination

2.47 If a party requests a final determination from an ombudsman, he will undertake an independent review of the evidence, perhaps asking for further evidence and giving directions in relation to evidence with which the parties must comply.[86] He may use his discretion as to what evidence he would like to see and which evidence he will admit,[87] and in what time frame, and his decisions about the provision of evidence may be different to a court's.[88] He will ensure that both parties have been given an opportunity to make representations, especially the complainant, when considering questions of jurisdiction, eligibility, or dismissal without consideration of the merits.[89] He will then send both parties a provisional assessment with his reasoning and a time limit within which either party must respond, before issuing a final determination[90] with a time limit within which the complainant may accept the decision and so bind both parties on awards up to £100,000 plus interest. The firm cannot attach any conditions of its own. If the complainant rejects the offer or remains silent until the time limit for accepting has expired, the firm is not bound and the complainant remains free to bring court proceedings against the firm.[91] An ombudsman's decision is final and cannot be appealed, even to another ombudsman. Once accepted by the complainant, a decision cannot be re-determined unless both parties agree, even if the FOS acknowledges it has made a mistake: if both parties do not agree in these circumstances, the appropriate remedy is judicial review.[92]

2.48 The FSA's rules require firms to comply promptly with an ombudsman decision accepted by the complainant, as well as with any settlement that may have been agreed earlier in the process. Both of these are enforceable by the courts.[93]

2.49 Excluding mortgage endowment complaints, on average about 40% of ombudsmen cases are decided wholly or partly in the complainant's favour,[94] although the 2008/9 and 2009/10 figures show for the first time a much higher overall figure, due in large part to payment protection insurance disputes with an unprecedented uphold rate of 89% in both years.[95]

THE INDEPENDENT ASSESSOR

2.50 Although there is no appeal of an ombudsman's decision, complaints can be made by either the firm or the complainant about the way in which the FOS has handled a complaint. Most complaints about the level of service provided by the FOS relate to FOS delays.

86. DISP 3.5.8R, 3.5.11G.
87. *Cf* DISP 3.5.9R, 3.5.10G and 3.5.12G.
88. DISP 3.5.13R, 3.5.14R, 3.5.15R. *Cf* paras. 4.2 and 4.3, below.
89. DISP 3.2.3R, 3.2.4R, 3.3.1R.
90. DISP 3.5.4R.
91. S. 228(6) FSMA and DISP 3.6.6R.
92. *R (on the application of Towry Law Financial Services plc) v FOS Ltd* [2002] EWHC 1603 (Admin). See further below "Judicial Review" at para. 2.70 for more details and cost consequences of such an action.
93. S. 229(8) and Sched. 17, Part III s.16 FSMA.
94. *Ombudsman News* Jan 2003; FOS Annual Reviews 2004/5, 2005/6 and 2007/8. The FOS Annual Review 2005/6 says that 59% of complaints dealt with by adjudicators and 51% of those dealt with by an ombudsman were rejected, and in a further 6% and 2% respectively, firms were found to have treated the customer's complaint fairly although the firm still agreed a goodwill payment.
95. Speech by Tony Boorman (Principal Ombudsman): PPI complaints and consumer confidence 24/02/09 and FOS Annual Reviews 2008/9 and 2009/10. However, insurance complaints excluding payment protection insurance remained at around the 40% mark in both 2008/9 and 2009/10.

Complaints should be made by phone or in writing in the first instance to the person dealing with the claim and if that person and their manager cannot sort it out directly, the complainant will need to write to the service review manager.[96] The FOS aims to conduct a review of its own case-handling and if appropriate issue an apology and/or compensation for damages and/or distress or inconvenience and provide a full written response within 20 working days. If the firm or consumer is still dissatisfied, he may complain within three months of the FOS written response to the FOS independent assessor,[97] who is appointed by the FOS board and has official terms of reference.[98] He will not investigate complaints about the merits of a decision, only the level of service provided by the FOS. He will have access to all the FOS files and may seek further information.

2.51 If the independent assessor upholds a complaint in whole or part, he may recommend to the Chief Ombudsman that the FOS makes an apology or pays compensation, or more compensation than that offered, for any damage, distress or inconvenience caused. The level of compensation is usually modest. The former assessor has noted[99] that where FOS delay results in the firm paying additional interest to the consumer, the FOS should pay compensation for inconvenience taking this into account, but without working out exactly how much should have been paid, for it is too difficult to estimate how long any particular investigation should have taken.

2.52 The assessor will write to the complainant and to the FOS with his findings from which there is no appeal by a complainant. If the Chief Ombudsman does not accept his findings (which in practice does not happen[100]), there is a process in place for the independent assessor to refer the matter to the Board of the FOS, who will make a decision at its next meeting. If the Board declines to accept the independent assessor's recommendation, it will inform the independent assessor and the parties and publish the result in its annual report.

2.53 The assessor has to report annually to the Board of the FOS. Complaints are made about the FOS's own service standards in only a tiny fraction of cases.[101] The statistics of complaints referred to the assessor have been broadly similar since 2004/5. The FOS Annual Review 2009/10 reported in that year 262 referrals,[102] of which he had to investigate 165.[103] Of the cases which did not require investigation, 45 were referred to the assessor too early in the process before the FOS service review team had been given the opportunity to deal with the complaint, 25 were general enquiries, seven were outside the independent assessor's jurisdiction as they were out of time or unrelated to the ombudsman and two were withdrawn by the complainant. The independent assessor upheld 67 complaints wholly or in part, of which distress and inconvenience was awarded, mostly between £50 and £500, in 60 cases. Twenty of the complaints were referred by businesses, all independent financial advisers or brokers and mostly relating to the case fee charged.

---

96. FOS Annual Review 2009/10 reported that the service review team handled 1,765 complaints in that year about the FOS service, which was about 1% of its total case load. The figures for 2008/9 were similar. Of these, 8% of the complaints were by firms, and 27% were upheld leading to a payment of £150–£200 for distress and inconvenience in 113 cases.

97. *Cf* FOS website "Our service standards".

98. To be found on the FOS website.

99. Michael Barnes CBE in FOS Annual Review 2006/7.

100. The FOS has to date accepted all the recommendations made by the independent assessor. Hopefully the position will be no different with the appointment of a new independent assessor in 2010.

101. In the FOS Annual Review 2008/9, the independent assessor calculated that complaints referred to him only represented 0.16% of the ombudsman's total workload.

102. Compared to 265 in 2008/9 and 281 in 2007/8.

103. Compared to 185 in 2008/9 and 170 in 2007/8.

2.54 It remains to be seen whether the appointment of a new independent assessor in May 2010[104] following the retirement of Michael Barnes CBE who had the role for the previous eight years, will make any material difference to these figure trends in future years.

REFERRAL TO COURT

2.55 Complainants with rejected complaints, whether they be consumers or small businesses, rarely reject an ombudsman's final determination and turn to the courts. This seems natural because:

(1) the ombudsman's decision may feel like a pseudo-appeal in itself as the case will have been reviewed at the FOS so many times before it reaches him;

(2) the costs and risks of litigation can be substantial, especially where an independent body has already determined that it is a losing case, and where the court would inevitably be shown the ombudsman's reasoned rejection of the complaint;

(3) many complainants will have had enough of the fight;

(4) some cases will be too big for the small claims court, but too small to be commercially viable to bring in the county or high court;

(5) where the law is applied strictly by the court, but not by the FOS, such as in non-disclosure cases, it may be less advantageous for the insured to bring a claim to court;

(6) many consumers will feel satisfied that they have already been heard and that an independent body has looked at the matter impartially, even if the decision has not gone their way. FOS customer surveys in 2003/4 showed that 80% of the consumers who replied were satisfied with the FOS, although only 60% had thought the decision had been reasonable. This may reflect the fact that more complaints are rejected than upheld. The FOS Annual Review 2005/6, shows that 96% of consumers who said they felt they had "won" were satisfied with the FOS handling of the matter, 64% of those who said they felt they had "lost" and 92% of those who felt that they had neither won nor lost. Interestingly, that Annual Review also reports that 75% of firms responding to the FOS survey thought that the FOS provides a good independent dispute resolution service. In the FOS Annual Review 2009/10, figures showed that 87% of customers who won and 46% of those who lost were satisfied with the FOS handling of their complaint, and 63% of firms responding thought that the FOS provided a good independent service.

2.56 There are only a handful of reported cases which began as complaints to either the IOB or the FOS and ended up in court. Of these, the insured failed to achieve a successful outcome both at the IOB/FOS and at court in all but two cases.[105] A common feature of these "failing" cases is the judge's criticism of the claimant's argument, conduct, attitudes and evidence, although only one went as far as calling the action frivolous and vexatious.[106] The two cases referred to above where the complaint failed before the FOS but succeeded before

104. Linda Costelloe Baker OBE.

105. E.g. *Clark* v *New Hampshire Insurance Company*, unreported, 27 June 1991; *Welch* v *Cunningham Hart (UK) Ltd & Another*, unreported, Court of Appeal, 26 July 1994; *Tucker* v *Abbey Life Assurance Co Ltd*, unreported, Court of Appeal, 4 October 1999; *Campbell* v *BMW Insurance Co* [2001] EWCA Civ 1660 and *Tonkin* v *UK Insurance Ltd* [2006] EWHC 1120 (TCC).

106. *Welch* v *Cunningham Hart (UK) Ltd & Another*, unreported, Court of Appeal, 26 July 1994.

the court are *Margate Theatre Royal Trust Ltd* v *White*[107] and *Lewis* v *Norwich Union Healthcare Ltd.*[108] The Technology and Construction Court's technical ability to deal with and cross-examine the expert evidence was probably what made the difference in the *Margate* case, which turned on the technical issues of whether work to a fire main at a theatre was included in the policy's description of the work for which public liability insurance was in place.

FOS DECISION-MAKING: FAIR AND REASONABLE

2.57 When considering evidence of fact and the evidence is contradictory, the FOS will decide what it thinks is most likely to have happened on the balance of probability. Although the FOS aims to be consistent in the way it deals with particular types of complaint, it is not bound by its own decisions and rarely, if ever, mentions in one case study the outcome of another.

2.58 One of the main differences between the FOS and a court is that the FOS decides each case in accordance with what it considers to be fair and reasonable in the circumstances of the particular case,[109] even if that is contrary to the way that a court would apply the law. However, in determining a complaint, the ombudsman must consider the matters set out in DISP 3.6.4R, which include the relevant law, regulations, regulators' rules, guidance and standards, relevant codes of practice and where appropriate, what the Ombudsman considers to be good industry practice at the relevant time.

2.59 What constitutes good industry practice at the relevant time? Even though many of the ABI and GISC codes of practice relating to how insurance is sold have been superseded by the introduction of the FSA's Insurance: Conduct of Business rules ("ICOB")[110] on 14 January 2005, itself superseded by the FSA's Insurance: New Conduct of Business source-book ("ICOBS") on 6 January 2008, the FOS still sees the former codes as evidencing good market practice, and so may still have regard to them. Although DISP 3.6.4R does not specify that the FOS must consider FSA approved "industry guidance" when it deals with disputes, it is expected that this may help the FOS establish what was thought to be good industry practice at the relevant time.[111] An ombudsman may also use his/her own knowledge of industry practice at the relevant period, as long as he/she is careful to guard against the use of hindsight.[112]

2.60 In *R (on the application of IFG Financial Services Ltd)* v *Financial Ombudsman Services Ltd (1) and Mrs Jenkins (Interested Parties)*,[113] the court expressly supported the right of the ombudsman to make an award which differs from that which a court would make, as long as it is fair and reasonable in all the circumstances of the case and provided he has

---

107. [2005] EWHC 2171 (TCC).
108. [2009] EW Misc 2 (EWCC).
109. S. 228 (2) FSMA; DISP 3.6.1R and 3.6.2G.
110. *Cf, supra* at paras. 1.5 *et seq* and 1.13 *et seq.*
111. *Cf* FSA Policy Statement 07/16 published in September 2007.
112. *R (on the application of Keith Williams)* v *FOS* [2008] EWHC 2142 (Admin). There it was held that, as long as he was not applying the advantage of hindsight, an ombudsman could use his own knowledge of traded endowment policies in 2002 and the attitude of the industry at that time to conclude that the investment in such policies was not suited to the particular circumstances of the independent financial adviser's client.
113. [2005] EWHC 1153 (Admin)—see below under "Judicial Review" at paras. 2.64 *et seq.*

considered the law and all the other matters set out in what was then DISP 3.8.1R(2), but which is now DISP 3.6.4R. There is no reason to think that the dicta would not apply to the updated version of DISP. The decision was approved by the Court of Appeal in *R (on the application of Heather Moor & Edgecomb Ltd) v FOS (1) Simon Lodge (2) (Interested Party)*,[114] where the relevant rule at the time was DISP 3.8.1R(2). There the Court of Appeal confirmed that the ombudsman could depart from the common law if he had considered the above factors, as long as he said in his final decision that he was doing so and why.

2.61 It is interesting that the Court of Appeal in *Heather Moor v FOS and Lodge* above found that the ombudsman had considered the relevant law through his reference to the appropriate test, even though he did not mention the case which set out the test. In deciding whether a financial investment adviser had acted negligently, the ombudsman explicitly referred to the question whether there was a respectable school of thought (as opposed to just some school of thought) amongst investment advisers at the time of the advice that would have done other than to advise the complainant to transfer his pension plan, and whether a letter from another financial investment adviser satisfied this requirement. This indicated to the Court of Appeal that the ombudsman clearly had the *Bolam*[115] test in mind, which was the appropriate law, even though it was not specifically mentioned. The ombudsman stated in his final decision that, "while I have taken into account the relevant law, I have determined this complaint based on what, in my opinion, is fair and reasonable bearing in mind all the circumstances of this case". The Court of Appeal found that he had set out his reasoning clearly in the rest of his determination.

2.62 It is not always clear from *Ombudsman News* reports whether the ombudsman has considered the law at every complaint as the ombudsman is meant to. It should be noted that the FOS internal information system may not be complete. The FOS Annual Review 2007/8 noted it covered only over 85% of the financial products and services about which the FOS commonly receives complaints. It is unclear how effectively it is updated, although the FOS Annual Review 2009/10 reported that over 1,000 new pages had been added to the staff intranet that year. Also, adjudicators and ombudsmen are not all lawyers, or may not have current experience or speciality in the field in question. This must make it harder for them to consider the law, especially if the internal information system is not sufficiently clear and comprehensive, and must make the FOS more vulnerable to judicial review. It would be wise therefore for parties to ensure that they set out whatever law they want the FOS to consider, as they probably should not assume that the FOS will know or apply it otherwise.

2.63 By comparison, most EEA countries which have ombudsman systems in place take a more legalistic attitude. Even where there may be leeway and they are not obliged to apply the law strictly, they do not seem to go as far as the FOS which actually makes its own policy in areas where it considers the law unfair, for instance in relation to non-disclosure and warranties.[116]

---

114. [2008] EWCA Civ 642.

115. *Bolam v Friern Barnet Hospital Management* [1957] 1 WLR 582 is authority for the proposition that a professional is not to be held negligent if what he did was in accordance with a practice accepted by responsible persons in his profession.

116. E.g., the Australian FOS does not have to follow law strictly (paras. 11.15–11.16 of its Terms of Reference), but it still applies the law on material non-disclosure, including those parts that are harsh on the assured. Rather than applying its own approaches instead of law, it publishes advice for consumers regarding certain common types of policy like travel insurance, telling them to read the policy and highlighting possible pitfalls and what might not be covered.

JUDICIAL REVIEW

2.64 Judicial review of an IOB decision was held in *R v IOB, ex parte Aegon Life Assurance Ltd*[117] not to be possible. For the IOB's powers were solely derived from contract between the IOB and member companies, not from statute and it could not be said that the IOB exercised any government functions. Although membership of the IOB might have been commercially advantageous to firms, Parliament had decided to make membership voluntary.

2.65 The position of the Pensions Ombudsman (before the combined ombudsman service of the FOS), was different. Its decisions were subject to a right of appeal from final determinations on a question of law only, under the pensions legislation[118] of the time.[119]

2.66 Now, at least under the compulsory jurisdiction of the FOS, applications may be made for judicial review of ombudsmen's decisions. However, there have only been a limited number of such applications,[120] presumably because the time and costs involved are prohibitive against the high risk of failure. There is a high risk of failure because, as confirmed in *R (on the application of IFG Financial Services Ltd) v FOS Ltd and Mr and Mrs Jenkins (interested parties)*,[121] as long as the ombudsman has considered the law and the other matters listed under what is now DISP 3.6.4R and as long as his reasoning is explained and is rational, he has a wide discretion to substitute his own values of fairness and reasonableness instead of law. In the *IFG* case, the ombudsman considering but not applying the law meant that an investment adviser had to pay even that part of the loss which was unforeseen and which a court would not have awarded.

2.67 A court will not interfere with an ombudsman's sense of what is fair and reasonable, unless the ombudsman has made such errors of reasoning as to deprive the decision of legal rationality. This was the position in *R (on the application of Garrison Investment Analysis) v FOS*,[122] where the investment adviser succeeded in the application as the court found the award irrational. The ombudsman had said he was putting the parties back into the position they would have been in were it not for the firm's error, but he had also found that the error had not caused the loss. There was no connection between the redress ordered and the error found. The ombudsman's decision was quashed and remitted back to him to determine the

---

117. [1994] CLC 88. Followed by *R v Deputy Insurance Ombudsman ex parte Francis* (unreported) 20 May 1998. Applied by *R v Panel of the Federation of Communication Services Ltd & Anr ex parte Kubis* (unreported) 3 September 1997; *R (on the application of Sunspell Ltd (t/a Superlative Travel)) v Association of British Travel Agents* (unreported) 12 October 2000; and *R v Personal Investment Authority Ombudsman Bureau Ltd ex parte Johannes Mooyes* [2001] EWHC 247 (Admin).

118. Part X of the Pension Schemes Act 1993. *Cf* in particular sections 146 to 151.

119. Examples of such cases are *Alfred James Duffield v The Pensions Ombudsman, The Times*, 30 April 1996; *Law Debenture Trust Corporation plc v The Pensions Ombudsman* [1997] 3 All ER 233; *Westminster City Council v Haywood* [1998] Ch 377; *Neil John Macaulay v The Pensions Ombudsman* LTL 04/02/98; *Legal & General Assurance Society Ltd v The Pensions Ombudsman* [2000] 2 All ER 577; *Alma Kearney Ewing v Trustees of the Stockham Valve Ltd Staff Retirement Benefits Scheme* LTL 01/03/2000; *Legal & General Assurance Society Ltd v CCA Stationery Ltd* [2003] EWHC 2989; *Michael Ward v South Yorkshire Pensions Authority* [2005] EWHC 2711 (Ch).

120. In September 2008, there were 15 current judicial review cases against the FOS. Compared to the number of complaints rejected by the FOS this is statistically tiny.

121. [2005] EWHC 1153 (Admin) and approved in *R (on the application of Heather Moor & Edgecomb Ltd) v FOS (1) Simon Lodge (2) (Interested Party)* [2008] EWCA Civ 642. There a financial investment adviser was applying for judicial review of an ombudsman decision that he should pay at least the £100,000 maximum that the FOS could order him to pay following advice about transferring a pension fund. The ombudsman was held to have considered the law even though he had referred to the relevant case law in substance rather than by name. See also above "FOS decision-making: fair and reasonable" at paras. 2.57 *et seq*.

122. [2006] EWHC 2466 (Admin).

appropriate redress in the light of his earlier conclusion as to the error. The ombudsman is entitled to adopt any test he wants to assist him in deciding whether something is fair.[123]

2.68 If an ombudsman makes a small mistake of fact in his determination, it has to make a difference to his decision before an application for judicial review will be successful.[124]

2.69 According to *R (on the application of Heather Moor & Edgecomb Ltd) v FOS & Simon Lodge*,[125] applying *R (on the application of Thompson) v Law Society*,[126] it is the ability to apply for a public hearing by way of judicial review which brings the whole FOS procedure within the oral hearing requirements of Article 6 of the Convention on Human Rights 1950.

2.70 If the FOS does not resist or defend judicial review proceedings, for instance because it acknowledges that it made a mistake in its determination, even a material mistake in law, it will not usually be ordered to pay the costs of those judicial review proceedings, unless it had acted improperly, i.e. perversely or with some disregard for the elementary principles which every court ought to obey, and even then only if it was a flagrant instance. So in *R (on the application of Towry Law Financial Services plc) v FOS Ltd*,[127] the FOS was not liable for the costs of the judicial review proceedings which quashed an ombudsman's decision. The FOS acknowledged that it had/may have made a mistake in relying upon a certain piece of evidence to prove a certain allegation, and offered a re-determination of the matter if both parties agreed. The court held that the FOS was right when it said that it could not re-determine the question which had already been accepted by the consumer complainant without both parties first consenting. Because both parties had not consented, Towry Law had no option but to bring judicial review proceedings. The consumer complainant was not asked to pay any costs of the proceedings because the judge felt that she had not been given any, or any adequate, warning by Towry Law that failing to consent to the re-determination could leave her exposed to the costs of the judicial review which would necessarily ensue if Towry Law pursued the matter. In fact, the court ordered Towry Law to pay the FOS costs of the judicial review costs hearing on the basis that it lost that application as the FOS was not ordered to pay any of the costs of the judicial review.

DEALINGS WITH CUSTOMERS WHILE THE FOS CONSIDERS THE COMPLAINT

2.71 In relation to matters other than the complaint, such as other insurance claims, a firm should continue to deal with a customer as normal whilst the FOS is considering the complaint. The firm may not take legal action against the customer in relation to the complaint while the FOS investigation is still pending. The firm will be prohibited from communicating directly with the insured on the subject matter of the dispute, and although it is free to make any offer or revised offer at any time, it should do so via the FOS. In practice, the insurer will have to submit its whole file to the FOS and the claims process will be frozen in relation to the particular complaint until a FOS outcome is reached. The

---

123. *R v FOS Ltd, ex parte Norwich & Peterborough Building Society & David Robert Jones* [2002] EWHC 2379 (Admin).
124. *R (on the application of Kenneth Green (t/a Green Denman & Co)) v FOS Ltd* [2003] EWHC 338 (Admin).
125. [2008] EWCA Civ 642 and also *R (on the application of Heather Moor & Edgecomb Ltd) v FOS & Ross* [2009] EWHC 2701 (Admin).
126. [2004] EWCA Civ 167.
127. *R (on the application of Towry Law Financial Services plc) v FOS Ltd* [2002] EWHC 1603 (Admin).

consequential delay may be significant to an insured, for instance, if he is awaiting insurers to agree a reinstatement to a damaged property, as was the factual situation in *Tonkin & Toureau* v *UK Insurance Ltd.*[128]

THE RELATIONSHIP BETWEEN THE FOS AND THE FSA

2.72 Part XVI FSMA provides for a statutory ombudsman scheme for financial services and sets out the framework for the scheme and the respective responsibilities of the FSA and FOS. In broad terms, the FSA is the regulator for financial services (but not for consumer credit[129]), and the FOS is an independent body set up to resolve disputes between those businesses and their customers. A Memorandum of Understanding exists between the FOS and the FSA[130] which confirms that both organisations are operationally independent,[131] but they need to cooperate. An example of cooperation is the format and content of the publication of complaints data from the respective organisations.[132] The FOS is accountable to the FSA in certain respects, although not in relation to individual complaint decisions, and the FSA is answerable to the Treasury and ultimately to Parliament.

2.73 Among other things, the FSA has certain financial responsibilities over the FOS and determines the scope of the FOS jurisdiction. It has to approve the FOS budget, make and approve rules about the scope of the FOS compulsory and voluntary jurisdictions, make rules about the funding of the compulsory jurisdiction, set the levy blocks and applicable tariffs and approve the FOS rules about case fees.

2.74 The FOS is responsible for operating its dispute resolution scheme, appointing the ombudsmen, making rules of procedure about dealing with complaints,[133] the award of costs and the levying of case fees and making arrangements for the voluntary jurisdiction. It must also recommend an annual budget for FSA approval and report to the FSA on the discharge of its functions.

2.75 There are circumstances where the FOS will call on the FSA to take regulatory action against, or at least investigate, a firm, and so will provide the FSA with further detailed and specific information about a complaint. These situations include where:

(1) the circumstances of the case call into question a firm's fitness and propriety, whether a person is "fit and proper" to carry out the relevant function or if a criminal offence or serious regulatory contravention has occurred;

(2) it appears appropriate for the FSA to consider using one or more of its regulatory tools;

(3) a firm has failed to comply with an award made by an ombudsman; or

(4) a firm has without reasonable excuse failed to comply with a requirement to provide information.

---

128. [2006] EWHC 1120 (TCC). There the FOS took over a year to reach the end of the adjudicator stage. The insured began litigation proceedings before the ombudsman became involved, so the FOS dismissed the complaint at that point. The court, rightly, did not make an interest award against the insurer in respect of this delay, which was caused by the insured insisting on bringing the complaint to the FOS, despite the insurer and the FOS warning that this would result in a delay in the insurer being able to deal with the claim.

129. See "OFT" below at paras. 2.79 *et seq.*

130. The current version can be found on the FOS website.

131. HHJ Davis QC confirmed the FOS independence from the FSA in *R (on the application of Heather Moor & Edgecomb Ltd)* v *FOS & Ross* [2009] EWHC 2701 (Admin).

132. *Cf, Ombudsman News* Oct/Nov 2008 and the FOS website.

133. FSMA 2000 Sched. 17, Part III.

2.76 The FSA tries to ensure that its rules or guidance are not inconsistent with the statutory objectives of the FOS, namely to resolve disputes quickly and with minimum formality, in a way that is fair and reasonable in all the circumstances. Sometimes the FOS will refer a matter to the FSA and ask whether it would like to consider it under the wider implications process, as it did in relation to payment protection insurance.[134] The FSA and FOS may also decide jointly that an issue raises wider implications. Such a referral would be based on whether it is a new issue, whether it affects a large number of consumers or firms, the financial integrity of a firm and/or the interpretation of an FSA rule or guidance or a common industry practice. The FSA may impose a regulatory solution, offer the FOS material for consideration, or it may decide that it does not need to be involved at all.

2.77 For instance, in the latter part of 2004, the FOS received a number of complaints about long-term care insurance, and raised the matter with the FSA under the wider implications process. The FSA decided that the mis-selling aspects of the problem were best dealt with by the FOS on a case by case basis, and that it would incorporate the FOS's findings into the FSA's normal supervisory work. It dealt with questions of whether the review clause in these types of contract was fair, by producing in May 2005 a Statement of Good Practice relating to the fairness of terms in consumer contracts with which it expects firms to comply. The FSA asked the FOS to report to it about the number and nature of the complaints received about these contracts and in relation to which firms, so that the FSA could take regulatory action against firms with poor standards of advice and complaints handling.

2.78 Another part of the wider implication process is where a firm, but not a consumer, requests that the matter be treated as a test case before the court under DISP 3.3.5R (see above).[135] If it does this, the entire case will be dealt with by the court, although any court decision on a test point will fall within the law which the FOS must take account of under DISP 3.6.4R.[136]

THE OFFICE OF FAIR TRADING ("OFT")[137]

2.79 The OFT is a non-ministerial government department. It was established by statute and is accountable to Parliament. It is the licensor and regulator for consumer credit, whilst the FSA is the regulator for other financial services. The Concordat between the OFT and the FSA sets out the division of responsibilities between them in relation to the Unfair Terms in Consumer Contracts Regulations 1999 ("UTCCR"). Both organisations consider the fairness of standard terms in financial services contracts, but the FSA considers those issued by FSA-authorised firms for FSA-regulated activities and the OFT considers all other financial services contracts. There is a Memorandum of Understanding between the OFT and the FOS.[138] The OFT joined the wider implications process in June 2007.[139]

---

134. See "Payment Protection Insurance" below at paras. 5.33 *et seq.*
135. FSA Policy Statement 05/10.
136. See also the collective court actions under ss. 18–25 Financial Services Act 2010 and consumer redress through the regulator under ss. 26–27, which Act received Royal Assent on 8 April 2010. See further the Memorandum submitted by the FOS to the Public Bill Committee (FS 02) 9 December 2009 on the effects of these sections, to be found at "House of Commons Public Bill Committee on the Financial Services Bill 2009/10—Associated memoranda" on www.parliament.uk.
137. *Cf* FOS website and www.fsa.gov.uk/pubs/other/oft_fsa_jap.pdf.
138. *Cf* www.financial-ombudsman.org.uk/about/other_bodies.html.
139. *Cf* www.wider-implications.info.

CHAPTER 3

AWARDS AND INTEREST

MONEY AWARDS

3.1 The aim of the ombudsman in making an award is to put the complainant back into the position he would have been in had it not been for the firm's actions. If it would be fair and reasonable, a determination may include a money award[1] to compensate for financial loss[2] or any other loss or damage of a specified kind,[3] including damages for distress or inconvenience, pain and suffering or damage to reputation, whether or not a court would award such or any compensation.[4]

LIMITS ON MONEY AWARDS

3.2 An ombudsman's award for financial loss is limited[5] to £100,000 (plus interest[6]), although the ombudsman can recommend an unenforceable, additional payment.[7] The FSA plans no change in the maximum figure at present,[8] but will review the position at regular intervals.

3.3 It was held in *Bunney* v *Burns Anderson plc*[9] that that part of an award which exceeds the FOS £100,000 limit is not enforceable, and that the firm is entitled to plead want of jurisdiction by way of defence to enforcement proceedings of any amount over £100,000, without seeking judicial review of the award itself. The court also said that the ombudsman did not have power to make a direction that would require a firm to make a payment that would exceed the statutory cap. If the cost of compliance with a direction was unknown at the time of the direction, it was subject to an implicit limitation that it would not be enforceable beyond the statutory cap, once reached.

3.4 Only a small percentage of FOS cases involve a loss greater than £100,000.[10] However, if the parties want a quick and relatively cheap dispute resolution, and they trust

---

1. S. 229(2)(a) FSMA.
2. S. 229(3)(a) FSMA.
3. S. 229(3)(b) FSMA.
4. DISP 3.7.2R.
5. S. 229(5) FSMA.
6. DISP 3.7.4R, 3.7.5G.
7. DISP 3.7.6G.
8. FSA/PN/138/2005 15 December 2005. In June 2006, the FSA confirmed that the £100,000 limit will be reviewed again in 2009. In 2010 it remained at £100,000.
9. [2007] EWHC 1240 (Ch).
10. FOS Annual Review 05/06 reports only 3% in that year.

that the FOS has enough technical and/or legal expertise to do the dispute justice, it might make commercial sense to put even a large claim before the FOS, perhaps agreeing in advance to be bound by a FOS recommendation above the £100,000 limit. Perhaps that explains Case Study 65/12,[11] relating to building repairs of at least £750,000 under a contractors' all-risks commercial insurance policy. The FOS felt that the claim was covered by the policy, and the insurer agreed to the FOS recommendation that it should pay the full amount due even if it came to more than the maximum award of £100,000. In Case Study 74/10,[12] the FOS contacted both parties before it had finished investigating the complaint and obtained confirmation from the insurer that it would pay any determination against it in full, even over the £100,000 limit. It is unlikely that an insurance company would renege on its agreement in these circumstances, but it would be optimum if such an agreement was recorded in writing and signed by the insurer.

INSURERS' LIABILITY IN LAW FOR DAMAGE CAUSED BY THEIR OWN BEHAVIOUR

3.5 Unlike the FOS, the law does not generally provide for damages caused by an insurer's own behaviour, for instance, in the late payment of an insurance claim, except to the extent that a court can make an award for interest following a judgment against an insurer from the date of the loss until payment. The court rate of interest awarded is usually 8% simple, although some commercial courts grant a more commercial rate. (In exceptional circumstances, the court can also make a costs order on an indemnity basis due to the conduct of the proceedings.) A court cannot make an award for damages for late payment of insurance monies, because there is a legal fiction that payment under an insurance policy is due the moment the insured event causes a loss, as the contract is considered to be an agreement by the insurer to prevent the harm from occurring, so that from the moment an insured event occurs, the insurer is in breach of contract. Damages are payable for a breach of contract, but in law there is no provision for damages for late payment of damages.

3.6 The leading case is *Sprung* v *Royal Insurance (UK) Ltd*,[13] where the result of the insurer delaying payment for four years or so whilst it investigated and then refused a claim following vandalism of Mr Sprung's factory, was that he went out of business. He could not afford to repair his factory himself, and he could not raise a loan, and he also lost the opportunity to sell his business. Yet the Court of Appeal found itself bound by precedent, and so could only give him an award of interest (simple) for the delay in payment, and not damages as well. The Law Commissions consider that this is unfair and have provisionally proposed changes which would result in damages being payable for late payment of a claim or if the insurer acts in bad faith, wrongly rejects a claim, or fails to respond to a claim.[14]

11. *Ombudsman News* Oct/Nov 2007.
12. *Ombudsman News* Dec 2008/Jan 2009.
13. [1997] CLC 70. *Sprung* applied *President of India* v *Lips Maritime Corporation* ("*The Lips*") [1988] AC 395 which related to demurrage under a charterparty. *Sprung* was followed in *Pride Valley Foods Ltd* v *Independent Insurance Co Ltd* [1999] Lloyd's Rep IR 120, *England* v *Guardian Insurance Ltd* [2000] Lloyd's Rep IR 404, *Normhurst Ltd* v *Dornoch Ltd* [2005] Lloyd's Rep IR 27 and *Tonkin* v *UK Insurance Ltd* [2006] EWHC 1120 (TCC) (*supra*). However *Sprung* has been criticised and the House of Lords in *Sempra Metals* v *Inland Revenue Commissioners* [2008] 1 AC 561, in the context of a tax overpayment to the Inland Revenue, cast doubt on the principle that damages (in the form of compound interest) is not payable at common law for late payment of a debt.
14. Law Commissions Issues Paper 6, "Damages for Late Payment and the Insurer's Duty of Good Faith", dated 24 March 2010.

3.7 Further, there seems to be no implied term that a claim will be paid within a reasonable time.[15] The Late Payment of Commercial Debts (Interest) Act 1998 which provides for interest to be payable outside of the court system where payments under a contract are unjustifiably withheld, probably does not apply to insurance contracts, as they are specifically excluded by the Directive[16] which underlies the Act. Following *Ventouris* v *Mountain ("The Italia Express") (No. 3)*,[17] there can be no damages for distress caused by maladministration of an insurance contract, because an insurance contract is not one which has as its specific objective the assured's peace of mind. Insurance policies only provide cover for such loss where the cover expressly extends to provision of peace of mind or freedom from distress of the insured.[18]

3.8 If insurers opt to reinstate, ancient case law has established that the insurance policy is treated as if it has always been a contract for reinstatement, and the legal fiction which results in there being no damages for late payment of damages would not apply. Insurers could therefore face liability in damages for distress or inconvenience, loss of profit or other consequential loss caused by failing to reinstate to a reasonable standard within a reasonable time. In *Axa Insurance UK* v *Cunningham Lindsey UK*,[19] the insurer sued its loss adjuster for professional negligence in the way that it had carried out the reinstatement of the insured's property. The insurer was trying to recover the amount it had paid its insured in a settlement, including £92,000 for distress and inconvenience. The judge found that although an award for distress and inconvenience was payable, this was too much, and should have been no more than £1,800 per person per year. He used as his guide the fact that the authorities for distress and inconvenience in the general law outside of breaches of insurance contracts, suggested a maximum of around £2,000 per person per year. For in the general law, distress and inconvenience is payable in two situations:

(1) There can be a relatively modest award for distress and inconvenience where a breach of contract has caused some physical inconvenience and discomfort as in *Watts* v *Morrow*.[20] There, £1,500 was awarded for the distress of a negligent residential purchase survey which resulted in the purchasers living with some physical inconvenience in their new home.

(2) Following *Farley* v *Skinner No. 2*,[21] damages for distress and inconvenience may be awarded if a major or important object of the contract is to give pleasure, relaxation or peace of mind. In that case the surveyor was particularly instructed by a potential house purchaser to survey the property with a view as to whether it would be disturbed by aircraft noise from the nearby airport. The claimant was in principle entitled to recover non-pecuniary damages for distress and inconvenience from that surveyor for his negligent failure to discover that the property was so affected.

3.9 In the hopefully rare instance where the insurer refuses or delays payment of a claim in bad faith, the law does not offer a satisfactory solution. The only remedy for a breach of

---

15. *Insurance Corporation of the Channel Islands Ltd* v *McHugh* [1997] LRLR 94 and *Tonkin* v *UK Insurance Ltd* (*supra*).
16. Directive 2000/35/EC on combating late payment in commercial transactions.
17. [1992] 2 Lloyd's Rep 281.
18. *Cf, England* v *Guardian Insurance Ltd* [1999] 2 All ER (Comm) 481 where a consumer's home insurance was not a contract for the purpose of the assured's peace of mind.
19. [2007] EWHC 3023 (TCC).
20. [1991] 1 WLR 1421.
21. [2001] UKHL 49.

good faith is avoidance under section 17 MIA, but this is unsatisfactory for an insured. Following *Banque Financiere* v *Westgate Insurance Co*,[22] breach of the duty of good faith does not give rise to damages. The Law Commissions would like to change the remedies available for a breach of the duty of good faith by an insurer.[23] The FOS will award damages if it is fair and reasonable to do so in the circumstances, whatever the position in law.

FOS AWARDS FOR DISTRESS AND INCONVENIENCE AND MALADMINISTRATION

In general

3.10 The above contrasts strongly with the ombudsman's power to make an award for distress or inconvenience caused by maladministration in the handling of a claim, whether through bad faith or not, and even outside of the situation of an inadequate reinstatement. It also sits against a background of many complaints reaching the FOS which include an element of claim maladministration.[24] According to the Law Commissions,[25] the FOS estimates that around one in 10 complaints contains a claim for a loss that would not have arisen had an insurer paid the claim within a reasonable time. The FOS deals with these in three ways, depending on the circumstances, by an award for distress and inconvenience, interest[26] or occasionally damages to compensate for financial loss.[27] The FOS may make such an award even if the complainant has not requested it or where the complaint is rejected.[28]

FOS distress and inconvenience for maladministration

3.11 The ombudsman will consider that distress will have been suffered if there has been embarrassment, anxiety, disappointment or loss of expectation. Inconvenience will include where the customer has expended time and/or effort. To merit an award, the distress and the inconvenience suffered must be as a result of a firm's conduct.

3.12 Maladministration or bad claims' handling includes the following:

(1) extensive delays;
(2) clerical or procedural errors;
(3) rudeness;
(4) incorrect or inadequate explanations;
(5) failure to respond to the customer's requests;
(6) requiring a customer to take additional and unnecessary steps to pursue a complaint;

22. [1991] 2 AC 249.
23. Issues Paper 6. "Damages for Late Payment and the Insurer's Duty of Good Faith", dated 24 March 2010, Part 4.
24. FOS Annual Review 2009/10 reports that an award for distress and inconvenience is made in 24% of cases upheld, which amounted to 18,511 cases in that year, usually between £150 and £500, and that the figures were similar in 2008/9.
25. Issues Paper 6. "Damages for Late Payment and the Insurer's Duty of Good Faith", dated 24 March 2010, at para. 6.1.
26. See below at para. 3.28.
27. See below at para. 3.25.
28. Briefing Note from the FOS November 2001; FOS Technical Note on Distress and Inconvenience (updated 13/11/09).

(7) refusing to settle a case at an early stage, despite knowing that the FOS has previously upheld similar complaints. This implies that the FOS expects insurers to know of its previous decisions and to keep up to date with its approach. So in Case Study 73/8[29] the FOS made the relatively large award of £750 when an insurer ignored the causation evidence of an expert engaged by the insured, which showed that the loss was covered under the policy in accordance with the FOS test for flood. And in Case Study 75/10,[30] insurers had to pay a modest amount for distress and inconvenience when they unreasonably required the insured to replace antique jewellery with modern pieces, and tried to deduct an amount from the alternative cash settlement to reflect the discounted price that the insurer could obtain if the insured had agreed to buy replacements at particular stores. All of this contravened the FOS's well-established views on what was reasonable in these circumstances and had been featured in *Ombudsman News* seven years earlier in October 2001; or

(8) refusing to accept that the repair or reinstatement provided is inadequate. In Case Study 79/7,[31] the insurer had been wrongly reluctant to accept that the work of its approved car repairer was unsatisfactory, or to approve the level of further repairs that were necessary, and had offered only £100 by way of compensation instead. The FOS awarded the insured £200 for distress and inconvenience in addition to the full repairs that she had requested.

3.13 Bad handling will not include:

(1) general distress which is inevitable, such as when dealing with a claim after injury or death;

(2) mere trivial annoyance, such as if a name is spelt incorrectly or the telephone line is sometimes busy;

(3) the insurer doing everything it should do, but the complainant still being inconvenienced. For instance, in Case Study 1/15,[32] no compensation was payable where an insurer kept trying to get a video repaired, but it still kept malfunctioning. Although the complainant was put to considerable inconvenience in the process, the insurer had provided a satisfactory standard of service because it had done all it could do. Similarly, in Case Study 68/9,[33] no compensation was payable for the delay caused when the insurer appointed a firm of engineers to inspect and report on flood damage. The insurer was entitled to do this due to the technically complex nature of the problem, and it had acted promptly both in appointing the engineers and in considering the claim once the report was ready.

The amount of a FOS award for distress and inconvenience

3.14 In considering the amount to award, the FOS will look at the severity of the distress or inconvenience caused by the firm's actions, the period of the problem, the nature of the inadequacy, whether any of it was caused by the customer's own actions and delays and, to a limited extent, the customer's own assessment of the distress or inconvenience suffered.

---

29. *Ombudsman News* Oct/Nov 2008.
30. *Ombudsman News* Jan/February 2009. See also below "Replacement" at para. 10.12.
31. *Ombudsman News* Sept/Oct 2009.
32. *Ombudsman News* Jan 2001.
33. *Ombudsman News* Mar/Apr 2008.

Most of the ombudsman awards in this category will be modest, usually not more than a few hundred pounds, as the award is meant to be compensatory, rather than penal. More recent examples show that the amounts awarded are not really changing dramatically over the years.

3.15 The FOS has produced a Technical Note on the topic headed "Compensation for distress, inconvenience or other non-financial loss" which makes a list of what sort of complaint will attract which level of award for distress and inconvenience[34]: awards can be modest (less than £300); significant (£300 to £999); or exceptional (£1,000 or more). However, this list does not give much detail and does not date the complaints. The examples which are relevant to insurance disputes are set out here, supplemented where marked by examples recently provided to the Law Commissions, and followed by more detailed examples from *Ombudsman News*.

Awards of modest compensation (less than £300)

3.16 The FOS has made modest awards in the following circumstances:

(1) Minor inconvenience caused by the financial business not getting the consumer's address right, despite a couple of requests, for two months.

(2) Minor administrative error by the financial business which caused the consumer to correspond/phone a few times before the problem was sorted out.

(3) Minor, but identifiable, delay by the financial business in paying out under a policy claim.

(4) Administrative error by the financial business which caused the consumer to correspond/phone a significant number of times before the problem was sorted out.

(5) The financial business lengthened by three weeks the time the consumer was unable to return home from alternative accommodation paid for by the financial business, following damage which had made the consumer's home uninhabitable.[35]

(6) Two-month delay by the financial business in providing the surrender proceeds of a policy.

(7) The financial business caused the consumer to be without transport for two weeks, when under the terms of the insurance it should have provided an alternative vehicle whilst the consumer's car was off the road as a result of an accident. (Travel costs incurred would be considered separately.)

(8) Failure by the financial business to provide information to the consumer, which it always knew it held, to enable him to sort the matter out with a third party. The issue remained outstanding for three months longer than necessary.

(9) Disappointment at being told that policy surrender proceeds were to be materially less than previously led to believe by the financial business.

(10) Material distress arising from the financial business's continued failure to deal with an apparently eligible and potentially meritorious complaint.

(11) Material delay arising from the financial business's failure to follow a settled FSA or ombudsman service approach, when it had every reason to believe it would be held liable.

34. Last updated on 13/11/09, and it can be found on the FOS website.
35. A similar example can be found in *Ombudsman News* 2008, and may be the same one.

(12) In Case Study 83/7,[36] a boiler broke down just before Christmas and then again on Christmas day. Although the insurer's engineer looked at the boiler two days later, he was unable to obtain a part due to closures over the holiday period. The insured found an independent contractor who had the part and fitted it, and the insurer agreed to reimburse the costs of this. The FOS ordered insurers to pay £250 in compensation for distress and inconvenience caused to the insured and the family staying with him (including young children and an elderly father), plus the full cost of hiring temporary heaters. The sum of £120 offered for distress and inconvenience was inadequate. It was noted that under the terms of the policy, the insured could have moved to and claimed for alternative accommodation.

(13) In Case Study 83/10,[37] the insurer's offer of £150 was enough for the distress and inconvenience of the insured waiting nearly two weeks before the insurer confirmed that it would not be repairing his boiler, as it was not economical to do so. He had been told that someone would call him back the same day.

Awards of significant compensation (£300–£999)

3.17 The FOS has made significant awards in the following circumstances:

(1) The financial business (or contractors it appointed) caused the consumer personally to carry out significant cleaning or decoration following repairs by the appointed contractors.

(2) Following the death of the consumer's husband, the financial business repeatedly wrote to her husband—rather than to her—about the insurance claim.[38]

(3) Material delay arising from the financial business's failure to follow settled FSA or FOS approach when it had every reason to believe it would be held liable, and every reason to know that the prospective policy shortfall would be distressing to the consumer.

(4) The financial business failed to arrange and pay for alternative accommodation for the consumer and his young children following insured damage, causing them to remain in their property for a month without essential facilities.

(5) Excessive intransigence by the financial business right from the start—i.e. failure to accept responsibility for its mistakes, frustrating the complaint process, and fighting the case through every stage in the FOS, despite the FOS pointing out at an early stage that the business was failing to follow a settled and published FSA or FOS approach.

(6) A woman had to pay for the cost of emergency surgery while abroad where her condition was life-threatening and the insurer had failed to give approval for the treatment within a reasonable time. Eventually the insurer reimbursed her.[39]

(7) The FOS considered that where a man had become seriously ill whilst on holiday and his treating physician had told the insurer that he needed to be repatriated urgently, it was unreasonable for the insurer to insist that a formal medical report would have to be produced in line with the policy wording before it would pay for

---

36. *Ombudsman News* Feb/Mar 2010.
37. *Ombudsman News* Feb/Mar 2010.
38. A similar example was given in *Ombudsman News* Aug 2008, and may actually be the same one.
39. This example is taken from examples provided to the Law Commissions and referred to in Issues Paper 6, "Damages for Late Payment and the Insurer's Duty of Good Faith", dated 24 March 2010, at para. 6.5.

repatriation. The man paid for the flights back himself and the FOS ordered the insurer to reimburse this, as well as pay for distress and inconvenience.[40]

(8) In Case Study 83/6,[41] the FOS awarded £350 for the delays in dealing with the repair of a boiler, resulting in the insured and her elderly mother suffering periods without any heating or hot water. In particular, once the problem had finally been diagnosed, it took the insurer's engineer over one week to come and fit a new valve. The insurer had offered £75, which was judged to be inadequate in the circumstances.

(9) The elderly widow in Case Study 83/9[42] was awarded £450 for distress and inconvenience caused by the insurer's first plumber. He said she had to replace the toilet (an uninsured expenditure which she told him she could not afford), before he could fix the leaking pipe. He did not mention any urgency. A few weeks later, she saw further signs of a leak, the same repairer attended and he flushed the toilet, even though she had told him not to, and it overflowed. He did not clear up the mess or repair the leak. The insured had to move in temporarily for a few days with a neighbour as the smell was so bad. Two days after she contacted the insurer again, they sent out a different contractor who repaired the leak and told her that the toilet had not needed replacing.

Awards of exceptional compensation (£1,000 or more)

3.18 The FOS has made exceptional awards in the following circumstances:

(1) The financial business wrongly disclosed the consumer's address to her violent estranged partner although it knew the circumstances, and about his violence. The partner subsequently broke into her home and assaulted her, causing her to spend several days in hospital.

(2) Repair work by the financial business (or its appointed contractor) exposed the consumer and his family to health risks (e.g. from asbestos).

(3) An elderly couple whose home had suffered from subsidence had to wait five years for their home to be repaired without alternative accommodation being provided.[43]

(4) In Case Study 18/18,[44] the FOS awarded £1,000 for the distress and inconvenience of living with a cesspit full of water, and the insurer refusing cover meant months of living without proper sanitary conditions.

(5) In Case Study 68/8,[45] the FOS awarded £1,000 for a couple who had to live in alternative accommodation for a further three months (after an initial nine months) whilst snagging was undertaken when insurers were repairing subsidence damage to their flat. This may be a surprisingly large award when compared to the examples above, and may have subconsciously been influenced by the fact that the insured were making a substantial claim for floor repairs which failed when they were given this award instead.

---

40. *Ibid* at para. 6.5.
41. *Ombudsman News* Feb/Mar 2010.
42. *Ombudsman News* Feb/Mar 2010.
43. *Ibid* at para. 6.5.
44. *Ombudsman News* July 2002.
45. *Ombudsman News* Mar/Apr 2008.

AWARDS FOR PAIN AND SUFFERING

3.19 Pain and suffering might arise in cases involving delays in arranging or paying for medical treatment. The FOS considers pain and suffering to be a more extreme form of distress and inconvenience and so will allocate to it a greater award. The law may allow compensation for pain, suffering and loss of amenity in these circumstances and does not treat it as an extension of an award for distress and inconvenience. The FOS provided an example to the Law Commissions where an ombudsman had awarded £2,500 for distress and inconvenience due to poor handling which caused the insured serious illness.[46]

DAMAGE TO REPUTATION

3.20 Damage to reputation may occur if a firm discloses to a third party incorrect information (e.g. relating to credit-worthiness) or private information (e.g. medical records). The level of any award, if any, will be based on how widely the information had been disseminated, its nature, its impact and the customer's previous reputation. It may be adequate for the insurer simply to correct the records in question. In Case Study 4/17,[47] one insurer passed on information about the insured's claim to another insurer without authorisation, and offered to pay £100 by way of compensation for distress and inconvenience. The FOS felt that this was enough, as there was no evidence that the disclosure had caused any loss or influenced the handling of the claim.

COMPLAINANT'S COSTS

3.21 The ombudsman has the power to award the complainant his administrative costs of complaining to the firm or to the FOS,[48] but does not usually exercise this power. If he did, the award would be extremely modest, and was £25 in Case Study 1/14.[49] The FOS may also make an allowance for the time the consumer needs to spend to put things right (excluding his time in dealing with the FOS), at a modest rate (around £50 to £100 a day, and not more than £10 per hour). Although a higher amount may be appropriate for business complaints, this would rarely be as much as the business's charge-out rate. However, there has been no insurance example in *Ombudsman News* where such an allowance has been made.

3.22 The FOS will not award the fees of a claims management company or solicitor,[50] because the ethos of the FOS, and indeed most other ombudsman organisations around the world, is that these services are not necessary for the fair and reasonable resolution of the complaint.[51] This is supported by the FOS statistics,[52] which show that there is no difference in outcome between complaints brought to it by claims management companies, and complaints brought directly by consumers. Walter Merricks, former Chief Ombudsman, commented[53] on the detrimental effect that claims management companies have had on the

---

46. *Ibid* at para. 6.20.
47. *Ombudsman News* Apr 2001.
48. DISP 3.7.9R.
49. *Ombudsman News* Jan 2001.
50. In Case Study 13/14 in *Ombudsman News* Jan 2002, the complainant was not awarded any of the legal fees she claimed: she did not need legal advice to be able to answer the insurer's arguments.
51. DISP 3.7.10G.
52. *Ombudsman News* July 2005.
53. Speech given on 4/10/05.

system, saying that there has been an increase in judicial review challenges made where increased claims management company involvement has made disputes more legalistic and hard fought, which challenges the level of informality in sorting out complaints that the FOS seeks to provide. The FOS regards the facts more than the presentation of the argument, and prefers to hear from consumers in their own words. Despite this, there is an increase in the number of claims management companies being instructed to bring a case on behalf of a consumer[54] and a small number of consumers will bring their complaints through solicitors and other fee-earning professionals.[55]

3.23 The FOS may order reimbursement of the costs of an expert which the complainant had to instruct in order to prove his point.[56] For instance, in Case Study 28/9,[57] the insured had to consult an independent engineer before the insurance company would accept that the car repairs it had approved were not satisfactory, and his fees were recoverable.

OTHER AWARDS/DIRECTIONS

3.24 The ombudsman can make other non-monetary awards or directions as appropriate, whether or not a court can,[58] such as ordering that an apology be made or flowers be sent. In Case Study 1/16,[59] there had been a series of oversights and mistakes which meant that a body had not been embalmed, so was too decomposed for viewing on arrival back in the UK. The complainant did not want a financial award to compensate for this. The insurer was asked to apologise, donate to the British Heart Foundation and set up a system so that the problem could not recur.

3.25 Sometimes the FOS will consider an award of compensation for further financial losses including business interruption and the cost the insured has incurred in having to borrow money at high rates. If these losses have been caused by the insurer's actions or inactions, for instance through delayed payment or non-payment, poor claims handling or poor repair, and the complainant can prove actual loss, an award may be made. The FOS gave two examples to the Law Commissions.[60] The first was where the FOS had awarded the maximum that it was authorised to award, £100,000, for the interruption of an insured's business, and recommended that the insurer should volunteer an additional amount. The second example was hypothetical and was that the FOS might require the insurer to pay the insured's additional costs, such as high credit card charges, where the insurer had failed to pay within a reasonable time the emergency medical costs incurred abroad, so the insured had been forced to pay them using his own credit card. The two bases on which these awards for financial loss are made by the FOS, are that insurers should pay for further losses flowing from a failure to pay a claim within a reasonable time or from failure to carry out repairs or

---

54. The FOS Annual Review 2009/10 noted that claims management companies brought 28% of all cases on behalf of consumers, an increase from 26% the year before, and two-thirds of them related to payment protection insurance claims.

55. The FOS Annual Review 2009/10 noted that 3.5% of all new claims were brought through professionals including lawyers and accountants, whilst only 2% were brought through free consumer advice agencies such as Trading Standards or Citizens Advice.

56. See also "Expert evidence" below at paras. 4.17 *et seq.*

57. *Ombudsman News* May 2003.

58. S. 229(2)(b) FSMA.

59. *Ombudsman News* Jan 2001.

60. *Cf*, Issues Paper 6 "Damages for Late Payment and the Insurer's Duty of Good Faith", dated 24 March 2010, at paras. 6.8 to 6.11.

reinstatement expeditiously and to a reasonable standard. Although the FOS requires insureds to mitigate such further financial loss as far as they can, it will not require them to mitigate when they cannot do so due to lack of resources, such as in the *Sprung*[61] situation.[62]

3.26 Although general contract law would only require compensation for loss foreseeable at the time the contract was made, the FOS has indicated to the Law Commissions[63] that in appropriate circumstances it would be prepared to compensate consumers for additional loss which was not foreseeable at the time of inception.

THE EFFECT OF AN EXCLUSION FOR CONSEQUENTIAL LOSSES AND POLICY LIMITS

3.27 If the insurer's handling of the matter is at fault, the FOS may give an award for consequential loss in spite of a clear policy exclusion. The FOS gave an example to the Law Commissions which illustrated that it would be prepared to award compensation for loss of profit, loss of rental income or loss of earnings if there was clear proof of such loss, even in the face of clear policy wording excluding consequential loss.[64] In another example, it was prepared to award £2,500 for distress and inconvenience due to poor handling which caused the insured serious illness, even though the policy excluded " . . . any cost or expense greater than that necessary to effect a workmanlike repair of the relevant defect or major damage . . . ".[65] Further, if alternative accommodation policy limits are exceeded, the FOS has said that it would not allow the insurer to cease paying if the excessive cost was due to the insurer's own delay.[66]

INTEREST

3.28 Interest may be awarded on a money award,[67] and will usually be the option that the FOS takes where a claim has been wrongly refused (rather than an award for distress and inconvenience). An award of interest is to compensate the consumer for being out of funds. For insurance complaints, the FOS usually applies a rate of 8% per year simple, in line with the rate used in the County Court.[68] For maladministration awards, this will be calculated from when the FOS considers that the firm's actions caused the problem until the date when payment is made. For awards relating to the proceeds of a policy, interest will be calculated from the date of the insured loss until payment. Occasionally it may award a different rate where this would more accurately reflect the consumer's loss, such as where the insurance was partly an investment.[69]

---

61. See above.
62. Note *Lagden* v *O'Connor* [2004] 1 AC 1067 where the road accident victim could recover from the wrongdoer in tort the cost of hiring a replacement vehicle as the victim was impecunious and unable to mitigate his loss.
63. This example is taken from examples provided to the Law Commissions and referred to in Issues Paper 6, "Damages for Late Payment and the Insurer's Duty of Good Faith", dated 24 March 2010, at paras. 6.12–6.16.
64. *Ibid* at paras. 6.18–6.20.
65. *Ibid* at para. 6.20.
66. *Ibid* at para. 6.21.
67. S. 229(8)(a) FSMA and DISP 3.7.8R.
68. Under s. 69 County Courts Act 1984.
69. Other rates may be used in some bad investment advice cases.

ENFORCEABILITY OF AWARDS

3.29 Firms are required to pay awards or comply with directions promptly,[70] and they usually do so. Courts will enforce money awards and interest.[71] Directions are enforceable by injunction.[72] If a complainant has any difficulty obtaining compliance, he should revert to the FOS in the first instance, as the FOS may be able to assist. The delay can be because the firm is trying to calculate the amount to be paid, based on a formula provided by the ombudsman and the FOS may have experts who can help. However, if the non-payment is due to lack of funds, the matter may need to be referred to the Financial Services Compensation Scheme.

THE FINANCIAL SERVICES COMPENSATION SCHEME ("FSCS")

3.30 If a firm goes into liquidation while the FOS is considering a complaint against it, the FOS will suspend its investigation, refer the case to the FSCS and inform the complainant. The FSCS will then contact the complainant to explain how it can help. If a firm goes into liquidation after an award has been made against it, the FSCS will step in to pay a proportion of the award.[73] However, the FSCS can only compensate for actual financial loss, not for distress or inconvenience.

IS COMPENSATION TAXABLE?

3.31 That part of an award which relates to the compensation for being deprived of money, usually the interest part, may be subject to income tax.[74] Insurers are meant to deduct this from source at the basic rate before the payment is made, and pass it on to the Inland Revenue. Any consumer who is not liable to income tax at the basic rate can reclaim it in the usual way from the Inland Revenue. Insurers can provide a certificate of tax deduction, although the complainant may have to request one if this is not done automatically.

---

70. DISP 1.4.4R.
71. S. 229(8)(b) and Part III Sched. 17 s.16 FSMA.
72. S. 229(9) FSMA.
73. Claims in respect of compulsory insurances are met in full; claims in respect of non-compulsory insurances are paid in full for the first £2,000, but are limited to 90% for any loss above this. See www.fscs.org.uk.
74. FOS website for Technical Briefing Note "Is Compensation taxable?"

CHAPTER 4

THE FOS APPROACH TO EVIDENCE

REQUIREMENT TO PROVIDE INFORMATION

4.1 The FOS may require a party to provide information and documents within a specified, reasonable period, manner and form.[1] Failure to comply without reasonable excuse can result in a court finding a party in contempt.[2] However, in practice, such a failure is more likely to result in the FOS finding against the party who does not provide the information, and there are no reported cases which resulted in contempt.

ADMISSIBILITY

4.2 The courts have developed systems for dealing with admissibility questions fairly and reasonably, and may impose costs sanctions on those who do not comply with the provisions of the Human Rights Act 1998 in obtaining evidence. For instance, in the personal injury case of *Jean F Jones* v *University of Warwick*,[3] the defendant's insurer entered the claimant's home by posing as a market researcher. The claimant was filmed with a hidden camera. The evidence was admitted, so that the claimant could not make an exaggerated claim, but the defendant was "punished" for obtaining the evidence in this underhand way by having to pay the costs of the admissibility question through to the Court of Appeal, even though it had won the admissibility point.

4.3 The FOS has no power to deal with admissibility in the same way and the FOS rules on this point are largely undeveloped, or if they have been developed, they are not publicly available. There is no provision in DISP which ensures that the person who decides the case has not seen evidence which is not admitted. Instead, the FOS is given a wide discretion to decide whether to admit evidence, and this decision may differ from a court's.[4]

STANDARD OF RECORD-KEEPING

4.4 The FOS will expect a higher standard of record-keeping from firms than from consumers. Firms should be able to produce records specific to the complainant as well as standard documents and marketing material. If a specific letter is unavailable, the FOS may accept a copy of the relevant standard letter with a computer record showing that it was actually

---

1. S. 231 FSMA and DISP 3.5.8R and 3.5.13R.
2. S. 232 FSMA.
3. [2003] EWCA Civ 151.
4. DISP 3.5.9R.

generated. In Case Study 13/7,[5] the complaint was upheld because the insurer could not produce the signed proposal, so could not prove its allegation of non-disclosure. This reflects the position at law, which requires the insured to prove his loss and the insurer to prove that the loss is not covered.[6]

4.5 However, the FOS stresses that a firm without documentation will not automatically lose the case.[7] The FOS will look at all available evidence to see what is most likely to have happened. Its approach is sensible, much as a court's. It will not allow a firm to put an insured to onerous levels of proof of loss, so in Case Study 69/1,[8] the request for original damp-proofing documentation, even if that had been a requirement of the policy, was too onerous when copies were available and there was no question of the claimant's entitlement to policy benefits.

REPLYING TO REQUESTS FOR INFORMATION

4.6 The FOS may fix and extend time limits for evidence gathering[9] depending on what the party is required to do, and expects firms to reply promptly. More recently, the FOS is imposing a 14-day time limit for both firms and complainants responding to its requests for information.[10] The aim is to speed up the complaints process. The FOS presumes that most of the information that it asks for will already be to hand as a result of the final response letter that the firm will have already provided to the complainant. A party who cannot comply with this or any time limit should notify the FOS immediately that it realises. Although an adjudicator will consider requests for more time than the 14 days sympathetically, a request will not automatically be granted, and he cannot amend a time limit set by an ombudsman. A firm's undue delays may mean that the FOS will make a decision without the additional information and if the delay causes distress or inconvenience, the FOS may award the consumer compensation, whether or not the rest of the complaint is upheld.[11] If the complainant fails to comply with a time limit, the FOS may proceed to the next stage of the process or dismiss the complaint.[12]

CONFIDENTIALITY

4.7 The FOS process is private. Any information published will hide the true identity of the parties. In contrast, the court process is public. Both systems have their respective merits, but the difference may influence an insured's choice of forum.

4.8 However, FOS confidentiality is limited. The FOS may need to consult and pass on details to any relevant third party who would be able to illuminate matters. It may pass information about firms to the FSA or any other regulatory or government bodies.[13] It will

---

5. *Ombudsman News* Jan 2002.
6. *Cf, Munro, Brice & Co v War Risks Association Ltd* [1918] 2 KB 78, where the insurer had to prove that the "loss by enemy action" exclusion applied.
7. *Ombudsman News* July 2006.
8. *Ombudsman News* Apr/May 2008.
9. DISP 3.5.13R.
10. *Cf, Ombudsman News* Apr/May 2010.
11. DISP 3.5.14R.
12. DISP 3.5.15R.
13. DISP 3.8.3R.

also disclose to the other party anything it receives about the complaint, unless it is asked to keep the information confidential and it considers that it should. It might keep a document confidential, for example, if there is a duty of confidentiality to a third party or the information relates to security precautions or is commercially sensitive. The FOS may decide to release to the other party an edited version or a summary or description of the document in question.[14] But it will bear in mind that its statutory right to demand information overrides a party's duty of confidentiality to any third party.

4.9 In Case Study 47/7,[15] legal expenses insurers settled a case before it got to an employment tribunal, although the insured did not want them to do this as she thought she would have achieved a better result at the tribunal. The FOS found that the insurers had acted reasonably in relying on the solicitors' advice in doing this, but kept from her the solicitors' assessment which influenced their advice, which was that she would have made a poor witness.

4.10 If a firm must keep information from the insured as a result of a report under the Proceeds of Crime Act 2002 (because money laundering is suspected), the FOS has a system set up to deal with this situation, and the FOS legal department should be contacted.

WRITTEN STATEMENTS BY INSURERS' EMPLOYEES

4.11 The FOS may ask the insurer to arrange for a signed statement to be taken from employees or ex-employees and the insurer must make reasonable efforts to comply. The statement should be in the employee's own words and should distinguish between what would usually have been done and what that employee remembers doing in the particular instance. If an important witness is unwilling to provide a statement, the FOS may dismiss the case on the grounds that a court may be the more suitable forum, because only a court can force a witness to give evidence.

RECORDINGS

4.12 The FOS regards the recording of critical telephone calls as good industry practice and expects to be able to resolve disputes about what was said on the telephone by referring to these. FOS case studies quite often refer to recorded telephone conversations and it seems that insurers and other financial institutions do now routinely record calls. Without such recordings, the FOS will require the firm to set out why, on the balance of probabilities, its version of events should be accepted, not the insured's. If a firm cannot show this, the FOS may give the insured the benefit of any doubt and/or conclude that there has been a genuine misunderstanding, in which case, the FOS will try to place the parties in the position they would have been in had the misunderstanding not occurred. So if a request for information or the response was uncertain, the FOS may review the claim as though the insured had given the correct information.

4.13 In Case Study 18/1,[16] the insurer alleged non-disclosure of seven previous claims, but the insured said that he was only asked about the last claim, which he disclosed. There

---

14. DISP 3.5.9R, 3.5.10G, 3.8.2B R.
15. *Ombudsman News* July 2005.
16. *Ombudsman News* July 2002.

was no tape recording of the relevant telephone conversation, so the insurer could not establish that it had asked him clear questions about the previous claims. The FOS found that the insurer's note of a subsequent telephone conversation, which said that the insured had denied making any previous claims, did not show what had happened at the sales point. The complaint was upheld. To a cynical insurer, it may be surprising that the insured was given the benefit of the doubt. However, this is really no more than a statement of the common law that the burden is on insurers to prove a non-disclosure.

4.14 Evidence of a telephone conversation taped by a consumer without the insurer's consent might not be admitted in court, but might by the FOS. In making its decision, the FOS would consider its relevance, how it was obtained, whether it breached a party's rights of privacy, whether participants were misled into saying something they would not otherwise have said and what was the other party's reaction to the evidence.

4.15 Similar considerations apply to video recorded evidence.[17] This is most often taken to assess an insured's medical symptoms. In Case Study 40/4,[18] the FOS told the insurer to show a video of the complainant to her doctors, who said she moved differently on the video to how she had moved in their consultations. This changed their conclusions as to what occupations she could undertake, and her complaint was rejected.

WRITTEN VERSUS ORAL EVIDENCE

4.16 Most of the evidence which the FOS considers is in written form. Although it can hear oral evidence, hearings are rare.[19] However, the FOS will speak by telephone or in person to the parties to try to clarify and resolve issues. The FOS cannot cross-examine witnesses, so if this would be necessary, perhaps to determine which of two parties is telling the truth, it will decline jurisdiction and suggest the insured takes the matter to court, as it did in Case Study 48/7[20] where fraud was alleged.

EXPERT EVIDENCE

4.17 The FOS will consider all expert evidence provided, although it would only be likely to award the complainant's costs in relation to expert fees if the loss could not have been proved otherwise.[21] However, insurers ignore an expert report provided by their insured at their peril and at risk of an award of distress and inconvenience being made against them. In Case Study 28/9,[22] the FOS made such an award, plus engineer's fees and interest, where the complainant had to instruct an engineer to prove that insurer-approved car repairs were not satisfactory. In Case Study 73/8[23] the FOS upheld the complaint and awarded the insured £750 for distress and inconvenience where insurers had with great delay continued to refuse the claim, even after receiving her expert's report as to cause of loss.

---

17. See also above "Admissibility" at paras. 4.2 *et seq* and below, "Assessing conflicting medical evidence" at para. 4.23(9).
18. *Ombudsman News* Sept/Oct 2004.
19. See above "Oral hearings" at paras. 2.42 *et seq.*
20. *Ombudsman News* Aug 2005.
21. See also "Complainant's costs" above at para. 3.23.
22. *Ombudsman News* May 2003.
23. *Ombudsman News* Oct/Nov 2008.

4.18 The FOS has a staff with varied backgrounds and expertise, and also a specialist medical insurance team. However, occasionally, as in Case Study 13/13,[24] it will not have sufficient expertise to determine a matter, and it will appoint an independent expert to report directly to it and to conduct either a paper review or an examination of the subject matter of the dispute.

4.19 The FOS takes more of an inquisitorial role than a court would, and will therefore review and question an expert's report, rather than simply accept its findings, adopting the causation test of what was the position "more likely than not". In Case Study 65/7,[25] its investigations directly contradicted the conclusions of the insurer's marine surveyor. The FOS had access in that case not only to the expert's report, but also to his subsequent correspondence with the insurer. In Case Study 79/6,[26] the FOS assessment of the insurer's independent engineer's report was that the car damage was more likely than not as a result of the accident, rather then mere wear and tear which the insurers claimed the report concluded. However, in Case Studies 79/8 and 79/9,[27] the FOS did not find that there was evidence to support the claims that certain additional car repairs were necessary as a result of the accidents in question, so rejected the complaints. The insured in Case Study 79/8 had refused to obtain a report from her own garage which she claimed had carried out the further work for her and this did not assist her position.

4.20 It may be sensible for the parties to agree to use an independent expert and accept his conclusions, with insurers bearing the costs. FOS adjudicators may make such a suggestion in any case. Insurers had offered this, and the adjudicator had concluded this was the best way to resolve the case of *Tonkin* v *UK Insurance Ltd*[28] before it went to court.

ASSESSING CONFLICTING MEDICAL EVIDENCE

4.21 The FOS specialist medical team, whilst being unable to diagnose a condition from assessing the medical evidence, will consider it to form a view about the insured's state of health and ability to work, and how these relate to the policy coverage. In Case Study 1/18,[29] the medical evidence was that 3% vision remained in the eye in question, so the insurer would not pay for "loss of sight" under a travel policy, even though the insured was blind in that eye for all practical purposes. The FOS found that this constituted loss of sight for the purpose of the policy. In Case Study 80/2,[30] the FOS concluded from its own assessment of the medical evidence that the insured's condition no longer fell within the policy's definition of incapacity for employment.

4.22 The FOS expects insurers to investigate cases thoroughly and to obtain any necessary medical reports before the complaint gets to the FOS. Occasionally it will still need to instruct its own medical expert as it did in Case Study 24/2,[31] in relation to what sort of work the insured was now capable of doing. The insured was awarded reduced, rather than no

---

24. *Ombudsman News* Jan 2002—the independent expert supported the insured's engineer; the cracks which appeared in the swimming pool were caused by an insured loss.
25. *Ombudsman News* Oct/Nov 2007.
26. *Ombudsman News* Sept/Oct 2009.
27. *Ombudsman News* Sept/Oct 2009.
28. [2006] EWHC 1120 (TCC).
29. *Ombudsman News* Jan 2001.
30. *Ombudsman News* Oct/Nov 2009.
31. *Ombudsman News* Jan 2003.

benefits as a result. And in Case Study 13/4,[32] the FOS expert report concluded that even though the insured was physically able to return to work, as it was such a stressful job, there was a very real risk of his heart problem returning. The FOS considered that this was a foreseeable result of returning to work, so he was not fit to do so and insurers should pay him the benefit under the policy plus interest on the back payments.

4.23 Where there is conflicting evidence, but no FOS-appointed expert, the FOS will weight different medical opinions as follows:

(1) A relevant specialist consultant commenting within his speciality will be preferred to a GP.

(2) A doctor involved with the insured for a period of time, trumps one who has seen him once or twice.

(3) A report based on a recent physical examination will be favoured over one based on a review of notes made after an earlier examination.

(4) More weight will be attached to a more recent report.

(5) Reports from independent commentators will carry more weight than those by the insurer's staff or observations by the insured.

(6) Any special circumstances surrounding the report will be taken into account.

(7) Reports from occupational physicians may help to form an overall picture, but are unlikely to overturn assessments made by consultants in the relevant speciality.

(8) Capacity evaluation tests try to measure the insured's ability to carry out various activities. They are not decisive and often produce findings inconsistent with other test results. It may be difficult to distinguish between an insured exaggerating the effect of physical symptoms, and someone in so much pain that he is wary of exerting himself fully in these tests. The FOS is unlikely to support insurers who, having agreed to pay benefits to an insured, subsequently use these test results as a sole reason to justify stopping payments.

(9) Serious inconsistencies between surveillance and other evidence will weaken the insured's case and reduce the weight of the medical reports. However, the FOS says that video evidence does not usually produce serious inconsistencies: it only shows activity over a limited period and is rarely directly relevant to the dispute. Performing one sort of activity does not mean that there is an ability to carry out another. Normally the FOS will favour medical evidence over video evidence. It may ask the doctor who carried out the independent medical examinations to view the video evidence and comment on any inconsistency.[33]

PAYING FOR MEDICAL REPORTS

4.24 In *Ombudsman News* July 2001, the FOS sought views as to who should pay for medical reports. In light of the responses, it reported in *Ombudsman News* January 2002 its general approach (subject always to the particular circumstances of the case in question):

(1) Firms' procedures should reflect the reality that delays can be expected in receiving reports from doctors.

---

32. *Ombudsman News* Jan 2002.
33. See also above "Recordings" at para. 4.15.

(2) Medical reports should only be requested where there is a clear need to confirm the policyholder's evidence.

(3) Firms should pay for medical reports which the policyholder has consented to release to them.

(4) However, a policyholder should pay for any medical report required primarily to prove that the claim is valid or should be validly continued, such cost to be reimbursed by insurers if the claim succeeds.

(5) Requests for regular reports for low value, ongoing claims may be onerous.

(6) Insurers should pay for evidence which helps them decide whether a claim is excluded (for instance because of a pre-existing medical condition). Insurers should handle such cases expeditiously, especially when the policyholder is being treated abroad, and sensitively.

(7) Where claims are rejected or terminated on reasonable grounds, the policyholder should produce and pay for any new medical evidence that could support their appeal against that decision, subject to reimbursement by insurers if they succeed.

4.25 The above points reflect the common law's burdens of proof (that the insured must prove a loss and an insurer must prove an exclusion) and seem both fair and sensible.

COMMENTARY

4.26 The FOS is a unique dispute resolution system, so it is right that it has its own rules of evidence, supported by the teeth of the courts. The point of the FOS as an alternative, quick and cheap dispute resolution service, would be defeated if it had to apply the Civil Procedure Rules and court standards of evidence. Where it considers that a case needs a formal system with cross-examination and witnesses compelled to give evidence, it will decline jurisdiction and suggest the matter is taken to court. Other alternative systems, such as (especially non-construction) arbitration under the Arbitration Acts are so saddled with procedural and evidential requirements that the practitioner will prepare much as for litigation, at similar cost, taking a similar time.

4.27 However, for the reasons set out above, it would be better if the FOS developed and publicised some rules on admissibility perhaps using those of a court as a base, which it could always choose not to apply in any particular circumstances in the exercise of its fair and reasonable discretion. Such rules would include who was allowed to consider the question of admissibility.

CHAPTER 5

POLICY CONSTRUCTION: LAW VERSUS FOS

PRECEDENT

5.1 In the interests of certainty, precedent will be followed by a court where the meaning of a term has been established by judicial decision, unless the wording or context in question can be distinguished. As Waller LJ said in *Ramco (UK) Ltd v International Insurance Co of Hannover Ltd*[1]:

"If a form of words has been in use for 80 years which describes one sort of insurance rather than the other, it would be meddlesome for this court to decide that the selected form of words do not achieve their intended purpose, unless there were some real reason for supposing that the form of words is unsatisfactory in practice. The fact that the form of words is the subject-matter of a previous decision of this court is a compelling reason why the courts should not depart from that settled meaning . . ."

5.2 Under the FOS regime, fair and reasonable in the particular circumstances is more important than certainty and following a court-set precedent (which it might not follow anyway, and in practice may not know about). Whilst the FOS aims at consistency, it is not obliged to follow its own decisions either. There are no reported examples where the FOS refers to a legal precedent on construction which it refuses to follow. But its reports generally do not refer to any precedents by name, although precedent forms part of the law which the FOS is obliged at least to consider. It is unclear how much legal precedent is set out in the FOS internal information system on which its officers rely and how effectively the system is updated. As noted above,[2] the FOS Annual Review 2007/8 admitted that the system covered only over 85% of the financial products and services about which the FOS commonly receives complaints, although the FOS Annual Review 2009/10 reported that over 1,000 new pages had been added to its staff intranet that year. If either party would like to rely on a precedent, they would be well advised to set out the details clearly.

ORDINARY AND NATURAL MEANING WITHIN THE FACTUAL MATRIX

5.3 A court should interpret a policy to give effect to the intention of the parties, assuming that the parties intend the words to be given their "ordinary and natural meaning" taking into account the factual matrix of the situation of the parties at the time of the contract.[3] So, for instance, "fire" will not include "explosion". Courts should not manipulate clear language

---

1. [2004] Lloyd's Rep IR 606.
2. In "FOS decision-making: fair and reasonable" at para. 2.62.
3. *Investors Compensation Scheme v West Bromwich Building Society* [1998] 1 All ER 98.

to repair a bad bargain, even if the result is harsh and technical. The court may imply a term if it is commercially necessary, unless an implied term would contradict an express one.[4] However, if it is clear from the background knowledge reasonably available to the parties that something has gone wrong in the drafting, so that the wording does not give the meaning intended, the court may also take account of other documents and market evidence (although not previous negotiations[5]). This is the so-called "factual matrix" surrounding the contract, the principles of which were set out in the leading case of *Investors Compensation Scheme v West Bromwich Building Society*[6] by Lord Hoffmann (giving credit to their development to Lord Wilberforce in *Prenn v Simmonds*[7] and *Reardon Smith Line Ltd v Yngvar Hansen-Tangen*)[8]:

" . . . (4) The meaning which a document (or any other utterance) would convey to a reasonable man is not the same thing as the meaning of its words. The meaning of words is a matter of dictionaries and grammars; the meaning of the document is what the parties using those words against the relevant background would reasonably have been understood to mean. The background may not merely enable the reasonable man to choose between the possible meanings of words which are ambiguous but even (as occasionally happens in ordinary life) to conclude that the parties must, for whatever reason, have used the wrong words or syntax.

(5) The 'rule' that words should be given their 'natural and ordinary meaning' reflects the common sense proposition that we do not easily accept that people have made linguistic mistakes, particularly in formal documents. On the other hand, if one would nevertheless conclude from the background that something must have gone wrong with the language, the law does not require judges to attribute to the parties an intention which they plainly could not have had. Lord Diplock made this point more vigorously when he said in The Antaios Compania Neviera S.A. v. Salen Rederierna A.B. [1985] 1 A.C. 191, 201:

'. . . if detailed semantic and syntactical analysis of words in a commercial contract is going to lead to a conclusion that flouts business commonsense, it must be made to yield to business commonsense.' "

5.4 This concept balances the interests of reliance on the ordinary and natural meaning of the words with interpreting the contract in a way that the parties intended. It also means that a contract only needs to be rectified if there has been a common mistake, that is a common continuing intention between the parties, an outward expression of that accord, the intention continued when the contract was executed and by mistake the instrument did not reflect that common intention.[9]

5.5 Usually the FOS applies the ordinary and natural meaning, even if the insured has not understood the position, as long as there has been no breach of a sales code. In Case Study 73/7,[10] the insured honestly misunderstood the extent of accidental damage cover, but there was no evidence of insurers misrepresenting the position at the point of sale, so the FOS agreed with insurers that accidental damage to a lawnmower was not covered, as it was not within the clear list of items included. In Case Study 74/10,[11] there was no clear definition in the policy of an exclusion for works carried out "on or at airports". It applied the ordinary meaning that a reasonable person would be likely to understand, rather than a statutory definition, and looked at the context of the wording to see what other exclusions were listed

---

4. *Andrews & Kern Ltd v CGU Insurance plc* [2007] EWCA Civ 1481.
5. *Hamishmar Insurance Agency Ltd v FirstCity Partnership* [2009] EWHC 256 (Comm).
6. *Supra.*
7. [1971] 1 WLR 1381.
8. [1976] 1 WLR 989.
9. *Cf, Chartbrook Ltd v Persimmon Homes Ltd* [2009] UKHL 38 which has more recently restated the *West Bromwich* approach.
10. *Ombudsman News* Oct/Nov 2008.
11. *Ombudsman News* Dec 2008/Jan 2009.

around it, so that "airport" did not include an RAF base. It is to be welcomed that these more recent case studies show the FOS focusing on the clear wording of the cover in a technical way, much as a court would.

5.6 The FOS may disregard the natural and ordinary meaning of a term in the interests of fairness in unusual situations, without referring to Lord Hoffmann's principles in *West Bromwich* to establish the mutual intention of the parties. Some examples of this are set out below.

5.7 In Case Study 7/10,[12] holiday cancellation cover clearly applied to illness of a relative, but the FOS required insurers to apply it to an unrelated next of kin when a priest was taken ill. In Case Study 13/9,[13] there was an exclusion for damage by animals, but the FOS felt that it should not apply when the insured's dog died and the carpet was stained. In Case Study 65/3,[14] insurers were asked to treat the person giving hydrotherapy to a dog as if he was a member of a particular organisation as was specified in the policy, because he was the only qualified person within some hours travelling time, the treatment had been recommended by a vet and the dog had responded well. And in Case Study 77/5,[15] the claim for the cost of medical treatment abroad was clearly excluded except in emergencies. Although the situation did not constitute an emergency, and despite the clear wording to the contrary, the FOS felt that it was fair and reasonable for insurers to pay the amount they would have had to pay under the policy if the assured had returned to the UK for treatment.

5.8 The result would probably have been different before a court in each of these examples. It does not seem right that the FOS should be able to override clear language when the insurer is not at fault, perhaps because it feels sorry for the insured. It must be trying to repair a bad bargain for the insured. It is going beyond the "factual matrix" principles of *West Bromwich*, which has not been mentioned in these or any other reported case studies, either by name or by reference to its principles, although that case is included in almost every legal judgment which involves construction.[16] It is unknown whether the case is mentioned in the FOS internal information system. FOS policy construction decisions, especially ones like these, seem to be based more on gut reaction than careful analysis. This may not give the fairest result. The FOS considering "all the circumstances of the case" is not enough guidance when trying to interpret policy wording, and its discretion would not be stifled if it referred to *West Bromwich* at each decision.

CONTEXT OF THE WORDING (AS OPPOSED TO CONTEXT OF THE SURROUNDING CIRCUMSTANCES)

5.9 The statutory context of compulsory insurances may be relevant, so "accident" in a motor policy has a broader meaning than in another type of policy, and will include a deliberately caused crash by an insured vehicle.[17]

5.10 The context of the position of the words within the policy will be important. Unless specifically excluded, the *eiusdem generis* rule will take effect. It limits the meaning of a

---

12. *Ombudsman News* July 2001.
13. *Ombudsman News* Jan 2002.
14. *Ombudsman News* Oct/Nov 2007.
15. *Ombudsman News* May/June 2009.
16. A recent example is *Durham v BAI (Run Off) Ltd* [2008] EWHC 2692 (QB). The factual matrix included the background to the relevant legislation and public policy.
17. *Charlton v Fisher* [2001] Lloyd's Rep IR 387.

general word if it is linked to a specific word, to the same genus as the specific word. So, (emphasis added) "*household* furniture, linen, wearing apparel and plate" was held to include household linen, but not linen drapery goods bought on speculation.[18]

5.11 The context of the type of insurance obtained will also be relevant, so that a clause in a property policy dealing with radioactive waste applied only to property damage, although out of context it might have seemed also to apply to consequential loss, which would have brought it outside of the insuring clause itself.[19]

5.12 The courts have used these tools over the decades to help construe terms. The FOS would find them similarly useful if it used them properly and consistently. In the reported case studies, there is little evidence of the FOS doing this, perhaps because it requires skills or experience which only the most senior insurance officers or lawyers experienced in the field might have, and these qualifications and experience are not required for FOS staff. In Case Study 73/9,[20] lead for household roof repairs and scrap metal were stolen from the insured's garden. The insurer said these were outside cover for "household goods, valuables, personal money, deeds and documents, business equipment and personal belongings". The FOS adjudicated a settlement whereby the insurer paid only for the loss of the lead. The FOS comment is that it was reasonable for the lead intended for household repairs to be covered under a household policy. It does not mention the *eiusdem generis* rule or comment about whether the lead was included as "household goods" and the scrap metal excluded. Without the context of the whole policy, it is not possible to comment on how the court would have interpreted this wording, but its approach would have been different, starting with the words, rather than the reasonableness of cover being provided, and dealing with the *eiusdem generis* rule.

TECHNICAL TERMS

5.13 In law, a technical or standard meaning in the relevant trade will usually apply to a technical term, even if it could also have an ordinary meaning, unless there is some contextual or other reason for a different approach, such as where the assured is situated outside of the jurisdiction. For example, the Court of Appeal in *Commonwealth Smelting* v *Guardian Royal Exchange Assurance Ltd*[21] gave "explosion" its technical meaning, so that there was no explosion where a piece of metal caused the outer casing to shatter, as there was no physical or chemical reaction.

5.14 The FOS is unlikely to uphold a special meaning which a consumer would not generally recognise, unless it has been brought specifically to the insured's attention before inception. In Case Study 7/3,[22] a bag with valuables was stolen from the locked boot of an unattended car. These valuables were excluded from cover due to a wide and unusual definition given in the travel policy. The FOS upheld the claim in part: the exclusion was unusually onerous and had not been specifically drawn to the insured's attention at the sales point.

---

18. *King* v *Travellers' Insurance Association* (1931) 48 TLR 53.
19. *Outokumpu Stainless Ltd* v *Axa Global Risks (UK) Ltd* [2007] EWHC 2555 (Comm).
20. *Ombudsman News* Oct/Nov 2008.
21. [1984] 2 Lloyd's Rep 608.
22. *Ombudsman News* July 2001.

REASONABLE CONSTRUCTION

5.15 There is an assumption in *West Bromwich*[23] that the parties do not intend an unreasonable result. The more unreasonable the result, the less likely it was intended. Although the law does not construe a policy in accordance with the reasonable expectations of the insured, the courts try to construe terms in a way which gives the policy the purpose for which it was entered into. Sometimes the wording will be so inappropriate that the court will have to construe a meaning which is not commercially sensible. The court will also try to construe a policy to make it an effective legal document, with a meaning for any obscure term so that a clause is not void for uncertainty.[24]

5.16 The FOS does not seem to struggle so hard to rely on the wordings, and will impose whatever meaning it considers fair and reasonable in the circumstances, even if that meaning is contrary to the obvious meaning of the wording. It will effectively re-write policies like this to repair a bargain. See the examples given above.[25]

CONTRA PROFERENTEM RULE

5.17 Where a term is ambiguous, the *contra proferentem* rule means that it must be construed against the party who drafted it, usually the insurer. This means that it will be construed narrowly. If the context, definitions or factual matrix make the meaning clear, it will not become ambiguous just because a literal construction would produce an unexpected and irrational result.[26] However, such a result might indicate that the meaning is not actually obvious and that looking at the policy as a whole, the *contra proferentem* rule should apply. This occurred in the Court of Appeal's interpretation of a warranty that the ship be crewed "at all times" in *Pratt* v *Aigaion Insurance Company SA (The Resolute)*.[27] The court at first instance[28] applied the obvious meaning, that there had to be a crew on board at all times, except when it was impossible. Although this might be expensive, commercial considerations were irrelevant. The Court of Appeal, overturning the decision, held that the primary purpose of the warranty was to protect the vessel against navigation hazards, so was only meant to operate when the ship was moving. It was common ground that the parties had not intended the warranty to be interpreted literally, but the qualification to the term "at all times" had not been defined. "At all times" was therefore an ambiguous phrase, to be interpreted *contra proferentem* against the insurers. So a crew member had to be on board "at all times" when the warranty was in effect and the ship was moving, but not when it was safely moored.[29]

---

23. *Supra.*
24. As illustrated by: *Smit Tak Offshore Services Ltd* v *Youell* [1992] 1 Lloyd's Rep 154; *Morley and Morley* v *United Friendly Insurance* [1993] 1 Lloyd's Rep 490; *Gan Insurance Co Ltd* v *Tai Ping Insurance Co Ltd (No 2)* [2001] Lloyd's Rep IR 291; *Charman* v *Gordian Runoff Ltd* [2004] Lloyd's Rep IR 373.
25. In the section on "Ordinary and natural meaning" at paras. 5.6 *et seq.*
26. As illustrated by: *Tarleton* v *Staniforth* (1974) 5 TR 695; *Sargent* v *GRE (UK) Ltd* [2000] Lloyd's Rep IR 77; *Drinkwater* v *London Assurance* (1767) 2 Wils 363; *Tektrol Ltd* v *International Insurance Co of Hanover Ltd* [2006] Lloyd's Rep IR 38; *GE Frankona Reinsurance Ltd* v *CMM Trust No 1400 (The Newfoundland Explorer)* [2006] EWHC 429 (Admlty); *Carlingford Australia General Insurance Ltd* v *EZ Industries Ltd* [1988] VR 349; *Hare* v *Barstow* (1844) 8 Jur 928.
27. [2008] EWCA Civ 1314.
28. [2008] EWHC 489 (Admlty).
29. See also warranties below "How the courts avoid the draconian effects of the law of warranties" at paras. 14.9 *et seq.*

5.18 The FOS seems to use the *contra proferentem* rule quite frequently without a particularly technical analysis of the policy, although often in circumstances where a court might apply the rule too.[30] Unlike a court, the FOS might also do this where the layout of a policy is confusing, for instance where exclusions are printed on different pages to the paragraphs they modify, or where wordings in schedules, policies and marketing material are contradictory.

5.19 In Case Study 18/15,[31] a baby-quad bike was stolen. The insured's assumption that the bike was covered under the household policy was reasonable in view of the explanatory leaflet, even though the policy contradicted this. She was entitled to the benefit of the wording that was most favourable to her.[32] This conclusion is surely "fair and reasonable", but the FOS report in *Ombudsman News* did not analyse the wordings in a legal or technical way. *Ombudsman News* reports rarely seem to and it is unknown whether ombudsman decisions in general do. A court might well have come to the same conclusion with a careful analysis, finding firstly that the leaflet formed part of the contract, then, looking at the policy as a whole, deciding that the leaflet should be given priority, and/or finally applying the *contra proferentem* rule in the insured's favour where the meaning of the policy was unclear, and maybe also considering whether there had been an estoppel—a misrepresentation by insurers as to what was covered on which the insured relied, and was entitled to rely upon, to her detriment.

5.20 Confusion as to which policy limits apply to which loss can result from poor sales performance and an unclear wording of the confirmation details, as in Case Study 4/9,[33] or because the policy wording is simply confusing, as in Case Study 4/14.[34] In both cases, the insurer had to meet the claim up to the highest limit. This is really no more than an application of the *contra proferentem* rule, and a court would probably have come to the same conclusions.

5.21 Even if a term is unclear, the FOS may require this to make a difference to whether the insured would have taken out the policy before it goes against the insurer. In Case Study 71/5,[35] the insured was likely to have taken out the policy however clear the particular term complained about was, so the complaint was not upheld. This would not be the court's approach. The natural and obvious meaning of a clear term, or adoption of the *contra proferentem* rule if the term is unclear, applies whatever the consequences, and whatever the motives for taking out the policy. If the complaint is that the term is unfair, then the FOS should look at the law on unfairness.[36]

POLICY TO BE LOOKED AT AS A WHOLE (INCLUDING HEADINGS)

5.22 A policy needs to be looked at as a whole to give effect to the plain and obvious intention of the parties and to try to give every clause some meaning, although a word may

---

30. E.g. Case Study 69/4, *Ombudsman News* Apr/May 2008, where the wording of an extended warranty for a leather sofa was so poorly worded that it was very unclear what was covered and excluded.

31. *Ombudsman News* July 2002.

32. See for comparison Case Study 73/6 in *Ombudsman News* Oct/Nov 2008, where there was no contradiction in the terms, and the FOS upheld the insurer's view that a "minimoto" powered bike was not covered under a household policy which excluded "motor vehicles, electrically, mechanically or power-assisted vehicles (other than domestic gardening equipment)".

33. *Ombudsman News* Apr 2001.

34. *Ombudsman News* Apr 2001.

35. *Ombudsman News* Aug 2008.

36. See further comment below in "Onerous and unfair terms" at paras. 5.52 *et seq.*

be ignored where it has plainly been included in error. This approach was key to the Court of Appeal decision in *Seele Austria GmbH & Co KG* v *Tokio Marine Europe Insurance Ltd*.[37] If there are conflicting or redundant clauses, a court will decide which should be given priority. Words specifically added will have priority over standard terms, and a later document will have greater weight where a contract is contained in more than one document. There is no rule that large print is to be preferred to small print or that a clause can be ignored simply because it is difficult to read, although this reasoning may now have been superseded by the principle that unusual or onerous terms must be brought to the attention of the other party (see *Interfoto* below at paragraphs 5.53 *et seq*). Recitals are relevant only to construe an ambiguous term.[38]

5.23 In practice, FOS policy analysis seems to be limited in this regard. However, it has set out its approach to misleading policy (or associated leaflet) headings, especially where less cover is provided than other policies with a similar title. Unlike a court, the FOS considers that the customer may rely, at least to some extent, on the policy headlines. The FOS will look at what a reasonable person would have concluded about the nature of the cover from the information available. If a wider cover could reasonably have been expected, it will conclude that the firm has not adequately explained the main features of the policy or ensured that it is suitable for the policyholder's needs, and will allow avoidance *ab initio* with a return of premium, or, where better alternative cover is readily available, tell the insurer to handle the claim as if the unusual and/or misleading restrictions did not apply.

5.24 An example is Case Study 18/13.[39] The upholstery on a sofa came loose. The description on the first page of the extended warranty was "for upholstery" but insurers said the terms only covered structural damage to the sofa. There was no special definition of "upholstery", and none communicated to the insured, so the FOS applied its ordinary meaning. The insured would not have bought the policy if he had realised how restrictive the cover was, so the FOS required insurers to pay the claim for upholstery as if the cover was not restricted, plus £100 for maladministration. It is unlikely that a court would have allowed reliance on a heading over the actual terms, and would not have awarded maladministration damages. Although unlikely, a court might have found a misrepresentation that the policy covered upholstery, coupled with reliance on that misrepresentation and an entitlement to rely on it, leading to the insured acting to his detriment in not taking out a different policy which would have given him the cover he wanted, which would estop insurers from refusing the claim.

5.25 However, the FOS will not permit an obvious "try-on" under this head. In Case Study 18/25,[40] the FOS found that the policy meaning was clear from the policy's title; that the policy covered road traffic accidents with motor vehicles. So it did not accept that because of a lack of explanation at the sales point, the insured thought that the policy covered any personal accident at all, rather than only injuries involving a motor vehicle, and insurers were

37. [2008] EWCA Civ 441. A clause providing cover for access damage intentionally and necessarily caused to the works to enable repairs, was interpreted to include work to replace leaking windows which had not yet caused damage, in light of the purpose of the whole policy, which was to provide an indemnity to the subcontractor against fortuitous damage to the works as a whole. The leaking windows would have caused a threat to the works as a whole sooner or later.

38. The above principles are illustrated in: *Commercial Union Assurance Co Ltd* v *Sun Alliance Insurance Group plc* [1992] 1 Lloyd's Rep 475; *Forsikringsaktieselskapet Vesta* v *Butcher* [1989] 1 All ER 402; *Beacon Life* v *Gibb* (1862) 1 Moo PCC (NS) 73; *Glen's Trustees* v *Lancashire & Yorkshire Accident Insurance Co Ltd* (1906) 8F (Ct of Sess) 915; *Eagle Star Insurance Co Ltd* v *Cresswell* [2004] Lloyd's Rep IR 537; *Kaufmann* v *British Surety Insurance Co Ltd* (1929) 45 TLR 399; *Blascheck* v *Russell* (1916) 33 TLR 74.

39. *Ombudsman News* July 2002.

40. *Ombudsman News* July 2002.

right to reject his claim after he suffered injury whilst riding his bicycle where no other vehicle was involved.

SUBSEQUENT CONDUCT

5.26 A contract must be construed as at the time it was made. Subsequent conduct, such as an endorsement, cannot be admitted as an aid to the original wording.[41] There are no published case studies which turn on this point. It is not clear that every FOS officer would be aware of this principle. In any case, the FOS would ignore it if it was unfair or unreasonable in the circumstances.

CUSTOM AND CODES OF SALE

5.27 The custom of the market may assist construction and cause a court to imply a term. A custom will be made out if it is notorious, universally followed and reasonable. Although it can explain express words or give them a less obvious meaning, it cannot be permitted to contradict them.[42] The FOS would probably treat a custom as it does a technical term. It is doubtful that the FOS would be aware of most market customs other than those reflected in the codes of sale.

5.28 Sales, including internet sales,[43] should conform with good practice as embodied in the FSA's ICOBS (and previously embodied in the ABI and GISC Codes, and ICOB). The courts are not required to take account of these codes, unless and to the extent that they set out a custom.[44] The court's tendency is not to focus much on sales at all, but more on the wording, unless dealing with misrepresentation and also in the few cases where *Interfoto* applies (where an unusual or onerous term should have been brought to the attention of the other party) (see below at paragraphs 5.53 *et seq*). However, this approach may be changing following David Steel J's reliance in *Jones v Environcom Ltd (No 2)*[45] on ICOBS, rather than copious case law, as setting out the duties of a broker to ensure that the policy is appropriate for the client's needs and to warn the assured of his duty of disclosure.

5.29 If poor marketing or sales techniques in contravention of the codes significantly reduces or changes the cover which the insured legitimately expects, and the insured is prejudiced (for instance if he could have found alternative cover in accordance with his expectations), the FOS may require the insurer to meet the claim even if the wording is clear, unless the insurer can show that it drew it to the customer's attention before the policy was

---

41. As illustrated in: *James Miller & Partners v Whitworth Street Estates (Manchester) Ltd* [1970] AC 583; *Absalom v TCRU Ltd* [2005] EWCA Civ 1586; *Bolton MBC v Municipal Mutual Insurance Ltd* [2007] Lloyd's Rep IR 233.

42. These principles are illustrated in: *Blackett v Royal Exchange* (1832) 2 G&J 244; *Goshawk Dedicated Ltd v Tyser & Co Ltd* [2005] Lloyd's Rep IR 379 and [2007] Lloyd's Rep IR 284; *Thor Navigation Inc v Ingosstrak Insurance (The Thor II)* [2005] 1 Lloyd's Rep 547; *Mander v Equitas Ltd* [2000] Lloyd's Rep IR 520.

43. *Ombudsman News* May 2006.

44. *Cf, Lewis v Norwich Union Healthcare Ltd* [2009] EW Misc 2 (EWCC), where the court specifically found that the ABI's SLIP was not incorporated into the policy and was not legally binding. It is of note that the Law Commissions have specifically refrained from including in the draft consumer insurance bill that the courts have to take into account any industry guidance. At paras. 4.55 and 10.42 of its Final Report 15/12/09, they explain that they did not wish to give the ABI or any other industry bodies the power to bind non-members if this is thought to be inappropriate.

45. [2010] EWHC 759 (Comm).

sold. The FOS will expect the insurer, rather than the insured, to produce contemporaneous information from the time of sale, including explanatory literature given to the customer before sale, a statement from the seller, a tape recording of any relevant telephone conversation or a saved web page from the time of sale. Telephone or online sales should preferably be followed by a completed form sent out for checking and signature. The FOS has said[46] that the ombudsman will assess the information provided and the context in which it was provided. So if the sale was made primarily by telephone, or at a meeting, and the evidence suggests failures in the oral disclosure by the firm, the FOS is unlikely to consider that subsequent written information automatically corrects previous shortcomings. At that point, the FOS will not consider it to be reasonable to expect the insured to read the documentation carefully and identify the important factors, and it will be even less reasonable to expect the insured to realise if the written position differs from the understanding gained during the previous oral communication. Where a customer has accepted an oral recommendation to buy a product based on inadequate information, there is a real risk that they will regard the written material as a mere formality and simply sign and return the documents. Whilst it is important that the customer has access to the full policy documentation, the firm will not satisfy its obligations by sending a copy to the customer and highlighting the customer's right to cancel the policy. Only recently has a court specifically acknowledged this. In *Jones* v *Environcom Ltd (No 2)*,[47] David Steel J relying on ICOBS as mentioned above, and referring to the duties of a broker said:

"I am not persuaded that it is sufficient simply to rely upon written standard form explanations and warnings annexed to proposals or policy documents . . . The broker must satisfy himself that the position is in fact understood by his client and this will usually require a specific oral or written exchange on the topic, both at the time of the original placement and at renewal . . . "

5.30 In Case Study 1/4,[48] an insured switched insurers when the salesperson assured her that the new cover would be the same as the old, and that her previous hip operation was irrelevant. The insurer later refused to pay for a hip replacement, saying it was excluded as a pre-existing medical condition. The insured said that she had never received any policy documents and was not aware of the exclusion. The FOS accepted her story and that she had been seriously prejudiced through bad sales as there was no sales point evidence from the insurer. Insurers were required to pay the claim as if the exclusion did not apply, with an additional £500 for distress and inconvenience.

5.31 In Case Study 13/8,[49] an insured purchased loan protection insurance for his car, pointing out that he wanted this because of a heart attack eight years earlier. He then suffered another heart attack and could no longer work. Insurers refused critical illness cover relying on an exclusion for pre-existing conditions. The insured had probably not read and understood the policy even though he had signed a declaration saying that he had. The wording was complex and the exclusion was not highlighted in the policy or customer leaflet or specifically drawn to his attention, as the FOS said it should have been, because it was particularly significant. If the insured had known, he would not have bought the car or would have made other financial arrangements. The insurer was required to pay the claim in full, along with the loan company's penalty charges and £300 for distress and inconvenience.

---

46. *Cf* FOS website under "Technical notes—online PPI resource".
47. [2010] EWHC 759 (Comm).
48. *Ombudsman News* Jan 2001.
49. *Ombudsman News* Jan 2002.

5.32 The FOS approach to these two case studies is more akin to misrepresentation and estoppel, although *Ombudsman News* does not use this terminology. A court would probably have concluded similarly using reasoning based on these legal principles rather than codes of sale, although a court would not have given awards for distress and inconvenience.

5.33 The FOS has noted particular sales and marketing problems with health-related products, extended warranties, payment protection and travel insurance. These products are often sold by untrained staff who do not understand or describe them properly, with unclear leaflets in support and without key features being pointed out to customers. The OFT investigated poor sales practice in payment protection insurance ("PPI") following a "super-complaint" by Citizens Advice[50] and the FOS referred it under the wider implications process in July 2008. Since September 2007, the FOS has received more than 500 of these complaints every week, of which the uphold rate is unusually high.[51] The complaints are mostly about sales suitability and information provided at the point of sale and mostly relating to single premium PPI sold alongside unsecured loans. In 2008/9[52] complaints about PPI reached more than 30,000, compared to around 800 in 2003/4 and 2004/5.[53] This largely unexpected and sudden increase in complaint volume has had a huge impact on the running and finances of the FOS. The FSA took action as a result of the FOS wider implication referral, and from 29 May 2009 banned the sale of single premium payment protection insurance sold alongside unsecured loans.[54] The FSA has also published two consultation papers[55] in response to the FOS referral and punished various companies. It fined Swinton Group Ltd for automatically including insurance quotes without first establishing that the customer had any real demand or need for the PPI cover, not making it sufficiently clear that PPI was optional, and not properly disclosing the cost of PPI at the point of sale.[56] The FSA fined Egg Bank plc for trying to persuade customers to take PPI on their credit cards when they did not want it and not obtaining a clear consent from customers to receiving only limited information about the PPI.[57] The FSA fined Alliance & Leicester plc for not giving customers details of the cost of PPI, not properly considering whether the customers needed PPI, not making it clear that PPI was optional, and training its staff to put pressure on customers to accept the PPI when they queried it or challenged advisers' recommendations.[58] The FSA also introduced a temporary suspension of the six-month time limit for bringing a

---

50. As reported in *Ombudsman News* Nov/Dec 2005.

51. Speech by Tony Boorman (Principal Ombudsman): PPI complaints and consumer confidence 24/02/09. The FOS Annual Reviews 2008/9 and 2009/10 both recorded uphold rates of 89%, compared to about 40% for other insurance complaints.

52. FOS Annual Review 2008/9.

53. FOS Annual Review 2009/10 noted that three in every 10 new complaints related to PPI, which in that year amounted to 49,196 or 71% of the insurance claims.

54. *Cf* Letter from FSA to FOS dated 8 April 2009 which can be found on the FOS website. See also the further measures unveiled by the FSA on 29 September 2009 to protect PPI consumers, to be found on the FSA website, document FSA/PN/129/2009 and the agreement for refunds etc reached between the FSA and Mortgage Payment Protection Insurance firms dated 7 October 2009, to be found on the FSA website, document FSA/PN/135/2009.

55. CP09/23 in September 2009 and CP10/6 in March 2010. At the time of writing this book, the FSA's final proposals were still awaited.

56. Swinton Group Ltd was fined £770,000, agreed to contact over 350,000 customers who paid for the PPI and offer a full refund, to pro-actively review previously rejected claims and pay compensation where appropriate and in March 2008 to exit the PPI market—FSA/PN/145/2009, 28 October 2009.

57. Egg Banking plc was fined £721,000 and agreed to contact all customers asking them to call a dedicated number if they have any concerns about their policy or the way it was sold, and to compensate them where appropriate—FSA/PN/149/2008, 10 December 2008.

58. Alliance & Leicester plc was fined £7 million and agreed to implement a substantial and comprehensive customer contact programme overseen by third party accountants and will review relevant rejected complaints to pay redress where appropriate.

complaint for some recent PPI complainants, so that they had more time to bring their complaint while the FSA worked to resolve a long-term solution to ensure the consistent and fair treatment of customers buying or complaining about the sale of a PPI policy.[59]

5.34 Examples follow of the way that the FOS has dealt with individual complaints. Part of the FOS response to this huge influx of payment protection cases has been to design two special, standard, comprehensive, forms to streamline and speed up the process for these cases; the consumer questionnaire to be used both for complaints brought to firms and for complaints to the FOS and a business response form.[60]

Payment protection insurance

5.35 The majority of PPI complaints are about sales, and usually relate to PPI which is paid for by a single premium funded up-front by being added to an unsecured or second-charge loan or credit card. In considering whether to uphold a complaint about these sales, the FOS takes account of the relevant regulatory, legal and other standards at the time of the sale. The relevant regulatory rules are[61]:

(1) ICOB or from 6 January 2008 onwards ICOBS and
(2) From January 2005 the FSA Principles or
    From 2005 to 2001 GISC Code or
    Pre 2001 the ABI and GISC codes.

Although the GISC and ABI codes no longer apply, the FOS considers that they still represent a helpful guide to good industry practice.

5.36 Whether or not the firm makes a recommendation for a customer to buy a PPI product, it is under a duty to provide adequate information about the product. As Principle 7 of the FSA's Principles says,[62] "A firm must pay due regard to the information needs of its clients, and communicate information to them in a way which is clear, fair and not misleading". Adequate information will include whether the customer was fully aware that the policy was optional, its price, duration, the nature of the single premium (where relevant), the impact of early termination of the policy, the requirements of eligibility and what are the significant policy exclusions/limitations and benefits. The overall impression left by the firm should represent a fair and balanced summary of the policy. The FOS will be looking, overall, to see if the customer was put in a position to be able to make an informed choice about the policy.

5.37 If a firm also gives a recommendation, it must in addition make reasonable enquiries to identify and consider the needs of the customer so that it can recommend a suitable policy.[63] Such enquiries will include the customer's financial and employment situation, whether early repayment is likely and how flexible the arrangement needs to be.[64] An example of an unsuitable cover can be found in Case Study 71/3,[65] where the policy provided only limited benefits for self-employed customers, yet the policy was sold to the assured who

---

59. See above "Time limits for bringing a complaint to the FOS—the six-month rule" at para. 2.30.

60. These were launched on 26 March 2010. The forms and guidance for completing them can be found on the FOS website under "Technical notes—online PPI resource".

61. For further details of the FOS attitude to PPI complaints, see the FOS website under "Technical notes—online PPI resource".

62. See FSA Handbook.

63. See also below "Unsuitable cover" at paras. 5.46 *et seq*.

64. For further detail as to whether suitability has been fairly assessed see the FOS website under "Technical notes—online PPI resource".

65. *Ombudsman News* Aug 2008.

was self-employed in circumstances where the lender knew that the assured was self-employed yet did not explain the limited benefits, other than in providing a written summary, which was not sufficient on its own. Where it is denied that there was a recommendation, the FOS will look at the evidence to decide whether it was most likely or not given. Actions which appear to the customer to endorse the product in the customer's particular circumstances would constitute a recommendation. On the evidence of most of the PPI complaints which the FOS sees, it considers that there has been a recommendation, as typically the customer is already engaged in a discussion with the firm about the loan and his or her personal finances; the firm has access to relevant information about the customer's circumstances; and the PPI is sold in discussion with the customer. In deciding whether there has been a recommendation, the FOS will consider sales process documentation; training manuals; sales scripts; the proportion of customers who took PPI in any one period; and relevant regulatory findings about past practice. Statements of customers and firm representatives can also be useful, but the FOS will bear in mind that subsequent events may have influenced these.

5.38 If a PPI policy has been mis-sold, the FOS will try to put the consumer back into the position he would have been in but for the failure of the financial business. This will typically mean assuming that the consumer would not have purchased the policy if the financial business had given a fair recommendation and/or had given appropriate information during the sale, and compensating the consumer if they have been out of pocket in the meantime. The calculation may be complicated, especially if the premium has been added to a loan and the interest for the premium and loan is being paid off together at monthly intervals. Various examples of the complicated arrangements which might be necessary to undo the sale can be found on the FOS website.[66] There may also be an award for distress and inconvenience in having to refer the complaint to the FOS if a firm has rejected the complaint without properly analysing the defects in its sales practices.[67]

5.39 In Case Studies 62/5, 62/6 and 62/8,[68] lenders mis-sold payment protection policies by not highlighting in the documentation their key features[69] and there was no record of the initial conversations. The lenders were required to refund the full amount of the premium plus all the interest that the complainants had paid on this amount. *Interfoto* (see below at paragraphs 5.53 *et seq*), mistake and misrepresentation arguments with all these cases studies may well have succeeded at court and produced a similar result. In Case Study 71/1,[70] insurers had to return the premium with interest where the insured said that he had not been told that the payment protection policy was an optional extra when obtaining his credit card or what the cost or benefit of the policy was. The FOS found no evidence that he had been told. The agent had filled out the application form, ticking the box that said that the insured wanted the insurance, and the insured said he had just signed where the agent had marked. The FOS noted that the insured's version of events was supported by the writing in different pens and styles in the application form and his age (19 years) and limited financial experience was relevant to what he would know. The fact that the premium was itemised on his monthly bank statements did not indicate that the insurance was optional. In terms of law, these factors

---

66. See FOS website under "Technical notes—online PPI resource".

67. In the examples on the FOS website under "Technical notes—online PPI resource" the amounts awarded for distress and inconvenience ranged from £200 to £400.

68. *Ombudsman News* June/July 2007.

69. These included that the premium was payable in a single lump sum at the beginning of the loan, to be funded by means of a loan on which interest would be payable and that no pro rata refund was payable if the policy was no longer needed.

70. *Ombudsman News* Aug 2008.

would all go towards questions of misrepresentation and reliance, and the result would probably have been the same, if this was the insurer's agent.

5.40 In Case Study 62/9,[71] insurers were required to pay the insured as if the misleading exclusion for unemployment caused by dismissal did not apply. Only unemployment through redundancy was covered. The insured had wanted, and believed she had obtained, cover for all types of unemployment. Although the position was clearly stated in the full terms and conditions of the policy, it was not highlighted by the insurer, and was not mentioned at all in the policy summary which referred only to unemployment, which the FOS found was misleading.

5.41 In three further examples provided by the FOS,[72] the different single-premium PPI policies sold with a loan to Mr and Mrs B, Mr A and Mrs C respectively were not suitable for their needs and the firms had not paid due regard to the information needs of their respective customers. The FOS found in each of these cases, the customers would not have taken out the PPI policy with the loans, so the appropriate remedy was cancellation of the policy without charges being incurred, re-configuration of the loans accordingly so that only the loan was being paid off (not the substantial PPI premium as well with its interest and charges), and repayment of all payments and interest made in relation to the PPI policy, plus simple interest at 8% on the repayments (calculated from the date that the customers had made each PPI payment until full settlement of the claim). In two further examples,[73] the firms in question did not take reasonable care to ensure the adequacy of the information provided respectively to Mr D and Mr E or have sufficient regard to their interests when PPI insurance was taken out with a credit card. The ombudsman concluded that they would not have taken out the policy and so needed to be put back into their respective positions had they been properly informed. In essence this meant a return of the PPI premiums and any interest or charges paid in respect of those premiums from the time the policy was taken out until cancelled, plus interest to compensate for being out of money from the point of payment to the time this award is paid, with a reconstruction of their credit card accounts accordingly.

Travel insurance

5.42 FOS examples of poor sales in relation to travel insurance include those where the insured is poorly advised or not advised at all, and so fills out the proposal form so that the insurance does not start until the first day of the holiday. Technically there will be no cover until then, not even cancellation cover. When the insured did this in Case Study 7/7,[74] the travel agent had not advised her about filling out the proposal. She wanted to cancel the holiday for medical reasons. The FOS asked the insurer to meet the claim without admitting liability, but without paying interest or her GP's fee for completing the claim form. By contrast, in Case Study 76/9,[75] the recording of the sale showed that the insurer had said that it was suitable for the insured to start the annual policy on the date of the start of the first trip, without explaining the consequences. The FOS required the insurer to pay the full holiday cancellation costs with interest.

---

71. *Ombudsman News* June/July 2007.
72. See FOS website (Technical notes—online PPI resource) to access a copy of the ombudsman's anonymised final determinations in these three examples dated November 2008.
73. See FOS website (Technical notes—online PPI resource) to access a copy of the ombudsman's anonymised final determinations in these two examples dated April 2009.
74. *Ombudsman News* July 2001.
75. *Ombudsman News* Mar/Apr 2009.

5.43 A court would have read the contract literally for both of the above case studies (subject to a possible misrepresentation by insurers in the latter case), and in the interests of certainty, the cover would not have started until the policy said it did.

5.44 Contrast again Case Study 36/10,[76] where cover ran from the day of travel, so did not cover the family for cancellation of the holiday when the father died. The online sales process was straightforward with clear instructions, and with a warning that cancellations would only be covered from the date that the insured asked cover to begin. Therefore the FOS felt that the insurer's offer of a goodwill sum towards the cancellation costs was more than fair. But was this offer made only in light of Case Study 7/7? Would the FOS have required anything to be paid if a goodwill offer had not been made?

Extended warranties

5.45 There is little case law on the meaning and operation of extended warranties. The FOS says that the sales process for these policies must make it clear exactly what the cover and restrictions are. See, for instance, the leather sofa and its upholstery example in Case Study 18/13.[77] Sometimes extended warranties come with a complex claims procedure with strict time limits. The FOS will consider these unfair if they have not been drawn to the customer's attention. In Case Study 1/14[78] the FOS found it unacceptable and inappropriate that largely procedural obstacles—a requirement to register within 21 days of purchase before a claim could ever be made—should be placed in the way of policyholders. The insurer was ordered to issue the insured with a certificate of registration and to pay the insured £25 for the costs of pursuing the complaint. This might be a classic *Interfoto* situation at law (see below at paragraphs 5.53 *et seq*).

Unsuitable cover

5.46 Care must be taken at the point of sale to ensure the suitability of policies and eligibility of prospective policyholders. In accordance with the relevant sales code, the FOS expects the seller to record what the insured discloses, ask questions to determine suitability and eligibility, and point out the main features and relevant restrictions of the policy. If the insurer fails to ensure that sellers meet these requirements, the FOS may consider that the insurer has waived any right it might have to refuse cover, especially if the insured could have obtained suitable cover elsewhere. Without saying so, this makes such a seller the insurer's agent, which may be contrary to the law.[79] In Case Study 1/5,[80] the insurer settled the claim as if the exclusion did not apply where a policy excluded medical treatment abroad, although the insurer knew that the insured lived abroad. In Case Study 76/8,[81] the applicant's travel companion was not eligible for cover under the terms of the policy because she lived abroad. However, the travel agent had not checked her eligibility and had not enquired further when her address was left blank, and nor had the insurer; the claim had to be paid as if there was cover. In Case Study 76/11,[82] the insured paid for an extension of cover which was unsuitable

---

76. *Ombudsman News* Apr 2004.
77. See above under "Policy to be looked at as a whole (including headings)" at para. 5.24.
78. *Ombudsman News* Jan 2001.
79. See "Intermediaries" above at paras. 2.9 *et seq* and "Non-disclosure by an intermediary" below at paras. 13.58 *et seq*.
80. *Ombudsman News* Jan 2001.
81. *Ombudsman News* Mar/Apr 2009.
82. *Ombudsman News* Mar/Apr 2009.

because they first needed to buy a base cover which they had not done. This was not clear from the documentation and nor had insurers explained the requirement. Insurers had to pay the claim as if the base cover had been purchased, subject to the additional premium of the base cover, as they should have ensured that the insured purchased the suitable policies in the first place.

5.47 However, if the insured had not been prejudiced by the mis-sale because he could not have obtained a suitable policy elsewhere, then the remedy may be to refund all premiums since inception of the first unsuitable policy, with interest, rather than to pay the claim. This happened in Case Study 24/4,[83] where the sale of an unsuitable income protection policy also resulted in an award of £250 for distress and inconvenience.

5.48 The problem of unsuitable policies occurs especially in the context of payment protection insurance for loans.[84] Case Studies 71/2, 71/3 and 71/4[85] provide examples. The policies' cost and flexibility were unsuitable in light of the financial circumstances and employment status of the respective complainants. With proper explanations, they might have realised this. A written summary is not enough on its own as it does not adequately highlight the limited cover.[86] The FOS required the loans to be recalculated as if the complainants had not bought the respective insurance, with the part of the premium already taken to be paid back with interest. In Case Study 71/2, the lender was also asked to look at assisting the complainants with a wider settlement of the debt, including waiving its fees for overdue loan repayments. In Case Study 71/4 the lender was also asked to pay a modest sum for distress and inconvenience. The FOS does not deal, in these or other cases, with the issues between the insurance company and the lender which result from the FOS determinations.

5.49 The law would be more likely to consider these situations and other FOS unsuitable cover/breach of sale code cases, under misrepresentation and estoppel.

INCORPORATION

5.50 An existing document may be incorporated into the policy by express or implied reference. A basis of the contract clause will incorporate a proposal form and turn the answers it contains into express warranties.[87] The FOS does not recognise basis of the contract clauses (see "Warranties" below at paragraphs 14.4, 14.25 and 14.28). If a point of incorporation arose before the FOS, it would be unlikely to refer to the pertinent case law, and would be more likely to decide the case on its facts according to what the reasonable consumer in those circumstances would have understood, and if the position was ambiguous, to apply the *contra proferentem* rule. An example would be Case Study 18/15[88] referred to above at paragraph 5.19.

DELETIONS

5.51 In a recent case on deletions, *Mopani Copper Mines plc* v *Millennium Underwriting Ltd*,[89] Christopher Clarke J concluded that the tenor of the diverse authorities was that it was

---

83. *Ombudsman News* Jan 2003.
84. See further "Payment protection insurance" above at paras. 5.35 *et seq.*
85. All to be found in *Ombudsman News* Aug 2008.
86. Case Study 71/3, *Ombudsman News* Aug 2008.
87. The criteria for incorporation were set out in *HIH Casualty and General Insurance Ltd* v *New Hampshire Insurance Co* [2001] Lloyd's Rep IR 234 and affirmed [2001] Lloyd's Rep IR 596.
88. *Ombudsman News* July 2002.
89. [2008] EWHC 1331 (Comm).

illegitimate to use deleted words as an aid to construction unless the deletion showed what the parties had agreed that they did not agree and there was ambiguity in the words which remained. There has been no FOS report on the point, so it is unlikely that it has developed its own approach. However, it may not be aware of *Mopani*, and would be more likely to decide the point on the basis of a subjective fair and reasonable gut reaction than on the law.

ONEROUS AND UNFAIR TERMS

5.52 The Unfair Contract Terms Act 1977 ("UCTA") does not apply to insurance contracts, although the FOS applies its spirit. However, insurance contracts are subject to the common law rule set out in the Court of Appeal in *Interfoto Picture Library Ltd* v *Stiletto Visual Programmes Ltd*,[90] and consumer contracts are also subject to the Unfair Terms in Consumer Contracts Regulations 1999 ("UTCCR").[91]

Interfoto

5.53 The *Interfoto* rule is that particularly onerous or unusual terms will not be given effect unless expressly brought to the attention of the other party. In *Interfoto*, transparencies were delivered in an envelope which also contained the delivery note setting out the terms. The onerous term charged £5 per transparency per day, whereas the normal rate would have been £3.50 per transparency per week. Bingham LJ said:

" . . . the more outlandish the clause, the greater the notice which the other party, if he is to be bound, must in all fairness be given."

5.54 Although the defendant would have seen the delivery note with its small but visible lettering and recognised that it probably contained contractual terms, this would only have bound it to conditions so displayed which were common terms regularly encountered in the business—even without reading them.[92] But the onerous terms in the delivery note were not binding, as they had not fairly and reasonably been brought to the defendant's attention and there had been no discussion of terms. Some clauses "would need to be printed in red ink on the face of the document with a red hand pointing to it before the notice could be held to be sufficient".[93] The defendant was required to pay only what the usual rate should have been, as determined by the evidence.

5.55 In practice, the courts tend not to apply *Interfoto*, but distinguish it saying that the term in question is not unusual or onerous enough for *Interfoto* to apply,[94] or finding that it

---

90. [1989] QB 433.
91. SI 1999/2083, implementing Council Directive 93/13/EC, and replacing the UTCCR 1994/3159.
92. *Parker* v *South Eastern Railway* (1876) LR 2 CPD 416.
93. Denning LJ, *obiter*, in *J Spurling* v *Bradshaw* [1956] 1 WLR 461 at page 466. See also Lord Denning MR and Megaw LJ in *Thornton* v *Shoe Lane Parking Ltd* [1971] 2 QB 163—a particularly onerous or unusual condition, or one of that particular nature, must be fairly brought to the notice of the other party (e.g. a term to exclude statutory occupiers' liability).
94. E.g. *Photolibrary Group Ltd* v *Burda Senator Verlag Gmbh* [2008] EWHC 1343 (QB); *Otto Chan* v *Barts & The London NHS Trust* [2007] EWHC 2914 (QB); *Berkeley Community Villages Ltd & Ors* v *Fred Daniel Pullen & Ors* [2007] EWHC 1330 (Ch); *Sumukan Ltd* v *Commonwealth Secretariat* [2007] EWCA Civ 243; *Shepherd Homes Ltd* v *Encia Remediation Ltd* [2007] EWHC 70 (TCC); *Euro London Appointments Ltd* v *Claessens International Ltd* [2006] EWCA Civ 385; *Debenhams Retail plc* v *Customs & Excise Commissioners* [2004] EWHC 1540 (Ch); *Director-General of Fair Trading* v *First National Bank plc* [2000] 1 All ER 240; *Carlsberg-Tetley Brewing Ltd* v *Gilbarco Ltd*, LTL 4/5/99, unreported elsewhere.

has in fact been expressly brought to the attention of the other party.[95] The courts seem to prefer the certainty of clearly expressed terms applying, especially when they can be found commonly in insurers' standard terms.[96]

5.56 In contrast, *Ombudsman News* often reports that a term is unfair and therefore onerous, especially if the average insured would not usually expect it, and however clearly expressed in the policy, it will require the term to be expressly brought to the insured's attention at the sales point before it takes effect. Highlighting the particular term may also include explaining its significance to the policyholder, which was how the duty was expressed in Case Study 85/1.[97] *Interfoto* is not usually expressly mentioned in *Ombudsman News* and the argument is usually about breach of sales code or good industry practice. The FOS expects insurers to provide evidence as to what information was given to the insured. Perhaps if this is effectively how the FOS treats unfair terms, it does not need to mention UTCCR and, indeed, hardly ever does, in its public reports.

5.57 Sometimes the FOS has indicated that it will generally find a particular sort of term onerous, and those instances are set out in this book, for instance with exclusions for unattended vehicles/keys left in cars.[98] However, in other cases it may not be clear in advance that the FOS is going to consider a term onerous. Case Study 76/12[99] may give some clues about what will make the FOS consider a term onerous—if it is unusual and unclear, and if the actual insured did not expect the condition. In that case, an insured had obtained "free" annual travel insurance when applying for a credit card, which insurance covered her husband as well, but only when he travelled with her. The FOS said that the term in question about whether the husband was covered when he travelled alone was not found to be onerous and did not need to be specially highlighted, as it was clear in the policy documents and the literature; it was not unusual for a policy of this type to limit cover the way it had; and the seller had not misrepresented the position. Also, the insured admitted to the FOS that she had never been entirely sure that the policy covered her husband travelling alone. Perhaps then the FOS may use the actual insured's understanding as a benchmark to test whether a term is onerous.

5.58 A claims condition may be onerous if not highlighted at the point of claim. For instance, in Case Study 65/5,[100] the FOS found that a 12-month limitation on the treatment of any one condition in a pet insurance was a significant term which should have been brought to the insured's attention at the claims stage. The insured said that it had not, and insurers could not prove otherwise. The insured had postponed the treatment until after this period, but because this had not prejudiced the insurer, the insured had renewed her policy each year and she was not trying to claim more than her original entitlement, the FOS told insurers to cover the cost of the late treatment, limited to what it would have cost if done within the original 12 months. It is arguable that a court might have stretched and applied *Interfoto* here to what conditions should be communicated to the insured at the claims stage, depending on how unusual and unexpected the 12-month limitation was.

95. E.g. *Ocean Chemical Transport Inc & Ors v Exnor Craggs Ltd sub nom The Julius Hammer* [2000] 1 Lloyd's Rep 446.
96. E.g. the alarm requirements in *Anders & Kern Ltd v CGU Insurance plc* [2007] EWCA Civ 1481, which were held not to be unreasonable or onerous, although *Interfoto* is not expressly mentioned.
97. *Ombudsman News* Apr/May 2010—see further below at para. 5.60.
98. See Chapter 9, below.
99. *Ombudsman News* Mar/Apr 2009.
100. *Ombudsman News* Oct/Nov 2007.

5.59 A term may be onerous according to the FOS if it imposes too wide an obligation on the insured. An example is the exclusion in the PPI policy of Case Study 80/1,[101] where unemployment claims were excluded if the policyholder became "aware of any increase in the risk of unemployment" within 90 days of the policy's start date. The FOS found this exclusion so broad that it was unfair, as on a strict reading this might include knowledge of any deterioration in the UK's economy. The FOS said that if the insurer wished to exclude cover if the policyholder's knowledge or circumstances changed within 90 days of inception, then not only did the term need to be drawn to the insured's attention at the time of sale, but the wording needed specifically to set out what change/s the insurer expected to be notified. The FOS believed that the insured had acted honestly and in good faith and had no particular reason to believe she was at risk of redundancy when she took out the policy, although she knew from the press that her employer was facing a difficult period, so it was not fair or reasonable for the insurer to reject the claim for unemployment benefit.

5.60 The FOS may find a term onerous if it simply puts a significant and non-obvious restriction on the cover. For this reason the exclusions in the equine cover in Case Study 85/1[102] were found to be onerous, as they excluded any illness suffered by the insured's horse either before the policy was taken out or more than once after the insurance had begun, in both cases unless the insurer agreed otherwise in writing. The horse insured had one minor episode of colic in the first year of cover which had not been disclosed to insurers at renewal. He died during the second year of insurance as a result of a serious bout of colic and the policyholder claimed for related veterinary fees. The FOS thought it highly likely that if the policyholder had known that the insurer would not cover future bouts of colic, she would have sought insurance elsewhere, and that as the previous bout of colic had not been serious, another insurer would have covered the horse for this condition and paid the veterinary fees claimed. The insurer was therefore told to pay the claim. It is interesting that the FOS does not deal with this case as a non-disclosure claim. If it had and the questions at renewal had been clear, it might not have been able to find that the policyholder's non-disclosure was innocent so that it could order her claim to be paid. It might have found her disclosure inadvertent, in which case the remedy would have depended on what the insurer would have done, which in this case would have been to exclude colic for the period after renewal, which means that her claim would not have been paid.

5.61 The FOS will also regard as onerous a term which requires the insured to exercise an excess of care over possessions or well-being beyond that which most people actually exercise. Examples are minimum security requirements for household and caravan policies, and the common exclusion for theft of items from cars left unattended or with keys left in the ignition (see Chapter 9, below). The courts do not deal with excess of care requirements specifically, except in as far as they might fall under *Interfoto* or UTCCR.

5.62 In *Interfoto* itself, the onerous term was treated as if it was substituted with the non-onerous term that the insured might have expected. The general remedy which the FOS seems to be adopting in these case studies seems to be slightly different. The FOS aim seems to be to put the insured back into the position he would have been in had the onerous term been alerted. If the result would have been that the insured would have been able to obtain full cover under another policy which did not contain the onerous term, the insurer will usually be asked to pay the claim as if the onerous term did not exist in its own policy. If the result would have been that the insured would not have taken out the policy had he known

---

101. *Ombudsman News* Oct/Nov 2009.
102. *Ombudsman News* Apr/May 2010.

of the onerous term, but would also not have been able to find alternative cover, then the appropriate FOS remedy will be to treat the policy as void *ab initio* with a repayment of the premium.

5.63 However, there is one example in *Ombudsman News*, Case Study 71/5,[103] which demonstrates that assessing what the insured would have done if the onerous/unfair term had been alerted, may not be the appropriate remedy. The term in question was about early repayment of a loan for a car purchase, but only receiving a refund for a small proportion of the premium for his related payment protection insurance. The FOS found that the terms were clear enough, but the insured was surprised by the early repayment charges which he thought were excessive. Even if the term had been onerous or unfair, the FOS did not uphold the complaint because it said that the insured would have taken out this, or indeed any suitable payment protection policy, whatever the detail of its standard early repayment terms, as he did not envisage the circumstances which resulted in early repayment. The circumstances were that his daughter dropped out of university and left the country, so no longer needed the car he had bought for her. However, considering what the insured would have done if he had known that the term was unfair or onerous does not make it any less unfair or onerous and should not be relevant to the question. The fact that the insured did not expect to have to rely on the term should not make it a fair term in the unexpected circumstances in which he finds himself having to rely on it. Reliance should not be a test of either an unfair or onerous terms. A better remedy would be to apply instead of an onerous term, the standard, non-onerous term that would be expected, as was the case in *Interfoto*. It is not clear from the report of the case study what the evidence was that if the insured had known of the onerous term, he would still have taken out the policy. Just because he did not envisage having to repay the loan early, does not mean that he would not have chosen a different policy with less onerous terms in this respect, just in case that unexpected possibility became a reality.

UTCCR

5.64 The protection of UTCCR only applies to consumers. A term judged unfair under UTCCR will not bind a consumer. The rest of the contract will be unaffected if it can exist without the unfair term.[104] A term is unfair if:

(i) it has not been individually negotiated,[105] as with standard insurance policies (the insurer has the burden of proving an individual negotiation[106]); and

(ii) "contrary to the requirement of good faith, it causes a significant imbalance in the parties' rights and obligations arising under the contract to the detriment of the consumer."[107]

5.65 Under Regulation 6(1), unfairness is to be assessed by taking into account the nature of the contract, the circumstances of its conclusion and its other terms. Schedule 2 sets out an indicative, non-exhaustive list of terms which may fall foul of the fairness requirement.[108]

---

103. *Ombudsman News* Aug 2008. See also below under "UTCCR" at para. 5.68.
104. Reg. 8.
105. Reg. 5(1).
106. Reg. 5(3).
107. Reg. 5(1).
108. *Cf*, *Colinvaux & Merkin's Insurance Contract Law*, para. B-0292 for examples of terms in the insurance context which might fall foul of UTCCR. These include a term which allows the insurer to terminate the policy at any time; one which makes the assured forfeit the premium if the policy is avoided; one which was not reasonably accessible to the assured pre-inception; one which makes the insurer's agent that of the assured for completing the proposal form; or one which restricts the limitation period.

Under Regulation 6(2), provisions expressed in "plain intelligible language", are excluded from judicial scrutiny if they relate either to:

    (i) the definition of the main subject matter of the contract; or
    (ii) the adequacy of the price or remuneration.

5.66 The premium, insuring and exceptions clauses will fall within Regulation 6(2), unless they are unclear, in which case they will be construed under Regulation 7 against the insurers. Regulation 7 applies to unclear written terms, not implied terms,[109] and is in effect a codified version of the *contra proferentem* rule as it usually applies against insurers. One of the few cases defining UTCCR is *Michael James Gillin* v *Lloyds TSB Bank plc*,[110] which held that if a term was clearly expressed, it could not be classed as unfair under UTCCR merely because the customer claimed the charges were excessive.

5.67 The OFT and FSA have a duty to consider a complaint made to them from within their respective jurisdictions, that a contract term drawn up for general use is unfair and may apply to the court for an injunction to prevent its further use.[111] An example is the litigation about the fairness of bank charges.[112] If the FOS sees certain unfair terms repeatedly, it might refer them to the FSA or OFT. This occurs infrequently.

5.68 For a court, the insured's reliance on the unfair term is not part of the test of unfairness, although judging from Case Study 71/5[113] it may, but should not be, for the FOS. Without knowing more detail, it is unclear whether the terms complained about in Case Study 71/5—early repayment conditions—might have been unfair under UTCCR.

5.69 The UTCCR are under-utilised and little understood and have had little impact on the insurance industry even though they have applied in their original form (now revoked and replaced by the 1999 version) to all consumer contracts entered into after 1 July 1995. Their profile would be raised if the FOS referred to them as often as it could, so that it applied its discretion as to fairness within the guidelines of these regulations, rather than at random setting its own criteria.

A CRITIQUE OF THE FOS APPROACH TO CONSTRUCTION

Overview of the FOS approach to construction

5.70 The FOS will support an insurer who rejects a claim on the grounds of reasonable restrictions and limitations stated clearly in the policy. It recognises insurers' commercial right to determine the limit of the risks it is prepared to cover. But it is concerned that insureds understand the cover, so the wording and layout of the policy must be clear and the policy headings must reflect the policy meanings. It wants marketing and sales of policies to be conducted in accordance with ICOBS, so that policies are suitable, and onerous or unusual terms are specifically explained.

---

109. *Cf, County Homesearch Co (Thames & Chilterns) Ltd* v *David Cowham* [2008] EWCA Civ 26; *Margaret Baybut & 73 Ors* v *Eccle Riggs Country Park Ltd*, *The Times*, 13 November 2006.
110. LTL 3/7/2007 (unreported elsewhere).
111. *Cf* Regs. 10–12. See also above "The Office of Fair Trading" at para. 2.79.
112. *OFT* v *Abbey National & Ors* [2008] EWHC 875 (Comm) and [2008] EWHC 2325 (Comm).
113. See para. 5.63, above.

Sales issues

5.71 In all public reports on a breach of sales code, saving a few examples of actual ombudsman determinations which the FOS gives on its website in relation to payment protection insurance, the FOS does not, but should for the sake of clarity and accountability, say which one or which part has been breached. Sales codes are not part of the law, and there are no plans for this to happen. It should be noted that in almost every sales example above, if the FOS had relied on legal principles like misrepresentation and estoppel rather than breach of a sales code, that would probably have given the same result. Notwithstanding the huge and noble contribution the FOS has made to fighting bad insurance sales practice, that should not be its job, but the job of the regulator, i.e. the FSA. The FOS could notify the FSA each time it discovers poor sales practice and the FSA could record the problem and take appropriate action against repeated offenders. This would help even those who do not or cannot complain to the FOS without having to wait for the problem to reach drastic proportions, which is what has happened with PPI. Perhaps there is a tacit understanding between the FSA and the FOS that the FOS will police ICOBS, or maybe it is just easier and cheaper for the FSA to rely on the FOS to do this.

Technical rules of construction

5.72 Even though the FOS results from relying on the sales codes may be fair, the above comparisons show that the FOS seems to construe terms with little or no careful analysis of the policy or consideration of each possibly relevant legal tool which might do the job just as well, with the same result. Of course it is possible that only the reports made public leave out a careful analysis of the construction of a policy, and that the actual determinations contain a full analysis. However, this is not the impression the combined reports give. Any lack of careful policy construction may be due to a lack of skill, experience or knowledge of the relevant FOS officer, who may not be legally qualified, or not legally qualified in the relevant field, or due to flaws in the internal information system. Instead, each case seems to be decided more on the FOS gut feeling based on the circumstances of the case. If that gut feeling dictates that the determination should be in favour of the insured, the FOS often relies on a breach of sales code when a legal tool might be just as effective. The technical rules of construction listed above have been developed over the years to help the process, and to prevent the collective thought process from reinventing the wheel each time and coming to inconsistent conclusions. They give flexibility to the law.

5.73 It is not advocated here that the FOS should be spending hours analysing the relevant wordings against a law textbook. But it should at least have a checklist of legal principles in its internal information system, if it does not already, which it should be required to tick off as it considers them. That would also reduce the chance of an application for judicial review succeeding on the basis that the law has not been considered.

5.74 This seemingly non-technical approach does the reputation of the FOS no favours in the legal world. It prevents it from being taken seriously by the courts or by lawyers, which means that it is less likely that a FOS approach, especially to something which has not yet reached the courts, will be considered or adopted by the courts.

Where the court results would be different

5.75 The main category where FOS cases are decided differently to a court is where the FOS chooses in the interests of fairness to disregard clear policy exclusions where the insurer's actions are not at fault. Contract certainty for the industry is compromised and the insurer in question is unfairly penalised. It might be better to have occasional harsh results for the consumer and not to stray from the strict legal interpretation, especially as these situations are not much reported in *Ombudsman News*, so it is assumed that they do not occur often. The FOS should not be able to force insurers to make payments outside of the terms of the contract when there is nothing inherently unfair about the contract terms or its sale process. Sometimes an event occurs which is bad for the claimant, but is simply uninsured. Sympathy for the claimant should not be relevant to policy construction.

Conclusion

5.76 In conclusion, if the FOS adopted a more technical approach to construction it would reduce the threat of judicial review proceedings and give confidence in the market about contract certainty, whilst making little difference to FOS results. Perhaps it should also refer more cases to the FSA to review the position in relation to that particular insurer, so that the FSA can carry out wider policing of ICOBS.

CHAPTER 6

TRAVEL INSURANCE

IN GENERAL

6.1 The courts interpret travel insurance in accordance with the principles of construction set out above, and apply no special rules. However, the FOS probably sees many more of these complaints,[1] and has developed some of its own approaches (as follows) where there is no case law on point, mostly based on standards it expects from the sales codes. The comments above in relation to sales codes apply here too.

6.2 Travel insurance is often sold as an add-on to another product, such as the holiday itself or other financial services product. In this situation, consumers are rarely focusing on the breadth of the actual cover and the quality of the claims administration, but more on the price. They are likely only to consider an explanatory brochure rather than the policy itself and to presume that the policy will cover them for every possibly travel eventuality. However, ICOBS must still be followed, and key and/or unusual features must be explained at the sales point and in the explanatory leaflets. Sending consumers a copy of the policy and expecting them to review its terms is not sufficient. The FOS will expect consumer travellers to rely heavily on the leaflets and what is said at the sales point. The presumptions that consumers make are not necessarily the fault of the insurer, although the FOS may expect the insurer to anticipate and actively neutralise the most common presumptions in its sales process and explanatory brochures.

RENEWAL

6.3 See below under non-disclosure at paragraphs 13.92 *et seq* for a discussion of renewal of annual travel policies and the need to disclose medical conditions.

CANCELLATION

6.4 Assuming that the policy is sold in accordance with the relevant code, the FOS tends to uphold strictly the limits on a travel policy's cancellation clauses, much as a court would. In Case Study 56/1,[2] the insured did not make suitable arrangements to obtain a visa in time, but cancellation cover was only available if cancellation was beyond the insured's control. The

---

1. Approximately one in eight complaints related to travel insurance in 2001 and 2004/5—*Ombudsman News* July 2001 and FOS Annual Review 2004/5—although in 2009/10 they accounted for only 3% of new claims—FOS Annual Review 2009/10.
2. *Ombudsman News* Sept/Oct 2006.

FOS agreed with insurers that it was not beyond his control. It was irrelevant to the exclusion that the travel agent had wrongly represented that if the insured cancelled the holiday when he did, insurers would refund 50%. A court would have agreed with the FOS, especially as the travel agent was probably the insured's agent, and the cancellation was unrelated to the misrepresentation, and indeed, had to occur whatever the travel agent said in view of the fact that the insured did not have his visa. In Case Study 7/11[3] the complaint was rejected when the insured missed his flight because of a traffic jam getting to the airport, and cancellation cover only applied under the policy if the flight failed or was disrupted.

CURTAILMENT WHERE THE POLICYHOLDER HAS NO FINANCIAL LOSS

6.5 If an insured has to curtail his holiday, insurers might consider that he has suffered no financial loss if they have paid for the return flight, or if the airline has allowed him to change his return date without additional charge. Either way, he has paid for and taken two flights. However, few would choose to pay for a return trip to Australia for instance, only to have to return home in a couple of days. There is an argument for which the FOS has said that it has considerable sympathy, that insurers should reimburse proportionately the cost of the flights, bearing in mind the number of days spent on holiday compared to the number of days originally scheduled. There has been no published case study on point, so it is not clear if this truly represents the current FOS position in practice. However, it is not clear why the FOS thinks it fair that the insurer should perform over and above the requirements of the policy just because the insured might suffer some non-financial loss for which he is not insured. A court would not.

CURTAILMENT BECAUSE OF ILL-HEALTH OR DEATH

6.6 If an insured does not consult the insurer's emergency helpline as required by most travel policies before curtailing a holiday because of ill health, the FOS does not generally accept that there was any need for the holiday curtailment. A court would also apply the requirement strictly. If a person is confined to his room due to illness, the FOS will uphold his partner's claims for holiday curtailment (maybe even without a call to the helpline) if there was a medical need for the partner to stay with the patient. In Case Study 56/2,[4] the FOS found that there was no such need for the wife to stay with her husband in his cabin after he broke his leg. It felt that the insurer's offer to pay for the cost of the cruise for the husband only from when he was laid up, was fair and reasonable, especially as the relevant clause in the policy only actually provided cover if the insured had been forced to return home.

    6.7 Curtailment of a holiday may also be necessary due to the death or ill health of a relative not on the holiday and the policy usually sets out the ambit of its curtailment cover. In Case Study 1/21,[5] the policy unambiguously covered holiday curtailment following the death of a relative resident in the UK. The relative in question had died in Kenya, so the insurer declined the claim. The FOS refused to apply the wording strictly, as the insured would have had to return home to the UK first wherever the relative had died. This is one of

---

3. *Ombudsman News* July 2001.
4. *Ombudsman News* Sept/Oct 2006.
5. *Ombudsman News* Jan 2001.

the rare examples of a case study where the FOS has decided the matter contrary to, and in spite of, the clear policy wording. Its reasons are understandable, and the results may be fair, but this goes against contract certainty. A court would not have been able to contradict the clear policy wording, but might have tried to employ a tool to circumvent the result, such as considering the term unfair or onerous and needy of express notification.

PRE-EXISTING MEDICAL CONDITIONS[6]

6.8 Although standard, the FOS views an exclusion for pre-existing medical conditions to be onerous, and therefore requires the insurer's exact requirements to be expressly drawn to the attention of any prospective policyholder. A signed declaration that the insured has read and understood the policy will not be enough to meet this requirement. By contrast, because it is in every standard policy, a court would be unlikely to consider such a term onerous,[7] and if it did, its decision would not be based on a breach of sales code. If the complaint reaches the FOS, it will make a detailed enquiry as to whether there was in fact a pre-existing medical condition which the policyholder should reasonably be taken to have known about and disclosed.

6.9 Non-disclosure of pre-existing medical conditions may result from an inadequate sales process, so that the insured does not realise that particular information is required. In Case Study 7/8,[8] the insured booked a holiday without disclosing an operation due to take place after the holiday. The operation was brought forward, the insured cancelled the holiday and the insurer refused cover. There was no evidence that the travel agent who sold the policy had made the insured aware of the need to disclose the operation and the consequence if he did not, so the FOS felt that the insured could not have been expected to do so. The insured's signed declaration that he had read and understood the policy terms did not affect the position. It seems that, probably without analysing the position, the FOS regarded the travel agent as the agent for the insurer. However, at the time of this case study, it had no jurisdiction over travel agents. In contrast, the complaint in Case Study 7/9[9] was rejected where the FOS could not fault the sale process or the clarity of the policy terms. It found the exclusion for pre-existing conditions and the advice to call to arrange cover for any pre-existing medical conditions to be clear. So the FOS supported insurers who refused to pay for the cancellation of a family holiday when there were problems with the daughter's kidney transplant operation. The girl had had kidney problems for years, but no mention of them had been made to insurers.

6.10 Non-disclosure can also occur if the insured does not realise that the medical condition is serious enough to warrant disclosure. That was the position in Case Study 76/10,[10] where the insured did not disclose his cough when he thought nothing of it and did not suspect that it would worsen so that he would have to cancel his holiday. The FOS found that it was not reasonable for him to be expected to disclose his cough in these circumstances.

---

6. See further below at paras. 7.14 *et seq* for pre-existing medical conditions in a non-travel context, for life insurance.

7. Although it is not a given that if a term is standard, it will also be fair. See for instance, *Munkenbeck & Marshall v Michael Harold* [2005] EWHC 356 (TCC), where some of the architect profession-wide standard terms were found to be onerous under UTCCR.

8. *Ombudsman News* July 2001.

9. *Ombudsman News* July 2001.

10. *Ombudsman News* Mar/Apr 2009.

6.11 Details of the respective sales evidence in these complaints is limited, and the FOS does not mention the concept of foreseeable loss, but it may be that the difference in outcome in the above cases might in reality be related to how foreseeable the FOS thinks the likelihood of cancellation was to the policyholder, rather than to how the policy was sold. Perhaps the father of the kidney transplant girl might not have booked a holiday if he had believed that he, rather than insurers, would be at risk of bearing the cancellation costs if there was a problem (and a highly foreseeable one at that).

MEDICAL CARE

6.12 Insurers are not responsible for the standard or availability of care in a holiday destination, decisions about repatriation from local practitioners, or if any medical decision about treatment or repatriation is incorrect. The FOS will not therefore hold them responsible for these things. They will be held responsible for paying for and sanctioning appropriate treatment, not to ensure that it is available or that it will meet UK standards. There is no reason to think that a court would approach these situations differently. However, the remedy that the FOS might award if the insurer does not comply with these duties might be different to a court. For instance the FOS might make an award for distress or inconvenience or refund other financial loss such as credit card charges if the insurer delayed sanctioning a required medical treatment abroad.[11]

HAZARDOUS ACTIVITIES

6.13 A standard travel policy will not generally cover medical expenses and personal accident for hazardous activities, but the exclusion must be clear about what activities will be regarded as hazardous, or the FOS will apply the *contra proferentem* rule, as would a court. The FOS will also expect it to be clear from the policy where the exclusions for hazardous activities are located. So if there was a list of hazardous activities which were excluded, the FOS might not allow insurers to rely on further relevant exclusions which were contained only in a different segment of the policy.

6.14 In Case Study 7/1,[12] insurers had not explained that motorbike travel was excluded as a hazardous activity in an annual travel policy. They delayed sending out the policy which meant that the family did not have a chance to check it was suitable before they left for the USA. The FOS said that as a result, the insurer would not have been able to rely on the exclusions if a claim had arisen during this US trip, although it could rely on the exclusion by the time of the trip by the son to Australia, by which time the insured had received the policy and had time to check it for suitability.[13] A court would probably agree, as a policyholder would need to read the policy or be told what was included within the hazardous

---

11. See above "FOS awards for distress or inconvenience" at paras. 3.14 *et seq* and "Other awards/directions" at paras. 3.24 *et seq*.

12. *Ombudsman News* July 2001.

13. The son died in a motorbike accident in Australia. The policy was due to lapse shortly after he had left for Australia. By the time he left, the FOS found that the family knew that the policy did not cover all hazardous activities, had had time to check it for suitability, and they had not checked that it would have covered the trip or the activities he had planned. The hazardous activities exclusions applied so the full death benefit was not payable. The insurers met the repatriation and funeral expenses as a gesture of goodwill in recognition of the problems at the sales point, and the FOS held that this was reasonable.

activities exclusion to realise that motorbike riding was excluded, as it is not necessarily obvious that it would be excluded. Indeed, the requirement of an insurer to communicate what is covered and excluded was the basis of the recent Court of Appeal decision in *Quantum Processing Services Co* v *Axa Insurance UK plc*.[14] There the travel policy excluded hazardous activities, but when the insured had disclosed that he was going scuba-diving, the insurer had agreed to cover him for this, without telling him that in fact it would not cover cave- or solo-diving. The court held that he was nonetheless covered when he went cave-diving. The insurer had not told him of any restrictions as to what he could do as a diver and the policy only made sense if the general conditions were read in context as covering all scuba-diving.

6.15 A court might also apply UTCCR to consumer contracts to determine whether an exclusion for a particular hazardous activity is fair.[15] One of the very few cases on UTCCR is *Bankers Insurance Co* v *South*.[16] Buckley J held that the exclusion for accidents involving "motorised waterborne craft" was in plain, intelligible language and was a core term to this travel insurance, so was exempt from scrutiny. He added that, anyway, it was not an unfair exclusion, as it was available to the holidaymaker to read if he had wanted to. He pointed out that the insurance was relatively cheap. These are sensible attitudes. Although in Case Study 7/1 above, the FOS required the insured to read the policy once he had received it, so that he knew whether motorbike travel was covered, the FOS has never mentioned in its reports the cost of a policy as being relevant to the question of what an insured can therefore reasonably expect it to cover.

BAGGAGE

6.16 Few insureds are aware of the standard exclusions for lost or stolen baggage (e.g. if they are left in an unlocked, unattended vehicle), that settlement is usually on an indemnity basis rather than as new, or that an excess will be deducted. There is a chance though, that the FOS may be more lenient than a court in interpreting these policy restrictions. In Case Study 63/8[17] baggage had to be kept in "locked accommodation" or in "a locked and covered luggage compartment/boot of a motor vehicle". The FOS decided that a camper van was more of a vehicle than an accommodation, but that as it did not have a luggage compartment or boot, securing the items out of sight within the locked van might have been enough to satisfy a valid claim. The complaint was rejected anyway, because the FOS did not believe that the items were secured out of sight as the insured had changed her story.

EARTHQUAKE

6.17 Typically, a travel policy will list circumstances in which it will respond, but usually earthquakes, terrorist attacks and epidemics are not included in the list. This leads to misunderstandings about policy coverage. If there has been no breach of sales code, the FOS will consider in the circumstances of the case what are the reasonable expectations of the policyholder.

14. LTL 15/12/2008, [2008] All ER (D) 152 (Dec).
15. See above "Policy Construction—UTCCR" at paras. 5.64 *et seq.*
16. [2003] EWHC 380.
17. *Ombudsman News* July/Aug 2007.

6.18 In Case Studies 1/19 and 1/20,[18] earthquakes were not included in the list of circumstances covered by the policy, although the FOS commented that they did not need to be specifically excluded. In Case Study 1/19, the FOS agreed with insurers that the policy covered curtailment due to a list of specified reasons (natural disasters were not among them), but did not cover relocation costs when the insured swapped hotels because of his fears about the cracks which had appeared in his original hotel after the earthquake. By contrast, in Case Study 1/20, the elderly couple were not allowed back into their hotel and flew home. Although curtailment for earthquakes was not actually covered, so that a court would have rejected the claim, the FOS upheld the claim for curtailment because it was fair and reasonable to expect curtailment for earthquakes to be covered, and its absence had not been highlighted in the policy material. The FOS was also influenced by the possibility that they might have ended up ill if they had slept out in the open for the rest of the holiday, so would have been eligible for curtailment due to illness. The law does not recognise cover for preventative loss.[19]

6.19 A cynic might comment that the case studies were decided differently due to the FOS having more sympathy for the elderly couple. But the facts are sufficiently different that a different outcome is understandable—stretching a curtailment cover in their case is not the same as inventing a relocation one in the other case.

COMMENTARY

6.20 In relation to travel insurance, the FOS continues to rely on breaches of sales code more than on technical and careful interpretation of wordings. However, it has considered situations which have not been before the courts. Hopefully, these FOS approaches might be useful to the court, but that would be dependent on them being more easily accessible in the public domain and available for a court to consider. Counsel do not usually refer to FOS approaches to bolster their arguments, and they are not usually within a judge's own knowledge.

---

18. *Ombudsman News* Jan 2001.
19. See below under "Household insurance—Preventative damage" at paras. 8.33 *et seq.*

CHAPTER 7

LIFE AND PERSONAL ACCIDENT

CHRONIC CONDITIONS

7.1 Private medical expenses insurance usually excludes "chronic" (i.e. not curable) conditions and limits cover to "acute" (i.e. treatable) conditions. The exact definition of what is included in each section may vary from policy to policy. The FOS considers these to be significant terms to be explained to insureds before inception, along with a warning that an acute condition can become redefined as chronic, and alleviation of chronic symptoms will not be covered. The FOS will look at the policy wording and the medical evidence to determine whether a medical condition falls within the chronic conditions exception.

7.2 In Case Study 1/1,[1] the insurer decided five days before scheduled open heart surgery that a heart condition had become chronic and therefore that the surgery was not covered. The FOS said that this was insufficient notice for the insurer to withdraw its support, and anyway, the medical evidence showed an uncertain prognosis and that the surgery might cure the patient, which made the condition acute, not chronic, so fell within the policy. In Case Study 1/2,[2] the insurer considered that further physiotherapy was not covered as the paralysed condition had become chronic. The FOS found that the medical evidence showed that the condition would continue to improve with further physiotherapy, so was still acute. "Acute" was not clearly defined in the policy and the insurer's apology and *ex gratia* payment of £1,800 towards the cost of home care was sufficient to cover the distress caused by the maladministration.

7.3 In Case Study 77/7,[3] the insurer found that a cancer had become chronic and refused to pay for a particular cancer drug partly because it did not think that it would have any impact on the underlying condition. The FOS looked at the evidence of the use of the drug. It concluded that the drug was a well-established (no longer experimental) and effective treatment for patients in a similar situation to the insured, and that it gave up to a 10% chance of complete remission and a 60% chance of partial remission. So the FOS felt that this meant that the drug could improve or at least stabilise the insured's condition, and the policy explicitly covered treatment "intended to stabilise and bring under control a chronic condition". Therefore, in view of the balance of evidence, the FOS told the insurer to authorise and pay for the use of the drug in this case. It also said that the insurer could exclude the cost of any treatment, medical attention or surgery that might arise in any future claims from this insured if they came about as a consequence of his undergoing treatment with this drug.[4]

---

1. *Ombudsman News* Jan 2001.
2. *Ombudsman News* Jan 2001.
3. *Ombudsman News* May/June 2009.
4. See also "Unproven and experimental treatment" below at paras. 7.5 *et seq*.

7.4 The courts would look at both the wording and the medical evidence as the FOS did in the case studies above, and the results might well be similar. There is no case law directly on point.

UNPROVEN AND EXPERIMENTAL TREATMENT

7.5 Unproven or experimental treatments are often excluded in medical insurance policies. However, where a condition is covered, the FOS considers that it will generally be fair and reasonable for the insurer to indemnify the insured's costs of a newer, untested treatment advised by a consultant, instead of an established one, up to the sum of the cost of the conventional treatment for which the insurer would have been liable. An example is Case Study 77/8,[5] where the insurer relied on findings of The National Institute for Health and Clinical Excellence about the status of the proposed treatment as being experimental. It would therefore only pay the insured the equivalent cost of the conventional treatment. The FOS endorsed both the evidence on which the insurer relied and the insurer's response. However, as Case Study 77/7[6] demonstrates, the FOS may not consider a treatment experimental if there is sufficient evidence to show that it could improve or at least stabilise a condition. And even if the FOS supports the insured wanting the experimental treatment, it may allow insurers to exclude the cost of any treatment, medical attention or surgery that might arise in any future claims from the insured if they came about as a consequence of treatment with the experimental drug in question.

7.6 There is no case law on point, and as this approach is fair, it would be good if the courts adopted the same reasoning if ever they had the opportunity.

MENTAL ILLNESS

7.7 Health policies usually exclude disability claims which arise from stress or other mental illness. They also usually require the insured to be in work when a disability arises and exclude a claim for employment benefit when the insured is not actively seeking work. The FOS regards these as significant limitations which must be highlighted to the proposer before inception. When looking at employment benefit, the FOS will consider whether any illness suffered by the insured was so severe that it would have prevented him from working and how likely it is that the insured would have found work were it not for the illness. Also, if an employment benefit would be payable but for a mental illness, or a disability benefit would be payable but for a redundancy, the FOS may allow all or part of the claim.

7.8 In Case Study 4/5,[7] the assured was made redundant and then suffered depression. The policy terms were clear. Because the assured would have been entitled to redundancy benefit if she was not depressed, the FOS felt that payment of 50% of the maximum redundancy benefit was appropriate. This seems a strange result and one with which a court, following the clear language of the policy, would not agree. It is odd that an insurer may be prevented from excluding, even with clear language, a common problem—depression following a redundancy, making it less likely that the insured will be able actively and

5. *Ombudsman News* May/June 2009.
6. *Ombudsman News* May/June 2009, also referred to above in "Chronic conditions" at paras. 7.1 *et seq.*
7. *Ombudsman News* Apr 2001.

effectively to seek and find work and come off the insurance benefits. Perhaps the FOS approach reflects a feeling that the exclusion of mental illness after redundancy needs to be highlighted to the insured at the sales point. No mention of the sale of this policy is made in the report. Perhaps instead the FOS simply considers an exclusion for mental illness following a redundancy to be inherently unfair, in which case surely it would have awarded 100% of the benefits. A court would have granted all or none of the benefits, rather than the 50% compromise, and would be more likely to have granted nothing unless it thought the exclusion an onerous or unfair term.

7.9 In Case Study 80/5,[8] the insured was suffering from an illness not specified in the report which prevented her from continuing to work. Her payment protection policy required her to be in employment before a claim would be paid. However, because she resigned from her job as a result of her illness two weeks before she was able to obtain an appointment with her GP and his medical certificate confirming her inability to work, insurers refused to pay the claim. The FOS felt that it would be fair and reasonable for the insurer to pay the claim even though she did not strictly meet the policy's continuing employment criteria. It was satisfied from the evidence that when she resigned, her health met the policy definition of "disability," so she would have qualified for benefit under the policy if she had been able to get an appointment with her GP within a reasonable time. She had been unable to get the GP appointment as he had been on holiday and fully booked before that and the FOS did not think it was appropriate for the insurer to take advantage of this. Without seeing the terms of the policy it is hard to say what a court would have done, but a court might not have been able to interpret the terms so flexibly.

CRITICAL ILLNESS COVER

7.10 Policies for critical illness usually list the illnesses which will trigger cover and any limitations on cover, such as a requirement for 28 days survival after diagnosis before a sum for care until death can be claimed. Each policy will have slightly different coverage so the FOS considers it important that exactly what is covered and any important limitations on cover are explained to the proposer before inception or his complaints have a greater chance of being upheld. The FOS will assess the medical evidence to determine whether a condition falls within the policy definitions or was pre-existing.

7.11 In Case Study 24/3,[9] the insured needed an angioplasty. The policy terms were such that the insurer would only pay if there was a 70% blockage in each heart artery. The insured's consultant said that the condition was very life-threatening, and the blockage was 95–99% in one artery but only 50% in the other. The FOS said that according to any ordinary definition, this would be a critical illness that needed urgent treatment. A strictly formulaic definition such as the one in this policy was an onerous condition which had not been made clear in the literature. The FOS commented that insurers should be cautious when relying on a formulaic basis for assessing how blocked an artery was, since this was not an exact science. Instead, insurers should look at the overall seriousness of the situation which here was too serious to rely on a strict formulaic interpretation. In any case, if the insured did not have the angioplasty, he would have had to have bypass surgery that would have entitled him

---

8. *Ombudsman News* Oct/Nov 2009.
9. *Ombudsman News* Jan 2003.

to claim under the policy anyway.[10] The FOS told insurers to pay £100,000 of the claim plus interest with a recommendation that they met the remaining £50,000.[11] The FOS was surely right to uphold this complaint, and it is likely that a court would have found a way of interpreting the policy similarly or relying on the onerous condition point of *Interfoto*.[12] The FOS comments indicate that the FOS would have found the formulaic definition unfair even if the insured had been warned of it before inception.

7.12 In Case Study 80/4,[13] the policy required a definite diagnosis of the multiple sclerosis before a pay-out of critical illness benefits. So insurers refused to pay the benefits during the period between the insured's consultant's diagnosis of probable multiple sclerosis and the confirmed diagnosis. The FOS supported insurers. A widely accepted diagnostic test existed for this illness, so the FOS felt that it was appropriate for the insurer to rely on the result of this test before it would provide cover.

APPROVED LIST OF DOCTORS OR HOSPITALS

7.13 The terms of private medical insurance usually limit the cover available to an approved list of doctors seeing patients in an approved list of hospitals. In certain circumstances, the FOS may force insurers to cover treatment from other doctors in other hospitals, subject to a limit on cover up to the cost that the approved hospital or doctor would have charged. In Case Study 77/6,[14] an insured wanted to see a consultant in her local hospital even though he was not on the insurer's approved list and even though he was more expensive than one on the list. The FOS required the insurer to allow this in view of the insured's mobility and other health issues, the lack of an alternative consultant in her town and the fact that the fees in question were not particularly high compared to those of other consultants in the area. However, the FOS limited the insurer's obligation to pay for this consultant to the amount it would have cost to see one of the insurer's approved consultants. In Case Study 85/3,[15] the elderly insured who lived in rural Scotland did not want to travel over 80 miles to a city hospital which was on the insurer's approved list for a cataract operation which she wanted to have in her local clinic which was not on the approved list. The conditions of the policy said that the insurer would reimburse the policyholder for the costs incurred in obtaining treatment at an approved hospital, so if the operation had been carried out an at approved hospital, it would have been reimbursed in full. In these circumstances, the insurer was asked to pay the insured the amount it would have paid if her operation had been carried out at the hospital on the approved list, which was slightly less than the amount she had paid for treatment at the local clinic. The FOS distinguished this sort of policy from one where the insurer offers to provide treatment at specific hospitals and will arrange payment direct with the hospital and consultant concerned. It is not clear why this would distinguish the case, and why the same remedy would not have existed in the same circumstances even if this had been the wording.

---

10. The law does not generally require insurers to provide cover for preventative loss unless such cover is expressed in the policy. See below at para. 8.36 for the FOS approach in household claims.
11. The upper limit for a FOS award is £100,000. See above for further details under "Limits on money awards" at paras. 3.2 *et seq.*
12. See above *Interfoto* at paras. 5.53 *et seq.*
13. *Ombudsman News* Oct/Nov 2009.
14. *Ombudsman News* May/June 2009.
15. *Ombudsman News* Apr/May 2010.

PRE-EXISTING MEDICAL CONDITIONS[16]

7.14 When consumers apply for a policy which excludes pre-existing medical conditions, the FOS[17] does not think they need to be asked about their medical history, as long as they are made aware that the policy contains such an exclusion and are given clear information about how it will operate. In Case Study 62/7,[18] the insured's incapacity related to an undisclosed pre-existing condition so was not covered under the payment protection policy, and the FOS rejected a complaint about non-payment of the sickness benefit. This decision seems sensible and in line with what a court would decide.

7.15 Unfortunately, insurers have acquired a bad reputation for trawling through medical histories at the point of claim to see if there has been a discrepancy between the medical history and the information disclosed at proposal or to see if a condition is pre-existing. There was concern that publicity about this was why the number of critical illness policies being sold halved between 2006/7 and 2007/8.[19] To prevent insurers behaving like this, the Association of British Insurers ("ABI") issued formal written guidance in January 2008 on non-disclosure in protection insurance.[20] It embodied the FOS categories of misrepresentations with alternative remedies to the law's avoidance of the policy.[21] The ABI upgraded this guidance to a Code of Practice[22] in January 2009, which means that it is compulsory for its members to follow. The FOS reported a significant fall in 2008/9 in these types of complaints since the ABI guidance was issued.[23]

7.16 When assessing whether a condition is pre-existing, the FOS continues the IOB's approach of following the House of Lords' definition of "condition" in *Cook v Financial Insurance Co Ltd*.[24] This requires a medical condition to be diagnosed as such by doctors before the policy is taken out, and some generalised symptoms occurring beforehand will not count. The FOS will review the assured's medical history and look at the position at the time when the policy was taken out including the:

(1) intensity of symptoms;
(2) seriousness with which the symptoms were regarded;
(3) diagnosis given, and when;
(4) treatment advised or given, and when;
(5) difference between the symptoms at inception and the medical condition which gave rise to the claim—the more remote the connection, the less likely the FOS is to accept that the condition existed at inception and
(6) assured's knowledge of the condition at inception.

---

16. See also "Travel" above at paras. 6.8 *et seq.*
17. *Ombudsman News* June/July 2007.
18. *Ombudsman News* June/July 2007.
19. The number of policies sold fell from 86,000 in 2006/7 to 44,000 in 2007/8: FSA, Pure Protection Contracts: Product Sales Data Trends Report (September 2008).
20. ABI Guidance, "Non-Disclosure and Treating Customers Fairly in Claims for Long-Term Protection Insurance Products" January 2008.
21. See below under "Non-disclosure and Misrepresentation—Fraudulent, deliberate, innocent, reckless or inadvertent non-disclosure" at paras. 13.28 *et seq.*
22. ABI Code of Practice, "Managing Claims for Individual and Group Life, Critical Illness and Income Protection Insurance Products" (January 2009.)
23. In 2006/7, the FOS closed 376 complaints where non-disclosure was the dominant issue in critical illness and income protection disputes, and in 2008/9, it closed 130 such cases. (Figures taken from the Law Commission's Final Report dated 15/12/09.)
24. [1998] 1 WLR 1765.

7.17 Case Study 80/3[25] applied the effect of *Cook* without the report actually mentioning the case. The insured suffered seemingly minor symptoms pre-inception which were in fact symptoms of a serious condition diagnosed after inception and which led to a claim for sickness benefit under payment protection insurance. The FOS obliged the insurer to pay the claim, as it concluded from the evidence that the insured did not know at inception that he was suffering from a serious respiratory condition. The evidence was that no definite diagnosis had been made before inception, although the insured had been referred to a consultant. The insured had not seen or been told about the notes made by the GP which speculated about several possible causes of the symptoms, one of which was this condition.

7.18 To avoid *Cook*, some insurers changed their wording to include symptoms which were apparent before inception, even if the condition was not diagnosed. An example is in Case Study 56/3,[26] but the FOS still applied *Cook*, and told the insurer that it was acting unlawfully in relying on the exclusion to refuse a claim for holiday cancellation. The insured had collapsed before inception and both he and his GP thought that this was migraine-related. The insured booked his holiday, but after a brain scan ordered by the GP as a sensible precaution, found out just before he left that he had in fact suffered a minor stroke. His doctor told him not to fly. The FOS also required the insurer to compensate the insured for distress and inconvenience caused by their refusal to pay the claim. A court would not have found that the insurer had been acting unlawfully, but might have found the terms unfair under UTCCR or onerous and un-notified under *Interfoto*.[27]

7.19 Other insurers try to get around *Cook* by providing for a moratorium exclusion. This excludes cover for a medical condition whose symptoms existed at inception until they have not been treated or advised about further for a set period, often two years after inception. There is no specific case law dealing with moratorium exclusions. A court would begin with the wording and interpret it in accordance with its usual principles. The FOS seems to accept moratorium exclusions and applied one in Case Study 13/3.[28]

7.20 A common question is whether high blood pressure at inception is a pre-existing condition for stroke so as to exclude stroke cover. In January 2002, the FOS reported that its initial view was that such an exclusion had the potential to be an onerous term which needed to be highlighted to the insured before inception. The FOS has not commented further as yet, although in Case Study 13/3 in the same edition of *Ombudsman News*, this situation arose, and it rejected the complaint without labelling the moratorium an onerous condition. The insurers had refused to pay the claim when the insured suffered a stroke during a two-year moratorium and had been treated for the previous few years for high blood pressure. A court would probably have agreed.

7.21 Another common question is whether early symptoms of multiple sclerosis, such as pins and needles or numbness were pre-existing conditions and whether they should have been disclosed when these symptoms were vague and at the time were dismissed as nothing. If the question was clear, the FOS will probably consider such non-disclosure as inadvertent, and apply a proportionate remedy, asking the insurer how it would have dealt with the proposal had it known the true information.[29] The Law Commissions cite[30] just such an

---

25. *Ombudsman News* Oct/Nov 2009.
26. *Ombudsman News* Sept/Oct 2006.
27. See "Onerous and unfair terms" above at paras. 5.52 *et seq.*
28. *Ombudsman News* Jan 2002.
29. See further "Inadvertent non-disclosure" below at paras. 13.50 *et seq.*
30. Final report 15/12/09, para. 3.30.

example taken from its 2009 survey of 47 FOS non-disclosure case studies, of which four out of 17 critical illness claims related to multiple sclerosis.

7.22 The common law, if referred to, might assist the FOS in these sorts of cases. For instance, in *Zeller* v *British Caymanian Insurance Co Ltd*,[31] a case decided under Cayman law which follows the English law approach, a consumer did not disclose that he had consulted a doctor and received a slightly raised cholesterol reading. The Privy Council found that he was still acting in good faith because he did not realise that the information was relevant. Lord Bingham commented that where a proposer is asked whether he has recently seen a doctor, "he is expected to exercise his judgment on what appears to him to be worth disclosing. He does not lose his cover if he fails to disclose a complaint which he thought to be trivial but which turns out later to be a symptom of some much more serious underlying condition".

7.23 In the Law Commissions' 2009 survey of FOS cases, they found an example of the proposer failing to mention her eating disorder in response to a question about psychiatric illness, because part of the illness was that she did not recognise it as such. She later developed multiple sclerosis. The FOS found that she had not been acting dishonestly or recklessly, but that if there had been full disclosure, the insurer would have excluded mental illness and increased the premium by 50%. The FOS asked insurers to pay two-thirds of the normal claim.

7.24 Many complaints to the FOS about pre-existing medical conditions are actually about non-disclosure, so the topic will be re-visited below at Chapter 13 under "Non-disclosure".

THE EFFECT OF A PRE-EXISTING CONDITION CONTRIBUTING IN PART TO THE LOSS

7.25 If a pre-existing condition has contributed to the loss, the law will not allow any of the claim, whilst the FOS may allow a proportionate recovery in accordance with common industry practice.[32] So if the medical evidence shows that an accident caused 10% of the injury, and the other 90% was due to degenerative change which was excluded under the policy, the FOS would usually ask the insurer to pay 10% of the benefit. The FOS view is that the mere presence of degenerative change should not exclude genuine personal accident claims to which policies are designed to respond. An example is in Case Study 13/18,[33] where an RAF engineer suffered back injury but had a history of such injury. The FOS felt that the insurer should pay 50% of the claim because the accident in question had significantly worsened the condition that had originated previously.

7.26 The FOS has not commented further following *Blackburn Rovers Football and Athletic Club plc* v *Avon Insurance plc*.[34] A footballer had a spinal injury. The Court of Appeal held that an exclusion for injury caused by degeneration applied whether or not the degeneration was normal in the population as part of the normal ageing process. If normal degeneration often led to injury, there was good reason to exclude it. If normal degeneration did not often lead to injury, then the law was unlikely to conclude that it had been a cause of injury induced by trauma on the sports field. The assured therefore could not recover if it

31. [2008] UKPC 4.
32. *Ombudsman News* Mar 2005.
33. *Ombudsman News* Jan 2002.
34. [2005] EWCA Civ 423.

could be shown that the player's disablement was attributable, even only in part, to the degenerative pre-condition, whether or not that pre-condition was normal. In the subsequent trial, Dobbs J found that the degenerative condition had been a cause of the injury, so on the Court of Appeal's reasoning, the assured could not recover.[35] The FOS would have probably awarded a proportionate recovery, saying that part of the injury related to the pre-existing condition, and part did not.

7.27 The FOS approach may seem fair. After all, the assured has suffered in part an insured loss. But what makes it unfair, is that it ignores the fact that insurers choose to exclude pre-existing disabilities for very good reason, precisely so that they will not be liable for an injury which is partly caused by that condition, which makes the total of the injury, and therefore the liability, greater. The premium for such a policy is set accordingly.

"ANY OCCUPATION" COVER AGAINST DISABILITY

7.28 In order of the most expensive type of disability policy first, cover can be obtained for (i) the insured being unable to continue his own occupation, (ii) any occupation for which he is suited because of education, training or experience, or (iii) any occupation whatsoever. The policy should state clearly what level of cover it offers, as the courts tend to interpret narrowly the third option. Insureds must continue to pay their premiums for whichever of the above policies they have, even if they have submitted a complaint to the firm or to the FOS. Premiums are usually waived during a time of incapacity when a claim is being paid, but should re-commence if the consumer returns to work and wants to keep the policy in force. If an insurer stops paying a claim, the onus is on it to show why the consumer no longer meets the necessary criteria.

"Any occupation"

7.29 The Court of Appeal in *Sargent* v *GRE (UK) Ltd*[36] held that "any occupation" is by itself an ambiguous term, and must be interpreted in context. The context of that case was that the policy was marketed to armed forces personnel, so the term was construed as referring only to the insured's occupation in the armed forces prior to his injury. He could recover under the disability policy even though he was fit for other work.

7.30 The FOS comments[37] that this judgment broadly corresponds with its own "fair and reasonable" approach. It views as harsh limiting benefits to those rare situations where an insured is unable to carry on any occupation at all, unless this has clearly been explained to the insured before inception. If there are no further qualifications or definitions, the FOS will interpret "any occupation" or "suited occupation" as meaning "any relevant occupation", or "any suited occupation", that is, any occupation for which the insured is suited by reason of his education, training, experience and social standing. So a painter and decorator who could no longer work on ladders could still do light duties, for instance working in a DIY outlet or builders' merchants where he could use his painting and decorating experience to advise customers. He did not therefore meet the "any occupation" definition of incapacity.[38] The FOS would not usually consider it reasonable to expect an unskilled manual worker to retrain

---

35. *Blackburn Rovers Football & Athletic Club plc* v *Avon Insurance plc* [2007] Lloyd's Rep IR 1.
36. [2000] Lloyd's Rep IR 77.
37. *Ombudsman News* Sept/Oct 2004.
38. FOS Consumer Factsheet on Income Protection Insurance on the FOS website.

as a skilled professional and vice versa. Probably, based on the *Sargent* context test, nor would a court.

Scope of the previous occupation

7.31 It may be necessary to determine the scope of a previous occupation which the assured can no longer carry out. The wording and context of every policy is different, but if there is a similarity to a decided case, there is also a thread of precedent for a court to follow. In *Johnson* v *IGI Insurance Co Ltd*,[39] the court found that a taxi-driver who could no longer drive could not undertake "similar gainful employment" simply because he could derive an income from renting out his taxis to other drivers. In *Hooper* v *Accidental Death Insurance Co*,[40] the assured could recover under the policy where he was *substantially* unable to "follow usual business or occupation", not only when he was *entirely* unable to. If the latter had applied, the court held that the policy should have expressly said so, and the FOS would have agreed wholeheartedly. In *Howells* v *IGI Insurance*,[41] a professional footballer was not permanently disabled from carrying on his "occupation" when injury forced him to drop from the Premier League to a lower division, since he was still a footballer.

7.32 Case Study 13/12[42] is the only one that the FOS has published on point. Insurers refused to pay income protection insurance because the insured's illness meant that she could no longer be a nurse, but she could still do her other stated occupation as housewife, as she could still undertake "normal pursuits". The FOS looked at the purpose of the policy as a court would, and upheld the complaint because the policy was meant to protect her from not being able to earn an income as a nurse. Insurers had not explained to her before inception that they would only pay under the policy if she could no longer do both nursing and housewifery. The wording was vague and there was no definition of "normal pursuits", so the FOS interpreted it *contra proferentem*. Even if the FOS did not look at the case law (and none is mentioned), it has still made a fair and reasonable decision which a court would also have been likely to make.

Scope of "any occupation whatsoever" and other common standard terms

7.33 The case law decides the scope of "any occupation whatsoever" on a case-by-case basis. In *Pocock* v *Century Insurance Co Ltd*,[43] the assured was no longer able "to attend to business of any kind" when he was carrying out different and part-time functions for the same employer, as this was only a minor contribution. In *Walton* v *Airtours plc*,[44] a pilot who could only undertake temporary employment was not capable of doing any occupation, as "occupation" implied full-time employment with an element of continuity rather than sporadic, part-time work, or work that could not be carried out without structured support. In *McGeown* v *Direct Travel Insurance*,[45] to fall within the wording "permanent disability which prevents you from doing all your usual activities", the insured had to be unable to carry on the normal incidents of living, including reasonable mobility and coping with

---

39. [1997] 6 CL 358.
40. (1860) 3 H & N 546.
41. [2003] Lloyd's Rep IR 803.
42. *Ombudsman News* Jan 2002.
43. [1960] 2 Lloyd's Rep 150.
44. [2004] Lloyd's Rep IR 97.
45. [2004] Lloyd's Rep IR 599.

domestic chores and personal care. Being unable to continue one pastime, in this case horse-riding, was not sufficient.

7.34 Case Study 40/5[46] is the only FOS one published on point. A professional dancer could no longer dance due to injury, but she could do other things. As the cover clearly related to "any occupation whatsoever" and the insured had signed a specific endorsement which said "any occupation whatsoever", the FOS supported insurers who rejected the claim. Although she was able to claim state benefits, the FOS rightly pointed out that qualification for these was different to qualification under the policy. A court might have come to the same conclusion on the basis of the clarity of the language, but it might have relied on *Pocock* and *Walton* to decide that in the context of the policy, the professional dancer should recover if she could no longer dance. The FOS does not mention any case law in its report of this case study.

7.35 The FOS will expect both the terms "any occupation whatsoever" and "activities of daily living" to be fully explained to the consumer before inception, as these are such broadly limiting terms. The activities of daily living should be clearly set out in the insurance policy. The words "total disability" or "total incapacity", without further definition in the policy clearly highlighted, may be interpreted to mean whether the consumer is totally unable to carry out the essential or substantial duties of his occupation, not whether he is totally unable to carry out all the duties required by his occupation. Total disability in relation to "own occupation" will be interpreted as meaning not being able to carry out the occupation, rather than not being able to carry on with a specific job at the consumer's actual employer, as long as they are not carrying out any other occupation. So although someone with certain skin conditions could no longer work for his employer in the oil industry, he could still carry out the same job in another industry. By comparison, a nurse could not return to her own occupation, as the medical evidence suggested that the material and substantial tasks involved were too much for her, and as the complex work she did was a material and substantial part of her occupation, she could not do that occupation.[47]

CAUSATION IN A PERSONAL ACCIDENT POLICY

7.36 For personal accident cover to apply, the assured's death or disablement must have resulted from bodily injury proximately caused by an accident, i.e. by an external, violent and visible cause. The courts tend to look at the immediate cause, and not to any earlier one in the chain. In *Winspear* v *Accident Insurance Co*,[48] the assured suffered a fit (excluded under "natural disease or weakness"), which meant that he fell into a stream and drowned (an accident, which fell within the policy cover). The court found that the cause of death was drowning, so was covered by the policy. In *Lawrence* v *Accident Insurance Co*,[49] the assured had a fit (not covered), which meant that he fell onto a railway line (an accident covered by the policy). The court found that the cause of death was being run over by a train, not the fit, so the policy responded.

---

46. *Ombudsman News* Sept/Oct 2004.
47. *Cf* FOS Consumer Factsheet on Income Protection Insurance on the FOS website, from which these examples have been taken.
48. (1880) 43 LT 459.
49. (1881) 45 LT 29.

7.37 The FOS case studies on point only relate to surgical complications resulting in patient death or bodily injury following surgery, and seem to adopt broadly the same approach as the law. The FOS splits these surgery cases into two types:

(i) Where the injury or death is a natural consequence of the risk of surgery and the patient was unlucky enough to suffer complications, it will reject a complaint about non-payment of an accident claim under a personal accident policy, as it did in Case Study 44/12.[50] There the patient had surgery to remove a lump from her neck, but unfortunately died as a result of complications, although the surgeons had not been negligent.

(ii) Where the injury or death is the result of something unplanned or negligent that happened before, during or after the surgery, and which although was a possibility, was not a natural result of the procedure, the FOS will require insurers to pay under a personal accident policy. In such a case the injury or death is as a result of an external, violent and visible cause. An example is Case Study 44/11,[51] where the patient died as a result of surgeon negligence.

7.38 Although the FOS does not use the law's wording in *Ombudsman News*, namely "immediate cause", these case studies show that actually, it is adopting the same approach. So in Case Study 44/11, the immediate cause of death was the surgeon's negligence (an accident), but in Case Study 44/12, the immediate cause was effectively the illness (not covered as an accident).

7.39 In law, if there are concurrent causes of loss, with an exclusion of liability for one of them, the exclusion prevails and the whole claim can be refused.[52] The FOS has commented[53] that, at least in the context of personal accident policies, it may not follow this practice, but may instead take a proportional approach.[54]

CALCULATION OF BENEFITS

7.40 Disputes arise as to calculation of benefits, particularly under income protection policies. The FOS will check the calculations are accurate and in accordance with the policy. It will consider any ambiguities in the wording, discrepancies between what was offered and provided and any over- or under-insurance, and will look at documents showing the insured's financial circumstances, demands and needs at the sales point.

7.41 Often in relation to income protection policies, the insured has not understood that:

(1) benefits are linked to earnings immediately before incapacity, which may be less than previous earnings;

(2) pre-disability earnings of a self-employed policyholder may be calculated on the basis of net profits, rather than turnover, and without including benefits-in-kind, bonuses, commission, drawings and dividend payments;

---

50. *Ombudsman News* Mar 2005.

51. *Ombudsman News* Mar 2005.

52. *Wayne Tank and Pump* v *Employers Liability Ltd* [1974] 1 QB 57; *Midland Mainline Ltd & Ors* v *Commercial Union Assurance Co Ltd & Ors* [2004] EWCA Civ 1042.

53. *Ombudsman News* Mar 2005.

54. See further above "The effect of a pre-existing condition contributing in part to the loss" at paras. 7.25 *et seq.*

(3) insurers may deduct disability benefits payable under a different policy, although unless clearly stated otherwise in the policy, the FOS will not interpret this to include benefits paid by a payment protection policy.

7.42 The FOS tries to deal with any unfairness. It interprets ambiguous wording contra proferentem. If the problem is a sales one, it may interpret the policy as if the insured purchased the policy he thought he had. If assessment of average income over the 12 months before the claim produces harsh results (for instance, if the insured has been struggling to cope with his disability for some time or if there has been a recent market downturn), the FOS may take an average of earnings over a longer period, say three years, unless the policy clearly restricts this.

7.43 The FOS will support an insurer who takes into account any income that a self-employed policyholder receives from the business during any period of incapacity, if the policy clearly allows this, as it did in Case Study 52/1.[55] In that case, despite his disability, the insured earned more from his business than he would have been entitled to in benefits, so insurers stopped paying the benefits altogether.

7.44 If the insured returns to work in a reduced capacity or to a different occupation, with reduced earnings, a policy may provide for a reduced benefit. If a policyholder's condition improves but he does not return to work, he may lose his entitlement to the full benefit and there may be no proportional or rehabilitation benefit. If the insured's condition improves so that he could go back to work, but in actual fact he cannot, perhaps because his business has failed, or he cannot return to a similar occupation, a proportional payment would be appropriate, depending on the policy wording.

7.45 There is little or no case law on this topic, and so the FOS setting out its approach is of potential usefulness to a court.

COMMENTARY

7.46 Breach of sales codes plays a large role in the FOS approach to interpreting life and personal accident cover, as it considers that consumers often believe that they have bought a wider cover. Comments above about this apply here too.[56] The FOS has developed policies for this cover where the courts do not seem to have encountered the issues, which is useful. However, the FOS does not seem to consider or adopt court precedents where they are available. The FOS departs from the law most significantly in its proportional treatment of pre-existing disabilities and concurrent causes.

---

55. *Ombudsman News* Apr 2006.
56. *Cf* paras. 5.27 *et seq* and 5.71 in "Policy construction: law versus FOS".

CHAPTER 8

HOUSEHOLD INSURANCE

STORM

8.1 Over the years, the courts have developed the definition of storm, beginning with the ordinary and natural meaning of the Oxford English Dictionary and refining it to include rain and wind.[1] The FOS seems to decide storm cases in the same way, although because it does not mention any case law, it is questionable whether this is only a coincidence most likely to happen because the court adopts an ordinary and natural meaning and because the FOS, especially with its non-legal staff, is unlikely to adopt anything else.

8.2 The reported FOS case studies on storm damage causation would be decided the same way in a court, even though the FOS applies an apparently different test. The FOS looks for the "dominant or effective" cause and applies a "but for" test, whilst a court looks for the "proximate" cause.[2] The FOS will investigate whether there was a storm, and whether and how much of the damage is as a result of that storm and so covered by the policy, or as a result of general wear and tear, as demonstrated in Case Studies 18/8 and 18/9.[3] This would also be a court's approach, the only difference being that the FOS has a wider ability to obtain informal evidence. In Case Study 18/8, it telephoned the glazier who had replaced the damaged windows to hear his views on the cause of the damage.

8.3 The FOS illustrates its approach to storm damage causation with two examples.[4] Firstly, it says that if there is evidence of a storm, but the roof tiles would have fallen off the house in a light breeze anyway sooner or later, due to poor maintenance, then the dominant or effective cause of the damage was wear and tear, not storm. The storm was merely the occasion of the damage rather than the cause. Requiring insurers to pay for such damage would be turning an insurance contract into a maintenance contract, which would not be fair or reasonable. In the second example,[5] the FOS concluded that the storm was the dominant or effective cause of the damage caused to the interior where water leaked through a poorly maintained roof during a rainstorm. The roof was not completely dilapidated and would have remained watertight during normal levels of rainfall, but it could not withstand the storm. Despite the lack of maintenance the water would not have entered, therefore, the damage in question was caused by the storm.

---

1. *S&M Hotels* v *Legal and General Assurance* [1972] 1 Lloyd's Rep 157, *Anderson* v *Norwich Union* [1977] 1 Lloyd's Rep 253, *Young* v *Sun Alliance* [1976] 2 Lloyd's Rep 189.
2. *Cf* s. 55(1) MIA 1906 and the leading House of Lords' case, *Leyland Shipping Co Ltd* v *Norwich Union Fire Insurance Society Ltd* [1918] AC 350.
3. Both in *Ombudsman News* July 2002.
4. Referred to in *Ombudsman News* May 2003.
5. Also referred to in *Ombudsman News* May 2003.

8.4 In Case Study 74/8,[6] the FOS applied these principles to a small business claim for storm damage and business interruption. It concluded that the water ingress was caused by the severe weather, not a supposed roof defect. It found no evidence of a roof defect as although there had been structural problems with the roof, there was evidence of repair with nothing to indicate that the repairs had been faulty.

FLOOD

The law

8.5 What constitutes a flood? The earlier cases, *Young* v *Sun Alliance*[7] and *Computer & Systems Engineering plc* v *John Lelliott (Ilford) Ltd*,[8] consider that flood must be caused by a natural, external source and is limited to inundations of water through severe weather conditions. In *Young*, the Court of Appeal found that there was no flood, when on a number of occasions there was a gradual seepage of a small amount of water into the ground floor lavatory of a house, once reaching a depth of 3 inches. In *Lelliott*, the Court of Appeal found that there was no flood when there was water damage caused by a negligent action breaking a pipe in an internal sprinkler system.

8.6 The later cases emanating from *Rohan Investments Ltd* v *Cunningham*,[9] give a wider definition, and consider that the impact of the water and the volume which ingressed, is more important than its source, so that heavy, abnormal rainfall lasting over a period of some days can also constitute a flood. In *Rohan*, the Court of Appeal found that there had been a flood when abnormally heavy rainfall lasting for some days resulted in a large volume of water (3–4 inches) accumulating on the flat roof, and an ingress of water to the assured's house. The Court of Appeal in *Rohan* decided that both *Young* and *Lelliott* were unusual cases and that neither court intended to set a definition of flood.

8.7 In *Tate Gallery (Trustees)* v *Duffy Construction Ltd*,[10] Jackson J attempted to reconcile the authorities. He found that there had been a flood when part of the Tate Gallery under construction became submerged under 1.4 m of water following the decoupling of a pipe from a water main. He concluded that flooding does not have to come from a natural source, does not need to involve a large amount of water accumulating rapidly, and said:

"In determining whether the unwelcome arrival of water upon property constitutes a 'flood', it is relevant to consider (a) whether the source of the water was natural; (b) whether the source of the water was external or internal; (c) the quantity of water; (d) the manner of its arrival; (e) the area and character of the property upon which the water was deposited; (f) whether the arrival of that water was an abnormal event. Ultimately, it is a question of degree whether any given accumulation of water constitutes a flood."

8.8 Jackson J regarded both *Young* and *Lelliott* as "fairly unusual". In *Tate* there was a significantly greater volume of water than in *Young*, in a larger area, the water had come from a source outside the insured premises and its arrival had been abnormal: it did not matter that the source was not natural. It seems then that *Young* should be limited to its specific facts—a

---

6. *Ombudsman News* Dec 2008/Jan 2009.
7. [1976] 2 Lloyd's Rep 189.
8. (1990) 54 BLR 1.
9. [1999] Lloyd's Rep IR 190.
10. [2007] EWHC 361 (TCC). Followed in *Tyco Fire and Integrated Solutions (UK) Ltd* v *Rolls-Royce Motor Cars Ltd* [2007] EWHC 137 (TCC) (the point did not arise on Tyco's appeal [2008] EWCA Civ 286).

gradual ingress by seepage of a small amount of water which was not the result of some form of external event will not constitute a flood.

The FOS

8.9 The FOS says it has changed its approach from its IOB days and now applies the *Rohan* definition of flood, as that is closer to the ordinary expectations of household policyholders. The FOS says that *Rohan* shows that a flood can originate from a slow and steady build-up of water, not necessarily from a natural phenomenon. It then applies this test to the case studies without referring to later case law. That might be reasonable if it said that it preferred *Rohan* as being *dicta* from a higher court than the later case law, but as it is never mentioned, it does not appear that the FOS is aware of this later case law. It gives the impression that once the FOS has decided the standard which it wants to adopt, it does not look any further and does not keep up with developments in the law. So applying its test in Case Studies 10/1,[11] 18/18[12] and 73/8,[13] the FOS found that there had been flooding from, respectively, a rise in the water table, rising ground water and rapid build-up of water behind a wall which collapsed. Only by the time of Case Study 73/8 had the cases later than Rohan been decided and could their *dicta* have been included. Jackson J's guidelines for looking at the circumstances of the case might have been particularly useful.

8.10 How would the courts have decided the same cases? In Case Study 10/1, a cellar filled with four inches of water due to a rise in the water table. The FOS commented that under *Young*, this might not have constituted a flood, but that the insured was entitled to the benefit of the more favourable case of *Rohan*, so that it was indeed a flood. We are not told the size of the cellar, but the volume of water involved—four inches compared to *Young*'s three inches—is greater, and would be significantly greater if the cellar was a lot bigger than the lavatory. It is unclear how much water got through the roof in *Rohan*, but Walker LJ estimated that the volume of water on the roof must have been significant, and also significantly more than in *Young*, if the water on the roof was three to four inches deep. Assuming that the water in the cellar in Case Study 10/1 was significantly more than in *Young*, under *Rohan* it would be possible to call it a flood. But if the ingress in the case study was a slow seepage or percolation as it was in *Young*, rather than involving something sudden or abnormal, as the build-up of rain during a period of about a fortnight was held to be in *Rohan*, it is questionable, even following *Rohan*, that the law at the time would find that this constituted a flood. However, the contrary is certainly arguable, so the FOS may have, as it claims, applied *Rohan*.

8.11 In Case Study 18/18, heavy rainfall over five months led to water entering a cesspit due to rising groundwater. The FOS determined that this was a flood in the ordinary and natural sense of the word with the *Rohan* judgment supporting a flood from a prolonged and steady rain or a steady, slow, build-up of water. Whilst the law might consider this a flood—assuming that there was lots of water and abnormal rains—it might not have found that there was a claim under the policy, depending on the wording, as the cesspit was not damaged, so the only loss was loss of its use.

8.12 Finally, Case Study 73/8 is most like *Rohan*, although it and subsequent case law is not mentioned in the case study. A garden wall collapsed after three months of exceptionally

11. *Ombudsman News* Oct 2001.
12. *Ombudsman News* July 2002.
13. *Ombudsman News* Oct/Nov 2008.

heavy rainfall, due not to the age and condition of the wall, but the build-up of water behind it. The FOS found that this constituted a flood which was covered under the policy. The relevant facts of this case study and *Rohan* are analogous, so a court would probably also have found there had been a flood.

Exclusions

8.13 Clear exclusions in flood cover seemed to be construed relatively strictly both by a court and by the FOS. In Case Study 58/1,[14] the FOS agreed with insurers that tracing, accessing and repairing the pipe which was the source of the leak was clearly excluded, but repair of water damage following an escape of water was covered. In Case Study 58/3,[15] the FOS found that the wording clearly covered an escape of oil, but not an accumulation of oil which had blocked a heating pipe and was a problem of maintenance or wear and tear, so was specifically excluded. In Case Study 58/4,[16] the FOS did not uphold a complaint about the rejection of a claim for a new bathroom suite and tiles. It found that the assured had been in breach of a clear notification and preservation of evidence condition when their plumber had allegedly removed and disposed of the items in order to locate a leaking pipe beneath the bathroom floor.

Commentary

8.14 Flooding is one of the few areas where the FOS has explicitly referred to in *Ombudsman News* and applied some legal case law, although it is not clear whether it has kept abreast of developments or whether there are internal FOS systems to enable it to do this. It has not stabbed at concepts of breach of sales code and fairness, and nor has it re-invented the wheel by coming to its own conclusions without considering carefully enough the position at law. In sticking to the law like this, the FOS position on flooding is clear and there is some certainty and consistency of approach. It has a firm and reliable anchor on which to base its own determinations, and this works well.

SUBSIDENCE

Meaning

8.15 Unless there is a history of subsidence, most buildings policies will cover it, although it is not usually defined. The ordinary meaning indicates a collapse or sinking of the property in a vertical direction. The case law[17] indicates that it can also include movement in a horizontal direction, i.e. settlement, but probably not heave, i.e. a bulging in the soil commonly caused by a chemical reaction. The National House-Building Council scheme mentions subsidence and heave separately, and covers both. The FOS says that unless the policy gives a clear definition of the term to the contrary, it will consider subsidence to include any downwards movement of soil, including, for instance, the compression of soil under the weight of a recently constructed building.[18] It would be strange if the FOS

---

14. *Ombudsman News* Dec 2006/Jan 2007.
15. *Ombudsman News* Dec 2006/Jan 2007.
16. *Ombudsman News* Dec 2006/Jan 2007.
17. *David Allen & Sons Billposting Ltd* v *Drysdale* [1939] 4 All ER 113.
18. *Ombudsman News* Jan/Feb 2007.

definition was narrower than a court's and did not include settlement, i.e. horizontal movement, so perhaps the FOS has not had to consider horizontal movement, or is unaware of the appropriate case law, or has simply not reported its approach fully.

What is included in subsidence works

8.16 As demonstrated in Case Study 59/10,[19] the FOS expects subsidence cover to include both the cost of repairs and stabilisation works. It will not accept that stabilisation should not be covered because it is preventative rather than restorative work. This is a practical and sensible response which the courts should support. However, like the court, the FOS will not consider that there should be coverage for uninsured perils discovered during the stabilisation works, such as the dry rot discovered in Case Study 10/2.[20]

Which insurer is responsible

8.17 In law, subject to the Latent Damage Act 1986,[21] a property insurer is only required to repair or pay for the repair of damage that occurred during the currency of its own policy.[22] The position changed in practical terms since the beginning of 1994, with the ABI Domestic Subsidence Agreement between property insurers. The Agreement says that if a claim is notified within the first eight weeks of a change of insurer, the previous insurer will deal with the whole claim; claims notified between eight weeks and one year from the changeover will be handled by the new insurer who will seek contribution from the previous insurer; and any claims made at least a year after the changeover will be dealt with by the new insurer alone.

8.18 The FOS says that it will take account of this ABI Agreement. Presumably this would be whether or not the insurer had signed up to the agreement, although in practice most of the relevant insurers will have. However, the FOS also comments that it will, in any case, expect an insurer to carry out stabilisation works to stop the movement in order to comply with the obligations to repair areas damaged during its policy coverage, and so should therefore be responsible for this work, even if the movement began when another insurer was on cover. This was the approach it adopted in both Case Studies 59/8 and 59/9,[23] where the claims were made over one year after a change of insurer. Presumably, the FOS comments only relate to claims made at least a year after the changeover and that for claims made earlier, its decisions would also reflect the ABI Agreement.

Delay in subsidence repairs

8.19 Often it is necessary to monitor a building to assess whether there is in fact subsidence and if so, what is the pattern and rate of movement. This may lead to delay in the works to stabilise the subsidence and repair the cracks. The FOS may award damages for distress or inconvenience if it considers that the insurer has caused any delay or has not taken a

---

19. *Ombudsman News* Jan/Feb 2007.
20. *Ombudsman News* Oct 2001.
21. Section 3—accrual of cause of action to successive owners in respect of latent damage to property. Through the Act, the owner of a building has the right to sue a builder or other person responsible for latent damage caused by their actions carried out before the current owner's purchase of that building.
22. *Wasa Insurance* v *Lexington Insurance* [2009] UKHL 40; [2009] Lloyd's Rep IR 675 (HL).
23. Both *Ombudsman News* Jan/Feb 2007.

reasonable and proportionate time to investigate and monitor the situation. It has hinted[24] that it might also grant such an award if insurers do not keep the insured properly informed of what is happening. The courts would not deal with delay like this, but through an award of interest.[25]

Commentary

8.20 The FOS and the law are broadly in line with each other in relation to subsidence. There is a difference in the definition of subsidence which might well fall away if and when the appropriate facts and case law came before the FOS, as there has been no criticism that the law is unfair in this regard. The FOS has given some guidance as to what works should be included in subsidence works, which seem reasonable and may prove useful to a court. Where there is possibly more than one insurer involved in subsidence damage, the FOS applies the ABI Agreement where a court cannot, but it is precisely because of the Agreement that the court should never have to decide the point.

PITCH-FIBRE PIPES

8.21 The FOS has developed its own approach as to whether damage caused through the use of underground pitch-fibre pipes would fall within a wear and tear exclusion (probably not) or might be covered as accidental damage (probably).[26] These pipes were often used in the 1950s and 1960s, unbeknown to the current house-owner, and are considered inherently defective as their inner surface is susceptible to delamination and they are more susceptible to collapse under applied loading than other pipes. The FOS says it continues the approach of the IOB. The relevant exclusions, such as for wear and tear, and any definition of accidental damage should be applied if they are fair and written in plain, intelligible language, and their effects were apparent to consumers or were adequately brought to their attention at the inception or renewal of the policy. The FOS would not expect accidental damage cover to apply to pipes which are discovered to be made of pitch-fibre, but which have not already distorted or collapsed, as preventative damage is not insured.[27] Nor will the FOS expect insurers to pay a claim for a blocked pipe, which was expected but not dealt with before the blockage, in the exceptional situation where the insurer can demonstrate that the policyholder ought reasonably to have realised the pipes were liable to fail, perhaps due to a CCTV inspection or the generally known history of the surrounding pipes. If an insurer or intermediary had and shared with the assured at inception or renewal knowledge of the pipes in the particular property or housing estate, the FOS will take this into account in deciding whether the assured has understood the significance of the relevant policy exclusions.

8.22 If an underground pipe is damaged when a worker drilled into the ground, that would constitute accidental damage and would be covered by a policy as the damage would be from a sudden external, visible and violent cause. The FOS says that it has seen very few complaints about loss or damage to underground pitch-fibre pipes where insurers have been able to demonstrate that the loss or damage should not be regarded as accidental. The FOS

---

24. *Ombudsman News* Jan/Feb 2007.
25. See "FOS awards for distress and inconvenience and maladministration" above at paras. 3.10 *et seq* and the Law Commissions' 6th Issue Paper, "Damages for Late Payment and the Insurer's Duty of Good Faith."
26. *Cf* FOS Technical Briefing Note 20 January 2009.
27. See further below "Preventative damage" at paras. 8.33 *et seq*.

says that where the policy does not contain a clear definition to the contrary, it is likely to regard unexpected collapses or blockages to these pipes as accidental damage in view of the ordinary usage of the words "accidental damage", even if the underlying cause occurred gradually, for example as a result of delamination of the inside of the pipes, encroachment by tree roots, or the passage of heavy vehicles. An ordinary policyholder would not expect underground service pipes to be sub-standard and consequently fail, and it is not usually something that the policyholder could know or do anything about until it is too late.

8.23 If the failure of the pipes is simply as a result of ordinary usage, the FOS is unlikely to agree that it is fair and reasonable for an insurer to reject a claim for their damage on the basis that it was caused by wear and tear, because often the failure will result from an inherent flaw in the structure of the pipes, a defect that was not known at the time of their manufacture and installation.

8.24 If the policy specifically excludes damage by gradual deterioration or a gradually operating cause, then the FOS will apply that exclusion to a claim for damage which has taken effect gradually over many years, if it was clearly worded and adequately brought to the assured's attention pre-inception. The same comments apply to exclusions for faulty workmanship, although the FOS says it has seen very few complaints where the insurer has been able to show that the loss or damage was caused by faulty workmanship. It also says that it has not been persuaded that failure of these pipes is as a result of faulty or defective design.

8.25 If there is a specific exclusion concerning pitch-fibre pipes, it will need to be both clear and adequately brought to the policyholder's attention pre-inception before the FOS will allow it to be relied upon.

UNOCCUPIED

The law

8.26 Often certain cover in household insurance is expressly excluded where the premises are unoccupied for a period of time, commonly 30 consecutive days. The case law defines "occupation" narrowly: although temporary absences are permitted, there must be a regular, actual, daily occupant, who not only attends as a night watchman but also enters the property,[28] and who not only attends by day to take care of the property, but also sleeps there at night,[29] and the property must be used as a dwelling house, not merely for storage.[30]

The FOS

8.27 The concept of "unoccupied" is rarely defined by the policy, so the FOS views it as ambiguous and will interpret it *contra proferentem*. The FOS may consider a property to be occupied if it is visited on a reasonably frequent basis, even if it is not being slept in every night, and even if a court would decide differently, although the FOS does not refer to any specific case law in its reports.

---

28. *Marzouca v Atlantic and British Commercial Insurance Co* [1971] 1 Lloyd's Rep 449 (Privy Council).
29. *Clements v National General Insurance Co* (1910) *The Times*, 11 June.
30. *Hussain v Brown (No 2)*, 1996, unreported.

8.28 In Case Study 34/1,[31] the exclusion was unclear, so the FOS decided that the house was occupied when the assured had visited almost every weekend to carry out renovations, sometimes staying there overnight. That would not have counted as occupancy under the above case law, because at no point was there a regular, daily attendant. In Case Study 34/3,[32] an elderly assured had unexpectedly been admitted to hospital and had remained there for more than a year without arranging for the house to be checked. The FOS rejected the complaint and found the house had been unoccupied. The courts would have agreed with that result, although checking a house would not be enough for occupancy under the case law, and nor should it. Insurance premiums are charged at a higher rate for unoccupied premises, and may have different conditions attached.

8.29 The FOS took a proportionate approach in Case Study 10/15,[33] where the assured did not inform the insurer that the house was unoccupied, but left the central heating on and inspected the property once a week, which is what the insurer would have asked him to do if it had known. Although the exclusion was clear and all reasonable steps had been taken to draw it to the assured's attention, the FOS felt that the claim for escape of water during this period should be covered. However, the FOS felt that the insurer should pay only 80% of the claim, less the excess, as it felt that 20% of the damage had been caused by the house not being checked for the two weeks when the assured was ill. The gap in the inspections had increased the damage. This is where the FOS's lenient interpretation of occupation does not quite gel together, because it appears that the insured could not take a holiday from his weekly inspections, even though the FOS found that weekly inspections equalled occupation, when he would have been able to take a fortnight's holiday without consequences if he had been living in the house. A court would have approached the case differently. Based on the case law, the property was not occupied, so the loss would not have been covered.

8.30 If a technical breach of an occupancy provision does not prejudice the insurer, the FOS does not consider it good practice for an unrelated claim to be rejected.[34] So the FOS has commented[35] that if damage to property occurs during a permitted period of un-occupancy, usually the first 30 days in a household policy, the damage should be covered even if the property was actually unoccupied for longer. An example is Case Study 58/2[36] where the assured were on a cruise and away from the property for more than the 60 days permitted, but the burst pipe probably occurred within the first 10 days, when the weather had been particularly cold, and they had not yet breached the occupancy provision. The FOS required insurers to meet the claim, but not that part of it which resulted from the extra time that the house was unoccupied but should not have been. The extra damage was the rot damage to the wooden floor which probably would not have occurred if the house had not been unoccupied for so long and the water damage could have been dealt with quicker, so would not have started to cause rot. The court would not have required insurers to pay the claim, which is arguably fairer, as it was not possible to prove when the damage actually occurred and the insured could and should have contacted insurers before they travelled, and if necessary, paid a higher premium.

8.31 The FOS is unlikely to permit an assured from taking advantage of a misrepresenta-tion about occupation when taking out or renewing insurance. Nor will the FOS support the

31. *Ombudsman News* Jan 2004.
32. *Ombudsman News* Jan 2004.
33. *Ombudsman News* Oct 2001.
34. See Warranties below at paras. 14.15 *et seq.*
35. *Ombudsman News* Jan 2004.
36. *Ombudsman News* Dec 2006/Jan 2007.

claim of an assured who abandons his property or so neglects it that it practically invites unwelcome attention, as was the situation in Case Study 34/2.[37] In that case, the house was in such a poor state of repair that the FOS felt that it stretched credibility that anyone would be able to live there, even for one night at a time as the insured claimed he did when he was in that town. A court would agree with the FOS on both these points.

Commentary

8.32 The FOS defines occupancy more widely than a court (when it is not clearly defined in the policy). The results must be unfair to insurers. When an assured only visits the property once every week, which is enough for the FOS for occupation, it is more likely that the event which causes the damage is going to occur whilst he is away from the property than when he is there. It is also statistically more likely than where the law's occupant who is there every night goes on a fortnight's holiday. Whatever the policy terms are, checking a property once every week is not the definition that an ordinary person would give to occupation. He is only checking the property because he knows that it is not occupied. In such circumstances he should either risk being uninsured, or tell insurers and comply with their requirements or pay a higher premium for them to continue to insure what may now be a greater insurance risk.

PREVENTATIVE DAMAGE

The law

8.33 Marine policies usually include a suing and labouring clause which makes recoverable the costs of preventing or mitigating damage, although probably only in relation to perils which have actually occurred. Non-marine policies rarely include such a clause. Without one, there will be no recovery for preventative action taken by the assured, even if such action might save the insurer from having to pay out on a large insured risk. Such a clause cannot be implied, as confirmed by the Court of Appeal in *Yorkshire Water* v *Sun Alliance & London Insurance Ltd*,[38] where the assured spent more than £4.6 million on flood alleviation works to prevent further pollution liability. The policy afforded protection not against the occurrence of an event but against any liability flowing from the occurrence of that event. There was an express duty to mitigate in that policy, but even without one, the Court of Appeal has confirmed in *Pilkington United Kingdom Ltd* v *CGU Insurance plc*[39] that a suing and labouring clause cannot be implied. There the assured's liability policy responded only to liability for personal injury and physical damage, not its prevention. To allow the assured to be able to recover the costs of preventing fractured glass panels in the ceiling from falling, would have converted a product liability policy into a general liability policy covering remedial costs.

8.34 *Gerling General Insurance Co* v *Canary Wharf Group plc*[40] was another recent case, this time about business interruption insurance, which produced the same result. Where a

---

37. *Ombudsman News* Jan 2004.
38. [1997] 2 Lloyd's Rep 21, followed in *Bartoline Ltd* v *Royal & Sun Alliance Insurance plc*, November 2006, unreported.
39. [2004] Lloyd's Rep IR 891.
40. [2005] EWHC 2234 (Comm).

self-climbing crane collapsed causing death, injury and property damage, the assured was not covered for thereafter using the other two cranes in a different, more expensive way to prevent any further such damage. The assured's action in diverting the cranes was part of its duties under the policy to take all reasonable precautions, at its own expense, to prevent or minimise any loss which might give rise to a claim. This was not emergency action, which would have been covered. A change in working methods to prevent a business interruption was not covered by business interruption insurers.

8.35 The law treats property insurance similarly. Most property policies only cover the physical loss of or damage to the insured subject matter. So unless explicitly included, there is no cover for economic, diminution in value,[41] or any other loss, and repairing/replacing a defect is not covered, unless it gives rise to an insured loss by causing damage to the property insured. So in *Shell UK Ltd* v *CLM Engineering Ltd*,[42] there was cover for replacing defective parts of an oil pipeline which had been physically damaged by an insured peril, but not for replacing undamaged, but defective parts. Courts sometimes find ways to interpret contracts so as to provide cover for replacing a defective item, but these cases can usually be distinguished on their facts and their wordings.[43]

The FOS

8.36 In relation to preventative damage in a household property context, the FOS comments that if a policyholder acts reasonably to prevent a much larger insured damage, which would have cost significantly more, it is reasonable to require the insurer to meet the costs, even though a court would not. It effectively implies a suing and labouring clause in direct contravention of the case law. So in Case Study 10/3,[44] the FOS required the insurer to pay a plumber's invoice (£70.50) for his time and the cost of a replacement to the blocked pipe he had deliberately broken to prevent flooding of the kitchen, which would have been more costly to the insurer. A blocked pipe was not an insured peril. A court would have treated it as a defective pipe like the pipe in the *Shell* case above, and not allowed a recovery for the preventative loss, without an insured peril occurring, which in this case study would have been an escape of water. However, the FOS has said that it would not expect insurers to pay for the replacement of pitch-fibre pipes (see "Pitch-fibre pipes" above at paragraphs 8.21 *et seq*), unless a blockage or damage had occurred. Perhaps the relative cost of the replacement of these underground pipes and the plumber's invoice above explains the difference in approach and is determinative of whether the FOS will allow preventative loss.

Commentary

8.37 Perhaps the FOS is right, and it would be sensible for insurers to have to pay for work in some circumstances which would prevent a much greater insured loss. But if the FOS is willing to imply a suing and labouring clause, is it also prepared to imply a duty on the insured to take preventative action? The law does not imply the latter duty unless the insured's actions are reckless, or in the few situations that they are so inexcusable that it is tantamount to the insured being the author of his own misfortune, as was the case in *James*

---

41. *Quorum AS* v *Schramm* [2002] Lloyd's Rep IR 292.
42. [2000] 1 Lloyd's Rep 612.
43. E.g. *Cementation Piling and Foundation Ltd* v *Commercial Union Insurance Co* [1995] 1 Lloyd's Rep 97; *Burts and Harvey* v *Vulcan & General Insurance Co* [1966] 1 Lloyd's Rep 161.
44. *Ombudsman News* Oct 2001.

v *CGU Insurance*,[45] where the assured failed to take simple steps to put out a small fire. And where will the FOS draw the line between general household maintenance which is not covered by property insurance and action which is preventative of certain insured loss? Much house maintenance could be argued to be preventative of insured perils, for instance expensive maintenance or installation of a damp proof course. Also, although an action might prevent an insured peril from occurring, it is not obvious that one particular insurer should pay for the preventative action when it might not still be on cover when the insured peril occurs. Perhaps on a practical note, insurers might be persuaded to provide *ex gratia* payments in relation to inexpensive, clearly preventative (as opposed to maintenance) work, and maybe that explains why the FOS has reported only one, early case study on this topic in relation to household cover.[46] It is not clear that the FOS has considered the case law carefully and thought through the consequences of a stance which supports payment of preventative losses in certain circumstances.

BUILDINGS OR CONTENTS COVER

The law

8.38 Generally, buildings insurance covers permanent fixtures and fittings which cannot reasonably be removed and taken to another home, and have essentially become part of the fabric of the property. Contents insurance covers items which can be reasonably removed. There is little case law on what falls under contents insurance and what buildings, but there is parallel case law on what constitutes a chattel and what constitutes a fixture.

8.39 *Botham* v *TSB Bank plc*[47] is a modern Court of Appeal case which summarises the position established through ancient case law[48] and which has been applied through the twentieth century.[49] The two tests are: (i) the method and degree of annexation and (ii) the object and purpose of annexation. Where an item is attached to the property by more than its own weight, if it was objectively intended to be permanent and to afford a long-lasting improvement to the building, it is a fixture. If the attachment is temporary and no more than necessary for the item to be used and enjoyed, then it remains a chattel. A relevant factor is whether or not the item can be removed without damaging the fabric of the building.

The FOS

8.40 The FOS will consider the individual circumstances of each case, but has set out the following guidelines, (with which a court applying the *Botham* tests would agree unless specified otherwise below). Buildings policies would usually cover:

(1) fitted wardrobes;

---

45. [2002] Lloyd's Rep IR 206.
46. See also above Case Study 1/20 discussed in "Travel Insurance—Earthquake" at paras. 6.17 *et seq*; the discussion of what the FOS considers should be covered within subsidence works at paras. 8.15 *et seq*; and Case Study 24/3 discussed in Critical Illness cover at paras. 7.10 *et seq*.
47. Unreported, CA, 30 July 1996.
48. Including *Holland* v *Hodgson* (1872) LR 7 CP 328.
49. By, for example, *Berkley* v *Poulett and Ors* (1977) 261 EG 911; *Hamp* v *Bygrave* (1983) 266 EG 720; *Dean* v *Andrews, The Times,* 25 May 1985; *Elitestone Ltd* v *Morris* [1997] 1 WLR 687; *Chelsea Yacht & Boat Co Ltd* v *Justin Pope* [2000] 1 WLR 1941.

(2) fitted kitchens and built-in appliances. However, contrary to its own guidelines which at least it is not blindly following, and without referring to any case law, the FOS found that the kitchen units installed by the council tenant in Case Study 30/3[50] were contents because she purchased them, they could easily be removed and the tenant claimed that she would take them with her if she moved. The FOS thought this was feasible, although it seems hard to imagine. Had she kept the old kitchen to re-install if she moved? Would the tenancy agreement have allowed her to leave this property with no kitchen? Would she really have ripped out any kitchen she found installed at a new premises, so as to install these particular kitchen units? Perhaps the FOS merely had sympathy with the complainant who did not have buildings cover, but had suffered damage to her new kitchen units through escape of water. The law would class kitchen units as fixtures, as it did in *Botham*.

(3) most laminate wooden flooring, where the individual planks are glued together and fixed under a skirting board or beading, as a fixture.[51] Unlike a carpet, they are difficult to remove intact and have essentially become part of the building.

(4) outside aerials fixed permanently to the roof, even if the policy lists them under contents. This is because few would remove them when moving house, most would regard them as part of the building and any damage caused would most likely be as a result of an insured event such as storm or lightning covered by buildings insurance. So in Case Study 30/2,[52] both the roof and the television aerial were damaged in a storm, and the FOS required the buildings insurer to pay for the repair of both of them, even though the wording clearly stated that the aerial was part of the contents cover which the insured had not taken out. The law would pay more heed to clear wording than the FOS does in this situation.

(5) parts of the building which have been temporarily removed and are then lost or damaged while being stored.

8.41 Contents policies would usually cover:

(1) furniture;
(2) appliances which are free-standing or easily unscrewed from the wall;
(3) fitted carpets.[53] The FOS says this is in accordance with industry convention. Although not mentioned, it is also in accordance with the case law.[54]
(4) re-useable click-together laminate wooden flooring, which is more like a fitted carpet than glued laminate flooring.
(5) new items which are damaged or stolen before being fitted, as they are the owner's transferable, personal possessions until they are fitted. Such items would include flat-packed kitchen units, laminate flooring, or the flat packed conservatory in Case Study 30/6.[55] This was stored in the garage and damaged when the roof collapsed and was part of the contents cover, where the insured only had contents cover.

8.42 Where there is real ambiguity in the wording about whether the buildings or contents insurer is responsible for a loss, the FOS considers that each should meet 50% of the claim.

---

50. *Ombudsman News* Aug 2003.
51. E.g. Case Study 30/4 *Ombudsman News* Aug 2003.
52. *Ombudsman News* Aug 2003.
53. E.g. Case Study 30/5 *Ombudsman News* Aug 2003.
54. E.g. in Botham (*supra*).
55. *Ombudsman News* Aug 2003.

It is understandable that the FOS should mediate in this way, although it means that it may not be in the interests of insurers to accept that they are on cover if there is a chance that the FOS will only hold them liable for half. A court would decide who was on cover, and if it was both of them, would consider if the liability was several or joint, and deal with any questions of contribution.

Personal possessions temporarily away from the home-contents cover?

8.43 Personal possessions temporarily away from the home will only usually be included in a contents policy if an additional premium is paid. Such cover is usually limited with lists of included and excluded items even in a supposedly "all risks" cover. The FOS considers that all this must be explained before inception, so an assured understands exactly what cover has been paid for. If the wording is unclear, the FOS will interpret it *contra proferentem*. If the policy has been explained and is clearly worded, the FOS acknowledges[56] that it is for an insurer exercising its commercial underwriting decision, not the FOS, to define the nature and scope of the cover.

    8.44 The FOS has considered whether satellite navigation equipment should count as part of a motor insurance policy or as personal possessions temporarily away from the home under a household policy. It has taken a common sense view.[57] Unless the insurer can establish a valid reason why not, if the device can only be used and is only used in a car, then the motor policy should respond, and if it can be and has been used outside the car, such as by walkers, the personal possessions section of a domestic contents policy should respond.

Double insurance

8.45 Under the law, double insurance is lawful, as long as there is no over indemnity.[58] The problem arises where both policies try to exclude their liability if another policy exists which could cover the loss. Neither the courts[59] nor the FOS will allow a self-cancelling situation. The courts will construe such a clause reasonably so as not to have been intended to apply to any cover which is expressed to be itself cancelled by such co-existence. Each insurer becomes potentially liable to the assured for the full amount of the loss, subject to any subsequent contribution claim. The FOS, encountering the problem in a household context, and without mentioning any case law, views this as a clause to prevent double recovery, not to prevent policyholders legitimately spreading their risk between insurers. In Case Study 35/1,[60] the insured accidentally dropped his camera. The FOS found that he could recover on his household contents insurance up to the limit on that policy, and then recover the rest from his purchase protection insurance which excluded loss covered by another policy or loss which would be so covered if it were not for a policy limit. The FOS does not discuss contribution between insurers, so nor will this work.[61]

---

56. *Ombudsman News* Oct/Nov 2006.
57. *Ombudsman News* Oct/Nov 2006.
58. *Cf* MIA 1906 s. 32(2).
59. E.g. *Weddell* v *Road Traffic & General Insurance Co Ltd* [1932] 2 KB 563, followed by *National Employers Mutual General Insurance Association Ltd* v *Haydon* [1980] 2 Lloyd's Rep 149; see also *National Farmers Union Mutual Insurance Society Ltd* v *HSBC Insurance (UK) Ltd* [2010] EWHC 773 (Comm).
60. *Ombudsman News* Feb/Mar 2004.
61. *Cf* Appendix B of the Law Commissions' Final Report 15/12/09 for a summary of how they would expect double insurance to work following a careless non-disclosure resulting in a proportional remedy, if the draft bill on consumer insurance contracts were enacted.

Commentary

8.46 The law and the FOS tend to decide whether something is covered by a buildings, contents or another policy, in the same way. But it is not clear whether the FOS approach is determined or influenced by the law, or simply by its application of common sense. No criticism is levelled at the law applied strictly on the subject, so there is no policy reason for FOS decisions to be different. The only obvious difference in approach is in relation to television aerials, which the FOS reclassifies in contravention of clear contract terms. It may be influenced by the fact of an insured not having contents insurance, as this was evident in all the case studies reported.

8.47 Hopefully, a court would find it useful where the FOS determines an issue which a court has not, for instance in relation to satellite navigation equipment.

8.48 In an ambiguous set of circumstances, the FOS will hold two insurers equally liable for paying for a loss. Whilst this is a quick and simple method of mediating an argument, it is not the same as a court decision which determines the question, and it might be better if an ombudsman would decide the actual issue.

CHAPTER 9

EXCLUSION FOR KEYS LEFT IN VEHICLE/ UNATTENDED VEHICLE

COMPLIANCE WITH A SALES/MARKETING CODE

9.1 The FOS regards an exclusion for theft if the keys have been left in or near the vehicle and/or it has been left unattended as a major restriction, which must be drawn to the proposer's attention before inception or it will not be applied. The FOS experience is that this exclusion is a shock to most insureds even though it is included in almost every motor policy. It says that most consumers realise that they should not leave their keys in the car, but do not realise that they will lose their theft cover if they do. The FOS wants these restrictions highlighted on the policy certificate, (which insureds have to possess by law), and on the policy schedule or summary, (which document insureds are more likely to read than the policy). It considers this to be good industry practice. The comments above at paragraphs 5.27 *et seq* in relation to breaches of sales code apply equally here. The latest FOS Technical Note on the subject[1] summarises the current FOS position and explains:

"Such exclusion clauses are not necessarily unfair or unreasonable—but the way they are applied could be, particularly if the policyholder was not made aware of the clause and its significance when the policy was sold (or when the clause was introduced)."

9.2 In Case Study 38/6[2] an insured parked opposite a letterbox, turned his back on the car without taking the keys and walked away to post a letter. While he was crossing the road, the car was stolen. The policy documents sent to him did not refer to the keys in the car exclusion, which was only mentioned in the policy booklet, and was not highlighted at the sales point. The FOS considered that it was fair and reasonable to assume that he had been prejudiced by these sales failures, and although he had not acted recklessly, if he had known, he might have acted differently. There is no mention of any evidence going to whether he would in fact have behaved differently. The complaint was upheld despite the clear wording of the exclusion which would have prevailed before a court.

9.3 This FOS reasoning does not at first glance hold together. If the insured in Case Study 38/6 would have left his keys in the car whatever the terms of the policy, then the breach of sales code made no difference. If he would have acted differently if he had known of the exclusion, is he recklessly taking a risk which he would not be prepared to take if he were uninsured or is he entitled to take some reasonable risks, knowing that he is insured? Perhaps it is unreasonable for him to leave his keys in the car in these circumstances. Presumably, insurers think it is, as this is not a risk they are willing to insure, and not one for which the insured has paid. So why should he be covered just because he did not know for certain whether he was? This may be an example of the FOS policing the sales codes, the point being

1. Dated October 2009—see FOS website.
2. *Ombudsman News* July 2004.

that it regards these conditions as unfair and onerous if not communicated to the assured pre-inception, and the assured's reaction to the term should not be relevant to the question of whether it is unfair or onerous.

9.4 By contrast, in Case Study 82/12,[3] a car was found to be unattended in similar circumstances,[4] even though the driver did not know of the exclusion. For the policy had been sold to his wife as the main driver, and the evidence was that she had been explicitly advised of this exclusion, which was also prominently and clearly set out in the policy document. The FOS thought that it was reasonable for insurers to have expected her to tell the named driver on the policy, in this case, her husband.

9.5 Once it is satisfied with the sales and marketing history, the FOS will look to see whether the driver was reckless and whether the exclusion applies in the circumstances of the case. Other than in relation to looking at the sales and marketing history, the court takes the same approach. Before considering which court precedents or FOS guidance to consider, it is important to look carefully at the exact wording of the exclusion. For instance, in Case Study 82/8,[5] the exclusion was for a vehicle left "unlocked and unattended" with the keys in or on the vehicle. The FOS found on the evidence, that the van had been locked with the spare key, so it did not have to consider whether it had also been left unattended when the other key was in the ignition and the driver had been making a delivery.

RECKLESSNESS

9.6 Insurers can refuse a claim if they can prove that the insured has been reckless and so breached the general condition to take reasonable care of the vehicle, which condition exists independently of any exclusions and any sales code. The FOS says that its approach in determining recklessness is consistent with the Court of Appeal test in *Sofi* v *Prudential Assurance*,[6] which defines reckless as recognising a risk but deliberately courting it.[7] The case studies below bear this out.

9.7 It is difficult for insurers to prove recklessness, as most people who leave their keys in the car or their vehicle unattended fail to recognise the risk, so do not have the requisite intent. If they had been aware of the risk, they might have acted differently. However, the FOS might expect the degree of attention required for a high value car to be greater than for a low value car.

9.8 In Case Study 1/10,[8] the FOS found the driver reckless when he saw a suspicious character loitering near his car at a petrol station, but still left the keys on the driver's seat when he went to the tap to wash his hands. The driver in Case Study 31/4[9] was found not to be reckless when he stopped at a petrol station to buy chocolate. He left the keys in the car with a lady whom he had met in a nightclub the night before and both she and the car had disappeared by the time he came out of the shop. He had not been reckless because he had trusted her, so had not appreciated the risk. Because she was in the car, it was clearly not

---

3. *Ombudsman News* Dec 2009/Jan 2010.
4. The car was stolen when parked in a busy road, with the keys in the ignition and the door unlocked, whilst the driver had nipped across the road to post a letter.
5. *Ombudsman News* Dec 2009/Jan 2010.
6. [1993] 2 Lloyd's Rep 559.
7. The FOS approach to recklessness is the same both in this and other contexts such as the installation of a gas heater in a boat in Case Study 65/7 (*Ombudsman News* Oct/Nov 2007).
8. *Ombudsman News* Jan 2001.
9. *Ombudsman News* Sept 2003.

unattended. The driver in Case Study 82/9[10] was also not reckless when he left his coat, with the keys to his car in the pocket, on a table close to the food counter of a fast food restaurant before going up to get his food, which took several minutes. He did not look over to the table to check his belongings, and it was only after he had eaten his meal that he found both his car and his car keys had been stolen. The FOS was satisfied that he had not recognised the risk of theft, especially as the restaurant was relatively quiet, he had expected to be served right away and the keys had been left just a couple of metres behind him.

9.9 In Case Study 63/7,[11] the FOS applied the *Sofi* test to the condition to "take all precautions to reduce or remove the risk of loss of the insured vehicle". This interpretation effectively softened the requirement so that the insured had to take only reasonable care rather than all precautions. The FOS concluded that the insured had not been reckless in leaving keys in his van whilst he was moving his tools into a residential garage, because he said that it had not occurred to him that he was taking a risk. On the *Sofi* test, the FOS conclusion must be right, but it is arguable that a court might have taken a stricter approach to the wording and said that recklessness was not the appropriate standard.

UNATTENDED VEHICLE EXCLUSION

A court's approach

9.10 To determine whether on the facts a vehicle has been left unattended and so breached an unattended vehicle exclusion, a court will apply the test formulated by Lord Denning in the leading authority of *Starfire Diamond Rings Ltd* v *Angel*[12]: whether there was "someone able to keep it under observation, that is, in a position to observe any attempt by anyone to interfere with it, and who is so placed as to have a reasonable prospect of preventing any unauthorized interference with it".

9.11 In *Starfire*, this question related to the exclusion in a jewellers' block policy for theft from cars which "not being garaged, are left unattended". The driver left the car parked in a lay-by off the road, locked the doors, took the key with him, walked some 37 yards up a track which led off from the road to go behind some bushes to urinate, keeping an eye on the car, before returning. The Court of Appeal found that the car had been left unattended given the distance between the driver and the car, the obscurity of his view, (he could only see the roof of the car from the bushes and he could not have been watching it the whole time that he was walking down the track away from it) and the fact that the driver was not able to prevent the theft. Also, as was emphasised by Lord Upjohn, during this time the thief managed to break the car window, open the door, snatch a suitcase of jewellery and start to walk away before the driver saw anything suspicious and could give chase to the thief, who escaped into a waiting car. If the car had been attended, the thief would not have been able to do all this. Lord Upjohn added that in approaching the question, one had to have in mind that this was a policy which insured jewellery, and that the insurer was not prepared to accept liability in respect of packets of jewellery which are so easily taken by a sneak thief in a very short space of time from a car left unattended.

9.12 Later cases followed and built upon *Starfire* and are set out in chronological order below.

---

10. *Ombudsman News* Dec 09/Jan 2010.
11. *Ombudsman News* July/Aug 2007.
12. [1962] 2 Lloyd's Rep 217.

Plaistow Transport Ltd v Graham[13]

9.13 Metal ingots were stolen from under the tarpaulin at the back of a lorry when the driver was asleep inside the cab in a lay-by on a night journey. A goods in transit policy excluded cover when the lorry was unattended. Nield J held that the lorry was not "unattended". One reason that the driver was not awakened by the thieves was that he had wrongly been driving for longer than he was meant to, so fell into a particularly deep sleep. But that did not mean that the lorry was unattended.

9.14 Although not expressed as such, the judgment seems to use the *Starfire* tests above. It notes that the driver was in a position to keep the lorry under observation (if the thieves woke him), and he was "so placed as to have a reasonable prospect of preventing any unauthorized interference" with his load, as he would have reasonably assumed that thieves would not be able to pilfer his load without him waking up and being able to stop them.

Ingleton v General Accident Fire & Life Assurance Corporation[14]

9.15 *Starfire* was expressly applied in this case, where the driver left his van unlocked, with the key in the ignition, outside the plaintiff's shop for 15 minutes while he made a delivery and chatted inside the shop. The van and contents were stolen, but only the van was recovered. There was a goods in transit policy which excluded theft cover from a vehicle if it was "left unattended in any public place" unless it was locked and there had been forcible entry. Phillimore J pointed out that from his position in the shop, the driver could not (and did not) see the driver's door or if anyone got into the driver's seat. He was therefore not in a position to observe any attempt by anyone to interfere with the van or able to have a reasonable prospect of preventing any unauthorised interference. He said that the best proof of the van being unattended, was that it was removed with all its contents without its attendant even being aware of what had happened.

Langford v Legal & General[15]

9.16 In a market traders' insurance policy, it was a condition precedent to liability for theft from a vehicle that it was attended by the insured or an employee of the insured. The plaintiff (the insured) parked her car in the driveway of her house, locked it and took the keys with her whilst she opened the porch and front door of the house and slipped inside to put her bag down in the hall. She ran out of the house when she saw through the kitchen window the shadow of a man, and heard the car alarm going. Thieves had broken the car window to get to her suitcases of jewellery. At the front door she came face to face with one man with one of her suitcases, but decided to try to save the second and more valuable suitcase which a second man was trying to take out of the car. She struggled with him and failed, and both men got away in another car with both the suitcases.

9.17 Judge Hawser QC found that the car was out of her view for only about five seconds, and that the distance from which she was away from the car was about 17ft (although the unobserved part of this was only 8ft). He said "one must take a practical, common-sense view of these matters". He was satisfied that "the vehicle was attended at this time in any sensible and practical meaning of those words". He also thought that the plaintiff was in a

13. [1966] 1 Lloyd's Rep 639.
14. [1967] 2 Lloyd's Rep 179.
15. [1986] 2 Lloyd's Rep 103.

position to be able to prevent a theft. She had locked her alarmed car and only left it for five seconds, and only been a short distance away. If she had been stronger, or perhaps an expert rugby tackler, she may have succeeded in preventing the theft of both the suitcases.

9.18 It may be that the situation was akin to being jumped whilst getting out of the car, and the insurers in that situation would not have been able to argue that the car was unattended, although the theft outcome would have been the same.

O'Donoghue v Harding[16]

9.19 In this case, the insured's salesman had left a case containing jewellery locked in his car, on the back seat, partially covered by his hanging suits, while he went to the kiosk at a quiet, self-service, petrol station to pay for petrol, keeping a reasonable look-out as he did this. He had parked at the petrol pump closest to the garage, and most of the car was visible to him except for a few seconds during which he was signing a credit card slip, and a few seconds when he had his back to the car while walking from the car to the kiosk and from the counter back to the door of the kiosk. He was away from the car for no more than two minutes, and no further than 14–16ft. He later discovered that the jewellery had been stolen. The jewellers' block policy excluded cover for theft from a vehicle "left unattended".

9.20 It was held on the balance of probabilities that a gang of professional thieves had probably targeted the salesman, tracked him for some days beforehand and obtained a duplicate key to his car. Then they must have crouched at the side of the car out of view, opened the door with the duplicate key, taken the jewellery case and shut and relocked the door, all within a matter of seconds.

9.21 Otton J held that the theft from the car had been carefully planned, that the salesman had acted in a thoroughly responsible manner, and that on the facts, it could not be said that the car had been left unattended. He commented that Lord Denning's observation requirement in *Starfire* did not mean that the driver had to keep the whole of the car, on all four sides, under observation for all of the time. What the salesman did in this case was sufficient. He added that "the fact that the case was stolen without the thief being observed is a fact to be taken into account but it is not conclusive". He did not think that the words "keep it under observation" did more than impose a duty of common care on the driver.

9.22 The second part of the *Starfire* test—being so close as to have a reasonable prospect of preventing an unauthorised interference with it—would be satisfied if the driver was so close that he would be able to prevent the interference, raise the alarm or take some other steps to lead to the apprehension of the thieves. Therefore, he concluded on the facts, that the driver did not leave the car unattended. He was closer than the driver in *Starfire* and could see more of the car for more of the time. He behaved in a "thoroughly responsible manner", unlike the driver in *Ingleton*. The chance that a sneak thief would come up during such a short period and be so skilful as to open the door with a duplicate key, remove the case and relock the car was extremely remote.

Sanger t/a SA Jewels v Beazley[17]

9.23 Here, the driver, also a jewellery salesman, stopped at a service station, got out of his car, locked it and then walked around the corner of the kiosk to wash his hands in the

---

16. [1988] 2 Lloyd's Rep 281.
17. [1999] Lloyd's Rep IR 424.

lavatory, from where he could not see his car. He then went into the kiosk, from where he had an obscured view of his car as there was another car parked in his way. He was not found to have kept looking at his car. While he was choosing a drink, someone came into the kiosk to say that a car had been broken into. He found that it was his car and that his jewellery bag which had been on the floor of the rear of his car, covered with a coat, had been stolen. The closed circuit television film showed that the theft had occurred during the 68 seconds when he was out of the picture and in the lavatory. Longmore J found that his car was unattended at the time of the theft, so insurers could rely on the exclusion.

9.24 This case was distinguished from *O'Donoghue* because the *Sanger* driver did not satisfy the *Starfire* tests, whereas the *O'Donoghue* driver had. The *Sanger* driver was not in a position to observe any attempt to interfere with his car, nor was he so placed as to have a reasonable prospect of preventing such interference. *Obiter*, the car was unattended even on the *Sanger* driver's own version of events, which was not accepted by the court; that he had not washed his hands in the lavatory, but by an outside tap adjacent to the lavatory, from which he would have been unable to see the car if he was crouching down to use the tap.

Hayward v Norwich Union

9.25 This case is different to those above as the exclusion in question was for keys "left in or on the car", as opposed to an unattended vehicle, it was a high value car that was stolen rather than the items contained inside and the wording in issue was that of car insurance rather than jewellers' block or goods in transit insurance.

9.26 The claimant filled up his Porsche with petrol at a service station, left the keys in the ignition but with the immobiliser on, and went to pay in the kiosk. He hid the control unit for the immobiliser under the seat. He was about 15–25 yards from the car which he could see and hear throughout, although he was not looking at it all the time. While waiting to pay, he heard the Porsche's engine being turned on. He ran to the passenger door, but found it locked from the inside. He saw a man inside fiddling with a gadget (later thought to be a scanning device to deactivate the immobiliser), who then drove away at high speed. The theft was planned and executed by professional thieves and the car was not recovered.

9.27 DJ Michael Tugendhart, QC at first instance,[18] found the word "left" to be ambiguous and interpreted it to mean "left unattended". He then applied the *Starfire* test to find that the keys had not been left unattended in the Porsche, as the petrol pump was reasonably near to the kiosk and, most importantly, the immobiliser was on. The driver believed that was enough to secure the car—and it would have been but for the remote chance that professional thieves would be able to override it. The immobiliser control was in the car, but it was adequately concealed. The doors were unlocked, but they would not have provided additional protection against someone who could override the immobiliser. The driver had kept a proper and reasonable lookout, was not absent for more than a few moments, and during this time he could see and hear the car. He was able to touch the car before it was driven off, and, but for the threat of force, he would have defended it. The judge likened this to a case of hijack.

9.28 The Court of Appeal[19] reversed the decision on 22 February 2001. "Left" on its plain and ordinary meaning did not need to be interpreted as "left unattended". Even if it did "it would not follow that the same test should apply to keys being left unattended as to vehicles being left unattended". The question was "whether the keys have been caused or allowed to

18. [2000] Lloyd's Rep IR 382.
19. [2001] EWCA Civ 243.

remain in or on the car by a person who has moved away from them, no one else being left in charge of the keys". Whether the person has moved away from the keys is a question of fact and degree, and "the test must be whether that person is close enough to make a theft unlikely".

9.29 On the facts, the Court of Appeal in *Hayward* decided that the keys had been "left". Moving 15–25 yards away from the car was too far to make the prevention of a theft unlikely, in circumstances where the driver did not see the thief open the car door, get into the car, shut the door, lock the doors and start the engine before being alerted. *Obiter*, had he left an adult passenger in the car with the keys, so that such a person stood in for the driver, he would not have "left" the keys in the car. Insurers accepted in argument that if the driver got out of a car to attend to a child in the back or to take something out of the boot, whilst leaving the ignition keys in the car, the driver would still be sufficiently proximate to the keys so that they had not been left.

Summary of a court's approach

9.30 The tables below show the key factors in a court's approach to the question of whether a vehicle has been left unattended. Whilst it is a combination of factors which determines the point, the feature which stands out as most likely to make a difference is the attitude of the driver and whether he kept a careful lookout. That is the only feature universally answered in the negative for unattended vehicles, and in the affirmative for attended ones.

Unattended

Case	Location	Item insured	Distance from vehicle	Vehicle locked	Key in vehicle	Vehicle visible	Proper lookout	Time away	Aware of theft
Starfire	Car: lay-by. Driver: walking on track leading off lay-by.	Jewellery.	37 yards.	Yes. Thief broke window to take jewellery case.	No.	Only the roof was visible when the driver was facing the car.	No – the driver's back was turned away from the car when he went down the track.	5 mins (estimated)	Yes when thief was already walking away with the jewellery. Driver could not catch him.
Ingleton	Car: parked in road. Driver: chatting in shop.	Van.	Distance btw road and shop.	No. Van stolen.	Yes, in ignition.	No.	No.	15 mins.	No.
Sanger	Car: petrol station Driver: lavatory then kiosk.	Jewellery.	Distance btw pump and lavatory/kiosk.	Yes.	No.	Not for the 68 seconds whilst the theft occurred, and the view from the kiosk was obscured.	No. Even when part of the car was visible, the driver did not keep looking at it when he went into the kiosk.	5 mins (estimated)	No

Not unattended

Case	Location	Item insured	Distance from vehicle	Vehicle locked	Key in vehicle	Vehicle visible	Proper lookout	Time away	Aware of theft
Plaistow	Lorry: lay-by. Driver: asleep inside cabin.	Goods in transit.	0.	N/A. Ingots stolen from under lorry tarpaulin.	Yes, along with the driver.	N/A	Yes – driver expected a theft would wake him.	0 mins.	No.
Langford	Car: house driveway. Driver: opened porch and front door and slipped inside house to put bags down.	Jewellery.	17ft, of which only 8ft was without view of the car.	Yes. Thieves broke in and stole two suit-cases of jewellery.	No.	Not for 5 seconds.	Yes, but could not see when in part of the house.	Moments.	Yes. Ran out of the house and confronted the thieves, but unable to stop them.
O'Donoghue	Car: quiet petrol station. Driver: kiosk.	Jewellery.	Petrol pump nearest kiosk. No more than 14-16ft.	Yes. Profes-sional thieves had probably been tracking the driver and broke in with own duplicate key.	No.	Most of car visible but for a few seconds when signing the credit card slip, walking to the kiosk, and walking from the counter to the door.	Yes.	Few moments.	No. Thieves on un-observed side of car, unlocked, stole and re-locked within a matter of seconds.
Hayward (first instance)	Car: petrol station. Driver: kiosk.	Porsche.	Petrol pump near kiosk. 15–25 yards.	No, but special immo-bilizer.	Yes.	Yes. Could see and hear car throughout.	Yes – proper and reasonable.	Few moments.	Yes. Touched car as it was driven away. Might have prevented theft if not for threat of force.

The FOS approach compared to a court's

9.31 Assuming that there are no sales code issues, the FOS will begin by applying all the circumstances of the case to the *Starfire* test, as a court would, to determine whether a vehicle has been left unattended. After the Court of Appeal ruling in *Hayward*, the FOS also said that it did not need to adjust its approach materially as a result. The FOS, making no distinction between exclusions for unattended vehicles and those for keys left in the car, has set out issues and guidelines which affect its decisions, some of which a court might not share. There is a danger that these will become rules of thumb which the FOS will follow whatever the circumstances and however the case law would respond, without referring to the original tests set out in the case law:

    (1) Was the driver in reasonable proximity to the vehicle or had he "moved away?" The nature of the location will be of prime importance to the FOS assessing this, as reasonable proximity will mean the driver will need to be closer to a car left in

a busy street or petrol station than to one left in the middle of an empty field. Someone leaving the engine running in the driveway whilst opening or closing his garage door (such as in Case Study 1/6[20]) has not moved away and is not necessarily reckless. But if this was done whilst the car was in the road, however close to the driveway or private property, and the driver turned his back on the vehicle or went inside to fetch something, then the insured might have "left" the car.

(2) Was the driver able to keep the vehicle under observation? However, the FOS notes that in some circumstances a vehicle can still be attended although not in view. A court would also take account of the obscuring of the view and the time during which it could not be observed.

(3) Would the driver have had a reasonable prospect of intervening? If a theft succeeds, it does not mean that the driver was not in a position to intervene. A driver standing next to his car can have a deterrent effect without having to be physically able to prevent a theft. A court would agree, but would also look, as it did in *Starfire*, at what was done in the driver's absence.

(4) The length of time the driver anticipated the car being unoccupied and unattended. A court might be more concerned with the actual time spent away from the vehicle, the distance and during how much of this time the vehicle was observed, as all the court cases mention these factors rather than the intention of the assured.

(5) The general attitude to the specific risk and whether the complainant's behaviour is likely to be regarded by other drivers as "reasonable". For instance in general, if the insured was standing only a few feet away from the vehicle, the FOS is likely to consider his behaviour reasonable and the vehicle attended. Following *Starfire*, the objective reasonableness of the behaviour is not really the point, and is not strictly part of the test, although it might go towards recklessness. The courts seem more concerned with carefulness and trying to keep the vehicle under observation.

(6) The car's value and its attractiveness to thieves. Following *Starfire,* a court would be more interested in the object of the policy, and would require a higher level of stringency in looking after high value goods such as jewellery. The FOS does not specifically note the object of the insurance as affecting its decisions.

9.32 The FOS has more recently published a Technical Note headed Motor Insurance: keys in car,[21] which correctly in this context refers only to the Court of Appeal decision in *Hayward* (and not to *Starfire*) and says that the FOS will follow this ruling. It is not impressive that the Technical Note only gives a Lawtel reference to this major Court of Appeal case. And then after quoting Peter Gibson LJ's interpretation in that case of what keys left in the car mean, bewilderingly asserts that it is clear that this means that even in law, insurers cannot enforce a strictly worded exclusion. The Note then goes on to say that the FOS takes a very similar approach. It can only be hoped that the FOS is following *Hayward* in practice.

9.33 In following the *Hayward* tests, the Note says that the FOS might ask two questions. These are also those that a court would ask:

---

20. *Ombudsman News* Jan 2001.
21. October 2009.

(1) Were the keys left in or on the car (either intentionally or inadvertently)? and

(2) If no responsible person was left in charge of the keys in or on the car, had the driver moved too far away from the keys to make the prevention of a theft unlikely?

9.34 The Note says that in determining the answers to this last question, it pays particular attention to where the car was at the time of the incident, whether the driver was in a position to deter the thief or make the theft unlikely, and any mitigating factors that caused the driver to leave the car. The Note adds that if the car is unlocked with the keys in or on it, and is on or close to private land, the FOS will ask:

(1) Was the car visible from and/or close to the public road?

(2) Were the driveway gates (if any) open?

(3) Were the doors or boot left open? and

(4) Was the engine running?

9.35 Then in deciding whether the keys were indeed left, the FOS will take into account the distance from the car, the length of time away, whether the driver went inside a building and whether the car was out of the driver's sight. It adds that if the car is on the public highway, a higher degree of care is required, however close to a driveway or private property it is. In a public place, if the driver has walked away from the car, the FOS is usually satisfied that the car has been left. If someone has acted reasonably in mitigating circumstances, such as an emergency, the FOS will expect insurers to pay a claim even if the exclusion was breached. (There are no example case studies which illustrate this last point.)

9.36 Although the FOS considers that it is following the Court of Appeal ruling in *Hayward,* the reasoning of some of the later case studies suggests that it may be applying the *Starfire* test for "unattended" to decide if an insured has "moved away" from the vehicle in a left keys exclusion. The FOS has commented[22] that it views the two tests as "very similar". The temptation to merge the tests is understandable, especially as many exclusions now include both unattended and left keys elements. However, this may not be a correct application of the case law in light of the comments referred to above made in the Court of Appeal's judgment.

FOS case studies involving unattended vehicles and/or keys left in cars

9.37 The Case Studies published in *Ombudsman News* illustrate the FOS approach to these clauses, although as mentioned above, there seems to be limited differentiation between unattended vehicle exclusions and keys left in cars. This is understandable for Case Studies 1/6 to 1/9 and 1/11 to 1/12[23] which were decided before the Court of Appeal had given its ruling in *Hayward* and differentiated between the two types of clauses. The FOS later commented that these case studies would not have had different outcomes even after this Court of Appeal ruling. With each case turning on its own facts, it is possible that if those cases had been decided by a court, the results would have been the same, except in Case Study 1/7 which turned on a sales point.

---

22. *Ombudsman News* May/June 2004.
23. *Ombudsman News* Jan 2001.

FOS not unattended vehicles

9.38 The FOS found that the vehicles in Case Studies 1/6, 1/8, 1/9[24] and 82/10[25] had been attended and that the drivers had not acted recklessly, recklessness seeming to be the factor that the FOS is actually using as a major part of the test to determine attendance.

9.39 In Case Study 1/6, the insured had stopped his car on his driveway and got out, leaving the engine running and the door open. Before lifting up his garage door, he put his briefcase in the unlocked porch adjacent to his garage. As he did this he heard a noise and turned round to see someone jump into his car and reverse away at high speed. Although he was very close to the car, he could not prevent it from being stolen. The insurer declined the claim on the basis of an exclusion for "losses arising from the use of keys which had been left in or around the vehicle". It is arguable that the driver in this keys-in-the-car case would not have satisfied the Court of Appeal's *Hayward* test, in that he may not have been sufficiently proximate to the keys so that a theft was unlikely.

9.40 In Case Study 1/8, the insured was picking up his children from school. He left his car in a busy street, with the door shut but the keys in the ignition, whilst he was speaking to his son about eight feet behind the car. Less than two minutes later, two youths ran up, jumped into the car and drove off, despite his best efforts to stop them.

9.41 In Case Study 1/9, the insured reversed his car out of his garage and got out of the car to return briefly to the house, leaving the car keys in the ignition and closing but not locking the car door. Although only away for about 30 seconds, the car was gone when he returned.

9.42 An example of a FOS case study on attendance post-*Hayward* is Case Study 82/10.[26] As is characteristic for FOS case study reports, no case law is mentioned. The FOS found that a man had not left a van unattended when he had left it with its rear doors open and the keys on top of his jacket which was on the ground next to the van, whilst he worked just a few metres away mending a digger on a building site. He had been working on private property that was sufficiently well secluded to prevent access by casual passers-by, and although he did not actually notice the theft of the van, the FOS accepted his view that he had been close enough to the van to be able to intervene if he saw anyone trying to steal it. The FOS also said that he had not been acting recklessly.

FOS unattended vehicles

9.43 The FOS found that the vehicles in Case Studies 1/11 and 1/12 had been unattended.

9.44 In Case Study 1/11,[27] the insured visited a house he was building to drop off equipment. He left his car off the road, leaving it unlocked and the car key among a bunch of keys in the lock on the front door of the house. The car was stolen even though it would have only been visible to someone close to the house.

9.45 In Case Study 1/12,[28] the policyholder's husband parked their Land Rover Discovery in front of a terraced house where he was working. He removed the keys from the ignition, but left the vehicle unlocked, with a spare set of keys in the pocket on the driver's side of the

24. *Ombudsman News* Jan 2001.
25. *Ombudsman News* Dec 09/Jan 2010.
26. *Ombudsman News* Dec 09/Jan 2010.
27. *Ombudsman News* Jan 2001.
28. *Ombudsman News* Jan 2001.

car. He entered the house to close windows upstairs and downstairs and to set the alarm, and returned to see the car disappearing up the road.

*FOS keys in the car cases, post-*Hayward

9.46 In Case Study 38/5,[29] the FOS thought that the insured had probably accidentally left the keys in the car when it was stolen from her driveway but parked close to the road. The FOS found it to be unattended as she was in the house so was too far away to prevent a theft and did not hear or see anything. Applying the Court of Appeal reasoning of *Hayward,* surely the keys were left in the car in the sense of their ordinary meaning, rather than needing to imply the words "left unattended". Were the keys left in the car? Yes. Had she moved away from them? Yes, because she was not close enough to make a theft unlikely. The position of where the car was parked seems irrelevant.

9.47 The same is true of Case Study 82/11,[30] where the FOS found that the vehicle had been "left unattended" and referred to the exclusion breached being an "unattended" one, and later as a "keys in car" exclusion. Perhaps both aspects were in the exclusion, or perhaps the FOS has fused the two types of issue. Either way, the FOS did not uphold the complaint and found that the vehicle had been "left unattended". The driver had left the car in her house driveway, with the keys in the ignition, the engine running and the driver's door open when she went back into the house. She returned to find the car gone. Neither she nor her husband, who was inside the house, had seen or heard anything, which meant that neither of them could have been watching the car, and also that she must have been in the house for longer than the 10 seconds she claimed. The result fits in with *Hayward,* although the case is not mentioned in the report. The keys were left in the car and the driver had moved away.

Car-jacking

9.48 Although there have been no reported FOS case studies relating to car-jacking, perhaps because the industry deals with these fairly, the FOS has commented that it would not let an insurer rely on a keys-left-in-vehicle exclusion, even where hijack was not specifically excepted from the exclusion. So probably would a court, based not on the FOS idea of fairness and reasonableness, but on LJ Gibson's *obiter* comments in the Court of Appeal in *Hayward,* that the duress in a hijacking situation would make the keys "taken" as opposed to "left".

Commentary on unattended vehicle/keys in car exclusions

9.49 The FOS is loosely following the case law in the way it is treating unattended vehicle and/or keys in car exclusion clauses. Any differences are more likely to be technical, with little or no difference in the outcome. The FOS example case studies show how it has decided various situations, but it must be remembered that the FOS does not follow its own precedents, and, although it aims for consistent decisions, it may not decide a similar case the same way, depending on all the circumstances of the case.

29. *Ombudsman News* July 2004.
30. *Ombudsman News* Dec 09/Jan 2010.

COMPENSATION FOR STOLEN CARS

9.50 The Technical Note referred to above specifies that if the FOS decides that insurers should pay the claim for a stolen car, it will direct the insurer to pay the market value of the vehicle assessed as at the date of the theft, plus interest at the simple rate of 8% per year (less any tax properly due), from the date of the theft to the date of actual settlement.[31]

---

31. See further below "Vehicle valuation: FOS" at paras. 10.20 *et seq.*

CHAPTER 10

MEASUREMENT OF LOSS, ABANDONMENT AND SALVAGE

INSURER'S OPTION TO REPAIR, REINSTATE, REPLACE OR OFFER A CASH SETTLEMENT

Reasonableness

10.1 Most household policies allow the insurer to opt to repair, replace, reinstate or offer a cash settlement to deal with the claim. The FOS says that the insurer must exercise this power reasonably, in the circumstances of the individual case. In Case Study 58/5,[1] following expert evidence and photographs of the units, the FOS found that it was not reasonable for the insurer to opt for repair instead of replacement. This requirement of reasonableness is a welcome feature which is not present in the law unless required by the wording of the policy.

Repair

10.2 The measure of loss for repair is normally the cost of restoring the goods to their pre-loss condition. The FOS seems to agree. If the assured intends the goods for resale, the measure is the market value of the goods before and after the loss.[2] The FOS has not published any material which tests this.

10.3 If the cost of repair is more than the market value of the goods prior to the loss, and only if the policy permits, an insurer may choose either to pay for a total loss or to indemnify the insured for the cost of repair. Motor insurers are most commonly affected by this matter and usually pay the market value prior to loss. The FOS seems to support that practice, although it is not clear whether it first requires the policy to include this option as the law does (see below "Vehicle valuation: FOS" at paragraphs 10.20 *et seq*). Without such policy terms, the law entitles the assured to an indemnity representing the reinstatement cost, although there is no modern case on point. In Case Study 83/10,[3] the insurer said that a boiler was uneconomical to repair and offered instead of repair a discretionary payment of £100 towards the cost of a new boiler. The policy stated clearly that the insurer could refuse to repair the boiler in circumstances where it decided it was not economical to do so. The FOS did not uphold the complaint.

10.4 The FOS considers that an insurer opting for repair (or reinstatement) must explain that if the insurer or its agent chooses or controls the repairer, then it is normally the insurer

---

1. *Ombudsman News* Dec 2006/Jan 2007.
2. *Quorum AS* v *Schramm* [2002] Lloyd's Rep IR 292. The assured intended to sell a valuable painting before it was damaged by heat. The measure of loss was therefore the difference between the pre and post-damage valuations.
3. *Ombudsman News* Feb/Mar 2010.

who will be liable to make good any deficiencies in the repair, even if this brings the claim above policy limits. If, however, the insured insists on a particular repairer, the insured will generally be responsible for the quality of the repairs, unless the insurer controls the work such as by requiring the repairer to cut his costs or to use particular materials or parts. The law would follow the rules of agency without requiring the insured to be notified of the consequences of his decision to use his own repairer.

10.5 In Case Study 68/7,[4] the FOS said that the insured could look to the insurers for the costs of remedying the defects in repairs of the insured damage, but would have to claim against the surveyor directly for remedying defects in additional work for which she had paid, even though insurers had paid for the surveyor overseeing all the work. In Case Study 83/9,[5] the insurer's repairer had not carried out the repairs to a toilet promptly when the insured first contacted the insurer, and then had pulled the toilet chain when the insured had warned him not to. On assessment of the evidence, the FOS thought that the damage to the bathroom floor and the ceiling of the room below more likely than not resulted from the repairer's actions, so insurers had to pay for the cost of these to be repaired, plus interest from the date that the insured first made her claim for the damage. A court would have agreed in both these cases with the FOS assessment of who was liable to pay for the repairs.

10.6 The obligation for insurers to pay for the repairs to their repairers' work extends to work that their repairers wrongly advised needed to be done. In Case Study 83/8,[6] the insurer's contractor advised that a boiler needed to be power flushed to sort out the problem, which work was not covered by the policy. The evidence was that it had not been necessary and had not resolved the problem. The FOS found that the insurers should be responsible for the cost of this power flush as it had been carried out on the advice of the insurer's contractor. The FOS also awarded interest from the date that the insured had put in a claim for this cost.

Reinstatement and under-insurance

10.7 When an insurer opts to reinstate, it is bound to replace as new with no deduction for wear or tear or depreciation. However, if there has been under-insurance, the law applies the principle of average to marine policies, under which the assured must bear the uninsured proportion of any partial loss.[7] The principle applies in non-marine policies usually only where an average condition is incorporated into the policy. Most fire policies contain one, and because they are so common in commercial fire policies, one may be implied with those. There is little authority on the application of average outside of marine and fire insurance, the assumption having been made in a number of ancient cases that average has no place outside of these categories. In any case, average is only required to ensure that the assured bears the uninsured proportion of a partial loss. For a total loss, insurers only have to pay up to policy limits, so the assured necessarily bears the uninsured balance.

10.8 The FOS supports insurers who adopt the principle of average when there has been under-insurance, as long as the reduction proposed by insurers is not communicated and imposed too late in the process. In Case Study 4/18,[8] the insurer agreed to reinstate in full an under-insured, fire-damaged property, as long as the policyholder increased the sum insured.

---

4. *Ombudsman News* Mar/Apr 2008.
5. *Ombudsman News* Feb/Mar 2010.
6. *Ombudsman News* Feb/Mar 2010.
7. S. 67(2) MIA 1906.
8. *Ombudsman News* Apr 2001.

The FOS would not allow the insurer then, in the middle of agreed works, to impose the sum insured as a ceiling on its liability, which would have left the first floor a shell. The law would not generally impose a time limit on applying average, although in the circumstances, insurers might have waived the average option or be estopped from asserting otherwise when they had agreed to reinstate in full.

10.9 Even where a building is adequately insured, it is possible, although unusual, that this will not be enough to cover reinstatement, as was the position in Case Study 4/20.[9] In these circumstances, the FOS does not believe it reasonable for the insurer to limit its liability to the sum insured. For it is this sort of unusual eventuality that insureds expect their insurance to cover. There is no recent case law on point, but the general principle applied by the law is the same: that a total loss is subject to the policy limits, but reinstatement is not. If an insurer discovers at the outset that the reinstatement costs are going to be more than policy limits, and if the policy so provides, insurers can choose to treat the loss as if it were total instead. They cannot make one representation at the beginning that they will cover the loss and then change their minds.

10.10 If the FOS considers that the householder has acted honestly in assessing the amount for which contents should be insured, but a loss adjuster later suggests that there has been under-insurance, the FOS will take a sympathetic line to the insured following loss, as valuation is not an exact science and can be difficult.

Replacement and cash settlements

10.11 There is no relevant case law on this topic, only guidance from the FOS as set out below, which it would be good for the courts to consider should the opportunity arise.

10.12 If the policy confers on the insurer a right to replace goods, the FOS will consider whether replacement is a reasonable option, and if it is not, the FOS will normally ask the insurer to agree a cash settlement. It will be a reasonable option if the object can be replaced, a suitable alternative is found (antique jewellery cannot be replaced by a modern piece) and the insured wants a replacement (personal circumstances may have changed his desire to own the item). The FOS may consider it unreasonable to limit the choice of replacement to a particular retailer or for the insurer to offer vouchers to the insured instead. Insurers would prefer these options as they can sometimes negotiate discounts as a result of their bulk business. As demonstrated in Case Studies 75/9 and 75/10,[10] the FOS would not regard it as reasonable for the insurer to make a deduction from the cash settlement to represent any discount it would have got if the policyholder had bought a replacement from one of the insurer's nominated suppliers.

10.13 Where there is a new for old policy (commonly in household insurance), both the law and the FOS will oblige the insurer to provide a new replacement or equivalent money, even if the damaged item had been subject to wear and tear, unless there is a clear exclusion for wear and tear. This overcomes the difficulties of calculating the amount of loss, although it might mean that the insured receives a windfall. In Case Study 58/5,[11] the FOS required the insurer to replace all the kitchen units, where all but one of them had been damaged by flood.

---

9. *Ombudsman News* Apr 2001.
10. *Ombudsman News* Jan/Feb 2009.
11. *Ombudsman News* Dec 2006/Jan 2007.

MATCHING SETS

10.14 There is no case law on matching sets, but policies usually exclude cover for replacing a whole set where only one part is damaged and a matching replacement cannot be located. Whilst the law might apply the exclusion strictly, the FOS typically awards 50% of the cost of replacing the undamaged items in buildings and contents insurance. This represents the FOS attempting to balance the unacceptable finish that the insured would have to his property if the wording was applied strictly, especially as he probably did not appreciate its meaning until that point, against the unfairness of distorting clear policy wording sold in line with the appropriate industry codes. In Case Study 10/8,[12] a dog knocked a tin of paint over a sofa, and the FOS asked the insurer to pay 50% of the cost of replacing the rest of the suite if a matching replacement could not be found.

10.15 The FOS will consider that the 50% approach is inappropriate where there has been no substantial loss, such as when only a few tiles in the whole room have been damaged. In such a situation, the FOS says that no compensation should be paid above the cost of replacing the damaged item/s. The 14 damaged bathroom tiles were enough to merit a 50% payment in respect of the undamaged tiles which the FOS felt was reasonable in the circumstances in Case Study 10/7.[13]

10.16 Where matching is intrinsic to the value of the objects, the FOS will make an award for full replacement of all the matching objects as well. So in Case Study 10/5[14] the FOS felt that it was fair and reasonable to treat the whole suit as a single item when only the trousers had been damaged. The wording was "We will treat an individual item of a matching set of articles . . . as a single item". The insurer was required to pay for the replacement of a whole suit. This seems a sensible way of dealing with the issue and a court might well have approached the problem in the same way in view of the wording.

10.17 In Case Study 75/6,[15] the sink was damaged, but insurers were not required to pay 50% of the cost of the matching bathroom suite that the assured had purchased as the assured had been clearly told to wait for insurers to see if they could find a matching sink first, although they thought it unlikely. This was evidenced in a tape recording of the relevant telephone conversation. In fact the insurer did find a matching sink, so there was no liability for them to pay for the cost of the matching suite. The insurer in Case Study 75/7,[16] by contrast, did have to pay for a replacement bath plus 50% of the rest of the bathroom suite the insured had purchased, even though the insurer had not given her express permission to obtain the replacements. The FOS felt that she had acted reasonably, as she had been given no clear explanation of how her claim would be progressed, and insurers' representatives who were meant to assess whether it would be possible to source a matching suite twice failed to turn up to appointments without contacting her to cancel them.

TOTAL LOSS

10.18 If goods are destroyed or cannot be reinstated or repaired, the assured will generally be entitled to their market value immediately before the insured event[17] up to policy limits.

---

12. *Ombudsman News* Oct 2001.
13. *Ombudsman News* Oct 2001.
14. *Ombudsman News* Oct 2001.
15. *Ombudsman News* Jan/Feb 2009.
16. *Ombudsman News* Jan/Feb 2009.
17. *Scottish Coal Co Ltd* v *Royal and Sun Alliance plc* [2008] EWHC 880 (Comm).

Unless specifically included in the policy, there will be no provision for consequential losses or loss of profits. Most consumer policies are unvalued, so the market value has to be calculated. It is common practice amongst insurers to judge the market value from the amount that the goods would have realised if sold, not the normally greater amount that they would cost to replace, which would be the tortious measure.[18] The sum is payable even if the assured has not replaced the chattel and has no intention of doing so. The price originally paid is not relevant in determining actual loss, so that if the claimant has had the good fortune to obtain the subject matter cheaply, he is nevertheless entitled to recover the market value.[19]

10.19 As a matter of practice, insurers often pay for a total loss following serious damage which renders repair uneconomic. The FOS allows this but has set out some further guidance in relation to vehicle valuation which the law does not have and a court might wish to adopt.

VEHICLE VALUATION: FOS[20]

Replacement value

10.20 In the more unusual case of a valued policy, both the FOS and the courts will only allow recovery of the value set out in the policy (assuming it is set out clearly), not the replacement cost, e.g. Case Study 66/4.[21] However, for unvalued motor policies at least, the FOS has taken the view that the tort measure of replacement value should prevail. So the market value of a written-off or stolen car would be the likely cost to the customer of buying a vehicle as near as possibly identical to the one that has been stolen or damaged beyond repair. This is not the same as the amount the vehicle was worth when purchased, although the purchase price will be relevant if the vehicle in question was recently purchased.[22]

10.21 The FOS expects insurers to know the FOS approach to vehicle valuation, as it says that it is like that of the IOB. This is one of the very few occasions where the FOS makes reference to IOB decisions. Perhaps it should therefore be inferred that usually IOB decisions/policy will not apply. If insurers do not assess vehicle valuations in line with good industry practice, the FOS might require them to and also to pay for distress and inconvenience. Following industry practice is not a requirement of the law.

The price guides

10.22 To establish a vehicle's true market value, the FOS will expect the insurer to consult trade guides and to adjust the price to allow for any unusual features in the vehicle's mileage or condition. The FOS forms an overall view by looking at all three of the major industry valuation guides, Glass's, Parker's and CAPcalc. If the guides show different values, the FOS will consider whether the insurer's offer is a reasonable one in light of the three guides. If one figure is significantly out of line with the other two, it is likely to be disregarded. If that one figure is significantly lower, an insurer's offer based on it is unlikely to be considered reasonable. What counts as a significant difference will depend on the circumstances,

---

18. *Aerospace Publishing Ltd* v *Thames Water Utilities Ltd* [2007] EWCA Civ 3.
19. *Dominion Mosaics* v *Trafalgar Trucking Co* [1990] 2 All ER 246.
20. *Cf* FOS Technical Note "Motor Insurance—Vehicle Valuation" dated 15/07/09.
21. *Ombudsman News* Dec 07/Jan 08.
22. See below "Forecourt prices and other factors" at paras. 10.25 *et seq.*

including the overall figure and the proportion it bears to the value of the vehicle. The FOS will not substitute its own judgment in place of the insurer's, if the insurer has behaved reasonably in consulting the appropriate guides and making appropriate adjustments to come to a market value within the range of what could be considered reasonable.

10.23 The insurer should usually refer to the guide retail price (the price a member of the public might reasonably expect to pay at a dealership). However, it may be suitable to use the guide trade value (the price that a motor trader might pay) if the vehicle was not in guide retail condition or where there is evidence that the insured intended to buy a replacement privately. The FOS would also expect the insurer to look at price guides available to the public, especially where they give significantly different prices to the trade guides. For the valuing of unusual, non-standard or classic vehicles, specialist publications and/or evidence from the firm's in-house engineer or an independent engineer might be necessary. If a vehicle has unusual features which makes its value not obvious from the standard guides, the FOS would expect insurers to contact the compilers of a relevant guide and make further enquiries. In Case Study 66/2,[23] it required the insurer to do this in relation to a car with a specialist sports body, and the result was a higher valuation. In Case Study 85/2[24] it told the insurer that it should have obtained accurate information from a specialist horse trailer manufacturer or dealer, and should not have based its offer on newspaper advertisements.

10.24 The FOS may make an award for distress or inconvenience if an insurer does not make a valuation on the basis of these guides or on any reasonable basis. An award of £150 was made where this happened in Case Study 66/1.[25] In contrast, a court could only penalise unreasonable behaviour through costs and interest awards under CPR.[26]

Forecourt prices and other factors

10.25 Forecourt prices advertised in local papers and internet sites are widely understood to be too high and only a starting point for negotiations. The FOS therefore does not place much weight on them. As pointed out in Case Study 66/1,[27] the information provided is often insufficient to ensure a like-for-like comparison of age, condition and mileage.

10.26 However, the FOS will take into account other factors if it seems sensible to do so, such as a recent purchase price from a reputable source. In Case Study 22/17[28] a car had been purchased new with only five miles on the clock from a reputable dealer, one month before it was stolen. The insurer said that the dealer's registration for five weeks before the purchase reduced its value but the FOS disagreed and said that there was no evidence of this. The FOS felt that the full purchase price was the appropriate market value and so asked the insurer to pay this with interest from the date of the theft.

10.27 As a fair market valuation will already have taken into account the condition of the vehicle, its owner's assessment of its usefulness or reliability will make no difference. However, an engineer's report can be useful evidence if he has actually inspected the vehicle. The FOS is likely to consider reasonable a deduction of up to 10% for the value of left-hand drives, unless is it a classic car and the left-hand drive of such is intrinsic to its character. Also reasonable would be a deduction of not more than 20% if the policyholder knew that the

---

23. *Ombudsman News* Dec 07/Jan 08.
24. *Ombudsman News* Apr/May 2010.
25. *Ombudsman News* Dec 07/Jan 08.
26. See above "Insurers' liability in law for damage caused by their own behaviour" at paras. 3.5 *et seq.*
27. *Ombudsman News* Dec 07/Jan 08.
28. *Ombudsman News* Oct 2002.

vehicle was a repaired write-off, but no such deduction if he did not know and the repairs were not obviously noticeable.

Accessories or modifications

10.28 Special features, accessories or modifications added or made by an insured may not add substantially to, or may reduce, a vehicle's market value. Where permanent modifications have been made, it may be appropriate to look at the closest equivalent vehicle and then make adjustments for the quality of the modifications. As long as the overall approach is reasonable, the FOS will not require the insurer to cover the policyholder for the precise mixture of features of the car in question. However, the market value (rather than the new value) of detachable accessories may have to be added to a settlement as was the position in Case Study 18/12[29] in relation to a CD player, roof bars and tow bar which had been on the damaged car, but did not fit on the replacement car. The FOS felt that the insurer had calculated the offer fairly. There will be consequences in accordance with the FOS' own non-disclosure scheme if there has been non-disclosure of relevant vehicle modifications at the proposal/renewal stage.[30]

Hidden defects: actual re-sale value

10.29 The market value of a vehicle which is found to have been clocked or imported from an unauthorised source, will be reduced. If the owner knew of such hidden facts, the insurer may be justified in rejecting the entire claim for fraudulently trying to obtain a benefit to which he was not entitled. An innocent victim of fraud should receive the vehicle's actual market value, but this will still not be as much as the value of the vehicle he thought he had bought, but only an equivalent replacement of the actual car that he did buy. These are faults which might have been reasonably discoverable from the sales documentation or the car itself. So in Case Study 22/18,[31] although a car had allegedly been purchased two months earlier for £25,000, it was a grey import and the FOS supported the insurer's valuation of £17,950 which was in line with the trade guide for grey imports. This approach is in line with the court, which might also require insurers to replace the item with a similar one representing its actual value, rather than the purchase price, following *Grimaldi* v *Sullivan*.[32]

10.30 In *Grimaldi*, the assured purchased Cartier watches for £57,000, but they proved to be fakes with a market value of about £3,500, and a scrap value of £750 and were seized by the police. The Court of Appeal held that the assured could not claim £57,000 from insurers of a policy covering defects in title, as that would have indemnified him for loss of genuine watches which he had not purchased. It also held that the scrap value was not appropriate as this disregarded the fact that fake watches had some resale value. The proper measure was £3,500, as this is the amount that could have been realised for the watches had the trade-mark owner granted permission for re-sale, so was the actual value of the watches. As it was the defect in title which allowed the trade-mark owner to prohibit re-sale, the loss was the amount which would have been realisable but for that prohibition.

---

29. *Ombudsman News* July 2002.
30. E.g. Case Studies 79/10 and 79/11 *Ombudsman News* Sept/Oct 2009, where there was innocent and inadvertent non-disclosure respectively. See below under "Innocent non-disclosure—the FOS" at paras. 13.39 *et seq* and "Inadvertent non-disclosure" at paras. 13.50 *et seq.*
31. *Ombudsman News* Oct 2002.
32. (Unreported 1997.)

Hidden defects: re-sale value as if no defect

10.31 Hidden rust and car cloning are two instances where the FOS may not adopt the replacement of actual equivalent approach, but rather the market value on re-sale as if there was no defect, as long as the insured is innocent and has taken all reasonable precautions on purchase. The difference between these and the clocking, grey imports or *Grimaldi* situations, is that the defects for hidden rust and car cloning may not be reasonably discoverable from the documents or vehicle itself on purchase and re-sale.

10.32 There is a New Zealand Court of Appeal judgment on hidden rust[33] which held that the assured was entitled to the re-sale value of the car, so the hidden rust could be ignored for valuation purposes because it would have remained hidden from a reasonable purchaser on re-sale. There is no English case law on point.

10.33 Car cloning is where the number plates, often of a stolen car, are changed to those of an almost identical car. The FOS will usually expect an insurer to pay a consumer's claim relating to a cloned vehicle if he had a comprehensive or third party motor policy with the premium paid and reasonably believed the purchase was legitimate. To establish the consumer's reasonable beliefs at the time of the purchase of the vehicle, the FOS will consider whether he:

(1) carried out an HPI check into a vehicle's history. The FOS regards this as a sensible precaution for any buyer of a second-hand vehicle, although the FOS appreciates that this check will probably not uncover cloning;
(2) had a vehicle registration form;
(3) received a purchase receipt showing the seller's contact details (even if these details are subsequently found to be false); and
(4) paid a purchase price comparable to that of other vehicles of a similar make, model and age.

10.34 If an insured acted in good faith and took all reasonable steps to ensure the vehicle's authenticity, the FOS will consider him to have a defeasible title and insurers should pay the full market value of a similar vehicle with an unblemished history, rather than the actual value of the cloned car. Some deduction might be appropriate where the buyer acted in good faith but failed to take reasonable steps which probably would have alerted him to the problem. Presumably the FOS would look to see if an insured has taken the above steps when looking at all hidden defect issues, not just car cloning.

10.35 The FOS has probably got the balance of interests right on hidden defects. For hidden rust and cloned car cases, insurers are basically paying out on what both they and the assured thought they were insuring and could not have reasonably discovered otherwise. It is to be hoped that a court faced with the same problem might come to the same conclusion. Instead, it might consider that the actual replacement value was appropriate, making analogies with *Grimaldi* in light of the paucity of other case law on the subject, and because *Grimaldi* is a Court of Appeal decision, even though it deals with defects in title of another type in a defects in title policy with defects that were reasonably discoverable.

Loss of use and courtesy cars

10.36 Only if provided for in the policy is a policyholder covered for the cost of a courtesy car, and most policies do not allow for one where a vehicle is written off. The FOS usually

---

33. *State Insurance Office* v *Bettany* [1992] 2 NZLR 275.

only awards an assured compensation for loss of use of a vehicle where the insurer unreasonably delays, wrongly declines the claim or misrepresents that a hire car would be available. Where the policyholder hired a car in these circumstances, the FOS might require the insurer to refund the hire-car charges plus interest. Where he did not, the FOS might require compensation for other reasonable transport expenses incurred plus inconvenience caused by lack of a car. An inconvenience award would usually be around £10 per day if it had a material effect on the policyholder and depending on the individual circumstances such as whether the policyholder had free access to another vehicle and the availability of public transport.

Payment of premium, excess and interest

10.37 An insured will still be expected to pay the whole term's worth of premiums, even if the car has been written off. The amount of the claim paid by the insurer will be subject to the policy excess. The FOS usually awards interest at 8% per year simple on the amount of the claim. Interest will be calculated from the date of the incident, not the date of the claim, to the date of payment: for the policyholder has not had the use of the vehicle during this time, but the insurer has had the use of the money.

ABANDONMENT AND SALVAGE

10.38 Ancient case law has developed the principles of salvage and abandonment primarily in relation to marine insurance, but they are equally applicable to non-marine insurance.[34] Abandonment is the transfer of the insured subject matter from the assured to the insurers, which takes place on payment of a total loss by the insurers. No notice of abandonment is required outside of constructive total losses in marine insurance. There is a right to be paid for a total loss only where the assured is willing to hand over what, if anything, remains of the insured subject matter to the insurers. Salvage is the insurer's right to claim for its own benefit the right of ownership of that subject matter where it has paid for a total loss and where the insured is not underinsured and has received a full indemnity. Once the insurer has agreed to pay for a total loss and to adopt the subject matter by way of salvage, it cannot thereafter seek to change its position and seek recovery of its payment should facts subsequently show that no loss has occurred.

10.39 It is commonly the case, particularly with cars, that the assured wishes to retain ownership of the property even though the insurer has classified it as a total loss. The insurer will usually be willing to sell the property back to the insured for its scrap value, although the insurer is not obliged to offer to do this, and the insurer may treat it as he wishes as soon as he has agreed to pay for a total loss. This is where the FOS begins to diverge from the law.

10.40 The IOB took the view that the insured had the right (in terms of good insurance practice, as opposed to the right at law), to repurchase the property, so the insurer should not dispose of it until the insured had been given an opportunity to repurchase.[35] Unusually, the IOB view may be relevant in this context, as the FOS has specifically said that the way it

---

34. *Kaltenbach* v *Mackenzie* (1878) LR 3 CPD 467.
35. IOB Annual Report for 1982 at p 13, IOB Annual Report for 1987 at pp 19–20.

deals with vehicle valuations after a total loss is the same as the way they were dealt with under the IOB.

10.41 The FOS says[36] that the salvage of a vehicle remains the insured's property until settlement has been agreed, so insurers will need the insured's express permission to dispose of it before this point, with an award against the insurer for distress or inconvenience if it does not adhere to this rule. Once settlement has been agreed, the insurer should consider a request from an insured who seeks to retain and repair the vehicle on the basis of the extent of repairs required. Where the damage is merely cosmetic, the FOS would think it reasonable for insurers to agree to the request, but it may not be so where the car has sustained structural damage and there are serious issues of road safety. The insurer is entitled to deduct from the settlement what it would have been able to sell the salvage for, although in the two examples that the FOS provides of the way it deals with car salvage, there is no mention in the reports of such a deduction of repurchase price.

10.42 In Case Study 7/22,[37] the insurer was found to have paid a reasonable amount for the replacement of a damaged car on a total loss basis and to have offered a reasonable amount (£500) for wrongly refusing to allow the insured to keep the salvage and other minor failings. The FOS required the insurer in Case Study 66/3[38] to pay the insured £400 for the distress and inconvenience of undervaluing a "write-off" car which was uneconomical for the insurer to repair and for selling it when the insured had made it clear at the accident report stage that he wished to repair it. The car was not so seriously damaged that it would have been dangerous if repaired, and had been regarded as a Category C in the Code of Practice for the Disposal of Motor Vehicle Salvage. In both these cases, the insurer could not have been forced under the law to give away the salvage, and a repurchase price would have been payable by the insured retaining the salvage.

COMMENTARY

10.43 The common law has long ago established rules about measurement of loss. In general, the FOS seems to accept and follow these. The main differences between the law and the FOS in this subject lie in the way that the FOS regards salvage and abandonment. Many of the problems which the courts have decided have not yet reached the FOS, or at least not the published FOS material, so are not mentioned above. But the FOS also gives some guidelines on matters on which the courts have not, for instance in relation to vehicle valuations, and these and any differences between the law and the FOS approach are set out above. It is to be hoped that a court would refer to and adopt such guidance as in general it is both reasonable and fair.

---

36. *Ombudsman News* July 2001 and Technical Note "Motor Insurance—Vehicle Valuation" dated 15/07/09.
37. *Ombudsman News* July 2001.
38. *Ombudsman News* Dec 07/Jan 08.

CHAPTER 11

PREMIUMS

NON-PAYMENT AND OVERPAYMENT OF PREMIUM

11.1 In law, if the premium is unpaid, there is no cover, but the FOS might find that there is if there has been an understandable, innocent oversight. For instance, in Case Study 23/14,[1] the insured thought his car insurance had renewed automatically. He had not noticed that the premium was no longer being taken from his bank account. The FOS found this understandable in view of the small amount involved, and found no evidence that he had cancelled the policy as the insurer alleged. The failure to renew and pay the premium was therefore an innocent oversight, and the FOS asked the insurer to reinstate the policy and pay for the car repairs with interest, subject to the outstanding premiums. In Case Study 31/1,[2] the cover for the assured had been cancelled by the time of a burglary, because the insured's bank had mistakenly cancelled the direct debit. The FOS attributed the blame for this as follows: 40% for the bank, 40% for the insurer (because it should have contacted the insured before cancelling cover) and 20% for the insured (because he should have noticed that no payments were being made over a six-month period). The insurer had to pay 40% of the claim less the outstanding premium. The bank had already offered £8,000 in full and final settlement in respect of its liability, which the insured had accepted, and the FOS was satisfied that this was fair and reasonable.

11.2 The FOS will try to remedy overpayment of premium where the insured is over-insured. In Case Study 4/17,[3] the insured was heavily over-insured and therefore paying too much premium because of an automatic annual premium increase over many years. The FOS thought that it would be fair if the insurer refunded 50% of the premiums paid over the previous five years plus interest.

11.3 All of the above show a sensible, practical and fair approach by the FOS, which a court might not be able to duplicate, although it might try to, based on who made the mistake, whether that party was an agent of the assured or of the insurer, and whether any term about the insurer's administration duties could be implied.[4]

REPAYMENT OF PREMIUM ON POLICY CANCELLATION

11.4 Where regulatory rules require "cooling-off" periods for contracts,[5] insurers cannot charge any fee for a policy cancellation which occurs during this cooling-off period. Other

---

1. *Ombudsman News* Dec 2002.
2. *Ombudsman News* Sept 2003.
3. *Ombudsman News* Apr 2001.
4. E.g. *Weldon* v *GRE Linked Life Assurance Ltd*, LTL 22 Jan 2001, unreported elsewhere, where an insurer could be liable in contract or tort where an insurance policy had lapsed because of its failure to collect premiums through the direct debit system.
5. E.g. ICOBS requires 30 days for pure protection contracts.

than in this situation, most policies stipulate that if sufficient notice is given of the insured cancelling a policy, he will be entitled to a pro rata refund of premiums paid, less a cancellation charge/administration fee reflecting the costs incurred in setting up and cancelling a policy. The FOS finds these requirements reasonable, so dismissed a complaint in Case Study 54/5[6] about a pro rata refund of premiums less £50 for administrative costs. The FOS also feels that it is fair for a term to stipulate that premiums for an annual contract are not refundable on policy cancellation if a claim has been paid.

11.5 However, the amount of some premium refunds may be unfair and inadequate. There is no case law on point, although for consumers a court, or indeed the FOS, should look at UTCCR (the relevant parts being Reg 5(1) and paragraph 1(d) of Schedule 2) which specifically deals with this situation. The FOS says it would ask the firm to explain how its approach complied with both UTCCR and the FSA publication "Challenging unfair terms in consumer contracts."[7] This says that terms which charge policyholders a disproportionately large sum if they do not fulfil their obligations under a contract or if they cancel it, are likely to be unfair. Where a policy provides that insureds will receive less premium refund if they cancel the policy than if the insurer cancels, the FOS[8] shares the FSA's view that this is likely to be unenforceable in law, as well as unfair and unreasonable.

11.6 It seems, however, due to the rarity of its mention in *Ombudsman News*, that in practice the FOS may not necessarily consider UTCCR without prompting. And it may have the concept of an unfair term wrong if it considers, as it did in Case Study 71/5,[9] that for it to be unfair, it also has to be relied upon by the insured. In that case the complaint about the insured only receiving back a small proportion of premium when he cancelled the 30-month policy after six months was not upheld, because the FOS decided that he would have taken out the insurance even if the terms had been highlighted. The point that this is not part of determining whether a term is unfair under UTCCR is discussed above (see "Policy construction—onerous and unfair terms" at paragraphs 5.63 and 5.68, above). Hopefully, this case study is nothing more than a FOS inconsistency.

11.7 The FOS recognises that a premium refund calculation will be affected by the particular circumstances of the policy. Whatever the calculation, the firm needs to have fair reasons for its approach which it can explain clearly to the insured. The insurer did not have fair reasons in Case Study 54/4[10] so as to justify how its costs could be so large that the policy provided that there would be no refund at all if an insured cancelled a policy more than four months after inception. The complaint was upheld.

6. *Ombudsman News* July 2006.
7. Available on the FSA website www.fsa.gov.uk.
8. *Ombudsman News* July 2006.
9. *Ombudsman News* Aug 2008.
10. *Ombudsman News* July 2006

CHAPTER 12

FRAUD/PROOF OF LOSS

WHAT CONSTITUTES A FRAUD

12.1 The Fraud Act 2006[1] defines fraud in the criminal law, although it does not seem to apply to the civil law. It is not mentioned in any relevant civil case, nor by the FOS, and as it post-dates both the most significant case law and all the FOS examples relating to fraud, it will not be mentioned further for the purpose of this discussion. The test of fraud in a general civil context was laid down by the House of Lords in *Twinsectra* v *Yardley*,[2] namely whether the conduct was dishonest by the ordinary standards of reasonable and honest people and the perpetrator himself realised that by those standards, his conduct was dishonest.

12.2 There has been a wealth of modern cases dealing with what constitutes fraud in the insurance context and what are its consequences on the claim and the policy. The four most significant, with a brief synopsis of each, are as follows:

Manifest Shipping Co Ltd v *Uni-Polaris Shipping Co Ltd (The Star Sea)* [2001] UKHL 1, decided on 18/01/2001

12.3 In this case, a fire on a ship resulted in a constructive total loss. In relation to a point unconnected to the fraud allegation, the vessel was found to have been unseaworthy, but the owners were not held to have had either actual or blind eye knowledge of this. The policy was a property insurance for hull and machinery, and the allegation relevant to this chapter, was culpable, but not fraudulent, non-disclosure at the claims stage and during the litigation. Reports had been made during the period of the policy which pointed to the vessel's deficiencies, although insurers had not been told of these when the claim was made. Also, during settlement negotiations, the owner's brokers had made statements which were allegedly misleading about the lessons learnt from recent fires on other vessels in the fleet. On the evidence, there was no actual fraud in the making of the claim. The House of Lords held that culpable non-disclosure during the currency of a policy was insufficient at the claims stage to attract the drastic consequence of avoidance of the whole policy under section 17 MIA 1906, which remedy would exist if there had been a material non-disclosure from inception or renewal. At the claims stage there was only a continuing duty of honesty. The continuing duty of good faith ceased to operate once litigation began, because the rules of court procedure took over. The shipowner could therefore recover under the policy.

---

1. Into effect on 15 January 2007.
2. [2002] UKHL 12.

K/S Merc-Scandia XXXXII v *(1) Underwriters of Lloyd's Policy and Ors (The Mercandian Continent)* [2001] EWCA Civ 1275, decided on 31/7/2001

12.4 This case was different to *The Star Sea*, because it related to liability insurance, rather than property insurance, and to fraudulent rather than culpable behaviour. Ship repairers in Trinidad (or rather their insurers) were liable to the claimant ship owners. It was a genuine claim, but the ship owners forged a letter to assist in the question of jurisdiction in the mistaken belief that this would be advantageous for both the insured and the insurer. The fraud was not material, in that it did not affect the ultimate liability of the insurer, and it was not so grave as to enable the insurers to terminate for breach of contract. As a result, the Court of Appeal found that it would have been disproportionate for insurers to have been entitled to avoid the policy under section 17 MIA.

Agapitos v *Agnew* [2002] EWCA Civ 247, decided on 06/03/2002

12.5 This was an appeal from an interlocutory decision. A ferry was lost when laid up for repairs for six months. In breach of warranty, substantive hot works had been carried out. After pleadings had been served, the claimant had made lying representations as to the date when the hot works commenced. Mance LJ held that this was a fraudulent means or device to promote a claim which might otherwise have been a good claim. As such, it was to be treated as a fraudulent claim might be, and so might result in forfeiture of that claim. Any lie that was intended to improve the insured's prospects of obtaining settlement or winning the case was relevant if it would, if believed, objectively yield a not insignificant improvement in the insured's prospects of obtaining a settlement or a better settlement, or of winning at trial. The making of a fraudulent claim fell outside of section 17 MIA, so no question of avoidance *ab initio*, such as that which might apply for pre-inception/renewal non-disclosure, would arise.

Axa General Insurance Ltd v *Gottlieb* [2005] EWCA Civ 112, decided on 11/02/2005

12.6 Various claims were made under a household insurance policy, some of which were fraudulently exaggerated. The questions were which claims should be paid, how forfeiture of the policy worked, and which interim or final payments could be reclaimed by insurers.

WHAT CONSTITUTES A FRAUDULENT CLAIM

12.7 Mance LJ in *Agapitos*[3] said that a fraudulent claim would exist when there had been:

(1) no actual loss;
(2) a substantial exaggeration of loss;
(3) fraudulent means or devices used to gain an advantage;
(4) a subsequent discovery that no loss, or lesser loss, had been suffered; or
(5) suppression of a defence.

The FOS broadly agrees with the first three situations, but has not reported in relation to the last two.

3. *Supra.*

LOSS AND PROOF

Proof of fraud

12.8 A claim for a loss which did not occur or which is self inflicted, is fraudulent. It is for the assured to prove ownership and loss. Insurers must prove fraud to the criminal standard of beyond reasonable doubt. Insurers must provide concrete evidence of inconsistent statements or acts of deception and show the appropriate dishonest intent to induce the insurer to pay more than the policyholder's entitlement. In *US Trading Ltd* v *Axa Insurance Co Ltd*,[4] insurers could not do this, and HHJ Simon Brown QC found that the supposed fraud was an honest mistake by the owners as to what was included in a quotation. Following *Yechiel* v *Kerry London Ltd*,[5] it can be an accumulation of evidential points which show that an assured's story ought not to be believed, even if none of the matters would be individually conclusive.[6]

12.9 The same burdens are applied by the FOS. It will expect careful investigations to have been carried out before the complaint reaches it, as by then it is unlikely that new evidence will be uncovered. It is presumed that insurers will not be penalised if they have good reason for not having all the evidence before the complaint reaches the FOS. Case Study 85/4[7] is an example where the FOS found that the insurer had carried out a careful and thorough investigation and produced convincing evidence to support its avoidance of the claim on the basis of fraud. The forensic evidence, the financial difficulties of the assured and other evidence which called into question the assured's credibility and integrity, pointed to the conclusion that the assured had started the fire in his hay barn which had destroyed most of the crop and justified the insurer's decision.

12.10 The FOS expects insurers to inform an assured if fraud is suspected, so that the assured can respond, and it is unlikely to support an insurer if, instead, it uses a separate and spurious reason to justify rejecting a claim. Although this sounds fair in view of the seriousness of the allegation and the possible police involvement, it may be impractical due to the difficulty in accumulating evidence. Notification to the assured too early may result in the evidence being destroyed or witnesses intimidated into refusing to give statements. It may be more practical for insurers to rely on another legitimate reason not to pay the claim, if any, even if it is not a strong reason, as it may be easier to prove, with a lesser burden. The law by comparison does not penalise insurers for bringing a fraud allegation late—unless perhaps it is a new allegation brought at a very late stage in proceedings, such as during the trial.

12.11 The case of *James* v *CGU Insurance plc*[8] shows how hard it can be for insurers to prove fraud, particularly fraudulent intent. There, insurers could not prove arson to business premises and Moore-Bick J found the evidence pointing towards an accidental fire, probably caused by the assured throwing a lighted cigar butt into the wastepaper basket. How could insurers possibly prove that the assured did this on purpose?

12.12 The fact that a policyholder has lied in another context (perhaps regarding a different claim under another policy), is not sufficient proof of fraud in the current claim

---

4. Unreported, 17 March 2008.
5. [2010] EWHC 215 (Comm) in the context of whether the insured had passed information to the broker as he said he had.
6. This contrasts to when dealing with material non-disclosure, each individual non-disclosure must be material, and the cumulative effect is not considered—see below under "Non-disclosure—materiality and inducement" at paras. 13.14 *et seq.*
7. *Ombudsman News* Apr/May 2010.
8. [2002] Lloyd's Rep IR 206.

(either before the court or the FOS), although it may raise doubts about the accuracy of the policyholder's version of events in the current claim.

12.13 There is no facility for the FOS to award insurers their costs of proving a fraud, although at law, if proceedings are issued and fraud is proven, such costs are payable by the insured on an indemnity, rather than standard basis.[9] It is a peculiar feature of the FOS system that it cannot make any financial award against a policyholder, even only in respect of the case fee, even in extreme cases where the policyholder has acted dishonestly or fraudulently, and so has wasted the time and resources of the FOS and insurers.[10]

Requiring proof of ownership and loss

12.14 Sometimes neither the insurer nor the FOS use the word fraud, as they will rightly refrain from such a serious allegation without sufficient evidence. However, a fraudulent claim will often flounder at the proof of ownership/loss stage and it is a wise insurer or practitioner who deals with a suspected fraud by first requiring the insured to prove ownership and loss. The FOS, without expressly saying so, seems to be in tune with this line of thinking. It supported insurers in Case Study 7/14,[11] where they refused to pay the claim, but promised to reconsider it if the complainant could provide proof that she had reported the loss to the police. This was reasonable in view of the alleged circumstances: that she had left her washbag containing jewellery in an aeroplane toilet and there was no police record even though she said she had reported the loss (although she had made a contradictory statement to the airline crew about this). A court would have responded similarly. Where in Case Study 75/8[12] the FOS supported insurer's request for proof of ownership of an allegedly lost designer watch, suggesting various ways of doing this, the complainant withdrew his complaint.

12.15 However, insurers should not be too difficult about requiring proof of loss. In Case Study 13/10,[13] a bag with a Game Boy and games inside had been accidentally left in a taxi on the way to the airport to catch a flight home. The FOS felt that the insured had done all he could reasonably be expected to do to get it back, so insurers were wrong to reject the claim for lack of a police report. A court would have agreed. And in Case Study 21/3,[14] the complainant was awarded £500 for maladministration for the insurer's late notification of non-renewal and poor claims handling in relation to the proof of loss. The insurer took nearly a year to investigate a burglary claim and then rejected it because the list of items stolen which was given to the police on reporting the burglary did not quite match the list given to the insurer a little later. The FOS felt that the insured had given a credible explanation for the discrepancy and had receipts for nearly every item claimed, so their burglary claim should be settled. Although a fair decision, a court would not have awarded damages for maladministration.

12.16 If a policyholder fails to resolve discrepancies or to cooperate with insurer's enquiries, both a court and the FOS will consider that insurers may be justified in refusing to meet the claim e.g. Case Study 13/17.[15]

---

9. *National Company for Co-operative Reinsurance v St Paul Reinsurance Co Ltd* 1998 (unreported).
10. See above "Funding: levies and case fees" at paras. 2.21 *et seq.*
11. *Ombudsman News* July 2001.
12. *Ombudsman News* Jan/Feb 2009.
13. *Ombudsman News* Jan 2002.
14. *Ombudsman News* Oct 2002.
15. *Ombudsman News* Jan 2002.

Unsuitable forum

12.17 The FOS can decline jurisdiction to deal with claims which are more appropriately dealt with by a court which, unlike the FOS, can compel witnesses to attend and can examine and cross-examine witnesses. The main examples in *Ombudsman News* of the FOS declining jurisdiction on this basis are in the context of suspected fraud claims. Examples are Case Study 7/13[16] where the complainant said that the receipt for a pendant had been altered not by her, but by her friend, and Case Study 48/7[17] where following a shop fire, there were allegations of fraud and conflicting evidence about the complainant's finances. A truly fraudulent claim would probably be abandoned at this point.

EXAGGERATED LOSS

Bargaining, innocent overvaluation and use of insurance monies, materiality and inducement

12.18 A substantially exaggerated claim will constitute fraud unless on the facts the court decides that it is merely part of a bargaining process, that there has been an innocent overvaluation, or if the insured is merely not using the policy monies to reinstate the damaged property. The FOS agrees and adds as examples that it would not be fraudulent to recall a purchase price inaccurately, give an exaggerated replacement cost mistakenly, or give an exaggerated view of a car's worth when the insurer would assess the market value independently. The FOS says that the last point goes to inducement, although it is not clear that the law requires inducement for fraud. The FOS classes this last point as an "immaterial fraud" (see below at paragraphs 12.29 *et seq*).

12.19 The application of the language of materiality and inducement to fraud is a result of early confusion in the law between fraudulent claims and the continuing duty of good faith (i.e. the continuing duty of disclosure of material issues). Since it has now been established that there is no continuing duty of good faith, the language about inducement for fraud should be obsolete, although the concept of materiality will still be important in that the fraud must be sufficiently serious and substantial to taint the entire claim. Inducement in fraud may have been brought back as a result of *Danepoint Ltd* v *Underwriting Insurance Ltd*.[18] There HHJ Coulson QC found that the lie (relating to the extent of necessary rebuilding work after a fire) was so blatant (because it would have been obvious to the loss adjuster that the amounts claimed did not match expenditure), that it was utterly disregarded by the insurers, who were therefore not induced by the fraud.[19] However, because the fraud on the loss of rent claim would not have been obvious to the loss adjuster, that part of the claim was fraudulent, and so tainted the rebuilding part. However, *Danepoint* does not stand with earlier authorities,[20]

---

16. *Ombudsman News* July 2001.
17. *Ombudsman News* Aug 2005.
18. [2005] EWHC 2318 (TCC).
19. See also *dicta* in the Court of Appeal of *Orakpo v Barclays Insurance Services Ltd* [1995] LRLR 443, that it is not fraudulent for a claim to be exaggerated if the exaggeration is just a starting point for negotiation, and the loss adjuster is in as good a position as the assured to form a view of the validity of the claim value.
20. Such as *Agapitos* which says that if there is a causal link between the fraud and the claim, whether or not the insurer was induced is irrelevant.

and has been subsequently undermined by the Privy Council in *Stemson* v *AMP General Insurance (NZ) Ltd.*[21]

12.20 The FOS comment on inducement occurred before *Danepoint*, so it is either ahead of its time, or, if *Danepoint* is wrong, operating a policy different to the law. Either way, it is not clear that the FOS has established its approach through a deep consideration of the case law, but rather through deciding somewhat arbitrarily that inducement is a fair requirement.

Partly genuine and partly fraudulent claims

12.21 The fraudulent part of a claim is not severable from a non-fraudulent part, so if the fraud is substantial, the entire claim will be tainted.[22] According to the Court of Appeal which was considering a burglary claim in *Galloway* v *Guardian Royal Exchange (UK) Ltd*[23] to determine whether a fraud is substantial, looking at the proportion it bears to the rest of the claim is not sufficient, as a small proportion of a large claim can still be large in absolute terms. The court should "consider the fraudulent claim as if it were the only claim and then to consider whether, taken in isolation, the making of that claim by the insured is sufficiently serious to justify stigmatising it as fraud". So a claim is fraudulent if the fraud is substantial either in proportion to the total claim or in absolute terms.[24] The following table of cases gives an indication of what the courts have decided constitutes a substantial fraud.

Name of Case[25]	Total claim (in rounded figures)	Of which, how much was fraudulent (in rounded figures)	Verdict
Nsubuga	£150,000 fire claim	£10,000 (goods which did not exist), £6,000 (altering an invoice), and £114,000 (failing to disclose in the business interruption part of the claim that the business was in difficulty and that distress for rates had been levied.)	Entire claim tainted. Thomas J commented that any one of the four instances of fraud would have been enough on its own to defeat the whole claim both under the policy terms or at common law.
Galloway	£16,000 burglary claim	£2,000 (computer which had not been stolen)	Entire claim tainted.

---

21. [2006] UKPC 30. There it was held on the facts that an assured had set fire to his own property in order to submit a fraudulent insurance claim, and that, independent of this finding, insurers had been entitled to reject the claim on the basis that the assured had also lied to them about his position and his state of mind in relation to any attempt to sell the property prior to the fire, without there being any requirement of inducement.

22. See for example *Nsubuga* v *Commercial Union Assurance Co plc* [1998] 2 Lloyd's Rep 682; *Galloway* v *Guardian Royal Exchange (UK) Ltd* [1999] Lloyd's Rep IR 209; *Baghbadrani* v *Commercial Union Assurance Co plc* [2000] Lloyd's Rep IR 94; *Direct Line Insurance* v *Khan* (first instance, not CA) [2001] EWCA Civ 1794; *Gottlieb* (*supra*).

23. *Supra*, rejecting support for apportionment by Staughton LJ in *Orakpo* (*supra*).

24. *Baghbadrani* (*supra*).

Name of Case[25]	Total claim (in rounded figures)	Of which, how much was fraudulent (in rounded figures)	Verdict
Baghbadrani	Fire claim. The figures are unavailable in the judgment, but represented damage to an Islamic school, and business interruption from 60 alleged new students having to be turned away as a result of the fire.	The whole business interruption claim. Also a sum in excess of £3,000, representing VAT on building costs which was fraudulently claimed to have been due.	Entire claim tainted by the false claim for business interruption. *Obiter*, the £3,000 VAT sum would have been enough on its own to taint the whole claim, for it qualified as a substantial fraud in absolute terms, as opposed to in proportion to the rest of the claim.
Khan	£69,500 fire claim	£8,250 in respect of the fraudulent alternative accommodation claim, supported by a fraudulently manufactured rental agreement and rent receipt.	Entire claim tainted.
Gottlieb	Claim: £40,000 dry rot plus £20,000 alternative accommodation.	The whole £20,000 claim for alternative accommodation.	Entire claim tainted.
Gottlieb	Claim 2: £14,250 escape of water	£1,200 false electrician's invoice	Entire claim tainted.
Tonkin	c £700,000	£2,000 or 0.3% of the reinstatement claim	Not enough to taint the claim (obiter, as the £2,000 in question was found not to have been fraudulent).

12.22 There is only one reported FOS case study on what constitutes "substantial" for fraud. The FOS found that the complainant in Case Study 10/6[26] was fraudulent when she was recorded in a telephone conversation with the insurer falsely claiming that all three pieces of her suite had been stained when the insurer had refused to clean any but the stained

25. Case references appear in the text or footnotes above.
26. *Ombudsman News* Oct 2001.

one. She was trying to gain an advantage by deception. In view of the case law above, it is likely that a court would agree. The fraud related to two thirds of the total claim, which is a high proportion, even if the actual amount involved was small.

12.23 This FOS case study was reported in October 2001, before *Agapitos* and *Gottlieb* had been decided, but there was still relevant case law on what constituted substantial fraud, most notably the Court of Appeal ruling in *Galloway*. Yet there is no reference to it, or to its test, either in the report of the case study or in any commentary to be found in any *Ombudsman News*. It seems that the FOS decision has been arrived at in an arbitrary, instinctive fashion, without consideration of the applicable law, which exposes it to risk of judicial review. It is of course possible that behind the scenes the FOS officers and internal information system has kept up with the case law, both now and when the case study was decided at the beginning of the FOS existence, but there is no evidence of this from *Ombudsman News*, which in a later edition, even with an abundance of relevant cases, only mentions *Merc-Skandia*.

USE OF FRAUDULENT MEANS OR DEVICES AND FOS "IMMATERIAL FRAUD"

12.24 Mance LJ in *Agapitos* said that insurers are entitled to treat even a genuine claim for an insured peril as fraudulent if it has been furthered by the use of fraudulent means or devices. This would include using forged documents or false statements in support of a genuine claim, although not every such document or statement will taint the entire claim. Mance LJ said that for there to be fraud, a false statement must be:

(1) directly related to the claim;
(2) intended to improve the assured's prospects of obtaining a settlement or winning the case; and
(3) if believed, objectively—prior to any final determination at trial—capable of yielding a not insignificant improvement in the assured's prospects of obtaining a settlement or better settlement.

12.25 This seems to mean that if there is a causal link between the fraud and the claim, whether or not the insurer was induced is irrelevant. It is to be noted that, following *Direct Line* v *Fox*,[27] if a fraudulent means—in this case a false invoice—is used to try to satisfy a condition in a settlement agreement already concluded with insurers, only that settlement agreement is affected from that moment on, but the underlying insurance contract is unaffected and the underlying insurance claim is not fraudulent.

12.26 Applying these principles, a property insurer could refuse to pay where the assured falsely stated that his burglar alarm was set at the time of the loss.[28] And insurers could deny a claim under a valued policy for a vessel lost through an insured peril, where forged documents gave its value as US$1.8 million, the sum for which it had been insured, rather than the actual value, which was US$150,000 for scrap.[29]

12.27 Even if the intention is not to make a profit, but only to ensure that the assured receives the full indemnity to which he believes he is entitled, it is still a use of fraudulent means or devices which will defeat the claim following the House of Lords in *Lek*

27. [2009] EWHC 386 (QB).
28. *Shoot* v *Hill* (1936) 55 Ll L Rep 29.
29. *Eagle Star Insurance Co Ltd* v *Games Video Co (GVC) SA (The Game Boy)* [2004] EWHC 15 (Comm).

v *Mathews*.[30] In the more modern day it will still be a fraud if there is also an *Agapitos* causal link between the use of fraudulent means and devices and the claim. In *Lek*, police recovered most of a stolen stamp collection under a valued policy (£44,000). In order to make up to £44,000 the difference between the value of the stamps that remained and those that were taken, the assured fraudulently claimed that he had owned various stamps that he had not. He wanted to ensure that he recovered the full amount that he thought was due to him.

12.28 Whatever the scope of the common law, the policy may expressly impose a condition upon the assured requiring him to submit full and accurate details of his loss to insurers. This will mean that any material fraud will defeat the claim even where it did not cause the insurer any loss, and even a minor fraud will defeat the claim if insurers have been prejudiced, for instance in relation to subrogation rights. In *Cox* v *Orion Insurance Co Ltd*,[31] a motor policy obliged the assured to submit particulars of an accident to the insurers. The assured damaged his car while intoxicated, but lied to insurers and said that it had been stolen and damaged by the thief. He was in breach of the notification clause so the Court of Appeal would not allow recovery, even though the policy would have responded if he had been truthful.

12.29 The FOS does not quite follow the law where it comes to the use of fraudulent means or devices in support of a genuine claim, as it requires an insured to have an intention of trying to obtain more than that to which he is entitled, contrary to *Lek*. The FOS is trying to prevent the harshness of a genuine claim not being paid or a policy forfeited where a policyholder is put under so much unreasonable pressure to provide receipts, that he forges an invoice to substantiate the claim. The FOS calls this an "immaterial fraud". If the insurer's ultimate liability to pay the claim is unaffected by the fraud, the FOS considers that it should, in effect, be disregarded. However, the FOS is ignoring the general policy point that the assured should be discouraged in the strongest way from producing a fraudulent document even in support of a genuine claim.

12.30 The FOS acknowledges that insurers may not wish to continue to insure someone who has committed an "immaterial fraud" and suggests that insurers can thereafter cancel the policy in accordance with the policy terms or not invite renewal. The FOS does not mention though, that with cancellation of a policy, rather than avoidance for fraud, there might have to be some return of premium.

12.31 Worse than the FOS creating a new category of "immaterial fraud", is its apparent reliance[32] on the law to do so, namely the Court of Appeal decision in *Merc-Scandia*, which it says has bolstered its view. The FOS says that Longmore LJ held that an insurer should only be able to avoid a policy for fraud if the fraud would have an effect on the insurer's ultimate liability and where the fraud, or its consequences, were sufficiently serious to entitle the insurer to repudiate the policy for fundamental breach of contract. However, the FOS has ignored the context of Longmore LJ's comments.

12.32 Firstly, *Merc-Scandia* did not involve a fraudulent claim, but the assured's breach of his cooperation obligations when it manufactured a letter to defeat a jurisdiction agreement in relation to the liability claim that insurers were defending on its behalf. Secondly, Longmore LJ's discussion of underwriters' lack of prejudice related to his finding that the cooperation obligation was a mere condition. In line with *Alfred McAlpine* v *BAI (Run-off) Ltd*,[33] which no longer applies, breach of that sort of condition was only repudiatory of the

---

30. (1927) 9 Ll L Rep 141.
31. [1982] RTR 1.
32. *Ombudsman News* Nov 2004.
33. [2000] 1 All ER (Comm) 545.

claim (as opposed to the policy) if it had caused insurers to suffer serious prejudice, which in *Merc-Scandia* it had not, as underwriters remained liable to indemnify the third party. This is not at all the same thing as saying, as the FOS does, that producing a fraudulent document in support of a claim has to have prejudiced insurers for it to have any consequences on the cover.

12.33 It is astonishing that the FOS did not refer to *Agapitos*, which the Court of Appeal decided after *Merc-Scandia* and more than two years before the relevant edition of *Ombudsman News*, and which was a case on point about a fraudulent claim. *Agapitos* flies in the face of the FOS approach, as it is authority for insurers' inducement to be irrelevant if there is a causal connection between the fraud and the claim.

12.34 The FOS applied its reasoning in Case Study 42/3.[34] The loss adjuster had over-zealously insisted on receipts for every item stolen from a van, so the assured's friend faked a receipt for him. As this was a genuine loss, the FOS asked the insurer to pay the claim. A court would not have decided the case in this way unless the amount of the invoice was an insubstantial part of the whole claim. As mentioned above, another example is where the policyholder is asked to substantiate the purchase price of a written-off vehicle, and produces a fraudulent document, when insurers do not use this information anyway when calculating the market value that they pay, e.g. in Case Study 10/10.[35]

CONSEQUENCES OF FRAUD UNDER THE LAW

12.35 The consequences of fraud are mainly the non-payment of the claim in question and not being liable for any future claims under the policy.

Express wordings

12.36 Policy wordings usually provide for the assured to forfeit all benefit under the policy in the event of a fraudulent claim or the use of fraudulent means or devices. Lord Hobhouse in *The Star Sea* and Mance LJ in *Agapitos* said that this means the loss of the right to claim for this and any future loss and does not imply avoidance of the policy *ab initio* (i.e. as if the policy had never existed). Sometimes the wording may add that the policy is to be treated as void, but it follows that this only means that the policy is brought to an end as from the date of the fraudulent claim, rather than from inception. In the absence of any express term setting out the consequences of a fraudulent claim, the common law takes effect.

Common law: basis of the insurer not paying a fraudulent claim

12.37 The obligation not to commit fraud is separate to the continuing duty of utmost good faith (i.e. disclosure).[36] So the remedy available in law for breach of the latter, namely avoidance *ab initio* which takes with it all previous valid claims and settlements, is not available in cases of fraud. The Court of Appeal in *Merc-Scandia* concluded that the continuing duty of good faith could only operate in the most exceptional cases, where the assured was under a contractual obligation to provide information to the insurers and had in bad faith failed to do so in a manner which amounted to a repudiation of the policy.

---

34. *Ombudsman News* Dec 2004/Jan 2005.
35. *Ombudsman News* Oct 2001.
36. *The Star Sea* overturning *The Litsion Pride* [1985] 1 Lloyd's Rep 437.

12.38 The true basis for the assured's inability to recover under the policy once he has committed a fraud is the common law principle that no man may profit from his own wrong.[37] In the words of Lord Hobhouse in *The Star Sea*:

"The fraudulent insured must not be allowed to think: if the fraud is successful, then I will gain; if it is unsuccessful, I will lose nothing."

Non-payment of any part of the fraudulent claim

12.39 The primary remedy for insurers is refusal to pay any part of a fraudulent claim, and reclaim of interim payments. In *Agapitos*, Mance LJ identified five types of fraud where this would be the remedy, where the assured had:

(1) suffered no loss;
(2) suffered a loss less than that claimed (and the additional amount claimed was significant);
(3) believed at the time of the claim that he had suffered a loss, but had failed to correct the position when he subsequently discovered that he had suffered no loss or a loss smaller than that claimed, (and the additional amount claimed was significant);
(4) suffered a genuine loss, but had suppressed a defence known to him that might be available to insurers;
(5) furthered a genuine claim by the use of fraudulent means or devices.

Repudiation of the policy so that future claims are not payable

12.40 Additionally, and certainly in relation to situations (1) to (3) above, insurers can repudiate the policy, i.e. terminate the policy so that future claims are not payable. In situation (5), Mance LJ felt that there was less of a case to be made for treating the policy as repudiated, so the only remedy was to refuse to pay the claim itself. Mance LJ did not elaborate in *Agapitos* or in *Gottlieb* whether situation (4) would allow an insurer to repudiate the contract. Perhaps the suppressed defence would be enough when used for insurers to achieve this or equivalent objective, and if it were not, such as if the defence were breach of a mere policy condition, maybe it would not somehow be a serious enough fraud.

Separate, genuine claims prior to the fraud are untouchable

12.41 A fraud cannot have a retrospective effect on prior, separate claims settled under the same policy before any fraud occurs. The right of insurers not to pay the claim backdates only to the date of the loss in question. Any right to treat the contract as repudiated in respect of future claims, arises only on the date of the fraud, thereby protecting earlier, genuine, accrued losses even if claims have not at that point been made in respect of them. Following *Gottlieb*, once the policy has reached the end of its natural life, it will be too late for the insurers to treat it as repudiated. In *Gottlieb*, although insurers could recover their interim payments on the fraudulent claims, they could not recover payments made in respect of other separate, genuine claims which were made after the fraudulent claims but before the fraud itself.

12.42 Before *Gottlieb* was decided, the FOS recognised that previous genuine claims were untouched (unless the fraud was at the proposal stage), and that insurers could refuse to pay

---

37. *The Star Sea* (HL), *Merc-Skandia* (CA); *Agapitos v Agnew* (CA).

all parts of a fraudulent claim, but could refuse future cover only from the date of the fraud. It has not published any case studies on point. The FOS was perhaps ahead of its time in deciding its approach, but now at least, perhaps coincidentally, the law agrees.

Premium is unaffected

12.43 With both non-payment of the claim and repudiation of the contract, insurers are entitled to retain the premium, and there has been no recent case in which the contrary has been held.

FOS APPROACH TO THE CONSEQUENCES OF FRAUD

12.44 Other than where there is an "immaterial fraud" on a genuine claim, the FOS approach to the consequences of fraud seem to parallel that of the law, even though it does not discuss the technical ambit of concepts such as repudiation, or refer, in public reports at least, to the policy wording in any detail or at all. Generally, it will not make an insurer pay a fraudulent claim and it is unlikely to expect an insurer to pay subsequent genuine claims, as it recognises that a fraudulent claim can rightly taint the future of the policy and insurers' wish to continue to insure that party. All the FOS material indicates that if there is proof of fraud or mere lies by the policyholder, the FOS will lose sympathy for the assured.

   12.45 Where the FOS treats the consequences of fraud differently is where a fraudulent document has made no difference to the amount properly recoverable under a genuine claim, so the insurer has not been induced by the fraud. It has therefore created a new category of "immaterial fraud". In these circumstances, the FOS considers that the harshness of the consequences in law of fraud cannot be justified, whilst in every other circumstance of fraud it can be. The FOS disagrees with the courts that as a matter of policy, all fraud is to be discouraged, and that it is unacceptable to make fraud acceptable even in limited cases.

COMMENTARY

12.46 The FOS approach to fraud now generally matches that of a court, although it has not developed in the same time-line as the law and little of the abundantly useful and recent case law is mentioned in public reports. It may therefore not have a good understanding of the law or have kept up with developments. The FOS recognises the severity of fraud and the need to make it unacceptable so as to deter future fraudsters, except in relation to its own concept of "immaterial fraud". This may be an unnecessary addition to the FOS repertoire and is contrary to recent carefully developed, considered and argued case law about the public policy issue of dealing harshly with fraud. The law itself has its own tools to soften the effects of fraud where fraud is not really intended, such as interpreting the statement as bargaining or an innocent overvaluation, but it is not clear that the FOS should soften the position any further with its use of the immaterial fraud category.

CHAPTER 13

NON-DISCLOSURE AND MISREPRESENTATION

A COMPARATIVE OVERVIEW OF THE LEGAL, FOS AND LAW COMMISSIONS' POSITIONS

The duty of disclosure

(a) The law

13.1 In insurance law, there is a duty of utmost good faith at the pre-contractual stage. This duty is derived from the Marine Insurance Act 1906,[1] and now applies to both marine and non-marine insurance. The duty means that before the assured takes out or renews a policy of insurance, he must voluntarily disclose all facts which an insurer might consider to be material, even if not asked. If he fails to do so, the policy will be void *ab initio*,[2] which means that it will be reversed as if there had been no contract in the first place. This would mean that the insurer could refuse to pay all claims under the policy, could recover any payments already made, and, unless there had been fraud,[3] would return the premium. These consequences of non-disclosure would be so under the law, even if the assured is unaware of his duty or which facts are material. The reason for the position at law is that the insured, rather than the insurer, is the one who knows the relevant information which the insurer has to trust the insured to share.

(b) The FOS

13.2 The FOS views the law as harsh in this respect, as it considers that insurers should make it clear in their proposal questions what information they consider to be important for their underwriting decisions. It imposes no duty of disclosure for all those under its jurisdiction, only a duty to answer clear questions. The current Law Commissions[4] propose that the law in this respect is changed for consumer insurance contracts to reflect the FOS approach.

---

1. S. 17 MIA 1906 "A contract of marine insurance is a contract based upon the utmost good faith, and, if the utmost good faith be not observed by either party, the contract may be avoided by the other party."
2. S. 18(1) MIA 1906 " . . . the assured must disclose to the insurer, before the contract is concluded, every material circumstance which is known to the assured, and the assured is deemed to know every circumstance which, in the ordinary course of business, ought to be known by him. If the assured fails to make such disclosure, the insurer may avoid the contract".
3. S. 84(3)(a) MIA 1906 "the premium is returnable, provided that there has been no fraud or illegality on the part of the assured".
4. *Cf* Issues Paper 1, 09/06, Consultation Paper 17/07/07 and Final report and draft bill 15/12/09.

(c) Law Commissions' proposals

13.3 The current Law Commissions have proposed a draft bill to amend the law of non-disclosure and misrepresentation in relation to consumers (only).[5] A copy of this draft bill can be found in the appendices to this book.[6] It is hoped that this bill might become law in the near future.[7] These proposals would bring the law in relation to consumers in line with current FOS practice. Clause 10 of the draft bill would nullify any attempt at contracting out of these rules so as to put the consumer in a worse position, or circumventing them by a choice of law clause where the law of England and Wales or the law of Scotland would otherwise have applied.

13.4 Possible amendments to the position in relation to non-disclosure and misrepresentation by businesses are being considered. For larger businesses, the Law Commissions have provisionally proposed[8] a default regime whereby a remedy would exist for a misrepresentation which induced the actual insurers in question, and which a reasonable person in the circumstances would not have made, but with rules about contracting out of the default regime. The reasonableness of a business insured will depend, for instance, on the type of market, whether the business received professional advice and the clarity of the questions asked. The Law Commissions are considering whether micro-businesses and/or small businesses should be treated like consumers or businesses for the purposes of pre-contractual information and unfair terms.[9]

13.5 The draft bill[10] defines a consumer insurance contract as "a contract of insurance entered into by an individual wholly or mainly for purposes unrelated to the individual's trade, business or profession". It also defines a consumer as "the individual who enters into a consumer insurance contract, or proposes to do so".

13.6 Although in substance the same, the proposed definition of a consumer is different to the definition of one under ICOBS: " . . . any natural person who is acting for purposes which are outside his trade or profession".[11]

13.7 The ICOBS definition reflects those used in EU consumer directives, and follows that used in the EU Directive on Distance Marketing of Consumer Financial Services.[12] The insurance must be taken out by an individual, not a company. The effective difference between the ICOBS/EU definitions and that of the Law Commissions, is that the Law Commissions include mixed use policies where the main use is a consumer one, for instance where a private vehicle insurance covers a limited amount of business use or a home contents insurance covers some business equipment. The Law Commissions have specified that they would consider that an individual who takes out income protection insurance for himself would be considered a consumer, but that letting a house commercially would be considered

---

5. Law Commissions' Final report and draft bill—Consumer Insurance Law: Pre-contract Disclosure and Misrepresentation published on 15 December 2009.
6. See Appendix H, below.
7. See above at paras. 1.32 *et seq.* Note that cl. 12(2) says that the Act would only come into force one year after it was passed, and cl. 12(3) says that it will not apply retrospectively to any contract or variation agreed before the Act comes into force.
8. Issues Paper 1 09/06 and Consultation Paper 17/07/07.
9. See Issues Paper 5, April 2009 and Summary of Responses to Issues Paper 5, November 2009.
10. Cl. 1.
11. ICOBS Rule 2.1.1(3).
12. Directive 2002/65/EU, art. 2(d).

a business even if it was not the landlord's primary business.[13] The Law Commissions would expect the courts to have regard to existing case law on the issue of whether someone was acting outside of his or her professional capacity, or as a consumer.[14]

13.8 By Clause 7 of the draft bill, the Law Commissions treat the beneficiary of a group scheme as a consumer for the purposes of pre-contract misrepresentation, where that beneficiary would have been a consumer had he taken out the insurance directly. The most common example is where an employer takes out a group health and life policy for the benefit of his employees. However, if the employer or other group policyholder is a business, its own non-disclosure will be treated under the business regime.[15]

13.9 Where a consumer insurance contract is taken out by a policyholder for life insurance on the life of another who is not a party to the contract, by clause 8 of the draft bill, information provided by that other is to be treated as if it were provided by the policyholder. So in effect, that non-party would become subject to the same duties as the policyholder to answer questions truthfully, and if there has been a non-disclosure or representation by that non-party, the question will be whether that non-party (rather than the policyholder) acted with reasonable care, carelessly, deliberately or recklessly.

(II) DUTY OF REASONABLE CARE NOT TO MAKE A MISREPRESENTATION

13.10 The draft bill would impose on the consumer before entering into or varying a consumer insurance contract, a duty "to take reasonable care not to make a misrepresentation to the insurer".[16] This duty would, for consumers, explicitly replace the section 17 MIA duty of pre-contract disclosure as described above.[17] It would mean in practice that consumers had to give full, honest and accurate representations at the pre-contract stage whether they were volunteering information or answering insurer's questions. This same duty would exist at renewal, as a renewal is regarded in law as a new contract.

13.11 The Law Commissions state[18] that they intend the concept of misrepresentation to be interpreted in accordance with the existing case law, which would mean that a true but incomplete statement would still be a misrepresentation.[19] The draft bill specifies in addition that a consumer's failure to comply with the insurer's request to confirm or amend particulars previously given is capable of being a misrepresentation for the purposes of the draft bill.[20] It envisages considering whether a reasonable consumer in the same position would have responded, based on factors such as whether the request was confused or unclear, or whether the insurer provided a copy of the information about which it is asking for confirmation.[21] The draft bill changes nothing in relation to post-contractual conduct, a subject saved for a later issues paper.[22] The Law Commissions comment that if insurers want the policyholder to inform the insurer about a change of circumstances during the period of the policy, they

---

13. Final report 15/12/09, para. 5.18.

14. Final report 15/12/09, paras. 5.14–5.16.

15. Final report 15/12/09, para. 7.20.

16. Cl. 2(2) of the draft bill.

17. Cll. 2(4) and (5) of the draft bill. Also, cl. 11 of the draft bill disapplies ss.18–20 MIA from consumer insurance contracts (see further below).

18. Final report 15/12/09, paras. 4.8 and 5.51.

19. E.g. *Winter* v *Irish Life Assurance plc* [1995] 2 Lloyd's Rep 274—where the proposer was held to have misrepresented her state of health through leaving one proposal question blank and not answering another fully.

20. Cl. 2(3) of the draft bill.

21. Final report 15/12/09, paras. 4.9 and 5.52–5.53.

22. Final report 15/12/09, para. 5.30.

need to make express provision for this, as they do under the current law, which will be subject to UTCCR 1999.[23]

13.12 It would be for the insurer to prove that there had been a misrepresentation, and then for the courts/FOS to decide how a reasonable person would have acted.[24] If there was a clear and specific question, the consumer would be presumed to know that the matter was relevant and the onus would be on the consumer to show that he/she did not act deliberately or recklessly in failing to give such information.[25]

(III) THE NATURE OF REASONABLE CARE

13.13 Clause 3(1) says: "Whether or not a consumer has taken reasonable care not to make a misrepresentation is to be determined in the light of all the relevant circumstances." Clause 3(2) goes on to give non-exhaustive examples of things which may need to be taken into account: "(a) the type of consumer insurance policy in question, and its target market, (b) any relevant explanatory material or publicity produced or authorised by the insurer, (c) how clear, and how specific, the insurer's questions were, (d) whether or not an agent was acting for the consumer". The standard is objective and is that of a reasonable consumer,[26] subject to whether the insurer "was or ought to have been aware of any particular characteristics or circumstances of the actual consumer".[27] The Law Commissions say that they intend this test to focus in a practical way on what the relevant insurance staff understood at the time, and not on information held by other departments unavailable to them at the time.[28] Clause 3(5) adds a proviso, that "a misrepresentation made dishonestly is always to be taken as showing lack of reasonable care".

Materiality and inducement

(a) The law

13.14 In law, a fact must be disclosed pre-inception if it is material. Under section 18(2) MIA,[29] it will be material if it would influence the judgement of a prudent insurer in fixing the premium or determining whether or not he will take the risk. The same test applies to the requirement of materiality for misrepresentation at section 20(2) MIA. The prudent underwriter test will be satisfied if the objective evidence of an independent insurer is that he would not have so granted the policy. In addition, the insurer has the burden of proving the actual inducement requirement imposed by the House of Lords in *Pan Atlantic Insurance Co Ltd v Pine Top Insurance Co Ltd*,[30] namely that the actual underwriter must show on the balance of probabilities, subjectively, that he would not have granted the policy at all or on the same terms if he had known the full facts.[31]

23. Final report 15/12/09, paras. 5.62–5.64.
24. Final report 15/12/09, para. 5.87.
25. Final report and draft bill 15/12/09, para. 5.35.
26. Cl. 3(3) of the draft bill. The FOS has commented in the Law Commissions' Summary of Responses —consumer issues 28/05/08, that this is harsher than the subjectively reasonable standard it applies.
27. Cl. 3(4) of the draft bill.
28. Final report and draft bill 15/12/09, para. 5.80.
29. "Every circumstance is material which would influence the judgment of a prudent insurer in fixing the premium, or determining whether he will take the risk."
30. [1995] 1 AC 501.
31. *Assicurazioni Generali v Arab Insurance Group* [2002] EWCA Civ 1642—though it may sometimes be possible to infer inducement from the facts in the absence of direct evidence.

13.15 As the case law develops, it provides further guidance as to what will be counted as objectively material,[32] although this does not feature in the FOS reports of case studies. The courts will not allow immaterial facts to be added together to produce a finding of collective materiality.[33] Each fact must be assessed individually for materiality. If a question is asked, it is presumed that the information requested is material. But a fact can still be material and there is no waiver of disclosure even if the proposal form does not ask the question.[34] However, it has been held recently[35] that if a question shows that the insurer had related issues in mind, but chose not to ask about them, the insurer will have waived the requirement of disclosure of that information, and the insured will not have made a non-disclosure if he answers the question accurately but without volunteering further information.

(b) The FOS

13.16 The FOS test does not mention materiality. Instead it considers firstly whether the question posed about the matter in dispute was clear (presumably implying that it was material if it was objectively clear), and secondly, whether the insurer was induced by the answer to enter into the contract at all or under terms and conditions that it otherwise would not have accepted.

(c) Law Commissions' proposals

13.17 The Law Commissions[36] criticise that, even with clear questions, in law the consumer has to guess what is material to the insurer. Instead, the Law Commissions favour the FOS approach of basing the disclosure obligation on one to answer questions honestly, rather than on the obligation to volunteer material information. The emphasis is on the insurer indicating by its questions, which could be general or specific, which information it considers material. Like the FOS, materiality is not mentioned. However, clause 4 of the draft bill requires actual inducement. The prudent underwriter test is not preserved and sections 18–20 MIA are disapplied in clauses 11(1) and (2) in relation to consumer insurance contracts. The misrepresentation will become a "qualifying misrepresentation" and so qualify the insurer for a remedy, if it has been made in breach of the duty of reasonable care set out in clause 2(2), and "the insurer shows that without the misrepresentation, that insurer would not have entered into the contract (or agreed to the variation) at all, or would have done so only on

---

32. E.g. the Court of Appeal in *North Star Shipping Ltd* v *Sphere Drake Insurance plc* [2006] EWCA Civ 378 commented, *obiter*, that overvaluation of the vessel was not material, and nor was non-payment of premium in an earlier policy. Waller LJ felt that the latter point went to the owners' credit risk, and not to the risk insured, and, if right, puts a gloss on the definition of materiality in s. 18(2), so that materiality should be confined to facts relating to the risk itself.

33. *North Star Shipping Ltd* v *Sphere Drake Insurance plc* [2006] EWCA Civ 378. Contrast this with the position in proving a fraud, where the evidence may be considered cumulatively. See above "Proof of fraud" at paras. 12.8 *et seq.*

34. *Noblebright Ltd* v *Sirius International Corporation*, 18 January 2007, unreported, Manchester Mercantile Court.

35. *R&R Developments Ltd* v *Axa Insurance UK plc* [2009] EWHC 2429 (Ch), adopting the *obiter* approach of the Court of Appeal in *Doheny* v *New India Assurance Co Ltd* [2004] EWCA Civ 1705. In *R&R* the proposal asked a question about the solvency of the company directors, but did not ask about the financial history of companies in which the directors had been involved. So there was no non-disclosure when it was not disclosed that one of the directors had been a director of another group of companies which had gone into liquidation some time before.

36. Issues Paper 1, 09/06 and Consultation Paper, 17/07/07.

different terms".[37] The insurer must show actual inducement on the balance of probabilities, although the case law is retained which will allow inducement to be inferred from the facts in the absence of direct evidence. The Law Commissions expect that insurers would usually provide underwriting guidelines or evidence from a particular underwriter to show what had been done in similar circumstances.[38]

13.18 The Law Commissions also expect the requirement of actual inducement to determine whether a beneficiary of a group scheme who had made a misrepresentation, should get his claim paid up to the limit of the so-called "free cover" which accompanies many large schemes. The free cover is the cover which is offered in any case, without requiring the beneficiary to give the insurer any disclosure. The ABI's 2009 Code of Practice[39] says that insurers should pay out the "free cover" in such circumstances. It is presumed that the FOS would enforce that aspect of the Code, and anyway, compliance with an ABI Code is meant to be compulsory for ABI members.[40]

Remedies

(a) The law

13.19 The remedy in law for misrepresentation or non-disclosure is avoidance *ab initio*.[41] There is no scope in law for any other discretionary remedy, even if the misrepresentation or non-disclosure is not that serious. Unless fraud is involved, the premium is usually returned. The only other option for the insurer would be to affirm the policy.

(b) The FOS

13.20 The remedy for insurers in law can be harsh for an insured if, for instance, the difference between a disclosed and a hidden fact would be a £20 increase in the premium, which was the position in Case Study 18/3.[42] So the FOS takes a more flexible approach, taking account of good industry practice, which it says[43] is reflected in the ABI Statements of Practice and the GISC Codes for Intermediaries (even though many of these no longer apply following the introduction of the ICOB on 14 January 2005) and ICOB/S.

13.21 In fact, the FOS goes even beyond the Codes/Statements in some circumstances, such as where they specifically permit insurers to avoid for all negligent misrepresentation, but the FOS allows avoidance only for serious negligence (which it calls recklessness), not for some minor negligence (which it calls inadvertence); the FOS approach is set out in detail below.

37. Cl. 4(1)(b) of the draft bill.
38. Final report 15/12/09, para. 6.9.
39. ABI Code "Managing Claims for Individual and Group Life, Critical Illness and Income Protection Insurance Products" (January 2009).
40. Final report paras. 7.24–7.27.
41. See definition above under "The duty of disclosure—The law" at para. 13.1.
42. *Ombudsman News* July 2002. The insured said that he had disclosed a speeding conviction, but it did not appear on the printed statement and he had not checked it properly before signing. The insurer would have charged and the insured would have paid an extra £20 premium if there had been full disclosure. The claim was to be paid subject to this extra premium. Later FOS case studies and commentary suggest that now it is more likely that the FOS would apply a proportionate remedy for this sort of inadvertent non-disclosure and require insurers to pay a proportion of the claim in the same ratio as the proportion that the premium actually paid bore to the premium which should have been paid had there been full disclosure. See further below for inadvertent non-disclosure and proportionate remedies.
43. *Ombudsman News* May/June 2005.

(c) Law Commissions' proposals

13.22 The Law Commissions' proposals mirror FOS practice. Clause 5(1) of the draft bill says that a qualifying misrepresentation can be either (a) deliberate or reckless, or (b) careless. It will be careless if it is not deliberate or reckless.[44] Under Schedule 1, an insurer may avoid for non-disclosure only of a deliberate or reckless misrepresentation, but the remedy for a careless misrepresentation will depend on what the insurer would have done had it received an accurate answer in the first place. Clause 5(2) defines deliberate or reckless as where the consumer knew that the misrepresentation was untrue or misleading, or did not care whether or not it was, and knew that it related to a matter which was relevant to the insurer, or did not care whether it was. This definition was intended to reflect the common law definition of recklessness in *Derry* v *Peek*[45] and society's disapproval of the morally reprehensible behaviour of lacking any interest in the truth of what one says.[46] So a consumer would be reckless if he must have known both that what he said was inaccurate and that the inaccuracy mattered, but careless if he should have known but did not.[47] It is for the insurer to show that a qualifying misrepresentation was deliberate or reckless.[48] But it is to be presumed, unless the contrary is shown, that the consumer had the knowledge of a reasonable consumer, and that the consumer knew that a matter about which the insurer asked a clear and specific question was relevant to the insurer.[49] Where these presumptions apply, the burden of proof is reversed.

THE FOS APPROACH IN DETAIL TO NON-DISCLOSURE/ MISREPRESENTATION

13.23 Taking account of the law and good industry practice, the FOS takes a three-stage approach, and has effectively removed the duty of disclosure from those whose complaints it considers.

(1) The clear question test

13.24 *When the customer sought insurance, did the insurer comply with good practice for instance in asking a clear question about the matter in dispute?*

The FOS will consider all the evidence of a sale, including proposal forms, tape recordings of telephone proposals or printouts of online applications, and/or a copy of the statement of facts that the insurer should probably have sent the customer after a telephone or internet sale. Without such evidence of the questions asked, the FOS may find a customer's credible account more likely than the insurer's version. Whilst the implication is that the FOS finds matters about which clear questions are asked to be material, it does not use this terminology. There are rare examples where the FOS will expect a disclosure without a clear question about the matter, but those will be the exception rather than the norm.[50]

---

44. Cl. 5(3) of the draft bill.
45. (1889) LR 14 App Cas 337 at page 350: "A man who makes a statement without care and regard for its truth or falsity commits a fraud". See also Law Commissions Final report 15/12/09, para. 6.31.
46. Final report 15/12/09, paras. 6.16 and 6.31.
47. Final report 15/12/09, para. 6.19.
48. Cl. 5(4) of the draft bill.
49. Cl. 5(5) of the draft bill.
50. See those examples below under "Renewals" at para. 13.94.

13.25 By contrast, the first question that a court would pose would be whether the fact was material and it would look to the evidence of a prudent underwriter in this respect, although it presumes materiality of the insurer's express questions put to the assured.[51]

(2) Actual inducement

13.26 *Did the answer to that clear question induce the insurer to enter into the contract at all, or under terms and conditions that it otherwise would not have accepted?*
    The FOS will apply the *Pan Atlantic*[52] test of actual inducement (probably without mentioning *Pan Atlantic*), but whereas a court would usually require evidence of the actual underwriter in each case, the FOS would only require this and/or a copy of the underwriting manual where the position is not clear cut. An example of a clear-cut case might be where a customer fails to disclose that his house has serious cracks. There the burden on insurers would not be high.

(3) The intention of the insured

13.27 *If the answer to either question above is no, the FOS will not support an avoidance and will require the claim to be paid. If the answer to both is yes, the consequences will depend on whether the FOS considers it to be fraudulent, deliberate, innocent, reckless or inadvertent.* Further details follow.
    In law, the insurer will only have two options: to avoid or affirm the whole policy. The Law Commissions propose in the draft bill[53] to adopt a similar approach to that of the FOS.

FRAUDULENT, DELIBERATE, INNOCENT, RECKLESS OR INADVERTENT
NON-DISCLOSURE

Fraudulent and deliberate non-disclosure

13.28 A deliberate non disclosure involves dishonestly providing information which the proposer knows to be untrue or incomplete. It will be fraudulent if coupled with the intention to deceive the insurer into giving the proposer an advantage to which he is not entitled. It will not be fraudulent if the intention is otherwise, for instance, merely to try to hide something embarrassing. However, both a deliberate and fraudulent non-disclosure will result in policy avoidance before the courts and the FOS. The FOS says[54] that only a small proportion of non-disclosing policyholders are found to have had any dishonest intent.
    13.29 The Law Commissions say that if a qualifying misrepresentation was deliberate, the insurer may avoid the contract and refuse all claims.[55] They do not make a distinction between fraudulent and deliberate misrepresentations—presumably on the basis that both are deliberate, both should be discouraged and fraudulent intent is so hard to prove that it is rarely alleged by insurers or specified by the FOS. The Law Commissions have noted that ombudsmen do not necessarily state the category of intent, are adverse to specifying that

51. *Dawsons* v *Bonnin* [1922] 2 AC 413.
52. See above "Materiality and inducement—The Law" at paras. 13.14 *et seq.*
53. 15/12/09.
54. FOS response to the current Law Commissions' 18 January 2006 Scoping Paper.
55. Sched. 1, para. 2(a) of the draft bill.

someone has acted with deliberate, fraudulent or even reckless intent, especially when writing to grieving relatives or terminally-ill patients, and instead talk of the policyholder not giving the questions and answers the care and attention required or not giving reasonable or accurate answers, or that the mis-statement was not innocent or inadvertent.[56]

13.30 An example of where the FOS found a non-disclosure to be deliberate is Case Study 61/6,[57] where on the balance of probabilities, the FOS felt that the assured could not have believed his answers to clear questions were accurate. He declared on the proposal form that his weight was 16 stone and his height was 6ft, although his actual weight was over 21 stone and his actual height was 5ft 9in. The disparity between the figures was too great. It is not clear why the FOS did not find that the proposer had a fraudulent intent.

13.31 There was a non-deliberate non-disclosure in Case Study 25/17,[58] where the assured deliberately did not disclose a consultation with a GP because he thought that the insurer already knew about it. The insurer had indicated that it had received the GP's notes after the time that the relevant information would have been included. The FOS required the insurer to meet the claim for prostate cancer and pay £200 for distress and inconvenience. The Law Commissions considered[59] providing for this sort of situation, but concluded[60] that the proposed reasonable consumer test was wide enough to protect the consumer in these circumstances. The law as it stands would be able to protect any insured in this situation if an estoppel could be made out, but the FOS rarely mentions, let alone relies on, such equitable remedies.

Can the premium be retained after a fraudulent or deliberate non-disclosure?

(A) THE LAW

13.32 Under the law, it is generally accepted that for fraud, the insurer can retain the premium[61] but risks waiving the non-disclosure if it keeps the premium in anything but a fraud situation.

(B) THE FOS

13.33 The FOS experience is that most insurers return the premium after avoidance of a policy following any type of non-disclosure. The FOS has not set out its stance on this. It would follow logically from the way that the FOS treats both fraudulent and deliberate non-disclosures that the premium could be retained on both types of non-disclosure. For it allows insurers the same remedy as the law for these two types of disclosures, namely avoidance *ab initio*, due to the dishonesty involved for both. Case Study 72/2[62] seems to show that without a dishonest intention being made out, the FOS will not allow the premium to be retained after a reckless non-disclosure, although it will allow avoidance in those circumstances, and it will order insurers to pay back the premium with interest. However, the FOS has not actually stated that if a dishonest intention is made out, the premium can be retained. And it is also not clear from Case Study 72/2 that it intended to send the message that a premium is

---

56. Consultation Paper 17/07/07, Appendix C.
57. *Ombudsman News* Apr/May 2007.
58. *Ombudsman News* Feb 2003.
59. Issues Paper 1, 09/06.
60. Consultation Paper 17/07/07 and Final paper 15/12/09, para. 5.71.
61. MIA 1906 s. 84.
62. *Ombudsman News* Sept/Oct 2008. See also below under "Reckless non-disclosure" at paras. 13.45 *et seq.*

returnable after a reckless non-disclosure. In Case Study 77/3,[63] there was a dishonest non-disclosure and the insurer voided the policy *ab initio* and returned the premium. The FOS supported the insurers' actions without commenting on, and perhaps not even considering, the return of the premium, but concentrating on the clarity of the structure and wording of the internet proposal form, and the mechanism of the form, which meant that the wrong information could only have been given intentionally. The evidence of the internet sale was that the insured had more likely than not intentionally misled insurers when she said that she had no penalty points on her driving licence, when in fact she had nine.

(C) LAW COMMISSIONS' PROPOSALS

13.34 The Law Commissions propose that where the consumer has made a deliberate or reckless misrepresentation, the insurer need not return any of the premiums paid, except to the extent that it would be unfair to the consumer to retain them,[64] in which case a court or ombudsman would have a discretion to order that some or all of the premium be returned to the consumer. The draft bill goes on to state that section 84 MIA would therefore be read subject to the exception in these provisions, so that the premium could be returned in more situations than that envisaged by section 84.[65] The Law Commissions give two examples of where it might be unfair for the insurer to keep all or some of the premium paid: where life insurance has an investment element, such as with an endowment policy,[66] or where there is a joint lives policy and only one person has made a deliberate misrepresentation.[67]

Innocent non-disclosure

(a) The law

13.35 Although the law's remedies for non-disclosure are not flexible, the law has adapted in some ways to make allowance for innocent non-disclosure (i.e. non-disclosure which is not the assured's fault), through construction of the proposal questions. If a question is ambiguous, so that the meaning intended by the insurer would not be readily apparent to a reasonable man it may apply the *contra proferentem* rule so that questions drafted at the proposal stage by insurers will be construed narrowly against them. The insured will still have to give accurate, complete and not misleading answers, and the FOS would expect the same. If an insured is dealing in Rolex watches, it is not accurate or adequate disclosure only to mention clocks.[68] The courts have typically been generous in construing an assured's answers as accurate.[69] The law will not allow the insurer to avoid the policy if the assured has misunderstood or misinterpreted the question in giving what he believed to be a truthful

---

63. *Ombudsman News* May/June 2009.
64. Sched. 1, para. 2(b) of the draft bill.
65. Sched. 1, para. 17 of the draft bill.
66. Final report 15/12/09, paras. 6.49–6.51.
67. Final report 15/12/09, paras. 6.52–6.53.
68. *WISE Underwriting Agency Ltd* v *Grupo Nacional Provincial SA* [2004] EWHC 1706 (Comm); [2004] Lloyd's Rep IR 764.
69. For instance, in *Friedlander* v *London Assurance* (1832) 1 Moo & R 171, it was accurate to describe one room occupied by a lodger as a "dwelling house", and in *Wulfson* v *Switzerland General Insurance Co* (1940) 67 Ll L Rep 190 it was accurate to describe furniture in lifts in a yard covered by tarpaulins as being "in store". Although a coffee house was not an "inn" in *Doe d Pit* v *Lanning* (1814) 4 Camp 73 and an unroofed yard was not a "garage" in *Barnett & Block* v *National Parcels Insurance* (1942) 73 Ll L Rep 17.

answer.[70] The law considers that a wide question is to be confined within reasonable limits[71] and that limited questions may waive otherwise material facts falling outside the precise scope of the questions,[72] the burden being on the insured to establish that the right to disclosure has been waived.[73]

13.36 There will be times where a matter is so glaringly important that it will be expected to be disclosed whatever the proposal questions, especially if there is a general declaration that all material information has been disclosed.[74] So the three serious armed robberies over a five-year period about which there had been no insurance claims in *Noblebright Ltd v Sirius International Corporation*[75] should have been disclosed, even though the proposal form only asked about claims in the previous five years and claims worth over £10,000. There are examples where the FOS takes the same approach.[76]

13.37 The law also allows five further exceptions to the duty of disclosure, where the facts:

(1) reduce the risk[77];
(2) are about which the insurer knows or is presumed to know[78] and has not specifically asked;
(3) are common knowledge;
(4) are about which the insurer has waived disclosure, for instance if the insurer has expressly limited its question, so the insured remains silent about that part of the information, or where an answer in a proposal form is left blank and the insurer makes no further enquiries; or
(5) could not reasonably have been discovered by the insured, and which he did not know or did not deliberately shut his eyes to.[79] This softens the insured's duty of disclosure under section 18(1) MIA. Section 18(1) is harsher for a business policyholder who is "deemed to know every circumstance which, in the ordinary course of business, ought to be known by him".

13.38 Although the law does not have any more official ways to prevent avoidance where the insured is "innocent", Staughton LJ noted in *Kausar v Eagle Star Insurance Co Ltd*[80] that the insurer's right to avoid liability for an "innocent" insured should be confined to "plain" cases. Presumably this means cases in which the evidence of materiality is overwhelming. Simon J has commented[81] that Staughton LJ was merely expressing "a broad caution against too readily accepting allegations of material non-disclosure".

---

70. *Yorke v Yorkshire Insurance Co Ltd* [1918] 1 KB 662.
71. *Connecticut Mutual Life Insurance Co of Hartford v Moore* (1881) LR 6 App Cas 644.
72. *Revell v London General Insurance Co Ltd* (1934) 50 Ll L Rep 114; *Taylor v Eagle Star Insurance Co Ltd* (1940) 67 Ll L Rep 136; *R&R Developments Ltd v Axa Insurance UK plc* [2009] EWHC 2429 (Ch).
73. *Noblebright Ltd v Sirius International Corporation Ltd* [2007] EWHC 868 (QB).
74. *Cf* paras. 17–17 to 17–19 of *McGillivray on Insurance Law*, 10th ed. (2003), which was expressly approved by Longmore LJ in *Doheny v New India Assurance Co Ltd* [2004] EWCA Civ 1705.
75. See above.
76. See below "Renewals" at para. 13.94.
77. Note that if the misrepresentation is in breach of warranty, these factors will not assist an innocent insured. In *Dawsons Ltd v Bonnin* [1922] 2 AC 413, an innocent misrepresentation about the garaging of lorries, the actual position was less risky than the one apparently insured and was still a breach of warranty which led to avoidance. See "Warranties" below at para. 14.6.
78. S. 18(3)(b) MIA.
79. *Carter v Boehm* (1766) 3 Burr 1905; *Economides v Commercial Union Assurance plc* [1998] QB 587.
80. [2000] Lloyd's Rep IR 154.
81. *WISE Underwriting Agency Ltd v Grupo Nacional Provincial SA* [2004] Lloyd's Rep IR 764.

(b) The FOS

13.39 The FOS will not allow avoidance of a policy following an innocent non-disclosure. It will require the insurer to pay the claim in full whatever it would have done had it known the true position, subject to policy terms and conditions. In deciding whether a non-disclosure is innocent, the FOS will take into account any explanation for the discrepancy which the insured gives. It will expect insurers to ask for and take into account such an explanation. In Case Study 18/21,[82] the FOS penalised an insurer for failing to ask why the insured had not disclosed tinted windows as a modification to the car. The law would not have required this. She genuinely did not realise she had to and the FOS felt this was an innocent non-disclosure. When the insurer cancelled the policy the insured had to get other insurance quickly and at a much higher premium. The FOS ask the insurer to cover her repair claim, with interest and pay £300 for distress and inconvenience.

13.40 Some difficulties with internet sales mean that the FOS might be more easily persuaded with these that there is an innocent reason for a non-disclosure where the proposer answers a question incorrectly. These difficulties include where the proposer did not see the question for long, did not write the answer down himself, did not get a chance to re-read the information and/or was not sent a document to read and sign at the end of the internet procedure.

13.41 The FOS will consider a non-disclosure to be innocent in three circumstances: where (1) the question was unclear, (2) the proposer should not reasonably have known the information, or (3) if it was reasonable for the proposer to have overlooked the information. Taking these each in turn:

(1) A non-disclosure will be considered innocent if contemporaneous evidence shows that the question was unclear or ambiguous, or did not clearly apply to the facts, e.g. Case Study 7/21.[83] Another example is Case Study 79/10,[84] where the insured had added a satellite navigation unit, Bluetooth kit, Playstation and CD changer to his car, but did not disclose these as modifications in answer to the proposal question. The FOS felt that the insured could not reasonably have been expected to realise from the wording of the proposal form and the other examples it gave that such disclosure was required. Insurers could not therefore void the policy for non-disclosure, and were told to pay the theft claim with interest from the date of the theft to the date of settlement of the claim. Without the report labelling it as such, this was treated as an innocent non-disclosure. Similarly, the Law Commissions point to a FOS example from their 2009 survey of FOS cases,[85] where the FOS found that the insured would not reasonably have deemed a single episode of lower back pain to be a disorder within the context of the proposal question for critical illness cover, as the other examples that the question gave were of significant medical conditions. The courts might come to the same conclusions in these examples using the *contra proferentem* rule of construction of the proposal questions.

Despite the FOS concentrating on the proposal questions, and saying that it bases the duty of disclosure on the questions posed before inception, there are

---

82. *Ombudsman News* July 2002.
83. *Ombudsman News* July 2001.
84. *Ombudsman News* Sept/Oct 2009.
85. In 2009 it reviewed 47 final ombudsman decisions involving consumer non-disclosure complaints.

examples[86] where it expects disclosure of a matter whether or not it is strictly within the ambit of the questions on the proposal form, if it is so obvious to the insured that it might influence acceptance or assessment of the proposal and if it relates to something about which the insured cannot seriously believe that the insurer would not want to hear. The courts will take this approach too.

(2) The FOS will find a proposer's non-disclosure innocent if he should not reasonably have known the relevant information. The questions should not relate to matters which the proposer could not possibly have known. The FOS does not refer to the law's parallel to this stemming from *Carter* v *Boehm*.[87]

(3) The FOS will also consider a non-disclosure innocent if it was reasonable for the proposer to have overlooked the information, for example, minor childhood ailments or minor motoring offences that occurred more than four years earlier.

13.42 The FOS does not seem to make use of the legal tools set out above to deal with an innocent non-disclosure. In Case Study 25/15,[88] the answer in the printed statement of facts was left blank. Instead of using the legal argument that the insurer had waived its right to object to the resulting non-disclosure, the FOS upheld the complaint on the grounds that it was not good industry practice that the insured had not been asked to check the statement or sign and return a proposal form.

13.43 The FOS may, however, use its onerous terms tool,[89] as it did in Case Study 85/1[90] to decide that the term which excludes a particular circumstance is onerous and should have been highlighted and explained to the policyholder before inception. So the question of non-disclosure in relation to that item never occurs.

(c) Law Commissions' proposals

13.44 If a consumer assured makes an innocent non-disclosure under the Law Commissions' proposed regime, he is unlikely to have breached his duty of reasonable care not to make a misrepresentation.

Reckless non-disclosure

13.45 If the non-disclosure is not fraudulent, deliberate or innocent, the proposer must have been negligent—either reckless in answering the questions or having made an inadvertent error. The law and the FOS allow avoidance for reckless non-disclosure, and view it as seriously as a deliberate non-disclosure. The Law Commissions also treat it the same as a deliberate misrepresentation.[91]

13.46 The FOS says that the meaning it gives to recklessness derives from Lord Diplock's test in 1967, "made with actual recognition by the insured himself that a danger exists, and not caring whether or not it is averted".[92] The FOS will consider a non-disclosure to be

---

86. See "Renewals" below at para. 13.94.
87. (1766) 3 Burr 1905; See above "Innocent Non-Disclosure—The law" at para. 13.37.
88. *Ombudsman News* Feb 2003.
89. See above "Onerous and unfair terms—Interfoto" at paras. 5.52 *et seq.*
90. *Ombudsman News* Apr/May 2010.
91. The claim would be refused and the policy avoided under Sched. 1, para. 2(a) of the draft bill 15/12/09.
92. *Fraser* v *Furman (Productions) Ltd* [1967] 2 Lloyd's Rep 1. This subjective test was formulated in the context of whether an employer had been reckless in his actions in interfering with certain machinery which resulted in an employee trapping her hand inside a machine. The purpose of the condition not to be reckless was to ensure that the insured will not, because he is covered against loss through negligence by the policy, refrain from taking precautions which he knew ought to be taken.

reckless where it finds it difficult to believe that the proposer could have overlooked a matter which is typically of significance and well known to him, but there is not enough evidence to show deliberate non-disclosure. The proposer must have given his answers without caring whether or not they were true or accurate. An example would be where a proposer signs a blank proposal form and leaves it to be filled in by someone who was not an intermediary whom he trusted to record his answers accurately. He must also have understood, if only in a limited way, that an answer was required, that it was important to the insurer and that there was a consequence to the answer.

13.47 In Case Study 61/5[93] the FOS found that the late proposer had been reckless. The proposal form asked clearly and specifically whether she had ever sought or been given medical advice to reduce the level of her drinking. She failed to disclose her alcoholism or her continuing treatment from a consultant psychiatrist in relation thereto. Although there was no evidence to show that she had deliberately given the wrong answer, it was unlikely that the non-disclosure had been innocent or inadvertent. For if she had properly considered the point, she would not have answered as she had, because the question would have raised issues that were fresh in her mind and that the FOS believed she knew were important to the insurer. It is not clear why the FOS found that this was a reckless and not a deliberate or fraudulent non-disclosure. What evidence could there ever be of a deliberate intent in these circumstances? What difference does it make if the non-disclosure was deliberate or reckless? Perhaps the FOS should merge this category with deliberate non-disclosure as the Law Commissions propose should be done with the law.

13.48 If Case Study 72/2[94] is indicative, it seems that the FOS will not allow the premium to be retained in the case of a reckless non-disclosure, although it might allow it to be retained for a deliberate or fraudulent non-disclosure.[95] In this case study, the FOS found that the non-disclosure of a claim for car theft within the previous three years and an accident in the previous year could not have been accidental or casual, although it found no evidence of dishonesty. So under which of the FOS non-disclosure categories did this case study fit? The report does not say. If the non-disclosure was not dishonest, it could not have been fraudulent or deliberate. Perhaps the assured's non-disclosure was reckless. It is unclear what would have convinced the FOS of the assured's dishonesty, especially as his premium would have been £1,000 more expensive with full disclosure. The FOS found the insurer was entitled to refuse the claim, but was wrong to retain the premium, which was to be returned with interest. The insurer seems to have quite reasonably considered the non-disclosure to be dishonest, acted accordingly and been penalised by the FOS. It is unhelpful that the report does not specifically categorise the non-disclosure as reckless, and it is not impressive as representing a weighty, thought-filled report as it refers to non-payment of the claim rather than avoiding the policy, the latter being the appropriate remedy even under its own scheme for deliberate, fraudulent or reckless non-disclosures.

13.49 The Law Commissions have criticised the FOS as it is unclear whether the FOS intends the recklessness to relate to the circumstances not properly disclosed or to whether the answer would affect the insurers' underwriting decision. Also, the FOS does not set out clearly upon whom the burden of proving the state of mind rests once the insurer has established a misrepresentation.[96]

---

93. *Ombudsman News* Apr/May 2007.
94. *Ombudsman News* Sept/Oct 2008.
95. See above "Can the Premium be retained after a fraudulent or deliberate non-disclosure?" at paras. 13.32 *et seq.*
96. Consultation Paper 17/07/07, Appendix C.

Inadvertent non-disclosure

13.50 For an inadvertent non-disclosure, the FOS will apply a proportionate remedy, based on putting the parties in the position they would have been in had there been no non-disclosure. This compares to the inflexibility of the law which requires avoidance of a policy if there has been a non-disclosure, whatever type of error led to the non-disclosure, or if the insurer does not wish to avoid the policy, it has to affirm it. See further "Remedies for Inadvertent non-disclosure" below at paragraphs 13.56 *et seq.*

13.51 Inadvertent means merely careless, but not reckless. Inadvertence is a case of minor negligence. The proposer unintentionally and not deliberately misleads the insurer through an understandable oversight or moment of carelessness relating to minor matters, distant in time or otherwise easy to overlook. The non-disclosure is not innocent because there is still some fault on behalf of the assured. In an innocent non-disclosure there would probably be some fault by the insurer through, for example, ambiguous questions. It will be more difficult for a proposer to prove inadvertence if he answered several questions badly, in which case he will probably have been reckless.

13.52 For instance, an assured would have made an inadvertent mistake if there was a clear question about motoring convictions, and he disclosed a drink-driving conviction, but not a less serious penalty points speeding conviction because he did not realise the latter type counted. In Case Study 48/1,[97] the proposer claimed on her policy following a breast cancer diagnosis, which the FOS found insurers should cover. This was even though she had inadvertently not disclosed back pain that she had suffered following childbirth more than five years before. She had failed to read and check the questions thoroughly enough. In Case Study 61/1,[98] even though the proposal question was clear and specific, the proposer did not disclose recurrent back and neck problems in response. The FOS found this an understandable error, and therefore an inadvertent non-disclosure, in view of the proposer's difficult family circumstances and because he had had only one orthopaedic consultation two years before the proposal. It was also an understandable oversight that he had forgotten to mention a health insurance application several years earlier which had been deferred when he did not have time to deal with the further enquiries due to the same difficult family circumstances. The FOS required a proportionate response, asking that the policy be rewritten as if there had been full disclosure. This meant cover for the insured's heart attack, although spinal conditions would have been excluded.

13.53 The FOS considers that policyholders should exercise a reasonable amount of care at the proposal stage. In determining inadvertence, the FOS will look at:

(1) The circumstances surrounding the proposal and whether the information was transcribed by an adviser.

The FOS will not say that there has been an inadvertent non-disclosure just because an intermediary acting as the insured's agent may have completed the form incorrectly. This was the situation in Case Study 27/6.[99] There the FOS could not deal with the dispute between the assured—a couple running a farm—and the broker as to the circumstances in which the proposal form was completed, signed and submitted, but saw no evidence that the insurer had been made aware of the farm's considerable claims history. In one of the few cases where the FOS has commented, it said that the intermediary was the agent of the insured (as he would

---

97. *Ombudsman News* Aug 2005.
98. *Ombudsman News* Apr/May 2007.
99. *Ombudsman News* Apr 2003.

have been in law), so any non-disclosure by him counted as a non-disclosure by the assured. The FOS therefore supported the insurer's avoidance of the policy following a fire claim. It seems to have been influenced by the substantial claims history that existed and had not been disclosed.

However, in Case Study 25/14,[100] non-disclosure where a broker completed a proposal form for the assured resulted in a finding of inadvertent non-disclosure of the assured's four speeding convictions and a proportionate settlement. The proposal question had been clear. The agency of the broker was not discussed and the paramount question that the FOS considered was whether the assured had acted inadvertently in her relationship with the broker. It looks as if the FOS considered that the broker was the insurer's agent, (which would be contrary to the position in law[101]—but at the time of the decision, the FOS did not have jurisdiction over intermediaries unless they effectively represented the insurer). The FOS treated inadvertent non-disclosures to this agent as inadvertent non-disclosures to the insurer. The assured here admitted to signing the proposal form without checking it. The FOS felt she should have checked it, but that her failure to do so was an oversight rather than a deliberate non-disclosure. The insurer said that it would still have offered her cover if the disclosure had been full, albeit with an increased premium, so the FOS felt that a proportionate settlement was appropriate.

In Case Study 61/3,[102] the report mentions that the broker was the insurer's representative. The FOS found that the non-disclosure of asthma was inadvertent where the assured claimed that the intermediary told her that its disclosure was unnecessary as her condition was mild. The FOS was uncertain whether this was true, but as the intermediary had made several other mistakes on the proposal form, and the complainant had disclosed her asthma in a subsequent application to the same insurer, it concluded that she had not intended to mislead the insurer. She had signed the proposal form assuming that the intermediary had recorded her answers accurately, but without recklessly not caring whether her answers were true. A proportional award resulted.

In Case Study 68/10,[103] one of the two joint insured was serving a prison sentence for a conviction that had not been disclosed to the insurer. However, they had told the mortgage department of their bank, and it was their bank which had sold them the policy along with their mortgage. They regarded the bank and the insurer as one. They had written to the bank in relation to the conviction asking about the mortgage and insurance position. A little later they had mentioned the conviction in their response to the bank's insurance renewal questionnaire, but no-one at the bank had thought to notify the insurer. Although this insurer said that it would not have offered cover if it had known, the FOS thought that it would have been possible for the insured to find cover elsewhere, with an additional premium. In an interesting development for the duties and liabilities of an intermediary, the FOS felt that the mortgage department should have passed the information to the insurer and that the bank should therefore pay what an insurer would have for the claim, deducting the cost of the additional premium. The insured's

---

100. *Ombudsman News* Feb 2003.
101. According to *Newsholme Brothers v Road Transport and General Insurance Co Ltd* [1929] 2 KB 356.
102. *Ombudsman News* Apr/May 2007.
103. *Ombudsman News* Mar/Apr 2008.

disclosure was treated as a disclosure to the insurer or its agent, and the FOS penalised the agent who was at fault in not passing on the information.

(2) How clear, concise and relevant the firm's questions were in relation to the issue.

The FOS will interpret narrowly and give little weight to "catch-all" questions, those which require significant and wide-ranging disclosure of minor matters that the firm knows will not be relevant to its assessment, or those where it would be impractical to expect a policyholder to provide a fully accurate response. A request for information about all visits to a doctor over the past five years would be an example.

(3) Whether the firm gave any or any clear warning about the consequences of giving false or incomplete information.

(4) The degree to which the policyholder should have been aware of the information and its significance to the firm. So the FOS would expect awareness of the insurer's likely interest in recent major illnesses for heath insurance, and significant convictions like dangerous or drink driving for car insurance.

(5) The more recent and significant an event is, the less likely the FOS is to consider its non-disclosure in response to a clear question to be inadvertent.

(6) If the non-disclosure relates to changes since a previous proposal, the firm should have provided a copy of that proposal.[104]

In Case Study 61/2,[105] the FOS considered the non-disclosure of a change in medical condition to be inadvertent where the insurer had not sent the complainant a copy of his original proposal with the letter confirming that cover would start shortly, so that he could assess what changes he had to disclose. This omission negated the warning which the insurer had put both on its proposal form and on the letter which reminded the complainant of his duty to inform them immediately if, as a result of anything that happened before the start of the policy, he needed to change his answers.

13.54 Even where a non-disclosure seems to be deliberate or reckless, in practice the FOS may consider it to be inadvertent if there is no evidence of a more culpable intention. For instance, in Case Study 79/11,[106] the assured did not disclose on a clearly-worded, online proposal the modifications that he had made to his car, but had no difficulty describing them when he reported its theft. As there was no evidence of a deliberate or reckless intention, the FOS treated his non-disclosure as inadvertent and asked the insurer to make a proportionate payment of the claim based on the premium that he should have paid with full disclosure.

13.55 In its final report and draft bill, the Law Commissions call this type of misrepresentation "careless" rather than inadvertent. By this they mean misrepresentations which are made without reasonable care, but which are not deliberate or reckless. In effect, they are negligent, but the Law Commissions were concerned that if they adopted the word "negligent" which is the word which appears in its consultation papers, people might charge it with characteristics or case law within the law of negligence when it is a new, stand-alone category.[107]

---

104. See further "Renewals" below at paras. 13.92 *et seq*.

105. *Ombudsman News* Apr/May 2007. This is different to the position where the original proposal information does not accompany a renewal notice, see "Renewals" below, at paras. 13.92 *et seq*, presumably because the time since the proposer last saw the information is different.

106. *Ombudsman News* Sept/Oct 2009.

107. Final report 15/12/09, paras. 6.54–6.57.

Remedies for inadvertent non-disclosure

13.56 Although the law would allow insurers to avoid the policy for all inadvertent non-disclosures which meet the test of materiality and inducement, both the FOS and the Law Commissions' proposals give insurers different remedies based on what they would have done if proper disclosure had been given.[108] This approach does not reflect the degree of carelessness or whether the non-disclosure related to the risk which is the subject of the claim. However, this may be one of the most useful and innovative policies which the FOS has adopted and it is mirrored in the Law Commissions' proposals.[109] There are four types of FOS remedy for an inadvertent non-disclosure:

(1) If the insurer would have declined the insurance had it known the true position, the FOS may support the insurers avoiding the policy *ab initio*, and so refusing all claims and returning the premium, e.g. Case Study 61/2.[110]

(2) If insurers would have offered the insurance but on different terms without increasing the premium, perhaps with an added exclusion, the FOS will expect it to re-write the terms as if there had been full disclosure, especially where the matter undisclosed is unrelated to the claim, and treat the claim as if that amendment or exclusion were in place, e.g. Case Study 48/1[111] where back pain would have been excluded if the previous back pain had been disclosed, but the breast cancer claim was unaffected. Similarly, in Case Study 27/5[112] the non-disclosure of ear problems was probably inadvertent, and its disclosure would have resulted in an exclusion for hearing related problems, leaving intact the leukaemia claim from which the insured died. The FOS asked insurers to pay the full critical illness benefits.

If the result of full disclosure would have been a reduced premium with more exclusions in the policy, the FOS might allow the insurer to add the premium refund to the settlement.

(3) Where the difference in the terms would be an increased premium, the FOS would adopt a proportional approach, where it calculates the proportion of the premium that was paid against the higher premium that would have been charged on full disclosure, and bases the settlement on that proportion. Examples are above at paragraphs 13.50 *et seq* in "Inadvertent non-disclosure". A specific example is Case Study 79/11,[113] where the insurer would have increased the premium by 75% if there had been full disclosure, so the FOS asked insurers to pay the car theft claim proportionately. The calculation is reached by taking the premium actually charged, dividing it by the premium which should have been charged, and then multiplying this number by 100 to reach the percentage of the claim that will be paid.

In a proportional settlement, it is not always clear from the report how the FOS has calculated the figures. In Case Study 25/14,[114] the insured was awarded 85%

---

108. Sched. 1, Part 1, para. 4 of the Draft bill 15/12/09.
109. *Cf* Schedule 1, Part 1, paras. 5–8 of the Draft bill 15/12/09.
110. *Ombudsman News* Apr/May 2007—see details of the case study at para. 13.53 above under "Inadvertent non-disclosure".
111. *Ombudsman News* Aug 2005—see details of the case study at para. 13.52 above under "Inadvertent non-disclosure".
112. *Ombudsman News* Apr 2003.
113. *Ombudsman News* Sept/Oct 2009.
114. *Ombudsman News* Feb 2003.

of the value of her claim, based supposedly on the proportion of extra premium she should have paid if there had been full disclosure, this being 12% more in the first year and 5% more in the second.

(4) A fourth possibility is a mixture of remedies (2) and (3) above. The Law Commissions quote in their Final Paper[115] a FOS example where the insured negligently had not fully disclosed an obsessive-compulsive disorder when he took out a protection plan covering life insurance and critical illness and which allowed him to waive the premiums in the event of serious illness. If the insurer had received full disclosure, it would have declined the latter of these cover options and increased the premium for critical illness by 25% and for the life cover by 75%. So the insurer was required to pay a proportion of the critical illness (cancer) claim, deducting the cost of the extra premiums from the settlement. The life cover continued, but on death, the pay-out would be proportionate.

13.57 If no claim has been made, can a policy be terminated if an inadvertent or careless non-disclosure is discovered? The point would not arise if the remedy for the non-disclosure is avoidance based on what the insurer would have done had it known the full details. For avoided policies are terminated from the start and, except in fraud cases, the premium is returned. Where the insurer would have offered the policy on different terms if there had been full disclosure, subject to the policy terms themselves, the FOS generally allows the consumer the choice of accepting those different policy terms or having the policy cancelled. The Law Commissions propose that, subject to waiver, either party to a non-life insurance should be able to cancel the policy with reasonable notice in such circumstances with that part of the premium relating to the future cover being returned to the consumer, but that for life insurance the insurer should be required to continue the policy on amended terms.[116]

NON-DISCLOSURE BY AN INTERMEDIARY

(a) The law

13.58 In law non-disclosure by an intermediary is taken to be the insured's non-disclosure when the intermediary acts as the agent of the insured, which is usually the case. Following *Newsholme Brothers* v *Road Transport and General Insurance Co Ltd*,[117] an intermediary who assists with the proposal form is the insured's agent for the purpose of filling out the form, even if he is a tied agent of the insurer in other circumstances. This means that an innocent insured would be penalised by the insurer avoiding the policy where it was the intermediary (acting as the insured's agent) who had been fraudulent or negligent in disclosing information to the insurer. However, the assured would have an action against the intermediary in such circumstances. Section 19 MIA enshrines that the agent has an obligation to disclose material information.

(b) The FOS

13.59 In a survey of FOS cases carried out by the Law Commissions,[118] 25 out of the 190 consumer (and eight out of the 12 small business) cases involving non-disclosure or

---

115. 15/12/09.
116. Final Report 15/12/09, paras. 6.88–6.100 and para. 9 of Sched. 1 of the Draft Bill.
117. [1929] 2 KB 356.
118. Insurance Contract Law Issues Paper 3: Intermediaries and Pre-contract Information March 2007.

misrepresentation involved allegations about what the intermediary said or did during the sales process. In the Law Commissions' further survey in 2009 of an additional 47 cases, nine of them, or almost one fifth, involved an allegation about the intermediary's actions.[119] The FOS does not seem to have a sct policy as to whether it will consider that the intermediary is the agent of the insured (as is usually the case in law). The position has not been set out in *Ombudsman News*, which also does not mention the relevant case law, and it was not clear to the Law Commissions when they examined a further sample of FOS cases selected specifically because agency issues had been raised.[120] However, the FOS has since set out its position more clearly in its Factsheet "Medical 'non-disclosure' in Insurance",[121] and states that a tied intermediary is likely to be the agent of the insurer and an independent one is likely to be the agent of the insured.

13.60 Especially before the FOS acquired jurisdiction over intermediaries, it seems usually to have looked at the position in the round, asking whether the insured was entitled to rely on the intermediary's information, as if the intermediary was the insurer's agent. In Case Study 23/12,[122] the FOS allowed the insured to rely on the intermediary's letter which confirmed that the policy covered the swimming pool dome against storm damage. The FOS said that it was not reasonable for the insurer to expect the insured to check the policy to make sure that the intermediary was correct. The insurer here met the claim, but refused to cover future loss. If the intermediary is not the insurer's agent, it is not fair and is contrary to the law that the insurer should effectively be held accountable for the intermediary's actions and mistakes.

13.61 Case Study 27/6[123] is an example of where the FOS treated the intermediary as the agent of the insured when the intermediary filled out the proposal form. This would be the position in law too, as set out above. Case Study 25/14[124] is an example of where the FOS seems to have treated the intermediary filling out the proposal form as the insurer's agent.[125] Both of these case studies were decided before the FOS acquired jurisdiction over general insurance intermediaries from 15 January 2005.

13.62 The Law Commissions' review of the sample of FOS intermediary cases referred to above[126] led them to the following conclusions:

(1) The FOS appeared to follow the legal position as far as independent intermediaries were concerned, so that those who searched the whole market or filled out a proposal form for the assured will normally be regarded as the insured's agent. An example given from the Law Commissions' survey was where the FOS supported the insurer who declined a breast cancer claim because of non-disclosure on the application form filled out by an independent financial adviser, of treatment for depression and a sore throat. The Ombudsman's final decision noted that the adviser was independent, not an agent or representative for whom the insurer was vicariously liable.

---

119. Final Report 15/12/09.
120. Issues Paper 3, March 2007.
121. *Cf* FOS website.
122. *Ombudsman News* Dec 2002.
123. *Ombudsman News* Apr 2003.
124. *Ombudsman News* Feb 2003.
125. For both of these case studies, see further detail under "Inadvertent non-disclosure" at para. 13.53.
126. Issues Paper 3, March 2007.

(2) However, the FOS told the Law Commissions that it often considered tied agents to be acting as the insurer's agent even in completing a proposal form, especially if the insurer in question considered them to be their agents.

(3) Sometimes the FOS treated the intermediary who completed a proposal form as the insured's agent because the insured had signed the form. An example is given of where the policyholder alleged that the medical information he had disclosed to an independent financial adviser who had completed the form, had been omitted. The ombudsman found that allegation unproven, because the policyholder had signed a declaration which said that the answers recorded were true and complete to the best of his knowledge and belief and that the policyholder had read and understood the application. Perhaps most damningly, the declaration specifically warned that if the application form had been filled in by someone else, the person signing must read all the answers to the questions on the form carefully before signing the declaration.

(4) However, there were many other cases where the FOS did not regard the signing of forms as conclusive, and as mentioned above, treated tied agents as acting for the insurer when filling out the proposal form, contrary to *Newsholme*. The Law Commissions did not find any specific mention of *Newsholme*. An example is given of a life and critical illness policy taken out jointly by a husband and wife who both signed the application form, although it was filled out by insurer's tied agent. When the wife died, the insurer avoided the policy for non-disclosure of various doctor's appointments made by the wife. The ombudsman found for the insured, and pointed out that the tied agent had made a large number of obvious errors in completing the form and concluded that some of the questions could not have been put to the couple and this led to non-disclosure of the wife's medical investigations. The ombudsman accepted that the assured should have read the application before signing it, but thought that it was most likely that they did not do so because the tied agent did not tell them how important it was for them to do this. Similarly, in another example where the tape of the telephone application for a critical illness application was available, the ombudsman ordered a proportionate remedy where the questions asked did not clearly relate to both the applicants, and where the representative said nothing about checking through the form or reading it carefully, but just told them to sign it and send it back.

13.63 Perhaps the fact that the FOS has not set out its policy in relation to intermediaries and agency is a good thing for allowing it flexibility in deciding each case fairly and reasonably in the circumstances of that particular case. This is at the cost of clarity and certainty. It is to be noted that the Law Commissions concluded from their survey that a consumer who takes an intermediary case to the FOS may have a better chance of recovering from the insurer than under the law.

(c) Law Commissions' proposals

13.64 The 1957 Law Reform Committee advocated that an intermediary should be deemed the agent of the insurers for the purpose of formation of the contract, to avoid unfairness to the insured. With the basic support of the FOS, the current Law Commissions originally proposed[127] that for consumers and small businesses, (a) an intermediary should be the

---

127. Consultation Paper on Insurance Contract Law 17/07/07.

insurer's agent for the purposes of obtaining pre-contract information, unless[128] the intermediary undertakes to search the market on the insured's behalf, and (b) an intermediary
completing the proposal form should be the insurer's agent for this purpose too[129] if they
would otherwise be considered the insurer's agent.

13.65 The Law Commissions' later Policy Statement[130] sets out a changed and much more
complicated position, which is mostly reflected in the draft consumer insurance bill.[131]
Clause 9 of the draft bill says that Schedule 2 determines for the purposes of this statute only,
whether an intermediary acts as the agent of the consumer or the insurer when collecting and
transmitting information from the consumer to the insurer at the pre-contract stage. Clause
12(4) preserves the normal agency rule that a person is responsible for the actions of their
own agent. So if according to Schedule 2 an intermediary acts for the consumer, his
knowledge and behaviour are considered to be the consumer's, and an insurer could have a
remedy against an honest consumer with a negligent, reckless or dishonest intermediary,
leaving the honest consumer to pursue the intermediary. The starting point of the draft bill is
that the intermediary acts for the consumer unless there are relevant circumstances to show
that he acts for the insurer.

13.66 Under Schedule 2, paragraph 2, an intermediary is to be taken as the insurer's agent
when the agent:

> (a) does something in the agent's capacity as the appointed representative of the
> insurer for the purposes of the FSMA (s. 39);
> (b) collects information from the consumer, if the insurer had given the agent express
> authority to do so as the insurer's agent; or
> (c) enters into the contract as the insurer's agent, if the insurer had given the agent
> express authority to do so.

13.67 In any other case, it is to be presumed that the agent is acting as the consumer's
agent unless, in the light of all the relevant circumstances, it appears that the agent is acting
as the insurer's agent.[132] It is common for intermediaries to change hats during the transaction, for instance acting for the consumer in advising on the choice of insurer, but for the
insurer in binding it to cover, but the Law Commissions envisage focusing on the intermediary's capacity at the time of the carelessness or wrongdoing in question. Paragraph 3(3)
of the schedule sets out indicative and non-exhaustive examples which might tend to confirm,
(but will not necessarily confirm) that the agent is acting for the consumer, namely if the
agent undertakes to give impartial advice to the consumer, or to conduct a fair analysis of the
market, or if the consumer pays the agent a fee. Paragraph 3(4) gives other indicative and
non-exhaustive examples which might tend to show that the agent is acting for the insurer,
namely if the agent places insurance with only a small proportion of the insurers who provide
insurance of the type in question; the insurer provides the relevant insurance through only a
limited number of agents; the insurer permits the agent to use the insurer's name in providing
the agent's services; the insurance in question is marketed under the name of the agent; or
the insurer asks the agent to solicit the consumer's custom. As a consequence of these
provisions, Clauses 11(1) and (2) disapply section 19 MIA to consumer insurance
contracts.

---

128. Summary of Responses—consumer issues 28/05/08 para. 5.47.
129. Contrary to the strict law position set out in *Newsholme* (see above).
130. 11/03/09.
131. 15/12/09.
132. Para. 3 of Sched. 2 of the draft bill.

13.68 Hopefully, the FOS would follow any changes made in the law in relation to intermediaries, especially as such change would be after years of discussion and consultation.

NON-DISCLOSURE RELATING TO GROUP POLICIES

13.69 The FOS treats beneficiaries under a group scheme as if they are insureds if the benefit is truly for them (see "Jurisdiction of the FOS—Intermediaries" at paragraph 2.9 above). This means that their non-disclosures can be treated like other consumer non-disclosures.

13.70 The FOS approach parallels the current Law Commissions' proposals[133] and draft bill[134] which say that if the insurance would have been consumer insurance had the beneficiary arranged it directly, any dispute about a misrepresentation by the beneficiary would be determined according to the Law Commissions' proposals for consumer insurance. It would cover typical employment schemes, as well as block building policies taken out by landlords for tenants, or buildings insurance taken out by freeholders for leaseholders. The draft bill adds[135] that if there was a misrepresentation by one beneficiary the policy would not be affected in relation to other beneficiaries. Presumably the FOS would also follow this line. However, non-disclosures by the company, rather than the beneficiary, would be dealt with under the business rules. The FOS would only deal with complaints from businesses if the business was small enough to fall within its jurisdiction.

CODES OF PRACTICE

13.71 The insurance industry, especially in relation to non-disclosure, is overlaid by a system of self-regulatory codes of practice.[136] The FOS applies its own criteria on top of these, may or may not apply the law and may have regard to a code which is no longer current. This may leave insurance claim handlers unclear about how they should decide matters, especially those relating to non-disclosure.

13.72 Courts cannot enforce the Statements/Codes which the industry never even made binding on itself and were only intended as statements of good practice. The court ruled in *Lewis v Norwich Union Healthcare Ltd*[137] that the ABI's SLIP 1996 was not incorporated into the policy and was not legally binding, so its terms were to be disregarded. However, in the later case of *Jones v Environcom Ltd (No 2)*,[138] David Steel J referred to the principles set out in ICOBS as setting out the duties of a broker, rather than citing copious authority, so it seems that the FSA rules are beginning to be recognised by the courts as authority for a standard of good industry practice.

13.73 Theoretically, a consumer can bring an action against an insurer under section 150 FSMA for breach of statutory duty in not complying with ICOB/S. The insured would have to ask for damages to compensate him for the loss he has suffered through a court having

---

133. Consultation Paper 17/07/07; Final Report 15/12/09.
134. Cl. 7 and Sched. 1, Part 3.
135. Cl. 7(4).
136. See also above "Self-regulation by the insurance industry" at paras. 1.13 *et seq* and "Custom and Codes of Sale" at paras. 5.27 *et seq*.
137. [2009] EW Misc 2 (EWCC).
138. [2010] EWHC 759 (Comm).

given judgment against him in accordance with the law which was harsher than treatment he could have expected under ICOB/S. Such an action is unlikely and impractical.

13.74 ABI Statements and GISC only require consumers to answer questions at the proposal stage to the best of their knowledge and belief. They state that the policy should not be avoided for non-disclosure unless:

(1) insurers have asked clear questions about facts they consider to be material;

(2) the proposal form sets out the consequences of failing to disclose all material facts;

(3) the proposal form warns that if the proposer is unclear about whether a matter is material, he should disclose it anyway;

(4) any intermediaries involved at proposal have explained the duty to give information and the consequences of failing to do so; and

(5) the non-disclosure or misrepresentation was deliberate or reckless, not innocent.

13.75 The ABI guidance/code of practice dealing with long-term protection policies[139] says that insurers should not avoid the policy where:

(1) the degree of materiality associated with the non-disclosure is relatively low (for example where it would have increased some part of the premium by no more than 50%);

(2) the information relates only to a "severable benefit" such as a Total Permanent Disability benefit, where the claim is for critical illness; or

(3) the insurer only knows about the incorrect statement because it has conducted an unjustified trawl through medical information.

13.76 The above three points go further than the Law Commissions' draft bill, which means that the codes would prevent an insurer from pursuing remedies which would be available to it under the draft bill. The Law Commissions did not want to make compliance with codes and other industry guidance compulsory, although it is likely that the FOS will enforce them. The Law Commissions did not think that it would be appropriate for the ABI and other industry bodies to have the power to bind non-members, it did not want to bring uncertainty into the legislation as to what constituted written guidance, and it did not want to discourage the industry representatives from putting guidance in writing.[140]

13.77 The ABI code also recognises the classification of misrepresentations as innocent, negligent and deliberate/reckless and accepts that for negligent misrepresentations a proportionate remedy should be applied.

13.78 These guidelines are reflected to some extent in ICOBS 8.1.1R, 8.1.2R,[141] and 5.1.4G,[142] which superseded the general ABI and GISC codes, but there are some important omissions. For instance, ICOBS does not require insurers to ask questions about matters which the insurer finds material. The part of ICOBS 8.1.2R which is relevant to non-disclosure is as follows:

---

139. The ABI Guidance was issued in January 2008, but was promoted to the status of a Code in January 2009 called "Managing Claims for Individual and Group Life, Critical Illness and Income Protection Insurance Products", and at the same time was extended to cover group schemes. Compliance with a Code is compulsory for ABI members.

140. *Cf* Law Commission Final Report paras. 10.29–10.43.

141. ICOB 7.3.6R had provisions in similar terms to ICOBS 8.1.1R and 8.1.2R.

142. See Appendix C.

"A rejection of a consumer policyholder's claim is unreasonable, except where there is evidence of fraud, if it is for:

(1) non-disclosure of a fact material to the risk which the policyholder could not reasonably be expected to have disclosed; or

(2) non-negligent misrepresentation of a fact material to the risk; ... "

13.79 If insurers cannot show the FOS that they have used reasonable endeavours to ensure good industry practice and compliance with the applicable statement/code, the FOS may support a policyholder who blames non-disclosure on his belief that he did not have to disclose the information, or that he was following an intermediary's advice. This elevates the status of the statements/codes, even though they are different to each other and some of the Statements are obsolete. The FOS is effectively acting as industry regulator and policeman, although that should be the role of the FSA. It is of note that Lord Mustill ruled in *Pan Atlantic Insurance Co Ltd* v *Pine Top Insurance Co Ltd*[143] that discipline did not form part of the law, which was only concerned as to whether there had been a distortion of the risk.

DISTRESS AND INCONVENIENCE

13.80 The FOS may award compensation for distress and inconvenience where it finds that an insurer has wrongly avoided a policy for non-disclosure, especially in a medical context, even if the insurer was entitled to avoid in law or under the codes. In Case Study 13/6,[144] £400 was awarded for distress and inconvenience. The insured developed skin cancer but in relation to specific questions about growths and doctors' treatments over the previous five years, she did not mention that she had recently asked her GP about a mole. The GP had said it was nothing to worry about, she had had it since birth, no treatment was given and she had only mentioned it casually at the end of a consultation about something else. The FOS said that this was not a consultation about the mole, so the proposal answers were correct. A court might have applied the *contra proferentem* rule and interpreted the proposal likewise, although it would not have made the award for distress and inconvenience. That award is all the more surprising as it is not obvious that insurers' initial refusal to pay the claim was unjustified.

13.81 It seems unfair that insurers should be penalised like this for following the law, or for being unclear as to what the current, relevant good practice is, or if they have followed ICOB/ICOBS, but the FOS standards are higher. But the point about the FOS is its flexibility to award what it considers fair and reasonable in the circumstances, and if it makes an award for distress or inconvenience when an insurer has "wrongfully" avoided a policy or refused a claim, then it can probably justify its reasons.

CONVICTIONS AND SPENT CONVICTIONS

13.82 Criminal convictions may be material in law depending on the questions asked, the type of policy, the seriousness of the offence and the time between the conviction and inception, but general dishonesty may always be material.[145] Through a series of recent cases, the courts have addressed whether rumours, charges and allegations of dishonesty might also be material.[146] The law is, in summary, that a rumour/criminal charge/suspicion of dishonesty

143. [1995] 1 AC 501.

144. *Ombudsman News* Jan 2002.

145. *Insurance Corporation of the Channel Islands* v *Royal Hotel (No 2)* [1998] Lloyd's Rep IR 151.

146. *Cf, Strive Shipping Corporation* v *Hellenic Mutual War Risks Association* [2002] Lloyd's Rep IR 669; *Brotherton* v *Aseguradora Colseguros SA* [2003] Lloyd's Rep IR 758; *Drake Insurance Co* v *Provident Insurance Co* [2004] Lloyd's Rep IR 277; *North Star Shipping Ltd* v *Sphere Drake Insurance plc* [2006] EWCA Civ 378.

is a material circumstance which should be disclosed at inception, along with any evidence which might disprove the allegation.[147] If it is not so disclosed, insurers will be able to avoid the policy, unless they first receive proof of the innocence.

13.83 It is to be hoped that the FOS, if it had to deal with the same issues, would follow the law which has now been so carefully developed. This is an area where its "clear question" approach might be inappropriate. For it would be disingenuous for an assured not to disclose a conviction or an allegation of dishonesty simply because the insurer has not asked exactly the right question, especially if it had occurred to him that the insurer would want to know about it. For if he was asked why he did not disclose or volunteer such information, if he responded truthfully, he might be likely to say that he was scared that the insurer would not grant him cover. Which is precisely why the fact should be disclosed. This was why the FOS in Case Study 23/15[148] felt that a policyholder should have disclosed on renewal of a motor policy, without specifically being asked, a drink-driving disqualification, even though the renewal notice said that he needed to do nothing. For the FOS thought that any driver should know that this was something that they would need to tell their motor insurers on renewal.

13.84 Notwithstanding this, however, the FOS would be likely to require the insurer to ask a clear question before it would expect convictions to be disclosed generally, and non-motor convictions to be disclosed for motor policies. For if it is important to the insurer, then it should be set out clearly in a question.

13.85 In law, under section 4 of the Rehabilitation of Offenders Act 1974,[149] a proposer does not have to disclose a spent conviction to insurers even if asked. A question about previous convictions, offences or proceedings is to be construed as not relating to spent convictions, and insurers are not permitted in law to try to avoid a policy through the rehabilitated person's failure to disclose them. The FOS seems to follow the law in this respect. It considers that if an insurer insists on asking about spent convictions, it must effectively ignore the answers it receives. Similarly, the FOS will uphold a complaint if a policy is voided for non-disclosure of a driving licence endorsement relating to a spent conviction.

13.86 The law will allow a spent conviction to be admitted in evidence at the discretion of the court under section 7(3) of the above Act if it goes to the credit of a party to the proceedings. The situation is unlikely to come before the FOS, and if it did, the FOS has a wide discretion as to admissibility of evidence, so it would decide the matter in accordance with the circumstances, rather than the statute.

PREVIOUS LOSSES AND PREVIOUS LOSSES BECOMING "SPENT"

13.87 In law, previous losses will be material where they indicate a lack of ordinary prudence on the part of the proposer, or where they show that the proposer's business or lifestyle makes him especially liable to suffer losses of the kind with which the policy deals.

---

147. Although in *Norwich Union Insurance Ltd* v *Meisels* [2006] EWHC 2811 (QB), Tugendhat J, *obiter*, thought that allegations of criminality might not necessarily be material, and it depended on a combination of dishonesty, age and importance, and also that exculpatory material would go both to materiality and to whether the insurers would have been induced by the facts in question had they been disclosed.

148. *Ombudsman News* Dec 2002; see also "Renewals" below at paras. 13.92 *et seq.*

149. S. 4(3)(a) "any obligation imposed on any person by any rule of law . . . to disclose any matters to any other person shall not extend to requiring him to disclose a spent conviction or any circumstances ancillary to a spent conviction (whether the conviction is his own or another's)".

Proposal forms usually ask questions about previous loss, although the duty of disclosure would still exist in law if they did not.

13.88 The FOS would usually say that if there is no question on the matter, the information does not have to be volunteered. Insurers would have to prove that the question was asked. In Case Study 1/23,[150] there was no tape-recording of the disputed evidence as to whether the assured was asked about his previous claims history. The non-disclosure of the assured's one previous claim was therefore found to be innocent, and insurers had to pay the claim in full with interest.

13.89 Sometimes policies, especially life insurance, include a term which waives insurers' right to avoid for non-disclosure of an event which occurred after a certain time from inception, typically five years in a life insurance policy. Without such a term, the law does not provide a general cut-off point after which a non-disclosure or misrepresentation at inception will have no effect.

13.90 The FOS goes further and implies a cut-off point after which a non-disclosure will not be material if the proposal question for any type of policy asks whether there has been a claim, loss or accident which occurred within a certain period. Proposal forms for household policies typically ask for a claims history for the last three years, implying that any loss etc which is older than three years is not important to that particular insurer. The FOS considers[151] that the claims history will therefore not be relevant to the insurer from the moment of each renewal which puts the loss older than the three years etc mentioned in the original proposal form. So in the typical three-year period above, a loss two-and-a-half years old will only be relevant if there is another claim in the first year of cover, but will be too old to be relevant after renewal as it will be three-and-a-half years old.

13.91 The Law Commissions[152] considered whether there should be a five-year cut-off point for non-fraudulent misrepresentations under life policies, but not for any other type of policy. They decided,[153] after consultation, not to propose such a change, as opinion was split as to whether it was necessary, and insurers generally opposed the measure. Insurers were concerned that such a measure might discourage insureds from taking care to fill out proposal forms properly and might provoke deliberate non-disclosure by insureds hoping that enough time would pass for the non-disclosure to become spent. In any case, insurers remain free to include such a term in their policies if they so wish.

RENEWALS

The duty at renewal and copies of relevant information

13.92 Policyholders should be notified in good time when a policy is about to expire.[154] The law requires disclosure on renewal of any change in circumstances which might be material, whether or not the renewal notice reminds the insured. The duty is the same as at inception and the insurer is not required to provide a copy of the proposal form. If an insured gives incorrect information at renewal because he cannot remember exactly what he said at

---

150. *Ombudsman News* Jan 2001.
151. *Ombudsman News* Jan 2001.
152. Issues Paper 1, 09/06 and Consultation Paper 17/07/07.
153. Law Commissions' Final report 15/12/09, paras. 10.20–10.28.
154. ICOB 5.3.18R suggested at least 21 days before expiry of the policy. ICOBS 6.1.5R only mentions "in good time" and ICOBS 6.1.8G does not give a specific time.

inception, even if he thinks he does, he is at fault for not checking first or requesting a copy of his original proposal and the law will hold him accountable for such a mistake, however innocent. This position is tempered by the fact that, unless there has been a factual misrepresentation, courts will not rush to find that there has been a non-disclosure at renewal. As Longmore LJ said in relation to misrepresentations of opinions and intentions in *Limit No 2 Ltd* v *Axa Versicherung AG*[155]:

"I do not, for my part, consider that a court should struggle to hold that everything said at inception is to be impliedly repeated on renewal."

13.93 In spite of this, the FOS considers the law's duty of disclosure at renewal is unfair. The FOS would only penalise a non-disclosure at renewal where the insurer clearly asked for details which the insured could reasonably be expected to possess and remember. The FOS considers that the insured cannot reasonably be expected to remember all information provided at inception, so expects the insurer to provide the insured with a copy of the original proposal form, which he should be asked to check and re-confirm, or ask all the questions afresh. Otherwise the FOS will not support an insurer who declines a claim based on non-disclosure following a general question about whether anything has changed from the previous year, or an unclear question, unless it is obvious that the new information needs to be disclosed.

13.94 There are two examples where the FOS found that the assured made a culpable non-disclosure on renewal without there being a direct and clear question on that point and without details of previously provided information being available. These situations are rare, as a clear, specific question will almost always be required. In Case Study 64/9,[156] there was a clear reminder at renewal to disclose any change of health since the previous year's annual travel policy. The assured failed to disclose a heart murmur. The FOS felt that this condition was so serious that even without being sent details of previously provided information, the assured should have realised that it needed to be disclosed. In Case Study 23/15,[157] the renewal letter said to "do nothing" if the assured wanted his policy to be renewed. That is exactly what he did. There was no clear or specific question about whether he had any convictions in the previous year, but the FOS felt that the assured should still have voluntarily disclosed on renewal a drink-driving disqualification. It felt that all drivers should know that this is something that they need to tell their insurers on renewal. Direct proof that the assured had not mentioned the disqualification was unavailable because there was no recording of the relevant telephone conversation, but the FOS felt it was improbable that the insurer would have ignored the information if it had been informed, as it would not have covered him on any basis if it had known.

13.95 The Law Commissions at first suggested that insurers should be required to provide consumers with the original proposal form on renewal.[158] However, they no longer consider that this is necessary in light of the draft bill whish says that there would only be a remedy for non-disclosure in relation to a general question if a reasonable consumer would understand that the question was asking about that information.[159]

---

155. [2008] EWCA Civ 1231.
156. *Ombudsman News* Sept/Oct 2007.
157. *Supra* at para. 13.83.
158. Issue Paper 1, 06/09.
159. Consultation Paper 17/07/07.

Insurers may refuse to renew

13.96 Insurers may make a legitimate commercial decision to refuse to renew a policy at all or on the same terms, especially if an insured discloses at renewal a material change in circumstances. As long as it makes this clear to the insured, the FOS will not interfere.[160] This is subject to the FOS requiring the insurer to pay for holiday cancellation charges if the insurer refuses to continue the cover at renewal of an annual travel policy due to the disclosure of a medical condition, where a holiday has already been booked. See further below.

Renewal of annual travel policies

13.97 If cover for a certain ailment is excluded following a disclosure at renewal of an annual travel policy, but a holiday has already been booked to commence after renewal, the insured may be in a predicament. There may be no policy grounds for cancelling the holiday before renewal, particularly if the insured does not know whether the ailment disclosed will affect the travel. But he may also want to cancel the holiday rather than take the risk that he would need that cover and not have it abroad. The law offers no remedy.

13.98 However, the FOS considers it neither fair nor reasonable that insureds should be placed in this predicament. Had they realised it was a possibility, they might have taken out a single trip policy the year before instead of an annual policy. So the FOS has decided that if insurers exclude the condition post renewal, the insured may cancel the holiday before renewal at insurers' cost whether or not the policy offers such cancellation cover. Examples are Case Study 49/1[161] where the assured disclosed a cancer diagnosis and the insurer said it would not cover cancer after renewal and Case Study 74/7[162] where the cover for stroke was excluded post renewal following disclosure of the same at renewal. The FOS will ask the insurer to reimburse these cancellation costs if the insurer does not offer to, as it did in Case Studies 49/3[163] and 74/7.[164] If an insured is reminded at renewal to disclose any material change of circumstances, but fails to do so and is not acting in bad faith, the FOS still expects insurers to pay for the holiday cancellation costs as they would have been at renewal, as if there had been no non-disclosure. However, if insurers fail to remind the insured to disclose any material change of circumstances at renewal, as in Case Study 49/2,[165] the insurer will have to pay the full holiday cancellation costs when the insured cancels the holiday after renewal, rather than the lesser amount it would have been at renewal.

IS THERE A CONTINUING DUTY OF DISCLOSURE AFTER INCEPTION?

13.99 There is generally no continuing duty of disclosure outside the process up to inception and acceptance of the risk, renewal or claims, unless the risk changes so fundamentally that

---

160. See also "Jurisdiction of the FOS—Legal proceedings and commercial judgement" above at para. 2.17.
161. *Ombudsman News* Sept/Oct 2005.
162. *Ombudsman News* Dec 2008/Jan 2009.
163. *Ombudsman News* Sept/Oct 2005.
164. *Ombudsman News* Dec 2008/Jan 2009.
165. *Ombudsman News* Sept/Oct 2005. The non-disclosure here where there had been no request for information at renewal related to a heart condition which resulted in a heart attack shortly before the trip. Compare this to Case Study 64/9 above at para. 13.94 where non-disclosure of a heart murmur in the face of a request for information at renewal was culpable, even though the previous proposal details had not been provided.

the subject matter of the insurance is completely different, such as with a new car or house,[166] in which case, it would be reasonable for the insurer to vary the terms of the policy. A condition such as the right to inspect and examine any property insured, or for the insured to provide any information requested, is an innominate term, not a condition precedent, as that would turn it into a continuing duty of disclosure.[167] Breach of an innominate term may only result in payment of (nominal) damages,[168] unless the contract itself sets out a specific remedy. Although avoidance may be included in the policy as a specified remedy, it is not the automatic avoidance of a breach of utmost good faith.[169] And both the condition obliging the insured to notify certain information during the currency of the policy and the remedy set out in the policy for breach will be subject for consumers to UTCCR.

13.100 The FOS may not consider such an information notification term to be fair and reasonable, especially if the duty was not highlighted at the sales point. The most common example is where an insured is required to notify insurers of a change in health between inception of a travel policy and the start of the holiday. In Case Study 36/9,[170] the FOS found such a clause arguably unfair and insurers met the holiday cancellation charges which they had originally refused to do because the cancellation related to a medical condition which occurred between inception and the start of the trip. The FOS said that it was acceptable to exclude pre-existing medical conditions, but unfair to exclude illness between inception and the start of the holiday. In Case Study 64/6,[171] the FOS found a similar notification of health changes condition too onerous, especially as the insurer wanted to withdraw cover for any claims arising from a newly disclosed medical condition. Therefore, the insured did not suffer a penalty for failing to disclose a temporary loss of vision which occurred between inception of the cover and the holiday, and the insurer was required to pay the medical expenses claim for a heart attack suffered abroad.

13.101 The FOS expects an annual policy to provide cover for the whole year, including cover for any condition notified during the policy period, even if this changes the risk during the currency of the policy.[172] The FOS generally finds a continuing disclosure obligation once a holiday has been booked so inherently unfair, that in Case Study 64/8,[173] insurers notified of cancer just before a holiday-wedding departure were penalised for refusing to cover any cancer-related illness during the trip and for offering instead to pay the holiday cancellation charges. Insurers were ordered to reimburse the cost of the alternative policy which the insured had to find at short notice, plus £200 for distress and inconvenience. However, if the insured travels against medical advice the FOS would support an exclusion for a new medical condition notified since inception.[174] And if people delay cancelling their holiday if they become too ill to travel, the FOS may allow an insurer to refuse to continue cover for the condition notified, to offer to refund a deposit for a holiday cancelled at the point the condition is (or presumably should have been) notified, and to refuse to pay any additional sum for later cancellation due to the condition notified. This was its approach in Case Study

---

166. In *Ansari* v *New India Assurance Ltd* [2009] EWCA Civ 93, the sprinklers being turned off was a fundamental change to a commercial property insurance which should have been notified under the continuing disclosure obligations of the policy.
167. *Scottish Coal Co Ltd* v *Royal and Sun Alliance plc* [2008] EWHC 880 (Comm).
168. See below "Breach of Warranty and Other Conditions—The law" at paras. 14.1 *et seq.*
169. *Hussain* v *Brown (No 2)* (unreported) 1996.
170. *Ombudsman News* Apr 2004.
171. *Ombudsman News* Sept/Oct 2007.
172. Presumably this would be so unless the change was fundamental.
173. *Ombudsman News* Sept/Oct 2007.
174. *Ombudsman News* Dec 2006/Jan 2007.

7/6[175] where a broken foot was notified but the insured refused to cancel the holiday until later, when the cancellation charges had increased.

13.102 The FOS does not discuss in its reports the basis for its assessment of unfair in the above case studies and does not mention UTCCR.

13.103 The FOS interpreted narrowly the obligation to disclose a "change in health" after inception of an annual travel policy, so that it did not include a change in medication.[176] (Even if it had, the FOS would have treated it as an onerous term which should have been specifically brought to the insured's attention before inception before it had any chance of being upheld by the FOS.) As there was no definition of the phrase in the policy, a court would probably have similarly interpreted the term strictly under the *contra proferentem* rule.

13.104 An example of the FOS approach outside of annual travel policies was included in the Law Commissions' 2009 survey of 47 FOS case studies.[177] An insured was convicted of common assault about half-way through the term of his household building and contents policy. The insurer had purported to avoid the contract for non-disclosure of the conviction, and so tried to avoid paying a water damage claim. The FOS required the insurer to reinstate the policy and deal with the claim, as the obligation to disclose the conviction was on renewal, not mid-term, and even then, only in response to a clear question.

NEW TERMS ON RENEWAL OR ON CHANGE OF INSURER

13.105 Insurers must notify an insured of any change of terms on renewal,[178] and the notification must be clear. Otherwise the FOS may not hold the insured bound by the change.[179] In Case Study 1/26,[180] the insured had been sent details of insurance cover being offered for his second year of owning a particular car, but without details of any differences from the original policy being drawn to his attention, and the covering letter had used the word renew. The FOS found that the insured had been misled into thinking that he was renewing on the same terms as his previous policy. The insurer had to deal with the claim for a written-off car as if the original policy applied. Therefore the insured received the cost of a new car in accordance with the terms of his original policy, rather than the market value for his old car in accordance with the terms of the new policy, plus interest and £25 for out-of-pocket expenses. In law, an estoppel might arise in this situation, where the actions of the insurer or his agent misrepresent the position to the insured, on which he reasonably relies to his detriment in that he takes out this policy rather than another.

13.106 The FOS expects insurers to play an active role in notifying employees, or requiring the employer to, of all changes in the terms of a group policy on renewal and if there has been a change of insurer. Insurers may not simply delegate this responsibility to the employer as they might be able to in law.[181] The FOS may not otherwise support insurers who refuse a claim based on a term which was changed at renewal but not highlighted for

---

175. *Ombudsman News* July 2001.
176. Case Study 64/7, *Ombudsman News* Sept/Oct 2007.
177. Final Report 15/12/09.
178. *Cf* ICOBS 6.1.5R and 6.1.6G.
179. For how the Law Commissions propose to deal with misrepresentations before a variation, see paras. 6.101–6.104 and Appendix B (B28–B45) of its Final Report 15/12/09 and Part 2 of Sched. 1 of the Draft Bill.
180. *Ombudsman News* Jan 2001.
181. *Cf* ICOBS 6.1.12G which states that the insurer should provide appropriate information to the employer and tell it to pass the information on to the relevant employees.

the employee. In Case Study 13/2,[182] the new insurer had to pay for the employee's elective caesarean, even though the new policy did not cover this, as the original policy did, and no one had told either the employee or the employer before the birth, of any differences in cover. The FOS is likely to find insurers responsible for notifying employees whom they are specifically told would be adversely affected by any change of terms. In Case Study 13/1,[183] a new insurer excluded mental ill-health without telling at least the one employee it had been informed would be affected, and without requiring the employer to tell him. The employee could have taken out his own policy which did cover him for mental illness if he had known he would not be covered under his employer's policy, so he had been prejudiced by the insurer's actions. The employee made a claim for mental illness in the first year of the new cover, and the FOS asked the new insurer to pay the benefits during the first year of cover.

MISREPRESENTATIONS

(a) The law

13.107 Misrepresentation of a material fact will afford grounds for avoidance under section 20(1) MIA, whether or not the proposer was aware that his statement was incorrect. The definition of materiality is the same as in section 18 MIA for non-disclosure. However, under section 20(5), a representation as to expectation or belief (as opposed to fact) is true if it is made in good faith, and following *Economides* v *Commercial Union Assurance Co*[184] it does not have to be based on reasonable grounds. In *Economides*, a 21-year old man had undervalued the contents of his flat when his parents moved in with him. The Court of Appeal found that his statement was one of opinion rather than fact, and so because it was honestly made in good faith, it did not have to be reasonable. The court here seems to be using the distinction between fact and belief to protect consumers who make an innocent and honest mistake.

(b) The FOS

13.108 The FOS approaches misrepresentations in the same way as non-disclosures, so the discussion above applies here. It looks at the sales position, determines on the evidence if there was a misrepresentation, decides if it was fraudulent/deliberate, innocent, reckless or inadvertent, and applies the remedies as it does for non-disclosure.

   13.109 Examples are where the insured falsely purports to be the main user of a car with a young driver as a named driver, so as to avoid the higher premium of insuring the young driver as the main user. In Case Study 7/18,[185] the FOS supported the insurer's avoiding of the policy *ab initio* in this situation, as the insurer would not have offered cover if it had

182. *Ombudsman News* Jan 2002.
183. *Ombudsman News* Jan 2002.
184. [1998] QB 587. See also the more recent cases of *Rendall* v *Combined Insurance Company of America* [2005] EWHC 678 (Comm), where an estimate of travel days on the basis of which reinsurance of business travel insurance was issued was not an assertion of specific fact but a representation of expectation or belief which was made in good faith; and *Zeller* v *British Caymanian Insurance Co Ltd* [2008] UKPC 4, where the assured was held not to have misrepresented his state of health because he did not know about the heart murmur and raised cholesterol that his doctor had never told him about. He had answered the proposal questions completely and correctly to the best of his knowledge and belief.
185. *Ombudsman News* July 2001.

known who was the main driver. In Case Study 7/19,[186] the insurer would have increased the premium if there had been a truthful representation at the outset, so the FOS thought that the insurer's offer of a proportional settlement based on the premium it would have charged if it had known the truth, was fair. So the insurer paid 52% of the total claim for the stolen car. It is not clear why these were not deliberate/fraudulent misrepresentations which would lead to avoidance under the FOS rules, rather than inadvertent ones, which would lead to a remedy based on what the insurer would have done if it had known the true facts. However, Case Study 63/9[187] is an example where the FOS found that there had been a deliberate/fraudulent misrepresentation. There the husband had been recorded as stating that his wife was going to be the main driver, with his daughter as a named driver. He made a claim following a minor accident during which his daughter had been driving. During insurer's investigations, she admitted that the car had been insured in her mother's name as it had been cheaper than insuring it in her own name. The law would have allowed insurers to avoid in all these cases.

(c) Law Commissions' proposals

13.110 The Law Commissions do not wish to retain the distinction between a misrepresentation of fact and one of expectation or belief for consumers. They want both statements of fact and those of opinion to be made with reasonable care. And they also want remedies other than avoidance to be available, depending on the type of misrepresentation. Clauses 11(1) and 11(2) of the draft bill therefore disapply sections 18 to 20 MIA 1906 to consumer insurance contracts.

COMMENTARY

13.111 The FOS has an innovative approach to non-disclosure and misrepresentation, and even where it could apply legal tools to minimise any harshness of result, it will apply its own approach instead.

  13.112 As the Law Commissions note,[188] the current position on non-disclosure and misrepresentation for consumers is "needlessly complex, confusing and inaccessible", with overlapping layers of law, regulation and ombudsman discretion. There is a need for reform and as Scottish Re put it,[189] "reform should also provide guidance to the FOS on what Parliament considers to be a reasonable balance between the interests of the consumer and the insurance industry". Perhaps even if the draft consumer insurance bill is never enacted, the Law Commissions' conclusions should be adequate guidance for the FOS as to where the balance should lie. The FOS agrees the need for statutory reform and is against the view that ombudsman discretion is adequate to ameliorate the harshness of the law.[190] In this context the Law Commissions quote it as saying:

"Our preference is for our decisions to be based on law and for our decisions on what is 'fair and reasonable' to coincide with the law. It is much easier to defend and justify our decisions when they are consistent with the legal position and it is advantageous to all our potential users if our decisions

---

186. *Ombudsman News* July 2001.
187. *Ombudsman News* July/Aug 2007.
188. Summary of Responses—Consumer issues—28/05/08.
189. Summary of Responses—Consumer issues—28/05/08, para. 2.3.
190. Summary of Responses—Consumer issues—28/05/08, para. 2.6.

can be predicted . . . . We also take the view that it is logically and morally unjustified to hang on to old law if it is widely agreed that the law is bad and no longer serves any useful purpose."

13.113 Some insurers argued[191] that once the law had been changed, the FOS should be required to make decisions that followed it rather than by reference to a wider concept of what is fair and reasonable. The Law Commissions reported that the FOS responded to this argument by stating that the industry had no reason to fear that it would use law reform as a stepping stone to make further changes in favour of consumers. The reforms by and large reflected its current approach and it had no reason to change this. In handling consumer credit, pensions and investment the FOS said that it strove to follow the law and regulations. If the insurance law were updated, it said that it would be able to follow the same approach in insurance.

13.114 However, as shown in this book there are other areas where the FOS does not follow the law, and may not even realise it.

13.115 It is telling that in another context,[192] the FOS commented that even if the Law Commissions decided not to include a certain judicial discretion in the new insurance statute, the FOS could and would operate such a discretion in light of its overriding obligation to reach a decision that is fair and reasonable. This shows that it has only a limited intention or ability to follow even an amended law.

191. Summary of Responses—Consumer issues—28/05/08, para. 2.8.
192. Summary of Responses—Consumer issues—28/05/08, para. 2.143, discussing a discretion to prevent an insurer avoiding a policy where it would not have taken the risk had it known of the matter in question, but where the policyholder's fault was minor.

CHAPTER 14

BREACH OF WARRANTY AND OTHER CONDITIONS

THE LAW

Term classification

14.1 Sometimes the policy itself will stipulate the effects of breach of any particular term. When it does not, the court will decide the type of term that has been breached, and apply the relevant consequences. Breach of warranty will discharge the insurer automatically from liability from the date of breach—see further below at paragraphs 14.5 *et seq*. A warranty has a special meaning in an insurance policy and is different to a warranty in a non-insurance context. Non-compliance with a condition precedent will, depending on the particular details of the requirements not complied with, prevent the risk from attaching, terminate the risk as a whole or prevent a claim being made. Serious breach of a fundamental term can lead to repudiation of the whole contract, but it is rare that any term is considered so fundamental. Any other condition is an innominate term, a breach of which can only lead to a claim in damages, although such damages are likely to be nominal as it is usually hard to prove that the breach caused any particular and quantifiable loss to insurers.[1] One other option put forward in *Alfred McAlpine plc* v *BAI (Run-Off)*,[2] is no longer good law.[3] That was that a serious breach of an innominate term, so as to seriously prejudice the insurer's position, could result in repudiation of the claim only, and not the whole contract.

Breach of a notification clause

14.2 Because of the harsh effect if a condition precedent has been breached, the courts will generally refrain from holding that a notification of loss provision amounts to a condition precedent, even in the face of express terminology.[4] And if it is held to be a condition precedent, its obligations will be interpreted loosely. So in *Loyaltrend Ltd* v *Creechurch Dedicated Ltd*,[5] a condition precedent to liability that immediate notice of any damage be given to the insurer was interpreted to mean that immediate notice should be given at the point that a reasonable assured would have been aware of the damage falling for notification. If the notification clause is not a condition precedent, the remedy for its breach under the current

---

1. *Friends Provident Life and Pensions* v *Sirius International Insurance* [2005] EWCA Civ 601.
2. [2000] 1 Lloyd's Rep 437.
3. *Cf, Friends Provident Life and Pensions* v *Sirius International Insurance, supra*.
4. *Re Bradley and Essex & Suffolk Accident Indemnity Society* [1912] 1 KB 415.
5. [2010] EWHC 425 (Comm) on the basis of *Laker Vent Engineering Ltd* v *Templeton Insurance Ltd* [2009] EWCA Civ 62.

law would usually be nominal damages under *Friends Provident Life and Pensions* v *Sirius International Insurance*.[6]

No materiality is required for a breach of warranty

14.3 The definition of warranties under section 33(1) MIA is wide and may apply to past or existing facts or to future conduct. Section 33(3) requires strict compliance with a warranty, whether or not it is material to the risk.[7] An example would be *Forsikringsaktieselskapet Vesta* v *Butcher*[8] where the breach of a warranty to provide a 24-hour watch on the fish farm was fatal to the unrelated claim for storm damage. By comparison, a non-disclosure or misrepresentation would have to be material before insurers could avoid a policy under sections 17–20 MIA.

Basis of the contract clauses

14.4 "Basis of the contract" clauses in proposal forms, once signed by the insured, turn all statements made on the proposal form into warranties whose truth the insured effectively guarantees. They typically say that the assured has answered all questions in the proposal form to the best of his knowledge and belief and that the answers form a basis of the contract of insurance or that the proposer warrants the truth of all answers given. These seemingly innocuous words create a warranty, which means that if there is a false statement in the proposal form, even if it is an innocent mistake, the risk will be automatically terminated. Most consumers would not understand the technical effect of such wording, and so these clauses have been banned in the appropriate industry codes for consumers and are rarely used in consumer insurance. It would be unlikely that the FOS would uphold them.

Automatic discharge from the date of breach of warranty

14.5 Section 33(3) MIA states that the insurer is discharged from liability as from the date of the breach of warranty. Under section 34(2) and *Bank of Nova Scotia* v *Hellenic Mutual War Risks ("The Good Luck")*[9] a contract will be automatically discharged from the date of the breach, even if the breach is later remedied before any loss.

14.6 An untrue warranty of fact at inception will result in a repudiated contract and repayment of the whole premium, even if the true statement would have decreased the risk insured.[10] This is contrary to the effect of a non-disclosure which decreases the risk. See paragraph 13.37 above under "Fraudulent and deliberate non-disclosure".

---

6. See term classification above at para. 14 1.
7. See Appendix G below for the text of the relevant parts of MIA.
8. [1989] 1 All ER 402.
9. [1992] 1 AC 233. There Lord Goff relied on the precise wording of s. 33(3) MIA to decide that a contract will be automatically discharged from the date of a breach of warranty. This was a marine case, but all subsequent non-marine cases have assumed that automatic discharge applies in the non-marine context too. This was expressly recognised by the Court of Appeal in *HIH* v *New Hampshire* [2001] EWCA Civ 735, which related to pecuniary, rather than marine loss.
10. *Dawsons Ltd* v *Bonnin* [1922] 2 AC 413. In this case, the proposal form for a furniture removal firm inadvertently said that the lorry would be garaged in a high risk theft area, when in fact it was garaged in the lower risk outskirts of the city. The proposal contained a basis of the contract clause, and the House of Lords held that this converted the statements into warranties, which meant that any mistake on the proposal form, whether or not material and however it affected the risk, could be used by insurers to refuse to pay all claims under the policy.

14.7 A warranty can turn a representation about the present position into a continuing obligation in the future, so that the risk incepts, but automatically terminates from the date of the breach, although the insurer retains and collects the full premium, e.g. *Hales* v *Reliance Fire Assurance*.[11] There the claimant said in the proposal form that the only inflammable material it stored on the business premises was fuel for cigarette lighters, but failed to mention that once a year they also bought fireworks for sale. McNair J held that this answer must be regarded as a warranty relating to the position at the date of the proposal as well as to the position throughout the insurance. Although the breach was material to the risk and relevant to the fire in question, the draconian effect of the law would have been the same if this had been otherwise.

Waiver only by estoppel for a breach of warranty

14.8 Because of the immediate and automatic effects of a breach of warranty, an insurer cannot waive the breach by electing to affirm the contract as it can for a misrepresentation.[12] It can only waive the breach by estoppel, where the insured shows that the insurer has made an unequivocal representation by words or conduct that it knew of its legal rights, but would not rely on them, and the insured relied on the representation to his detriment, for instance by not taking out another policy. In *HIH* v *AXA*[13] there was no waiver by estoppel because it was not until the Court of Appeal in *HIH* v *New Hampshire Insurance Co*[14] ruled that the term relating to the number of films which would be made was in fact a warranty, that the reinsurers appreciated that they had a defence based on breach of warranty.

How the courts avoid the draconian effects of the law of warranties

14.9 The above outline on the law of warranties shows that the effect of a breach can be harsh, especially if the breach was not material or related in any way to the claim, or if it rests on the technical effects of a basis of the contract clause about which the insured had no idea.

14.10 Through UTCCR, a court can consider unfair and refuse to give effect to a term which has not been individually negotiated in a consumer contract and causes a significant imbalance in the parties' rights and obligations. It may be that many warranties will cause such an imbalance, especially those created through basis of the contract clauses.

14.11 Where UTCCR does not apply, the courts may use policy construction to protect against draconian effects. The courts construe warranties strictly against the party who has put them forward, usually the insurer, as follows:

(1) A warranty could be interpreted as only applying to past facts or those at inception, but not to the future. In *Hussain* v *Brown*,[15] a warranty that the premises were fitted with an intruder alarm needed only to be true at inception. The court refused to imply a continuing warranty from a statement of fact at inception, so it held that the warranty was not broken when the alarm was not actually set.

---

11. [1960] 2 Lloyd's Rep 391.
12. *The Good Luck (supra)*; *HIH Casualty & General Insurance Ltd* v *AXA Corporate Solutions* [2002] Lloyd's Rep IR 325, as approved by the Court of Appeal [2003] 1 Lloyd's Rep IR 1.
13. *Supra*.
14. [2001] EWCA Civ 735.
15. [1996] 1 Lloyd's Rep 627.

(2) The wording could be interpreted as requiring the insured to know of the situation and fail to remedy it promptly before that insured could breach the warranty. In *Melik* v *Norwich Union*,[16] Woolf J held that a warranty which required that a burglar alarm be kept in full operation at all times when the property was unattended implied that before there could be a breach, the insured must be aware of the facts which gave rise to the alarm not being in efficient order. The judge distinguished the obligation to keep the alarm in a certain way to the obligation for it to be in that way, which wording might have had a stricter interpretation. So when the alarm became disabled following the cutting of telephone wires outside the premises, there was no breach of warranty, because the duty to keep the alarm in efficient working order did not extend to protecting it against external interference with the system. The requirement in the warranties in *AC Ward & Sons Ltd* v *Catlin (Five) Ltd*[17] promptly to remedy any defects in the burglar alarm and other protections, *obiter*, had the same effect as "kept" in *Melik*. So there was no breach of warranty when in that case the alarms and protections were not activated due to various technical faults when a robbery of commercial premises occurred, as the wording imposed no more than an obligation promptly to remedy defects known to the assured and on the facts the insured had not known of the defects.[18]

(3) In *US Trading Ltd* v *Axa Insurance Co Ltd*,[19] HHJ Simon Brown QC stated, *obiter*, that a warranty was generally to be construed as satisfied if the assured puts in place arrangements to have work done even though the work is not actually done.

(4) The warranty might be interpreted as relevant only to some sections of a severable policy. In *Printpak* v *AGF Insurance Ltd*,[20] the court found an alarm warranty only applied to the theft not the fire risk, so that the fire was still covered.

(5) The clause may not be a true warranty but merely descriptive of the risk. In *Farr* v *Motor Traders Mutual Insurance*,[21] cover only existed when the risk was as described (when the taxi was only used for one shift a day), and was suspended on the limited occasions when the warranty was not adhered to.

(6) The wording of the warranty may not apply to the facts in question. In *Provincial Insurance Co* v *Morgan*[22] the insured had warranted that their lorry would be used for coal, although on the day in question, but not at the time of the incident, it had been used to transport other goods. The warranty was held to mean only that transporting coal was to be the normal use, which was the case, and transporting other goods would not terminate liability under the policy.

(7) If a term is a warranty, it will be interpreted very narrowly and *contra proferentem* even in a commercial situation, so as to escape having a draconian effect, following *Pratt* v *Aigaion Insurance*.[23] The idea is that the more unreasonable the result,

---

16. [1980] 1 Lloyd's Rep 523.

17. [2009] EWHC 3122 (Comm). The same was held by HHJ Mackie QC in the application for summary judgment he refused at [2008] EWHC 3585 (Comm) which decision was upheld by the Court of Appeal at [2009] EWCA Civ 1098.

18. Another finding of fact was that some of the protections said to be defective were not protections that existed when the insurance incepted, so they fell outside the scope of the warranty.

19. Unreported 17 March 2008.

20. [1999] Lloyd's Rep IR 542.

21. [1920] 3 KB 669.

22. [1933] AC 240.

23. [2008] EWCA Civ 1314.

the more unlikely it was that the parties could have intended it. In *Pratt,* a crewing warranty on the face of it required the vessel to be manned at all times. Sir Anthony Clarke MR found that because it was common ground that the parties could not have intended the warranty to be interpreted strictly, and could not have intended the crew to be in literal continuous presence, even when the vessel was docked, the parties had intended the warranty to be qualified. The precise scope of this qualification was unclear, so the warranty was ambiguous and should be interpreted *contra proferentem.* It was not clear that the warranty was intended to apply when the vessel was safely tied up alongside the quay with its generator running, as was the case when the fire occurred, and so it should not be construed as doing so. This is not so much the court re-writing the contract, but investigating what the parties must have intended by the words they used. If they had intended a draconian effect, then the court said that it was up to the parties to stipulate for it in clear terms. In order to try to avoid a strict interpretation like this being applied following *Pratt,* the insurers in *AC Ward & Sons Ltd* v *Catlin (Five) Ltd*[24] unsuccessfully argued that terms relating to burglar alarms and other property protections were not warranties but suspensory conditions, so that the cover did not apply when the burglar alarms etc were not working. HHJ Mackie QC found that the clauses were true warranties and not suspensory conditions as they were labelled warranties,[25] and in this case that was all that was required. He added that the draconian effect of a provision will be relevant to the factual matrix within which the policy was to be construed. Rather than interpret the warranties, the Court of Appeal, ruling on the summary judgment application, pointed out where the warranties lacked clarity, the implication being the expectation of an interpretation in line with *Pratt* when the matter reverted to the High Court for a decision on the substantive issues.

(8) At its most extreme, a court might disregard clear language and call a warranty a suspensive condition in order to avoid a draconian result. In *Kler Knitwear* v *Lombard General Insurance Co,*[26] a sprinkler system was not inspected 30 days after renewal as warranted, but 60 days late, although it was working at the time of, and unconnected to, the storm damage claim. The court held that the policy coverage was suspended until the sprinkler system was inspected, but was in place thereafter.

14.12 The court's approach should discourage insurers from taking purely technical points or using warranties unreasonably, although it cannot protect against every harsh decision and the Law Commissions propose amendments.[27]

THE FOS APPROACH

Term classification

14.13 The FOS approach is entirely different to that of a court. It does not ask how a term should be classified—as a condition precedent, an innominate term or a warranty—and then

---

24. [2008] EWHC 3585 (Comm)—application for summary judgment not granted, and this decision was upheld by the Court of Appeal at [2009] EWCA Civ 1098. Also see *supra.*
25. Although that had not helped the position in *Kler Knitwear* v *Lombard General Insurance* below.
26. [2000] Lloyd's Rep IR 47.
27. See below at paras. 14.27 *et seq.*

apply the appropriate consequences of breach. It would be clearer if it did. Instead, it concentrates on what it thinks the effect should be of the breach in question and then whether the complainant qualifies for the extra protection as a consumer that ICOBS and/or the relevant industry guide provide.

14.14 So in Case Study 31/5,[28] it effectively found that providing a death certificate for a parrot was a condition precedent to liability. Instead of saying this, it said that the insured breached "an important and material condition", by not providing a death certificate, which meant that the insurer could not verify the cause of death for the accidental death benefit, and so did not have to pay the claim. Under the terms of the policy in Case Study 79/6,[29] the insured should have obtained his insurer's approval before allowing and paying for repairs to his car. The FOS did not think his failure to do so was enough in the circumstances to prevent the claim being met. The issue for the FOS was whether the damage was an insured loss or not. Again there is no discussion about the type of term breached and whether it was a condition precedent to liability. In Case Study 74/9,[30] it ignored the label of condition precedent to certain security conditions for a property, and went on to consider its own test of causal connection between breach and loss which it applies to consumers facing allegations of breach of any type of term.

Causal connection between breach and loss: consumers

14.15 Another major difference between the way that the FOS deals with a breach of a term (whatever its categorisation) and how a court would, is that the FOS requires a causal connection for consumers between breach of any term and the loss. This is an additional protection which the FOS only applies to consumers. A "consumer" is defined[31] as "any natural person who is acting for purposes which are outside his trade or profession". Anyone else is a "commercial customer".[32]

14.16 Clause 2(b)(iii) of SGIP (one of the ABI's Statements of Practice now obsolete) says that unless fraud is involved, the loss must be connected to the breach of warranty or condition before the insurer can repudiate liability to indemnify a policyholder. SLIP for long-term insurance or COB/S have similar provisions, as do ICOBS 8.1.1R and 8.1.2R(3):

ICOBS 8.1.1 Rule:
An insurer must:

(1) handle claims promptly and fairly;
(2) provide reasonable guidance to help a policyholder make a claim and appropriate information on its progress;
(3) not unreasonably reject a claim (including by terminating or avoiding a policy); and
(4) settle claims promptly once settlement terms are agreed.

ICOBS 8.1.2 Rule:
A rejection of a consumer policyholder's claim is unreasonable, except where there is evidence of fraud, if it is for:

---

28. *Ombudsman News* Sept 2003.
29. *Ombudsman News* Sept/Oct 2009.
30. *Ombudsman News* Dec 2008/Jan 2009.
31. A "consumer" under ICOBS 2.1.1G is equivalent to the "retail customer" of ICOB 7.3.
32. The "commercial customer" of ICOBS was basically a "retail handler" under ICOB.

. . .

(3) breach of warranty or condition unless the circumstances of the claim are connected to the breach and unless (for a pure protection contract[33]):

    (a) under a "life of another" contract, the warranty relates to a statement of fact concerning the life to be assured and, if the statement had been made by the life to be assured under an "own life" contract, the insurer could have rejected the claim under this rule; or

    (b) the warranty is material to the risk and was drawn to the customer's attention before the conclusion of the contract.

14.17 That the insurer can repudiate a contract does not fit with the legal concept that an insurer is automatically discharged from liability for breach of warranty. In any case, the codes/statements will not protect an insured from an insurer repudiating on technical grounds and without a causal connection, as it is entitled to under the law, if it suspects but cannot prove fraud. It is uncertain how the FOS would respond to such a scenario.

14.18 In Case Study 4/22,[34] the FOS applied SGIP and required the insurer to meet the claim because there was no evidence of a causal connection between the caravan owner's failure to comply with all the required security conditions, and this particular theft. The report does not mention what sort of term this was. A court would have established this first. If it was not a warranty or a condition precedent to cover, then it was a mere innominate term, breach of which might result in a claim for damages by the insurer only if there was a causal connection between the breach and the theft so that insurers could argue that they had suffered a loss as a result of the breach.

14.19 By comparison, in Case Study 4/23,[35] there was a causal connection between the breach (failure to buy a lock for the caravan) and the theft, and because the insured knew of his obligation but had failed to deal with it, the FOS rejected his complaint. Does this mean that over and above the requirements of the relevant statement/code, the insured has to be aware of his obligations? Again there is no mention in the report as to what type of condition this was, but a court would have been likely to end up with the same result.

Treating businesses like consumers

14.20 The FOS realises that if it only followed the statements/ICOBS, its approach to breaches of warranty/condition would protect consumers but not those small businesses who within its own logic would also need protection. So it treats some businesses as consumers in this context. However, until the FOS decides, no-one knows for sure whether a business is going to get the added consumer protection, namely in this context, that the loss must be related to the breach of warranty or condition before the breach will affect policy coverage.

14.21 The FOS looks at the nature and resources of a business to decide whether its understanding of insurance issues is similar to that of a consumer, and expects the insurer to do the same.[36] A business is more likely to obtain consumer protection if the interest disputed is commonly covered under personal insurance, the policyholder is self-employed, without

---

33. I.e. a payment protection policy—a single premium policy providing benefits on death or incapacity. See above "payment protection insurance" at paras. 5.35 *et seq.*

34. *Ombudsman News* Apr 2001.

35. *Ombudsman News* Apr 2001.

36. Case Study 74/9, *Ombudsman News* Dec 2008/Jan 2009.

experience in financial and legal matters and/or without any easy access to expert advice (e.g. from brokers) on insurance matters, and it should have been clear to the insurer or intermediary that the business was an unsophisticated buyer of insurance. A business is less likely to be treated as a consumer if it is a limited company, employs a number of staff, rents substantial business premises, has detailed legal agreements with suppliers and/or could reasonably be expected to have a greater understanding of business issues than a private individual, for instance in view of the director's previous employment, perhaps as a solicitor or insurance broker.

14.22 In Case Study 39/1[37] a small café was burgled. The FOS treated it as a commercial entity as it employed four full-time staff, was a limited company and had access to expert advice from insurance brokers through whom it bought the policy and made the claim. The claim for the loss, including part which was not caused by the breach of security warranty, was not paid and the complaint was rejected. By comparison, in Case Study 74/9,[38] the FOS found that a small graphic design business should be treated as a consumer, as it had a modest turnover and only two part-time employees. So the claim had to be met because the breach of a condition precedent (that the doors should be made of solid wood) was unconnected to the theft (the front door was forced off its hinges, so ingress would have been achieved regardless of the construction of the door).

14.23 However, these tests do not consider the business's actual knowledge and understanding, only what the FOS would expect from them. There are many large, well-resourced companies, who are clueless about insurance and do not employ brokers. Even if a business does understand the effects of a warranty or basis of the contract clause, it may not have the bargaining power to exclude warranties from its policy, so is subject to the same harshness of the law which the FOS is trying to avoid. Should a knowledgeable consumer be treated as a business? If the FOS is going to apply its own rules, perhaps it should apply them to everyone over whom it has jurisdiction in the interest of certainty. It is strange that the FOS will treat the same claim differently according to whether it is made by a commercial entity. The law of warranties does not try to find a dividing line between different types of businesses.

Contra proferentem

14.24 None of the warranty case law referred to above is mentioned in any of the *Ombudsman News* reports. Perhaps ombudsmen never refer to it at all. However, the FOS uses the same tool as is used in the case law, namely interpreting a warranty *contra proferentem*, that is, interpreting the wording narrowly as against the party who was responsible for its drafting. An example is in Case Study 7/23[39] where the FOS had to decide whether a commercial contractor had satisfied the policy condition of "suitable fire extinguishing appliances to be kept available" by the provision of a spray bottle. There was disagreement on the evidence about the spray bottle's precise size, but the FOS considered that whichever it was of the two sizes alleged, it satisfied the terms of the condition. For the policy did not contain any guidance on the insurer's criteria and the FOS did not agree that the bottle was so obviously inadequate that it was unsuitable as a fire-extinguishing appliance.

---

37. *Ombudsman News* Aug 2004.
38. *Supra.*
39. *Ombudsman News* July 2001.

Basis of the contract clauses

14.25 Although the industry guides SGIP and SLIP banned basis of the contract clauses, the FSA did not in either its ICOB or ICOBS. There is no explanation and reasons of freedom of contract are unlikely. There have been no reported FOS cases involving basis of the contract clauses, possibly because insurers do not in practice tend to use or rely on them in consumer contracts. However, it is unlikely that the FOS will uphold the draconian effects of a technical breach based on a basis of the contract clause either for general or life insurance, which approach would therefore be stricter than both the law and the FSA, although in line with industry practice for consumers.

Late notification of claims conditions

14.26 In Case Study 39/2[40] a self-employed forest management adviser with no employees gave late notification to insurers of a public liability claim made against him. The notification was given 18 months after a third party was injured by a falling tree. This was when the assured first realised that the owner of the estate was passing on the claim to him, as it was spelt out to him in a letter from the estate owner's insurers that he received. The FOS felt that in view of his circumstances, he should be treated as a consumer, and that it was not reasonable to expect him to know that he was potentially liable and so to notify insurers any earlier. Insurers had to ignore the late notification and deal with the claim. The FOS report does not explore the type of term that was allegedly breached or mention any case law. Nor does it discuss whether there should be a remedy for the late notification, although perhaps it did not need to if it considered that there had been no late notification at all.

LAW COMMISSIONS' PROPOSALS

14.27 There is much wrong with the law of insurance warranties. It may be unfair that compliance must be strict and cannot be remedied in retrospect, and that materiality to the risk and causation of the loss are irrelevant. It is a "major mischief",[41] that general statements in a proposal form can be turned into warranties through a basis of the contract clause, and that the consequences of even an entirely innocent breach are draconian and probably unexpected by most insureds.

14.28 There has been much past and recent discussion to amend the law relating to warranties.[42] The only proposal that is included in the Law Commissions' draft bill is the abolition of basis of the contract clauses in consumer contracts.[43] The Law Commissions felt that that the law on consumer warranties should be consistent with the law on business warranties, and so should be dealt with together in a separate bill still to come.

14.29 Some of the Law Commissions' ideas in relation to warranties include[44]:

(1) abolishing basis of the contract clauses in business contracts as well;

40. *Ombudsman News* Aug 2004.
41. The 1980 Law Commission.
42. E.g. Law Commission Issues Paper 1 (28/09/06) and 2 (28/11/06), Consultation Paper 17/07/07 and Final report and draft bill 15/12/09. In some countries like Australia and New Zealand, the law relating to warranties has already been reformed. See Professor Merkin's report for the Law Commission, "Reforming Insurance Law: Is there a Case for Reverse Transportation?" published in 2007 and available through the Law Commission's website.
43. *Cf* Final report and cl. 6 of the draft bill 15/12/09.
44. Consultation Paper 17/07/07.

(2) treating pre-inception statements of past or current facts as representations, rather than warranties, with any remedy for a misrepresentation depending on whether it was made deliberately, recklessly, negligently or innocently;

(3) enshrining into mandatory law the existing FOS guidelines for consumers relating to warranties as to the future (not mere exceptions), namely that:

   (i) a warranty should be set out in writing;

   (ii) an insurer may only refuse a claim for a breach of warranty if it has taken sufficient steps to bring the requirement to the consumer's attention; and

   (iii) the consumer's claim should be paid if he can prove on the balance of probabilities that the breach did not contribute to the loss.

(4) for businesses, the default rules should not be those set out in MIA, but instead:

   (i) a warranty should be set out in writing;

   (ii) subject to the parties making express agreements to the contrary (which would in turn be subject to controls if they appeared in insurers' standard term contracts), a business's claim should be paid if it can prove on the balance of probabilities that the breach did not contribute to the loss; and

   (iii) a breach of warranty would give the insurer the right to terminate cover for the future, rather than an automatic discharge from liability.

CHAPTER 15

LEGAL EXPENSES INSURANCE

DEFINITION

15.1 Legal expenses insurance, defined in FSMA 2000,[1] is a before-the-event insurance against the costs of litigation. Typically, it covers the legal expenses that a policyholder may incur in an action and for any award against him of the other party's legal costs. It is relatively new, but increasingly used. There is little case law on the topic, other than relating to the possibility under section 51 Supreme Court Act 1981 of insurers having to pay costs above policy limits, but there is no FOS material on that.

REASONABLE PROSPECTS OF SUCCESS

15.2 Insurers usually require any legal action to have a "reasonable prospect of success" before they provide cover. The courts have not yet considered this phrase in this context, but the FOS has and interprets it to mean a 51% or better chance of success. A claim will be assessed to see if it meets this 51%, usually firstly by insurers' own staff, who may or may not be legally qualified, and then if they consider a claim should be pursued, by their panel solicitors.

15.3 The FOS will look at whether the firm has given the matter proper consideration, rather than the merits of whether a case has reasonable prospects of success. An insurer will have given the matter proper consideration if it has adopted the advice of legal experts. Notwithstanding this, the FOS may uphold the complaint if a complainant can show a legal opinion which "trumps" that obtained by insurers. The FOS considers that an expert opinion from a barrister is highly persuasive and is likely to trump other opinions. It should only be disregarded if it is obviously erroneous and/or based on factual mistakes. So in Case Study 47/8,[2] the FOS felt that the opinion of the complainant's barrister, who was a specialist in the field, trumped the opinion of the insurer's panel solicitor. If a privately funded case with worse prospects than 51% ultimately succeeds, that does not prove that the insurer was wrong to deny funding, as long as the insurer acted on legal advice. In any case, where cover is not provided or is withdrawn, a typical policy will allow the assured to recover from the insurer any of his reasonable costs which he is not able to recover from the other party to the litigation if he ultimately wins.

---

1. In Class 17 of the classes of General Insurance Business.
2. *Ombudsman News* July 2005.

COMMERCIAL JUDGEMENT

15.4 In cases where the costs of the claim make it uneconomical to pursue, the FOS supports policy terms which allow the insurer instead to opt to pay the consumer the sum of money at stake. If the insured wants an injunction which is uneconomical to pursue, the insurer will assess the costs of such an action against the damages that a court is likely to award rather than granting an injunction.

WHO SHOULD BE APPOINTED AS THE LEGAL REPRESENTATIVE

15.5 Where the insurer accepts liability under the policy, the insured has a right under the Insurance Companies (Legal Expenses Insurance) Regulations 1990[3] to nominate a solicitor to act on his behalf. Regulation 6(1) provides:

"Where under a legal expenses insurance contract recourse is had to a lawyer . . . to defend, represent or serve the interests of the insured in any inquiry or proceedings, the insured shall be free to choose that lawyer . . . ."

15.6 Under Regulation 6(3), this right should be written in the policy. It arises out of an EC Directive[4] to ensure that there can be no conflict of interest where the third party's liability insurer is also the insured's legal expenses insurer. The limited exception to this right is set out in Regulation 7 and involves a motor claim where neither the motor insurer nor the legal expenses insurer carry out liability business and there are arrangements to ensure that if both parties have the same insurer, completely independent legal advice is provided for each. Regulation 3 sets out the limited circumstances in which the regulations do not apply: they include legal expenses insurance for marine risks, proceedings which are also in the insurer's own interest and foreign travel assistance where the traveller falls into difficulties whilst abroad.

15.7 The European Court of Justice has recently considered the Directive in another context.[5] It ruled that Article 3 of the Directive confers upon member states the choice of three mechanisms to prevent conflicts of interest; preventing the same staff from within the insurer from handling legal expenses insurance and other claims, entrusting legal expenses insurance to a separate undertaking, or affording the assured the right to choose his own lawyer from the moment he has the right to claim from the insurer. However, the court found that Article 4 conferred a right for an insured to choose his own lawyer once proceedings had been initiated, irrespective of any conflict of interest, and subject only to one express exception for motor insurance. Therefore the court concluded that there could be no further derogations from the insured's right to appoint his own lawyer where proceedings had been initiated, even with express policy wording. This meant that in this Austrian case, one insured could appoint his own lawyer in a group action, even if that meant that insurers might have to fund more than one similar claim arising out of the same event.

15.8 The FOS mentions the above regulations in passing. It says[6] that insurers can appoint solicitors when a claim is notified, but that the regulations entitle insureds to choose their own solicitor only once administrative or legal proceedings have started. It would not require an

---

3. 1990/1159.
4. Council Directive 87/344/EEC.
5. *Eshig* v *UNIQA Sachversicherung AG* [2009] EUECJ Case C-199/08.
6. *Ombudsman News* Mar 2003.

insurer to offer the insured a choice of solicitor at the pre-action stage unless or until the courts support such an interpretation of the regulations. For it is unclear whether the word "inquiry" in Regulation 6(1) is enough for this.

15.9 The FOS adds that if it considers that the panel solicitors acted incompetently at the stage of determining whether there was a reasonable chance of success, it may allow the insured to instruct his own lawyers from that point onwards, funded in accordance with the policy terms. For instance, in Case Study 47/8,[7] the FOS found the insurer's advisers to be incompetent because they had not found that there was a reasonable prospect of success, although the insured's specialist barrister had, and the insurer had not instructed its own barrister for an opinion. The FOS asked the insurer to pay for the insured's legal costs to date, which included her instructing a solicitor and that solicitor instructing the barrister, with interest, and to fund the reasonable costs of litigation in accordance with the usual policy terms and conditions. The FOS also felt that it would be fair and reasonable for the insurer to allow her to continue with her own solicitors (and barrister) even though proceedings had not yet been issued. The conclusion of incompetence on these facts does not necessarily follow, especially as it cannot be reasonable to expect insurers always to obtain Counsel's opinion. Does this mean that an insured should always try to find a second opinion from Counsel when insurers decide that the case has no reasonable chance of success, and if it is favourable, require insurers to fund that opinion?

15.10 The FOS gives further examples[8] in addition to where panel solicitors have shown themselves to be incompetent, where it might support insureds choosing their own representation. Although it does not say, presumably the FOS means from the stage before proceedings have been issued (as the regulations grant that right from the stage after proceedings are issued). This would be in cases:

(1) that involve large personal injury claims;
(2) that are necessarily complex, (e.g. medical negligence);
(3) that involve significant boundary or employment disputes (especially those with a considerable history);
(4) where the policyholder's own solicitors have had considerable involvement and knowledge of the issue or related matters; or
(5) where there is a suggestion of conflict of interest and there was a reasonable prospect of success, the solicitor and insurer agreed fees and arrangements for monitoring the conduct of the claim, and the chosen solicitor had the necessary experience. The FOS comments that such a conflict might exist in the *Imran Sarwar* v *Muhammad Alam*[9] sort of case, where it was not reasonable for the claim of a car passenger to be conducted by his opponent's, the driver's, insurers and the Court of Appeal gave guidance for similar future cases.

15.11 The FOS says that apart from the above sorts of cases, it is not inherently unreasonable or unfair to policyholders for insurers to require them to use the legal services of its own appropriately trained staff or a pre-selected panel, so long as appropriate arrangements are made to handle conflicts of interest. It has seen no evidence of any systematic difference in quality between the work of panel and non-panel solicitors, except in the occasional case where the panel does not include solicitors with the relevant expertise or

---

7. *Ombudsman News* July 2005.
8. *Ombudsman News* Mar 2003.
9. [2001] EWCA Civ 1401.

specialist knowledge. So the FOS concludes that, in general, policyholders making claims in connection with motor accident disputes, minor personal injury claims and routine consumer disputes are unlikely to suffer any significant prejudice if the insurer simply appoints a solicitor for them from its own panel. This finding may affect an insured's decision to appoint his own solicitor, rather than his right to do so.

15.12 The policy should set out clearly whether the insurer will fund all or any part of a claim handled by the insured's solicitor, otherwise insureds may be prejudiced if they incur fees. The FOS considers it fair and good industry practice for the insurer to pay such fees. The regulations do not mention fees. Perhaps the FOS is also saying when it produces the above list of circumstances in which the insured should be entitled to choose its own representation, that those are also the circumstances in which the FOS would consider that insurers should pay for the insured's choice of legal representation, even pre-proceedings, whatever the policy terms. If that is indeed the case, then it is not clear from the reports in *Ombudsman News*, although it would be a fair and sensible guideline.

HANDLING OF THE CLAIM

15.13 The FOS will reject a complaint about whether the insurer should have settled a case if it acted on solicitors' advice and there is nothing to suggest that the advice is wrong, e.g. Case Study 47/7.[10] There the case was settled but the insured thought she would have got a better result if the matter had proceeded to an employment tribunal and so complained to the FOS. Whilst policies usually provide for insurers to pre-approve any proposed settlement, the FOS expects the insurers to exercise reasonably their discretion not to cover a settlement made without its permission. In Case Study 26/12,[11] the settlement in question was made without the insurer's permission, but was the best outcome for the claim. The FOS required the insurer to reimburse the insured with the amount of the agreed settlement plus interest from the date that the insured had made the payment. A court would not be able to require the insurer to act outside of the policy terms, however unreasonable the insurer.

COMMENTARY

15.14 Some of the FOS approach is not set out clearly. This might be because of the context of its comments, which were in response to a question about its position following the Court of Appeal decision in *Sarwar* v *Alam*.[12] From its comments in *Ombudsman News*[13] it is not clear that the FOS was already aware of the case or that it was familiar with the regulations.

---

10. *Ombudsman News* July 2005.
11. *Ombudsman News* Mar 2003.
12. *Supra.*
13. March 2003.

OMBUDSMAN NEWS: INSURANCE CASE STUDIES*

Issue Number	Date	Case Study Numbers	Page
Issue 1	January 2001	1/1 to 1/26	
Issue 4	April 2001	4/1 to 4/23	
Issue 7	July 2001	7/1 to 7/23	
Issue 10	October 2001	10/1 to 10/15	
Issue 13	January 2002	13/1 to 13/18	
Issue 18	July 2002	18/1 to 18/25	
Issue 21	October 2002	21/1 to 21/4	
Issue 22	November 2002	22/15 to 22/18	
Issue 23	December 2002	23/11 to 23/15	
Issue 24	January 2003	24/1 to 24/4	
Issue 25	February 2003	25/14 to 25/18	
Issue 26	March 2003	26/12	
Issue 27	April 2003	27/5 to 27/6	
Issue 28	May 2003	28/7 to 28/11	
Issue 29	July 2003	29/1 to 29/7	
Issue 30	August 2003	30/1 to 30/6	
Issue 31	September 2003	31/1 to 31/5	
Issue 32	October 2003	32/7 to 32/11	
Issue 34	January 2004	34/1 to 34/3	
Issue 35	February/March 2004	35/1 to 35/6	
Issue 36	April 2004	36/9 to 36/12	
Issue 38	July 2004	38/5 to 38/7	
Issue 39	August 2004	39/1 to 39/2	
Issue 40	September/October 2004	40/4 to 40/6	
Issue 42	December 2004/January 2005	42/3 to 42/5	
Issue 44	March 2005	44/11 to 44/12	
Issue 47	July 2005	47/7 to 47/8	
Issue 48	August 2005	48/1 to 48/7	
Issue 49	September/October 2005	49/1 to 49/3	
Issue 52	April 2006	52/1 to 52/3	
Issue 54	July 2006	54/4 to 54/5	
Issue 56	September/October 2006	56/1 to 56/5	
Issue 58	December 2006/January 2007	58/1 to 58/5	
Issue 59	January/February 2007	59/8 to 59/11	
Issue 61	April/May 2007	61/1 to 61/6	
Issue 62	June/July 2007	62/5 to 62/9	
Issue 63	July/August 2007	63/7 to 63/9	

ISSUE 1: JANUARY 2001

1/1 medical expenses—exclusion—chronic conditions—formerly acute condition—whether insurer required to notify policyholder when condition considered chronic

The policyholder suffered from heart disease and received various treatments between 1998 and 1999. The insurer met his claims for the cost of these treatments, making payments of approximately £40,000. Open heart surgery was recommended in August 1999 but, for reasons which were unclear, the insurer did not receive the claim form until 20 September 1999.

The insurer made enquiries and, on 8 October, notified the hospital that it had decided the policyholder's condition was chronic so it would not meet his claim. The policy specifically excluded 'treatment of a chronic condition'. It defined 'chronic' as 'a disease where you need observation or care, and treatment will only relieve or control the symptoms but not cure the medical condition'. The policyholder was informed of this decision either that day or on 9 October. Nevertheless, surgery was performed as scheduled on 13 October. The policyholder did not survive and his widow claimed £11,595 to meet the cost of surgery.

Complaint upheld

The operation was clearly a serious one and the prognosis was uncertain. But there was some significant prospect that the operation would successfully arrest the decline in the policyholder's condition without the need for further extensive treatment.

Whether this would have amounted to a 'cure' was debatable. However, the insurer failed to give the policyholder any notice that it had decided his condition had become chronic. Given the conflicting medical evidence and the need for urgent action in September 1999, the insurer should have accepted the claim. It might then have explained that any further treatment would be excluded. We required the insurer to meet the cost of the treatment.

1/2 medical expenses—acute illness or injury—'occurrence of brief duration'—meaning of 'brief duration'

The policyholder was involved in a motor accident in May 1999 and sustained serious injuries, leaving her paralysed below the waist. She was hospitalised for three months. The insurer met all her medical costs. The policyholder continued to receive physiotherapy as an outpatient until December 1999. The insurer then decided her condition was no longer acute and terminated payments. It relied on the policy definition of 'treatment'. This provided that benefit was only payable for 'surgical or medical procedures the sole purpose of which is the cure or relief of acute illness or injury. An acute illness or injury is characterised by an occurrence of brief duration, after which the insured person returns to his/her normal state and degree of activity'.

The policyholder argued that further physiotherapy was essential for her recovery and cited her consultant's opinion that her condition was still acute. He considered she would continue to improve and expected her to achieve 90% of her previous functional abilities within one to two years. The insurer maintained it had always intended to transfer the policyholder's treatment to the NHS. However, it produced no evidence to prove her condition was no longer acute.

Complaint upheld

Although the policy only covered 'acute' illness or injury, this was not clearly defined. We considered that the phrase 'occurrence of brief duration' should be interpreted according to the extent of the injury. For example, a broken finger might mean a few days' disability, whereas a broken back—as in this case—would mean many months'.

The medical evidence established that the policyholder's condition would continue to improve as a result of treatment. We were therefore satisfied that it was still acute and thus covered under the policy. We also agreed with the policyholder that her claim had not been administrated properly. However, the insurer's apology and its *ex gratia* payment of £1,800 towards the cost of the policyholder's home care were sufficient compensation for the distress caused.

1/3 medical expenses—exclusion—pre-existing condition—whether undiagnosed condition excluded

The policyholder submitted a claim under his company medical scheme for his daughter's tonsillectomy and adenoidectomy. The insurer rejected the claim on the ground that the daughter's GP disclosed that she had suffered from tonsillitis since 1991, almost seven years before the policy was purchased.

The policyholder complained about this decision. He stated that surgery had not been recommended until February 1999 and contended that his daughter's consultations had been for illnesses typical of childhood, not indicative of a serious condition which had not been diagnosed.

Complaint rejected

The clinical notes revealed a long history of bouts of tonsillitis which were not indicative of ordinary childhood infections. The policy clearly excluded claims for treatment of any illness or related condition which originated prior to the policy cover. The insurer was therefore fully entitled not to accept liability for the daughter's operations.

1/4 medical expenses—exclusion—pre-existing condition—representations by insurer's agent—whether insurer estopped from relying on exclusion

In December 1998, when the policyholder decided to switch insurers, she had had medical expenses cover for over 20 years. She discussed her situation with the new insurer's agent, who completed an application form for her. Details of previous medical problems were recorded on the form. Before she signed the form, she asked the agent to double-check her position and ensure she would maintain her existing level of cover.

In October/November 1999, the policyholder began experiencing pain in her hip and requested a claim form. She saw her consultant the following month and he recommended a complete hip replacement without delay. The insurer refused to meet the cost of surgery on the ground that it was due to a pre-existing medical condition.

The policyholder contended that she had informed the agent of a previous hip operation in February 1996, with further surgery in December 1996. She said the agent had advised her that the insurer did not consider as relevant any operations which took place more than two years before the start date. He had also confirmed that her level of cover would remain the same. She said she had never received any policy documents and was not aware of an exclusion for pre-existing conditions.

The insurer agreed to meet the consultation fee and X-ray costs and to return the premiums paid by the policyholder, but refused to reimburse the £12,000 cost of her private operation.

Complaint upheld

We were satisfied that the policyholder had the highest possible level of cover under her first policy. The insurer no longer employed the agent and was unable to investigate how the subsequent policy had been sold. As there was nothing to rebut the policyholder's allegations, we accepted her version of events.

The actions of the insurer and/or its agent had seriously prejudiced the policyholder's position and we did not agree that a premium refund was an acceptable settlement. The insurer accepted our recommendation that the policy should be reinstated—subject to payment of the outstanding premiums—and that the claim should be met, in accordance with the level of cover originally selected. It also agreed to pay £500 compensation for distress and inconvenience.

1/5 medical expenses—group scheme—provision of medical services in UK—policyholder resident abroad—whether overseas medical expenses covered

The policyholders retired in 1989 and moved to Mallorca. They had been allowed to continue as members of their employer's private medical insurance scheme after their retirement, paying the premiums personally. It was not drawn to their attention that cover was restricted to 'medical services specified in this Policy if they are provided in the United Kingdom, Channel Islands or Isle of Man'.

Their employer asserted that it had written to them in 1994, explaining that cover was not provided for people residing abroad. The policyholders did not receive that letter as it was sent to the wrong address. In any event, the employer continued to collect premiums and renew the policy.

One of the policyholders needed dental surgery and part of the treatment was carried out in Mallorca. He submitted a claim for the cost of this and also for further treatment he required. The insurer rejected the claims on the ground that there was no cover for treatment performed abroad.

Complaint upheld

There was no formal agency agreement between the employer and the insurer. However, we considered that by confirming the policyholders' membership of the scheme after they retired and collecting their premiums, the employer was acting as the insurer's agent. Given that the policy was clearly unsuitable for the policyholders, we decided the claims should be settled without reference to the restriction on where treatment could be performed.

The policy included cover for 'oral surgical operations', so the policyholder's claims were valid if the territorial restriction were ignored. We required the insurer to meet the cost of both treatments.

1/6 motor—theft—exclusion for theft if keys left in car—whether policyholder in breach of exclusion

The policyholder stopped his car on his driveway and got out, leaving the engine running and the door open, in order to lift up his garage door. However, before doing so he stopped to put his briefcase in the unlocked porch adjacent to his garage. As he did this he heard a noise and turned round to see someone jump into his car and reverse away at high speed. He was very close to the car but could not prevent it from being stolen.

The insurer declined the claim on the basis of exclusion for 'losses arising from the use of keys which had been left in or around the vehicle'.

1/7

The policyholder arranged cover for her Fiat Marea, over the telephone, on 9 August 1999. The next day the vehicle was stolen while she was paying for petrol. She said she had inadvertently left her keys in the ignition.

The insurer rejected the claim, relying on a policy term excluding theft 'if the insured vehicle has not been locked, windows and sunroof closed and keys removed, when left unattended or unoccupied'. The policyholder maintained that when she telephoned to arrange the insurance she had been told all the good points of the policy but not about the restrictions, and the policy did not arrive until after the car was stolen.

1/8

The policyholder was picking up his children from school. He left his car in a busy street with the door shut but the keys in the ignition while he went to speak to his son, about eight feet behind the car. Less than two minutes later, two youths ran up, jumped into the car and drove off, despite the policyholder's best efforts to stop them. The youths were involved in an accident and the policyholder's car was a total write-off.

The insurer refused payment on the ground that the policy excluded claims for theft if 'the car is left unattended or unoccupied and the doors and boot are not locked or any window or roof opening/hood has not been secured closed or if the keys are not removed from the car'. It said that the policy wording was clear and that the commentary in the policy also explained that theft was not covered 'unless the car is fully locked and the keys are removed when it is left unattended or unoccupied'. The policyholder argued that he had left the car on the spur of the moment because he needed to speak to his son; he had been only feet away and the car had been in sight the whole time.

1/9

The policyholder reversed his car out of his garage and got out of the car to return briefly to the house, leaving the car keys in the ignition and closing but not locking the car door. He said he had only been away from the car for approximately 30 seconds but came back out of the house to find the car had been stolen. The insurer declined the claim on the ground that the policy excluded theft 'if the car is left unattended or unoccupied and the doors and boot are not locked or any roof opening/hood has not been secured closed or if the keys are not removed from the car'.

Complaints upheld

We considered the four complaints above were valid. We interpreted these exclusions as removing theft cover only when the car driver has clearly gone away from the vehicle. This applies regardless of whether the exclusion referred to leaving the vehicle 'unattended' or simply stated there was no theft cover if the keys had been 'left'. This interpretation required evidence that the driver had either gone a significant distance from the vehicle or had left it for an extended period. It was not sufficient for the driver merely to have turned his back or gone inside his home briefly. While we would not generally interpret such exclusions in a wide sense, we would not require insurers to meet this type of claim if we were satisfied the driver had behaved in a reckless fashion.

1/10 motor—theft—lack of reasonable care—policyholder aware of risks—whether loss excluded

In May 1999, the policyholder paid £17,000 cash for a Volkswagen Golf GTI turbo to be imported from Belgium. He arranged insurance to take effect on the anticipated delivery date. Nine days after accepting the car, he filled it with petrol. Later that afternoon, he returned to the filling station to put the car through the jet wash.

Leaving the key on the driver's seat, he went to the tap to wash his hands. The policyholder noticed a man who did not appear to have a car and who was standing in front of the jet wash.

However, the policyholder did not feel particularly concerned. As he was washing, he heard a car revving up. At first he did not realise the car was his, but then he saw it being driven out of the garage by the man he noticed earlier. The insurer rejected the theft claim on the ground that the policyholder had breached the duty to take reasonable care of his car.

Complaint rejected

The courts had decided that the duty of reasonable care was breached if the individual acted 'recklessly'—meaning that the individual recognised a risk but deliberately took no steps to avoid it or took steps that were clearly inadequate.

In this case, the policyholder saw someone loitering near his car but had left the car unlocked with the keys on the driver's seat. We were satisfied he had taken no steps to protect his car from a known risk of theft.

1/11 motor—theft—exclusion for car left unattended and doors unlocked—whether car left unattended

The policyholder was building a house and, in January 1999, visited it to drop off some equipment. He parked his Mazda off the road, leaving it unlocked and the car key among a bunch of keys in the lock on the front door of the house. The car was stolen and was later recovered in a damaged condition, requiring nearly £3,000 to repair.

The insurer rejected the claim. It explained that the policy excluded liability for thefts if 'the car is left unattended or unoccupied and the doors . . . . are not locked'. The policyholder argued that he had acted reasonably and he produced photographs showing that the car would have been visible only to someone close to the house. He also pointed out that his household insurer had met his claim for tools and equipment stolen with the car.

Complaint rejected

We were satisfied that the car was both unattended and unoccupied at the time of the theft. We accepted that the household insurer was satisfied that the policyholder had behaved reasonably, but that was not the motor insurer's reason for declining liability and was therefore not relevant in this situation.

1/12   motor—theft—exclusion for theft if keys left in unattended car—whether car unattended

The policyholder's husband parked their Landrover Discovery in front of a terraced house where he was working. He removed the keys from the ignition, but left the vehicle unlocked. A spare set of keys was kept in the car in the pocket on the driver's side. The driver entered the house to close windows upstairs and downstairs and to set the alarm. He returned to the pavement to see the car disappearing up the road.

The insurer rejected the policyholder's theft claim on the ground that the policy excluded any claim for 'loss or damage if the Motor Car has not been locked, with the windows closed and ignition key removed, when left unattended or unoccupied'.

Complaint rejected

The case law established that an item was 'unattended' if someone was not in a position to observe any attempt to interfere with it, and was close enough to have a reasonable prospect of preventing any unauthorised interference. It was clear that the husband had not been in any position to observe the attempt to interfere with the vehicle. We were satisfied that the car was 'unattended' and therefore within the scope of the exclusion.

1/13   extended warranty—option to repair or replace—extent of insurer's obligation if repair or replacement impossible

The policyholder paid £300 for a five-year warranty in July 1997, covering her new suite of furniture against a number of eventualities including staining. An armchair was stained in February 1999 and the policyholder put in a claim. The insurer sent her a stain removal kit, but this did not successfully clean the chair.

After making two unsuccessful attempts to remove the stain, the claims administrator finally advised the policyholder that the fabric would have to be replaced. The policyholder was asked to submit a fabric sample for matching. Four months passed but the administrator failed to obtain new fabric. Given the lack of progress, the policyholder demanded that her policy be cancelled and that she should get compensation and a refund of the premium. The insurer cancelled the policy and returned the premium, but did not offer any compensation. It stated that the premium refund was the full extent of its liability.

Complaint upheld

The insurer's decision to allow the policyholder to cancel as if this brought its liability fully to an end was disingenuous. It had already accepted the claim and, as it had been unable either to remove the stain or replace the fabric, the insurer was required by the terms of the warranty to replace the damaged furniture if no other solution could be found.

The insurer accepted that the policyholder had not been adequately compensated. It acknowledged that she might have felt less aggrieved and frustrated, and therefore less likely to cancel, if it had kept her informed of the progress of her claim. Following our involvement, in addition to the premium it had already agreed to refund, as compensation for distress and inconvenience, the insurer offered to pay the cost of re-dyeing the suite (subject to a limit of the full cost of replacing it). We considered this the appropriate response.

1/14   extended warranty—cashback offer—time limit for registration—policyholder in breach of time limit—whether insurer entitled to refuse to register policyholder

The policyholder took out a five-year extended warranty when she bought a teletext televideo in October 1997. One of the features was a cashback offer, described as 'Make a claim or your money back!' Policyholders could obtain a full premium refund if they made no claim during the period. However, the terms of the policy stated that this offer only applied if policyholders registered for the scheme within 21 days of purchasing the policy. The policyholder did not register until January 1999. The insurer refused to accept her registration. It argued that she had not complied with the policy terms and that her breach had prejudiced its position. It contended that it was essential to have accurate information about the potential risk in order to make adequate reinsurance arrangements.

Complaint upheld

The cashback offer was one of the elements of cover provided for the purchase price of the policy. It was emphasised in the marketing material as a significant benefit. We appreciated that the insurer wanted information regarding potential claims. However, it was not acceptable that largely procedural obstacles should be placed in the way of policyholders, primarily to minimise the number of otherwise justifiable claims. 'Small print' procedural requirements such as this were wholly inappropriate and might well be considered unfair contract terms.

We therefore required the insurer to issue the policyholder with a certificate of registration and to pay her £25 to compensate her for her costs in pursuing her complaint. We noted that the policy also stipulated that a cashback claim would only be valid if the policyholder returned the certificate to the insurer within 30 days of the end of cover. Although this clause had not formed any part of this complaint, we considered it likely that a claimant's failure to meet the insurer's strict deadline would not be sufficient ground for rejecting the claim.

1/15 extended warranty—repairs—delay—whether policyholder entitled to compensation

The policyholder began to experience problems with his video cassette recorder (VCR) in May 1999. He notified his insurer, in accordance with his extended warranty, and his VCR was taken away for repair. It was returned in mid-June but broke down again in late August. It was taken away again but the tester was unable to trace the fault until it had been returned once more to the policyholder. It was eventually restored to full working order in November. The policyholder sought compensation from the insurer for six months' loss of use, poor claims handling and inconvenience. He said he had to make at least 50 calls to the insurer and had been visited 25 times by technicians. He had been given a replacement VCR while his was undergoing repairs, but only for two weeks. He also claimed that his warranty period should be extended for a further six months.

Complaint rejected

While we did not doubt that the policyholder had experienced much inconvenience, we did not agree that the insurer or repairer had failed to provide a satisfactory standard of service. The fault was difficult to diagnose and only became known when the VCR was replaced in its usual cabinet.

It could not be said that the policyholder had lost the benefit of six months' cover under the warranty. If another fault had appeared, the insurer would have met a claim. The insurer was not obliged to arrange for the loan of equipment while repairs were being carried out, or to offer compensation for inconvenience.

1/16 maladministration—travel—repatriation—failure to embalm body before repatriation—whether insurer responsible for failure

The complainant's son and daughter-in-law went on holiday to Madeira, where the son died following a heart attack. The widow contacted the assistance company appointed by the insurer to arrange repatriation of the body and local funeral directors were instructed.

When the mother went to view her son's body in the UK, she was not allowed to see it as it had not been embalmed before repatriation and had deteriorated badly. The mother was greatly distressed. She complained to the insurer, which undertook extensive enquiries and liaised with the local British Consulate. It was established that the funeral directors were not on the assistance company's approved list.

The funeral directors explained that they would not normally carry out embalming unless they received specific instructions to do so. The Consulate confirmed that embalming was not the usual practice in Madeira. The mother considered that the failure to ensure the body was embalmed resulted from the insurer's wish to cut costs.

The insurer stated that embalming expenses were reasonable and necessary and that it would have met the charges. It contended that only an error had prevented its general practice being followed in this case. Normally, the assistance company would have contacted local funeral directors. They did not do so in this case because the funeral directors were not on its approved list. It could not be established who had appointed them. And the insurer was not able to identify who had been responsible for the decision not to embalm to body.

Complaint upheld in part

The failure to embalm the body resulted from a series of oversights and genuine errors on the part of a number of organisations. These oversights and errors did not seem part of any attempt by the insurer, or /any of the other parties, to avoid their proper responsibilities. However, we concluded that the insurer, through its agents—the assistance company and funeral directors—had failed to provide the service it should have done. All of these had also failed to give the mother's initial concerns the attention they deserved.

The insurer confirmed it would implement steps to ensure that, in future, embalming would always be specifically requested. It would advise all its assistance companies that it would meet the cost of preparing a body for repatriation. The mother had made it clear that her complaint was not about financial compensation. Nevertheless, we required the organisations concerned to provide a full apology and to make donations to the British Heart Foundation.

1/17 travel—cancellation—duty of disclosure—change in medical condition—whether policyholder under continuing duty to disclose any change in medical condition

In June 1999, the policyholder booked a cruise for himself and his fiancée from 5–20 March 2000 and took out insurance. He signed a declaration relating to himself, anyone travelling with him and anyone else whose health might affect the trip. This stated that no one was waiting for an operation, hospital consultation or other hospital treatment or investigations. The declaration stated that—

'If there is a change in your medical condition or the medical condition of anyone who the trip depends on (after you take out this insurance, but before you travel) and you can no longer agree with the declaration, you must contact [the insurance company]. We will then tell you if cover can continue. If we cannot continue cover, you can claim for the cost of cancelling your holiday at that time.'

'If you do not tell us about anything we have asked for above, we may not pay your claim.'

The fiancée's mother was diagnosed with cancer in December 1999. She underwent surgery in January 2000 but was told in February that further treatment would be required. The policyholder cancelled the cruise then and claimed reimbursement under his travel insurance.

The insurer settled the claim by paying £250—the cost of cancelling in December 1999. The policyholder sought reimbursement of the full cancellation charge of £1,394.

Complaint upheld

The declaration imposed two duties of disclosure on the policyholder, the second of which was an extended or continuing duty that applied to the period—just over eight months—immediately before departure. We regarded the continuing duty of disclosure as both unusual and unduly onerous. It was not inconceivable that, after a policyholder had notified a change in someone's medical position, the policyholder and insurer might hold conflicting views about whether cancellation was necessary at that stage.

The practical effect of the declaration was to make the insurer the sole arbiter of whether any policyholder should cancel the holiday. We considered this inherently unfair and a possible contravention of the Unfair Terms in Consumer Contracts Regulations 1999.

We were not persuaded that the policyholder should have cancelled in December 1999. There was no evidence that he and his fiancée had realised at that time that they should cancel the cruise immediately, even though it was not due to take place for 11 weeks. The insurer accepted our recommendation and paid the balance of the charges plus interest.

1/18 travel—personal accident—total and irrecoverable loss of sight—policyholder retaining 3% vision—whether loss of sight claim valid

The policyholder went on holiday with her family to Florida on 1 January 1998. Three days after arriving, they were involved in a serious road accident. They contacted the assistance company and the policyholder and her daughter were hospitalised.

The policyholder submitted a claim for loss of sight under the personal accident section of the policy. She said she had no useful vision in her left eye and there was no prospect of improvement.

The insurer insisted on obtaining additional medical evidence. The insurer's consultant concluded that the policyholder had lost all central vision but retained a small amount of peripheral vision, which he estimated at 2–3%. In his opinion, 'In theory, [the policyholder] had retained sight in the left eye. However, it was so minimal, it [would] be of no practical use to her. For practical purposes, [the policyholder] had lost all sight with the left eye'. The policy stipulated that the £25,000 benefit was payable only for 'total and irrecoverable loss of all sight in one or both eyes'. The insurer contended that this provision should be interpreted literally and that therefore the claim was not valid. However, following our involvement, it offered an *ex gratia* payment of £12,500. The policyholder considered her claim should be met in full.

Complaint upheld

We noted that the World Health Organisation defined 'profound blindness' as the inability to distinguish fingers at a distance of 10 feet. The Royal National Institute for the Blind advised that only about 18% of blind people were classed as totally blind and the majority of those could distinguish between light and dark. We concluded that 'sight' implied an ability to discern objects. On this basis we were satisfied that the policyholder had, for all practical purposes, suffered a total loss of sight. We required the insurer to meet the claim in full, together with interest, from the date of the accident.

1/19   travel—curtailment—requirement that policyholder return home—earthquake —policyholders relocating at holiday destination—whether holiday curtailed— whether assistance company authorised expenses

The policyholder and his family were on holiday in Cyprus when, on 11 August, there was a series of earthquakes, one of which shook their holiday apartment so violently that the occupants were evacuated. They returned to the apartment for the next two nights but by 13 August cracks had appeared. The family was frightened, tremors were continuing and the policyholder decided to move them out of the apartment. He claimed the cost of re-arranging his family's holiday.

The insurer rejected the claim. It explained that curtailment of a holiday was only covered if the policyholders returned to the UK. The policy did not cover relocation at the holiday destination. The policyholder maintained this was unfair as the policy did not exclude earthquake.

Complaint rejected

Earthquakes were not excluded by the policy but they did not need to be—they were not covered in the first place. The nearest section of the policy to the policyholder's circumstances was curtailment. This provided that the insurer would pay if the holiday was curtailed by a policyholder's returning home before the end of the holiday because of specified reasons such as death, illness, etc. But it did not include curtailment following a natural disaster in the holiday destination.

We were required to look beyond the strict legal position and to make a decision which was fair and reasonable in all the circumstances. Had the policyholder returned home, matters might have been different. In this case, whatever the policyholder's fears, they were not sufficient to cause him to return home before the scheduled date. We concluded that the insurer had acted reasonably.

1/20   travel—curtailment—cover limited to disaster at home—earthquake at resort— whether policyholders' claim covered

In October 1999 the Turkish holiday of these policyholders (aged 74 and 76) was disrupted by a severe earthquake. Their tour operator offered to fly them home immediately but they decided to remain. They slept that night on the beach but changed their minds about continuing the holiday when the magnitude of the disaster became clearer. The hotelier was unwilling to allow guests to sleep in the hotel and suggested they slept instead on loungers by the pool. Further earth tremors could not be ruled out, so the tour operator flew the policyholders home at no cost.

The policyholders made a claim for curtailment. This was refused on the ground that the policy did not cover curtailment following an earthquake. The policyholders argued that this was unfair, as Acts of God were not excluded.

Complaint upheld

If a particular risk was not covered by the policy in the first place, it was irrelevant whether or not it was excluded. So far as cutting short the holiday was concerned, the policy covered curtailment in the event of the death, injury or illness of the policyholders etc, or if the policyholders had to return home because of burglary, fire, etc affecting their home in the UK. There was no cover for curtailment following a natural disaster in the holiday destination.

However, we were required to make a decision which was fair and reasonable in all the circumstances. In our view, when they took out the travel insurance as part of the holiday package, the policyholders would have envisaged that it would cover them for exactly the type of problem they had encountered. The absence of cover for events giving rise to a real need to curtail the holiday restricted the cover and had not been highlighted in the policy material. According to the insurer's position, the policyholders would only have had a justifiable claim if they had become ill or been injured. It was arguable that this was a significant possibility, given the policyholders' ages and their having to sleep in the open. Taking all these points into consideration, we decided the fair and reasonable solution was for the insurer to meet the claim.

1/21 travel—curtailment—death of relative—relative resident abroad—whether policyholder's return to UK covered

Following the death of his mother in Kenya, the policyholder and his wife had to return home to the UK from their holiday in Amsterdam. The insurer refused to meet the claim as the policyholder's mother was not resident in the UK. It referred to the policy section which covered curtailment due to 'the death, severe injury or serious illness of an immediate relative resident in the United Kingdom'.

Complaint upheld

Although the policy wording was unambiguous, we considered that its application was unfair in the circumstances. The country in which the policyholder's mother was resident at the time of her death did not seem relevant, as he and his wife had first to return home to the United Kingdom. The insurer agreed to meet the claim.

1/22 motor—non-disclosure—'accidents or losses'—whether policyholder required to disclose unsuccessful claims

The policyholder applied for motor insurance. The proposal form asked: 'Have you or anyone who will drive been involved in any motor accidents or made a claim (fault or non-fault including thefts) during the last five years?' His answer was 'No.'

When the policyholder's car was stolen, the insurer learnt that he had made a theft claim under his previous motor policy within the five year period. The insurer voided the policy from its start date and rejected the policyholder's claim. The policyholder argued that he did not have to disclose his previous theft claim because the insurer concerned had decided not to meet it.

Complaint rejected

The policyholder's answer on the proposal form was incorrect. Although the question was confined to claims and did not extend to losses not claimed for, it was clearly worded: it was not limited to successful claims, nor did it ask what the outcome was. The policyholder had pursued his previous claim all the way to a conclusion and ought to have disclosed it. The insurer was fully entitled to treat the policy as void.

1/23 motor—non-disclosure—mistake—whether insurer entitled to cancel policy

In June 1999 the policyholder applied for motor insurance over the telephone. The insurer's standard practice was to ask about claims made within the previous three years. The policyholder remembered that he had made a claim, but was not sure whether it fell within that time span. He maintained that he mentioned this to the insurer's telesales operator, who told him she would check the position. When the proposal form arrived without any mention of the claim, the policyholder signed it, assuming the insurer's investigation had revealed it was more than three years old. In reality, the insurer had not carried out any investigations, and the claim was not noted on its records.

A few weeks later, the policyholder's car was stolen. On investigating his claim, the insurer discovered he had made a motor theft claim previously, in August 1997. The insurer refused to indemnify the policyholder for his loss, on the ground that he had failed to disclose the earlier claim on the proposal form.

Complaint upheld

There was no tape-recording of the policyholder's initial telephone call, so it was difficult to know exactly what was said. At worst, however, it seemed to us that the non-disclosure resulted from a misunderstanding, and—on a balance of probabilities—we were satisfied the policyholder had acted innocently. The insurer would only have charged a small additional premium had it known about the previous claim. In the circumstances, we asked the insurer to meet the present claim in full, with interest.

1/24   motor—non-disclosure—'accident or loss'—named driver—whether policyholder obliged to disclose named driver's loss

The policyholder applied for motor insurance, answering 'no' to the following two questions on the proposal form:

'Has the car been altered/modified from the maker's specification (including the addition of optional fit accessories such as spoilers, skirts, alloy wheels etc.?)
Have YOU or ANY PERSON who will drive . . . during the past five years been involved in any accident or loss (irrespective of blame and of whether a claim resulted)?'

When the insurer investigated a new claim, it came to light that the car had been fitted with oversized alloy wheels, spoilers, and chrome wheel arches, and that the policyholder's husband, a named driver on the policy, had made two significant claims in the previous five years. The insurer refused to meet the claim and cancelled the policy from its start date.

The policyholder stated that she had bought the car with the all the modifications already fitted, and she assumed they were all part of the car's original specification. She further explained that she did not realise her husband had made one of the two earlier claims, and that his other claim had been rejected because he had only third party cover at the time.

Complaint rejected

On the evidence presented, we accepted the policyholder genuinely believed the car was not modified when she bought it. The fact remained, however, that she failed to disclose her husband's previous claims. The question in issue was clear and unambiguous, and asked for details of any 'loss' irrespective of whether a claim was made. The policyholder ought, therefore, to have appreciated the need to disclose those previous incidents. By not doing so, she misled the insurer into accepting a risk it would only otherwise have agreed to cover, if at all, in return for a substantially higher premium.

1/25   household contents—non-disclosure—'property stolen, lost or damaged'—whether policyholder liable to disclose attempted break-in

The policyholder applied for household contents insurance. His local bank manager completed a proposal form on his behalf, which he signed. One of the questions asked was:

'Have you or any member of your household . . . had any property or possessions stolen, lost or damaged or had any claims made against you, in the last three years (whether insured or not)?'

The policyholder remembered telling the bank manager of an attempted break-in which occurred some months previously.

The advice he said he was given in reply was that, because the intruders had not gained entry into the house or stolen anything, the incident did not count as a burglary and need not be mentioned on the form.

This previous incident came to light when the insurer appointed loss adjusters to investigate two burglaries. The insurer refused to pay either claim, and voided the policy from its start date. The policyholder was aggrieved, and sought reinstatement of the policy, payment of both claims and compensation for inconvenience suffered.

Complaint upheld

On the question as worded, the policyholder had not supplied an incorrect answer. The question would have had to be phrased differently to elicit disclosure of an attempted burglary which did not result in any quantifiable loss. Even if there had been quantifiable loss, and the policyholder had declared the attempted break-in, it was apparent from the insurer's underwriting guidelines that it would still have been prepared to accept the risk. The insurer agreed to reinstate the policy, deal with both claims, and pay compensation of £250.

1/26   motor—renewal—policy replaced—insurer failing to notify policyholder of new policy terms—whether insurer entitled to rely on new terms

The policyholder bought a new car in April 1998. He was given a year's free insurance as part of the purchase arrangements. The policy provided, amongst other benefits, that if the car were damaged beyond economic repair within two years, the insurer would replace it with a new car of the same make and specification. The policy was due to expire on 23 April 1999. On 1 April, the policyholder received a letter from the dealer offering to renew the policy. The letter enclosed a new proposal form and details of the new cover but did not draw attention to any differences. The policy had a new title but was underwritten by the same insurer. The policyholder was involved in an accident in December 1999 and his car was written off.

The insurer settled his claim by paying the market value, but the policyholder contended he was entitled to a new model. The insurer explained that this benefit had been limited to the first policy and was not included in the terms of the second policy. The policyholder argued that he had been misled.

Complaint upheld

The insurer had offered two years' free insurance to some purchasers, but this was not available to purchasers of the model bought by the policyholder. He was therefore not offered renewal of his policy, only the option of taking out a new policy. However, the same policy booklet was given to both types of purchaser.

We were satisfied that the policyholder had not understood that cover under the new policy was different from that under the first one. The insurer's agent's offer to 'renew' the policy on behalf of the insurer had led the policyholder to misunderstand the nature of the cover being arranged. The insurer's duty to notify changes in cover had not been met, so the insurer should deal with the claim as if the original policy terms applied.

The insurer accepted our view that the policyholder was entitled to be paid the balance of the cost of a new car, plus interest, together with his out-of-pocket expenses of £25.

ISSUE 4: APRIL 2001

4/1   loan protection—joint insureds—calculation of benefit—whether each insured entitled to full monthly benefit.

Mr and Mrs H took out insurance to protect their joint mortgage repayments, choosing a monthly benefit of £500. In October 1998, Mrs H became unemployed and submitted a claim. The insurer made monthly payments of £250. Mrs H and her husband argued that she was entitled to £500 per month. In their opinion, the policy covered each of them for that amount. They said this was what they were told when they bought the policy and it had been confirmed in the insurer's letter accepting the claim.

The insurer did not accept this argument, stating that the policy explained clearly how benefit would be calculated. However, it offered £50 compensation 'for the errors and incorrect advice'.

Complaint upheld

Neither the application form nor the insurance certificate explained the amount of monthly benefit that would be paid in the case of joint applicants. Both documents showed the amount of the monthly benefit required as £500 and contained no more than a general reference to the booklet which detailed the conditions. There was no specific reference to the limitation of cover in the case of joint borrowers.

The layout of the conditions booklet was confusing and unlikely to help anyone wishing to ascertain the position for joint borrowers. On Page 4, 'monthly benefit' was defined as 'the amount you have agreed with us as specified in your certificate of insurance' but there was no reference to the limitation that applied to joint borrowers. The sections of the booklet, 'What we will pay', 'What we will not pay' and 'How to claim' also failed to reveal the relevant limitation.

The limitation was, in fact, set out under the heading 'Eligibility'—'If the mortgage has been taken out by joint borrowers who are all eligible for cover . . . each borrower's cover is limited to an equal share of the monthly benefit, eg if the monthly benefit is £600 and there are three borrowers eligible for cover, each would be covered for £200'.

The insurer appeared to have accepted at an early stage that there was some substance in the complaint. It accepted our recommendation that it should make an additional payment to Mrs H on the basis that her true entitlement was to benefit payments of £500, plus interest. It also increased its compensation offer to £200.

4/2   loan protection—accidental death—meaning of 'accidental'

A young couple, Mr and Mrs R, had mortgage payment protection insurance which included accidental death cover. When Mrs R died suddenly, her husband claimed the policy benefit. The insurer made enquiries and was advised that the cause of death was pneumococcal meningitis and pneumonia. It rejected the claim on the ground that the death was not caused by an accident.

Mr R argued that the policy defined 'accident' as 'a sudden unforeseen unintentional violent external event' and that his claim was therefore valid, particularly as the policy did not exclude death by sickness or disease.

Complaint rejected

An exclusion for death by sickness or disease would only be necessary if the definition of 'accident' were wide enough to include such deaths. It was not. Mrs R's death resulted not from an accident but from a viral infection. We accepted that the death was accidental in the sense that it was not anticipated. However, it could not be regarded as due to a 'violent external event' in any ordinary use of that term. We did not agree there was any ambiguity in the policy terms and we considered the insurer was entitled to reject the claim.

4/3   loan protection—eligibility—self-employed insured on 'maternity leave'—whether 'actively working at her business'

Mrs M was a self-employed dietician for a dieting organisation. After the birth of her child in February 1998, she did not return to work for some months. In June 1998, while she was still unemployed, a lender telephoned to offer a loan to her and her husband, who was in full-time employment. She was also offered insurance to cover the repayments and she agreed to take out both the loan and the insurance. The paperwork named only Mrs M as the borrower but she did not consider this important.

Mrs M returned to work in September 1998, but was offered less work than previously and her earnings were only £12 per week. Her husband fell ill in November and was diagnosed as having a brain tumour.

When the couple put in a claim for disability benefits, they were told the policy did not cover him. Mrs M contended that when the policy was sold she had provided full details of her husband's earnings and her own status, and had discussed the recent birth of their child.

Complaint upheld

It was up to the insurer to prove that the policy had been properly sold and that the sale complied with the provisions of the ABI Code. The insurer was clearly aware that Mrs M was both self-employed and on 'maternity leave'. Since she was not 'actively working at her business' she was not eligible for the policy. However, we did not consider that the insurer's refunding the premium constituted an appropriate resolution of the dispute.

We accepted the insurer's contention that the policy could have been transferred into the husband's name at Mrs M's request. However, we did not agree that her failure to make such a request meant she had deliberately chosen not to take out cover for her husband. We were satisfied that the policy had not been properly explained at the time of the sale.

The appropriate outcome was for the insurer to amend its records to include the name of the husband on the policy and to meet his disability claim.

4/4   loan protection—unemployment—fixed-term contract—whether claim for unemployment at end of fixed-term contract valid

A university lecturer, Dr J, took out a loan with loan protection insurance in May 1999. On 1 October that year, he became unemployed and claimed benefit under the insurance. The insurer rejected his claim, stating that the policy did not cover unemployment occurring at the end of a fixed-term contract.

Dr J maintained that his claim was covered, as the policy stated that the exclusion did not apply because he had been 'in continuous work for the same employer for at least 24 months, and [his] contract has been renewed at least twice and [he had] no reason to believe that it would not be renewed again'.

However, Dr J's employer stated that his contract had been from 20 January 1997 until 1 October 1999 and that he had been told on 27 October 1998 that it would not be renewed.

Complaint rejected

It was clear that Dr J had been aware before taking out the loan that he would become unemployed on 1 October 1999. There were no grounds for requiring the insurer to make any payment to him. Moreover, on the facts, Dr J did not meet the other conditions of the exception as there was no evidence that his contract had been renewed twice.

4/5   loan protection—disability—exclusion for any mental or nervous disorder—insured made redundant and affected by stress—whether insurer liable for disability or unemployment benefit

Miss K was made redundant in January 1999. She subsequently became unwell and her GP signed her off with depression. When she submitted a claim for disability benefits under her loan payment protection insurance, the insurer rejected it on the ground that the policy specifically excluded claims 'caused or aggravated by any psychiatric illness or any mental or nervous disorder'. She was unable to claim unemployment benefit because her illness prevented her from signing on. She was not therefore 'actively seeking new employment'. Miss K maintained it was unfair to deny her benefit on either ground because of her circumstances.

Complaint upheld in part

We were concerned about the impact of the two exclusions on the claimant. Redundancy is likely to be a difficult time for anyone and stress and/or depression can be common. The policy clearly excluded any claim for mental illness, so Miss K was not entitled to disability benefit.

However, since she would have been entitled to redundancy benefits if she had not been signed off with depression, we did not consider it would be fair for her to forgo all benefits. In the circumstances, we concluded that payment of 50% of the maximum benefit was appropriate.

4/6   loan protection—unemployment—exclusion for employees working outside UK— insured employed abroad but registered as unemployed in UK—whether claim valid

Mr D worked as an oil industry welder in the UK. In March 1999 he bought a car on hire purchase and took out insurance to cover the loan repayments. In June 1999 his employment was terminated. He obtained work as a welder through an agency in Manchester and was employed in Belgium from August 1999 until January 2000, when that job was terminated. He then returned to the UK and signed on as unemployed.

The insurer rejected his claim for unemployment benefit on the ground that the policy contained an exclusion for anyone working outside the UK.

Complaint upheld

Mr D was a UK citizen who had returned to the UK and was registered for employment here. This was not a case where there was a need for the insurer to make enquiries of the relevant authorities abroad to see whether he met foreign criteria for state benefits. We considered that Mr D had complied with the spirit of the policy terms, if not with the strict wording. The insurer agreed to our recommendation that it should meet the claim and reimburse any penalties charged by the lender.

4/7 loan protection—unemployment—insured unable to sign on as disabled—whether unemployment claim valid—whether payment of disability claim reduced entitlement to unemployment benefits

Mr E was employed as a courier/driver from November 1998 until spring 1999. He submitted disability claims for benefits under a number of loan payment policies, stating that he had been signed off work by his GP from 13 April 1999 for whiplash injuries and anxiety.

When the insurer asked for confirmation of Mr E's employment, his employer stated that his last day at work was 11 April 1999, although on Mr E's P45 the employer had given the date as 31 March. The employer refused to answer all further enquiries from the insurer.

The insurer rejected the claim on the ground that Mr E had ceased working before becoming unwell. However, after Mr E won a claim for unfair dismissal at an industrial tribunal it agreed to review the claim. The insurer paid Mr E disability benefits under the three policies from 13 April until 12 December 1999, the date when his GP said he was fit for work.

Thereafter, Mr E submitted an unemployment claim and was paid benefit under one of his policies for the balance of the policy maximum of 360 days. The insurer rejected Mr E's claims on the other policies because he had cancelled the policies. Mr E said he had only done this because the insurer had refused his disability claims.

Complaint upheld

Mr E had taken out protection against both disability and unemployment and both these misfortunes had befallen him at the same time. His first sick note was dated 12 April, immediately after his employment was terminated.

We therefore considered that a separate maximum benefit period applied for the unemployment claim and that the insurer should not have combined this with the disability claim. Both policies clearly provided for a maximum unemployment benefit of 360 days. So Mr E's claims should not have been limited by the payment of the earlier disability benefits and his unemployment benefit should have run from the date he was first able to sign on.

With respect to the two cancelled policies, we put it to the insurer that Mr E had cancelled them simply because of justifiable frustration at the handling of his claims, not because he no longer wished the insurer to consider claims under those policies. The insurer agreed to treat the claims as if the policies had continued in force.

4/8 legal expenses—policy covering 'any acts affecting policyholder's legal rights'— policyholder claiming cover to determine his legal rights—whether claim valid

When Mr and Mrs G bought their house in July 1997, they found their drive obstructed by a fence panel which their neighbours had erected. They could not reach agreement with their neighbours as to the correct boundary and, in February 2000, the neighbours issued proceedings.

Mr and Mrs G notified their legal expenses insurer that they were claiming indemnity for their legal costs. The insurer rejected their claim, stating that the policy only covered 'any act which affects [their] legal rights arising out of or to do with [their] living in or owning [their] home'. The insurer contended that until Mr and Mrs G had proved that their rights had been affected by the neighbours' action, it had no liability to provide any indemnity.

Complaint upheld

If the court decided that Mr and Mrs G were wrong, then it could not be said that the neighbours' act had affected their legal rights. Nevertheless, it could not be correct that cover only operated after the issue in dispute had been determined.

The insurer was, of course, entitled to receive sufficient evidence to show that a *'prima facie'* case existed, but in our view the policyholder could establish his 'rights' by producing evidence, such as documents, before the case had come to court.

In this instance, in April 2000 the policyholders' solicitor had sent the insurer documents which established that Mr and Mrs G had a *prima facie* case, and the insurer had not explained why the claim was not covered. We upheld Mr and Mrs G's complaint and the insurer agreed to provide indemnity for all 'reasonable and necessary costs' they had incurred since 28 February 2000, the date when it had rejected the claim.

4/9 household contents—policy limits—limit for high risk items—whether insurer making limits clear to policyholder

The insurance Mrs M arranged for her household contents had a standard limit of £7,500 for high risk items. She was sent confirmation of her policy details which stated:

'Your policy will be issued with a limit of £11,500 for High Risk Items and a High Risk Item single article limit of £1,000. If you require the total High Risk Items limit to be increased, please state the amount required. If there are any High Risk Items which exceed £1,000, please provide the descriptions and values in the box below.'

Mrs M provided the insurer with details of a number of items she wished to specify separately. When she was burgled, the loss adjusters recommended settlement of her claim at £11,504.09 for the high risk items and £7,179 for the specified articles. The insurer refused to make these payments, stating that Mrs M was under-insured. It said the values she stated for the high risk Items should have been sufficient to include all the specified items as well as those not specified.

Complaint upheld

The insurer had failed to make the policy limits clear to Mrs M. The wording of the confirmation details was not plain and Mrs M and the insurer had different recollections of their conversation before the policy was issued. We were not satisfied that the insurer had asked clear questions, as it was required to do under the ABI Statement.

We concluded it was not appropriate for the insurer to reduce the claim because the high risk items limit was insufficient to include the items specified separately. We considered it should meet the claim in full, subject to deduction of the additional premium it would have charged.

4/10 household contents—policy limits—valuables—conflicting limits—whether both limits had to be drawn to policyholder's attention

Mrs L had a collection of ornaments and claimed £1,200 under her household insurance when her granddaughter accidentally damaged some of them. Initially, the insurer rejected her claim, stating that she had not chosen the optional accidental damage policy extension to her contents cover. She disputed this and the insurer accepted that the ornaments came within the definition of 'valuables' for which she was covered. However, it sent her a cheque for only £500, the maximum payable. This was because the policy stated that the single article limit applied to 'any item, collection or set'.

Complaint upheld

There was no doubt that the damaged items were part of a collection or set. However, we agreed with the policyholder that there was a discrepancy in the policy wording. The schedule simply referred to the single article limit and did not mention collections or sets. That limit appeared only on page 21 of the policy.

Moreover, this was a significant restriction which should have been clearly drawn to Mrs L's attention. It would not be difficult for the £500 limit to be exceeded by almost any collection of jewellery, pictures or works of art. The insurer accepted our view that the claim should be met in full.

4/11 personal possessions—cover for lost property—exclusion for unattended property—whether exclusion a significant restriction on cover

Mr B bought a mobile telephone and insured it. The policy provided an indemnity if the phone were lost or stolen. However, it specifically excluded 'theft or damage arising where equipment is left unattended by the insured . . . in any property, place or premises or in or on any form of public conveyance'.

After a shopping trip, Mr B reported that his phone had been lost or stolen, probably after he had left it on a shop counter. The insurer repudiated liability, in accordance with the exclusion. It also contended that Mr B was in breach of a policy condition to take all reasonable precautions to prevent loss or damage.

Complaint upheld

Within 20 minutes of realising that he did not have his phone, Mr B returned to the shop where he thought he had left it. The phone had clearly been 'unattended' during his absence. However, by applying the exclusion to losses as well as to theft claims, the insurer had severely restricted the cover it purported to provide. This exclusion should therefore have been drawn to Mr B's attention before he bought the policy. Since the insurer could provide no proof that this had happened, we did not consider it could rely on the exclusion.

As to lack of reasonable care, the insurer had to prove that Mr B had been reckless and there was no evidence of this. Mr B had acted inadvertently and had not exhibited any lack of care. We therefore required the insurer to reimburse the cost of the phone and to add interest to its payment.

4/12 household buildings—landslip—exclusion for 'faulty design'—boundary fence failing to prevent landslip—whether design of fence 'faulty'

The house Mr A bought in 1992 was part of a new development whose back gardens overlooked a railway embankment. His garden was separated from the top of the embankment by a large fence, set into the embankment with tall posts similar to telegraph poles.

By the following year, the fence was leaning outwards over the embankment and a fissure appeared in the lawn. Mr A replaced the fence and built a patio over the lawn. But by 1995, both were showing signs of downward creep. A new fence was put up in 1997, but did not remedy the problem, so Mr A claimed for the cost of stabilising his property.

The insurer refused indemnity. It concluded that the original fence was built to retain the embankment and its replacement had failed to prevent movement of the site. As the policy excluded damage due to 'faulty design', it said it had no liability for the cost of repairs.

Complaint upheld in part

We appointed a surveyor to advise whether the original fence had been constructed in order to retain the embankment. He concluded that the builder had not taken the possibility of landslip into account and that the design of the fence could not be regarded as faulty. In any event, we were not persuaded that a fence could 'retain' an embankment which lay below it.

We required the insurer to deal with the damage to Mr A's property. However, it did not have any liability for stabilising the embankment. The embankment was not part of Mr B's property and such works would constitute significant betterment.

4/13 travel—cover terminating on return home—policyholder returning home before end of trip—whether cover in force

Mr and Mrs N took out holiday insurance to cover them from 6–30 October 1998. They spent the first part of their holiday in Italy, where they met an old friend, Mr G. They decided to return home earlier than they originally intended—on 26 October. They planned to collect fresh clothes and provisions before setting off for Wales with Mr G. However, after Mrs N had dropped off her husband at home, together with Mr G, while she went to fill up the car with petrol, she was killed in an accident.

Mr N made a claim under the policy for death benefit of £60,000. However, the insurer said the policy stated that cover 'finishes immediately [they returned] to [their] home . . . for any reason'. Mr N argued, first, that his wife had not returned home since she had merely dropped him off there with Mr G before going to the filling station. Second he contended that the insurance had not expired because the policy was due to continue until 30 October.

Complaint upheld

The personal accident section of the policy stated that benefit was payable while the policyholders were on their 'trip'. This was defined as 'any journey or holiday . . . which starts and finishes in the United Kingdom . . . for which [the policyholder has] paid the premium'.

We considered the word 'trip' was wide enough to cover a two stage holiday, even though that holiday was broken by a stopover at the travellers' home, provided that it was over by 30 October. The insurer accepted that Mr N had a valid claim for benefit and interest.

4/14   travel—policy limits—loss or theft of cash—whether limits clear

Mr T took out 'gold plus' travel insurance to cover his holiday in Corfu. The policy included cover for loss of money. A table on the front of the policy stated that the limit of cover was £500, although it also said 'This is a guide only. Please read the terms and conditions of this insurance'.

The policy terms provided: 'We will pay up to £500.00 for the loss or theft of cash or travel cheques, if you can give us evidence that you owned them and evidence of their value. We will pay up to £300.00 for cash for travel outside Area 1 and up to £150.00 for places within Area 1 for gold plus cover, winter sports cover and multi-trip cover only.' Area 1 was defined as Europe.

Mr T's money was stolen while he was on the way to Corfu. The insurer settled his claim subject to the £150 gold plus cover limit. Mr T argued that the proper limit was £500, which the insurer had several times confirmed as applicable.

Complaint upheld

The policy document was confusing. The first line stated that the insurer would pay up to £500 if a claimant could provide evidence of ownership and value. Mr T had done this. However, the insurer argued that the rest of the section contained a limitation. This was not clear to the reader. Indeed, it was not clear whether the insurer would ever pay up to £500 if the upper limit outside Area 1 was set at £300.

We were satisfied not only that the limit had not been pointed out to Mr T, but that he had been assured there was cover for up to £500. We recommended that the insurer should pay Mr T the outstanding balance between its settlement and his loss, up to £500, and it agreed to do this.

4/15   medical expenses—exclusion for treatment related to engagement in professional sport—meaning of 'professional sport'

The policyholder had insurance to cover his family's medical expenses and submitted claims for the cost of treatment for his daughter, a member of the Great Britain Ladies Hockey Team. The insurer made enquiries and established that she had been given an award from the Sport England Lottery Fund (World Class). It considered that treatment of her sports injuries was excluded under the policy. This was because it decided the treatment consisted of 'care and/or treatment arising from or related to engaging in professional sport'.

The policy defined 'professional sport' as 'a sport where a fee or benefit in kind is received either directly or indirectly for playing or training'. The policyholder stated that the Inland Revenue did not treat the lottery grant as 'income'. He said the insurer had not notified him when it added this restriction to the policy and he denied his daughter was a 'professional' player.

The insurer did meet the claims, but it did not admit liability. The policyholder was dissatisfied with the way the insurer had handled matters and claimed compensation for the distress and inconvenience caused by the insurer's disputing liability.

Complaint upheld in part

The insurer seemed to have interpreted its definition of 'professional' sports people as including those who were seriously committed players. This extended the definition beyond its generally accepted meaning. The lottery grant was not directly related to past or future appearances, performance or training requirements; it could more properly be described as a charitable donation. We did not agree that it was a 'fee or benefit in kind' or that receiving this payment had altered the status of the policyholder's daughter from amateur to professional. We agreed with the policyholder that the insurer was liable for the cost of his daughter's treatment.

However, the insurer's handling of the claims was not unacceptable. We had not agreed with the insurer's interpretation of the exclusion, but the judgment was a fine one and the insurer's position was not without merit. Any annoyance the policyholder had experienced did not amount to material maladministration. We therefore concluded it would not be right to award any compensation.

4/16   household—sum insured—inflation-linking causing policyholder to be over-insured—whether policyholder entitled to premium refund

Mrs G and her aunt had, for many years, held household buildings and contents insurance for their two-bedroom terraced house in Wales. The policy was inflation-linked and premiums increased by 15%

annually. Mrs G did not query the sums insured until 1999, when her daughter began managing her affairs. The annual premium had increased by then to £1,674.91. The contents were insured for £141,488 and the buildings sum insured was £212,042. The correct amounts should have been £40,000 and £55,000 respectively.

The insurer accepted that the values for both buildings and contents were far too high and it offered a rebate of £1,000 and a further year's cover without charge.

Complaint upheld

Although it was the policyholder's responsibility to assess the replacement cost, the consequence in this case of the firm's applying an automatic annual increase was an insured value which was totally unjustified. If the policyholder submitted a total loss claim, the sums insured would have had no bearing on the insurer's liability.

We considered a fair result would be achieved if the insurer refunded 50% of the premiums paid over the previous five years, with interest, and it agreed to do this.

4/17   household contents—minimum security requirements—policyholder noting requirements before start of insurance—whether policyholder entitled to compensation for distress and inconvenience—maladministration—distress and inconvenience—whether cancellation of policy by policyholder justified compensation

Mr C telephoned the insurer on 12 June to ask about household insurance. He wanted the cover to start on 1 July. When he received the policy documents, he was dismayed to learn that cover depended on his complying with a minimum security condition. He protested, saying no one had mentioned this when he enquired about the policy, and he cancelled the policy on 21 June. The insurer returned his premium in full but rejected his demand for a payment of £3,000 as compensation for the inconvenience he said the insurer had caused him.

Complaint rejected

The insurer recorded most calls made to its call centres and we were able to listen to tape recordings of Mr C's conversations with the insurer's staff. On several occasions, matters of security had been discussed at considerable length. We were therefore surprised that Mr C alleged he had not been told of the insurer's requirements. He had not been put to any unnecessary inconvenience and we agreed that the insurer was fully justified in refusing to pay compensation.

4/18   household buildings—sum insured—reinstatement—whether insurer entitled to limit cost of reinstatement to sum insured

Following a serious fire at Mrs Y's house in March 1999, the insurer appointed loss adjusters to assess the damage. They considered that repairs would not exceed the sum insured of £110,000. They also calculated that the sum insured was too low and that the cost of rebuilding would be £135,000. Mrs Y increased the sum insured to the amount they recommended.

The insurer paid over £7,000 for emergency works to make the property safe, but there was bad weather in April and further damage occurred. When tenders for the repairs came in, however, the lowest was for £139,250. The insurer agreed to reinstate the property, but it limited repair works to a total of £103,000—the sum insured less the cost of emergency work. This was sufficient to rebuild the property, but left the first floor a shell.

Mrs Y said she had been promised that if she increased the sum insured to the amount the loss adjusters recommended, the insurer would meet the claim in full and would make no deduction for under-insurance.

Complaint upheld

The policy gave the insurer the option of making a cash settlement, repairing, replacing or reinstating. The insurer had clearly opted to reinstate and was therefore bound to replace as new, with no deduction for wear and tear or depreciation. The cost was accordingly not limited to the sum insured.

If the insurer wished to impose a ceiling of £110,000 on its liability, it had to communicate that to the policyholder. It had not done this until after the house had been demolished and it could not impose the limit in the middle of agreed works. We required the insurer to meet the full cost of reinstatement.

4/19 maladministration—confidentiality—insurer disclosing information in breach of policyholder's instructions—whether compensation payable

Mr D insured his house and garage with one insurer, while the business property, which he stored in the garage, was insured by a different insurer. When he made a claim under the business property policy, the loss adjusters appointed by that insurer wrote to Mr D's household insurer, seeking information. The household insurer responded, confirming that it insured the house and garage, giving the policy number, and stating that no claim had been received.

Mr D was extremely aggrieved to learn that his household insurer had provided information to the loss adjusters, asserting that this was in breach both of his specific instructions and the Data Protection Act. He demanded £60,000 compensation for damage to his stock. The household insurer accepted that it should not have released information to the loss adjusters. It offered Mr D £100 in recognition of the distress and inconvenience it had caused.

Complaint rejected

There was no link between the household insurer's unauthorised disclosure of information to the loss adjusters and any loss by Mr D. No evidence had appeared which indicated that the disclosure had influenced the loss adjusters' handling of the business insurance claim. In the circumstances, we were satisfied that the insurer's offer was appropriate and we stated that we would not require it to increase its offer or to contribute to Mr D's alleged losses.

4/20 household—sum insured

Mr J insured his house for an index-linked sum—£285,000—when he renewed the insurance in 1993. In February 1995, he discovered landslip damage to his tennis court. He appointed an engineer and notified the insurer. It became apparent almost immediately that the damage was progressing rapidly and, in March 1995, the insurer agreed to pay for emergency work to stabilise the site.

This work did not halt the slippage and a meeting was held in June 1995 to discuss possible remedies. Mr J asked the insurer to settle his claim by declaring the property a total loss and paying the full sum insured. However, the insurer's loss adjusters were of the opinion that the insurer's liability was limited to underwriting the cost of remedial work up to the sum insured.

Work continued, becoming more complicated as time went on, until eventually the site was stabilised. The insurer informed Mr J that the sum insured had been exhausted. He complained, asserting that the insurer had elected in June 1995 to reinstate the property instead of making a cash settlement, and that it was therefore bound to meet the balance of the full cost of repairing his house. This was estimated at £145,000.

Complaint upheld

Cases of catastrophe such as this are fortunately very rare. The sum insured had been correctly calculated and was sufficient to cover the rebuilding and associated fees, as stipulated in the policy. However, it was not sufficient to cover the additional cost of stabilising the site. Although insurers are generally aware there is a theoretical possibility of rebuilding costs exceeding an adequate sum insured, the insurer in this case had not advised Mr J of this possibility.

The insurer had never agreed to reinstate the property regardless of cost. However, we did not accept it was appropriate for it to limit its settlement of this claim to the sum insured. The insurer had been closely involved in approving repairs and, once they had begun, both the insurer and the policyholder had effectively been committed to their completion. It was reasonable for Mr J to believe his property would be fully reinstated and he could not be said to have been indemnified if he was left with a badly cracked house on a stable site.

More generally, Mr J was not in a position to assess the likelihood of such rare combinations of events when he decided on the sum insured. The sum insured was generally accepted to be appropriate and we concluded that, in such cases, the sum insured should not act as an absolute cap on the insurer's liability. We therefore required the insurer to pay £100,000 towards Mr J's repair costs. We also recommended the insurer to meet the balance of his costs, although we had no jurisdiction to make a binding award for any amount in excess of £100,000.

4/21 **household buildings—cover dependent on satisfactory survey—delay by insurer in arranging survey—whether policyholder prejudiced by cancellation of cover**

Miss F had a mortgage valuation survey carried out in November 1998 before she purchased her rented property. The surveyor noted the presence of minor hairline differential cracking and a slight bulge in one wall. He concluded there was no indication of recent or continuing movement and suggested the most likely cause was historic bomb damage. Miss F telephoned the insurer asking for insurance cover. Policy documents were issued on 15 December, with the proviso 'Cover is provided subject to a satisfactory building survey.'

The insurer did not have the survey carried out for two months, but progressive movement was then identified and the insurer cancelled the policy. Miss F was dissatisfied and asserted that the insurer's delay in carrying out the full survey had prejudiced her. The insurer maintained that she was advised during her initial telephone conversation that cover was conditional on a satisfactory survey and it stated that the risk did not meet its underwriting criteria. However, it agreed to extend cover until May 2000. Miss F remained dissatisfied and sought compensation.

Complaint upheld

It was not possible to determine whether Miss F was advised of the need for a full survey during the telephone conversation. Even if she was, she might not have acted any differently. She was clearly aware of the cracking and did not consider it significant. Moreover, she had the opportunity of cancelling the policy when she received confirmation of the proposal, highlighting the insurer's requirement. However, the delay in carrying out the survey was regrettable and the insurer's decision to cancel the policy meant Miss F would almost certainly be unable to find alternative cover.

The insurer accepted that its delay had prejudiced Miss F. It would now be extremely difficult for her to go back to her last insurer or to find another. We considered the insurer should reinstate the policy without conditions, which it agreed to do. However, we did not think there was any justification for awarding compensation in addition to reinstating the policy.

4/22 **caravan—minimum security requirements—theft—whether theft linked to breach of requirements—whether insurer entitled to reject theft claim**

Mr J submitted a claim for the theft of his caravan and its contents. The insurer rejected the claim on the ground that he had not complied with the policy's security requirements. The caravan's storage facility did not have security lighting and the gate to the caravan park had been unlocked.

Mr J pointed out that he had fitted the caravan with a hitch lock and wheel clamp and that the park had some 25 other caravans. Although he accepted that there was no security lighting, he stated this was usual and that, in any event, lighting would not have deterred the thieves.

Complaint upheld

There was no evidence as to whether the theft had taken place at night or in the daytime or whether the gate was open or merely unpadlocked. In the circumstances, we were not persuaded that Mr J's failure to comply with all the security requirements was linked to the theft. The ABI Statement says that insurers will not reject claims on the ground of a breach of condition unless the loss is connected with the breach. We therefore recommended that the insurer should meet the claim in full and it agreed to do so.

4/23 **caravan—minimum security requirements—theft—whether policyholder's failure to secure caravan justified rejection of theft claim**

Mr S purchased a caravan on 20 June 2000. He took it on a trip on 10 July and brought it back on 13 July, when he left it at a friend's house for four days. He was aware that he needed to buy a wheel clamp and other accessories, but on 16 July, before he had done so, the caravan was stolen.

The insurer rejected Mr S's theft claim on the grounds that he had failed both to exercise reasonable care and to safeguard the vehicle, because it had no wheel clamp and was neither attached to a hitch post nor stored in a secure compound. Mr S explained that he had been about to comply with the insurer's requirements but the caravan was stolen before he could do so.

215

Complaint rejected

Although the caravan had been left unsecured for only a short period, the policy endorsement applied regardless of the length of time. We were satisfied that Mr S knew which precautions he was required to take and had simply failed to secure the vehicle when he left. In the circumstances, we were satisfied that the insurer's rejection of his claim was justified.

ISSUE 7: JULY 2001

7/1 travel—accidental death benefit—exclusion for 'hazardous activities'—whether exclusion brought to insured's attention

Mr H took out an annual travel policy for his two adult sons before they went to America in May 1999. The insurer took approximately three weeks to issue the policy and then sent it to Mr H. As he was away at the time, the sons were unable to check—before they set out on their trip—whether the policy was suitable for their needs. In fact, it was not. It restricted cover for individual trips to 30 days, whereas they planned to be away for 74 days, and it did not cover claims arising from hazardous activities, including riding motorcycles over 125cc.

The following April, one of Mr H's sons went out to Australia. Whilst there, he had a fatal accident riding a 600cc motorcycle. Mr and Mrs H put in a claim for repatriation and funeral expenses and for the accidental death benefit of £30,000.

The insurer explained that, because of the motorcycle exclusion, the policy did not provide any cover. However, it accepted that it had not sold, issued or explained the policy correctly. It therefore met the repatriation and funeral expenses as a gesture of goodwill. Mr and Mrs H did not accept that the motorcycle exclusion was valid, since it had not been drawn to their attention, and they felt they were entitled to the full death benefit.

Complaint rejected

Mr H bought the policy specifically for the trip to America and had decided to buy an annual policy because of the length of the trip. The insurer had accepted that the policy had not been properly sold and it confirmed that it would not have relied on the exclusions or restrictions to repudiate any claims arising during the trip to America.

However, by the time of the second trip, the family was aware that the policy did not cover all hazardous activities and the policyholders had had ample opportunity to check whether the policy was appropriate for their needs and to request an amendment if necessary. The policy was, in any event, due to lapse shortly after the son's departure to Australia yet they had not checked that it would cover the trip or the activities he planned. In these circumstances, we took the view that the insurer's offer to pay the repatriation and funeral costs was reasonable and that it had no liability for the death claim.

7/2 travel—baggage—temporary loss—meaning of 'temporary'

Mr and Mrs N flew to Barcelona to join a cruise and the airline lost Mr N's baggage. He notified the cruise operator and was advised that the insurer would reimburse emergency purchases. He bought some shirts and, some days later, other clothing. His bag was found fairly quickly and was sent to the ship when it docked at Athens.

Mr N claimed £345 from the insurer. It sent him a cheque for £150, explaining that this was the maximum payable for temporary loss of baggage. The insurer submitted a claim to the airline and in due course received £150, which it regarded as reimbursment of its payment to Mr N.

Mr N argued that his claim should not be limited because the loss was not 'temporary'. He had restricted his purchases until the ship had left port and had no means of knowing when or if his bag would be found.

Complaint upheld in part

We accepted that a claimant could not know for some time whether the loss of baggage was temporary and that Mr N had taken all reasonable steps to minimise his expenditure. However, he had received his bag within a week and the policy terms made the limited nature of this cover clear. The insurer was justified in limiting its payment to £150.

However, Mr N was entitled to payment from the airline in priority to the insurer's right to recover its payment to him. We decided the insurer should not have kept the airline's payment and should send it to Mr N, giving him a total recovery of £300.

7/3 travel—baggage—theft—exclusion for theft at night from unattended vehicle—whether exclusion onerous

Miss H went on holiday with her partner to Crete. They left a beach bag containing a camera, two mobile phones, a tape player and some cash, in the locked boot of their hire car. The car was broken into and Miss H claimed for theft of the bag. The insurer rejected the claim on the ground that all the items were within the policy definition of 'valuables' and therefore excluded from cover in unattended motor vehicles.

The policy defined 'valuables' as 'photographic and video equipment, camcorders, radios and personal stereo equipment, computers, computer games and associated equipment, hearing aids, mobile telephones, telescopes and binoculars, antiques, jewellery, watches, furs, precious stones and articles made of or containing gold, silver or other precious metals or animal skins or hides'.

Miss H argued that the policy was self-contradictory, in that another exclusion stated that the insurer would not be liable for 'any theft from motor vehicles left unattended at any time between 10 pm and 8 am'.

Complaint upheld in part

We did not agree that there was a contradiction between the two exclusions; the more onerous exclusion applied only to valuables and meant that they were not covered at any time in an unattended car.

However, that exclusion was unusually onerous and required Miss H to take specific action in order to maintain cover under the policy. The insurer should therefore have drawn it to her attention at the time she bought the insurance. There was no evidence that the insurer had done so.

The fact that she had been given time to read the policy and the option to cancel it was not sufficient for the insurer to comply with its duty to draw such exclusions to the attention of anyone purchasing the policy. We required the insurer to deal with the claim. However, the policy contained a limit of £200 for all valuables and an excess of £45 for cash. These meant that Miss H and her partner would not be reimbursed for the majority of their losses.

7/4 travel—cancellation—disability—cause known to policyholder when buying insurance—whether claim valid

On 28 January 2000, Mr A booked air tickets for his family to travel from Manchester to Saudi Arabia on holiday from 8 to 30 March. On 26 February, he bought insurance to cover their travel. He cancelled the flights on 2 March, stating that Mrs A was suffering from complications of her pregnancy and that travel was inadvisable for her.

The insurer's investigation established that Mr A had tried unsuccessfully to amend the air tickets on 7 February and that his wife's GP had made a formal diagnosis a week later. The insurer rejected the claim, explaining that the policy did not include cover for any medical condition which existed when the policy was issued on 26 February. Mr A argued that they had no reason to believe that the trip might have to be cancelled when they bought the tickets and he said the sales operator had told him he would be reimbursed if Mrs A became ill. However, the insurer would only refund the premium, not meet the claim.

Complaint rejected

We accepted that Mr and Mrs A did not know that the pregnancy was subject to complications when the flights were booked. However, they had been aware of the problem for two weeks before they bought the insurance. The insurer was therefore fully justified in refusing to meet the claim.

7/5 travel—cancellation—disability arising after start of insurance—whether insurer liable for cancellation cost

In January 2000, Mr W and Mrs G arranged to go on a holiday in July. Mrs G's son was admitted to hospital in April and underwent a series of tests. Mr W and Mrs G paid the balance of the holiday costs on 5 May. The son was discharged in the middle of that month but was referred back to a consultant on 24 May, readmitted to hospital a few days later, and died on 13 June, one day after his illness had been diagnosed.

Mr W and Mrs G claimed reimbursement of the cost of cancelling their holiday, but the insurer refused to make any payment beyond the £200 deposit. It relied on a condition in the policy which required policyholders to notify the insurer's helpline if an immediate relative was 'receiving, recovering from, or on a waiting list for, in-patient treatment in a hospital' or 'waiting for the results of tests or investigations or referral for an existing medical condition'.

Complaint upheld

We interpreted the requirement as applying only at the time the policy was issued in January 2000, as is usual with this type of wording. If the insurer had intended this requirement to cover the whole period until the date of departure, that would be an onerous obligation and the insurer would have had to have made it much clearer in its documentation, as well as drawing it to the attention of potential policyholders.

Moreover, even if we considered it reasonable to treat the condition as if it applied when the balance of the money was paid, the claim would still be valid. Although Mr G was in hospital when the payment was made on 5 May, the insurer accepted that it would have provided full cover after his discharge from hospital in mid-May. He would therefore not have come within the terms of the condition when he saw the consultant on 24 May or was readmitted to hospital on 28 May. The insurer agreed to pay the balance of the holiday cost, which the couple had forfeited when they cancelled.

7/6 travel—cancellation—disability arising after start of insurance—whether insurer liable for full cancellation charge

In February 2000, Mr and Mrs T booked a holiday in Florida for May and paid a deposit. On 17 March, Mrs T fell off a ladder, breaking bones in her foot.

The foot did not heal well and, when the balance of the holiday cost was due to be paid, Mr T telephoned the insurer for advice.

The insurer would not take responsibility for deciding whether the couple should go ahead with the holiday. It told Mr T that if they went ahead and then found Mrs T was not well enough to travel in May, it would only reimburse the deposit, not the balance of the holiday cost. Mrs T's foot was not sufficiently recovered before departure and they cancelled the holiday. Mr and Mrs T claimed the full cost of the holiday, but the insurer refused to pay more than the deposit.

Complaint rejected

It was Mr T's decision to pay the remaining balance, trusting that his wife's foot would have recovered before the holiday started. We were satisfied that the additional expenditure he incurred when paying the balance of the cost of the holiday was a risk he had personally agreed to take. In these unusual circumstances, the insurer was justified in refusing to indemnify him.

7/7 travel—cancellation—event leading to cancellation pre-dating insurance—policyholder choosing date of departure as start date of policy—whether insurer liable for cancellation due to event occurring after insurance bought but before start date

On 9 February 2000, Miss S bought insurance to cover her holiday, which was to begin on 20 February. On 17 February, she injured her back and had to postpone the holiday. A month later, she gave up hope of being fit to travel and cancelled the holiday. She submitted a claim for the cancellation cost, but the insurer refused to make any payment. It explained that she had asked for the policy to come into force on 20 February, which was after her injury had occurred. Even though the cancellation date was after the policy's start date, the insurer considered that the event leading to cancellation had pre-dated the insurance.

Complaint upheld

It is normal practice for policyholders to ask for their insurance to start on the date they book a holiday so that cancellation cover operates immediately. Miss S had bought the policy from her travel agent, but he had apparently not given her any advice as to how she should complete the application form. She had not intentionally inserted an incorrect date for the policy to start, but it was not the insurer's fault that she had asked for cover to begin only on the date of departure. On a strict interpretation, Miss S was not entitled to reimbursement of the cancellation charges. However, owing to the unusual circumstances, we asked the insurer to meet the claim without admitting liability and it agreed to do so. We could not agree that Miss S was also entitled to interest, or to reimbursement of the fee her GP charged for completing her claim form.

7/8 travel—cancellation—exclusion for pre-existing medical conditions—need for exclusion to be drawn to policyholder's attention

Mr R booked a week's holiday in January 2000, with a departure date of 12 May. He knew he was due to undergo surgery for his hernia and the operation was scheduled for June. When Mr R was told the operation would be performed in April, his daughter asked the travel agent what alternatives were available. The travel agent said that the insurer would meet the cost of cancelling the holiday.

However, when Mr R cancelled, the insurer said it was not liable to make any payment, since Mr R had known about his operation since October 1999. The policy excluded any claim arising out of a medical condition which the policyholder was aware of before buying the insurance. Mr R contended that he had not had any reason to expect the surgery would interfere with his holiday. He also said that, had the travel agent not misled his daughter, he would have rearranged the holiday or transferred it to someone else.

Complaint upheld

Mr R could not have been expected to disclose his operation to the insurer unless the travel agent had made him aware of the need to do so, and had explained that the insurer would not otherwise cover any claim resulting from his medical condition. The insurer did not comply sufficiently with the industry selling code by simply requiring the person applying for the insurance to sign a declaration that they had read and understood the policy terms.

Unless there was evidence that the exclusion for pre-existing medical conditions had been drawn to Mr R's attention before he bought the insurance, we considered that the insurer had to meet the cancellation claim. It accepted our view.

7/9 travel—cancellation—exclusion for pre-existing medical conditions—whether complications of surgery a pre-existing medical condition

Mr D booked a holiday for himself, his wife and daughter to start in August 1999. In June, his daughter underwent a kidney transplant and suffered complications, Mr D cancelled the holiday and claimed reimbursement of the cost.

The insurer rejected the claim because Mr D's daughter had suffered from kidney problems and been on dialysis for some years.

Mr D argued that they had not cancelled because of his daughter's kidney problems but because of complications that had arisen after her operation. The operation had not been planned when they booked the holiday, but was a one-off life-saving opportunity that they could not pass up.

Complaint rejected

The policy excluded any condition 'which [they] knew about at the time [they] bought the insurance . . . unless [the insurer] agreed to cover it in writing'. This clearly excluded liability for the claim, even though we acknowledged that the reason for cancelling the holiday was because of deterioration in Miss D's condition.

Although Mr D denied that this exclusion had been discussed with him, he had signed a declaration that he was aware of it. There was clear advice to call the insurer's helpline to arrange cover for any pre-existing condition. However, Mr D had not done so. We considered that the insurer's rejection of the claim was fully justified.

7/10 travel—cancellation—illness of relative—definition of 'relative'—whether illness of next of kin covered

Mrs and Miss M were due to fly to Rome on 6 August 2000. In July, their parish priest was admitted to hospital as an emergency case and put in intensive care. Mrs M cancelled her holiday to stay by his bedside. The insurer rejected her claim for the cost of cancelling the holiday since the policy stated that benefit would be paid for cancellation 'because of the death, injury or illness of a relative, travelling companion or a business colleague', and the priest did not come into any of these categories. The policy definition of 'relative' listed various blood relations. Although the priest was not a blood relation, Mrs M produced proof that she was specifically named as his next of kin.

Complaint upheld

Although the policy definition of 'relative' was clear and the priest did not come within it, the situation was highly unusual and not one which a policy could be expected to mention. In the circumstances, we considered that anyone who is named as 'next of kin' for someone hospitalised on an emergency basis should be treated as a 'relative' of that person. We required the insurer to meet the claim in full.

7/11 travel—cancellation—missed departure—failure or disruption of pre-booked public transport—'additional expenses'—whether cancellation claim valid—whether cost of taxi to and from airport 'additional expenses'

Mr D booked a flight to Malta for a week's holiday and arranged for a car to take him to the airport. A motorway accident, causing serious congestion and tailbacks, meant that he missed the plane. The next flight was not for more than 25 hours and would have cost a further £115, so Mr D decided to give up his holiday and return home.

The insurer refused to reimburse the cost of the flight (£173) because the policy only covered cancellation in the event of 'failure or disruption of the pre-booked public transport service in which the insured is due to depart from the UK'. As the flight had not failed or been disrupted, Mr D's claim was not covered.

Mr D then contended that the insurer should reimburse the cost of the car taking him to the airport as 'additional expenses' for missed departure due to failure of his 'pre-booked connecting public transport'. He produced a taxi receipt for £90 for the return trip.

Complaint rejected

The insurer correctly rejected the cancellation claim. However, Mr D's claim for missing the plane's departure would have been valid, if he could have proved he had incurred additional expenses.

Mr D had not mentioned the costs of the 'taxi' until three months after his claim had been rejected, having previously indicated that a friend drove him to the airport as a favour. And despite the receipt, we were not persuaded that he had actually made any payment.

In any event, we considered that Mr D had not proved that he had incurred any 'additional' expenses as a result of missing the flight. He would have had to meet the cost of travel to and from the airport, even if we accepted that he had agreed to pay the driver. We therefore rejected the complaint.

7/12 travel—exclusion for unattended baggage—policyholder sitting next to bag but distracted by thief—whether bag 'unattended'

Mr N was on holiday in New York. While he was sitting on a subway platform bench waiting for a train, another traveller started a conversation with him. When Mr N looked around a minute or two later, he found his rucksack had been taken from the seat beside him. He claimed for theft of £2,000 of personal belongings and about £400 cash. The insurer rejected the claim on the ground that the rucksack was 'unattended' and therefore specifically excluded from cover.

Complaint upheld

It could not be said that the bag was unattended when Mr N was in reasonable proximity at the time. Indeed, this was borne out by the circumstances of the theft. There would have been no need for one of the thieves to distract Mr N by engaging him in conversation if the bag had been unattended: the thieves could just have taken it.

The mere fact that a theft had occurred did not prove that property was 'unattended'. If there had been any indication that Mr N had walked away from his bag and returned to find it stolen, it would have been different. The insurer accepted our view that it should meet the claim, subject to the policy limits of £1,500 per bag and £400 total cash, less the policy excess.

7/13 travel—fraud—burden of proof

Mrs B's handbag was stolen when she was on holiday in Spain. She claimed for the bag and contents, including a neck pendant. The insurer asked her to provide receipts and the receipt for the pendant showed a price of £474. After making enquiries, the insurer established that the receipt had been altered. The true cost was £74.

The insurer rejected the claim in full, quoting the policy provision that it would not pay for any claim 'if it is either in whole or in any part fraudulent'. Mrs B asserted that she had bought the pendant from a friend and had not altered the receipt, although her friend might have done. The insurer was unable to make contact with the friend and Mrs B could not produce anything from him to support her story.

Complaint rejected

There was no evidence or other information to support Mrs B's assertion. Although she alleged that her friend had defrauded her, there was no evidence she had bought the necklace from the friend and she had not initiated any legal action against her friend. Whilst she might be entirely innocent of any attempt to defraud the insurer, our informal procedures were not suitable for the full examination of witnesses that would be necessary to try and establish all the facts of the case. We recommended Mrs B to consider pursuing her claim through the courts, where witnesses could be compelled to attend and undergo a thorough cross-examination.

7/14 travel—loss—proof—policyholder failing to provide police report—whether insurer liable for claim

Miss K left her wash bag in the aeroplane toilet when travelling to Spain. She submitted a claim for make-up and jewellery valued at £3,200. The insurer rejected her claim on the ground that she had not obtained a written police report of the loss, as required by the travel policy terms. She argued that a report was unnecessary since the police would not be interested, but she stated that she had informed the police.

This statement was contradicted by the claim form, in which she said only that she had told the airline crew and ground staff. The insurer made enquiries with the Spanish police. However, they did not recognise the police reference number Miss K had quoted and there was no mention of Miss K in the police records. Nevertheless, the insurer agreed to reconsider the claim if Miss K could provide any evidence that she had reported the loss to anyone.

Complaint rejected

The burden of proving a loss which is covered by the policy rests with the claimant in the first place. We could not say the insurer was unreasonable in refusing to accept Miss K's account without independent verification. It was somewhat unusual that she had no other insurance, such as a household policy, to protect such valuable items, and her word alone was not sufficient to validate the claim.

7/15 travel—loss—proof—written police report—whether report essential to validate claim

Mrs M's ring was damaged while she was on holiday in Malta. She made a claim for £124, the cost of repairing it and replacing one stone. The insurer refused to make any payment, citing the policy wording which stated that it would not pay 'for loss or theft of valuables . . . and any item valued over £100 not reported to the police'. Mrs M argued that the requirement was not appropriate in her case, as the police would not have been prepared to document the damage to her ring.

Complaint upheld

The policy defined valuables as 'items containing precious or semi-precious stones'. Although the ring came within the definition, Mrs M had not lost the ring, only one stone. The estimate for replacing it was less than £100 and therefore it was neither a 'valuable' nor 'any item valued over £100'.

One of the reasons insurers require police reports is to provide independent evidence that a loss has occurred. In addition to submitting an estimate, Mrs M had provided a letter from the holiday group leader confirming that the ring had been damaged. The insurer agreed to meet the cost of replacing the stone and repairing the ring, less the £35 policy excess.

7/16   **travel—medical expenses—exclusion for pre-existing medical conditions—policyholder required to obtain permission to travel—whether permission could be given retrospectively**

Mr M went on a long cruise. He was robbed in Singapore and then, two weeks later, became ill with chest pains. He was transferred to a hospital in Jordan, where he was found to be suffering from unstable angina. Subsequently he was repatriated. When the insurer carried out medical enquiries it learnt that Mr M had an extensive history of heart problems. It referred him to the policy conditions and to a declaration he had signed on the policy application form saying he was in good health. These conditions provided that the insurer would not be liable for claims if the policyholder had 'during the 12 months prior to taking out this policy suffered from any chronic and/or recurring illness of a very serious nature which has necessitated consultation or treatment, and has not obtained permission from their doctor that he/she is fit to travel . . . '.

The insurer rejected Mr M's claims for medical expenses and curtailment of his holiday. Mr M acknowledged that he had had cardiac problems for many years, but asserted that he was in good health when he embarked on the cruise. He provided letters from his consultants to confirm this.

Complaint upheld

The wording of the application form did not require Mr M to inform the insurer or the intermediary of his pre-existing medical history, as the insurer had argued. It simply required him to obtain permission to travel from his doctor. The policy document contained similar wording. The exclusion stated that the insurer would not meet a claim from someone who had suffered from a chronic or serious condition in the previous 12 months unless the person's doctor had given them permission to travel. There was no requirement that this permission had to be in writing or presented to the insurer before the holiday.

It was clear that Mr M had seen his GP a week before his cruise. Although it was not clear that Mr M's reason for visiting his GP was to obtain permission to go on the holiday, his GP was certainly of the opinion that Mr M had been fit to undertake the holiday. In the circumstances, we considered Mr M had satisfied both the policy condition and the declaration he had signed on the application form. The insurer accepted our view and agreed to meet both the medical expenses and curtailment claims.

7/17   **travel—non-disclosure—pre-existing condition—insurer repudiating liability for medical expenses—delay in communicating repudiation—whether insurer liable for expenses despite non-disclosure**

Ms S and Mr C were on holiday in America when Mr C injured his leg. He was hospitalised with deep vein thrombosis, but his condition was exacerbated by liver cirrhosis, hepatitis and alcoholism. Ms S notified the insurer, but after several days it refused indemnity.

Ms S argued that the insurer's delay had resulted in large medical bills. She said that if it had notified them of its decision more quickly, she could have given Mr C an alcoholic drink and his withdrawal symptoms would have stopped. They could then have taken their flight home.

Complaint rejected

It was clear from Mr C's medical notes that he had a long history of alcoholism, fairly severe liver disease and thrombocytopenia. His GP had only reluctantly agreed that Mr C was fit to travel and had advised him to declare his medical history to the insurer. Despite plain warnings in the policy, Mr C had not done so. We considered that he had accepted responsibility for the risk of travelling.

We did not agree that stopping treatment and giving Mr C a drink would have been acceptable. Mr C was not fit to fly and no doctor would have certified him as fit. There was no unreasonable delay on the insurer's part in deciding whether to accept the claim. It had made the necessary enquiries as quickly as possible. In any event, the seriousness of his illness meant that Mr C could not have flown home as quickly as Ms S later suggested, regardless of the insurer's decision.

7/18   **motor—misrepresentation—owner of vehicle—father insuring son's car—whether insurer entitled to cancel policy**

Mr H insured his car, with his son as a named driver. After the car was stolen from a supermarket car park, the insurer investigated Mr H's theft claim and discovered the car was, in fact, registered in the name of the son, and the son was also responsible for the financing arrangement. The insurer refused to meet the claim and cancelled the policy from its start date.

Mr H admitted that he had taken out the policy in order to reduce the premium by using his no claims discount, but he argued that his son was the main user of the car.

Complaint rejected

We accepted that the fact the son was the registered owner of the car was not conclusive. However, the evidence showed clearly that the son—rather than Mr H—was the main user. Mr H had misrepresented the position to the insurer and its decision to treat the policy as if it had never come into force was fully justified.

7/19 motor—misrepresentation—whether innocent—whether insured entitled to full indemnity

Mr L insured his car in April 2000, with his wife and son named as 'additional drivers'. The car was stolen a few days later, after being driven by the son. The insurer concluded, after investigation, that contrary to his declaration on the policy application form, Mr L was not the car's main user. However, the insurer did not cancel the policy. Instead, it offered to pay a proportional settlement. This was based on the premium it would have charged if it had known the son was the main driver and it was calculated at 52% of the total claim.

Mr L denied that his son was the main user of the car and he argued that the insurer's investigators had misunderstood the answers he and his son had provided. He contended that the claim should be settled in full.

Complaint rejected

There was sufficient evidence to satisfy us that Mr L's son was the main user of the car and that the insurer had not misunderstood the answers. Both the son and Mr L had told the insurer that the son was the main user. Moreover, there were a number of discrepancies and inconsistencies in Mr L's accounts. The strict legal position was that the insurer was entitled to treat the policy as if it had never come into force and to reject the claim, subject to refunding the premium. Its offer of a proportional settlement, based on the assumption that all the misrepresentations were innocent, was a fair and reasonable response to the dispute. We were not satisfied that the misrepresentations were innocent and there was no ground for requiring the insurer to increase its offer.

7/20 motor—misrepresentation—whether named driver was 'owner' of car—whether insurer entitled to cancel insurance

Mr D, a police officer who had taken early retirement on medical grounds, took out motor insurance for his new car. He stated that he owned the car and that his family did not own or use any other car. His adult son was named as a driver.

Two days after Mr D took out the insurance, the car was stolen. On investigating the claim, the insurer learnt that the purchase receipt was in the son's name, as was the finance agreement and the direct debit mandate for the premium payments. The personalised registration number corresponded with the son's initials. When questioned, both Mr D and his son agreed that the son's old car had been sold in part exchange towards the purchase price. They did not dispute that Mr D also had another car.

The insurer cancelled the policy, on the ground that both the answers Mr D had given on the proposal were untrue. Mr D argued that his son was only an occasional user of the car and that the investigation did not prove otherwise.

Complaint rejected

It was very difficult to believe that Mr D, rather than his son, was the car's owner and main driver. Mr D had not been able to explain why it was necessary for him to use the car extensively when he had the use of another car, or why his son would use the car only occasionally when there were two cars in the family. We were satisfied that Mr D had not answered the questions on the proposal form correctly.

If the insurer had known the son was the car's owner, it would not have issued this policy, since it was a policy offered only to retired police officers to cover their own cars. In the circumstances, the insurer was entitled to treat the policy as if it had never come into force.

7/21 motor—non-disclosure—whether clear questions asked—whether insurer entitled to cancel policy

Mrs B took out insurance for her car, with her son as a named driver. She was asked various questions, one of which was whether she had 'use' of another car. She later received a printed 'Statement of Facts' which recorded her answer to that question as 'No'.

Almost two years later, her son was involved in an accident. Mrs B completed a claim form, on which she stated that she had 'access' to another car. The insurer cancelled the policy, rejecting the claim and denying liability for damage to the third party vehicle, on the ground that Mrs B had misrepresented the risk. Mrs B explained that she did not normally drive the other car, which belonged to her husband and that she was the main user of this car. However, the insurer contended if it had been aware she had access to another car, it would only have covered this car for a premium of £4,319.

Complaint upheld

There was no evidence of the questions the insurer had asked Mrs B at the outset, other than the Statement of Facts. We were not satisfied that asking Mrs B if she had 'use of another car' was a clear question. The insurer had issued no guidance as to the meaning of the question and Mrs B had interpreted it as asking whether she wanted the policy to cover more than one car.

We did not accept that the fact of Mrs B's having access to another car made a material difference to the risk she had represented to the insurer when she took out the policy. We were satisfied that she was the main user of the car and that the son was an occasional user. The situation was not altered because she occasionally drove her husband's car. We therefore required the insurer to deal with Mrs B's claim. In addition, we awarded Mrs B £200 compensation for the mishandling of her claim.

7/22 motor—total loss—salvage—whether insurer entitled to retain salvage—compensation for wrongful disposal of salvage

Miss G's car was damaged in an accident and the insurer settled her claim on a 'total loss' basis. She wanted to keep the salvage, but the insurer refused and passed the car to salvage agents. Some months later, Miss G learnt from the Driver Vehicle Licensing Agency that someone had applied to re-register the car, apparently with a view to repairing it and putting it back on the road. She complained to the insurer and demanded compensation for the additional cost she had incurred in having to buy a new vehicle, plus interest.

The insurer explained that it was unwilling to allow its policyholders to keep cars which were unroadworthy. In this, it believed it was acting both in the public interest and in accordance with industry and government guidelines. However, it accepted that, on this occasion, it should have allowed Miss G to keep her car. In recognition of its error and other minor failings, the insurer offered her £500 compensation.

Complaint rejected

The salvage of a car remains the policyholder's property until settlement has been agreed. Insurers are not entitled to dispose of the salvage without the policyholder's express permission. Where there is some unusual delay in reaching agreement, the insurer could ask for the policyholder's permission to dispose of the salvage. This would prevent storage charges accruing, particularly where the only point in dispute is the amount offered.

If a policyholder seeks to retain and repair a car, the insurer should consider the request on the basis of the extent of repairs required. Where the car has sustained structural damage which cannot be repaired economically, then there will be serious issues of road safety to resolve. However, where much of the damage is cosmetic, it would not be unreasonable to agree to a policyholder's request to keep their car.

In this instance, we were satisfied that the insurer's compensation offer was reasonable, in the absence of any evidence that Miss G had suffered financial loss, distress or inconvenience except as a result of the insurer's retaining and disposing of the salvage. The offer was in line with awards we had made in similar situations. By settling Miss G's claim on a 'total loss' basis, the insurer had already paid her enough to enable her to replace her car with a similar one.

7/23 commercial—contractor's liability—policy condition—'suitable fire extinguishing appliance'—whether spray bottle met terms of condition

Mr S, a contractor, took out liability insurance. In 1997, while two of his employees were working on the exterior of a building, using a blowtorch to burn paint off a window frame and doorframes, the window frame caught fire. They tried to put out the fire with a 5-litre spray bottle of water. This was insufficient to extinguish the fire, so they broke down the door and covered the flames with a duvet. However, their efforts were unsuccessful and extensive damage had been caused by the time the fire service arrived and put out the fire.

Investigation established that the window was not fully sealed, as it had appeared to be. At some time a hole had been drilled through the sealed, double-glazed aluminium frame and subsequently concealed with filler. Mr S stated that the fire would not have spread to the curtains inside the building if this hole had not been there. He provided an expert's report supporting his argument. The insurer repudiated liability on the ground that Mr S had not complied with a policy condition which required 'suitable fire extinguishing appliances to be kept available'. It argued that the 5-litre spray bottle did not meet this condition as it would only damp down a fire. It also contended that the bottle's capacity was only 1.25 litres.

Complaint upheld

We had to consider whether the spray constituted a 'suitable fire extinguishing appliance' in accordance with the policy condition. There was insufficient evidence to determine the spray bottle's precise size, but we considered that it satisfied the terms of the condition. The policy did not contain any guidance on the insurer's criteria and we did not agree that the bottle was so obviously inadequate that it was unsuitable as a fire-extinguishing appliance.

ISSUE 10: OCTOBER 2001

10/1 household buildings—flood—rise in water table—whether 'flood'

During heavy rainfall in November 2000, Mr B's cellar filled with around four inches of water. He claimed under his household buildings insurance, which included cover for accidental damage. The insurer concluded that the damage was due to a rise in the water table and informed Mr B that this was not covered by the policy.

Mr B argued that the damage was clearly due to a 'flood' and that therefore it was covered under his policy.

Complaint upheld

Although in the past we had held that such claims were not covered, the 1998 decision by the Court of Appeal referred to above (*Rohan Investments Ltd* v *Cunningham*) indicated that they might be valid.

We considered that, as a result of this decision, the complaint should succeed. This was partly because the wider interpretation of 'flood' was closer to the ordinary expectations of householders. The decision in this court case was contrary to a previous Court of Appeal ruling (*Young* v *Sun Alliance*) in 1977, but we considered Mr B was entitled to the benefit of the more favourable case.

10/2 household buildings—exclusion for dry rot—rot discovered in course of subsidence repairs—whether exclusion applied

Mr N's household buildings insurer agreed to repair his property when it was affected by subsidence. The property was underpinned and superstructure repairs were undertaken. However, the repairer then found rising damp and stopped work until it had been rectified. While installing a damp-proof course, workmen found widespread woodworm and dry rot.

Mr N accepted that his policy did not cover the cost of eradicating either woodworm or dry rot and he arranged for the additional work to be carried out. However, his contractor discovered that the bearer wall supporting the infected timbers along the flank side of the house had collapsed in several places.

The insurer accepted this was further subsidence damage and it paid for rebuilding the wall. But it refused to meet the cost of removing and replacing the timbers and joists, maintaining that it was not liable, even though this work was required in order to carry out the subsidence repairs. This was because the timbers and joists were affected by dry rot, which was excluded from cover.

Mr N argued that the insurer should at least pay the proportion of the costs which related to the damaged part of the wall.

Complaint upheld in part

The insurer was responsible for repairing property damaged as a result of an insured peril. Had the insurer noticed the damage to the bearer wall at a different time, it would have had to remove and replace the floor in order to complete the repairs. We concluded that the fact the damage was only noticed in the course of other repairs did not affect the insurer's liability.

However, that liability was limited to the section of the floor affected by the insured damage. The insurer accepted our view that it was liable for the cost of removing and refitting the timbers adjacent to the damaged part of the bearer wall.

Mr N argued that the insurer should reimburse the full cost of removing the floor. We did not agree. It was clear that the timbers were rotten and could not be replaced. The cost of putting in new boards and joists was not covered by the policy and the insurer was not liable. Moreover, the replacement wood meant that Mr N was in a better position after the repairs than before.

10/3   household buildings—deliberate damage—damage caused deliberately to limit greater loss—whether policyholder covered for deliberate damage

When a blocked pipe caused water to flow back up into Mr J's kitchen, he quickly called out a plumber. The plumber broke the pipe and diverted the water before it caused any damage. However, when Mr J put in a claim for reimbursement of the plumber's charges (£70.50), the insurer rejected the claim on the grounds that the policy did not include any cover for accidental damage. Damage due to escape of water was covered under the policy, but Mr J had not claimed for any damage to his property other than the broken pipe. He argued that it was only the plumber's prompt action that prevented damage from occurring.

Complaint upheld

We agreed with Mr J that the plumber's actions were a direct and necessary consequence of the escape of water and were consistent with his duty under the policy to take all reasonable steps to prevent loss. The insurer did not dispute that the plumber's action had prevented considerable damage to the cupboards and floors. This damage would have been covered under the policy and could well have exceeded the cost of fracturing and repairing the pipe.

In such cases we would not consider it reasonable to require an insurer to reimburse the cost of deliberately-caused damage unless the claimant satisfied us that:

- he had acted reasonably and in order to prevent damage which was covered under the insurance policy; and
- the damage he was acting to prevent would cost significantly more than the damage deliberately caused.

Mr J satisfied both elements of this test and we therefore required the insurer to reimburse him for the plumber's bill.

10/4   household buildings—subsidence—preventative work—whether insurer liable for cost

In 1997, Mr and Mrs L noticed cracking in their garage. The loss adjusters appointed by their insurer concluded that it was caused by conifer trees owned by Mr and Mrs L's neighbour—Mr G. Mr G's insurer also appointed loss adjusters. They did not think the conifers were to blame, but they recommended the removal of several other trees.

Mr and Mrs L's loss adjusters monitored the property for the next twelve months and were satisfied that it had stabilised. The couple's insurer offered to carry out repairs but, after consulting a solicitor, Mr and Mrs L rejected the offer.

Both insurers agreed that three of the conifers would be removed, the remainder kept at their existing height, and that a new fence should be constructed. Mr and Mrs L said that Mr G's insurer should pay for the work. They argued that Mr G was benefiting whereas they had been unfairly obliged to pay the £1,000 policy excess towards the cost of the work. They sought compensation for their insurer's delay of three and a half years in progressing matters and said that this, in addition to their being subjected to Mr G's 'foul and abusive' language, had made them ill.

Complaint rejected

Mr and Mrs L's insurer was not obliged to force Mr G to remove all his trees, as the couple required, nor did it have any duty to fund the legal proceedings they wished to undertake. Mr and Mrs L were unable—or unwilling—to take legal action at their own expense and had not chosen to include legal expenses cover in their insurance.

We considered that the insurer had dealt with the claim properly and was justified in deciding not to have repairs carried out until the property had stabilised.

10/5 household contents—exclusion for undamaged items—matching sets—clothing—business suit—whether separate 'items'

Mr C bought a suit in the summer sales, which was a real bargain. Three weeks later, he accidentally leant on a bleached surface and the trousers were discoloured. He claimed under his household contents insurance and the insurer agreed to pay for a new pair of trousers. As they were not sold separately, it offered him £206, which was 40% of the cost of the suit, less the policy excess of £50.

Mr C complained that he could not replace the trousers on their own and said he was entitled to the cost of a new suit (£515). The insurer increased its offer to include a contribution of 50% of the cost of a replacement jacket, but it refused to pay the full cost of a new suit. It said the policy stated:

'We will treat an individual item of a matching set of articles or suite of furniture or sanitary fittings or other bathroom fittings as a single item.

We will pay for damaged items but not for the other pieces of the set or suite which is not damaged.'

Dissatisfied with the insurer's response, Mr C brought his complaint to us.

Complaint upheld

We did not accept that the insurer should regard the suit as 'a matching set of articles'. The jacket and trousers could only be purchased together, so we did not agree that—individually—they were 'single items'. On the contrary, the two pieces were together a 'single item' and we considered that settlement should be reached on that basis. The clause the insurer had relied on was not appropriate in these circumstances and we required the insurer to pay the balance of the claim, plus interest.

10/6 fraud—household contents—damage to one part of three-piece suite—whether claim that all of suite damaged was 'fraud'

Mrs M telephoned her insurer to notify it of damage to an armchair, which was part of a three-piece suite. She said that dye from her husband's trousers had stained the fabric. The insurer agreed to clean the chair, but Mrs M insisted that the whole suite would have to be cleaned, otherwise the chair would no longer match the other items in the suite.

After the insurer explained that it had no liability for the undamaged furniture, Mrs M said that all three pieces of furniture had been stained in the same way. The investigator appointed by the insurer to assess the damage reported that only one chair was stained.

The insurer then told Mrs M that it was cancelling her policy because she had 'used fraud to gain a benefit'. Mrs M explained that she had no intention of defrauding the insurer and had only said the other furniture was damaged because she was dissatisfied with the insurer's decision not to pay for the whole suite. The insurer sent her a tape recording of the telephone conversation in which she said all three items were stained, but she maintained she had only been joking.

Complaint rejected

The insurer's tape made it clear that Mrs M had stated there was damage to all three pieces of furniture. She did not seem to be joking. Moreover, she had allowed the insurer to arrange for an investigator to visit her rather than simply arranging for the chair to be cleaned. This indicated that she was pursuing her claim that all three parts of the suite were stained and should be cleaned.

Mrs M had attempted to gain an advantage by deception and the policy terms clearly entitled the insurer to cancel the policy. We were satisfied that the insurer had treated her fairly and in accordance with the policy terms.

10/7 household buildings—replacement—loss of match—tiles—whether policyholder entitled to compensation for loss of match in replacement of damaged tiles

Fourteen tiles in Mr and Mrs J's bathroom were damaged. The insurer agreed to replace these tiles but refused their request to re-tile the entire room. It explained that the policy specifically excluded 'the cost of replacing any undamaged item or part of any item solely because it forms part of a set, suite, or one of a number of items of similar nature, colour or design'.

After the couple expressed their dissatisfaction, the insurer made an additional payment representing 50% of the cost of re-tiling the remainder of the room.

Complaint rejected

The insurer had drafted its policy carefully. There was no reason why the policy should be disregarded or distorted simply because Mr and Mrs J had not appreciated that the wording might not allow them to claim for re-tiling the whole room. On the other hand, strict application of the terms would leave many householders—if not most—with a finish they would regard as unacceptable. The insurer's payment of 50% of the cost of total re-tiling was in line with our usual approach and we were satisfied it was reasonable in the circumstances of this case.

10/8 household contents—accidental damage—lack of reasonable care—burden of proof

While Mr M was touching up the paintwork on his sitting room wall, there was a knock at the front door. He put the tin of paint on a table and went to the door. As he opened it, a gust of wind blew through the house and the kitchen door swung open, letting his dog loose. The dog rushed into the sitting room and knocked into the table, tipping the tin of paint over the sofa—part of a three-piece suite.

Mr M claimed under the accidental damage section of his household insurance. The insurer rejected his claim, on the ground that he had not complied with the policy condition to take reasonable steps to prevent damage. It considered he was negligent because he had not covered the sofa before starting to paint.

However, after Mr M explained that he had not been redecorating—only touching up some marks on the wall, the insurer made an offer of £600 towards the cost of replacing the three-piece suite. Mr M refused this offer and referred the complaint to us.

Complaint upheld

To prove the alleged lack of reasonable care, the insurer had to show that Mr M had been reckless. That meant proving that he had recognised there was a risk of damage but had failed to take reasonable precautions to prevent it.

There was no indication that Mr M had been reckless and we considered the insurer should meet the cost of replacing the damaged sofa. If the sofa could no longer be replaced, then the insurer should also pay 50% towards the cost of replacing the other matching parts of the suite.

10/9 household buildings—repairs—failure to repair properly—policyholder suffering distress and inconvenience—appropriate compensation

After Dr I's flat was seriously damaged by fire in October 1997, the insurer appointed loss adjusters and builders to handle his claim. Extensive work was necessary, but the flat was expected to be ready for Dr I to move back into by May 1998.

In the event, the work was not carried out to an acceptable standard and a second firm of builders had to be brought in to put matters right.

For the first few months, Dr I lived in rented accommodation but he then moved in with his father. Repairs were finally completed in December 1999. Dr I complained about the insurer's failure to get the work done properly in the first place, and he sought compensation in excess of £309,000. This included £216,000 for 20 months of distress and aggravation; reimbursement of various costs including telephone bills, legal expenses, and mortgage charges; payments for his time spent supervising and reporting on the work; and finally a payment in recognition of his inability to sell the flat while the work was in progress.

Complaint upheld in part

The insurer acknowledged that it failed to ensure the original repair work was up to standard, but we were satisfied that it took appropriate steps to remedy the situation. What we had to decide was how much compensation the insurer should pay to reflect the added inconvenience to Dr I, and any expenses he incurred, over and above what he would have had to endure anyway as a result of the fire.

We took the view that whatever had happened, he would still have had to pay his mortgage and other property-related costs. We were not persuaded that he would have sold the flat, had it not been for the problems encountered; nor were we satisfied that he needed to involve solicitors to progress the remedial work. In our opinion, the insurer had already paid Dr I at least £4,000 compensation for alternative accommodation costs while he was living with his father. Taking this into account, we awarded Dr I a total of £3,750 compensation. This comprised £1,000 for the time he spent in overseeing and reporting on the work, £750 for distress and general inconvenience, and £2,000 for loss of use and enjoyment of his flat for the period between the expected and actual completion dates.

10/10 fraud—motor—policyholder submitting false receipt in proof of purchase—whether insurer entitled to reject damage claim

Miss F submitted a claim after her car was damaged by thieves. The insurer's engineer decided the car was beyond economical repair and the insurer would not settle the claim without proof of the amount Miss F had paid for the car. In fact, Miss F's boyfriend had given the car to her, but she produced a receipt showing she had paid £3,800.

The investigator appointed by the insurer discovered that it was the boyfriend who had purchased the car and that he had only paid £2,700. The insurer advised Miss F that it would not make any payment because she had presented false evidence in support of her claim. It explained that the policy terms justified its rejecting a claim entirely if a claimant submitted any forged or false document. Miss F argued that her boyfriend had given her the receipt and that she had no reason to believe it was not genuine.

Complaint upheld

The insurer's liability under the policy terms was limited to settling the claim by paying the car's market value. The insurer's aim in asking to see the receipt was not to establish the car's value but to obtain proof that Miss F had owned the car and to confirm its make, model and age. There was independent proof both of the car's existence and of Miss F's ownership of it. Clearly, we would not support any customer who produced fictitious evidence to gain more than their just entitlement, but that was not the situation here. The insurer's liability would have been the same even if Miss F had told the truth and said the car was a present from her boyfriend.

In the circumstances, we were satisfied that Miss F had suffered a genuine loss and that she had not attempted to claim more than her proper entitlement under the policy terms. We concluded that the insurer should pay Miss F the car's market value, plus interest.

10/11 personal accident—quadriplegia—policyholder disabled in four limbs—policy definition of 'quadriplegia' more restrictive—whether policyholder entitled to benefit

An extremely serious accident left Mr F with a major permanent disability. He was covered under a personal accident policy and the insurer made a payment of £125,000, the policy benefit for para-plegia—paralysis of the lower part of the body.

Mr F claimed he was entitled to a total payment of £250,000 on the ground that he was disabled in all four limbs. The insurer rejected his claim. It stated that Mr F did not fit its policy definition of 'quadriplegia'—'permanent and total paralysis of the two upper limbs and two lower limbs'. The insurer relied on a medical report it had obtained. This stated that Mr F retained 'gross motor function in terms of shoulders and arms' and could 'form a primitive handgrip', even though he had lost the majority of his hand function and his 'pincer grip' was dramatically reduced.

Complaint upheld

When Mr F took out the policy in March 1996, it did not include cover for either paraplegia or quadriplegia. These benefits were added in June 1998, but this 're-launch' of the policy had not included the definition on which the insurer relied. In the circumstances, we considered the claim should be assessed in the light of the ordinary meaning of the word 'quadriplegia'. Mr F's own medical advisers were satisfied that—in general medical terms—he was 'quadriplegic'. We therefore considered it unreasonable for the insurer to use a narrower definition. After our involvement, the insurer agreed to pay Mr F the balance of £125,000.

10/12   extended warranty—theft—exclusion for claims without proof of 'forced and violent entry or exit'—whether proof of theft sufficient

Among other items stolen in a burglary, Mr O lost his 'surround sound' television speakers. Mr O had extended warranty insurance for the speakers, but this only included cover for theft so long as the product had 'been stolen by forced and violent entry or exit'. The insurer repudiated the claim because Mr O could not provide evidence of 'forced and violent entry or exit'.

After the burglar had been caught and convicted, Mr O asked the insurer to reconsider his claim. He asserted that the burglar had gained entry to his flat by damaging the front door, its frame and lock. The insurer checked with the police, but rejected the claim again on finding none of this damage was mentioned in the crime report.

Complaint rejected

There was a clear distinction between 'forced' and 'violent' entry. Unless the burglar had entered through an open door or window, his entry was doubtless 'forced'. However, 'violent' required proof of some physical damage to the property. Mr O could produce no evidence of this, so the insurer was justified in rejecting the claim.

10/13   personal accident—loss of fingers—assessment of compensation

Mr J made a claim under his personal accident policy after cutting three of his fingers with a knife. He was dissatisfied with the insurer's offer of £4,221.30, based on loss of function of the affected fingers, and instead sought the full permanent total disablement benefit of £105,000. He maintained that his injuries meant he could no longer use his left hand well enough to continue his job as a sheet metal worker. He also sought compensation totalling £125,000. This comprised: £25,000 for time off work and loss of potential earnings, £20,000 a year for having to seek employment with lower earning potential and £80,000 for loss of the projected value of his company pension scheme.

Complaint upheld in part

We did not consider Mr J was entitled to permanent total disablement benefit. This benefit was only payable to those whose injuries prevented them 'from engaging in any occupation for which he/she is fitted by reason of education, training or experience for the remainder of their life' and the medical evidence available did not justify this conclusion. Indeed, Mr J had retrained to work as a clerk. The policy did not provide cover for the other consequential losses for which he sought compensation. The policy did provide for 10% of the sum assured to be paid for the loss of use of any finger and we were satisfied the insurer was correct in approaching Mr J's claim on that basis. However, following a reassessment of the medical evidence, we decided the insurer should increase its offer to £5,171.09.

10/14   household contents—non-disclosure—convictions—whether insurer entitled to avoid policy

In 1999, Mr N—a gardener—took out household insurance through his bank. He signed a form stating that he had no criminal convictions. However, when he made a theft claim the following year, the insurer learnt that he had been sentenced to four years' imprisonment in 1985 for theft from commercial premises. As this conviction was still not 'spent' in 1999, the insurer treated the policy as if it had never been issued.

Mr N argued that his previous insurance company had been aware of his conviction and had covered him regardless, telling him the conviction was 'spent'. He also asserted that his bank manager knew of his conviction. However the bank manager was certainly aware that policy applications from anyone with a conviction were unacceptable and there was no record of his having any conversation with Mr N about this.

Complaint rejected

Mr N did not provide us with any details of his criminal record, though it seemed surprising that he received such a long sentence for a relatively minor offence. We invited him to clarify this but he failed to respond. We were therefore satisfied that there was no ground for requiring the insurer to alter its decision. Mr N had not provided a correct answer to a clear question and we were unable to accept his contention that the insurer had been made aware of the true facts.

10/15 household buildings—escape of water—exclusion if property unoccupied—whether insurer would have covered unoccupied property

Mr D was trustee of a trust whose property included a house that he insured under a standard buildings policy. After the house became vacant on 25 October 1999, he left the central heating on and inspected the property once a week, but did not tell the insurer that the house was unoccupied. During December 1999, he was ill for a fortnight and unable to visit the house as regularly as before. When he next inspected the house, at the end of December, he discovered that a pipe had burst, causing extensive water damage.

The insurer rejected Mr D's claim, stating that the policy did not cover damage caused by escape of water if the property was unoccupied for more than 30 days.

Complaint upheld in part

It was clear that the house had been unoccupied for more than 30 days when the damage occurred. And we were satisfied that the insurer had taken all reasonable steps to draw Mr D's attention to the exclusion.

However, when we asked the insurer what steps it would have required Mr D to take if he had told it the house was unoccupied, it said it would have required him to keep the central heating on and to inspect the property at weekly intervals. As Mr D had—in fact—complied with these requirements, until he became ill, we considered the insurer should deal with his claim. But because Mr D's illness had prevented him from inspecting the house every week, and this gap in inspections had increased the amount of damage, we decided the insurer should pay 80% of the claim, less the excess.

ISSUE 13: JANUARY 2002

13/1 private medical expenses—transfer of cover to new insurer—exclusion for 'mental illness'—insured not advised of change in terms—whether claim valid

Mr B had the benefit of an employer's group medical expenses scheme. He suffered from intermittent mental ill-health and the insurer had paid for his treatment. In January 2000, his employer changed insurers. The terms of the new policy excluded 'treatment of psychiatric and mental disorders unless your company has specifically applied to include this benefit'. The employer had not paid the additional premium required for this benefit.

In May 2000, Mr B was hospitalised for mental problems. The new insurer refused to cover the cost of treatment, relying on the policy exclusion. Mr B argued that he had not been made aware of the change in policy cover. The new insurer said that the employer had made a specific enquiry about continuing mental health benefits for Mr B and it contended that the employer was under a duty to advise Mr B that it had decided not to pay for this extension.

Complaint upheld

The new insurer had taken no steps to ensure that employees such as Mr B were aware of the new policy terms. And despite being informed of Mr B's situation, the insurer did not make any effort to notify him of the change, nor did it require the employer to provide him with this information.

If Mr B had been told of the restricted terms of the new insurance, he could have chosen to continue cover for himself under the old policy. The failure to give him correct advice had prejudiced his position.

We required the new insurer to deal with any claims Mr B made during the first year of cover, if these claims would have been valid under the terms of the old policy. However, we did not agree with Mr B that he was entitled under the new policy to indefinite mental illness cover.

13/2   private medical expenses—transfer of cover to new insurer—exclusion for 'elective' surgery—whether new insurer entitled to rely on exclusion

Mrs L was an employee of JI, which provided private medical insurance for its staff. When she became pregnant, her doctor told her that her baby would have to be delivered by Caesarean section. This was because Mrs L had undergone uterine surgery some years previously. She telephoned the insurer for advice and was told the operation would be covered.

In March 2000, JI transferred the insurance to a different insurer. Mrs L's baby was born the following month and she submitted her claim to the new insurer. It refused to make any payment, explaining that the policy specifically excluded 'elective sections' for maternity claims. It concluded that the Caesarean was 'elective' because the pregnancy was normal and there was no emergency relating to the delivery.

Mrs L complained that no one had told her that the change of insurer meant that, despite the previous insurer's decision, she was no longer covered for the operation. She noted that the company secretary had told her that the new insurer had not asked him any questions about the health of employees or the treatment proposed for any of them. Instead, it had told him that the transfer of cover between insurers was 'on protected underwriting terms', although these were to be based on the new policy wording.

Complaint upheld

We accepted that the surgery was 'elective', but we did not agree that the limitations on cover had been made clear. The brochure referred to the employer's need to ensure any difference in cover was explained to staff, but there was no evidence that the insurer had drawn those differences to the attention of the company secretary.

Although the policy had been transferred 'on protected underwriting terms', the meaning of this phrase was not clearly defined. In our opinion, it indicated continuous cover. No policy document had been sent to employees by the time the surgery was performed and Mrs L could not have known of the exclusion.

In the circumstances, we decided that the insurer was liable for the cost of the surgery.

13/3   private medical expenses—moratorium—whether emergency condition exempt from moratorium—whether blood pressure 'related to' stroke

Mr and Mrs L took out insurance in May 1999 to cover the cost of private medical treatment. The policy included a moratorium exclusion. This excluded treatment 'of any illness or injury . . . which existed or was foreseeable prior to or which recurs after the Insured Person's Date of Entry, until a continuous period of two years has gone by'.

In February 2000, Mrs L suffered a stroke and was admitted to hospital. Her claim under the insurance was rejected. The insurer said that her stroke was related to the high blood pressure for which she had been treated during the past few years. As the two-year moratorium period had not passed, she was not entitled to any benefit. Mr and Mrs L argued that the insurer should meet her claim, since she had been admitted as an emergency patient and the insurer did not require prior authorisation in such circumstances.

Complaint rejected

It was true that emergency admissions did not require pre-authorisation in the same way as other claims, but when Mr L notified the insurer of the claim, it explained that he and his wife would be liable for all expenses if it did not accept the claim.

Mrs L was receiving treatment for hypertension at the time the policy came into force, so hypertension would not be covered until two years had passed without her needing any treatment for it. This exclusion covered not just the condition itself but also 'any other illness . . . related to it'. Hypertension was a contributory factor for strokes and Mrs L's stroke was therefore covered by the exclusion. The insurer was entitled to reject the claim.

**13/4   income protection—'totally disabled'—disability due to stress—policyholder
physically well—whether possible future stress sufficient to render policyholder
'disabled'**

On holiday in France, Mr N had a transient ischaemic attack. He was subsequently diagnosed as suffering from heart disease and he gave up work. He claimed benefits under his permanent health insurance on the ground that his state of health totally prevented him from working. The insurer made medical enquiries and found that although Mr N's GP and his consultant neurologist had both recommended he should give up work, they agreed that he was physically fit to resume work. His occupation, as managing director of the company he had started many years before, was highly stressful. The insurer maintained that there was no physical reason why Mr N should not return to work.

The medical evidence was inconclusive. So we arranged for Mr N to undergo an independent examination. The independent consultant considered there was no medical reason why Mr N could not return to work, but that he should not do so because of the risk to his health. The consultant felt that Mr N's occupation involved such a degree of stress that the risks of further disability would be increased if he went back to work, and there would be a very real risk of his illness recurring.

Complaint upheld

This was an unusual case. Generally, a person with a stable medical condition who is fearful that returning to work may aggravate their condition—perhaps through stress—will have difficulty demonstrating they are not able to work. Here, however, the medical evidence pointed strongly to a worsening of the policyholder's condition being not just a worry but a foreseeable result of returning to work. So although Mr N's position had clearly stabilised after he gave up work, that was not sufficient justification for rejecting his claim. The medical evidence made it clear that he was only well so long as he did not work. Returning to work would put his health at risk, so it was not right to conclude that he was not 'disabled'.

We required the insurer to meet Mr N's claim from the end of the deferred period of six months, and to add interest to the back payments.

**13/5   critical illness—misrepresentation—underwriting limits—proposer outside
underwriting limits—whether misrepresentation justified cancellation of policy**

A salesman called on Mr L, a pub landlord, and recommended that he should take out critical illness insurance. This would pay him £10,000 if he were diagnosed with any of the conditions listed in the policy. The salesman completed the application form and Mr L signed it. The form stated that Mr L's height was 6' 1" and his weight, 17 stone.

The policy was issued in November 1999. In December 2000, Mr L was diagnosed with cancer and he submitted a claim. The insurer's enquiries revealed that Mr L had mis-stated his height (he was actually 5' 10"). It therefore cancelled his policy on the ground that he had misrepresented his measurements. It told Mr L that it would not have insured him if it had known his actual height as, combined with his weight, it put him outside its underwriting guidelines.

Complaint upheld

Mr L's mis-statement was innocent and not an unusual mistake for someone to make. The difference in height was within a 3% margin and the insurer ought to have made an allowance for such a minor error. The insurer conceded that if it had known Mr L's correct height—and his weight had not exceeded 17 stone—it would have covered him. The difference between his actual weight and that stated was also within a 3% margin.

The policy had been sold to Mr L in person. The salesman should therefore have appreciated that Mr L's size brought him close to the insurer's underwriting limits, and he should have stressed to Mr L the importance of giving accurate measurements. There was no reason why Mr L should have been aware of the insurer's underwriting limits. It was irrelevant whether Mr L gave the salesman inaccurate information, or had simply failed to notice that the salesman had recorded the information incorrectly.

In the circumstances, we concluded that the insurer was not justified in relying on the misrepresentation to cancel the policy. It accepted our conclusion that it should pay the £10,000 policy benefit.

233

13/6   critical illness—non-disclosure—whether insurer entitled to cancel policy because of innocent non-disclosure

Mrs C applied for life assurance and critical illness insurance in May 1999. One of the questions she was asked was whether she had a 'lump, growth or tumour of any kind'—she answered 'No'. She was also asked whether she had 'consulted, or been prescribed treatment by a doctor during the last 5 years'. She answered 'Yes' and listed what she and her GP considered relevant information from her medical records.

In July 2000, Mrs C claimed benefit under her critical illness policy as she had been diagnosed with a malignant melanoma. The insurer sought information from her GP and discovered that, in March 1999, Mrs C had asked her GP to look at a mole that had been on her left thigh since birth, and was starting to bother her. The insurer accepted that Mrs C's failure to tell it about this incident was innocent, but it cancelled both her policies. It considered that she should have disclosed this particular GP 'consultation' in response to its direct question about 'growths' and that by failing to do so, Mrs C had prejudiced its position.

Mrs C disputed this decision. She said her GP had told her the mole was nothing to worry about and she had not sought further advice or treatment for it until May 2000. Her GP's notes confirmed that the mole was only mentioned casually at the end of a consultation for an unrelated matter, and that Mrs C was told it was benign and had no sinister features.

Complaint upheld

A brief mention of a minor problem was not a 'consultation' and we did not consider that Mrs C had provided an incorrect answer to the question about consultations. The GP had not organised any further investigation of the mole or made any recommendation about it. It seemed only to have been included in the GP's notes in case a problem occurred in future.

As to the question about lumps, growths or tumours, Mrs C had acted reasonably in answering 'No'. She had to answer the insurer's questions only 'to the best of her knowledge'—and—to the best of her knowledge, she did not have any condition that she needed to tell the insurer about. Her GP had told her the mole was inconsequential and since it had been present all her life, and was apparently not a matter of any concern, she could not have been expected to mention it.

We did not consider the insurer had sufficient grounds for cancelling the policies and we said it should reinstate them and assess the claim. We also awarded Mrs C £400 for distress and inconvenience.

13/7   pension—non-disclosure—questions regarding current consumption of tobacco and alcohol—whether proposer required to disclose past excesses

In June 1998, Mr S took out a personal pension which included death benefit. He answered questions on the proposal regarding his past health, his weight and his cigarette and alcohol consumption.

In December 1999, Mr S died and his widow applied for the death benefit. As a result of its enquiries, the insurer concluded that Mr S had not given truthful answers to its questions. In particular, it was satisfied that he had failed to disclose episodes of bronchitis and had not given correct information about his weight, smoking and drinking habits. Mr S was obese, according to his GP, and had smoked 30 cigarettes and drunk about a bottle of vodka every day. He had suffered several episodes of bronchitis between 1970 and 1975.

Mrs S disputed this evidence and asserted that although Mr S had been a heavy drinker and smoker, he had changed his habits after the birth of their first child in 1984. She said that his height and weight had been correctly recorded.

Complaint upheld

The insurer was unable to produce the signed proposal and this omission had undermined its case. There was no evidence that Mr S had not answered the questions truthfully. Moreover, from a sample proposal form that we obtained from the insurer, it seemed that the questions all related to the current health and consumption of the person wanting to obtain the critical illness cover, not to their past history or old habits.

So far as could be ascertained from the medical evidence, Mr S had changed his habits by the time he signed the proposal. There was no reference to his drinking or smoking after 1988. He did not seem to have consulted or been treated for bronchitis after 1975.

We decided that the insurer was not justified in concluding that Mr S had failed to provide correct answers to its questions. The insurer agreed to pay Mrs S the death benefit of over £30,000.

13/8 loan protection—exclusion for pre-existing medical conditions—failure to highlight exclusion—whether customer prejudiced by failure

Mr G purchased a car from his local garage. He took out a hire purchase agreement and a loan protection insurance policy—both purchased at the garage. Nine months later he suffered a major heart attack and he has not worked since. The firm rejected his claim for the critical illness benefit because he had suffered previously from angina and generalised chest pain. The policy excluded any medical conditions for which the policyholder had sought advice in the 12 months before starting the policy. A 'condition' was defined as including 'any symptom of [any sickness]'.

Mr G said that he had wanted cover as he had suffered a heart attack eight years previously and was concerned about his ability to continue working if he was ill again. He said he had explained this to the car salesman, but the exclusion was not pointed out to him.

Complaint upheld

The firm's reliance on the exclusion for pre-existing conditions was questionable. Mr G had suffered in recent years from some generalised chest pain symptoms but his condition appeared to have been minor and reasonably stable. It was perhaps debatable whether such relatively minor symptoms could reasonably be described as symptoms of the heart attack that followed. However, this was not a matter we needed to resolve in this particular case because the main dispute rested on whether the policy had been sold properly.

Mr G had signed a declaration that he had read and understood the policy. In fact, it seemed highly unlikely that he had read and understood it. The policy wording was complex and little or no effort had been made to draw the important provisions to the attention of policyholders. In particular, the exclusions for pre-existing conditions were not highlighted in any way (either in the policy or in a customer leaflet).

Exclusions for pre-existing conditions are recognised both by the industry and by customer groups as being particularly significant and needing to be explained and drawn clearly to policyholders' attention. In this case, this clearly didn't happen and advice was either not given or misleading. Overall, the sale did not meet the requirements set down in the codes of either the General Insurance Standards Council or the Association of British Insurers.

Our general approach in these cases is to put customers back into the position they would have been in had the firm not made an error. This will often be achieved by returning the premium, as many of these customers would not have bought the policy if they had been correctly advised. In other cases, we may conclude that the customers suffered no material detriment from a mis-sale, as they would probably have purchased the policy in any event. Conversely, if the unexplained exclusion is unusual or onerous, we may require the firm to meet the claim in full, as alternative policies with wider cover may have been available.

In Mr G's case, the exclusion itself was not unusual. But we were satisfied that if he had been aware of the true nature of the policy, he might well not have bought the car at all, or he might have made more cautious financing arrangements.

On this basis, we required the firm to meet the claim in full; to meet any costs arising from Mr G's inability to make the loan repayments since the claim was made; and to pay him £300 for distress and inconvenience.

13/9 household contents—accidental damage to carpets—exclusion for damage caused by domestic animals

Ms E's dog died in her lounge. As it was some time before the unfortunate dog was found, the carpet was badly stained. Ms E arranged for the carpet to be cleaned but without success. The staining and foul odour was permanent. Ms E claimed under the accidental damage section of her policy for replacement carpets—valued at about £1,100—as well as for the initial cleaning costs. The firm declined to meet the claim on the basis of an exclusion that covered damage caused by domestic animals.

Complaint upheld

This was scarcely a case of damage caused by a badly housetrained animal. The dog was dead when the accidental damage occurred. It did not seem reasonable to apply the exclusion in these circumstances and we required the firm to meet the claim in full.

13/10 travel—loss of goods when location known—reasonable steps to recover—whether gameboy game a 'disk'

Mr H's son left a bag containing his 'gameboy' and associated games on the back seat of the taxi that took the family to the airport on their way home from the Canary Islands. Mr H contacted the taxi firm through the resort and the missing bag was located. However, the taxi driver concerned had not returned to the airport with the bag by the time the family had to board the plane. Back in the UK, Mr H again tried (through the holiday resort) to get the bag located and returned. He had no success, so he claimed £305 for the 'gameboy' and games under his travel policy.

The insurer rejected the claim—initially on the basis that the loss had not been reported to the police. It then claimed that the bag was not, in fact, lost and that Mr H had not taken 'adequate steps to recover the goods' (as required by the policy). As a subsidiary point, it argued that the games should be considered as 'cassettes or tapes or disks', which were excluded from cover under the policy.

Complaint upheld

It seemed to us that Mr H had made appropriate and—in the circumstances—more than adequate efforts to recover the goods. It was not reasonable of the firm to require him to do more. Equally, we did not accept the insurer's argument that since the location of the goods was known, the goods were not lost. Just as if the items had been dropped from a boat and were now at the bottom of the ocean, there was no practical prospect of recovering Mr H's lost goods. Goods can be 'lost' if their location is known but they cannot—for practical purposes—be recovered.

The list of exclusions from cover was lengthy. It therefore seemed appropriate to interpret the provisions narrowly and, in case of doubt, to favour the customer's interpretation. A 'gameboy' game was not, strictly speaking, a disk (cassette or tape) and we therefore required the firm to meet the claim in full.

13/11 personal accident—specified injuries—whether other injuries also covered

On the flight home from a family holiday, Mrs M's toddler son hit her in the face, breaking her nose. She submitted a claim to her travel insurer for the policy benefit of £20,000. The insurer rejected her claim, stating that the benefit was only payable in three situations: death, loss of one or more limbs or eyes, and permanent total disablement. As none of these had occurred, it maintained it was not liable for Mrs M's injury.

Mrs M argued that the policy wording did not make it clear that only three events would give rise to the benefit. She also felt that she was entitled to be indemnified under the personal liability section of the policy. This provided a maximum payment of £2 million for any personal injury.

Complaint rejected

The policy wording was unambiguous and provided for payment of the personal accident benefit only if one of the three specified events occurred. There was nothing in the policy to suggest that any other personal injury would give rise to a benefit entitlement.

As to the liability section, we did not accept that a two-year-old was capable of being held liable for the injury by a court. The insurer therefore had no responsibility for indemnifying the child against any liability to his mother. Moreover, the policy specifically excluded liability to family members.

13/12 income protection—disability from 'normal pursuits'—meaning of 'normal pursuits'

Mrs B took out income protection insurance in 1981. This protected her dual occupations of nurse and housewife and would provide a weekly benefit of £50 if she became too ill or disabled to continue work.

When she became ill, the insurer rejected her claim on the ground that she was not disabled from 'the normal pursuits' of a housewife. Mrs B protested, arguing that her disability prevented her from continuing with her nursing work, and that this was the situation she had intended the policy to cover. She pointed out that the policy did not define 'normal pursuits' and therefore she could not tell whether her claim met the policy criteria. The insurer still maintained that no benefit was payable unless Mrs B was unable to follow the normal pursuits of a housewife. It said that this must have been clear to Mrs B because all the usual references to income had been deleted from the policy.

Complaint upheld

Mrs B had clearly purchased the policy to protect her income, which was solely derived from nursing. The policy was called an 'Income Protection Policy' and the the fact that it would only pay a benefit if she was also unable to perform a housewife's normal duties had not been explained to her. The wording of the policy was vague, at best, and where an insurer has drafted its contract terms ambiguously, we take the interpretation least favourable to the insurer.

Moreover, since the policy contained no definition of 'normal pursuits'—it was reasonable to interpret it as referring to her occupation of nursing. Mrs B derived no income from housework and it was unreasonable to interpret the policy as meaning that benefit was not payable unless she was unable to perform housework.

We required the insurer to pay benefits to Mrs B from the date of her disability, subject to any deferred period, and to add interest to the amount it paid her.

13/13 household buildings—heave—exclusion for damage to swimming pool when house not damaged—damage resulting from previous subsidence repairs—whether insurer entitled to rely on exclusion in relation to heave damage

Mr E's house was affected by subsidence in 1996 and his insurer dealt with the claim. Its loss adjusters decided to stabilise the property by removing and reducing trees on both Mr E's and the next-door properties. Superstructure repairs were completed in 1998, after the property had stabilised. In 1999, Mr E noticed that his swimming pool was seriously affected by heave, which had pushed up the underlying soil and cracked the pool. There was no damage to the house.

Mr E notified the insurer and it appointed the original firm of loss adjusters and an engineer to investigate. The engineer concluded that the cracking of the swimming pool was not connected with the removal of the trees. The insurer rejected the claim. It did not accept that the damage was a continuation of the 1996 claim. The claim was therefore for new damage and only covered under the policy if the house were affected at the same time.

Mr E obtained his own engineer's report. This concluded that the damage to the swimming pool was a direct consequence of the tree management programme implemented by the insurer. However, the insurer refused to alter its decision.

Complaint upheld

We appointed an independent engineer to assess the damage, and the insurer agreed to accept his conclusions. The independent engineer advised that the tree reductions had most likely caused heave of the site. He accepted that the reduction programme had been undertaken in good faith, but he was concerned that no heave predictions had been made and that the heave consequences of removing the trees had been largely ignored. In the circumstances, he did not think it would be fair for the insurer to rely on the exclusion.

The insurer accepted that it should deal with the claim and agreed that the independent engineer should take over management of the claim from the loss adjusters. It also agreed to reimburse Mr E's engineer's fee.

13/14 motor—driving other cars—extension of cover for driving abroad—whether driving other cars abroad covered

For many years Mrs H had held motor insurance with the same insurer. She had family in Northern Ireland and her policy covered her for driving in the Republic of Ireland and for driving other cars. In September 1999, she had an accident, hitting another vehicle while driving her brother's car in the Republic of Ireland.

Mrs H claimed indemnity under her policy against a third party claim. However, the insurer rejected the claim, saying that her brother's insurer should deal with it. It referred her to the policy, which stated: 'Cover for driving other cars does not apply . . . in any country outside the United Kingdom'.

Mrs H argued that this was overridden by the extension, noted in the Statement of Insurance, that permitted her to drive in the Republic of Ireland. However, the insurer explained that this extension was limited to her car only. She also contended that the insurer was in breach of the law that required insurers to provide minimum cover throughout the European Union.

Complaint upheld

It was only by reading the policy document in conjunction with the schedule and the Statement of Insurance that it was clear that Mrs H was not covered for driving other cars outside the UK. However, none of these documents made it plain that all three documents had to be read together. We accepted Mrs H's argument that the policy was not clear and that she should therefore be given the benefit of the doubt. She had believed she was covered for driving other cars in the Republic of Ireland and that belief was not unreasonable. We therefore required the insurer to deal with the third party claim.

As to the legal position, the legislation required insurers to provide minimum insurance cover, but did not state whether—in this type of situation—it was the insurer of the car or the insurer of the driver which should deal with any third party claim. The Road Traffic Act 1988, as amended, referred to the obligation to insure 'such person . . . as may be specified in the policy'. In the light of this, it might be reasonable to expect the driver's insurer to accept liability. However, we did not need to determine this point as the first argument succeeded.

Mrs H had also claimed compensation for the fees her representative charged for pursuing the complaint. We only award these in very rare cases, for example, where the policyholder required legal advice in order to respond to an insurer's arguments. This was not such a case so we did not award any additional compensation.

13/15 motor—non-disclosure—policyholder stating he had not been asked about ownership or use of car—whether insurer entitled to cancel insurance

Mr O applied over the telephone for motor insurance for his son's car. He answered a series of questions and the insurer then sent him a statement of facts, for checking, based on the answers he had given. The statement showed that there were two drivers, Mr O and his son.

A few months later, the car was stolen and Mr O claimed compensation. The insurer's enquiries revealed that the car was registered in the son's name. Mr O and his son said they had bought the car jointly and that the son was the main user. The insurer then cancelled the policy, telling Mr O that if it had known these facts, it would have charged a premium six times higher.

Complaint upheld

The insurer did not ask Mr O to sign a proposal and it did not keep any record of his answers to its questions. Although it maintained that Mr O had described himself as the 'main user', this information was not recorded in the statement of facts and it was impossible to verify whether he had been asked this question. We required the insurer to deal with the claim on the ground that there was insufficient evidence that Mr O had failed to disclose all relevant information.

13/16 livestock—cost of veterinary treatment—exclusion for illnesses arising within 14 days of cover—whether insurer's failure to highlight exclusion prejudiced policyholder

Over a period of several years, Mrs S had insured a number of different horses. These horses did not belong to her, but were lent to her by their owners for long-term use. On 13 March 2001, one of these horses—Chino—was due to be returned to its owner. Mrs S telephoned the insurer that morning to transfer the policy cover from Chino to another horse—Sparky. The insurer agreed to do this immediately.

Later that day, Mrs S's daughter found that Sparky was unwell. The vet diagnosed colic and the total cost of treatment came to over £4,000. Mrs S claimed under the policy but the insurer rejected her claim on two grounds. It stated that the policy:

- did not cover any horse which the policyholder did not own; and
- excluded claims for any illness that arose within 14 days of the policy's start date.

Mrs S argued that she had not owned any of the horses she had insured, and she pointed out that the insurer had never raised this matter before. She also said that the insurer had failed to mention the

14-day exclusion, and she presented evidence that Sparky had been in good health on the morning she arranged the insurance for him.

Complaint rejected

The insurer conceded that it would cover horses on long-term loan to a policyholder, so that issue was no longer relevant. However, even if we accepted Mrs S's assertion that the exclusion had not been drawn to her attention, it was hard to accept that that failure had prejudiced her position. Sparky had been well when the insurance was taken out, so even if the insurer had pointed out the exclusion, we believe she would still have gone ahead and obtained cover from this insurer.

13/17   household contents—proof of loss—policyholder failing to cooperate with insurer's enquiries—whether insurer justified in rejecting claim

On 8 May 2000, Mr S took out household contents insurance, with additional cover for specified personal belongings, including legal textbooks and a computer. Two weeks later, he set out to travel by train to Glasgow, where he was due to catch a flight to Frankfurt. As he had a few minutes before the train went, he left the station to buy food from a supermarket and was mugged. He submitted a claim for the computer and textbooks; a silver cigarette case; £300 cash; clothing and his air ticket (a total of some £5,000).

The insurer's enquiries revealed numerous discrepancies. The film from the CCTV cameras in the station did not support Mr S's account of the mugging, although he provided more than one version of events. Mr S refused to sign the statement taken by the insurer's investigator and instead submitted his own summary. The insurer refused to make any payment, stating that Mr S had failed to prove that the incident had occurred or that he had owned the items claimed for.

Complaint rejected

It is a claimant's responsibility to prove that a loss has occurred and that the loss is covered by the insurance policy. There were several unsatisfactory aspects to Mr S's account that he had failed to resolve. This, together with Mr S's failure to cooperate with the insurer's enquiries, justified its refusal to meet his claim.

13/18   personal accident—permanent total disablement—accident occurring after policy start—disablement due to combined effects of two accidents—whether benefit payable

Mr M was an avionics engineer with the RAF. In 1990, he injured his back but recovered after treatment. He took out personal accident insurance in December 1993. In November 1994, Mr M had another back injury, again returning to work after a temporary absence. However, following a further injury in May 1996, spinal instability was diagnosed. An MRI scan in 1997 showed that he had a prolapsed intervertebral disc. Several operations were performed but Mr M did not recover and he was discharged from the RAF on medical grounds in January 2000.

Mr M submitted a claim under his personal accident insurance for the lump sum, permanent total disablement benefit of £10,000. The insurer accepted that Mr M was permanently disabled, but concluded that it was the accident in 1990 that had caused the disability. As this had occurred before the insurance came into force, his claim failed.

Complaint upheld in part

The consultant had concluded that 'on a balance of probability, [Mr N] did have a prolapsed disc following the incident that occurred in 1990', even though Mr N had been passed fit for work by the RAF after recuperation. We were satisfied that the injury which eventually resulted in Mr N's disablement was in 1990 and that the incident in 1996 simply made it worse.

However, Mr N had not been given a copy of the full policy terms, merely a brochure describing the cover. This began with the words 'If an accident were to happen to you, how would your finances cope?'. The benefits were said to be payable 'If you are disabled by an accident'. This wording implied that a policyholder would be entitled to benefit if he were disabled by an accident after the policy had been issued.

The incident in 1996 had, according to the consultant, made the original condition significantly worse. We therefore put it to the insurer that it should make a payment of £5,000—in other words 50% of the full benefit. It agreed with our conclusion.

ISSUE 18: JULY 2002

18/1 household—non-disclosure—proposal—proof of non-disclosure

Mr B's lender sent him a leaflet advertising premium discounts for new household buildings and contents insurance policies. He applied for a policy by telephone and it was issued on 1 March 2000.

In November the following year, after settling a claim from Mr B for water damage, the insurer searched the industry database. It discovered that—between February 1995 and August 1999—Mr B had made eight claims of which it had no record. The insurer had been aware of only one previous claim and said it would never have agreed to insure him if it had known he had made so many previous claims. It cancelled his policy and offered to pay him the difference between the premiums he had paid to date and the amount it had paid to settle his water damage claim.

Mr B said that when he applied for the policy, the member of staff he had spoken to had said she required details only of his most recent claim. However, the lender said it had a note made by another staff member that, in a later conversation, Mr B had denied making any previous claims. He had also refused to provide confirmation from his last insurer about his claims history.

Complaint upheld

There was no recording of the telephone conversation when Mr B applied for the policy. So the insurer could not prove that it had asked him clear questions about matters it considered important for assessing his application. There was nothing to support its argument that he had failed to disclose all the information it considered material and it could not prove that Mr B misrepresented the details of his claims history.

We took account of the lender's note of Mr B's subsequent telephone conversation. However, we did not agree that this was sufficient to demonstrate either that the sales staff had asked him clear questions about relevant matters or that he had given misleading information. We decided the insurer was not entitled to cancel the insurance or to recover its payment of the water damage claim.

18/2 travel—exclusion for pre-existing medical conditions—exception for conditions agreed by insurer—whether insurer agreed to cover policyholder's heart condition

Mr and Mrs W's son invited them to join a family holiday in Las Vegas and he paid for their trip and insurance. The travel agent said that Mr and Mrs W should call the insurance company's medical advice line to discuss their health. Mrs W did this and told the adviser that her husband had suffered from diabetes and angina for some years.

While in Las Vegas, Mr W had a heart attack and was admitted to hospital. The family notified the insurer's emergency medical service. After some confusion about the policy cover, the emergency service told the hospital that there was no cover for Mr W's heart condition and that it would not meet his expenses.

Mrs W said she had been told that the insurer would cover both of Mr W's conditions. The insurer said it had agreed to cover the diabetes without charge. But it had said it would cover the heart condition only if the couple paid a further premium of £33.60 and agreed an excess of £350. As they had not paid, the heart condition was excluded. The insurer said that the policy terms excluded Mr W's heart condition from cover, so it had not needed to send the couple written confirmation of this.

The insurer paid for Mr W to return to the UK, but it rejected the claim for his hospital fees of about £250,000. Mr W died shortly after his return home.

Mrs W maintained that her claim was valid and said she would have made the additional payment if she had been asked to do so.

Complaint upheld

We generally settle complaints based on the paperwork and other evidence that the firm and the customer provide, rather than at a hearing, where both sides to the dispute meet face to face. However, we decided that a hearing would be helpful in this case, so that both parties could put forward their versions of events.

The insurer based its position on a computer note made at the time of Mrs W's call. This said 'not interested in cover for heart'. Mrs W was firm in her conviction that she had not been asked to pay an additional premium to cover her husband's heart condition.

We found Mrs W's account generally convincing, particularly since she had taken the trouble to telephone the advice line before the holiday. The insurer had an obligation to check that Mrs W understood the implications of not paying the additional premium it said it had quoted her. She might not have agreed to pay, even if she had understood clearly that this meant she could not make any claim arising from her husband's heart condition. However, we decided this was unlikely. It seemed possible that there had been an innocent misunderstanding.

It was unfortunate that the insurer did not record telephone conversations with its policyholders and had not sent the couple any written confirmation of what had been agreed. It left the position regarding Mr W's heart condition open to misunderstanding. It also meant that—had there been any dispute about the insurer's agreeing to cover the diabetes without additional charge, and amending the terms of the policy—there was no evidence other than the insurer's computer record.

We required the insurer to put Mrs W back in the position she would have been in if:

there had been no misunderstanding;
and
she had paid the additional amount required to cover her husband's heart condition.

We awarded her £100,000—the maximum amount we can order a firm to pay. However, we accepted that if the firm met the balance of the claim, it could deduct the amount she would have paid for the additional premium and the £350 excess.

18/3   motor—non-disclosure—innocent non-disclosure—whether insurer treated non-disclosure as serious

Mr C arranged motor insurance over the telephone for himself and for his wife as a 'named driver'. The insurer sent him a printed statement of the questions and answers on which it had based its decision to offer him insurance. It asked him to check the statement and let it know if anything needed correcting. One of the answers confirmed that neither he nor his wife had any motoring convictions in the past five years.

Some time later, after Mr C had put in a claim for damage done to the car during an attempted theft, the insurer discovered that both Mr and Mrs C had convictions for speeding. So it told Mr C it was treating the policy as void and would not deal with the claim.

Mr C insisted that he had disclosed his conviction when he telephoned for a quotation. But he admitted that he had not checked the statement carefully before he signed it. The insurer conceded that Mrs C's conviction was not important. However, it said it would have increased the premium by about 5% if it had been aware of Mr C's conviction.

Complaint upheld

We accepted Mr C's assertion that his failure to disclose his conviction was not deliberate and that he had genuinely overlooked the mis-statement on the pre-printed form. The firm told us that if Mr C had disclosed the convictions, it would have offered cover for a minimal premium increase—about £20.

Non-disclosure is a serious matter. But in the circumstances of this case, it seemed to us unreasonable for the firm to avoid meeting the claim on the grounds of Mr C's non-disclosure. We thought it likely that if Mr C had told the firm about the convictions, he would have accepted the quotation and the firm would subsequently have met the claim. So we required the insurer to reimburse the cost of repairs, after recalculating the premium to include the increase, and deducting this recalculated premium from the total sum it paid Mr C.

18/4   household—non-disclosure—oral representations—burden of proof

Mr O applied by telephone for household insurance. He answered various questions and the insurer then sent him a statement of the facts it considered relevant to his application. It asked Mr O to check the statement and let it know if any of the facts had been recorded incorrectly. The statement read in part: 'Neither you, nor anyone normally living with you, have ever been convicted of, or have any prosecutions pending for, any criminal offence (other than motoring offences).' Mr O did not make any corrections.

Some time later, Mr O needed to make a claim. In response to a question about convictions, he stated on the claim form that he did not have any. However, when a claims investigator interviewed him, he said he had been convicted only once—for theft—when he was 18. The insurer made further enquiries and found that more recently—in 1997—Mr O had been convicted for causing criminal damage.

The insurer cancelled Mr O's insurance and said it would not have issued the policy if it had been aware of the conviction. Mr O insisted that he had told the telesales operator about it, even though he did not consider it relevant to his household insurance.

Complaint rejected

Given Mr O's incorrect statement on the claim form, we were unable to accept his assertion that he had disclosed his conviction when he applied for the insurance. We considered the insurer had been fully justified in treating the insurance as if it had never been issued. It therefore had no liability for meeting Mr O's claim.

18/5   motor—non-disclosure—call recorded by insurer—whether proof of non-disclosure

Mr A's son telephoned the insurer to arrange motor insurance for himself and his father. After receiving the policy, he telephoned the insurer again to say it had made a mistake. He said his father, rather than himself, should be named as the policyholder and main driver. He stated that his father was the registered owner of the car. The insurer then issued new papers.

When the car was reported stolen, the insurer investigated the claim and found that it was the son who was the owner and main user, not the father. Mr A confirmed this. He said they had registered the policy in his name because the premium was cheaper this way. The insurer then cancelled the insurance, saying it would not have issued this policy if it had known the true situation.

Mr A argued that the car belonged to the whole family and had been a joint purchase, even though it was registered in the son's name. The insurer had recorded the calls and produced a transcript of the son's second call, in which he said the firm had made a 'mistake' in naming his father as the policyholder.

Mr A then argued that he did not speak or read English and he claimed that the investigator had not recorded his statement correctly.

Complaint rejected

We were not satisfied that Mr A had given the insurer correct information when it agreed to issue this policy. Mr A's son stated clearly that he was not the main user and that it was a mistake to issue the policy in his name. Mr A's first statement to the investigator confirmed that his son was the car owner and main user. Mr A subsequently contradicted this, but we noted that his signed statement included numerous alterations which he had added and initialled.

We concluded that the insurer was fully entitled to cancel the insurance and reject Mr A's theft claim.

18/6   travel—cancellation—cancellation as a 'direct consequence of compulsory quarantine or subpoena'—whether claim by policyholder held on remand valid

Mr H took out a single trip travel policy for his holiday to Benidorm. However, he was unable to take the holiday. Three days before he was due to travel he was arrested and kept in custody for seven days.

The insurer rejected his cancellation claim. It said that the policy covered cancellation only in certain specified circumstances and this was not one of them. Mr H argued that his claim was valid because cancellation as a 'direct consequence of compulsory quarantine . . . [or] subpoena' was covered.

Complaint rejected

We did not agree that Mr H was in 'compulsory quarantine' while he was held on remand. His detention may have been similar to being subpoenaed to appear in court but it was not the same. The reason he was unable to travel was because he was in prison, not because he was required to appear in court. In the circumstances, the insurer was justified in rejecting Mr H's claim.

18/7   payment protection—insured increasing loan but not insurance—how insurer should calculate benefits

Mrs E arranged a mortgage in 1995 and took out payment protection insurance through the lender to cover her repayments. On three occasions during the next six years, she arranged remortgages of her property with the same lender.

In 2001, Mrs E was made redundant and submitted a claim under the policy. The insurer accepted her claim, but it calculated the benefit that was payable to her each month on the basis of her monthly mortgage payment in 1995. This was insufficient to cover the increased repayments that resulted from the later remortgages.

Mrs E argued that the benefit payable under the policy should have increased each time she remortgaged her property, to protect the revised monthly payments. The insurer said it had been her responsibility to ensure the policy cover was adequate.

Complaint upheld

In our view, each time the remortgage was arranged, the insurer should have suggested to Mrs E that she should increase her policy cover. It should also have drawn her attention to the inadequacy of the benefit payable under the policy unless she did so. This would have been good insurance practice, since insurers and intermediaries arranging insurance policies have a duty to ensure that the policy is suitable for the policyholder's needs and resources.

The insurer agreed to recalculate Mrs E's benefits as if she had increased the cover each time she remortgaged her property. It backdated this additional payment to the start of her claim, deducting the amount she would have paid in premiums for the increased cover.

18/8   household buildings—storm—proof of storm

Mr M, whose house is on top of a mountain in South Wales, submitted a claim for storm damage to the rear windows. He said that in July 2001, storm force winds had caused serious damage to all the windows at the rear of his house. However, he did not submit the claim until October 2001 and by then he had replaced all the windows and doors.

The loss adjuster appointed by the insurer to inspect the damage had found nothing left to inspect—the glazier had disposed of the old windows and doors. The insurer rejected the claim on the basis that there was no evidence of storm damage. Mr M sent the insurer a letter from the glazier stating that the windows were replaced because they were in a 'very weatherbeaten state, particularly those at the rear'.

Complaint rejected

We spoke to the glazier, who indicated that the windows had not been damaged during a single incident of stormy weather, but were in a state of general decay resulting from the normal weather conditions in that area.

Weather reports recorded strong winds during July 2001, but there was insufficient evidence to indicate these had been 'storm force'. We concluded that the windows had not been damaged by storm force winds and we rejected the complaint.

18/9   travel—non-disclosure—exclusion for pre-existing medical conditions—whether insured required to disclose treatment for related conditions

Mr N took out insurance to cover his holiday in Canada in May 2001. The policy included a declaration that he 'had not suffered from or received treatment for . . . a heart-related condition, hypertension, or a stroke . . . [or] received in-patient treatment, has been prescribed medication or has had a change of medication during the last 12 months . . . '.

Mr N told the agent that he had 'dormant' angina and disclosed his age. As a result, the insurance premium was doubled. He did not mention any other conditions. While on holiday he suffered a stroke and incurred substantial medical costs. The insurer would not reimburse Mr N's medical expenses. It said this was because of his failure to disclose that, in 2000, he had suffered from mild hypertension and had been referred to a consultant for 'intermittent claudication' (leg cramps).

Mr N disputed this decision. He submitted evidence from his doctor that the episode of hypertension had 'resolved spontaneously'. Although Mr N had received antihypertensive treatment, this was for ankle oedema (related to the claudication) and not for hypertension.

Complaint upheld

We concluded that the evidence did not support the insurer's decision that Mr N had failed to disclose a medical condition he was required to make known. The medical evidence confirmed that the antihypertensive treatment Mr N received was not for hypertension.

His condition of claudication/ankle oedema was not directly related to the disability that led to his claim—the stroke—so the insurer was not entitled to reject the claim. Mr N had not failed to disclose hypertension; he had not received treatment for that condition within the excluded period.

The insurer agreed to meet the claim and to add interest.

18/10   extended warranty—proof—policyholder claiming for second of two identical losses—evidence required to prove loss valid

Mr D had two fridge-freezers. When one of them broke down and had to be replaced, he took out extended warranty insurance to cover both the new fridge-freezer and the one he already had. Unfortunately, just three weeks later, the old fridge-freezer broke down and that too had to be replaced. Mr D submitted a claim for a replacement and for compensation for the food that had been spoilt. He also claimed for the cost of other food that he had intended to store in the fridge-freezer which broke down, and that he had since had to throw away because it would not fit in the remaining freezer.

The insurer rejected Mr D's claim on the ground that it related to the earlier incident, that took place before the start date of the insurance. Mr D refuted this and insisted that the second breakdown was covered.

Complaint upheld in part

Mr D produced evidence showing that when the first fridge-freezer had broken down, it had been removed and replaced. This proved that he had owned two identical models.

The insurer agreed to deal with the claim and also to pay £130 for the spoilt frozen food. However, it refused to reimburse the cost of the food that Mr D had intended to store in the freezer. We agreed that there was no cover under the insurance for this part of his loss.

18/11   household buildings—non-disclosure—cancellation—whether insurer entitled to refuse to meet cost of work completed before policy cancelled

Mr J applied for household insurance in January 2001. When asked about his insurance history, he disclosed three previous claims, for which he had been paid a total of £2,800. The insurer sent him a statement of facts for checking, together with a direct debit mandate for the payment of premium instalments. One of the statements confirmed that no insurer had ever refused to cover Mr J.

In June 2001, Mr J's pigeon loft caught fire and was damaged beyond repair. He submitted a claim form and two estimates for replacement of the loft. The insurer accepted his claim and told him to proceed. However, it then made enquiries. It found that Mr J had failed to disclose that two insurance companies had refused to insure him. It also discovered that he had not disclosed all his previous claims, for which he had received a total of £24,000.

The insurer refused to pay for the new pigeon loft. It cancelled the insurance and refunded the premiums Mr J had paid. Mr J asserted that he had never received the statement of facts, although he had signed and returned the direct debit mandate. He denied giving incorrect information to the insurer. He claimed he had read out over the phone to the insurer a letter from his previous insurer, saying it would no longer continue to insure him.

Complaint upheld in part

Non-disclosure is a serious allegation. The information that a proposer (someone applying for insurance) provides to an insurer is the basis of the contract and only the proposer can answer the insurer's questions. If Mr J had given false information to the insurer, it would have been fully justified in cancelling the policy.

But we were not satisfied that Mr J had provided incorrect information. He had not been asked to give written answers to the insurer's questions, or even to sign the form on which the insurer had recorded the information he had provided. It was possible that he had not received the statement of facts or that he had failed to check it carefully. The statement of facts was the only record of his telephone conversation with the insurer.

We accepted that the insurer would have refused to issue this policy if it had been aware of Mr J's claims experience. The contract had therefore been agreed on the basis of a fundamental mistake, so the insurer was entitled to cancel it. However, we thought it would be unfair to allow the cancellation to prejudice Mr J. He had started work on the replacement loft on the clear understanding that the insurer had accepted his claim. The insurer agreed to meet the cost of all the work that had been carried out up until the time it notified Mr J that it was cancelling the insurance.

18/12   motor—accessories—valuation—whether policyholder entitled to cost of new replacement

Mr F was involved in an accident with a third party. Both cars were insured with the same company. The third party was 100% liable for the damage to Mr F's car and the insurer settled Mr F's claim on a 'total loss' basis. Mr F also received further payments from the insurance company on behalf of the third party.

The insurer agreed to Mr F's request to retain the car's CD player and roof bars. Mr F thought he might also want to keep the tow bar, although he did not mention this. However, when he got his replacement car, he found that it was a different model and that the old CD player and roof bars did not fit. So he told the insurer he was claiming the cost of a new CD player, roof bars and tow bar.

The insurer said there was no cover for these losses, but it agreed to increase its settlement to reflect their market value, since he could not use them in his new car. It paid Mr F a further £140 for the CD player and £50 for the tow bar. It made no payment for the roof bars, but offered to assess their value if Mr F sent them in.

Complaint rejected

We did not agree that Mr F was entitled to the cost of a new CD player, roof bars and tow bar. His insurer's liability was limited to the market value of the car's accessories, adjusted for 'wear, tear and loss of value' due to their age. The insurer had calculated its offer fairly and we did not consider there were any grounds for increasing it.

18/13   extended warranty—upholstery—meaning of 'upholstery'

When Mr V bought a sofa in 1997, he took out extended warranty insurance to protect it. The policy was headed—'A Five Year Policy for Upholstery (excluding leather)'. The following year, he found that a section of the upholstery was coming loose and separating, so he claimed the cost of repairs. The insurer told him that the cover was limited to 'structural defects' and did not provide indemnity for problems with the upholstery.

Complaint upheld

There was a clear conflict between the actual terms of the policy and the description of the policy cover on its front page. Mr V said that the name of the policy was misleading and that he would not have bought the policy if he had understood how restricted the cover was.

We did not accept the insurer's argument that the policy only covered 'structural defects' with 'upholstery'. The policy did not define 'upholstery', and its ordinary meaning is the fabric that covers furniture. If the insurer intended the word to be defined in a more restricted way, it should have made this clear.

Since the insurer was unable to show that the limited nature of the policy cover had been made clear to Mr V, we concluded it was not justified in rejecting his claim. We also awarded Mr V £100 compensation for the insurer's poor claims handling.

18/14   travel—driving—breakdown and recovery insurance—whether providing comprehensive motor cover

Mr I took out holiday motoring insurance specifically to cover his European motoring holiday. He had an accident while on the holiday, which resulted in his car being written-off. His travel insurer refused to meet his claim, on the ground that the policy only covered 'breakdown and recovery' of his car. It told him he should claim under his UK motor insurance.

Mr I was dissatisfied with this response. He argued that he had been led to believe that the travel insurance provided him with the same level of cover—abroad—that he held in the UK (fully comprehensive motor insurance). If he had been correctly informed about the policy, he would not have purchased it, particularly since his motor insurer would have provided fully comprehensive cover in Europe if he had paid an additional premium.

Complaint upheld

We were not satisfied that the insurer had used its 'best endeavours' to ensure the policy was suitable for Mr I's needs, as it was required to do under the terms of the Association of British Insurers' Code for the Selling of General Insurance. The insurer accepted our recommendation that it should deal with the claim as if the policy covered the full loss, and that it should refund the storage charges Mr I had paid, together with interest.

18/15   household contents—limit of cover—brochure promising wider cover than policy terms—whether insurer entitled to rely on policy exclusion

Mrs K took out the household insurance recommended by her lender and chose the top of the range offered—'Supercover Special'. The brochure described it as 'unlimited contents cover—accidental damage and personal possession cover outside the home' and 'one of the most complete covers available'. It confirmed that personal possessions, including sports equipment and children's bikes, were covered up to £1,500 for any one article.

The explanatory leaflet stated that the policy did not cover 'motor vehicles, caravans, trailers, aircraft, watercraft or spare parts and accessories'. However, it warned—'This leaflet is just a guide and does not summarise all aspects of the cover; only the policy document does this.'

When Mrs K made a claim for the theft of her son's baby-quad bike, the insurer rejected it, citing the policy exclusion for 'mechanically propelled vehicles'. It said the quad bike should have been covered by motor insurance. Mrs K objected, arguing that she had never received a copy of the policy document and that the leaflet suggested that the bike was covered. She also pointed out that her son was only seven years old and could not have used the bike on the road or taken out motor insurance.

Complaint upheld

Whether a baby-quad bike was a 'motor vehicle' or a 'mechanically propelled vehicle' was debatable. However, we did not need to decide that point. There was a clear contradiction between the policy exclusion and the wording of the leaflet. Not only did it expressly include 'children's bikes', but it stated there was 'unlimited' contents cover. It did not seem reasonable to assume Mrs K should have known that the insurer did not consider her son's bike to be part of the 'contents' of her house.

The insurer had not worded its policy leaflet in a clear and unambiguous way, so Mrs K was entitled to the benefit of the wording that was most favourable to her. We required the firm to meet her claim.

18/16   household contents—renewal—notification of new restriction on benefits—whether leaflet documenting change constituted sufficient notification

Mrs H had household insurance for some years. In March 2001, her car was broken into while she was visiting a hospital and possessions were stolen from the locked car boot. She submitted a claim for £2,385 and provided receipts.

The insurer accepted her claim, subject to the policy limit of £1,000, and it deducted the policy excess of £50 from its settlement. Mrs H complained, saying her policy did not refer to such a limit. The insurer said it had imposed the limit when the policy was renewed in 1999.

The changed terms introduced at that time meant that the insurer would not meet claims for—'Theft from unattended road vehicles other than from a locked, concealed luggage boot . . . following a forced and violent entry to a securely locked vehicle. The most the insurer will pay for any one event is £1,000.'

Mrs H denied receiving any information about the change of terms. Although she had moved house in 1999, she had kept all the documents that the insurer had sent her. The insurer produced computer records to prove it had sent Mrs H notification of the change.

Complaint upheld

We could not determine whether Mrs H had received the insurer's notification. However, even if she had, we did not consider the notification was sufficient to draw her attention to such an important change in the policy cover. Any significant restriction in benefits needs to be highlighted but the leaflet did not do this adequately. So it was not reasonable for the insurer to rely on the restriction when it calculated its settlement of her claim.

In addition, we considered the wording of the exclusion ambiguous. It could be argued that the phrase 'any one event' did not refer to thefts from a locked, concealed luggage boot. However, in view of our first conclusion, we did not need to make a decision on this point.

Finally, the insurer had not calculated its settlement correctly. It should have deducted the excess before it applied the policy limit. We were surprised that the insurer had not noticed this error when it reviewed the complaint. We required the insurer to waive Mrs H's excess—as compensation—and to pay the balance of the amount she had claimed, together with interest.

18/17   household contents—renewal—change of policy terms—need to highlight change

Miss L's golf clubs were too big to fit in the boot of her car so she folded down one of the back seats and placed the clubs there. When she returned from an afternoon's play, she forgot to bring the clubs indoors. By the next morning, they had been stolen. The insurer rejected her claim. It said that her household contents insurance only covered thefts 'from a locked, concealed luggage boot' of an unattended car.

Complaint upheld

We agreed with the insurer that Miss L's loss was caught by the wording of the exclusion. As at least parts of the golf clubs were visible, they had not been taken from a 'concealed' luggage boot.

However, we were concerned that the policy terms did not contain this exclusion. The insurer explained that it was added to the policy with effect from the date of renewal in August 1999 and it said it had sent Miss L documents explaining this at the time. Miss L said she had not received any such documents.

The insurer claimed to have sent Miss L:

a standard letter referring to the renewal;
a page setting out the premium and direct debit details;
a schedule providing a general breakdown of the cover;
an advertisement for travel insurance; and
the policy update entitled 'important changes to your home protection policy'.

We did not consider that this set of papers—noting the restriction on cover in the middle of the 'update'—was adequate to draw Miss L's attention to the change. There was no warning that part of the existing cover had been withdrawn and we decided that this fact had not been sufficiently highlighted or properly explained. It is important that adverse changes are prominently announced. We required the insurer to meet Miss L's claim in full and to add interest.

18/18   household buildings—flood—rising water table—cesspit—whether 'damage' caused to cesspit by 'flood'

Mr G's house was 150 years old and served by a cesspit, not connected to mains sewerage. Following unusually heavy rainfall between September 2000 and February 2001, the cesspit was becoming full of water within hours of being emptied. Mr G's sanitary and washing facilities became unusable. He submitted a claim under his household buildings insurance for the cost of remedial work, claiming the cesspit had been damaged by 'escape of water' or 'flood'.

Mr G's insurer rejected his claim, explaining that damage due to escape of water was only covered if water had escaped from a fixed water system. In Mr G's case, the reverse was true, since water appeared to be entering the cesspit from the outflow pipes. And the insurer said that 'flood' only occurred if there was a 'rapid accumulation or sudden release of water from an external source'.

Complaint upheld

According to a recent decision by the Court of Appeal, the word 'flood' should be construed in its ordinary and natural sense and can include prolonged and steady rain or a steady, slow build-up of water.

In this case, the cesspit had been affected by rising ground water. It was not an 'escape of water' but could be described as a 'flood'. The water had not caused physical damage to the cesspit but it had prevented Mr G from using it as usual. This was a 'loss' and it was therefore covered by the insurance.

We put it to the insurer that Mr G's claim was valid and that he was also entitled to compensation for the insurer's delay in accepting liability. This had meant that Mr G and his family were left without proper sanitary facilities for some months. The insurer accepted our conclusions and agreed to meet the claim and to pay £1,000 compensation for distress and inconvenience.

18/19   household—storm—proof of storm—proof that damage caused by storm

Mr S noticed damage to his roof tiles and internal decorations. He had the damage repaired and submitted a claim to the insurer. The insurer rejected the claim after the repairer it sent to look at the damage noted that there were visible signs of wear and tear on the roof.

Mr S submitted a report from his builder, denying any wear and tear and saying the damage was due to a storm. The insurer obtained weather reports that showed there were no storm conditions at the time Mr S noticed the damage. Mr S then conceded that he did not use the damaged bedroom often, so he was unsure when the storm had occurred.

Complaint rejected

It was up to the claimant to show that the damage was due to a particular storm and not merely to poor weather over a period of time, or to general wear and tear. We did not require the insurer to meet the claim. There was no evidence that the damage to the roof had been caused by a storm, or even that there had been a storm around the time of the claim.

18/20   personal accident—motor accidents—policyholder assaulted when getting into car—whether assault covered under policy

Mr Y submitted a claim under his '4-Way Accident Cash Plan', when he was assaulted outside a food and wine shop by the shop owner, and injured his knee.

The insurer rejected his claim on the ground that the policy only covered him if he sustained an accident when he was getting into or out of a private car or public conveyance, or if a vehicle struck him when he was walking on a public road. Mr Y argued that his claim was valid because he had been assaulted while he was getting into his car, after leaving the shop.

The insurer refused to make any payment. It referred to Mr Y's initial statement about the injury, which had not mentioned his car at all.

Complaint rejected

Mr Y was unable to produce any evidence to support his amended description of the incident. Given that he had not originally mentioned the car, we were not convinced that the incident occurred as he claimed. Even if we had been convinced about this, the claim still did not meet the strict criteria of the policy, which limited benefits to injuries sustained as a result of a motor accident.

18/21   motor—non-disclosure—clear questions—modifications—whether tinted windows a 'modification'

When Miss M took out motor insurance, she was asked to disclose any modifications that had been made to her car, such as changes 'to engine, body, wheel, suspension'. She informed the insurer that the car had a body kit but she did not mention any other modifications.

Some time later, after she put in a claim for theft damage to the car, the engineer appointed by the insurer to inspect the car noted that it had tinted windows. The insurer rejected her claim and immediately cancelled her insurance from the start date. It said she should have mentioned the tinted windows, since they constituted a 'modification' and it would not have issued the policy on any terms if it had known about them. Miss M then had to act quickly to obtain insurance with another firm, and she had to pay a much higher amount for it.

Complaint upheld

It was debatable whether the windows were part of the car's 'body' and whether tinted windows were a modification that Miss M was required to disclose. We were satisfied that she had genuinely not realised that she needed to tell the insurer about the windows. We thought the insurer should at least have asked her to explain why she failed to mention the windows, instead of just cancelling her insurance without warning.

We decided that the firm had not been justified in cancelling the insurance. Miss M had by this time taken out an alternative policy with a different firm. So we suggested that the earlier policy should be treated as having been cancelled by her rather than by the insurer. She should give back to the insurer part of the premiums it had refunded, from the policy start date until the new insurance began. In any event, we decided that the insurer had to reimburse Miss M for the cost of repairing the car, plus interest. We also decided that the insurer should pay her £300 compensation for the distress and inconvenience it had caused.

18/22 mechanical breakdown warranty—exclusion for external oil leaks—meaning of 'external'

The camshaft oil seals on Mr R's car broke down and oil leaked on to the cam belt, which was contained in housing at the end of the engine, the housing being sealed with a gasket. Mr R arranged for the necessary repairs—steam-cleaning of components and replacement of the cam cover gasket and the oil seals. He then claimed back the cost of the repairs from his insurer.

The insurer rejected the claim on the ground that the policy excluded 'external oil leaks'. It explained that it would cover internal oil leaks, such as a leak into the cylinders from a blown head gasket. However, it would not pay for any leak outside the main engine block, sump and cylinder head. Mr R argued that the wording of the exclusion was ambiguous.

Complaint upheld

We concluded that the insurer had interpreted the exclusion too restrictively. We did not think it was reasonable to expect policyholders to appreciate the narrow distinction it was making between different types of oil leaks. And we did not agree that an oil leak into a housing, due to the failure of the oil seals, would generally be regarded as 'external'. We therefore required the insurer to meet the claim in full, plus interest.

18/23 medical expenses—transfer from 'a similar existing plan'—whether previous insurance arrangements were 'a similar existing plan'

Mr T was a member of his employer's private medical expenses insurance scheme until 1 September 1993, when he transferred into a personal scheme with the same insurer. Then in September 1999, he cancelled that policy and took out a similar policy with a different firm, whose explanatory literature promised that 'cover may be transferred from a similar existing plan and future claims made for acute conditions originating at the time you were participating in a previous plan will be honoured. No health questions will be asked or medical examinations required.'

In July 2000, Mr T saw a consultant about recurrent groin pain and underwent investigations and a colonoscopy. However, after making enquiries, the insurance company rejected his claim to have his costs reimbursed. It said Mr T had not been entitled to an automatic transfer because his previous insurer had not asked him any questions about his health before it issued him with cover. It also concluded that his illness had 'originated' before he had taken out the personal insurance cover in 1993, because he had received the same treatment in 1987. It did not accept that Mr T's corporate membership was relevant.

Mr T argued that his 1987 claim had been met by the insurance company that covered him at that time and also that his current claim was for a different illness, even though the treatment was the same. He pointed out that the current insurer had not told him that his cover could only be 'transferred' if his previous insurer had asked questions about his health before offering him insurance. In response, the insurer said that Mr T should have understood the terms on which it would allow cover to be transferred.

Complaint upheld

The condition on which the insurer relied in rejecting Mr T's claim stipulated that cover could only be transferred 'from a similar existing plan'. It did not define this term or make it clear that the previous scheme would not qualify unless it had been underwritten on the basis of questions about the policyholder's health.

We concluded that it would have been difficult for anyone to understand the insurer's requirements. Moreover, the explanatory literature only emphasised the ease of transfer, not the insurer's restrictions.

We considered that the insurer should have asked Mr T specific questions on any matters it regarded as vital, before agreeing to provide cover. We decided that all Mr T's previous insurances—both the corporate and the personal schemes—should be treated as 'a similar existing plan'.

We also concluded that the 1987 illness was too remote to be considered as 'an illness that . . . originated before the enrolment'. The insurer was not entitled to reject Mr T's claim on either of the grounds it cited. We required it to reimburse Mr T in full and to add interest to its payment.

18/24   payment protection—unemployment—unemployment defined as redundancy— whether policy restriction made clear to borrower before sale of policy

Mr B took out insurance to protect his loan repayments. His lender arranged a 'Life, Disability and Unemployment' policy. When Mr B became unemployed, he made a claim. The insurer refused to meet his loan repayments, stating that the policy only provided benefits if he became redundant. The policy defined 'unemployed' as 'being without work due directly to your redundancy or business failure'. It also relied on the policy definition of 'redundancy': 'employment being terminated due solely to your employer ceasing or reducing the activities for which you were engaged'.

Mr B argued that he was redundant because he had received a redundancy payment, but the insurer did not agree. It pointed to evidence from Mr B's former employer, showing that he had been dismissed because he was incapable of performing his duties satisfactorily.

Complaint upheld

The policy title referred to 'unemployment' cover, but the policy did not include this benefit and restricted cover to redundancy situations. This restriction was only apparent after a close reading of the policy, including the definitions section. However, the insurer had named and marketed the insurance as if it covered all unemployment. It did not do this, so the insurer had to ensure that the lender selling the policy made the actual scope of the cover clear to potential purchasers before they committed themselves.

There was no evidence that the lender selling this policy had drawn Mr B's attention to the limitations of cover and we accepted on balance that the policy had been mis-sold. We did not consider that it would be fair merely to give Mr B a premium refund—if he had known the policy did not cover all unemployment, he could have bought wider cover from another insurance company. He had been prejudiced by the lender's failure to explain the terms of this insurance.

We were satisfied that Mr B had become unemployed through no fault of his own. So we required the insurer to meet his claim and to pay any interest or arrears charges he had incurred.

18/25   personal accident—mis-sale—road and travel plan—bicyclist—whether policy misrepresented to policyholder

Mr M and his partner took out a 'Road and Travel Plan' in 1996. The policy benefits were set out in a table. Shortly before taking out this plan, Mr M's partner had been involved in a road traffic accident and had been distressed to find that the insurance she had at the time did not provide any cover for her injuries.

In 2001, Mr M was injured while riding his bicycle. No other vehicle was involved in the accident. He submitted a claim, but the insurer refused to make any payment. It told him the policy only covered accidents involving motor vehicles or public transport. Mr M said this restriction had not been explained to him and he asked for a full refund of his premiums.

Complaint rejected

The policy's title indicated that it was concerned with road accidents involving motor vehicles. In fact, it only provided cover for policyholders injured in accidents if they were in a vehicle or if they were a pedestrian, pedal cyclist or passenger on public transport and had an accident with a vehicle.

We were unable to accept Mr M's allegation that he was led to believe that the policy covered any personal accident. Nor did we agree that the policy was unsuitable for his needs and was mis-sold to him. He was not entitled to a full premium refund.

21/1   household contents—exaggerated claim—whether insurer entitled to reject claim in full—whether policyholder pressed to disclaim part of loss

When Mr J was burgled, he notified the police and put in a claim to the firm. His claim—totalling £3,000—included a DVD player, 14 DVD discs, other audio-visual equipment and jewellery.

When the firm questioned Mr J, it emerged that although he initially said that he had bought one of the stolen items (a hi-fi) for £150, he had actually bought it from his brother for £60.

The firm's investigator noticed that some of the DVDs he had listed in his claim had not yet been released in the UK. Mr J was unable to explain how he had bought them. He then admitted he had never owned a DVD player or discs, and he said he wished to withdraw that part of his claim.

The firm rejected Mr J's claim, citing the policy exclusion that enables it to do this if any part of a claim is false or exaggerated.

Mr J's solicitor then said that Mr J had been told by the firm's investigator that if he said that he had never owned a DVD player, the rest of the claim would be paid more quickly. The solicitor also said that Mr J had reported the theft of the DVD player to the police and this proved it was a valid claim.

Complaint rejected

We were unable to reconcile Mr J's statement with his solicitor's assertions. It was hard to believe that, merely to progress payment for the rest of his claim, Mr J was willing to admit he had claimed for something he did not own. The only logical explanation was that Mr J had deliberately exaggerated his loss. So the firm was entitled to refuse to make any payment.

21/2   permanent health—'disabled'—evidence that policyholder engaged in activities inconsistent with his statements—whether insurer justified in ceasing claim payments

Mr G received monthly benefits from the firm after it accepted his disability claim in March 1992. His case was reviewed periodically and his disability was described as a 'non-specific' problem, which caused him to feel unwell and lethargic, with aching muscles and weakness. His GP confirmed that his condition remained static and that he was suffering from 'psychogenic pain unspecified'.

The firm arranged for another doctor, Dr L, to examine Mr G at home. Mr G told Dr L that he spent most of the day either sitting in a chair and staring into space or sitting outside in the garden. Mr G also said that he needed help to load shopping into the car and had not been able to drive for two to three months. However, Dr L could find nothing wrong with him.

The firm's investigators filmed Mr G in the weeks before and after Dr L's visit. These videos showed Mr G getting out of his car, opening the boot without difficulty, pushing a supermarket trolley and loading shopping into his car. They also showed him jet-washing and drying his car and driving long distances.

The firm concluded that Mr G did not satisfy the policy definition of 'disabled' and it stopped the benefit payments. In response, Mr G presented the firm with a letter from his GP saying that his condition had deteriorated. The GP did not appear to have been aware of the video evidence of Mr G's activity, or of why the firm had stopped the payments.

Complaint rejected

We were satisfied that the firm had acted fairly. We did not think Mr G was medically unable to perform his normal occupation. He had been unable to explain either the level of activity shown in the videos or the disparity between this activity and his statements to Dr L about what he could—and could not—do.

21/3   household contents—fraud—police not informed of full loss—whether sufficient reason for rejecting claim

Mr and Mrs B returned home from an evening out to find they had been burgled. They notified the police right away and rang the firm the next morning. The claim form they sent the firm listed 63 stolen items, with a total value of over £20,000.

The firm's investigator was suspicious about the claim and his enquiries continued for the next eleven months.

During the enquiries, the couple's insurance came up for renewal. The firm took more than two months to consider the matter and then refused to renew. The couple were unable to obtain any replacement insurance.

Almost a year after the loss, the firm rejected the claim. It said that when Mr and Mrs B reported the loss to the police, they had not mentioned all the items they later claimed for. It also said that Mr and Mrs B had not provided all the help and information it needed.

Complaint upheld

Mrs B said that she had still been in shock when she reported the burglary to the police and she had only mentioned the most obvious items that were missing. This explanation was entirely credible. Theft victims may well not be aware of the full extent of their loss within a few minutes of discovering it. In any case, Mrs B had mentioned most of the missing items when she telephoned the firm the morning after the burglary. And the couple had receipts for nearly everything.

We required the firm to settle the claim and to pay £500 compensation for its maladministration. We did not think it had handled the claim well, and it had not given Mr and Mrs B sufficient notice that it would not renew their insurance.

21/4   motor—proof of purchase—cash purchase—lack of substantiation—conflicting information—whether claim valid

Miss D insured her campervan in June 2000. A few weeks later, on 12 July, she went on holiday to Grenada. When she returned on 28 August, she reported the campervan missing, presumed stolen. It was never found.

When the firm questioned her about the claim, Miss D said she had bought the campervan on 10 May 2000 and had paid £9,700 in cash. She said it had been advertised for sale in a newspaper and that she and a friend, Mr W, arranged to meet the seller in a pub. She said she had bought the campervan on the spot and had driven it home. She later explained that most of the cash for the campervan had come from the sale of her previous car for £6,250 some six months earlier. She said she had kept that cash in her flat until she bought the campervan. She could not explain how she obtained the balance of £3,450.

The firm was unable to contact Mr W, any of his neighbours, or the previous owner of the campervan. It discovered that the dealer to whom Miss D claimed to have sold her car did not exist. A jeweller had been operating for the last six years from the address she gave as the car dealer's. The firm also found that the campervan had been written off in 1990.

Complaint rejected

It is not normally the business of a firm to investigate how a policyholder has financed the purchase of a vehicle. But it is legitimate for the firm to make enquiries when there is doubt about the vehicle's ownership. No one else beside Miss D had claimed to own the vehicle, but there were many conflicting details in the case and Miss D was unable to explain them. The firm was therefore justified in refusing to pay the claim.

ISSUE 22: NOVEMBER 2002

22/15   motor—valuation—unusually low mileage

Dr M's insurer valued her car at £2,040 after it was seriously damaged in an accident. She disputed this, saying that she had bought the car new eight years before for £7,500 and that it was now worth £4,500. The firm increased its offer to £2,500. Dr M refused to accept this. She said that the firm had failed to take account of the fact that the car had only 6,000 miles on the clock.

Complaint rejected

Even considering the unusually low mileage, the firm's offer seemed to us to be quite generous. It was more than the car's 'market value' so there was no reason for the firm to increase its valuation.

22/16   motor—valuation—proof of condition

Miss W insured her car in January 2001 and told her insurer that it was worth £10,000. After the car was stolen in June that year, the firm offered her £2,600. She objected—saying she had paid £9,500 for the car. When the firm looked into the matter further, it found that the car's previous owner had bought it as a wreck and then sold it to her for £1,000.

When challenged about this, she said further work had been done on the car after she had bought it, to restore it to 'pristine' condition. Although Miss W was unable to produce the car's service history and had no purchase or repair receipts to support her statement, the firm increased its offer to £4,100. It had referred to the published valuations for 'classic' cars, even though she had not taken out 'classic car' insurance. Miss W refused the firm's offer, saying she was prepared to accept £7,500. But the firm would not budge, so she brought her complaint to us.

Complaint rejected

The firm was not liable for the £10,000 Miss W had said the car was worth. The firm's policy documents made it clear that if the car was stolen, the firm would assess and pay the car's 'market value'. This was the amount it would cost to buy a similar vehicle of a similar age and condition. In our view, the firm had valued the car properly. In fact, it had valued it as if it was in excellent condition, despite its high mileage and the lack of any service history. There was nothing to support Miss W's claim that the car was in 'showroom condition', so we were satisfied that the offer was very fair.

22/17   motor—valuation—evidence of value—whether purchase price an accurate indicator of value

Mr Q's car was stolen just over a month after he had bought it. Since he had paid £18,495 for the car, he was extremely upset when the firm valued it at just £15,564.

He pointed out that his policy contained a promise that the firm would replace new cars if they were stolen or became a 'total loss' within the first 12 months. However, the firm said the car had not been 'new'. It said the car had been registered in the dealer's name before Mr Q bought it, and that this affected the car's value.

Eventually, the firm agreed to increase its offer to £16,524. Mr Q refused to accept this, arguing that the car had only five miles on the clock when he bought it. The firm would not change its stance, so Mr Q brought his complaint to us.

Complaint upheld

The firm had no evidence to support its claim that the registering of the car in the dealer's name, only five weeks before Mr Q bought it, would have affected its value. We required the firm to increase its offer to the full amount Mr Q paid for the car, and to add interest from the date of the theft.

22/18   motor—valuation—grey import—evidence of value

Mr T bought a new car for £25,000. It was a 'grey import'—in other words, a car that had been imported by a supplier who was not authorised by the manufacturer.

Just over two months later, after leaving the car in a public car park, Mr T was arrested and taken into custody. The following day, a fixed penalty notice was put on the car, which was still in the car park.

Some time later the car was stolen. The theft was eventually reported to the police in November by Mr T's friend, Mrs C. She subsequently made the insurance claim on Mr T's behalf in January 2001.

The firm valued the car at £17,950 and agreed to add interest to this amount. Mr T said the firm should pay him the full purchase price.

Complaint rejected

In making a valuation, the firm had consulted a specialist trade guide for valuing 'grey imports'.

We were satisfied that the insurer's offer reflected the car's full market value, particularly since there was evidence that the car had suffered some damage before it was stolen. We thought the insurer's offer to add interest to the amount it paid Mr T was very fair, since much of the delay was caused by his being detained after his arrest.

We thought it probable that he had paid more than the car's market value when he bought it and we recommended that he should accept the firm's offer.

ISSUE 23: DECEMBER 2002

23/11   household contents—renewal—change of policy terms—whether sufficient to note amendment on renewal documents

In 1984, Mr K took out index-linked household buildings and contents insurance. This included cover for his personal possessions, which were valued at £9,150 in total. He renewed the insurance every year. However, when he was burgled in 2001, the firm rejected most of his claim. It said that some of the personal possessions that had been stolen were worth more than £500 each and that such items were not covered unless they were insured separately.

Mr K was very surprised by this. He said he had no reason to think these possessions were not covered, as they were items of jewellery that his wife had owned since he first took out the insurance in 1984. He pointed out that the firm's promotional literature stated 'New for Old Replacement means exactly that' and that it promised 'Reimbursement in full at today's prices, whatever the original cost'. The literature also said that index-linking 'automatically takes account of inflation when assessing claims and renewal premiums'. Since none of the stolen items of jewellery had been worth more than £500 in 1984, he considered that they should all still be covered.

The firm based its rejection of the claim on the renewal notices that, since 1991, had stated, 'any item worth more than £500 is not insured at all unless specified'. The firm said that Mr K should have noticed this and made sure that each item of expensive jewellery was individually specified.

Complaint upheld

We considered that the firm's decision to exclude all personal possessions worth more than £500 constituted an unusual and onerous policy term. And such policy terms should be clearly drawn to the attention of policyholders. It is not sufficient for firms merely to print them on the renewal notice without giving policyholders any explanation or notice of the change. Most insurance policies contain a price limit on claims for any single article but it is not common for a firm to withdraw all cover for such items.

The firm knew that Mr K had over £10,000 worth of personal possessions and it should have made it clear to him that he had to specify any item over £500. We concluded that the firm was unreasonable to limit its settlement of Mr K's claim on the grounds that the claim did not meet strict policy terms that the firm had not made clear to him. We required it to meet his claim in full, although we said it could deduct the additional premiums it would have charged for the past five years if Mr K had specified the valuable items.

23/12   household buildings—change of policy terms—need for clear notification—swimming pool dome—dome specifically excluded from policy—intermediary stating policy covered dome—whether insurer entitled to reject claim for storm damage to dome

Before Mr and Mrs A took out household insurance with the firm in 1994, they asked their intermediary if the policy would cover the PVC dome over their swimming pool. The intermediary wrote to them confirming that the dome would be covered 'at no extra cost' so they took out the insurance and renewed it each year.

In October 2001, a storm damaged the dome and Mr and Mrs A made a claim. However, the firm told them the policy specifically excluded swimming pool covers. Mr and Mrs A disputed this and said that if the policy wording had been amended, the firm should have informed them.

The firm argued that swimming pool covers had probably been excluded even in 1994, although it could not produce a copy of the original policy to confirm this. It said Mr and Mrs A should have checked the policy terms at the outset to see if the policy was suitable for them. Dissatisfied with this response, the couple brought their complaint to us.

Complaint upheld

Mr and Mrs A had specifically asked whether the policy would include their dome and in our view they were entitled to rely on the intermediary's letter as confirmation that the dome was covered. It was not reasonable of the firm to expect the couple to have then checked the policy terms to see if the intermediary's statement was true.

The couple had every reason to believe that the dome was covered when they first took out the policy. There was nothing to suggest that the firm had subsequently altered the policy terms and notified its customers that it had done this, so we did not agree that it should have rejected the claim.

The firm agreed to meet the claim, but said it would not cover the swimming pool dome against any loss after Mr and Mrs A's current insurance expired.

23/13 motor—renewal—firm choosing not to invite renewal—whether policyholder entitled to compensation when policy not renewed

Shortly before Mr E renewed his car insurance in February 2002, the firm wrote to tell him that it was transferring customers to a subsidiary. It said Mr E would not be able to renew his policy. The subsidiary had different underwriting criteria and was not prepared to insure him because of the number of claims he had made.

Mr E was upset about this decision, saying it was a 'one-sided variation' of his policy. He did not think the subsidiary was reasonable to have counted windscreen damage as a 'claim'. He said he was entitled to £300 for distress and inconvenience and he asked for his policy to be reinstated.

Complaint rejected

The insurance contract was an annual policy and the firm was entitled to decide not to offer renewal. It was also entitled to decide how many claims policyholders could make before it would decline to insure them. We did not agree that the firm had exercised its discretion unreasonably or that Mr E's complaint was justified.

23/14 motor—renewal—automatic renewal—failure to pay premiums—whether policy should have been renewed—whether subsequent loss covered

Mr H had insured his car with the same firm since 1994. He renewed his policy every year and, from 1997, the firm had renewed the policy for him automatically.

So after he had an accident in October 2001, he was shocked when the firm rejected his claim, telling him he was no longer insured. The firm said that Mr H had telephoned in April 2001 to say he had decided not to renew. It said it had subsequently written to him to confirm his instructions.

Mr H denied this. He said he had no idea that his insurance had lapsed and he had not noticed that the monthly premiums were no longer being deducted from his bank account. The firm told him he should have realised he did not have a valid policy.

Complaint upheld

We asked the firm to send us a recording of the telephone conversation in which Mr H had said he would not renew his policy. But it could neither do this nor supply any notes of the conversation. Nor could it produce a copy of the letter it said it had sent Mr H, acknowledging his decision to cancel the policy.

As the monthly premium was small, we were not surprised that Mr H had failed to notice that the deductions from his bank account had stopped. We thought he should have noticed that he had not received a new certificate, but we accepted his statement that he believed the policy had been renewed automatically, as usual.

We put it to the insurer that Mr H had intended to renew his insurance and his failure to do so was an innocent oversight. It agreed to reinstate the policy and to reimburse the cost of repairs plus interest, subject to his paying the outstanding premiums.

23/15 motor—renewal—non-disclosure—automatic renewal—whether firm made policyholder aware of need to disclose change of circumstances

Mr J's motor insurance was due for renewal on 30 January 2001. The firm sent him renewal papers, including a letter that opened with the line 'If you want to renew then do nothing, it's that easy'. Further on, the letter said, 'If your details aren't the same, then please ring us'.

The letter referred to the premium being based on 'the details we already have on file for you. These are listed for you on the enclosed renewal notice'. However, the renewal notice did not include any information about driving offences or accidents. At the end of the letter, there was a checklist that included a request to call the firm if any details such as 'convictions or prosecutions' had changed.

Mr J's car was stolen in July 2001 and the firm found out that he had been convicted of a drink-driving offence on 11 January that year. So it told him that it would not meet the claim and that it was cancelling his policy from the date of the renewal.

Mr J said he had been away from home until February 2001, but that he had called the firm then and disclosed his conviction. The firm agreed that he had called, but it said he had not mentioned his conviction. It said he had only asked about reducing his cover from comprehensive to third party, fire and theft.

Complaint rejected

We did not think that the firm's renewal invitation made it clear that policyholders had to disclose new information to the firm. So we did not think it was entitled to decline to meet claims on the grounds that a policyholder had failed to disclose routine information, including minor offences.

It was regrettable that the firm did not record its telephone conversations with customers, since a recording would have resolved the dispute. In the absence of a recording, we had to decide what had occurred on a balance of probabilities.

We thought it highly improbable that any member of the firm's staff would have overlooked the significance of Mr J's being disqualified from driving. If he had mentioned it, we thought the firm would have said it was not prepared to offer him cover on any basis.

We also thought that any driver would know their insurer would consider the conviction and disqualification highly significant and would realise they had to disclose this when renewing their insurance. So we decided that in this particular case the firm acted reasonably in cancelling the insurance from the date of renewal.

ISSUE 24: JANUARY 2003

24/1   income protection—disability—policyholder disabled from original occupation but not disabled from 'any' occupation—policyholder's condition deteriorating—whether firm entitled to terminate benefits

Mr B, an electrician, took out an income protection policy. This would provide him with benefit for up to 24 months if he were unable to carry out his normal occupation due to disability caused by accident or sickness. The benefit would, however, stop after 24 months unless he was medically unable to perform 'any' occupation for which he was suited.

In May 1997, Mr B was injured in a road traffic accident. As a result, he suffered severe back, neck and arm pain and saw a consultant orthopaedic surgeon, who identified a degenerative condition. Mr B made a successful claim under the policy and his benefits continued after the initial 24-month period.

However, in January 2001, the firm arranged for Mr B to be examined by a consultant neurosurgeon, who concluded that Mr B might be able to undertake a 'desk job'. In November of that year, the firm appointed an investigator to carry out some video surveillance of Mr B. This showed him bending, lifting, crouching and driving without any apparent restriction. In December 2001, on the strength of this video, the firm terminated his benefits.

In response to this, Mr B produced further medical evidence in support of his claim for 'total disability'. Although, as the video showed and his doctor's report confirmed, he was able to carry out some activities, he said this was only possible at the risk of his health, and that undertaking a job would aggravate his condition.

Complaint rejected

We accepted that Mr B's condition had continued to deteriorate and that he was now incapable of any work. What we had to decide was whether he had met the policy definition of 'total disability' in December 2001, when the firm had stopped paying his benefit.

The medical evidence that Mr B provided at that time suggested that there were some jobs involving only 'light' duties that Mr B could undertake. In order to continue receiving benefits after the first 24 months, Mr B needed to meet the policy definition of 'disabled'—'unable to perform any occupation'.

Since he did not satisfy these criteria, we concluded that the firm had been right to withdraw his benefits.

Although we did not uphold the complaint, the firm agreed to refund the premiums Mr B had paid after December 2001.

24/2 income protection—disability—policyholder disabled from original occupation but able to undertake part-time work—whether entitled to any benefit—method of calculation of benefit

Mr G, a self-employed butcher, developed disabling back pain and claimed under his income protection insurance policy. In December 1990, the firm accepted his claim and started paying him benefits.

By 1996, Mr G was still unable to work. The firm offered to make final settlement of the claim by paying him a lump sum of £167,376. Mr G did not accept the offer and he continued to receive monthly payments.

In 1999, the firm required Mr G to attend a 'functional capacity' examination by a physiotherapist. She concluded that Mr G had not been exerting himself in the tests to his full ability, and that it was impossible to determine whether he was physically capable of returning to his former occupation. The firm had also obtained video evidence. On the basis of this and the test results, it stopped paying Mr G's benefits.

Complaint upheld in part

We appointed an independent consultant orthopaedic surgeon to examine Mr G and to consider the video evidence. This showed Mr G playing golf, driving and gardening. The consultant concluded that Mr G was not fit to carry out the work of a butcher and was unemployable in that capacity. However he might be able to undertake some part-time work in a butcher's shop if it only involved—for example—serving customers and handling cash.

The policy definition of 'disability' was very strict. Taken literally, it might mean that a policyholder's ability to carry out a minor administrative element of an otherwise physically demanding job would justify a firm's rejection of a claim. However, it is accepted market practice to treat someone as 'disabled' if they are unable to perform the 'material and substantial' duties of their ordinary occupation.

As a butcher, Mr G's main duties involved heavy physical work, with much bending and carrying. He spent most of the day on his feet. As well as preparing food, he had to lift heavy carcasses and to spend a considerable time standing behind the counter, serving customers.

When he first applied for the policy, Mr G had described his normal day's work as being split equally between 'jointing' and 'selling/serving' and the firm had insured him on this basis. The type of part-time work that the consultant had suggested he might be able to do was markedly different from this. Any difficulty Mr G might encounter in finding such work was not relevant to an assessment of his disability.

We accepted that Mr G was capable of performing some part-time work, but only in a limited and lower-skilled role. The duties involved would be materially different from his original occupation and less remunerative.

The policy did not deal clearly with this type of situation, but it did provide for the payment of a reduced benefit. We concluded that the firm should reinstate Mr G's claim and pay him benefits calculated at 66% of the full rate. It should also make him backdated payments at this reduced rate, plus interest, from the time when it had stopped his benefits.

24/3 critical illness—definition—angioplasty—whether claim invalid unless meeting strict definition of condition

Mr T took out life assurance to cover his £150,000 mortgage. The policy benefit was payable if he died or was diagnosed with a 'critical illness'. Some weeks after he took out the policy, he was diagnosed with atherosclerosis. He was advised to have balloon angioplasty to correct the narrowing of his arteries.

After Mr T submitted a claim for the policy benefit, the firm wrote to his consultant asking whether the blockage was 'at least 70% in two or more coronary arteries'. This was the policy definition of 'angioplasty'. The consultant confirmed that one artery was 95–99% blocked and another was 50% blocked. He said that this was a particularly serious and life-threatening condition and would have been fatal if left untreated.

Mr T was dismayed when the firm then wrote to him saying it would not pay the claim because it did not meet the terms of the policy.

Complaint upheld

Insurers are, of course, entitled to decide what conditions they wish to cover. But they are obliged to make the terms of their policies clear to customers. Mr T had taken out a policy to cover him for critical illness. By any ordinary definition, he had experienced a critical illness that required urgent treatment. If his doctor had not performed balloon angioplasty, Mr T would have required bypass surgery, which would also have entitled him to claim under this policy.

Assessing the extent to which an artery is blocked is not an exact science. Firms should exercise caution in assessing cases on such a formulaic basis and should normally take account, instead, of the overall seriousness of the condition claimed for. Moreover, the firm's decision to pay benefit only to patients whose arteries were blocked by more than a specific percentage constituted an 'onerous' policy condition, so the firm should have made this very clear in its literature.

We concluded that Mr T's condition was so serious that it was not appropriate for the firm to rely on a strict, formulaic interpretation of the policy. We required it to pay the maximum we can award, £100,000 plus interest, but we recommended that the firm should also pay the balance of the claim.

24/4   income protection—'income'—self-employed policyholder—benefit assessed on earnings—policyholder not informed of restriction—whether assessment of benefit a significant restriction—whether insurer liable to assess benefit on turnover not earnings

Mr C, a self-employed catering machine repairer, took out an insurance policy in 1993 through his bank. This would pay him a monthly income if he became too ill to work. The policy said it would provide a weekly income benefit of £90 if he suffered a disability that lasted more than 13 weeks.

However, when he submitted a claim in 1999, the insurer turned it down. It said it would not pay him anything, because his earnings were not high enough. It explained that the benefit payable under the policy was based on the amount of profit he made, not on his turnover. So, since Mr C had not made any profit in the previous year, the firm said he was not entitled to receive anything.

Mr C was very surprised to hear this. He said that the bank had not properly explained how the policy worked and that the examples it had shown him to illustrate the potential benefits of the policy had been misleading. The bank denied that its salesman had made any error in recommending the policy. And in response to Mr C's complaint that the bank had not told him that payment of benefit depended on his earnings, it said it was not part of the salesman's responsibility to go into such matters.

Complaint upheld in part

The bank had plainly failed to ensure that the policy it sold to Mr C was suitable for his circumstances. It had also failed to draw his attention to the way in which benefits would be calculated. If the policy had been explained properly, he would never have bought it, since he could not have made a successful claim unless his earnings increased significantly. He could not have obtained a policy that calculated benefits on the basis of turnover, so we did not consider the insurer was liable to meet the claim.

However, since he would not have bought the policy if the bank had explained it properly to him, we decided that the bank had to:

- reimburse Mr C the full cost of all the premiums he had paid, plus interest; and
- pay him £250 compensation for distress and inconvenience.

ISSUE 25: FEBRUARY 2003

25/14   motor—non-disclosure—negligence—whether negligent non-disclosure justified cancellation of policy—whether proportional settlement fair

Mrs A insured her car through an insurance broker in August 1999. When her car was stolen in June 2001, she contacted the firm to make a claim. The firm discovered that she had a total of four convictions for speeding. In September 1994, September 1995 and April 1996 she had been convicted for driving at over 30 mph in a 30 mph area. In March 2000 she was convicted for exceeding a 60 mph limit.

The firm refused to meet Mrs A's claim because she had not mentioned the convictions. It said that both when she first applied for the insurance, and again when she renewed the policy in August 2000, it had specifically asked whether she had received any convictions in the previous five years.

Mrs A said that the broker had completed the proposal form for her and she had simply signed it. She said she had not intentionally concealed any information from the firm. However, since her offences were relatively minor, she considered that even if she had told the firm about them, it would still have insured her.

Complaint upheld in part

The question on the proposal form about convictions was clearly worded. And even though it was the broker, not Mrs A, who had completed the form, Mrs A should have checked the answers carefully before she signed it. However, we considered that her failure to do so was an oversight, rather than a deliberate attempt to conceal the convictions from the firm.

The firm agreed that the convictions were relatively minor. It also agreed that it would still have insured her if it had known about them. But it said that it would, initially, have charged her 12% more for her premiums. It would then have charged a further 5% when she renewed the policy in 2000. So her failure to disclose her convictions meant that she had paid less than she should have done.

In the circumstances, we felt that a fair and reasonable settlement would be for the firm to meet the claim on a proportional basis. The firm agreed and paid Mrs A 85% of the value of her claim.

25/15   household contents—non-disclosure—clear question—no evidence question asked—whether incorrect answer entitled firm to cancel policy

In September 2001, Mr C arranged household contents insurance through an insurance broker. Several months later, Mr C was burgled and made a claim under his policy.

In the course of the firm's enquiries, it discovered that, following a domestic dispute in January 2001, Mr C had been convicted of three offences of causing actual bodily harm to police officers.

The firm said it would not have issued the policy if it had been aware of these convictions and it cancelled the policy. Mr C complained unsuccessfully to the firm and eventually he came to us.

Complaint upheld

After Mr C had visited the broker, the broker sent him a printed statement. This incorporated the questions the broker had asked and Mr C's replies. The statement included a heading 'Non-motoring convictions (relating to you or any other permanent resident)'. The space under this was left blank.

When we asked Mr C why he had not disclosed the convictions when he applied for the policy, he said he had told the broker about them. The broker denied this.

We accepted that the existence of the convictions constituted material information that the firm needed in order to assess whether it would insure Mr C. We also accepted that the firm would not have insured him if it had been aware of his convictions. However, there was no evidence that he had deliberately withheld information when he applied for the insurance.

There was a space for details of non-motoring convictions on the printed statement that the broker sent Mr C. But there was no evidence that the broker had asked about convictions during their meeting.

Mr C had not been asked to check the statement, or even to sign and return it. And neither the broker nor the firm had asked Mr C to sign a proposal form. We therefore considered the sale to have fallen short of good industry practice.

Mr C had not attempted to conceal his convictions from the firm's investigator when the firm was looking into his claim. We concluded that his failure to tell the firm about the convictions when he applied for the insurance was innocent. So we required the firm to meet the claim and to pay him £200 for maladministration, since it had cancelled his insurance without having any proof that he had failed to answer its questions.

**25/16   income protection—non-disclosure—duties of a 'company director'—whether firm
entitled to cancel insurance for non-disclosure of manual duties**

When Mr F applied for income protection insurance, he said he was a 'company director' and described
his work as 'inspecting construction sites and training workers in health and safety awareness'. Asked
whether his job involved 'manual or outdoor duties', he answered 'no'.

A year later, poor health forced him to stop work and he made a claim on the policy. In answer to
a question on the claim form about the physical requirements of his work, Mr F said that 30% of his
normal working day consisted of driving, 30% climbing ladders, 5% carrying heavy items, 5% lifting
heavy items, 10% crawling or kneeling and 20% other physical activity. The firm cancelled the policy.
It already knew that Mr F had a heart valve disorder and it said it would never have issued the policy
if Mr F had disclosed the true extent of his physical activities at work.

Complaint rejected

Mr F admitted that he did carry out all of the physical activities he mentioned on the claim form. But
he said that—on reflection—when he had completed the form, he had overestimated the amount of time
he spent on these activities.

In our view, the way in which Mr F answered the firm's questions when he first applied for the policy
gave the clear impression that he was not involved in any outdoor or manual work. Mr F had given
minimal information about his work, even though the form included a space for applicants to describe
their duties fully.

Because of Mr F's medical history, if the firm had known that he was involved in heavy manual
duties on construction sites, it would not have provided insurance. We concluded that his answers had
misled the firm and that it was justified in cancelling the policy from its start date.

**25/17   critical illness—non-disclosure—continuing duty of disclosure until policy in
force—whether failure to advise firm of medical referral innocent—whether firm
took sufficient steps to make assured aware of continuing duty**

In March 2000, Mr M applied to the firm, through a financial adviser, for life assurance to protect his
mortgage. He rang the firm on 9 May, as he still had not heard whether his application had been
successful. He was told there had been a delay as the firm was still waiting for his medical records from
his GP.

The firm finally wrote to Mr M's adviser on 23 May, saying it had accepted the application and
enclosing a letter of acceptance. This letter reminded Mr M that he had a duty to notify the firm if there
had been any change in his details since he applied for the policy.

The policy took effect on 12 June 2000. Some nine months later, Mr M contacted the firm to say that
he had been diagnosed with prostate cancer and that he wished to claim under the policy for the full
critical illness benefit of £30,000.

When the firm obtained a report from Mr M's GP, in connection with the claim, it saw that Mr M
had consulted his doctor on 3 May 2000 with symptoms for which he was referred to a cancer specialist.
The firm cancelled Mr M's policy. It said that when he received the acceptance letter, he should have
disclosed the fact that his GP had referred him to a specialist.

Mr M said that he had never received an acceptance letter. He also argued that, since the firm had
not received his GP's notes until after the consultation had taken place, he had assumed it was aware
of the situation.

Complaint upheld

We were satisfied that Mr M had not received the acceptance letter. The adviser had failed to forward
it to him and it was later found in the adviser's files.

The firm insisted that it was irrelevant whether or not the adviser had sent Mr M the letter. It said
its application form made it clear that anyone applying for insurance had to tell the firm of any change
of circumstances that arose after they had completed the form. We did not agree that the application
form made this sufficiently clear.

We also noted that although the firm had told Mr M on 9 May 2000 that it was still waiting to receive
his records from his GP, it had actually received them in early April, some weeks before the
consultation in question took place.

We considered that the firm's practice of sending the acceptance letter to the customer's adviser, without requiring the adviser to post it on, was likely to cause confusion and was not consistent with good industry practice.

We concluded that Mr M had not deliberately failed to disclose details of his referral to a specialist. We required the firm to meet the claim and to pay Mr M £200 compensation for distress and inconvenience.

25/18 household buildings—non-disclosure—subsidence—whether policyholder's answers were to 'the best of his knowledge'

When Mr W took out a new household insurance policy in March 2001, he stated, in response to a question from the firm, that his house had never been affected by movement of any kind, such as subsidence, heave, landslip or settlement.

In August that year, Mr W notified the firm that cracks had developed in the walls of his house. The firm's loss adjuster concluded that the damage was due to subsidence. The firm asked Mr W for a copy of the structural survey he had obtained before he bought the house in 1997. The surveyor's report concluded 'The property is affected by structural movement evident in severe cracking to the gable elevation. This appears significant and likely to be progressive.'

During the firm's enquiries, it also became aware of a report on the house that had been prepared in 1996, shortly before Mr W bought the property. Although this recommended repairs to the drains, they had never been carried out.

The firm cancelled the policy, saying it would never have been issued if the firm had known about the existing problems.

Mr W said the firm should not have done this, as he had answered the questions on the application form correctly, to the best of his knowledge.

Complaint rejected

When we inspected the application form, we noted that the firm had asked a very clear question about any incidence of subsidence or other kinds of movement. However, Mr W's reply had not fairly represented the true picture and had made no reference to the findings of the surveyor he consulted before he bought the house.

We concluded that the firm had acted correctly in cancelling the insurance.

ISSUE 26: MARCH 2003

26/12 commercial legal expenses—compensation payable under any settlement—firm entitled to approve settlement—whether firm entitled to withhold approval despite legal advice

Ms D put in a claim on behalf of her swimming club under its legal expenses insurance when the club's coach issued legal proceedings for unfair dismissal. She told the firm that as the coach was employed under contract and was not an employee, the club's legal advisers did not think he had a case for unfair dismissal.

The firm accepted Ms D's claim and instructed solicitors to represent the club. The solicitors obtained counsel's opinion that there was a better than 50% chance of defending the coach's allegations, so the firm funded the cost of defending the action. However, the employment tribunal concluded, as a preliminary issue, that the coach was an employee of the club.

Ms D then asked the firm if it would reimburse the club for £5,000 (the cost of settling the claim out of court). The solicitors had recommended this as the best course of action. However, the firm refused, saying the policy terms gave it the right to approve any proposed settlement. Ms D then brought the complaint to us.

Complaint upheld

Under the terms of the policy, the firm did not have to meet the cost of settling any claim unless it had approved the settlement. However, we expected the firm to exercise its discretion reasonably. The settlement in this case was agreed on the advice of the solicitors and, once the tribunal had established that the coach was an employee, it was the best outcome possible for the claim. We required the firm to reimburse the club for the £5,000, together with interest for the period since the club had made the payment.

ISSUE 27: APRIL 2003

27/5 critical illness—non-disclosure—inadvertent—whether proportional settlement appropriate

Mr C's wife had suffered from a series of ear infections that resulted in some loss of hearing. She wore a hearing aid and had seen a consultant. Both she and the consultant viewed her condition as a minor disability.

When Mr C applied, through an intermediary, for a critical illness policy for himself and his wife, the form included the following questions.

'Have you, within the last five years, seen a doctor or been recommended to see a doctor for any of the following: a medical or surgical investigation or operation, treatment, test or advice?'

'Are you aware of any condition for which you may need to see a doctor?'

'Have you ever suffered from or had investigations for: eye disease, loss of speech, loss of hearing or ear trouble, disorder of the brain (including benign brain tumour), disease of the nervous system, anxiety, depression, back or spinal trouble, joint problems, arthritis or any form of paralysis?'

The intermediary completed the form on behalf of the couple, answering 'no' to all of these questions, and the firm issued the policy.

Just over a year later, Mrs C was diagnosed with leukaemia and she died shortly afterwards. The firm rejected the substantial claim that Mr C made under the policy. Its reason was that when Mr C applied for the policy, he had not disclosed his wife's ear condition. The firm said that if it had known about this it would have imposed an exclusion relating to her hearing.

Complaint upheld

We concluded that Mr C's failure to disclose the ear condition probably resulted from an inadvertent oversight. We thought it would be unreasonable and disproportionate for the firm to reject the claim. The exclusion would not, in any event, have affected Mrs C's ability to claim following the discovery of her leukaemia. In the circumstances we required the firm to meet the claim in full.

27/6 farm buildings/machinery/produce—fire damage claim—non-disclosure of previous losses/claims—whether firm justified in voiding the policy and not accepting the claim

In July 2002, Mr and Mrs J arranged farm insurance cover through an intermediary. In answer to a question on the proposal form about previous losses or claims, they disclosed one claim (for losses following a straw fire in 2000). The firm issued the policy.

Only a month later, Mr and Mrs J made a claim when a fire resulted in extensive damage to their farm buildings, machinery and produce.

The firm's investigations revealed that Mr and Mrs J had a history of losses and claims in recent years. They had made a number of claims during the period from October 1993 to February 2001. And they had a total of four substantial losses and claims within the previous five years (one being the straw fire in 2000 that they had disclosed). The firm viewed the couple's failure to provide full disclosure of their losses and claims history as a misrepresentation, entitling it to cancel the policy.

Complaint rejected

Mr and Mrs J were in dispute with the intermediary about the circumstances in which the proposal form was completed, signed and submitted. It was beyond our role to determine that dispute. However, we did conclude that, in completing part of the proposal form and sending it to the firm, the intermediary was acting for Mr and Mrs J, and not as the firm's agent.

We saw no evidence that, at the time of proposal, the firm was made aware of the couple's history of losses and claims, other than the one incident Mr and Mrs J disclosed.

It was Mr and Mrs J's responsibility to ensure that they gave complete and accurate information in response to the questions in the proposal form. We concluded that their failure to provide the full history of their substantial losses and claims within the previous five years had induced the firm to provide cover. So the firm was justified in cancelling the policy from its start date and rejecting the claim.

ISSUE 28: MAY 2003

28/7   causation—damage to carpet caused accidentally rather than by flood—customer had no accidental damage cover under household policy

When a sewer became blocked, effluent threatened to flood Mr B's home. He called the fire brigade and they managed to stem the flood but, in the process, they soiled Mr B's carpet.

Mr B put in a claim under his household policy. However, his policy did not include cover for accidental damage. The firm said that, strictly speaking, it was not liable to pay him anything because the damage was accidental—not caused by an event that he was insured against. However, it agreed to pay the claim on an *ex gratia* basis.

Mr B was dissatisfied with this. He insisted that his policy had covered him for the damage and he said that the firm should also pay him compensation for distress and inconvenience.

Complaint rejected

We concluded that flooding—something that Mr B's insurance covered—was not the cause of the damage. The damage had been caused accidentally in an emergency situation when the fire fighters had failed to remove their soiled footwear or put down protective covering before walking over Mr B's carpet.

So the flooding was merely the 'occasion' of the damage; the fire fighters would not have been in his house if it had not happened. Flooding was not the dominant or effective cause of the damage and no water had, in fact, entered the property. We considered that the firm had not been obliged to pay the claim and that its *ex gratia* offer was more than reasonable in the circumstances.

28/8   causation—furniture warranty—whether recliner chair damaged by insured event of structural fault or by wear and tear/neglect

When Mr G bought a recliner chair, it came with a five-year warranty. Among other things, the warranty covered structural faults, which were defined as including 'breakage of metal components, including recliner and sleeper mechanisms'.

Shortly before the warranty expired, the chair collapsed when Mr G used the recliner mechanism. The firm rejected his claim on the basis of a report from its upholsterer. This said the chair 'has obviously had very heavy use and has not been looked after'. So the firm said the cause of the damage was 'wear and tear and/or neglect, rather than any event covered by the warranty'.

Complaint upheld

The warranty contained no exclusion clause for wear and tear—only for neglect, abuse or misuse. The chair had simply been used. It had not been misused or abused. And we did not consider that there was anything Mr G could reasonably have done to maintain or service the internal recliner mechanism in order to prevent its failure.

Given that the warranty expressly defined 'structural faults' as including the breakage of recliner mechanisms, we concluded that the firm should pay the claim.

28/9   motor insurance—whether damage to insured car caused by inadequate repairs or by some other event

While driving home from work one evening, Mr H was involved in an accident. After he put in a claim, the firm's approved engineers carried out repairs.

However, nine months later Mr H discovered that the front offside tracking (the area of impact in the accident) appeared to be faulty and was causing undue wear to the front offside tyre. Mr H complained to the firm that the approved repairs had been unsatisfactory.

The firm rejected the complaint, saying there was no evidence to support his view. It said that the damage to the front tyre must have been caused by a separate, 'intervening', incident that occurred after the accident.

Dissatisfied with the firm's response, Mr H consulted an independent engineer, who concluded that the damage had happened in the original accident, but had not been seen to as part of the approved repairs. The engineer supported his conclusions with geometric reports made before and after these repairs.

Following a joint inspection of the car by the independent engineer and an engineer appointed by the firm, the firm agreed to pay for the damage to be repaired. However, it refused to reimburse Mr H for the cost of the independent engineer's report, or to pay Mr H any compensation.

Complaint upheld

Mr H had produced persuasive expert evidence to support his view that the damage was caused by the original accident and/or by the inadequate repairs that followed it.

Following the joint inspection, the firm had already effectively conceded liability. So we felt it was unreasonable for it not to reimburse Mr H for the engineer's fee. Despite having no basis for disputing the cause of the damage, the firm had maintained its allegations long after it was reasonable for it to do so.

Mr H had proven his case on the balance of probabilities. We awarded him the cost of obtaining the engineer's report (with interest) plus compensation for distress and inconvenience.

28/10 motor trade policy—whether damage to machinery caused by accidental damage or whether the damage pre-dated the insured event

Mr N, who owned a vehicle repair workshop, had a motor trade policy that covered accidental damage at his premises. Following a break-in, during which the workshop roof was damaged, Mr N put in a claim to the firm. He said that rain had entered through the damaged roof and seriously affected two machines.

The firm rejected the claim, saying there was no evidence to show that the machines had been damaged accidentally.

Complaint rejected

None of the evidence we examined—which included correspondence from the machine suppliers, an independent engineer's report, and weather reports—supported Mr N's view that the damage was caused accidentally, following the actions of a burglar or burglars (an 'insured event').

The letters from the suppliers were inconclusive, but the report from the independent engineer clearly indicated that the damage had been caused by internal faults, not by rainwater entering the machines accidentally. The weather reports did not indicate any significant rainfall during the relevant period.

We concluded that the dominant cause of the damage appeared to be mechanical failure and/or wear and tear over a long period. These causes were not covered under the terms of the policy.

28/11 household buildings policy—whether damage caused by storm or lack of maintenance

Mr K submitted a claim for storm damage to his home after water had leaked in through the roof. The firm rejected his claim on the basis that:

- there was no evidence of storm conditions at the relevant time; and
- the roof was in such a poor state of repair that water would have entered the property in any event.

However, as a goodwill gesture, the firm offered Mr K 10% towards the cost of replacing the roof. He rejected this, saying he was entitled to the full amount.

Complaint rejected

We studied the loss adjuster's report and photographs, together with the estimates provided by Mr K's contractors. This evidence indicated that the property was in a very poor state of repair. No recent maintenance had been carried out to the exterior and even Mr K's own estimates indicated that the roof needed replacing.

Given the absence of stormy weather on or around the period claimed for, we concluded that the dominant or effective cause of the damage was lack of maintenance, rather than storm or any other insured event. Even light rainfall would have caused the roof to leak.

We considered that the firm had been correct in rejecting Mr K's claim and that its *ex gratia* offer had been very fair.

ISSUE 29: JULY 2003

29/1 curtailment claim—firm rejects on basis of policy's general exclusion clause about claims arising directly or indirectly from alcohol

Mrs D had to curtail her holiday and fly home when she got news that her father had been unexpectedly admitted to hospital. He was suffering from liver disease—the result of years of alcohol abuse.

She put in a claim under her travel policy for the cost of return flights and unused accommodation. However, the firm rejected her claim on the basis of the following general exclusion clause:

'[We will not pay for] claims arising from the influence of intoxicating liquor or of a drug or drugs unless prescribed by a registered medical practitioner.'

The firm said this clause excluded all alcohol-related claims, however they were caused. It said it took the view that it would be unreasonable to expect insurers to cover any claims arising directly or indirectly from the effect of alcohol or drugs, whether their use was long- or short-term.

Dissatisfied with this, Mrs D brought her complaint to us. She said it was unfair of the firm to apply the exclusion clause in this case, since her father had not been drinking (and was not drunk) when he was admitted to hospital.

Complaint upheld

We did not think there was anything inherently unreasonable or unfair about the exclusion clause. But we decided that the firm had been unfair to apply it in these particular circumstances.

The clause was intended to remove cover where a named individual, covered by the policy, bore some culpability for the loss or damage for which they were claiming. We interpreted the phrase 'influence of intoxicating liquor' as indicating a state of drunkenness and/or lack of control over one's actions. It was designed to exclude claims that arose from the insured person being drunk, not from the mere consumption of alcohol.

It appeared that the firm had only cited this clause because its policy made no adequate provision for excluding claims that arose from a pre-existing medical condition (which is what had really led to the curtailment in this case).

We considered that if the firm's interpretation of the clause in question were upheld, the exclusion would be unreasonably wide and would exclude all sorts of situations for which most people would expect to be covered. For example, it would exclude a claim where a drunken driver injured a holidaymaker.

We concluded that the firm could not have intended to exclude claims where policyholders were merely innocent victims of chance events beyond their control. So it should not apply the exclusion clause in cases such as this, where claims arose because individuals other than the insured person were 'under the influence of intoxicating liquor'.

29/2 cancellation claim—policyholder's father-in-law committed suicide—whether claim should be excluded

Mr G cancelled his holiday just a week before it was due to begin, when his father-in-law committed suicide. The firm rejected his claim for the cost of the holiday. It said that the policy contained a general exclusion clause relating to claims that arose from suicide or attempted suicide.

Unhappy with the firm's decision, Mr G came to us.

Complaint upheld

We thought the firm had behaved unfairly in applying the exclusion clause in these circumstances. Mr G's father-in-law was not one of the named individuals covered by the policy and his suicide was an unexpected event beyond Mr G's control.

In our view, it was unreasonable of the firm to interpret the exclusion clause as applying to uninsured individuals, including those whose death or serious illness might give rise to a legitimate claim, such as close relatives, business associates, travelling companions, etc.

We were also satisfied that the suicide was a wholly unexpected event so far as Mr G was concerned, and that his late father-in-law had not been suffering from any pre-existing condition. The firm agreed to pay the claim.

29/3   medical emergency and repatriation—firm rejected claim—exclusion clause related to alcohol—medical evidence indicated history of alcohol abuse and causal link with claim

Mr T had to be repatriated to the UK after he collapsed and was taken to hospital as an emergency case while he was on holiday in Tenerife.

The firm rejected his claim for medical and associated expenses. It cited an exclusion clause in the policy that said it would not meet 'any claim resulting from being under the influence of or in connection with the use of alcohol or drugs'.

Mr T said the illness had not been caused by alcohol or drugs but by a prawn curry he had eaten. He said he had suffered a severe stomach upset and breathing difficulties before finally collapsing.

Complaint rejected

The medical evidence from the doctors who had treated Mr T in Tenerife indicated that his illness had been caused by his severe and chronic alcoholism, and by the fact that he had been bingeing on whisky for five days while on holiday. This had led to acute alcoholic pancreatitis. We were satisfied that there was a direct causal link between Mr T's abuse of alcohol and his claim. We rejected his complaint.

29/4   accidental bodily injury claim—whether deep vein thrombosis constituted 'bodily injury' under the terms of a travel policy

Mrs W's husband collapsed and died shortly after their plane arrived at Heathrow airport, on their return from a trip to Australia. The cause of death was determined as 'deep vein thrombosis' (DVT).

Mrs W made a claim under her travel policy, which included cover for 'Accidental Bodily Injury'. The firm rejected the claim on the basis that Mr W's death had been 'caused by a naturally occurring condition and was not accidental'. The policy stated that bodily injury 'does not include sickness and disease unless resulting from a mishap, pregnancy or childbirth or other naturally occurring condition'.

Mrs W insisted that her late husband had been in good health before the trip. She said his death must therefore have been caused by external factors, such as the cramped conditions on the aircraft.

Complaint rejected

We acknowledged that, despite the medical debate that continues to cloud this issue, there is widely thought to be a link between long-haul air travel in cramped conditions and some instances of DVT. But many people who have not flown recently, or who have flown in business or first class, where the conditions are less cramped, also suffer DVT. And each year large numbers of people make long-haul flights in economy class without developing the condition.

We concluded that Mr W could not be said to have died as a result of 'accidental bodily injury', rather than from sickness, disease or some other naturally occurring condition. We also had regard to a recent court ruling (in *re Deep Vein Thrombosis and Air Travel Group Litigation*, TLR 17/01/03) in which it was decided that DVT was not an 'accident for the purposes of article 17 of the Warsaw Convention'. In other words, DVT was not an unexpected or unusual event or happening external to the passenger. We therefore rejected the complaint.

29/5   cancellation claim—firm rejected due to pre-existing medical condition and/or exclusion clause relating to anxiety, depression or psychiatric disorder—whether firm's decision infringed the policyholder's human rights

Mr B cancelled his holiday just a couple of days before 15 May—the date it was scheduled to begin. He said that he had become too unwell to travel. The firm rejected Mr B's cancellation claim, citing two clauses in the policy. These were:

- an exclusion clause relating to claims where the insured person was aware of any existing medical condition or set of circumstances that might reasonably be expected to give rise to a claim; and
- an exclusion clause relating to claims arising from anxiety or depression, or from any previously diagnosed psychiatric disorder.

Mr B's GP had certified that the condition that had given rise to the claim was 'acute stress reaction with anxiety' and that this condition had started on 13 April. Mr B had not booked the holiday until the end of April.

When the firm rejected Mr B's complaint and told him that it would report him to the police for his 'threatening behaviour' towards its staff, he said the firm had infringed his human rights and he brought his complaint to us.

Complaint rejected

We noted a discrepancy between the original medical certificate that the firm had asked for when it was considering the claim and the copy that Mr B subsequently sent to us. The original clearly showed that Mr B's medical condition pre-dated the booking of his holiday and the start of the policy. The copy had been altered to show that the illness began at a later date.

We decided the firm had been correct in excluding the claim on the grounds that Mr B had a previously-diagnosed psychiatric disorder. And since we were satisfied that Mr B had been aware of his illness before he took out the insurance, we agreed with the firm's rejection of the claim on these grounds too.

We did not consider that there had been any infringement of Mr B's human rights, not least because the firm was not a 'public authority' within the meaning of the Human Rights Act 1998. The firm was a private limited company and therefore not bound by the Act.

29/6   medical emergency claim—whether policyholders were using travel policy as private medical expenses insurance

Mr and Mrs M were a retired couple who owned a villa in Spain. They had purchased an annual multi-trip travel policy that provided cover for up to 31 days per trip from the start of each trip.

On 1 March, Mr and Mrs M travelled out to their villa using cheap one-way airline tickets. On 24 March, Mr M fell ill and was admitted to hospital as an emergency case. When the couple subsequently returned home, they made a claim under their travel policy for Mr M's emergency medical expenses.

The firm rejected the claim. It noted that Mr M had become ill towards the end of the 31-day period of cover and that, at that stage, the couple had still not booked their return flights. It therefore concluded that the couple had intended staying for a longer period, incorrectly using their travel policy as a medical expenses policy.

Mr and Mrs M denied this. They said that although they had still not bought their return flights at the time Mr M was taken ill, they had been intending to do so around that date. They said they had always planned to return to their home in the UK before the end of the month, when the 31-day limit on their travel insurance policy expired.

Complaint upheld

It was possible that Mr and Mrs M had effectively been treating their travel policy as a medical expenses policy. However, Mr M's illness had arisen within the period of valid cover and there was no evidence to suggest that the couple were not planning to return to the UK before the policy expired.

Cheap flights are widely available these days and people like Mr and Mrs M, who can be relatively flexible about dates, sometimes prefer to travel out on a one-way ticket, only buying the ticket for their return shortly before they fly home.

We pointed out to Mr and Mrs M that their complaint would not have succeeded if Mr M's illness had occurred after 31 March (the expiry for the 31-day period of insurance) and they had still been in Spain at the time. However, in the circumstances we felt that the fair and reasonable solution was for the firm to pay this claim.

29/7   cancellation claim—whether illness of pets is covered—whether pets are 'family members'

When four of Mr and Mrs C's eight dogs fell ill, shortly before the couple were due to go abroad on holiday, Mr and Mrs C cancelled the trip. They put in a claim under their travel policy but the firm rejected it, saying the policy did not cover them for cancellation in these circumstances. The couple then brought their complaint to us.

Complaint rejected

The policy provided cover for up to £5,000 in relation to the unrecoverable cost of unused accommodation and travel expenses (plus up to £250 for unused kennel or cattery fees). But it only did this if the cancellation was caused by, among other things, the 'serious illness of a relative'.

The policy did not define the term 'relative' and the couple argued that their pets were 'family members' so should be covered. The couple noted, too, that although the policy expressly excluded cancellation claims arising from the death of a 'pet or other animal', it did not expressly exclude claims that arose from a pet's illness.

We did not uphold the complaint. Although Mr and Mrs C felt their dogs were 'family members', the policy did not refer to 'family members' at all—only to 'relatives'. And we did not consider that a pet could reasonably be considered a 'relative' of its owner or owners. Although the term 'relative' was not defined in the policy, in our view it could only properly mean other human beings.

The policy did not provide cover for cancellation caused by the illness of a pet or other animal. The fact that the policy did not specifically exclude this occurrence did not imply that it would be covered. Insurance policies only cover those 'perils' that are expressly set out in the policy and that are not subject to any specific restrictions or exclusions (also stated in the policy).

ISSUE 30: AUGUST 2003

30/1   contents cover only—fire—whether council tenant liable to pay own cost of internal redecoration

A fire damaged some of the contents of Mr J's flat, together with the wallpaper and paintwork. He assumed that the council from which he rented the flat would be responsible for redecorating it after the fire. However, the council said this was his responsibility, so he did the work himself and added the cost of the materials to his claim for the damaged contents.

The firm dealt with part of Mr J's claim—for the damaged contents. However, it said that his contents-only policy did not cover the flat's internal decorations.

Complaint upheld

We pointed out to the firm that its policy defined 'contents' in such a way as to include the internal decorations for which Mr J was liable as tenant. We therefore asked it to reimburse the money Mr J had spent on redecorating the flat.

30/2   buildings cover only—storm damage—whether TV aerial insured as 'buildings' or 'contents'

Mr W had buildings insurance but had not taken out a policy to cover his household contents. After a storm damaged the roof of his house, he put in a claim under his buildings policy.

The firm agreed to repair the roof, but told him the policy did not cover his television aerial, which was fixed to the roof and had been damaged during the same storm. The firm said that aerials were only covered under its 'contents' policy, which Mr W had not bought.

Complaint upheld

We concluded that it was neither fair nor reasonable to treat a permanently fixed aerial, such as this one, as 'contents', even though (in keeping with widespread industry practice) the policy wording clearly stated that aerials were 'contents'. Most people would regard such an aerial to be part of the building, because it is permanently fixed and not readily removable. Moreover, an external aerial is far more likely to be damaged by the type of 'insured event' that affects the structure of the building, such as lightning or a storm, than by the type of event that might damage contents. We therefore required the firm to meet the claim.

30/3 council tenant—contents policy only—escape of water—whether kitchen units were 'fixtures and fittings' or personal possessions

Mrs C, a council tenant, bought some new kitchen units and had them fitted at her own expense. When the units were damaged by an escape of water, she put in a claim to the firm under her 'contents-only' policy. However, the firm told her it could not meet the claim. It said the damaged units were not 'contents' but 'fixtures and fittings', so they would only be covered under a buildings policy.

Mrs C complained that this was unfair, since the units were her personal possessions, not part of the property. When the firm rejected her complaint, she came to us.

Complaint upheld

We agreed with Mrs C that the kitchen units, though fitted, could fairly be regarded as her personal possessions. They belonged to her, not to the council. The units could easily be removed without substantially affecting the fabric of the building. And Mrs C said that if she ever moved house, she would remove the units and take them with her. This seemed entirely feasible and we therefore asked the firm to meet the claim.

30/4 laminate wooden floor accidentally damaged—whether floor covering was 'buildings' or 'contents'

After Mr K's shower leaked, damaging his laminate wooden flooring, he put in a claim to the firm. Mr K had both buildings and contents cover with the firm, but it said it was unable to meet his claim. It told him the damage would only be covered under the buildings section of his policy if he had taken out 'extended accidental damage cover'. Mr K only had this for the contents part of his policy. When the firm refused his request that it should meet the claim under the contents part of the policy instead, Mr K came to us.

Complaint rejected

We agreed with the firm that Mr K's laminate flooring could not properly be described as part of the 'contents'. It was glued together and fixed under beading to the skirting board. It would be very difficult to lift and relocate the flooring without substantially damaging it. In our view, the flooring had effectively become part of the fabric of the building. Mr K did not have accidental damage cover in the buildings section of the policy, so the firm was not liable to pay the claim.

However, we suggested that Mr K might have a valid claim under the buildings section for damage caused by 'escape of water'. The firm acknowledged this and subsequently settled the claim.

30/5 buildings policy only—fire—carpets purchased with property—whether carpets 'contents' or 'buildings'

Mr F had buildings insurance, but no cover for the contents of his property. So when a fire damaged his carpets, the firm rejected his claim on the basis that carpets were 'contents'. Mr F insisted that the carpets were not 'contents', but 'fixtures and fittings' and that they should therefore be covered under his buildings policy. The reason he gave was that the carpets were fitted and had been in place (and included in the purchase price), when he bought the property.

Complaint rejected

We referred to the Court of Appeal's judgment in *Botham* v *TSB Ltd*, which stated that it was doubtful that carpets could ever be regarded as 'fixtures'. So we concluded that the firm had correctly rejected Mr F's claim. He had not bought contents insurance, so the carpets were not covered. We did not agree with Mr F that his having 'paid stamp duty in respect of the carpets' was relevant to the outcome of his complaint.

30/6 contents policy only—storm damage to garage—whether flat-packed conservatory 'household goods'

Mr and Mrs D put in a claim under their 'contents-only' policy after their garage roof collapsed in a storm and damaged a number of items that had been kept in the garage. The firm agreed to pay for all the damaged items except for a flat-packed conservatory, which the couple had recently bought but not yet assembled. The firm insisted that the conservatory was a 'building' and was therefore only covered by its buildings policy, which the couple did not have.

Complaint upheld

In our view, the unassembled conservatory could properly be said to be part of the couple's 'household contents'. It had not yet been erected and comprised a collection of separate components, stored in boxes. We therefore required the firm to pay the claim.

ISSUE 31: SEPTEMBER 2003

31/1 household insurance policy—mistaken cancellation of policy—no cover for theft claim—multiple parties—shared liability

Mr I put in a claim to the firm after his home was burgled. He was shocked when the firm said it was unable to pay out, as he no longer had any cover. The firm said it had cancelled his policy six months earlier because he had failed to pay his premiums. It had been informed by Mr I's bank that he had cancelled the direct debit.

Mr I complained to the firm, saying it should have contacted him to let him know it had not received his premiums. He also complained to his bank, asking why it had misinformed the firm about the direct debit. Unhappy with the responses he received, Mr I came to us.

Complaint upheld in part

We established that Mr I's bank had been responsible for incorrectly cancelling the direct debit. And although the insurance firm should have contacted Mr I when it noticed his premiums had stopped, there was no evidence that it had done so.

But we thought that—over a period of six months—Mr I should have realised the direct debits were not leaving his account. We decided that although the bank and the firm were equally to blame for the problem, Mr I's failure to notice what was going on made him partly responsible too. We therefore apportioned liability between all concerned: 40% to the firm, 40% to the bank and 20% to Mr I.

We required the firm to deal with the claim in accordance with its usual policy terms and conditions. However, we said that (provided the claim was successful) the firm should only pay 40% of it, less an amount equalling the premiums that Mr I had missed. The bank had already offered £8,000 in 'full and final settlement'. Mr I had accepted this offer and we were satisfied that it was fair and reasonable. The bank was prepared to run the risk that Mr I's claim might ultimately be rejected (under the policy's terms and conditions) or be adjusted down, in which case it would have overpaid him.

31/2 legal expenses—reasonable prospects of success—whether supplier of secateurs liable for failing to warn about danger of personal injury

After Mr B's wife accidentally cut off the tip of her finger while she was pruning her rose bushes, Mr B decided to take legal action against the shop where they had bought the secateurs. He thought that the retailer should have ensured that safety warnings were printed on the packaging and he obtained advice that supported this view.

Mr B had assumed that he would be able to claim back the costs of the legal action through the legal expenses policy he had with the firm. So he was very disappointed when the firm rejected the claim, saying the proposed action had no reasonable prospect of success. After complaining unsuccessfully to the firm, Mr and Mrs B brought their complaint to us.

Complaint rejected

In cases where a firm has said the policyholder's proposed legal action has no chance of success, it is not for us to try to reach a conclusion on the merits of the proposed action. Instead, we need to establish whether the firm gave the claim proper consideration. We therefore look at the steps the firm took before it rejected the claim.

Legal expenses insurers are entitled to rely on the professional advice of their legal experts. So if an insurer has obtained independent legal advice from suitably qualified lawyers—whether they were panel solicitors, non-panel solicitors or counsel—and has acted on that advice, then we will not generally question the advice.

In this instance, the firm sought advice from two firms of solicitors and from counsel before it concluded that Mr B's proposed action had no reasonable chance of success. None of these legal experts considered that a court would hold the retailer liable. Mr B had, in part, based his decision to take action on the opinion of an 'accident expert' who cited the General Product Safety Regulations 1994. These regulations include a requirement that consumers should be given relevant information to enable them to assess the inherent risks in a product.

However, the counsel consulted by the firm pointed out that there was an important qualification to this regulation—the requirement only applied 'where such risks are not immediately obvious'. In the counsel's view, 'it should be immediately obvious that if you put your hands too close to cutting blades, you are in danger of injury'.

We were satisfied that the firm had taken appropriate steps to determine whether the proposed action had a reasonable prospect of success. We therefore rejected the complaint.

31/3   commercial policy—whether appropriate to decide case on 'fair and reasonable' basis

Mr C was a self-employed forest management adviser. In December 1999, a tree on land owned by one of his clients, Mr A, fell down and injured a third party, who was driving on a nearby main road. The third party made a claim against Mr A.

It was nearly 18 months later when Mr C discovered that liability might be passed to him. He notified his professional indemnity insurer of the situation, but the insurer said it would not meet the claim. It said Mr C was in breach of contract because he had taken so long to inform it that a claim was likely to be made against him. It also said he had prejudiced its position. The firm cited several legal cases in support of its stance.

Complaint upheld

We established that Mr C had been told of the injury caused by the tree almost as soon as it happened. And he was told a couple of days later that the third party was taking legal action against Mr A. However, there was nothing to suggest that Mr C had any idea that he might be held liable until he received a letter to that effect from Mr A's solicitors on 9 May 2001.

Mr C's policy required him to notify the firm as soon as he became aware of any potential action being brought against him. In this particular case, however, we did not think it was fair or reasonable to have expected him to know he was potentially liable until this was spelt out to him.

We also considered that the firm should have had regard to the Association of British Insurers' Statement of General Insurance Practice. Strictly speaking, the Statement applies only to non-commercial policies. But since Mr C was a sole trader, he was, effectively, in the same position as a private individual with a personal policy. The Statement says that 'an insurer will not repudiate liability to indemnify a policyholder . . . on grounds of a breach of warranty or condition where the circumstances of the loss are unconnected with the breach unless fraud is involved'.

We did not accept that the firm had been prejudiced by the length of time that had elapsed after the accident before Mr C told it that a claim might be made against him. And none of the correspondence that Mr C had entered into regarding the claim had constituted an offer, promise or admission of liability.

We therefore required the firm to deal with the claim, subject to the other terms of the policy.

31/4   motor policy—car stolen from garage forecourt—whether 'lady friend' was responsible for theft—reasonable care—keys in car—theft by deception—multiple reasons given for rejecting the claim

Mr K met a young woman in a nightclub and took her back to his place. The following morning, he offered to drive her home. He said that—on the way—she gave him some money and asked him to buy her some chocolate.

Mr K stopped at a petrol station and left her in the car, with the keys in the ignition, while he went to buy the chocolate. When he returned, both the car and the woman had vanished. The car was later recovered burnt out.

The firm rejected Mr K's claim for the theft of his car. Initially, it said that this was because he had breached the policy condition that required him to take 'reasonable care'. After Mr K challenged this, the firm said there was a policy exclusion that meant it could not pay out if the keys were left in the car. Finally, after he challenged this, it told him that there was a policy exclusion covering 'theft by deception'. It considered that this applied here because the woman had set out to deceive Mr K in order to steal his car.

Unhappy with the firm's stance, Mr K brought his complaint to us.

Complaint upheld

The onus was on the firm to give evidence backing up its reasons for declining the policy. It was unable to do this.

We did not consider that Mr K had failed to exercise reasonable care. He had not acted recklessly by 'deliberately courting a risk of which he was aware'—see *Sofi* v *Prudential Assurance* [1993] 2 Lloyd's Rep 559. On the contrary, the very fact that he had left his car and keys in the care and custody of the woman indicated that he trusted her. It never occurred to him that there was a risk of theft.

The 'keys in car' exclusion could not properly apply because the policy was worded in a way that meant the exclusion only applied if the car was left unattended. In other words, the case was similar to that in *Starfire Diamond Rings Ltd* v *Angel* [1962] 2 Lloyd's Rep 217 CA, rather than *Hayward* v *Norwich Union Insurance Ltd*. The car had not been left unattended—there was someone inside it.

And we were not satisfied that there was a 'theft by deception'. In order to reject the claim on these grounds, the firm would have had to show that when the woman asked Mr K to buy her some chocolate, she had already decided to use this as a ruse to enable her to steal the car. In fact, there was no evidence that she had stolen the car. For any number of reasons she may have abandoned the scene, leaving the car unattended, and an unknown third person may then have stolen it.

In the circumstances, we felt that the fair and reasonable solution was for the firm to meet Mr K's claim. We pointed out that the way in which it had handled the claim, citing different reasons in turn for rejecting it, did the firm no credit and suggested that its aim was to avoid payment at all cost.

31/5   pet insurance—breach of condition—whether death benefit payable—whether valid claim for 'personal accident' to bird

When Mr E's prize-winning parrot died, Mr E put in a claim to the firm for accidental death benefit of £1,200. He also claimed damages of £12,000 for 'personal accident' to the parrot. He said it had accidentally crashed into the toys in its cage and became dizzy before it collapsed and died.

The firm rejected the claim. It was a condition of the policy that Mr E should provide a vet's report, certifying the cause of death, but he had failed to do so.

Complaint rejected

We agreed with the firm that in failing to obtain a vet's report, Mr E had breached an important and material condition of the policy. Without this information, the firm was unable to verify the cause of death and establish whether the accidental death claim was valid.

As far as the claim for personal accident was concerned, we pointed out to Mr E that his policy did not provide personal accident cover and that this type of insurance was only available for human beings.

32/7   jurisdiction decision—group PHI policy—whether complainant eligible

XYZ Ltd held a group personal health insurance policy with the firm and offered health insurance to its staff. In July 2001, one of its employees (Mr W) made a claim under this policy, but the firm turned it down. When Mr W said he would take his complaint to the ombudsman, the firm told him the complaint was outside our jurisdiction. The reason it gave was that XYZ Ltd, not Mr W, was the policyholder, and XYZ Ltd had not given consent for us to consider the complaint.

Despite this, Mr W decided to refer his complaint to us.

Complaint outside our jurisdiction

While firms do sometimes express a view to customers about whether or not they think a complaint is within our jurisdiction, this is ultimately a matter for us to determine. In this particular case, we decided that the complaint was indeed outside our jurisdiction.

This was a relevant new complaint—one where:

- the matter complained about occurred before the Financial Ombudsman Service effectively existed (that is, before 1 December 2001); but
- the complaint was not made to us until after 1 December 2001.

Under our rules, we therefore had to look at how the relevant predecessor scheme—in this case, the Insurance Ombudsman Bureau (IOB)—would have treated the complaint.

Mr W was complaining about the fact that the firm had turned down his claim. It did this in July 2001, which was before the Financial Ombudsman Service effectively existed. The IOB's terms of reference said it could not consider a complaint unless the complainant was the policyholder, or the policyholder had given express permission.

The policyholder in this case, XYZ Ltd, had not given us permission, so we were unable to look at the complaint.

32/8   jurisdiction decision—whether employee was eligible complainant—was key man policy taken out for his benefit?

DP Ltd was a company with an annual turnover of over £1million. When Mr A (one of its employees) was off sick for some time, DP Ltd made a claim to the insurance firm on his behalf. The firm turned down the claim. It told DP Ltd that the complaint could not be referred to us. It said the matter would be outside our jurisdiction because the size of DP Ltd's turnover made it ineligible to complain to us. Mr A subsequently brought the complaint to us himself.

Complaint outside our jurisdiction

The firm had been correct in telling DP Ltd that it was not eligible to complain to us. But we needed to establish whether Mr A was an eligible complainant.

When we asked for further information about the policy, we discovered it was not a personal health policy as we had been led to believe. It was a 'key man' policy (insurance taken out on the life of an individual—in this case, Mr A—whose serious illness or death would create a loss of earnings for the company).

The policy was not taken out for Mr A's benefit, but for the benefit of DP Ltd. It was not designed to pay salary or sick pay to Mr A and there appeared to be no direct or indirect link between any payments the firm was liable to make and any payments that Mr A might receive.

We therefore concluded that the complaint was outside our jurisdiction.

32/9   jurisdiction decision—commercial policy—whether event pre-dated 1 December 2001—what is the relevant 'event'?

Mr D was the owner of a hotel that was badly damaged during an arson attack in August 2000. A couple of months later, he put in a claim under his commercial policy. The firm paid it. However, it turned down a further claim that Mr D made in September 2001 for business losses and sundry expenses in connection with the fire.

When the firm rejected Mr D's complaint about this, he came to us.

Complaint outside our jurisdiction

The firm argued that Mr D's complaint was outside our jurisdiction because the fire had occurred in August 2000, before the Financial Ombudsman Service effectively existed.

We came to the conclusion that the complaint was outside our jurisdiction, but not for the reasons given by the firm.

This was a relevant new complaint about a commercial policy. It therefore needed to be looked at in accordance with the Ombudsman Transitional Order. The relevant date was not the one on which the fire had taken place—August 2000—but the date when the firm turned down Mr D's claim—over a year later. However, in this particular case, this was still before 1 December 2001, so the complaint was outside our jurisdiction.

32/10   group PHI policy—whether case within jurisdiction—employer was policyholder— whether employee an 'eligible complainant'

Mr H worked at GJ Ltd, a large supermarket that offered private health insurance to its staff. After a period of ill health, Mr H put in a claim to the insurance firm. When the firm refused to pay, Mr H referred his complaint to us.

Complaint within our jurisdiction

The firm argued that the complaint was not one we could deal with because neither GJ Ltd nor Mr H were eligible complainants; GJ Ltd because it was a commercial customer with an annual turnover of over £1million, and Mr H because the policyholder was GJ Ltd, not him.

We found that the complaint was within our jurisdiction. It was true that, because of its size, GJ Ltd was not an eligible complainant. However, Mr H was. Under the rules (DISP 2.4.12R), we were able to look at this complaint because ' . . . the complainant [was] a person for whose benefit a contract of insurance was taken out or was intended to be taken out'.

It was clear that the policy was taken out for the benefit of GJ Ltd's employees, including Mr H. For the complaint to be within our jurisdiction, it was not necessary for Mr H to be the only person to benefit from the policy. The fact that the employer also benefited was immaterial.

32/11   jurisdiction decision—complainant resident in Jersey—firm based in Jersey— territorial scope of our jurisdiction

Mrs S, who lived in Jersey, rang us to ask if we could look into her complaint against a financial services firm based in the Channel Islands.

Complaint outside our jurisdiction

Under the rules (DISP 2.7.1), the territorial scope of the Financial Ombudsman Service 'covers complaints about the activities of a firm . . . carried on from an establishment in the United Kingdom'. The Channel Islands are not part of the UK and therefore not subject to the regulatory requirements of UK financial services law.

If the firm complained about had a registered office in England, Wales, Scotland or Northern Ireland, and the transaction complained about had been carried out there, then we might have been able to help. As it was, however, the complaint was outside our jurisdiction. We suggested that Mrs S should contact the Jersey Financial Services Commission to see if it could help with her complaint.

ISSUE 34: JANUARY 2004

34/1   buildings policy—policyholder claims for fire damage after arson attack—firm voids policy on grounds of misrepresentation—says property was 'left unoccupied'

Mr S, who worked in London, bought a house near his parents' home in Cardiff. His mortgage lender arranged the buildings insurance and was aware that Mr S had bought the house with the intention of renovating it and then letting it out.

Mr S visited the property almost every weekend to work on it, sometimes staying there overnight and sometimes sleeping at his parents' house. One weekend, he arrived at the house to find it had been damaged by fire. He later found this had been a case of arson.

When he put in a claim, the firm refused to pay out. It said it had 'voided' the policy (cancelled it from the outset) on the grounds that Mr S had misrepresented the position when he took out the insurance. The firm said Mr S had not made it clear that he did not intend to live in the property long-term. Mr S then brought his complaint to us.

Complaint upheld

The firm agreed to reinstate the policy after we pointed out that there had been no misrepresentation. Mr S had made his intentions perfectly clear when he asked the mortgage lender to arrange the policy. However, the firm still rejected the claim, citing the policy exclusion relating to properties that were left 'unoccupied'.

We did not consider that the firm had acted fairly or reasonably in rejecting the claim. The house had minimal furniture and lacked adequate facilities, such as a lavatory and a working kitchen. However, Mr S was able to provide ample evidence to show that he had visited it frequently to carry out work and to check up on the property. The house was neither abandoned nor neglected and Mr S had not applied for a council tax discount on the grounds that it was 'unoccupied'.

Because we considered the wording of the policy exclusion to be unclear and ambiguous, we interpreted it in favour of Mr S. We concluded that the property had not been left 'unoccupied' for more than 30 days, even though it had not been lived in and was not yet habitable on a long-term basis.

34/2 buildings policy—firm refuses claim for damage following break-in—considers property 'unoccupied'

Mr K lived in London but owned a house in Belfast, where he had been a student and where his girlfriend lived. His insurer turned down the claim he made after he discovered the house in Belfast had been broken into and extensively damaged. He then came to us.

Complaint rejected

The firm had rejected Mr K's claim because of the exclusion clause in his policy that said it would not meet claims if the property was 'left unoccupied'.

Mr K told us that he visited Belfast periodically to see his girlfriend and to check up on the house. There was a small amount of evidence that he had visited Belfast occasionally, but we concluded he had simply been staying with his girlfriend. It was doubtful whether he had checked on the property at all.

The house was in such a poor state of repair that it stretched credibility that anyone would be able to live there, even for one night. We considered that the firm's position had been prejudiced by the fact that the house was not lived in.

We did feel that the exclusion clause could have been written more clearly. However, in the circumstances of this case, we thought it reasonable for the firm to cite the clause in order to reject the claim.

34/3 buildings policy—firm refuses claim for water damage after pipes burst—property left unlived in for over a year

Miss Y, an elderly woman, was unexpectedly admitted to hospital and she ended up spending more than a year away from her home. During that period, she had made no arrangements for anyone to visit or check the property.

She subsequently discovered that her home had been damaged when some water pipes had frozen and burst. She put in a claim, but the firm rejected it because she had 'left her house unlived in for more than 30 days'.

Complaint rejected

The property had effectively been abandoned for a very long period and this had led directly to the damage. We established that it would have been relatively easy for Miss Y to have ensured the property was looked after while she was away. We therefore concluded that the firm had acted reasonably in rejecting her claim.

ISSUE 35: FEBRUARY/MARCH 2004

35/1   customer unable to recover full amount of claim under contents insurance policy—value of damaged property exceeded the policy limit—whether firm right to reject customer's claim for the balance under his purchase protection policy

Mr K accidentally dropped and damaged his new camera one afternoon when he was taking pictures of his family at a local carnival. The camera was worth about £4,000 and Mr K put in a claim under his household contents policy. He had paid an additional premium on this policy to obtain cover for his personal possessions while they were outside the home.

Mr K's contents insurer accepted the claim. However, it only paid him £1,500, as this was the policy limit. Mr K then tried to obtain the balance from his purchase protection insurer (firm C). Firm C rejected the claim on the grounds that its policy contained the following exclusion: 'This policy does not cover . . . loss or damage insured under any other policy or which would have been insured under another policy but for the application of a policy excess.' Mr K then complained to us.

Complaint upheld

The clause in this particular policy was similar to that found in many types of policy. We consider the purpose of such clauses is to prevent policyholders making a 'double recovery' (claiming for the full amount of the same claim—from two different insurers). We did not consider the clause to be inherently unfair or unreasonable, provided the firm applied it appropriately, so as not to exclude genuine losses that were otherwise uninsured.

Mr K had recovered only part of his actual loss from the contents insurer. We therefore considered that it was fair and reasonable for him to ask firm C to cover the balance—and for it to do so, subject to the policy excess and limit.

35/2   whether electricity generator came under policy's definition of 'personal possessions'

When Mr J's electricity generator was stolen from a local stable, where it was being kept temporarily while in use, he made a claim under his household policy.

The firm rejected the claim. It said the generator was not covered when it was outside the home. The only 'personal possessions' that the policy covered outside the home were 'Items which you . . . would wear or carry around for personal use, adornment or convenience . . . '. Mr J then complained to us.

Complaint rejected

We felt that the firm's policy definition was worded sufficiently clearly to exclude Mr J's claim. The firm intended only to cover certain sorts of items—those that were portable. It could not reasonably be said that a bulky electricity generator was an item that you would carry around for 'personal use or convenience'.

We therefore rejected the claim.

35/3   customer's claim for stolen computer—whether firm correct to say computer did not fall within policy description of 'personal belongings'

Miss G took her personal computer with her when she went to stay with a friend for a few weeks. The computer was a standard desk-top model, not a laptop. There was a break-in at the friend's house shortly after Miss G arrived and the computer was stolen.

Miss G put in a claim under the 'personal possessions' section of her household policy but the firm turned it down. It said that her computer did not fall within the policy definition of 'personal belongings' which listed 'Clothing and Personal Effects (including clothing, jewellery, watches, furs, binoculars, musical, photographic and sports equipment)'. Miss G then complained to us.

Complaint upheld

We decided that if the firm intended only to cover personal belongings that were designed to be portable, or that were customarily carried about the person, then it should have said so in plain language.

We pointed out that the policy definition included musical instruments. Some musical instruments, such as pianos, are not usually considered 'portable'. However, the policy did not make any distinction between 'portable' and 'non-portable' instruments. So non-portable items could fall within the policy definition of 'personal belongings'. The computer was a possession that was personally owned by Miss G. Since the policy did not specifically exclude computers, we decided the fair and reasonable solution was for the firm to pay the claim.

35/4   customer's furniture destroyed in fire at 'storage facility'—whether firm correct in rejecting claim on grounds that items were stored in a 'furniture depository'

Mrs A put her furniture into storage while she was having renovations carried out after moving home. Unfortunately, all her furniture was destroyed when the storage facility burnt down. The owners of the facility held no insurance and had been declared bankrupt, so Mrs A put in a claim under her household insurance policy for £50,000.

Her policy covered her against loss or damage for 'personal possessions temporarily away from the home'. However, there was an exclusion that said items were not covered while they were stored in a 'furniture depository'. The firm cited this exclusion to turn down Mrs A's claim.

Mrs A argued that the storage facility was not a 'furniture depository', but the firm still refused to pay the claim. However, it did offer her a goodwill payment of £5,000.

Complaint rejected

We decided that a 'storage facility' fell within the ambit of the phrase 'furniture depository'. It was a place where furniture was deposited. We did not agree with Mrs A that because items other than furniture could be stored there, it could not be defined as a 'furniture depository'. We concluded that the firm was not liable to meet the claim and that its goodwill payment had been very fair.

35/5   bag stolen from parked car when left covered with a coat on front seat—whether firm right to dismiss complaint on grounds that bag had not been 'concealed'

Mr D and his wife left their car in the car park while they were visiting a stately home one afternoon. They returned to the car later in the day to find that a thief had broken into it and stolen Mrs D's handbag. She had left the bag on the front seat, covered with a coat.

Mr D made a claim under the personal possessions section of his household insurance policy. However, the firm said it would not meet the claim because the handbag had not been left in 'a locked and concealed boot, concealed luggage compartment or closed glove compartment', in accordance with the terms of the policy.

Complaint rejected

The policy exclusion had been very clearly stated and it was evident that the bag had not been left in a 'secure concealed compartment'. The handbag could easily have been left in the boot. Even though the bag had been covered with a coat, it would have been obvious to an opportunistic thief that the coat could be hiding something worth stealing. We decided the firm acted reasonably in turning down this claim and we rejected the complaint.

35/6   firm turns down claim for sunglasses stolen from car—whether sunglasses had been 'effectively concealed from view'

When Mrs M returned to her parked car after a brief shopping trip, she found that a thief had broken into her car. The designer sunglasses that she had left in the pocket of the door nearest the driver's seat had gone.

Mrs M put in a claim under the personal possessions section of her household policy but the firm turned it down. It said this was because the sunglasses had not been left in 'a concealed luggage compartment or closed glove compartment'. Mrs M then complained to us.

Complaint upheld

We considered that, strictly speaking, Mrs M's claim fell foul of the exclusion clause. However, we felt the firm's decision was less than fair and reasonable because the sunglasses had effectively been concealed from view. They would not have been visible to a passing thief and the door pocket was, in many ways, similar to a glove compartment. This thief just happened to strike lucky when he broke into the car. We therefore decided that the firm should pay the claim.

ISSUE 36: APRIL 2004

36/9   travel insurance policy—customer cancels holiday—whether customer breached the terms of the policy by not disclosing information

Early in the New Year, Mr C decided to arrange his summer holiday. He booked two weeks in Tenerife for that August. At the same time, he took out a travel insurance policy with the firm.

In February, Mr C's mother was diagnosed with cancer. However, it was only a few weeks before Mr C was due to travel that she was told her illness was terminal. As soon as he discovered this, Mr C cancelled his holiday and put in a claim to the firm for the cost of the trip.

The firm refused to pay out. It said that Mr C should have got in touch when his mother's illness was first diagnosed. Mr C argued that he had not known at that stage that her condition was terminal, or that her failing health would mean he had to cancel his trip. The firm was insistent that because he had not disclosed this information at the earliest possible stage, he had breached the terms of the policy. Mr C then came to us.

Complaint upheld

The firm said the policy imposed an 'ongoing duty of disclosure' on policyholders. In other words, it said that policyholders had to inform the firm of any illnesses or other 'relevant matters' that occurred after they had taken out a policy. If policyholders failed to do this, then it could refuse to pay a claim.

We acknowledged the general point the firm made to us that customers should not delay in cancelling their holiday if a situation arose where there was clear medical evidence or advice that they should not travel. However, that was not what had happened in this case.

We felt the firm's clause arguably amounted to an unfair contract term. It is acceptable for policies to exclude claims from cover if they arise from 'pre-existing conditions'—medical conditions that pre-date the start of the policy. But in this case, the firm excluded not only illnesses known about in the three years before the start of the policy, but also those that occurred 'before the trip started'.

In our view, in turning down a claim because of circumstances that arose between the time Mr C took out the policy and the date when his holiday began, the firm was acting unfairly. Its clause effectively relieved it of any obligation to pay health-related claims. By seeking to remove the element of risk, the policy undermined one of the fundamental principles of insurance. We upheld Mr C's complaint and told the firm to meet the claim.

36/10   annual travel policy bought online—cover to start from a specified date—customers cancel holiday before cover starts—whether firm should pay cancellation costs

Mr and Mrs B bought their annual travel policy online in March, but specified that the cover should not begin until 1 June, the day they were due to fly to Malta for a holiday.

At the end of May, Mr B's father died and the couple cancelled their holiday. When they put in a claim to the firm, they were dismayed to be told that they were not covered. The firm explained that the policy had not yet come into effect because the couple had chosen 1 June as its start date.

As a gesture of goodwill, the firm offered the couple a sum towards the costs of the cancelled holiday, although it refused to pay the whole of the claim. Dissatisfied with this, the couple complained to us.

Complaint rejected

We felt that the firm's offer had been more than fair. The online sale process was very straightforward, with clear instructions. The firm's website explained that if customers asked for the cover to begin at a future date, rather than from the time of the sale, the customers would not be covered if they cancelled their holiday before the cover began.

This was not a case of the firm varying the terms of the policy after it had come into effect. The policy had not been in force when the couple made their claim. We therefore rejected their complaint.

36/11   house insurance policy—unoccupied house burns down—whether firm right to reject customer's claim

Ms G left her home unoccupied while she was working abroad for six months. While she was away, her house was broken into and set on fire. The house was so badly burned that it was beyond repair.

Ms G was covered for 'malicious damage' to her property and she put in a claim to the firm. However, it told her it was not liable in cases where the property had been 'left unoccupied' and it said she should have notified it when she moved abroad.

Complaint upheld

We agreed with the firm that it was not obliged to pay Ms G's claim for any 'malicious damage' to her home. The policy clearly defined the term 'left unoccupied' in relation to this type of claim, and it did not cover claims for this kind of damage to unoccupied properties. However, the primary cause of the damage to Ms G's house was a separate, insured event—'fire and explosion'. There was no general or specific reference to the firm not being liable for such an event if the house was unoccupied.

While acknowledging that this was the case, the firm insisted that Ms G should have told it when she moved out of her house. The firm said this had changed the 'nature of the risk' and that, because she hadn't disclosed the fact she had moved out, it was entitled to vary the terms of the policy and cancel it.

We disagreed. We did not feel that Ms G had been obliged to disclose this fact to the firm, in the way she would have had to do if—say—she had sold the property and bought another house. We thought that by attempting to vary the policy after Ms G took out her house insurance, the firm had acted unfairly. We upheld Ms G's complaint and told the firm to meet her claim.

36/12   travel insurance—customer disclosed medical condition after taking out policy—whether firm right to invalidate policy

In February, Mr and Mrs J took out a travel policy to cover the holiday they had booked for May.

Mrs J was unexpectedly admitted to hospital in April for a clot on the lung. Her treatment was successful and her consultant said there was no reason for the couple to cancel their forthcoming trip.

When she was double-checking all the arrangements the day before the holiday, it occurred to Mrs J that she ought to ring the firm just to update them on what had happened. She was shocked when the firm told her it would have to invalidate the policy and refund the premium.

As there wasn't time for Mr and Mrs J to arrange any alternative cover, the couple felt they had no option but to go on holiday without any insurance. When they returned home, they complained to the firm about its actions and about the 'unnecessary distress and inconvenience' they had suffered as a result. When the firm dismissed their complaint, they came to us.

Complaint partially upheld

This was not a case where the policyholders had failed to disclose a material fact. At the time the couple took out the policy, Mrs J had not been suffering any ill health. And in any event, the firm had never asked the couple any questions at all about their health.

The firm told us it had invalidated the policy because there was a 'continuing duty of utmost good faith' that required policyholders to 'notify the firm of any change to the risk' after the policy was taken out.

We cited Professor Malcom Clarke's *Policies and Perceptions of Insurance*, together with Ivamy's *General Principles of Insurance Law*, to support our view that—generally—there is no duty on a policyholder to disclose 'material facts' once the firm and policyholder have agreed on the contract.

In addition, we noted that there was nothing in the terms of the policy that entitled the firm either to 'avoid' it (in other words, to treat it as though it had never existed) or to cancel it. Although there was no claim to consider, we required the firm to pay Mr and Mrs J modest compensation for the distress and inconvenience they had been caused.

38/5   **car stolen from driveway—whether firm was right to reject complaint on the grounds of customer's 'carelessness'**

Miss L's car was stolen from the driveway of her home while she was inside the house. She neither saw nor heard the theft. When she put in a claim to the firm, it asked her to send it her car keys. However, she was only able to produce the spare ignition key.

Taking this as evidence that the key had been in (or on) the car when it was stolen, the firm rejected Miss L's claim. It said that by failing to 'exercise reasonable care in safeguarding her car' she had breached a general condition of her policy.

Miss L objected to this. She said that the key had definitely not been in the car when it was stolen. She had lost the key a month earlier and had been using the spare. She was adamant that she had not been 'careless', as the firm had suggested. After the firm rejected her complaint, she came to us.

Complaint rejected

We agreed with Miss L that she had not been 'reckless'. As we noted in our last issue, someone is reckless if they recognise a risk, but deliberately 'court' it. Miss L had not done this, so the firm was wrong to say that she had breached the 'reasonable care' condition.

However, the firm's policy also contained a specific (and very comprehensive) clause that excluded claims for cars stolen when the keys were left in them. The firm had specifically highlighted this clause when it sold Miss L the policy. And as we were not satisfied with Miss L's explanation that she had lost the original car key, we concluded on balance that it was likely that she had left the key in, or on, the car.

We were satisfied that the circumstances of this theft did fall within the scope of that exclusion. She could be said to have 'left' the keys in the car because she had gone into the house, and was too far from the car to be able to prevent it being stolen. In addition, the fact that the car was parked so close to the road meant it was relatively vulnerable to an opportunistic thief. We therefore rejected the complaint.

38/6   **keys left in ignition—firm rejects claim—whether firm had highlighted exclusion clause**

Mr A parked his car opposite a letterbox and jumped out to post a letter, leaving the key in the ignition. While he was crossing the road to reach the letterbox, someone stole his car.

Mr A was horrified when the firm rejected his subsequent claim on the grounds of its 'keys in car' exclusion clause. He said that the firm had never told him the policy included such a clause and, eventually, he complained to us.

Complaint upheld

By turning his back on the car and walking away from it, Mr A had fallen foul of the 'keys in car' clause in the policy. In legal terms, he had left the car 'unattended'—in other words he was not close enough to the car to make prevention of the theft likely, as established in *Starfire Diamond Rings Ltd* v *Angel*, (reported in 1962 in Volume 3 of the *Lloyd's Law Reports*, page 217); and in *Hayward* v *Norwich Union Insurance Ltd*, (reported in 2001 in the *Road Traffic Reports*, page 530).

Mr A accepted that he had left the car unattended. But he claimed that none of the policy documents that the firm had sent him (such as the policy schedule and certificate) referred to the 'keys in car' exclusion. The firm had set out the exclusion in the policy booklet but had done nothing to draw Mr A's attention to it when it sold him the policy, as it should have done in accordance with industry guidelines. We therefore felt it was fair and reasonable to assume that Mr A had been prejudiced by the firm's failure to highlight the clause. If the firm had clearly referred to the clause on the policy certificate or schedule, Mr A might well have acted differently.

And we were satisfied that Mr A had not acted 'recklessly'. Applying the test of 'recklessness' as set out in *Sofi* v *Prudential Assurance* (1993)—he had not even recognised that there was a risk, let alone deliberately courted it. We therefore required the firm to pay Mr A's claim.

38/7 key left in car—theft recorded on CCTV—whether firm right to use 'key in car' exclusion to refuse claim

Mr H drove to the council-run tip to get rid of an old carpet. While he was disposing of the carpet, someone stole his car. He had left the keys in the ignition and, although he hadn't walked far from the car, he did not hear or see anything suspicious. He only realised that his car was gone when he turned back towards where he had left it. The firm turned down Mr H's claim because he had left his keys in the car. When it rejected his complaint about this, Mr H came to us.

Complaint rejected

The firm's decision not to pay the claim was based on CCTV footage that it obtained from the council. This showed Mr H walking away from his car with the carpet. It also appeared that he had left the car's engine running.

We agreed that the firm had been correct in turning down the claim on the grounds of its 'keys in car' exclusion. Mr H had turned his back on the car after leaving it in a public place and he was completely oblivious to the theft until after it had happened. He had walked a fair way from his car, so he was unlikely to have been able to prevent the theft.

In this instance, Mr H had no excuse for not being aware of the policy exclusion. The firm had highlighted it very clearly on the policy certificate, a document that every motorist is required to have by law. We therefore rejected his complaint.

ISSUE 39: AUGUST 2004

39/1 commercial policy—firm rejects claim for theft from café on grounds that policyholders breached warranty

Mr K and Mr L were business partners who ran a small café. One morning they arrived at the café to find that someone had broken in, stolen some cash and damaged the safe.

They put in a claim under their premises insurance but the firm turned it down. It told them this was because they had been in breach of the policy warranty, as they had left cash in the till overnight, had not fitted a specified type of lock on the café windows, and had not taken adequate security measures in relation to the siting of their safe.

The policyholders said that they had not been aware that their policy required them to comply with specific security requirements. They argued that these requirements were largely immaterial to the incident in question, since the thieves had entered and left the premises by breaking down the front door, not via the windows, and the till had only contained a small amount of loose change.

They insisted that they had done all that they reasonably could have done to leave the premises secure, and that the firm should therefore accept the claim. When the firm refused to reconsider the matter, Mr K and Mr L came to us.

Complaint rejected: principles of the Statement not applied

In our view, the evidence made it clear that, regardless of whether the policyholders had complied with the security measures set out in the warranty, the thieves would still have gained entry to the premises. However, we thought that the thieves would probably not have been able to get into the safe. So although the loss would still have occurred, the amount lost would probably have been smaller.

If we applied the principles of the Statement, we might have decided that the firm should pay for the part of the loss that would still have occurred even if the policyholders had complied with the warranty.

However, we noted that the café employed four full-time staff and was run as a limited company. And although Mr K and Mr L told us they had no knowledge of legal and insurance matters, they clearly had access to expert advice because they had bought their policy through a firm of insurance brokers and that firm had represented them when they made a claim for the break-in.

We concluded that the nature of the business, and the resources available to the policyholders, meant that it would not be appropriate to apply the principles of the Statement. We therefore rejected the complaint.

39/2   **commercial policy—firm refuses to accept claim arising from a legal action against the policyholder, on grounds of breach of warranty**

Mr C was a self-employed forestry consultant. While he was working on a large estate, a tree fell down and injured a third party. A few days later, Mr C heard that the third party was planning to put in a claim to the estate owner for the injuries caused by the fallen tree.

Nearly 18 months after that, the estate owner's insurer told Mr C that it would be passing on to him the third party's claim for his injuries. Mr C then contacted his insurer right away, but was shocked when it told him it would not meet the claim. It said that by waiting so long after the accident before contacting it, he had breached the condition in his policy that said he must notify it immediately, in writing, of 'any occurrence which may give rise to a claim'.

It also argued that its position had been prejudiced by Mr C's failure to notify it as soon as the accident had occurred. It said the delay meant it had lost the opportunity to obtain any evidence from the time of the accident that could have given it a better chance of successfully defending the claim.

Complaint upheld: principles of the Statement applied

When Mr C referred his complaint to us, we noted that he was a self-employed contractor with no employees. His policy did require him to notify his insurer as soon as he became aware of any potential action being brought against him. However, we did not think it was fair or reasonable to have expected him to know he was potentially liable until this was spelt out to him, by the estate owner's insurer, nearly 18 months after the accident happened.

We concluded that this was a situation where a commercial policyholder was, effectively, in the same position as a private individual with a personal policy. It was appropriate to apply the principles of the Statement and we therefore upheld his complaint and required his insurer to deal with the claim.

ISSUE 40: SEPTEMBER/OCTOBER 2004

40/4   **critical illness—'any occupation' cover—whether firm correct to reject claim solely on the basis of video evidence**

Mrs T put in a claim under her critical illness policy for permanent total disability resulting from fibromyalgia. The insurer rejected her claim, saying she was not disabled from carrying out 'any occupation'. It based its view on the video surveillance it had carried out. This showed Mrs T walking and moving normally. Mrs T was unhappy with the firm's decision and she complained to us.

Complaint rejected

We did not think it was fair for the insurer to reject the claim solely on the basis of a short piece of video footage, so we asked the insurer to show the video to Mrs T's doctors.

The doctors agreed that the way in which Mrs T was seen to be moving on the recording was not consistent with the manner in which they had seen her moving during consultations. This cast some doubt over Mrs T's claim.

The policy covered Mrs T if illness prevented her from performing 'any occupation'. We were satisfied that, even applying the more generous 'Sargent' interpretation, the weight of the medical opinion established that Mrs T's condition did not prevent her from performing any occupation for which she was suited by reason of her education, training or experience. We therefore rejected her complaint.

40/5   **personal accident—'any occupation' cover—whether policyholder 'unable to carry out any occupation whatsoever'**

Miss G, a professional dancer, suffered a serious injury while performing in a West End show. The injury effectively ended her career as a dancer and she put in a claim under her 'any occupation' cover.

Although Miss G was receiving state incapacity benefits, the insurer refused to pay her disability claim. It said that she did not fulfil the policy definition of disability: 'unable to carry out any occupation whatsoever'. Miss G then complained to us, arguing that the insurer's decision was unfair and discriminatory.

Complaint rejected

We noted that, unlike some policies, this one was written in very clear terms. Indeed, because of the nature of her occupation, the firm had required Miss G to sign a specific endorsement as part of her application for the policy. This confirmed that 'benefit will only be payable if Miss G is unable to perform any occupation whatsoever'.

Having carefully reviewed all the medical evidence and 'functional capacity' reports, we concluded that Miss G was certainly so disabled that she was unable to continue working as a dancer. However, she was an educated and intelligent person, and was not disabled from any occupation for which she was suited, let alone from any occupation whatsoever.

The fact that Miss G was classed as 'disabled' for the purpose of state benefits did not necessarily mean that she was also disabled within the terms of the policy. We decided that the insurer's decision was neither unfair nor unreasonable in all the circumstances. There was no evidence to support Miss G's allegation that the insurer had contravened the Disability Discrimination Act 1995. We therefore rejected the complaint.

40/6 personal accident 'own occupation' insurance—whether insurer's actions after receiving consultant's report were correct

Mr D, a motor mechanic, developed a phobia about germs. He felt compelled to wash his hands so frequently during the day that, eventually, he was unable to complete any of his tasks and he had to give up work altogether.

He was covered for illness that prevented him from carrying out his 'own occupation', and he put in a claim to his insurer. The insurer paid him disability benefits for a few months. However, it stopped these payments as soon as it received a report on Mr D's condition from a consultant psychiatrist.

The insurer told Mr D that it would not pay him any further benefits because the psychiatrist had concluded, ' . . . once Mr D receives cognitive behavioural treatment for his phobia, it is likely that he will be able to return to work and have a relatively normal life within six months of the start of the treatment'.

Mr D felt his benefits should continue, at least for the time being, but the insurer disagreed, so Mr D complained to us.

Complaint upheld in part

We felt that the insurer's interpretation of the medical evidence was rather harsh. We were satisfied that, at present, Mr D's illness was preventing him from carrying out his 'own occupation' of motor mechanic.

The psychiatrist had not said that Mr D could now return to work. She had said that it was likely he would be able to return to work:

- if certain conditions were satisfied (about the overall hygiene standards of the workplace); and
- after he had successfully completed six months of cognitive behavioural treatment.

The consultant indicated that a premature return to work would probably cause a recurrence of Mr D's underlying depression and anxiety.

We were satisfied that, at present, Mr D's illness was preventing him from carrying on with his occupation as a motor mechanic. We decided that the fair and reasonable solution was for the firm to reinstate benefits, at least until Mr D had completed the six months' cognitive behavioural treatment. After that, Mr D would have a medical reassessment. Future benefits would depend on the outcome of that reassessment and of the cognitive behavioural treatment.

ISSUE 42: DECEMBER 2004/JANUARY 2005

42/3   **policyholder forges documents in the course of making a valid claim—insurers wrongly attempt to 'avoid' entire policy**

Mr H was a self-employed plumber. In January, his home was burgled and he made a claim under his home insurance policy, which the firm duly paid. In May, his van was broken into and a number of personal possessions were stolen, including the tools he used for his work. He made another claim to the firm under the personal possessions section of his home contents policy.

During the course of its enquiries, the firm's loss adjusters insisted that Mr H substantiate all his losses with original purchase receipts. Mr H was unable to find all the receipts, so he asked a friend to fake one for him.

When the firm discovered the forged receipt, it 'avoided' the policy—in other words, cancelled it from the start. The firm not only refused to pay for the items stolen from the van, it also tried to recover the money it had previously paid out to Mr H for his earlier burglary claim. After complaining unsuccessfully to the firm, Mr H came to us.

Complaint upheld

The firm accepted that the theft from the van was genuine. Mr H had been foolish to obtain a forged receipt but he was not dishonestly trying to obtain something to which he was not entitled. The loss adjusters had, in fact, been rather overzealous in insisting on strict proof of purchase for all the items stolen.

We applied the rationale of '*The Mercandian Continent*' case (reported in [2001] Volume 2 of *Lloyd's Law Reports* at page 563) which concerned the principle of 'utmost good faith'. Ultimately, the case held that insurers should only be able to 'avoid' a policy for fraud where the insurer's ultimate liability was affected, or when the fraud was so serious it enabled the insurer to repudiate the policy for fundamental breach of contract.

Following this rationale, we concluded that the fair and reasonable solution was for the insurer to reinstate the policy and pay the claim. In any event, it was unlikely that the firm's ultimate liability would be affected by the fraud, as Mr H's work tools were specifically excluded from the home policy. Home policies often exclude cover for contents or possessions that are for business rather than personal use.

We also pointed out to the firm that even if Mr H had been guilty of fraud, it would only have been entitled to 'forfeit' the policy from the date of the current claim, leaving the earlier burglary claim intact. It was not entitled to recover previous payments for valid claims.

42/4   **policyholder supplies misleading and fraudulent documents in the course of making a valid claim—insurers able to 'forfeit' policy from the date of the claim**

Miss J made a claim under her general household policy for 'escape of water' damage. As the damage was reasonably limited, the firm simply asked her to send in repair estimates. She provided three. The firm discovered that all three estimates—purporting to come from different contractors—were fraudulently produced by one contractor who had carried out extensive works for Miss J in the past. The firm considered Miss J to be guilty of fraud. It cancelled her policy and refused to deal with the claim. Miss J then bought her complaint to us.

Complaint rejected

Miss J had already admitted supplying false information to the firm, and in an attempt to resolve the matter, had produced further—genuine—estimates from independent contractors. However, these merely served to show the extent to which the prices quoted in the fraudulent estimates had been exaggerated.

Once again, we applied the principles of '*The Mercandian Continent*' case (see case 42/3). If the fraud had not been discovered, the firm would have ended up paying more in compensation than was properly required of it, and more than Miss J was legally entitled to. To this end, the fraud affected the firm's ultimate liability and was a fundamental breach of contract.

Having applied that rationale, we decided that the firm had been entitled to 'forfeit' the policy from the date of the claim.

42/5 **policyholder purposefully gives wrong details of stolen items—insurers able to 'forfeit' policy from the date of the claim**

Mr G made a claim for goods stolen from his home during a burglary. Among the many items he claimed for were some Star Wars DVDs. This alerted the firm's loss adjusters to the possibility of fraud, since at the time of the burglary the films in question had not been released on DVD. The firm rejected the claim and 'forfeited' Mr G's policy from the date of his claim. Mr G complained to us, arguing that he must have mistakenly claimed for pirated copies of the DVDs, and that this mistake did not warrant 'forfeiture' of the policy.

Complaint rejected

We were satisfied that this was a clear attempt to defraud the firm. There was evidence that showed 'beyond reasonable doubt'—more than the usual civil requirement of 'balance of probabilities'—that Mr G was claiming for something that he could never have owned. This higher standard of proof indicated that Mr G would still be guilty of fraud, even if the pirated DVDs did exist, since he had attempted to claim for legitimate copies.

The value of the DVDs was relatively small compared with the overall size of the claim, but we did not feel this was a case of 'innocent and minimal exaggeration'. Mr G had dishonestly claimed for something he was not entitled to. This went to the very root of the insurance contract, and was a breach of the policyholder's duty to act in 'utmost good faith' when submitting a claim.

We also felt that this fraud, and Mr G's subsequent attempt to cover it up, cast doubt on the validity of the entire claim. The firm's decision to 'forfeit' was therefore fair and reasonable.

ISSUE 44: MARCH 2005

44/11

Mr T underwent minor surgery to correct a prolapsed disc. The operation appeared to be uneventful. However, during recovery Mr T complained of tightness in his neck and eventually he was rushed to intensive care, where he died. The coroner concluded that the cause of death was haemorrhaging from a vertebral artery. When the insurer rejected the personal accident claim brought by Mr T's widow, she complained to us.

Complaint upheld

The weight of the medical evidence indicated that the surgeon had negligently torn or cut the artery during the surgery. We felt that this was not a natural consequence of the risks inherent in surgery. Something had gone wrong and this was not what any of the parties to the surgery had anticipated.

The injury was not the natural result of the procedure as it was solely and directly caused by external, violent and visible means. The injury therefore fell within the scope of the policy. When we put this argument to the insurer, it agreed to meet the claim.

44/12

Mrs G had an operation to remove a lump from her neck. During recovery, the wound started to bleed profusely, resulting in a massive haemorrhage. As a result of this, Mrs G died.

The insurer rejected a claim made by Mrs G's husband on their personal accident policy. It said that Mrs G's death had resulted from the complications of planned surgery—rather than from an accident. Mr G then brought his complaint to us.

Complaint rejected

There was nothing to suggest that this was an accident. The medical reports and the coroner's inquest cleared the surgeons of any wrongdoing. No error had occurred during the operation. Mrs G was just one of the very few unfortunate patients who react badly to this type of surgical intervention.

The bodily injury here was a natural, though tragic, consequence of the surgery. It was an anticipated risk which Mrs G had consented to, insofar as the general risks of surgical complications had been explained to her. So despite sympathising with Mr G's situation, we could not agree that the insurer had acted unfairly or unreasonably.

47/7 **legal expenses insurance—insurer's panel solicitors obtain out-of-court settlement in unfair dismissal case—policyholder thinks she would have received more if insurer had taken case to an employment tribunal**

After Mrs T lost her job, she made a claim under the legal expenses section of her household policy as she wanted to pursue an action for unfair dismissal against her former employer.

The insurer agreed to investigate the claim. It instructed one of its panel solicitors to review the evidence and give an opinion on the merits of Mrs T's proposed action. The solicitors concluded that the case had reasonable prospects of success, so they entered into pre-action negotiations with the other side. These resulted in an out-of-court settlement, which was endorsed by the employment tribunal.

Mrs T felt that she would have received a higher amount if the dispute had been fought out face-to-face before the tribunal. She therefore complained to us that the insurer and/or its solicitors had prejudiced her case by refusing to provide the further funding that would have been needed for this.

Complaint rejected

We were satisfied that the insurer had acted on the independent advice of legal professionals. There was nothing to indicate that the advice was patently wrong or based on factual errors.

The solicitors had settled for less than their original estimate, but this was because their assessment of the prospects of success had changed as the case proceeded. New evidence and arguments had become available which had influenced the solicitors' opinion about the case. Such a change of view is not unusual or improper, given the complex and uncertain nature of litigation.

Moreover, although we did not reveal this to Mrs T, the solicitors' files indicated real concerns that she would make a poor witness. In our view, this was a legitimate consideration for the solicitors when deciding whether or not to settle out of court.

47/8 **legal expenses insurance—unhappy with insurer's rejection of claim, policyholder obtains separate and more favourable legal advice, but insurer refuses to reconsider**

After injuring herself at work, Miss E made a claim on her legal expenses insurance as she wished to pursue a case against her employers for negligence. The insurer's panel solicitors advised the insurer to reject the claim, on the basis that it had no reasonable prospects of success. Miss E felt that the insurer's legal advice was flawed. She therefore instructed her own solicitors, who obtained a favourable opinion from a barrister. However, the insurer refused to consider the matter further, so Miss E complained to us.

Complaint upheld

While acknowledging the generally subjective nature of legal opinions, we felt Miss E had shown—on the balance of probabilities—that her employers did have a case to answer concerning their alleged negligence.

Given that the barrister was a specialist in the field of personal injury litigation, we considered that her opinion tipped the balance in favour of Miss E. We therefore asked the insurer to:

reimburse Miss E's legal costs to date (with interest); and

fund the reasonable costs of litigation, in accordance with the usual policy terms and conditions.

We also felt that it would be fair and reasonable for the insurer to allow Miss E to continue with her own solicitors (and barrister) even before proceedings were issued. This was because the panel solicitors had been shown to be incompetent, in that they had failed to consider all the relevant legal issues or obtain a second opinion from counsel.

ISSUE 48: AUGUST 2005

48/1 **life assurance—inadvertent non-disclosure**

In December 2002 Mrs D applied to the firm for life assurance cover of £100,000 and for £35,000 critical illness cover. Two years later she was diagnosed with breast cancer. The firm refused to meet her claim. It said this was because she had not disclosed that for most of the early 1990s she had been suffering from, and received treatment for, back pain following childbirth. It considered the fact that she had not revealed this information to be reckless non-disclosure.

Mrs D told the firm that she had not thought she needed to disclose this information. She had thought the question on the firm's application form referred only to illnesses that had resulted in her taking time off work during the previous five years. It was more than five years since she had suffered from the back pain and she had never needed to take time off work because of it.

In response, the firm pointed out that it had asked whether she had 'ever suffered' from 'back or spinal trouble'. Mrs D said she did not believe that back pain due to childbirth was 'back or spinal trouble'. Unable to reach agreement with the firm, Mrs D came to us.

Complaint upheld

After studying the questions that the firm put to Mrs D when she applied for insurance, we noted that—in answer to most of the questions—Mrs D needed to give information only about any medical consultations that had occurred during the previous five years.

However, the firm's question about 'back or spinal trouble' was not limited to that five-year period. We felt that the wording of this question was potentially misleading. We accepted that Mrs D had genuinely misunderstood the question and that any non-disclosure was inadvertent.

However, we thought that a careful reading should have made it clear that the firm wanted to know about all back and spinal trouble, regardless of how it occurred or when she had sought treatment for it. We took the view that Mrs D had been slightly careless in completing the application.

Slightly careless or inadvertent non-disclosure entitles an insurer to rewrite the insurance policy. It should do this on the terms that it would have offered originally, if it had been fully aware of the applicant's medical history. In this case, the firm would have offered full cover except for back and spinal problems.

We required the firm to reinstate Mrs D's policy—adding the exclusion for back and spinal problems—and to deal with the claim on those terms. There was no connection between Mrs D's breast cancer and the exclusion clause so the firm had to meet her claim in full, together with interest.

48/2   motor insurance—deliberate non-disclosure

Mrs G took out motor insurance by telephone. In answer to one of the firm's questions she said that she was the owner and keeper of the car. Mrs G asked for her son, A, to be added to the policy as a named driver.

The firm sent Mrs G details of all the information she had given and that it had relied on when deciding the terms of her insurance policy, asking her to let it know if anything was incorrect. Mrs G did not make any changes.

A few months later, after A was involved in a road traffic accident, the firm discovered that the car was registered in his name, not his mother's. The firm also found that the receipt for the car named A as the purchaser.

When the firm declined to meet the claim, Mrs G insisted that she was indeed the real purchaser and owner of the car. She said that the registration documents had been issued in her son's name by mistake. The firm told her it would not have insured the car at all if it had known that A was the owner. Unable to reach an agreement, Mrs G came to us.

Complaint rejected

In our view, the questions that the firm had asked Mrs G when she applied for insurance were clear and unlikely to be misunderstood. And the firm had specifically drawn Mrs G's attention to the importance of accurate information and records.

Her failure to reveal that the car was registered in A's name had induced the firm to offer insurance. As it would not have insured the vehicle if it had been aware of the true position, the firm was entitled to avoid the policy (treat it as though it had never existed). We rejected the complaint.

48/3   life and critical illness insurance—innocent non-disclosure

In January 2005, Mr E was diagnosed with lung cancer and put in a claim to the firm. Over six years earlier, in November 1998, he had taken out life and critical illness insurance cover worth £150,000.

After carrying out enquiries, the firm found that in September 1997 Mr E's GP had recorded that Mr E was consuming approximately 80 units of alcohol a week (21 units is the recommended maximum weekly amount for men). In February 1998 Mr E's alcohol consumption was up to 84 units a week but by July of the next year it had gone down to a more moderate 40+ units a week.

The firm said this differed greatly from the declaration Mr E made when applying for insurance. He had said then that his average alcohol consumption was five units a day (35 per week). The firm told him that if it had been aware of his drinking habits, it would have increased his premium by 200–300%. It refused to pay the claim and it returned his premium, avoiding the policy from its start date.

Mr E was extremely angry with the firm's response. He said that when he applied for the insurance he had answered all the firm's questions accurately. He pointed out that he had, at that time, been the sole carer for his newly-born daughter and could not have handled his responsibilities if he had been drinking as heavily as before. The firm still maintained that he was likely to have been drinking more than he had claimed.

Complaint upheld

When the complaint was referred to us we found no evidence concerning Mr E's drinking habits at the time he applied for the insurance. The amount he had said he was drinking (five units a day or 35 units a week) was close to the 40+ units a week that his GP had recorded eight months later. Mr E had given a plausible explanation for his answer and the firm had no justification for disregarding it.

As there was no evidence of non-disclosure or misrepresentation, we required the firm to reinstate the policy and meet the claim. The firm agreed to pay the full sum of £150,000, plus interest.

48/4   household insurance—deliberate non-disclosure

Mr A applied for household insurance. After receiving his completed questionnaire, the firm agreed to put the policy into effect from 28 June 2002. They also sent him a statement of facts, setting out the information he had given. In response to a question asking whether he had any 'non-motoring convictions' he had replied 'none'.

The following day, Mr A contacted the firm to say that his house had been burgled. However, the firm was unable to get any response when it tried to arrange for its investigator to visit him at home. It heard nothing more until January 2003, when it was informed that Mr A was in jail.

In the course of the firm's subsequent investigations, it discovered that—at the time Mr A took out his policy—he had a criminal record for possession of drugs and resisting arrest. After making the burglary claim, Mr A had again been found in possession of drugs and was fined for resisting arrest. Finally, three months after the burglary, he was remanded in custody on a murder charge.

The firm told Mr A that it would not have insured him if it had been aware of his criminal record. It said it would avoid his policy and refund the premium. Mr A complained to the firm, saying he had not been asked about his criminal record. When the firm rejected his complaint he came to us.

Complaint rejected

Unfortunately the firm was unable to produce the questionnaire that Mr A had completed when he applied for the insurance. It had only kept a copy of the statement of facts. This established that the firm was likely to have asked Mr A whether he had any non-motoring convictions.

Mr A admitted that he had kept a copy of the application form. However, he would not let us see it.

We concluded that although the firm was remiss in not keeping all the original paperwork, it had still been entitled to decide that Mr A had not answered its questions accurately, and to avoid his policy for deliberate non-disclosure.

48/5   household insurance—deliberate non-disclosure

Mr M's home was broken into in October 2002. The burglars had kicked in a panel in his back door and stolen many of his possessions. After accepting his claim for the stolen contents, the firm arranged for one of its approved contractors to replace the back door, even though the council owned the property and was responsible for repairing the damage.

Early the following year, shortly before Mr M's policy was due to expire, the firm sent him a renewal questionnaire. This asked for details of his current security arrangements. Mr M completed the form, confirming that his external doors had 'a mortise deadlock and security bolts or a key-operated locking system'.

The firm renewed the policy, but within a month Mr M's property was broken into a second time. Again, the thieves had kicked in the rear door panel. When the firm discovered that the back door did not, in fact, have security bolts or a key-operated locking system, it refused to meet Mr M's claim. After complaining unsuccessfully to the firm, Mr M came to us.

Complaint upheld

We accepted Mr M's explanation that he had assumed the firm's contractors had installed a door that met the firm's own security requirements. It was careless of him not to have double-checked this. However, given that his other answers were accurate, we were satisfied that he had not deliberately or recklessly supplied an incorrect answer.

We also took two further factors into account. First, even if Mr M had realised that he needed to fit bolts, we did not believe they would have impeded the burglary. This was because the burglars had entered the house by kicking in the door panel. Second, even if Mr M had answered the question correctly, the firm would still have allowed him a reasonable period of time in which to change the locks. The burglary occurred within this timescale.

We upheld the claim. We did not think Mr M's failure to comply with the security condition was connected with the loss and we pointed out to the firm that it was good insurance practice to meet claims in such circumstances.

48/6   term life assurance and critical illness insurance—reckless non-disclosure

In December 2001, Mr and Mrs W applied for term life assurance and critical illness insurance. This included own occupation cover, which paid benefits if either of them was unable to continue with their own occupation because of permanent total disablement.

In response to the firm's questions they both stated that they were not 'currently receiving any medical treatment or attention or awaiting any medical or surgical consultation, test or investigation' and had 'never had any medical or surgical treatment, including investigations, tests, scan or X-rays for any... mental or nervous illness (including depression) lasting for more than 3 months and/or requiring more than 10 consecutive days off work'.

The firm accepted the application on the condition that, since signing the application, Mr and Mrs W had not 'suffered any illness or required any medical attention or changed occupation'.

Two years later, Mrs W submitted a claim for rheumatoid arthritis but the firm refused to meet it. It said her medical records showed that she had been consulting a doctor for carpal tunnel syndrome and depression for about eight years before the date when she applied for the policy. She had not disclosed this.

In addition, she had never disclosed that—after she had submitted her application but a few days before it was accepted—she had seen her doctor for pain and swelling in her ankle. And she had failed to tell the firm that, before she received the firm's offer of acceptance, she had changed her occupation.

The firm said that although it was entitled to treat the whole policy as void from the start, it would not do this. However, it would exclude claims for Mrs W's previous health problems and would no longer provide the own occupation cover. Unhappy with this, Mr and Mrs W referred the complaint to us.

Complaint rejected

We did not consider there to be any basis for requiring the firm to pay the sum insured for Mrs W's rheumatoid arthritis. We accepted that there was no link between her carpal tunnel syndrome and depression and the onset of her rheumatoid arthritis. However, this did not change the fact that, in response to clear questions, she had failed to disclose information about her health.

In our opinion it was fair and reasonable of the firm to offer to rewrite the policy on the terms it would have offered originally—if it had been given the correct information. Mr and Mrs W appeared to have given very little thought to the accuracy of their answers, and their non-disclosure appeared to be at least reckless, which would have entitled the firm to void the policy.

48/7   commercial insurance—non-disclosure

In January 2001, there was a serious fire at Mrs Y's shop, which was insured with the firm under a commercial policy. The fire brigade thought the fire might have been caused by an electrical fault.

The firm made an interim payment to Mrs Y of £10,000 and appointed loss adjusters. In the course of their investigations the loss adjusters discovered that Mrs Y's business owed its suppliers £70,000. Mrs Y had borrowed almost £100,000 from her bank over the previous two years and had made incorrect statements when applying for the bank loans. The loss adjusters also discovered that, in her original insurance application, Mrs Y had failed to disclose that the ground floor of her shop unit was unoccupied and was not properly secured.

The firm told Mrs Y that it was treating her policy as void. This was because she had failed to disclose that the building was not secure and that her business was in difficulty, even though it had questioned her directly about these matters. The firm also believed that Mrs Y had committed a criminal offence in misrepresenting the purpose of the loans. Unhappy with the firm's actions, Mrs Y referred her complaint to us.

Complaint dismissed

Mrs Y denied that her business was in difficulty. She said the money she had borrowed from the bank had originally been intended for home improvements, but she had later changed her mind.

We noted that Mrs Y had run her business for several years and claimed to have run a previous business overseas. So the firm was entitled to treat her as a commercial customer and not a consumer. This meant that the firm was entitled to rely on the strict legal position. In the circumstances of this case and because of the fraud allegations, we concluded that the dispute was not suitable for our informal procedures and would better be dealt with in a court.

ISSUE 49: SEPTEMBER/OCTOBER 2005

49/1   annual travel policy—policyholder discloses newly-diagnosed illness when renewing policy—firm offers right to cancel

In April 2004, Mr A booked a holiday to Cyprus, departing in March the following year. His annual travel policy was due to be renewed on 30 December 2004.

In July 2004 he was unexpectedly diagnosed with cancer and began having treatment. This was still ongoing when the time came to renew his policy. The prognosis was good, however, and he expected to be well enough to travel in time for his holiday.

When the firm sent Mr A his renewal documents, which clearly outlined the policyholder's duty to disclose any change in health since the policy was last renewed, Mr A told the firm about his cancer. The firm responded right away, saying that—as from the renewal date—his policy would exclude any claims resulting from the cancer.

After Mr A complained to the firm about this, it told him that if he cancelled the holiday it would meet his claim for the cancellation costs. Unhappy with this, Mr A brought his complaint to us, saying he did not want to cancel his holiday, but was uneasy about travelling without full insurance cover.

Complaint dismissed

There had been a material change in Mr A's circumstances since his policy had started. This meant that the firm was not obliged to offer to renew the policy on the existing terms. It is not our practice to interfere with firms' legitimate commercial decisions, such as the one it faced here regarding the underwriting risks.

The firm had offered Mr A the option of cancelling the holiday without any cost to him. We considered this to be fair and reasonable, in the circumstances. Under our rules we may dismiss a complaint if the ombudsman is 'satisfied that the firm has already made an offer of compensation which is fair and reasonable in relation to the circumstances alleged by the complainant and which is still open for acceptance' [DISP 3.3.1(4)]. We therefore dismissed the complaint.

49/2 policyholder with pre-existing medical condition denied fair opportunity to make pre-emptive cancellation claim at the date of renewal

Miss J was a member of her employer's group annual travel policy that was renewed in June each year. In January 2004 she booked a holiday for that September. Unfortunately, however, in April she was diagnosed with a minor heart condition. The condition was controlled with medication and her doctors were satisfied that she would be fit to travel by September. Miss J did not mention the heart condition to the firm when the policy came up for renewal, not least because all the renewal documentation was processed by her employer.

Shortly before her trip, Miss J suffered a heart attack and had to cancel. The firm rejected her claim for the unused cost of travel and accommodation, citing the exclusion clause in the policy that related to pre-existing medical conditions. Miss J then complained to us.

Complaint upheld

There was no evidence of any bad faith on Miss J's part—or of deliberate non-disclosure. She had simply not appreciated the nature of her travel insurance: that it was an annual, discrete contract.

The renewal documentation that Miss J received did not make it clear that she was under any duty to disclose any changes in her medical circumstances. And there was nothing that might have alerted her to the possibility that the holiday she had booked before her illness was diagnosed might not be covered after the annual renewal date.

We asked the firm to pay the full cancellation costs that Miss J incurred, rather than the (cheaper) costs she would have incurred if she had cancelled some months earlier, at the time the policy was renewed. This was because we were satisfied that the firm had breached its duty to inform customers of the need to notify it of material changes of circumstance. Miss J had never been given the opportunity to make an informed decision about cancelling at an earlier stage, before it was medically necessary.

49/3 policyholder became ill after booking holiday—firm should have offered to pay cancellation costs under the expiring policy from the date of renewal, even though cancellation was not medically necessary at that date

Mr G's annual travel policy came up for renewal each March. Towards the end of January 2004, just a couple of weeks after he had booked a trip to South Africa for that December, he became ill with angina.

When the firm sent Mr G the policy renewal documents he told it about the change in his health. As a result, the firm added an exclusion clause to the new policy. This stated that the policy would not cover any claims arising directly or indirectly from angina. Unwilling to travel without cover for his angina, Mr G thought he had no option but to cancel the holiday, which he did (at his own expense) in April 2004.

Unhappy with the situation, Mr G complained to us. He said he resented having being 'forced' to cancel his holiday and he wanted the firm to re-issue the policy on the same terms as before.

Complaint partially upheld

The firm was entitled to impose an exclusion clause for a pre-existing medical condition which Mr G had disclosed in accordance with his duty of utmost good faith. That was a legitimate underwriting decision.

But we did not think it was fair and reasonable to leave Mr G with no cover at all for the holiday he had already booked. We felt that the firm should have given him the opportunity to cancel the holiday and claim under the expiring policy. Mr G did not have to take up this offer, but he would still be aware that his trip would proceed at his own risk. We therefore asked the firm to reimburse Mr G for the costs of cancelling his holiday.

ISSUE 52: APRIL 2006

52/1   income protection—calculation of benefit where earnings unaffected by disability

Mr G, a self-employed IT consultant, took out an income protection insurance policy. The policy had a limitation of benefit clause restricting the amount of benefit he could be paid to 75% of his normal earnings.

Several years later Mr G made a claim under the policy, on the grounds that repetitive strain injury was affecting his ability to work.

The firm reviewed Mr G's business accounts to see whether his medical condition had affected his income. It noted that he had not recorded payments he had made to a sub-contractor. It also found that the accounts did not show all of Mr G's income and expenditure. So it decided the accounts were unreliable. It did, however, agree to pay the claim until it was able to review Mr G's audited accounts, when it would re-consider the position.

When it examined the audited accounts, the firm compared Mr G's pre-disability earnings with his net income and 'drawings' for the period after he made his claim. It concluded that he had not suffered a loss of income because of his disability, so it stopped his benefit payments.

Complaint rejected

When a self-employed policyholder makes a claim, the firm must be satisfied there was an actual loss of income. In this case, Mr G's audited accounts did not show a loss. Despite his disability, Mr G's business remained profitable. Indeed, the business had made a significantly higher net profit in the period after his claim than in the year in which his illness began.

Mr G disagreed with the firm's assessment. He said the accounts showed an artificial profit and that he had been forced to borrow money to remain trading. But the turnover figures suggested that sales sustained profits, rather than just borrowings.

In any event, under the limitation of benefit provision in his policy, Mr G wasn't entitled to benefit unless his earnings were less than they had been before his disability. Mr G had continued to earn more than he would have been entitled to in benefits. We rejected his complaint.

52/2   income protection—calculation of increases in benefit

Mr M took out an income protection policy in October 1991. He selected an option that protected him against the effects of inflation by increasing his benefit by 7.5% each year. This option was subject to an annual increase in premium.

In 1994, Mr M became disabled and made a claim on his policy. The firm wrote to tell him how his benefit would be calculated. The standard policy restricted benefit to two-thirds of the amount the policyholder was earning immediately before becoming disabled. However, because of the option he selected when he took out the policy, Mr M's benefit payments were more than this.

For several years, Mr M's benefit payments continued to increase at the rate of 7.5% per year. But then the firm reviewed its policies. It decided the standard policy condition, which limited benefit to two-thirds of the policyholder's salary, over-rode the increases arising from the inflation-protecting option. When the firm rejected Mr M's complaint about its subsequent reduction of his benefit, he came to us.

Complaint upheld

It was clear from the policy documents that the option Mr M had selected:

- was intended to offset the effects of inflation; and
- had been sold to Mr M on this basis.

Neither the policy itself, nor any of the associated promotional literature, made it clear whether the benefit cap applied to the option. We decided it was reasonable for Mr M to have assumed the two-thirds cap would not have applied in his case, since it appeared to apply only to the 'standard' policy.

Selecting the option would have been pointless for Mr M if the cap had been applied from the outset of the claim, as the firm said it should have been. At the outset of his claim, Mr M's benefit was already two-thirds of his pre-disability earnings. So despite paying higher premiums for the option he could never have benefited from the increase it was designed to provide.

The way in which the policy had been sold and/or represented did not make it clear that the benefit cap would limit any increase arising from the option. We decided it would be unfair of the firm to restrict Mr M's claim to the original benefit limit. We told the firm to reinstate the increases arising from the option and to backdate any payments owing to Mr M, plus interest.

52/3   income protection—calculation of benefit against continuing income

Mr J, a self-employed architect, had been unable to work because he was suffering from stress. He made a claim for income replacement benefit under his income protection policy. The firm accepted his claim but said he would not be paid any benefit because he was continuing to receive earnings from his business.

The firm calculated Mr J's entitlement to benefit in accordance with the policy terms, which required it to take continuing income into account. Mr J's continuing income from his business was £55,000. This was more than the maximum allowable benefit, calculated as 75% of the first £50,000 of his annual earnings immediately before the start of his disability.

Mr J said that when he arranged the insurance he had provided the firm with copies of his accounts. The firm's adviser had not based his calculations on Mr J's annual earnings (including both 'drawings' and share of profits) but only on his annual 'drawings'. So Mr J said the level of earnings that needed replacing (£50,000) had been undervalued at the outset.

Complaint rejected

There was no evidence that Mr J had supplied his accounts at the time he took out the policy. And the firm's adviser had based his calculation of the appropriate level of benefit on Mr J's gross earnings, as declared on the application form. On this basis, we determined that the income replacement benefit provided was likely to have been appropriate at the time of sale.

Even if this were not the case, the claim was not affected. Mr J had not suffered a sufficient reduction in income to justify a payment of benefit, so we rejected the complaint.

ISSUE 54: JULY 2006

54/4   cancellation of motor insurance by policyholder—whether firm correct in refusing any refund of premiums

Mr A took out the firm's standard motor policy in February 2005 and paid the annual premium in full. Five months later, he decided to sell his car as he no longer needed it. However, when he returned his policy to the firm, it refused his request for a refund of some of the premium.

The firm said that if it cancelled a policy, then it would normally make a pro rata refund of the amount the customer had paid. However, when a customer cancelled the policy it did not refund any premiums if the cancellation was made four or more months after the start of the policy. When the firm rejected Mr A's complaint about this, he came to us—saying he thought the firm was 'grossly unfair'.

Complaint upheld

We asked the firm for a copy of the policy conditions. These included the following:

'cancellation by us

. . . If you return your certificate . . . to us we will refund the part of your premium which applies to the period of insurance you have left. If we cancel this insurance because you have not paid the full premium, we will work out the refund using the rates shown below. We will not give you a refund if anyone has claimed in the current insurance period.

cancellation by you

If you have not made any claims in the current period of insurance, and you are not going to make a claim, we will work out a charge for the time you have been covered using our short-period rates shown below. We will refund any amount we owe you.

Period of time you have had the cover	Refund of up to
one month	70%
two months	60%
three months	50%
four months	40%
more than four months	0%

Any refund made to you for any reason above will only be provided if your annual premium per vehicle exceeds £150.'

We asked the firm to explain why it had made these particular conditions. It said its main concerns had been to discourage customers from cancelling their policies and to recover the costs it incurred if they did so.

We then asked the firm how its costs could be so large as to justify its making no refund at all to customers cancelling more than four months after taking out a policy. The firm was unable to do this.

We concluded that the policy condition was unfair and contrary to the UTCCR. So we told the firm it should make a pro rata refund, after deducting a reasonable administration fee.

54/5 cancellation of house insurance by policyholder—whether firm correct to charge an administration fee

Mr Y insured his house with the firm in June 2005. When he married in December that year, he sold the house and cancelled his policy. In accordance with the cancellation condition in the policy document, the firm made a pro rata refund of his premiums, less a sum of £50 to cover its administration costs.

Mr Y thought it unfair of the firm to levy an administration fee, since he considered that administrative costs should already have been built in to the amount he had paid for his insurance.

Complaint rejected

We agreed with Mr Y that the firm had allowed for administration costs when it calculated the price of its policy. However, since the policy had only—in the event—lasted for six months, the firm would not have recouped all of these costs; it had only received half the annual premium. And we were satisfied that it had also incurred additional and unexpected costs in cancelling the policy. We therefore rejected the complaint.

ISSUE 56: SEPTEMBER/OCTOBER 2006

56/1 travel insurance—whether cancellation caused by events outside the policyholder's control

In mid-April Mr G, an investment banker, visited his local travel agent and booked a week's holiday to Moscow, departing three months later, on 16 July. At the same time, the travel agent sold him travel insurance to cover the trip.

Five days before the holiday, Mr G realised that he had not yet obtained a visa. He knew this shouldn't be a problem because, for an additional fee, the Russian consulate offered a 'fast track' service with a 24-hour turn-around.

As he was very busy at work, Mr G gave the completed visa application to his mother and asked her to send it off for him. Unfortunately, Mrs G enclosed the fee for the 3–5 working day turn-around, not for the 'fast track' service her son needed.

Becoming extremely anxious when—the day before his holiday was due to start—the visa had still not arrived, Mr G phoned the Russian consulate and Royal Mail. Neither could help him, so he called round to see the travel agent.

The travel agent told Mr G he would be able to claim a 50% refund from the insurer if he cancelled the holiday immediately—but would get nothing if he left it any later. Mr G cancelled.

Half an hour later he got home to find the visa had arrived. It was too late to reinstate his booking. And in due course the travel insurer told him he was not entitled to claim back any of the money he had paid for the holiday. The insurer pointed out that Mr G was only covered if he was forced to cancel for reasons beyond his control. It did not consider his failure to obtain a visa in time to be a matter outside his own control.

Mr G disputed this—saying that the cancellation had been caused by 'an unforeseeable mix-up' between him and his mother—and that this 'mix-up' had been outside his control. When the insurer rejected Mr G's complaint, he came to us.

Complaint rejected

We looked at the wording of Mr G's policy. Under the heading, 'cancellation cover—what you are covered for', it said:

'If you have to cancel or curtail your trip through your inability to travel for reasons beyond your control following an event that happened after the commencement date of this Certificate we will pay up to the amount shown above in respect of . . . travel costs which you have paid or are contracted to pay and which you cannot recover from any other source . . . '.

It was clear that Mr G's reason for cancelling the holiday was not outside his control. He had left it until the week before his departure before applying for his visa. And he had then chosen to delegate to his mother the task of arranging payment and sending off his application. In our view, it was his responsibility to ensure the correct fee was enclosed with his application. We rejected the complaint.

56/2   travel insurance—whether insurer should pay curtailment claim when policyholder was taken ill but did not return home before scheduled end of the holiday

In April 2003, while on a cruise with his wife to celebrate their silver wedding, Mr B tripped on some steps and broke his leg. After his leg had been put in plaster, Mr B was prescribed strong painkillers and spent the remainder of the cruise—a total of 11 days—in his cabin.

When the couple returned home, Mr B submitted a claim under his travel insurance policy for medical expenses and for the curtailment of his and his wife's holiday. The insurer settled the medical expenses claim. However, it rejected the curtailment claim in its entirety, on the grounds that Mr and Mrs B had not left the ship and returned home before the scheduled end of their holiday.

After Mr B disputed this decision, the insurer agreed to meet half of the curtailment claim. It paid the cost of the final 11 days of the cruise (less the policy excess)—but only for Mr B, not for his wife.

Mr B said the insurer should pay for his wife as well, because after his accident she had remained in the cabin to look after him. However, the insurer disagreed, so Mr B came to us.

Complaint rejected

The travel policy provided cancellation cover ' . . . if you are forced to curtail your trip and return home after departure as a direct and necessary result of any cause outside your control . . . '.

There had been no medical reason for Mr B to leave the ship and return home before the end of the cruise. He and his wife would have preferred to return home, but this was not the same as being forced to do so. We were satisfied that the insurer's payment of half of Mr B's curtailment claim was fair and reasonable, and we rejected the complaint.

56/3   travel insurance—whether an insurer correctly relied on policy exclusion to refuse cancellation claim resulting from policyholder's ill-health

Mr K occasionally suffered from migraines but was otherwise in excellent health. So he was somewhat concerned when, for no apparent reason, he collapsed and briefly lost consciousness.

He soon recovered but 'just to be on the safe side', as he later told us, he made an appointment with his GP. Mr K saw the doctor four days later—on 30 August 2005—and told her he had felt perfectly well until immediately before he passed out. At that point he had started to feel dizzy and had then found himself unable to stand.

The doctor told Mr K that his collapse had in all probability been related to a migraine. However, the doctor thought it would be a sensible precaution to have a brain scan, just to rule out any possibility that Mr K might have had a minor stroke.

In her referral letter to the hospital, which we later asked to see as part of our investigation, the doctor stressed that she did not think Mr K had suffered a stroke. But she said she wanted Mr K to have the scan in order to 'completely rule out this possibility'.

Mr K's appointment for the scan was on 27 September 2005. A couple of weeks before this—on 14 September—he booked and paid for a holiday and bought a travel insurance policy. The holiday was to start on 30 September, a few days after he was due to have the scan.

The result of the scan came back on 28 September and revealed that Mr K had suffered a minor stroke. His doctor told him he should not fly for at least three months, so Mr K cancelled his holiday.

The insurer rejected the claim Mr K made under his travel insurance policy. It pointed out that the policy contained an exclusion from cover for:

' . . . any condition of which the policyholder was aware at commencement of the policy or for which he received advice, treatment or counselling from any registered medical practitioner during the 12 months preceding the commencement date, whether diagnosed or not'.

Complaint upheld

There was clear evidence that—at the time Mr K had taken out the policy—both he and his doctor had thought that the dizziness and resultant collapse had been caused by a fairly minor ailment—not by a stroke.

So we told the insurer that it its reliance on the policy exclusion in order to reject the claim was neither fair nor reasonable. And citing the legal case, *Cook v Financial Insurance Co Ltd* [1998] 1 WLR 1765, we told the insurer that it had not acted in accordance with the law.

We said the insurer should meet Mr K's claim, less any excess, and pay him interest from the date of the cancellation. We also said it should compensate him for the distress and inconvenience he had been caused.

56/4 travel insurance—whether insurer correct in refusing to pay repatriation expenses for policyholder taken seriously ill on holiday

Mr C, a 45-year old landscape gardener, was taken seriously ill while on holiday in West Africa. It was clear that he would require major surgery. And it seemed probable that he would need a blood transfusion during or after the operation.

The treating doctor thought Mr C should be flown home to the UK for the operation, despite the risk that he might suffer further problems while waiting for this to be arranged—and during the flight itself.

Mr C contacted his insurer to explain his predicament. He asked for assistance in arranging his flight home but the insurer said it could not help. It insisted that flying was too risky for him.

The doctor treating Mr C had provided an oral assurance that Mr C was fit to fly, and had explained why repatriation was in his best interests. But the insurer said it would need a written report to this effect before it could reconsider the matter.

Mr C argued, unsuccessfully, that the insurer's insistence on a written report was unreasonable, bearing in mind the urgency of the situation and the doctor's view that it was in his best interests to be repatriated. Anxious not to delay matters any longer, Mr C arranged and paid for the flight home himself.

Once Mr C had recovered from his operation, he complained to the insurer about its handling of the matter. The insurer rejected his complaint, arguing that its representative had acted in Mr C's best interests because she genuinely believed he had not been fit to fly home.

Complaint upheld

In medical cases, the evidence of the treating doctor is normally very persuasive. The doctor is generally best placed to assess their patient's situation at the time the problem arises. This was such a case, and we agreed with the treating doctor's assessment of the risks in flying Mr C home, when set against the risks associated with carrying out his operation in West Africa.

The doctor who subsequently operated on Mr C in the UK confirmed that, in the circumstances, it had been the best course of action for Mr C to return home for surgery. Most medical facilities in West Africa are still fairly basic. And the risk of contracting HIV as a result of a blood transfusion is much higher there than in countries where there is an effective donor-screening programme.

We felt that in this particular case the insurer's insistence on a written report had been unreasonable. The Insurance Conduct of Business Rules state that an insurer should not reject a claim on the basis that a policy condition (such as having to provide a written report) has been breached, unless the circumstances of the breach are connected to the loss. In other words, the insurer's position must have been prejudiced as a result of the breach.

Since the treating doctor in Africa had given an assurance that repatriation was in Mr C's best interests (even though he had not put this in writing), we did not think it a material factor that Mr C had not provided the insurer with a written report.

We upheld the complaint and required the insurer to reimburse Mr C for the expenses he had incurred in returning to the UK. We also said it should pay him a significant amount for the distress and inconvenience he had experienced because of its refusal to assist with his repatriation.

56/5   travel insurance—whether insurer right to reject policyholder's cancellation claim after her father became ill

In October 2004, Miss J visited a travel agent and booked to go on holiday to Greece in June the following year. The travel agent also sold her an insurance policy to cover the holiday.

In January 2005, Miss J's father was diagnosed with a heart problem. He responded well to treatment and soon appeared to be back to normal. However, in May—just a few weeks before the start of Miss J's holiday—his condition suddenly deteriorated. Miss J found she needed to look after him almost full-time.

She tried to arrange some respite care, so that she could get away for her holiday as planned. However, it proved impossible to find a suitable carer at such short notice. Miss J cancelled the holiday and submitted a claim under her travel insurance policy for the full cost of cancellation.

The insurer rejected her claim. It referred to the following provisions:

'Cancellation:
Cover applies if You have booked a Trip to take place within the Period of Insurance, but You are forced to cancel Your travel plans because of one of the following changes in circumstances, which is beyond Your control, and of which You were unaware at the time you booked the Trip . . .

- Unforeseen illness, injury or death of a Close Relative as confirmed to Our medical staff by the treating doctor, who will deem whether it is necessary for You to cancel or curtail Your Trip . . .

To declare a Pre-existing Medical condition or a change in Your state of health or prescribed medication, You should contact the Medical Screening Helpline . . . '.

The insurer said that Miss J had been aware of her father's illness in January and could have cancelled the holiday at that stage for only 15% of the cost. It also said she should have contacted its helpline in January (to declare the change in her father's state of health), and again in May (when his condition worsened and she had attempted to obtain respite care for him).

Complaint upheld

The medical evidence we obtained confirmed that:

- Mr J's condition had responded very well to treatment in January and
- there had been no reason at that time for Miss J to believe her father's state of health would force her to cancel her holiday.

It was the unexpected change in Mr J's health in May, and Miss J's inability to find respite care, that meant she had to cancel the holiday. We found that Miss J had acted reasonably and promptly in seeking respite care, and in notifying the insurer and cancelling the holiday when this proved impossible.

We did not believe the policy imposed a duty on the policyholder to call the insurer's medical screening helpline if there was a change in the health of anyone on whom the holiday might depend. Any such duty would constitute an 'onerous' term, and would have to be made very clear to the customer before the policy was sold. The insurer had made no effort to do this through its own policy summary or sales documentation, or through the efforts of the travel agent.

We upheld the complaint and required the insurer to reimburse Miss J for the full cost of cancelling her holiday.

ISSUE 58: DECEMBER 2006/JANUARY 2007

58/1   whether policyholders are covered for 'trace and access' work and/or pipe repairs

When a maturing insurance policy produced a larger sum than expected, Mr G decided to spend part of the money on a cruise. He had recently taken early retirement on ill-health grounds and his wife thought a trip to the Caribbean over Christmas and New Year would boost his spirits.

Before the couple left home, they turned off their central heating. They were anxious to save on their gas bill while they were away.

Three weeks later, Mr and Mrs G returned home to find their kitchen flooded with water from the bathroom above. The weather had been particularly cold while they were away and the water in the pipes had frozen, expanding and cracking the metal. As the temperature rose, the ice melted and water flooded out of the pipes, causing extensive damage to the kitchen ceiling, walls and carpet.

The insurer accepted the claim and arranged to put right the damage caused by the flooding. But it would not reimburse Mr G for the cost of calling out the emergency plumber to find the source of the leak and fix it. After complaining to the insurer about this without success, Mr G came to us.

Complaint rejected

Details of the cover were set out very clearly in the policy. Mr and Mrs G were covered for loss or damage caused by 'escape of water'. But they were not covered for 'trace and access'—the cost of finding and repairing the source of the damage.

This restriction on the scope of the cover was neither unusual nor significant. So it was not something the insurer needed to have highlighted in its policy summary, given to customers at the point of sale.

As with most home insurance policies, the 'trace and access' cost and the plumber's fees for replacing the damaged pipe were uninsured losses, which had to be borne by the policyholder. We rejected the complaint.

58/2   whether there is cover for 'escape of water' when insured premises are left unoccupied

After a major lottery win, Mr and Mrs W decided to spend some of the money on a three-month cruise. Before they set off on their trip early in the New Year, they switched off their heating and hot water.

The couple returned home at the beginning of April to find that burst internal water pipes had caused a significant amount of damage to their home. As well as the initial problems caused by the flood, the resulting damp had caused the wooden floor to start rotting.

Understandably, Mr and Mrs W were very distressed by what had happened. But they were even more upset when their insurer rejected their claim. The insurer said an exclusion clause in the policy meant there was no cover for 'escape of water' if the insured property had been left unoccupied for 60 or more consecutive days.

It had never occurred to the couple that they might not be covered for the situation they were now faced with. And after complaining unsuccessfully to their insurer, Mr and Mrs W came to us.

Complaint substantially upheld

Technically, there had been a breach of the policy conditions, since the couple had left their property unoccupied for more than 60 days. However, the insurer's own evidence had established that the area where Mr and Mrs W lived had suffered particularly cold weather in the first 10 days of January. So the flood had almost certainly occurred well within the period during which the property was covered, even if it was unoccupied.

That meant that the 'circumstances of the claim' (the burst pipes) were not connected with the breached policy condition. We explained to the insurer our long-established approach to such cases, as set out in issue 34 of *Ombudsman News* (January 2004):

'We do not consider it good practice for insurers to decline to pay out where the policyholder's breach of a policy condition has been only a technical breach that has not prejudiced the firm's position in any way . . . '

We also pointed out that the Insurance: Conduct of Business Rules (which came into force on 14 January 2005) state: 'An insurer must not . . . except where there is evidence of fraud, refuse to meet a claim by a retail customer on the grounds . . . of breach of warranty or condition, unless the circumstances of the claim are connected with the breach.' (Rule 7.3.6).

We said the insurer should meet the claim. However, we accepted the insurer's argument that it should pay only part of the cost of replacing the wooden floor. If Mr and Mrs W had not left their home unoccupied for so long, the water damage could have been dealt with more quickly and the floor would probably not have started to rot.

58/3 whether a blocked oil-pipe is covered

Miss J awoke one morning in early February to find her cottage was unusually cold. The central heating had failed to come on. She was unable to get it to work, so she called out an emergency plumber.

It took the plumber some time to discover the cause of the problem. The outlet pipe from the oil storage tank to the boiler had become blocked with sludge and oil deposits that had built up over the years. The plumber eventually managed to unblock the system and to get it up and running. But Miss J was left with a bill for almost £1,000.

When she submitted a claim to her insurer for damage to the oil tank and pipes, the insurer refused to pay out. It told her this was because there had been no physical damage to the tank or pipes and no 'contamination of the surrounding site'. The unblocking of the system was simply a matter of maintenance, for which no insurance cover was available.

After arguing unsuccessfully against the insurer's decision, Miss J brought her complaint to us.

Complaint rejected

We sympathised with Miss J's predicament. However, it was clear that her policy did not cover loss or damage caused by blocked pipes; it only covered loss or damage caused by escape of oil. Fortunately, there had not been any escape of oil.

In principle (and in certain circumstances) 'damage' can be interpreted to include loss of function. However, this was not the case here since the 'insured peril' (escape of oil) had not occurred in the first place.

In any event, damage resulting from 'wear and tear' or lack of maintenance was specifically excluded from the scope of cover. We therefore rejected the complaint.

58/4 whether insurers should pay for replacing a bathroom suite and wall tiles, removed when plumber traced the source of a leak

Mr C's sitting room was badly damaged when water leaked through the ceiling from his bathroom. He called a plumber, who located the source of the leak and fixed it. In so doing, the plumber apparently had to rip out the entire bathroom suite, including the wall and floor tiles.

The insurer accepted Mr C's claim for 'escape of water' and it paid the cost of repairing the water damage to the sitting room and replacing the bathroom floor tiles. But it would not cover the cost of replacing the bathroom suite and the wall tiles. It told Mr C it did not think it had been necessary for the plumber to remove these items in order to 'trace and access' the burst pipe.

Unhappy with the insurer's response, Mr C brought his complaint to us.

Complaint rejected

We were satisfied that the insurer's offer had been fair and reasonable in the circumstances. It was a clearly-stated condition of the policy that policyholders should:

- notify the insurer immediately of any situation that was likely to give rise to a claim and
- preserve relevant information and evidence.

Mr C had not contacted his insurer to report the damage until after the plumber had ripped out and disposed of the bathroom suite and wall tiles.

We accepted the evidence provided by the insurer that it had not been necessary to remove the entire bathroom suite and all the wall tiles in order to locate a pipe beneath the floor. In the circumstances, we thought the insurer's offer to pay for Mr C's actual, proven, losses was fair and reasonable. We rejected the complaint.

58/5   **whether insurers should pay for new kitchen units, following flood damage**

When a mains pipe burst underneath Ms K's kitchen sink, water flooded everywhere. There was a great deal of damage, particularly to the kitchen units.

Ms K's insurer accepted the claim, but offered her only 50% of the cost of replacing the kitchen units. It pointed out that the units were quite old and had probably already suffered a fair degree of wear and tear before the flood damage occurred.

Ms K said this was unfair, as she could not afford to replace her kitchen units for the amount the insurer had offered.

Complaint upheld

When we looked into Ms K's complaint, we felt the insurer had not handled the claim fairly and reasonably. Like most home policies, this provided 'new for old' cover. The policy did not contain any exclusion for items that had already suffered some degree of 'wear and tear'. And there was no doubt that Ms J's units had been damaged as a result of a genuine incident.

'Indemnity' policies simply require the insurer to put the policyholder back to their pre-incident position (so far as reasonably possible). But as this was a 'new for old' policy, the insurer was required to replace the damaged items with new ones, or to give the policyholder enough money to cover the cost of buying new items.

The insurer pointed out that the terms of the policy gave it the discretion to arrange repair rather than replacement in certain circumstances. However, expert evidence, together with photographs of the units, convinced us that repair would not be a reasonable solution in this case.

Regardless of their previous condition, all but one of the units had been severely damaged by the escape of water. So we said it was fair and reasonable for the insurer to meet the cost of a complete set of new units.

ISSUE 59: JANUARY/FEBRUARY 2007

59/8   **insurer denies liability for subsidence damage on the grounds that it occurred before its own policy came into force**

Mr K complained to us when his insurer rejected his claim for subsidence damage. The insurer thought Mr K's house had been exhibiting cracks and distortions for many years, long before its own policy came into force. So it did not consider it had any liability for the claim.

Following our usual approach in such situations, we set about trying to establish whether the damage continued to occur after the start of the policy under which the claim was now being made. The evidence was that the movement (and damage) was progressive. That meant that the property had been damaged by an insured event during the period when Mr K was insured. As is the case under most policies, this triggered the insurer's liability.

Strictly, under most policies, the insurer's liability is to repair (or pay for the repair of) damage that occurred after the start of its policy. This does not include any damage that pre-dates the policy. If the insurer is able to distinguish between the two sets of damage, it is entitled to do that. However, it is often impossible to distinguish the two sets of damage. That was the situation here.

If stabilisation is necessary to stop a property moving, then we believe it is needed just as much to repair damage that occurred during the insured period as it is to repair earlier damage.

Complaint upheld

We said that in order to meet its liability for the damage that had occurred since it had started to cover the property, the insurer would have to pay for the repair of all the damage. This would include the cost of stabilisation if necessary.

59/9   **insurer says it is not liable for subsidence damage that occurred before it took over responsibility for insuring the property**

When Mr and Mrs E bought their terraced house in 1988, they took out buildings insurance through the bank that provided their mortgage. Ten years later, a different insurer took over the provision of insurance. The following year (1999), Mr and Mrs E made a claim for subsidence.

The insurer thought that most of the damage had happened before it started providing insurance for the property. It said that settlement/subsidence had been affecting the terrace as a whole for some years. This had caused long-term distortion and fracturing to the couple's house. And while there was some slight general continuing movement, subsidence movement of the floor had occurred before it had started to insure the property.

The insurer said it was liable only for damage that had occurred when its own policy was in force. So the schedule of repairs prepared by its engineers was restricted to damage thought to have occurred after 1998, and omitted general significant distortion to the property. The insurer considered this distortion to be historic, rather than the result of the recent subsidence. It said the fact that 'corrections' had been made in the past confirmed this.

Mr and Mrs E said that substantial movement had occurred since they bought the property, and it had caused considerable distortion. They said that cosmetic repairs and decorations had been carried out from time to time, when damage and distortions became visible. They were aware that floorboards and joists had been replaced in 1980, before they bought the house—but they understood that this work had been carried out because of woodworm and rot.

The insurer did not consider the ABI's Domestic Subsidence Agreement to be relevant in this case, because it excluded damage that had 'occurred before an insurer took on an insured risk'.

Complaint upheld

We established that there was no relevant period when the property had not been covered by buildings insurance. While some of the distortion was thought to have occurred after 1998—when the insurer changed—it seemed likely that much of it had occurred before 1998, but after Mr and Mrs E first moved in and took out insurance.

We therefore said that the ABI's Agreement was relevant in this case. The property had been continuously insured, so we said the insurer should deal with the entire claim and could not exclude damage that pre-dated its own policy.

59/10   insurer refuses to pay for stabilisation because it says it is not liable for any preventative work

The insurer agreed that subsidence was the cause of the damage Mr C claimed for under his buildings policy. However, it refused to pay for any stabilisation work. Mr C felt this work was essential to put matters right and prevent future problems.

The report prepared by the insurer's engineers stated that minor movement would probably continue unless the foundations of the house were stabilised. The insurer said it would pay for any superstructure repairs and redecoration that might be necessary, as and when further movement occurred. But it argued that stabilisation was not strictly part of its liability, since its policy only covered the cost of repairs and it considered stabilisation to be 'preventative, not restorative'.

Complaint upheld

After complaining unsuccessfully to the firm, Mr C referred the matter to us. Following our usual approach, we considered the insurer's contractual obligation under the terms of its policy. As is usual in buildings policies, the insurer was obliged to repair (or pay the cost of repairing) the subsidence damage.

In our view, the proper repair of a building requires something more long-lasting than a temporary patch-up. Filling cracks and repainting cannot properly be regarded as repairing subsidence damage if, within a relatively short time, those same cracks are likely to reappear. The expert evidence had indicated that, without stabilisation, the movement that had caused the damage would continue. So we said the insurer should meet the cost of stabilisation.

59/11   difficulties in dealing with subsidence claim from owner of a semi-detached house—when the entire house is affected, but the owner of the other half refuses to cooperate with remedial work

Mrs B, who lived in a semi-detached house, put in a claim for structural damage. Her insurer confirmed that subsidence was the cause of the damage—and that it affected the entire property, not just her half of it.

Mrs B's insurer did not cover the other half, owned by a Mr J. And Mrs B was unable to persuade Mr J even to discuss the situation with her.

After obtaining expert advice, the insurer decided to proceed with the normal remedy in cases where both sides of a semi-detached property are affected. This involves carrying out work to the foundations of both parts of the property.

If the insurer treated only half of the house, then any future movement between the two parts might result in a recurrence of the damage to Mrs B's property. Future movement might also create new damage to her property—or indeed damage her neighbour's property, leaving open the possibility that he would then hold her responsible.

The insurer spent a number of months trying to persuade Mr J to cooperate with the planned works. It even threatened him with legal action. Meanwhile, frustrated that nothing was being done to remedy the problems in her own part of the property, Mrs B complained—first to her insurer and then to us.

Complaint upheld

This was a difficult situation all round. Persuading Mr J to cooperate represented the best hope for a solution that was both structurally sound and likely to maintain neighbourly relations. But there seemed little likelihood of obtaining Mr J's agreement.

Mrs B was contractually entitled to have the damage to her property repaired properly. The insurer had insisted that its proposed course of action was the only viable solution. However, the expert evidence that we obtained confirmed there was an alternative approach. This would not require access to Mr J's property. And it would stabilise the building—in a way that would probably prevent the subsidence causing further damage.

This alternative approach was technically much more difficult than the insurer's preferred solution. It was also very much more expensive. However, we told the insurer that, in the circumstances, it was the only reasonable and realistic way to settle the matter.

ISSUE 61: APRIL/MAY 2007

61/1 life and critical illness insurance—back and neck problems—inadvertent non-disclosure

Mr F took out life and critical illness cover in June 2002. Just five months later, in November 2002, he suffered a heart attack and submitted a claim to the insurer.

However, the insurer refused to meet the claim, on the grounds that Mr F had been reckless in failing to disclose basic information on the application form. It said that after reviewing his medical records, it had discovered that Mr F failed to disclose recurrent problems with his back and neck. He had also failed to disclose that he had made a previous application for similar cover, from a different insurer. That application had never gone ahead but had been deferred, as the insurer had asked for further information which Mr F had never provided.

Mr F complained that the insurer's stance was unreasonable. He said he had simply forgotten that he had made the earlier application. And he had forgotten to mention that he had been referred to an orthopaedic consultant two years earlier for back and neck problems. He pointed out that he had mentioned on the form that he suffered from depression. He had also disclosed that his mother had heart problems. And he added that, at the time he had applied for the policy, he had been going through a particularly traumatic period caring for his wife and son, both of whom had been seriously ill.

Complaint upheld

We established that Mr F's back and neck trouble had arisen after his wife had become quadriplegic, following an accident, and he had started having to lift her. And around the same time that Mr F had been referred to an orthopaedic consultant for his neck and back problems, he had been having to accompany his young son (who had a rare disease) on a number of hospital appointments.

Mr F had only the one consultation with the orthopaedic consultant, who had advised him to continue for a time with physiotherapy and medication. We accepted that, in the circumstances, Mr F had simply forgotten to mention the consultation on his application form. And we thought it understandable that Mr F had not thought he had needed to mention these back and neck problems when answering a question on the form about 'back, spine or recurrent joint disorder'. So we accepted that his failure to disclose this information had been inadvertent.

Mr F did not dispute that he had failed to disclose the earlier insurance application. He said he had simply overlooked this. At the time of this earlier application (1998), he had been fully occupied caring for his wife and family. He had not had time to follow up the insurer's queries and to provide the clarification it needed before it could proceed with his application.

In support of his case, Mr F provided a letter from his cardiologist. This said that if Mr F had been asked to undergo a medical examination when he applied for his current policy in 2002, it was unlikely that this would have led to a diagnosis of coronary heart disease.

We decided that Mr F had not shown a reckless disregard for his answers—his oversights had been inadvertent. In the circumstances, the insurer needed to make a proportionate response. In other words, it should rewrite the policy on the terms it would have offered Mr F if it had known the full facts at the outset. In this particular instance, it would have excluded spinal conditions from the disability benefits provided under the policy. It would not have excluded heart attacks or refused to cover Mr F at all.

So we said the insurer should reinstate Mr F's policy—adding the spinal condition exclusion—and deal with the claim. Since no exclusion applied to Mr F's heart attack, the firm had to pay the claim in full (less any premium refund), with interest.

61/2   income protection insurance—non-disclosure after application had been made

In April 2002, Mr J applied for income protection insurance. He answered 'no' in response to a question on the application form about whether he had received any medical treatment or had any medical consultations in the previous two years. He gave the same answer when the question was put to him during the medical examination that the insurer arranged for him in June 2002.

The application form contained a warning, reminding him he had a duty to inform the insurer immediately if—as a result of anything that happened before the start of the policy—he needed to change any of his answers.

In August 2002 Mr J developed a serious condition which he had not suffered from before. He had a number of consultations about it with his doctor, who prescribed treatment in September 2002 and certified Mr J as unfit to work for the next two months.

The insurer said it sent Mr J a letter in October 2002, confirming its acceptance of his application and asking him if there had been any change in his medical condition since he completed the application form. The policy started a week later.

Just over a year later, Mr J developed leukaemia. The insurer rejected his claim, saying he had been reckless in failing to disclose the medical condition that had arisen in August 2002. The insurer said it would not have been prepared to cover him if it had known about this condition.

Mr J said he never received the insurer's letter in October 2002. And he said that, in any event, the medical condition that had arisen in August 2002 had nothing to do with his claim for leukaemia. Unable to reach agreement with the insurer, Mr J referred his complaint to us.

Complaint rejected

We thought it probable that the insurer had sent the letter in October 2002, even though Mr J could not recall receiving it. So we considered that by sending this letter, and by including the warning on its application form, the insurer had given Mr J adequate warning of the need to disclose any changes to his health since he had applied for the insurance. However, we noted that the insurer had not sent him a copy of his original application form with this letter, so that he could assess what changes were relevant to the insurer.

We decided that Mr J had not intended to mislead the insurer. We took into account how close—in time—the emergence of the new medical condition in August 2002 and the outcome of the consultations were to:

- the date when he applied for the insurance
- the acceptance letter and
- the start date of the policy.

Although, in the light of the warning letter, he should have understood the need to disclose his new condition, we recognised that a duty to disclose information after an application has been accepted is a particularly onerous requirement that few consumers anticipate.

In this case we considered that, despite the insurer's warnings, Mr J had not fully understood the need to inform the insurer of any changes to his health. So his non-disclosure had been inadvertent rather than the result of a reckless disregard for the truth of his answers.

The usual remedy for inadvertent non-disclosure is to allow the insurer to rewrite the policy on the terms it would have imposed, had it known the full facts. In this case we were persuaded by the insurer's evidence that it would not have offered Mr J any cover at all, had it known about his new medical condition. So we concluded that it was fair for the insurer to:

- refuse to consider the claim
- cancel the policy from the outset and
- refund the premiums that Mr J had paid.

61/3   life and critical illness insurance—asthma—inadvertent non-disclosure

Mrs B applied for life and critical illness cover in March 2000 during a face-to-face meeting with a representative of the insurer, who completed the application for her.

Several years later, after Mrs B developed breast cancer, the insurer declined her claim on the grounds of reckless non-disclosure. And it avoided the policy (in other words, treated it as if it had never existed).

The insurer said this was an instance of reckless non-disclosure because Mrs B had failed to mention that she suffered from asthma, even though several of the questions on the application form should have prompted her to disclose this. It said that if it had it known about her asthma, it would have increased the premium.

Mrs B challenged the insurer's decision. She said she had informed the representative about her asthma at the time she applied for the policy. He had said the insurer was not interested in such 'run of the mill' matters. He had told her there was no need to mention the condition because it was fully controlled by an inhaler and she had never had to use a nebuliser or go into hospital because of it. The insurer disputed this—and said it had a statement from the representative confirming that he would never have suggested that an applicant omitted details of any health matter, however trivial.

Complaint upheld

We found that Mrs B had disclosed her asthma on a separate application she'd made to the insurer a few months later, through a different representative. It was clear from her medical records that Mrs B's asthma was well-controlled, and she had never needed to use a nebuliser or go into hospital because of it.

We also noticed that the application form, which the insurer's representative had completed for Mrs B, contained several mistakes. These included the fact that he had ticked the box indicating that Mrs B was a non-smoker but had also stated that she smoked an average of five cigarettes a day.

Mrs B had disclosed her asthma in a subsequent application to the same insurer, so we accepted that she had not intended to keep quiet about the condition. And in view of the mildness of her asthma, it was plausible to believe that the representative might have told her there was no need to mention it.

We could not be certain what had happened during the meeting between Mrs B and the insurer's representative. It was clear that the representative had guided her through the application. The mistakes on the form suggested that he might not have captured accurately all the information that she gave him. However, he insisted that he had followed the correct procedure. We thought it likely that there had been a misunderstanding about what information needed to be disclosed on the form.

Mrs B had signed the declaration stating that the information on the form was true, to the best of her knowledge and belief. We were persuaded by the evidence that she had assumed the representative had recorded her answers correctly, so she had not thought she had any reason not to sign it. In any event, she had not been given a copy of the answers to check before signing.

In the circumstances, we were unable to conclude that Mrs B had been reckless in her approach to the application. There was nothing to suggest that she had not cared whether her answers were true or false. So we concluded that any non-disclosure was likely to have been inadvertent.

We required the insurer to meet the claim on a proportionate basis. In this case, that meant the insurer should calculate the premium that Mrs B would have been charged, if her asthma had been disclosed on her application form. It should then pay a proportion of her claim, equivalent to the proportion of this premium that she had actually been charged. It should also pay her interest on this amount.

61/4 life and critical illness insurance—smoking—monitoring of blood pressure—no non-disclosure

When Mr L applied for life assurance in July 2005 he stated that he had not smoked within the previous 12 months. Asked about any medical consultations, he said he had sought advice about a hernia that had subsequently required surgery. He also disclosed that there was a history of hypertension in his family.

Five months later he submitted a claim for oesophageal cancer. The insurer rejected the claim, on the grounds of reckless non-disclosure, and it avoided the policy. It said that when looking into his claim it discovered that he had previously been a heavy smoker. It accepted that he had now stopped smoking. However, there was a record of his regularly having smoked one cigar a day at the start of the 12-month period in question. The insurer said Mr L should also have disclosed that his blood pressure had been monitored in the period between 8 June and 18 July 2005.

Mr L said he had only smoked cigars very occasionally since giving up heavy smoking in 1994. And he insisted that he had accurately stated on the application form that he had not smoked at all in the previous 12 months. He did not deny that his blood pressure had been monitored for a few weeks. But he said this had only been done in advance of—and in connection with—the hernia operation.

Complaint upheld

On his application form, Mr L had provided clear details of his impending hernia surgery and also the family history of hypertension. He had obviously given some attention to the application form and taken it seriously in this respect. The insurer had not sought any additional information about these matters, either on the form or subsequently.

The blood pressure monitoring had clearly been simply a preparatory step before the surgery for his hernia. It had been considered a necessary precaution because of the family history of hypertension. Mr L had disclosed both the surgery and the history of hypertension, so we did not consider that he had also been obliged to disclose the blood pressure monitoring. There was no separate question that would have required specific disclosure of it, and in any event the results of the monitoring had not merited any medical follow-up.

Mr L submitted evidence from his GP, who said he could not recall his conversation with Mr L and accepted that he might have misunderstood Mr L's history. The GP also said that the computer system on which he entered details of patients' tobacco consumption was unable to record a minimum consumption of less than one cigar or cigarette per day. We were satisfied, on a balance of probabilities, that Mr L had told the truth when he stated that he had not smoked in the 12 months before July 2005. So we concluded there had not been any non-disclosure in relation to his smoking. We required the insurer to meet Mr L's claim in full.

61/5 life assurance—alcoholic counselling—reckless non-disclosure

Mrs M took out two life assurance policies in November 2002. One was in her sole name and the other was a joint policy with her husband. Both application forms contained the questions:

'Do you consume alcoholic drinks?'
   'Are you currently receiving any medical treatment or attention?'
   'Have you ever sought or been given medical advice to reduce the level of your drinking?'

Mrs M answered 'No' to each question.

Several years later Mrs M died. The insurer would not meet Mr M's claim because it said Mrs M had failed to disclose that, since 2000, she had been receiving treatment from a consultant psychiatrist in relation to 'cessation of drinking'. She had also failed to disclose that she had been attending Alcoholics Anonymous meetings. The insurer regarded Mrs M's non-disclosure as deliberate or reckless, and it avoided both policies.

Mrs M's representatives argued that she had stopped drinking in 2002. The consultant psychiatrist stated that he had been monitoring Mrs M's abstinence and not giving 'medical advice' about reducing her drinking. He also said that he had advised Mrs M that her alcohol dependency should not be considered as an illness. However, the insurer contended that Mrs M should have realised that her history of drink problems was relevant to the insurance.

Complaint rejected

We decided that Mrs M had been entitled to answer 'No' to the question, 'Do you consume alcoholic drinks?' She was not consuming alcohol at that time. On the question 'Are you currently receiving any medical treatment or attention?' we were satisfied that she had been receiving medical treatment or attention from her consultant psychiatrist in relation to drinking. However, we recognised that her consultant's approach was to minimise any suggestions that his role was medical, and we accepted that her incorrect answer to the question had probably been made innocently or inadvertently.

We accepted that Mrs M had stopped drinking before 2002, but it was clear that she had continued to seek regular advice to support her decision to eliminate alcohol. So we thought her answer to the question, 'Have you ever sought or been given medical advice to reduce the level of your drinking' was incorrect. We did not agree with her representatives that advice on maintaining her abstinence was not advice 'to reduce the level of her drinking'. We concluded that there was no evidence that Mrs M had deliberately given the wrong answer to this question. But neither was it likely that her answer had been innocent or inadvertent.

In our view, she could not have stopped to properly consider the question or her answer. Had she done so, we thought it unlikely that she would have given the answer that she did; the question would have raised issues that were fresh in her mind, and that we believed she knew were important to the insurer. We therefore regarded Mrs M's answer as reckless non-disclosure.

We accepted that the insurer would not have issued either policy if it had been aware of the true facts. Its decision to decline the claim and avoid both policies had therefore been justified.

61/6   life assurance—incorrect height and weight given—deliberate non-disclosure

When Mr K took out life assurance, he stated that he was 6 feet tall and weighed 16 stone. Following his death from a blood clot at the age of 37, just five months after taking out the policy, the insurer discovered that Mr K's actual height was 5'9" and his weight was over 21 stone. Mr K had also failed to inform the insurer about his kidney stone and gout. The insurer said that if it had known the full facts, it would have loaded the premium by 275%. It considered that his answers amounted to either reckless or deliberate non-disclosure and it avoided the policy.

Complaint rejected

We had no reason to suppose that Mr K had not understood the form he was completing. We noted that, in response to clear questions about his health, he had failed to provide relevant information. As far as the information about his height and weight was concerned, the evidence suggested that he was aware that he was obese. We established that his weight had been recorded as 25 stone in May 1999, 24 stone in September 1999 and 21.2 stone at the post-mortem, less than five months after he had stated on the form that his weight was 16 stone.

We were satisfied, on a balance of probabilities, that at the time Mr K signed the application form he could not have believed his weight was only 16 stone. Nor could he have believed he was 6 feet tall. The disparity between his actual weight and height and the information he gave on the form was so great that it was difficult to accept that he had been unaware of it. We decided that the insurer was entitled to avoid the policy on the grounds that Mr K's non-disclosure had been deliberate.

ISSUE 62: JUNE/JULY 2007

62/5   whether bank followed correct process in selling payment protection insurance to cover customer's loan repayments

Mr F took out a loan from his bank to consolidate his debts, which included an existing loan with the bank. The bank also offered him payment protection insurance to cover his monthly loan repayments if he became unemployed or incapacitated. The insurance premium was payable as a lump sum of £1,700. The bank added this to his loan for £7,800, which was to be repaid—with interest—over 60 months.

Mr F's financial situation improved over the next year and he asked the bank if he could pay off the entire amount outstanding on his loan. The bank agreed, but told him he would not be entitled to any pro-rata refund of the amount he had paid for the insurance.

He later told us that it was only as a result of this conversation that he realised just how much the insurance had cost him. And he said it was only at this stage that he discovered the insurance had been optional, as the bank had told him he could only have the loan if he also took the insurance.

The bank rejected Mr F's complaint about its sale of the policy and its refusal to give him a pro-rata refund, so he referred the matter to us.

Complaint upheld

The bank denied there had been anything wrong with the way in which it had sold the policy. And it said it had been correct to refuse Mr F a pro-rata refund of his premium. This was because the policy contained a valid and enforceable term saying that customers were not entitled to a pro-rata refund if they cancelled their policy before the end of the term.

The bank could not produce any record of the meeting at which Mr F claimed he had been told that taking the insurance was a necessary condition of getting the loan. However, the bank said it never insisted on a customer taking out payment protection insurance with a loan. The representative concerned no longer worked for the bank and was not available to comment.

The bank could not find a signed copy of its agreement with Mr F, detailing his acceptance of the loan and the payment protection policy. It did, however, produce a copy of the standard agreement that it said Mr F would have been asked to sign, as part of its normal procedure.

In our view, in selling the payment protection insurance, the bank was acting as an insurance intermediary. It therefore had a responsibility to ensure Mr F was able to make an informed choice about whether or not to take out the policy. It also had a responsibility to draw his attention to significant features of the policy. We thought that in this instance it should have stressed that:

- the policy was to be paid by a single lump sum premium covering the whole of the policy term
- no pro-rata refund was payable if the policy was no longer needed and
- the cost of the lump sum premium was to be funded by means of a loan, on which interest would be payable.

We saw no evidence that these features had been specifically drawn to Mr F's attention, either during the sales process or in any of the documents he was given. The bank said that Mr F had taken payment protection insurance on the two previous occasions when it had given him a loan, so he must already have been fully aware of how these policies operated. However, it was clear to us from Mr F's response to our questions that he had no understanding of how the policies worked.

We accepted Mr F's evidence that he had wanted the loan in order to consolidate his debts and reduce his outgoings, and would not have added to the overall cost of his loan by taking the insurance if he had realised it was optional.

We decided that the bank's sales process in this case had been flawed, and that the bank had failed to bring significant features of the policy to Mr F's attention. We upheld the complaint and required the bank to refund the full amount of the premium, plus all the interest that Mr F had paid on this amount.

62/6 whether lender mis-sold payment protection insurance in connection with a loan

Some eight months after he had taken out a loan, together with payment protection insurance, Mr M asked the lender to clarify details of the policy benefits and restrictions. As a result of what he was told, he asked the lender to cancel the policy and refund all the money he had paid for it.

Mr M had concluded that the policy was unlikely to be of any value to him. He was 66 years old and the loan ran until he was 71. Although the policy offered cover for death, temporary total disability and hospitalisation, any pre-existing medical conditions were excluded from cover and the death benefit only covered policyholders up to the age of 70.

The lender was only prepared to offer Mr M a refund equivalent to 75% of the cost of the policy. He insisted that he should have a 100% refund and eventually he referred the dispute to us.

Complaint upheld

Mr M had arranged the loan over the telephone. He said he had thought the insurance was compulsory, as the cost of the premium had been automatically included in the details quoted to him over the phone.

He had not been asked any questions about his health and had not been told that the policy would not cover him for any pre-existing medical conditions.

The lender said it had no record of the specific telephone call during which the loan was arranged. However, it sent us a copy of the script that it said its representative would have followed. We considered the exclusion from cover for a pre-existing medical condition to be a significant feature of the policy. It therefore needed to be drawn specifically to consumers' attention. However, the script made only a passing reference to the fact that 'entitlement to benefit could be affected' if the consumer suffered from a pre-existing medical condition. This was not given any particular prominence.

We noted that Mr M had asked the lender to cancel the policy as soon as he realised the implications of the exclusion for pre-existing medical conditions. So we accepted that he was unlikely to have taken the policy if he had fully understood the significance of the exclusion at the time of the sale.

The script did mention that the insurance was not compulsory. However, it did not highlight that:

- the cost of the premium was payable up-front and was added to the loan,
- policyholders were not entitled to a pro-rata refund if they cancelled the policy after the initial 30 days; and
- the death benefit applied only until the policyholder reached the age of 70.

In the circumstances, we decided that the policy had been mis-sold. We required the lender to refund the whole of the insurance premium, together with all the interest charged on the premium from the outset of the policy.

62/7 insurer rejects claim for sickness benefit made under a payment protection policy because the policyholder's incapacity related to a pre-existing condition

Mr J arranged a personal loan from his building society and took out a payment protection policy to cover his repayments for periods of sickness or unemployment.

Six months later he had an accident at work and put in a claim under his policy for sickness benefit. However, the insurer refused to meet it. It said the accident was related to a pre-existing medical condition and that such conditions were not covered by the policy. Mr B then referred his complaint to us.

Complaint rejected

The insurer said Mr J's medical records showed that on several occasions before he had taken out the policy he had received treatment for his knee. It was this same knee that Mr J injured in the accident that gave rise to his claim. After making further enquiries, we were able to confirm that this was indeed the case.

Mr J did not think the insurer's stance was fair. He accepted that the building society had told him there was a policy exclusion for pre-existing medical conditions. However, he said that since the building society had not asked him any details about his health, he had not understood how the exclusion would affect his own particular circumstances.

We explained that we do not consider it necessary for consumers to be asked about their medical history when they apply for a policy that excludes pre-existing medical conditions. It is enough that they are made aware that the policy contains such an exclusion—and are given clear information about how it will operate. We accepted that Mr J had acted in good faith. However, we felt that in the circumstances it was fair and reasonable for the firm to refuse the claim. We rejected the complaint.

62/8 whether bank mis-sold payment protection policy in connection with a loan

Ms B applied for a bank loan in order to consolidate her existing debts and reduce her monthly outgoings. The bank agreed to lend her the sum she needed. It also arranged payment protection insurance to cover her monthly loan repayments if she became unemployed or incapacitated.

There was a one-off premium for the payment protection policy, amounting to just under £3,000. This sum was added to the underlying loan of just over £11,000, which was to be repaid—with interest—in 84 monthly instalments.

Two years later Ms B asked her father's advice on cutting her expenditure, as she was still experiencing financial difficulties. She later told us that it was only at this stage, after her father had looked closely at her loan arrangement, that she realised how much she had been paying in total for the insurance. It was also at this stage that she discovered the insurance had been optional.

When the bank refused her request to cancel the policy and give her a pro-rata refund of the premium, Ms B brought her complaint to us.

Complaint upheld

Ms B insisted that she would never have agreed to take the insurance if she had known how expensive it was. She said the bank had been aware she had only taken the loan because she was anxious to try and manage her existing debts. So she did not think it should have made her add to her outgoings by taking the insurance.

The bank was unable to provide evidence that the adviser who sold the policy had told Ms B the insurance was optional. However, it said the adviser would have followed its normal sales process, which included an explanation of the implications of opting for the insurance cover.

The bank pointed out that Ms B had signed a loan agreement which included a full breakdown of the figures. She had also been given 30 days in which to study the details of the policy and cancel it without penalty if she was not happy with it.

After reviewing the evidence, we came to the view that there was nothing in the bank's sales process that drew consumers' attention to significant features of the policy. These features included the onerous cancellation conditions and the fact that payment for the policy had to be made up-front by means of a single premium, funded out of a loan on which interest would be charged.

It was evident that Ms B had no experience or knowledge of how insurance worked. There was nothing in the bank's documented sales process that explained—in basic terms—how the policy operated. And the sales process did not allow for any response to situations such as this, where the consumer had expressed a particular need to reduce her outgoings as far as possible.

In the circumstances, we took the view that the policy had been mis-sold and that Ms B was entitled to a refund of the full amount she had paid for the insurance, plus the interest she had paid on this amount.

62/9 insurer refuses to pay claim made on a payment protection policy as it says unemployment benefit is payable only in cases of redundancy

When Ms G took out a loan to buy a new car, she also bought a payment protection policy to cover her repayments in the event of her unemployment, disability or death.

Some three years later, after losing her job, Ms G put in a claim under the policy for unemployment benefit. However, the insurer refused to pay out. It said the policy only provided cover for unemployment that was the result of redundancy. Ms G had not been made redundant but had been dismissed from her job for under-performance.

Ms G said that the possibility of unemployment had been a particular concern when she took the loan. When she had taken out a mortgage a few years earlier, she had checked that her mortgage payment protection insurance covered her in case she lost her job. She had wanted similar cover when she took out a loan to buy her car and had thought the policy she was offered covered any period of unemployment, irrespective of the cause.

In the circumstances, the insurer offered to refund the insurance premium in full. However Ms G objected strongly to this. She said the insurer should instead pay her the unemployment benefit. Unable to reach agreement with her insurer over this, Ms G brought the dispute to us.

Complaint upheld

The insurer pointed out that it had sent Ms G a copy of the full terms and conditions as soon as she had said she would take the policy. This document stated clearly that the policy only provided unemployment cover for instances of redundancy.

Ms G admitted that she had not read the full policy terms and conditions. She said she had relied solely on what she had been told when she was sold the insurance, and she had not been told there were any restrictions on the circumstances in which the unemployment cover was provided.

After reviewing the evidence, we accepted Ms G's argument that she had been specifically seeking cover for unemployment before agreeing to borrow the money to buy the car.

We noted that the insurer's summary of the policy terms, which had been shown to Ms G at the time of the sale, referred several times to the fact that the policy covered unemployment. However, the summary did not mention that this cover was only available for unemployment resulting from redundancy. We thought this was misleading.

The document that Ms G was sent after the sale, containing the full policy terms and conditions, only mentioned once that unemployment cover was limited to instances of redundancy. And it did not give this information any prominence.

We upheld Ms G's complaint and required the insurer to pay her the full amount of benefit she would have received under the policy if her unemployment had been caused by redundancy.

ISSUE 63: JULY/AUGUST 2007

63/7   commercial motor insurance policy—keys left in the vehicle—whether the policyholder had taken reasonable care

Soon after starting work as a trainee electrician, Mr A bought a second-hand van. When he returned from work each evening, he parked outside the house where he lived with his mother. Even though this was in a residential area with a relatively low crime rate, he was always careful not to leave his tools in the van overnight, but to move them into his mother's garage.

Unfortunately for Mr A, his van was stolen one evening while he was unloading it. There was subsequently some confusion about the exact sequence of events. However, it was generally accepted by both Mr A and the insurer that Mr A had left the keys in the van while he was moving the tools into the garage. While he was in the garage he suddenly heard the van being driven away.

The insurer rejected Mr A's claim for the stolen van, saying he had not complied with the policy condition to 'take all precautions to reduce or remove the risk of loss of the insured vehicle'.

Complaint upheld

In rejecting the claim, the insurer was relying on a 'reasonable care' condition in the policy, rather than on a specific exclusion of cover that said the vehicle would not be covered if the keys were left in it.

Our approach in dealing with the complaint closely followed the line taken in the Court of Appeal case of *Sofi* v *Prudential Assurance* [1993] 2 Lloyd's Rep 559. The test established in this case is relatively simple—in order to show there was a lack of reasonable care, you must first demonstrate 'recklessness'. This is generally defined as recognising that a risk exists, but deciding to take it anyway. So we believed that in order to exclude Mr A's cover, the insurer would need to show he had deliberately courted the risk of having his van stolen.

We accept that the recklessness test is subjective, and that some people might consider Mr A's actions to be foolhardy. Mr A told us it had not crossed his mind that he was taking a risk, and we were satisfied that this was the case. He had been fully engaged in unloading the tools and happened to leave the van unattended for longer than he had anticipated. We had no reason to believe that Mr A had acted recklessly and we required the insurer to meet the claim in full, adding interest calculated at our normal rate.

63/8   travel insurance policy—theft of personal possessions from a camper van while travelling

During her gap year, Miss H went travelling across New Zealand. She had been there for three months when a number of her possessions were stolen from her camper van. She had been careful to take out full travel insurance before she left the UK, so she was very surprised when her claim was refused.

The insurer told her there was an exclusion in her policy that said claims for theft of property would only be covered if the stolen items had been kept in 'locked accommodation' or in 'a locked and covered luggage compartment/boot of a motor vehicle'.

Miss H challenged the insurer's decision. She said her camper van was her accommodation—and as it had been locked at the time of the theft, she should be covered by the policy. She also said that the insurer was treating her unfairly because camper vans do not have separate, lockable luggage areas.

After the dispute had been referred to us, Miss H told us that she had kept the possessions in question in nine padlocked storage boxes in the back of the camper van. This was a significant departure from her original statement on the claim form, where she had said the items had been 'all over the place'. It also differed from another statement she had made, in which she had said that she kept the items in a box under the bed in the van.

Complaint not upheld

We accepted that Miss H had been sleeping in the camper van and that it was partly designed for this purpose. But we had to consider whether it could reasonably be classified as 'accommodation'. We concluded that the most reasonable and appropriate definition of a camper van was as a 'motor vehicle'—and this would apply over and above any other definition.

In this situation, we were satisfied that the accommodation exclusion applied, so her possessions should have been placed in a locked boot or locked and covered luggage compartment in order to comply with the policy.

In our view, securing the items out of sight within the camper van could possibly be enough to satisfy a valid claim. However, when the claim had first been presented to us, Miss H said that the items had been 'all over the place . . . ' within the camper van. Although she later changed her story, we thought it reasonable to conclude that the first report was the most believable. We concluded that, in the circumstances, it was fair and reasonable for the insurer not to accept the claim.

63/9 motor insurance policy—daughter was 'named driver' on parents' car

Mr J and his wife bought a second family car soon after their daughter passed her driving test. He arranged the car insurance over the phone and—as is standard practice for many insurers—the call was recorded.

When asked if he was the 'owner and keeper' of the vehicle, Mr J said that he was. He also confirmed that he was the principal driver of the car. The insurer then pointed out that Mr J was the principal driver of another vehicle it insured. Mr J said he had been mistaken and that it was his wife who would be the principal driver of the new car. He asked to add his daughter to the policy as a 'named driver'.

While driving the new car a couple of months later, Mr J's daughter had a minor road traffic accident, which meant that the car needed some small repairs. Mr J submitted a claim to his insurer but it was rejected because the insurer believed this was an instance of 'fronting'. In other words, it thought the car had been insured in the name of an experienced driver—Mr J's wife—because it would be too expensive to insure in the name of the real principal driver—his daughter.

The insurer reached this conclusion after Miss J had given the insurer a statement in which she said, 'It's insured in mum's name I think. Dad did it because it was too expensive to have me named as the main driver . . . '

Mr J did not dispute that his daughter had made this statement. The insurer therefore 'avoided' the policy (treated it as if it had never existed) and declined to deal with the claim. Mr J then referred the matter to us.

Complaint not upheld

We considered this to be a prime example of 'fronting'. Mr J had misrepresented the risk when he took out the policy—as his daughter later confirmed.

As the information on which the insurer had agreed to provide the policy was incorrect, the insurer was entitled to 'avoid' the policy from the beginning—and to decline to pay any benefit that would otherwise have been due under the policy.

ISSUE 64: SEPTEMBER/OCTOBER 2007

64/6 ongoing travel insurance—insurer rejects claim because policyholder failed to disclose a change of health

Mr K had an ongoing travel policy that his bank had provided, free of charge, as one of the benefits of his current account. Under the terms of the insurance, the cover remained in operation as long as he retained the account.

In October 2006, Mr K and his wife booked to go on a cruise, departing early in the New Year. A few weeks after making the booking, Mr K suffered a temporary loss of vision and was referred to a specialist. Mr K's vision had returned to normal by the time of his consultation with the specialist, but she suspected that he might have had a minor stroke.

She therefore made a small adjustment to the medication he had been taking since he had suffered a blocked artery and heart attack four years earlier.

Mr K had no further problems with his vision and appeared to be in good health when he and his wife set off on the cruise towards the end of January. However, several days before the end of their holiday, Mr K had a heart attack.

Once he had returned home and his condition had stabilised, his wife submitted a claim under their travel policy for the expenses they had incurred while away—as a result of his illness. To the couple's dismay, the insurer said it was unable to accept the claim. It pointed out that the policy contained a condition requiring policyholders to report any changes in their health. Mr K had not reported the loss of vision he had experienced after booking the cruise.

The couple disputed the insurer's decision. They considered that they had complied with the policy condition requiring them to declare health changes. This was because they had sent the insurer full details shortly after Mr K had suffered his first heart attack in 2001. They said that since Mr K had very quickly recovered from the temporary loss of vision, they had not thought it sufficiently significant to be worth mentioning.

Complaint upheld

We looked closely at the policy condition cited by the insurer when it rejected the claim. We also examined the overall effect of the way in which the insurer applied this condition. The insurer told us it required policyholders to report all changes of health. Depending on the individual case, it would then consider whether or not to withdraw cover for any claims arising from that new medical condition.

The insurer said that because many apparently minor ailments or problems could be symptoms of a serious condition, it was impractical to provide policyholders with guidance about how significant a change in health needed to be before it should be reported.

In our view, this approach meant that the policy condition was a very onerous one. Requiring policyholders to contact their insurer every time they suffered any kind of ill-health placed a heavy responsibility on them. It also meant that policyholders could never be certain exactly what cover was available under the policy. If, each time a policyholder experienced any change in their health, the insurer could simply withdraw cover, it was difficult to see how a claim for ill-health could ever be made, unless the illness arose entirely without warning or as a result of an accident.

We noted that the insurer had agreed at the outset to offer cover against the risk of ill-health affecting a policyholder's travel plans. So Mr K was relying on the policy for the peace of mind of knowing he was covered for any financial loss he might incur if he was taken ill after booking a holiday.

We do not consider it fair for an insurer to use a policy condition to achieve an effect that would not be apparent to a reasonable policyholder, and that would place onerous demands on them.

If claims resulting from a change in health are not covered, then the benefit of the cancellation cover is severely limited. So we did not consider in this case that the insurer was entitled to rely on its policy condition to reject Mr K's medical expenses claim. We upheld the complaint.

64/7   annual travel policy—insurer rejects claim because policyholder fails to disclose change of health

When she applied to buy an annual travel insurance policy, Mrs C told the insurer that she suffered from angina. It agreed to cover her for this condition.

Several months later, her GP made a small alteration to the medication she took for her angina, as she had begun to experience some minor side-effects with the original dosage.

Mrs C had no further health problems until six months later, when she was admitted to hospital while on holiday in Florida. She was suffering from chest pains, linked to her angina.

Fortunately, Mrs C recovered fairly quickly and was soon able to return home. It had never crossed her mind that there would be any difficulty in claiming back from her insurer the medical expenses she had incurred while on holiday. However, the insurer refused to meet her claim. It said she had failed to comply with its policy condition requiring her to inform it of any changes in her health. After complaining unsuccessfully to the insurer, Mrs C contacted us.

Complaint upheld

We noted that the policy condition in question was not stated clearly in the policy document. And it had not been specifically pointed out to her when she bought the insurance. Moreover, the policy gave no explanation of what it meant by a 'change in health'. There was nothing to indicate that policyholders should tell the insurer about any change in medication.

We were satisfied that if the position had been clearly explained to Mrs C at the outset, she would have told the insurer that her medication had changed. If the insurer had then said it could no longer provide cover for this condition, she would have arranged alternative cover. In the circumstances, we did not think it was fair for the insurer to reject the claim. We upheld the complaint.

64/8 annual travel policy—insurer refuses to provide cover for medical condition that arose after the policyholder booked a holiday

Three months after Mr G had taken out an annual travel insurance policy he booked a trip to the Bahamas, departing in January 2006. He and his partner, Miss K, planned to get married during the trip.

Unfortunately, only a few weeks after booking the holiday, Mr G was diagnosed with cancer and underwent urgent surgery, followed by radiotherapy. It was not until three days before he was due to travel that he was well enough for his doctor to declare him fit for travel. He called his insurer straight away to check that he would be covered if he experienced any problems linked to his cancer while he was away.

The insurer promised to get back to him urgently. However, it was not until the afternoon before he was due to set off that the insurer contacted Mr G. It told him it would not cover any claims resulting from his cancer. The insurer did offer to meet Mr G's cancellation claim if he decided to cancel the holiday at this point. Understandably, however, Mr G did not want to cancel his wedding. Instead he spent several hours ringing round other insurers until he was eventually able to arrange a new policy that gave him the cover he needed.

On his return from holiday, Mr G complained to the original insurer and asked for compensation for the distress and inconvenience it had caused him. He had found himself effectively uninsured, less than 24 hours before he was due to depart. When the insurer rejected his complaint, Mr G came to us.

Complaint upheld

When rejecting Mr G's claim, the insurer had cited a clause in the policy that gave it the right to alter the policy terms if the policyholder's health changed before a holiday started, but after it had been booked. As in case 64/6, we did not consider this to be fair. Policyholders could not ever be certain exactly what cover was available under their policy.

It had clearly been distressing for Mr G to be told so close to his departure that his policy would not provide the cover he needed. And he had been put to considerable inconvenience—and some additional expense—in arranging the new policy. So we said the insurer should reimburse the cost of the new policy and pay Mr G £200 in compensation.

64/9 ongoing travel policy—insurer refuses to meet a claim when the policyholder ignores a reminder about the need to declare any new medical condition

Mr G had an ongoing travel policy, provided by his bank as part of a package of benefits attached to his current account. Every year, the insurer sent policyholders a letter reminding them to report any changes in their health that had arisen over the past year. The policy excluded any claims relating to such changes unless, before booking a holiday, the policyholder contacted the insurer and the insurer specifically agreed to cover the new medical condition.

Mr G failed to tell the insurer that he had been diagnosed with a heart murmur, shortly before he had booked a trip to Greece. He had also failed to check with his doctor that he was fit to travel and there seemed to be real uncertainty about that.

Unfortunately, while he was in Greece Mr G suffered a heart attack. When he subsequently claimed for the medical expenses incurred while he was on holiday, the insurer refused to pay up.

It said he should have provided details of the heart murmur before he went ahead and booked the holiday. If he had done this, the insurer would have excluded cover for any heart conditions. Mr G considered this unfair and referred his complaint to us.

Complaint not upheld

We were satisfied that the insurer had stated clearly—in its policy summary—the need for policyholders to declare any changes in their health. It had also made it clear what it meant by 'changes in health'.

And it sent policyholders a clearly-worded reminder each year, pointing out the need to inform it of any changes in health that had arisen over the previous twelve months. We noted that the insurer did not send policyholders any details of the health information they had provided in earlier years. We thought that in some instances this could make it difficult for policyholders to distinguish between 'new' medical conditions and those they had already told the insurer about.

In this particular case, however, we did not think Mr G should have had any difficulty in knowing that the heart murmur was a new condition and that he needed to disclose it. If he had disclosed that he had been diagnosed with a heart murmur, the insurer was entitled—under the policy conditions—to exclude cover for heart conditions that affected any travel plans he made after disclosing this health problem.

Mr G had gone ahead and booked his holiday without telling the insurer that he had been diagnosed with a new and serious heart condition. He had also failed to check whether he was 'fit to travel'. We felt that in the circumstances of this particular case, it was fair and reasonable for the insurer to reject the complaint.

ISSUE 65: OCTOBER/NOVEMBER 2007

65/1 **pet insurance—incorrect date of diagnosis on claim form results in insurer refusing claim**

Mrs F had been worried about her dog, Herbie, for some time. In early July 2005, after a number of visits to the vet, Herbie was diagnosed with arthritis. Mrs F submitted her pet insurance claim immediately, and it was accepted under the terms of the insurer's 'premium policy'. This was the cover Mrs F held at the time, and it provided a maximum benefit of £4,000 (less any excess).

In July 2006 the vet gave Mrs F a continuation claim form to send to the insurer—for Herbie's long-term treatment. This said the condition had first been treated in November 2004.

The insurer refused to pay the claim. It said that in November 2004 Mrs F had only a basic insurance policy in place (with a maximum benefit of just £1,500). The insurer had already paid out more than this, so it said it could not make any further payments for Herbie's arthritis treatment—and that any future arthritis-related claims would be excluded from the policy.

Mrs F was unhappy with this. She said Herbie's condition had not been diagnosed until July 2005. By then, she was covered by the premium policy, so she thought the insurer should continue to cover Herbie's arthritis.

She backed up her complaint with a detailed letter from the vet, confirming that Herbie had not been diagnosed with arthritis until 22 July 2005.

The insurer still insisted the claim should be dealt with under its basic policy. It said it would not ask for the 'over-payments' it had already made to be returned, but it refused to make any further payments or to meet any further claims for the cost of the arthritis treatment. Mrs F then brought her complaint to us.

Complaint upheld

When we investigated the case, we found that the second claim form—sent to the insurer in July 2006—had been completed by the head veterinary nurse, not by the vet who had actually treated Herbie and who had completed the earlier forms. Mrs F said the nurse had clearly made a mistake when giving the date of the diagnosis.

The evidence suggested that although Herbie was indeed first seen by the vet in November 2004, no diagnosis had been confirmed at that stage. It was not until the return visit in July 2005 that further investigation led to the diagnosis of arthritis.

Having considered all the evidence, including correspondence from the vet, we believed that Herbie had been diagnosed with arthritis in July 2005. We asked the insurer to review Mrs F's claim under the terms of its premium policy and to pay her any amount it owed her under the terms of that policy.

65/2 **pet insurer refuses claim on grounds that policyholder 'failed to take reasonable care'**

Mrs D was a keen fund-raiser for a local charity, and often took her horse to various outdoor fund-raising events for children to ride. Unfortunately, on the morning of the town's summer fair, Mrs D's horse-box overturned after becoming detached from the vehicle towing it. The horse was seriously injured, and after it had been examined by two vets it had to be put down.

Mrs D later submitted a claim for the veterinary fees she had incurred—and for the value of her horse. Initially, the insurer made an offer which would only cover the veterinary fees. However, when it received its loss adjuster's report, the insurer discovered that the horse had injured his leg in a similar accident two years earlier.

The insurer then withdrew the offer (which had not yet been formally accepted). It said it doubted Mrs D's trailer had been roadworthy and it believed she was in breach of the policy condition 'to take reasonable precautions to prevent accidents, illness, loss or damage'. It also stated that she should have disclosed the first accident at the time she renewed her policy.

Mrs D was unhappy that the insurer had withdrawn its offer. She thought it should meet her claim for both the veterinary fees and the value of her horse, so she brought her complaint to us.

Complaint upheld

We had to consider whether Mrs D had breached the policy condition that required her to take 'reasonable care'. In order to reject the claim on these grounds, the insurer had to demonstrate that Mrs D had been 'reckless'. It had to show that she had realised there was a risk involved in transporting her horse but had either taken no steps to avert it, or taken steps she knew were inadequate.

We found no evidence that she had been aware of the problem—that the tow-bar was corroded. Showing the trailer to be unroadworthy would not be sufficient to demonstrate Mrs D's recklessness. The terms of the insurance policy did not require her to keep the vehicle in good condition. And in any event, she had borrowed the vehicle—it was not hers. We accepted that Mrs D had not appreciated the trailer was in a poor state of repair.

We noted that when Mrs D renewed the policy, the insurer had asked her to disclose 'any material fact'. Mrs D told us that the earlier injury to the horse had been so minor that it had never occurred to her to disclose it. In our view, her failure to disclose the injury had been inadvertent, rather than reckless.

We told the insurer it should meet Mrs D's claim for both the veterinary fees and the value of her horse.

65/3 **pet insurer refuses to meet hydrotherapy claim because treatment not carried out by a vet or registered member of a relevant association**

Mr and Mrs J's dog, Ruby, was very fit and active until November 2003, when she suffered a prolapsed disc. Her veterinary surgeon recommended a course of hydrotherapy. This would help Ruby to regain the use of her hind legs as well as assisting with her rehabilitation in general.

Mr J told us that he had checked the proposed treatment with the insurer and was told it would be covered. Ruby responded very well to the hydrotherapy. However, when Mr and Mrs J submitted the claim, the insurer refused to meet it.

It said that—unless the treatment was carried out by a vet or a member of the Canine Hydrotherapy Association (CHA) or other relevant association—the policy specifically excluded 'the cost of hiring a swimming pool, hydrotherapy pool or any other pool or hydrotherapy equipment'. The insurer said that although it had previously paid similar claims, it would not do so in this case as neither the hydrotherapist nor the veterinary nurse were members of the CHA.

Complaint upheld

We understood why the insurer did not routinely approve all hydrotherapy claims. However, we noted that Ruby's treatment had been recommended by a qualified veterinary surgeon. The clinical evidence made it clear that the hydrotherapy had contributed to her recovery and that she had derived significant benefit from it. We also noted that the therapy had been administered by an experienced veterinary nurse—the only qualified hydrotherapist within some hours travelling time from Mr and Mrs J's home.

It was true that the veterinary nurse was not a member of the CHA. However, we were satisfied that she was sufficiently well qualified and experienced to provide an appropriate level of treatment.

We believed that the fair and reasonable outcome in this case was for the insurer to act as if the treatment had been carried out by a member of the CHA. So we instructed the insurer to meet Mr and Mrs J's claim.

65/4   pet insurance—claim rejected because it related to a pre-existing condition

After visiting a friend whose cat had recently had kittens, Mr and Mrs W became besotted with the runt of the litter. They were offered the kitten and—against the advice of their vet—decided to keep her. Mr and Mrs W named the kitten 'Pepper' and insured her straight away.

Pepper had suffered from serious health problems since her birth and eventually had to be put down. When Mr and Mrs W later came to claim £2,000 for the cost of her treatment, their insurer refused to pay. It said that the policy they had taken out excluded any pre-existing conditions.

Mr and Mrs W argued that Pepper's initial problems had been fully dealt with while she still lived with their friend. They indicated that they had phoned the insurer before taking Pepper to an animal hospital after she had become seriously ill. And they suggested that the insurer had said it would meet all veterinary and hospital charges.

The couple said these were expenses which they would not otherwise have incurred, as they would have had the kitten put down immediately rather than getting her treated at the hospital.

The insurer did not accept that it had agreed to cover all the costs. However, it said that as there might have been some misunderstanding about this, it would pay 50% of the veterinary costs as a goodwill gesture.

Complaint not upheld

The vet's notes showed clearly that Mr and Mrs W had been aware, when they were first offered the kitten, that she had serious unresolved health problems. There was no doubt that the exclusion for pre-existing medical conditions applied.

The evidence did not support Mr and Mrs W's claim that the insurer had said it would cover all the fees. They had made only a very brief call to the insurer before taking the kitten into hospital. This call was not long enough for them to have raised any significant issues. They had a more detailed conversation with the insurer four days after the kitten went into hospital—by which point most of the costs had already been incurred.

Mr and Mrs W were told by the insurer that the claim would be covered if it was an 'ongoing problem which had previously been met'. We thought it possible that the couple had simply misunderstood the position. In the circumstances, we considered the insurer's offer to pay 50% of the charges was both fair and reasonable, and we advised Mr and Mrs W to accept it.

65/5   pet insurance—claim rejected because policy limited cover for treatment of any one condition to a 12-month period

Mrs G's three-year old beagle, Jasper, was diagnosed with a condition where his rear kneecaps were constantly dislocating or slipping out of position. This was very painful and Jasper suffered to the extent that he had difficulty walking. Surgery was needed and Jasper's rear right leg was operated on in December 2001.

The vet recommended that Jasper's rear left leg should also be operated on, ideally in the first few weeks of February 2002. But Mrs G did not arrange any further treatment until September 2005. When she then submitted a claim for the cost of the final operation, the insurer rejected it. It pointed out that Jasper's treatment had begun in 2001—when his condition was first identified. The policy terms clearly stated that any condition would only be covered for 12 months after the initial treatment began. Unhappy about the insurer's decision, Mrs G brought her complaint to us.

Complaint upheld

The insurer told us that, at the time of the initial claim, it would have made it clear that there was a 12-month limitation on the treatment of any one condition. Unfortunately, the insurer was unable to produce any evidence to support this.

Mrs G insisted that the limitation had not been brought to her attention. She said if she had been told she needed to have all Jasper's treatment carried out within 12 months, she would have done this. The only reason she had waited so long was that Jasper was still very young and the leg did not appear to require immediate treatment.

We decided that the policy limitation was a significant term that the insurer should have brought to Mrs G's attention. However, we could not be sure that this had happened.

Mrs G's decision to postpone the treatment had not prejudiced the insurer. Mrs G had renewed her policy each year, and was not attempting to claim for more than she would have originally been entitled to. So we instructed the insurer to reimburse Mrs G for the cost of Jasper's surgery—although we did agree to it applying a limit to the claim, based on what the treatment would have cost in 2002.

65/6   pet insurance—administrative error prevents policyholder renewing policy before it lapses

Mr T's pet insurance policy gave comprehensive cover for his expensive pair of breeding cockatiels, Rosie and Jim. The insurer who arranged the policy did not itself offer this sort of specialist cover and instead acted as an intermediary for the actual underwriter.

Towards the end of 2005, the underwriter notified the intermediary of its intention to terminate the pet insurance scheme. The intermediary arranged, at short notice, to contact all policyholders and advise them of the situation.

Cover had already been arranged with a second underwriter, and the intermediary told existing customers that while most of them would be covered by the new policy, some would not be eligible. These customers would continue to be covered under the existing arrangements with the original underwriter.

At the time Mr T's policy was due for renewal—in December 2005—one of his cockatiels, Jim, was undergoing long-term treatment for a skin condition. Because of that ongoing claim, Rosie and Jim were not eligible for cover under the new scheme and would continue to be covered by the original policy. Unfortunately, an administrative error meant that the renewal letter that contained this information was not sent to Mr T. By the time the error came to light, Mr T's renewal date had passed and the policy had lapsed.

Following negotiations with the underwriter, the original insurer offered to accept liability for the continuation of Jim's treatment. This would apply from the date Mr T's policy lapsed until the treatment was completed, or the policy limit for that claim was reached.

The insurer also offered Mr T £100 for the distress and inconvenience he had been caused. Mr T was unhappy with the situation. He wanted to receive indefinite cover for Jim's treatment on the same terms he had enjoyed previously.

Complaint not upheld

When we considered the case, it was evident that even if Mr T's policy had not lapsed, he would only—at best—have been able to secure the continued benefit of cover for a further twelve months —and up to any applicable policy limit. We noted that Jim had been in the middle of treatment for his skin condition when the policy was nearing the end of its annual contract. This meant that if the policy had been renewed on the same terms, cover for his treatment would have continued either until its completion or until the relevant policy limit had been reached.

The original insurer would not have been obliged to continue to provide the same level of cover at the next policy renewal. Equally, no other pet insurer would have been under any obligation to offer the same terms as those held under the original policy. In the circumstances, we told Mr T that we were not able to require the intermediary—or either of the insurers—to provide indefinite cover for the treatment of Jim's skin condition.

65/7   marine insurance—whether explosion and resulting damage caused by policyholder's 'recklessness' while installing gas heater in cabin of his boat

Mr A was devastated when he had a phone call to say his boat had been badly damaged by an explosion in the cabin. Since buying the boat a year earlier he had put a great deal of money and effort into renovating it and had spent almost every weekend—and most of his annual leave—on the boat.

After inspecting the damage, Mr A put in a claim under his marine insurance policy. However, the insurer refused to pay out. It said that, in installing a gas heater in the cabin, Mr A had 'knowingly taken insufficient measures to avert the risk of a faulty and dangerous installation'. The insurer said that this constituted 'recklessness' and was therefore a breach of a policy condition.

The insurer based its view on a report prepared by the marine surveyor it had appointed to inspect the damage. The surveyor concluded that the cause of the explosion was the gas heater Mr A had installed in the cabin.

Mr A disputed the surveyor's conclusions. He was not convinced that the heater had caused the explosion and he put forward several alternative theories. He strenuously denied that he had acted recklessly in installing the heater, and said that he had considerable experience in installing such appliances correctly and had taken appropriate care.

When the insurer insisted that the circumstances of the case meant that it was not obliged to meet Mr A's claim, he brought his complaint to us.

Complaint upheld

To decide whether the insurance company was entitled to refuse Mr A's claim, we needed to consider whether Mr A had been reckless when he installed the gas appliance. In other words, we had to try and establish whether he failed to take adequate measures to avert the risk of a faulty and dangerous installation.

In reaching its conclusions on the case, the insurer had relied heavily on the advice of the marine surveyor. So we reviewed the surveyor's report and his subsequent correspondence with the insurer.

We were concerned by some of the surveyor's findings. For example, he had noted that the heater was not of a type intended for use 'in a marine situation'. However, our investigations showed that this was not the case.

We also noted that in response to a written query by the insurer, the surveyor had said that he did not feel Mr A had been 'reckless' when installing the heater, merely that he had 'probably been unaware of the perils involved'.

In the light of the available evidence, we concluded that Mr A had understood the risks and had taken appropriate steps to ensure the heater was installed safely.

He had not, therefore, acted 'recklessly'. We told the insurer it should deal with the claim, in accordance with the terms of the policy.

65/12 contractors' all-risks commercial insurance policy—liabilities to third parties—claim for serious fire damage during renovation work—whether claim can be dismissed on grounds of contractor's carelessness and breach of policy condition

Mr K bought a large house that needed major restoration. It was while this work was taking place that there was a serious fire, thought to have been caused by a blowtorch used by one of the builders. The estimate for repairing the damage looked like totalling at least £750,000 and the building contractor, Mr B, put in a claim under his contractors' all-risks commercial insurance policy for liabilities to third parties.

Mr B was extremely surprised when the insurer rejected the claim. It said he had breached a specific policy condition regarding the preparations necessary during the use of heat in building works. The insurer said that it could also dismiss the claim on the grounds of the builder's carelessness.

Mr B complained to the insurer that the specific policy condition it said he had breached had not been part of his insurance contract, so he could not be bound by it. The insurer disagreed. After a lengthy dispute about which of several slightly different versions of the policy condition applied in this case, and about the precise legal interpretation of these different versions, Mr B referred the complaint to us.

Complaint upheld

We concluded that the policy condition could properly be considered a part of Mr B's insurance contract. The differences in the wording of the various versions of the policy condition were immaterial as far as this specific dispute was concerned. That was because none of the versions explained exactly what policyholders were expected to do—over and above taking standard fire-prevention precautions—in order to comply with the policy condition. We were satisfied from the evidence that Mr B had ensured his staff had taken all standard precautions. There was nothing to substantiate the insurer's view that it could also reject the claim on the grounds of the contractor's carelessness. So we said the insurer should deal with the claim. It agreed to our recommendation that that it should pay the full amount due, even if this came to more than £100,000—the maximum award we have the power to insist on in any individual case.

ISSUE 66: DECEMBER 2007/JANUARY 2008

66/1   motor vehicle insurance—dispute over insurer's valuation

After Mr W's 1989 Saab saloon was badly damaged in a road traffic accident, the insurer offered him £700, which it said was the car's pre-accident value. The insurer had calculated that repairing the car would cost considerably more than the car's market value.

Mr W was far from happy with the insurer's offer. He thought it was based on an inaccurate valuation and failed to take the car's particular features into account. He sent the insurer details of these features and suggested that £2,600 was a more realistic figure.

The insurer subsequently increased its offer to £1,040. Mr W still thought this was inadequate. He complained to us about both the valuation and the poor service he felt he had received from the insurer. To support his view of the car's value he sent us copies of a number of newspaper and magazine advertisements for the sale of similar vehicles.

Complaint upheld

The advertisements Mr W had sent us were not particularly persuasive. Apart from anything else, they featured many different models—including convertible and turbo Saabs. We pointed out to Mr W that a number of apparently minor details—for example in the model type or mileage—can significantly affect value. And sellers usually inflate the price they state in such advertisements, to allow for a degree of negotiation. So advertisements rarely provide sufficient detail for an accurate 'like for like' comparison, such as that needed to provide a proper valuation.

We explained to Mr W that our usual approach when assessing the value of vehicles is to consult the major motor-vehicle trade-guides. These guides are published regularly and provide detailed information on the market valuation of most makes and models.

In this particular instance, we noted that the trade guides showed a value that was significantly higher than the £1,040 that the insurer had offered Mr W. However it was less than the £2,600 Mr W felt the vehicle was worth.

We had been surprised by the amounts the insurer had originally offered Mr W, as we could not see that they had any reasonable basis.

We told the insurer to offer what we considered to be a fair amount, based on the trade guides we had used. We said it should also pay Mr W £150 to compensate him for the distress and inconvenience it had caused him.

66/2   motor vehicle insurance—dispute over insurer's valuation

Mrs B paid £7,995 for a second-hand 2006 Vauxhall Corsa which had a specialist sports body. Ten days after she bought the car, it was badly damaged in an accident. The insurer declared the car to be a total loss, as the estimated cost of repairs exceeded £7,000. So it offered Mrs B £6,900, which it said was the fair pre-accident retail value of the car.

After Mrs B rejected this offer, insisting that the insurer had not taken the car's special features into account, the insurer offered her £7,175. Mrs B felt this was still not a fair offer, so she brought her complaint to us.

Complaint upheld

Because Mrs B's car had fairly unusual features, it was not as quick and easy as is usually the case with more standard models to just check in the trade guides for a guide retail price.

However, we told the insurer that if it had contacted the compilers of these guides and made some further enquiries, it should have been able to obtain an accurate guide price for Mrs B's exact model.

The insurer then made the enquiries we said it should have undertaken when Mrs B first made her claim. As a result, it established that the guide price was higher than either of the amounts it had offered Mrs B. We said it should settle the complaint by paying Mrs B the correct guide price.

66/3   motor vehicle insurance—dispute over insurer's valuation and its sale of car for salvage

Mr G's 1999 Daewoo was damaged in an accident in July 2006. When he contacted the insurer to make a claim, he stressed that even though the car was badly damaged, he wanted the insurer to return it to him in due course, so he could get it repaired.

However, after deciding that the car was a total loss, the insurer immediately sold it on for salvage. The insurer then offered Mr G £2,125—representing what it said was the car's pre-accident market value.

Mr G was extremely unhappy to discover that the insurer had disposed of his car, even though he had specifically asked it not to do this. He also complained that the amount he was offered did not accurately reflect the car's value.

The insurer refused to comment on its sale of the car, and it would not reconsider its offer, so Mr G referred the complaint to us.

Complaint upheld

Mr G pointed out that the car had benefited from the liquid petroleum gas (LPG) conversion he had carried out just over two years earlier, at a cost of £2,000. He was firmly of the view that the car could have been repaired, allowing him to retain the benefit of the LPG conversion. He said that the insurer had not only prevented him from attempting a repair, it had also failed to take the LPG conversion into account when it valued the car.

We agreed with Mr G that the insurer had not valued the car correctly. And the insurer did not dispute that Mr G had made it very clear, when he reported the accident, that he wished to have the car repaired.

The car had been regarded as a Category 'C' in the 'Code of Practice for the disposal of motor vehicle Salvage'. This meant that although it was uneconomical for the insurer to repair the car, the car was repairable.

We said that the insurer had clearly acted incorrectly. Mr G was still the owner of the car at the time the insurer disposed of it. And he had asked the insurer to return the car to him, so that he could arrange a repair.

We told the insurer it should pay Mr G £4,125. This was £2,000 more than the amount it had offered him, and would enable him to buy a car with LPG conversion, to replace the vehicle the insurer had disposed of. We said the insurer should also pay Mr G £400 for the distress and inconvenience it had caused him.

66/4   motor vehicle insurance—dispute over insurer's valuation—classic car insured on 'agreed value' basis

When Mr H bought a classic car, he took out a motor insurance policy on an 'agreed value' basis rather than on the more usual 'market value' basis.

Such policies are generally taken out only by owners of classic or particularly valuable cars, where the value is unlikely to depreciate substantially—if at all.

The value of the vehicle is agreed in advance and insurer is then obliged to pay that amount if the car is lost or damaged beyond reasonable repair. However, the insurer is not obliged to pay for the replacement cost of the vehicle.

Mr H agreed the value of his classic car under this policy was £2,500. Unfortunately, the car was badly damaged when Mr H was involved in an accident. The insurer took the view that it would cost more than £2,500 to remedy the damage, so it offered him £2,500, in settlement of the claim.

Mr H thought that this figure was far too low. He told the insurer that, bearing in mind the good condition of the car before the accident, it would cost between £4,000 and £5,000 to replace. He therefore wanted the insurer to pay that amount.

Complaint not upheld

We noted that Mr H had renewed his annual policy twice—on the 'agreed value' basis—before the claim in question. The policy terms, which had been clearly stated in the policy documents, said that Mr H was entitled to receive the 'agreed value' of the car—not the cost of replacing it. So we told him we could not uphold his complaint.

68/7   **whether insurer responsible for cost of remedying faults in building work carried out as part of a claim for flood damage**

Mrs C lived in an old mill house which was badly damaged by winter floods, following prolonged rain and storms. She was insured by the same firm for both buildings and contents and she submitted claims under both policies.

The insurer accepted liability and appointed contractors to carry out repairs to the property. After a few weeks, however, Mrs C concluded that the contractors were making unreasonably slow progress. She discussed the situation with the insurer and said she would like to appoint a local surveyor to represent her and supervise the work. The insurer agreed to her proposal and confirmed that it would pay the surveyor's fee.

During the course of the subsequent works, Mrs C's surveyor replaced the existing contractors with a new firm of builders. And Mrs C asked for some additional work to be carried out, at her own expense.

As time went on, Mrs C became increasingly dissatisfied—both with the surveyor and with the standard of the building work. When all the work was eventually completed, she hired a different surveyor to prepare a report on what had been done. He identified a number of faults in the building work and estimated that it would cost just under £50,000 to remedy matters.

Mrs C sent the report to the insurer, together with a claim for the cost of putting things right. However, the insurer refused to meet the claim. It said that as Mrs C had appointed a surveyor to oversee the work, responsibility for any faults lay with him. Mrs C then brought her complaint to us.

Complaint upheld in part

It was clear that there were a number of problems with the building work. Some of the faults listed in the report related to the additional work that Mrs C had asked the builders to carry out. We agreed with the insurer that it was not responsible for putting right any defects in this additional work.

However, we said that the repair work relating to the flood damage was a different matter. The insurer had authorised and paid for the work. And it remained responsible for ensuring that the work was completed satisfactorily, regardless of the fact that—with its agreement—Mrs C had appointed a surveyor to oversee the builders.

We said the insurer should pay Mrs C £20,000 to cover the cost of remedying the defects in the work carried out to repair the flood damage.

68/8   **whether uneven concrete flooring resulted from subsidence or poor construction**

Mr and Mrs B contacted their insurer when they first suspected that their flat had been affected by subsidence. The insurer appointed a firm of surveyors to inspect and monitor the situation.

It became clear that subsidence was affecting the entire block of flats and that a significant amount of work would be needed to remedy matters. The insurer paid for Mr and Mrs B to move into alternative accommodation for eight months, while work was carried out on their flat.

In the event, it was over nine months before the work was finished. And when Mr and Mrs B visited the flat, they concluded that it was still not in a fit state for them to return to. They told the insurer that the uneven state of the concrete floor was unacceptable. They also submitted a long list of 'snagging' items that they said needed to be fixed before they could move back home.

The surveyors said that the poor state of the floors was nothing to do with the subsidence or the repair works. It was attributable to the age of the property and the poor quality of its original construction. The surveyors did, however, agree that the 'snagging' items needed attention.

The insurer agreed to pay for Mr and Mrs B to continue living in alternative accommodation for a further three months. At the end of that time, the couple returned home. However, they remained unhappy about the state of the floors. Unable to get any further with the insurer on this matter, they referred the dispute to us.

Complaint upheld in part

In our view, the insurer had acted reasonably in carrying out the repairs and then extending the period during which it paid for the couple to stay in alternative accommodation. We accepted the surveyors' evidence that the poor state of the floors did not result from subsidence, the repair works, or any other insured 'event'. So we agreed with the insurer that it was not responsible for any work that was needed to restore or improve the state of the floors.

We did, however, conclude that Mr and Mrs B had been caused additional and significant inconvenience and distress by the need to extend their stay in alternative accommodation. We therefore required the firm to pay them £1,000 for this.

68/9   claim for flooding and damp in basement after exceptional rainfall—whether policy also covered cost of repairing damaged damp-proofing in walls

After a period of exceptional rainfall, Mr and Mrs D discovered that the basement of their house had suffered flooding and damp. They put in a claim under their household insurance policy.

After sending an engineer to inspect the basement, the insurer agreed to pay the cost of repairing the flood damage. However, it said it would not meet the cost of making the walls of the basement watertight. The engineer had reported that the damp-proof membrane protecting the walls was in a poor condition and that this had contributed to the problems in the basement.

The couple thought it unreasonable of the insurer not to pay for all the repairs. However, the insurer insisted that it was not liable for the cost of repairing the damp-proof membrane or providing an alternative solution to keep the basement water-proof and damp-proof. It said the damage to the membrane must have been caused by defective design or poor workmanship or by very gradual movement in the surrounding earth.

The insurer pointed out that the policy did not cover such matters. Mr and Mrs D then brought their complaint to us.

Complaint upheld in part

The evidence from the engineers suggested that the damage was likely to have been caused by ground movement rather than by any defect in workmanship or design. The insurer said that this type of ground movement constituted a 'gradually-operating process'—something that was not covered by the policy.

After reviewing the evidence, we concluded that the ground movement that had, in all likelihood, caused the damage was covered by the policy.

We therefore required the insurer to pay for the cost of installing a new system to replace the damaged membrane and protect the basement.

Mr and Mrs D had also asked to be compensated for the insurer's 'undue delay' in dealing with the claim. We did not agree that it was appropriate in this case for the insurer to make such a payment. In view of the technically complex nature of the problem, the insurer had been entitled to appoint a firm of engineers to inspect and report on the damage. The insurer had acted promptly, both in appointing the engineers and then in completing its consideration of the claim, once the report was ready.

68/10   insurer refuses to pay claim for storm damage when it discovers that policyholder is serving a prison sentence

Mr and Mrs T put in a claim under their buildings insurance policy after their small, sea-front house was badly damaged in a storm involving wind speeds of up to 100mph and exceptionally high tides.

While it was looking into the claim, the insurer discovered that Mr T was serving a prison sentence. It told the couple it would not have offered them any cover at all if it had been aware of Mr T's conviction. It said that it would not pay the claim and that it was 'avoiding' the policy (treating it as if it had never existed).

Mr and Mrs T insisted that they had told the insurer about the conviction. However, the insurer refused to reconsider the matter so the couple brought their complaint to us.

Complaint upheld

Mr and Mrs T had been sold the policy by their bank and regarded the bank as their insurer. There was clear evidence that the bank had been fully aware of Mr T's circumstances. In fact it had written to him at his prison address. However, it had not passed on any information about his conviction to the insurer.

The bank admitted that it had received a letter from Mr T in which he had given details of his prison sentence and asked about some concerns regarding both his mortgage and his household insurance. However, it said that Mr T had addressed his letter to the bank's mortgage department—and the correspondence had all been dealt with within that department, not in the insurance part of its business. It said that it was not fair to imply that the one part of the business would automatically be aware of what went on in other departments.

In our view, the staff in the mortgage department of the bank should have realised that they needed to pass on to the insurer the information that Mr T had provided about his conviction and imprisonment.

We noted that a few weeks after the bank's mortgage department had replied to Mr T, the bank had sent him the standard questionnaire it sent all policyholders when their insurance was due for renewal. When he completed the questionnaire, Mr T referred to his recent correspondence with the bank about his 'changed circumstances and conviction'. However, it appeared that no one at the bank had passed on to the insurer what Mr T had written on the questionnaire.

We did not think it likely that Mr T, or his wife, would have been unable to obtain insurance cover—either from the same insurer or from a different one—if the details of his conviction had been known. However, the couple would probably have had to pay an additional premium because of the conviction.

We upheld the complaint. We said the bank should pay the couple the same amount that the insurer would have paid them in settlement of the claim. However, we agreed that it could deduct the cost of the additional premium that the insurer would have charged, if it had been aware of the conviction.

68/11 whether problem with floorboards was caused by a relatively recent flood or by rot that had been spreading for some years

While Mr H was visiting his elderly mother he became aware of a problem with the flooring. After removing the carpet, he discovered that the wooden floorboards and joists were suffering from extensive rot. Acting on his mother's behalf, Mr H then put in a claim under her buildings insurance policy for the cost of replacing the wooden timbers and floorboards.

After investigating the claim, the insurer refused to pay out. It cited an exclusion in the policy that meant it did not cover 'loss or damage . . . resulting in wet or dry rot'.

Mr H complained to the insurer about its decision. He said that the damage must have been caused by a leak at the property four years earlier that had led to the installation of a new water meter and stopcock. As the policy had been in force since that time, and it covered liability for 'escape of water and flooding', he said the insurer should pay up.

Complaint rejected

We examined all the evidence, including the independent reports that both the insurer and Mr H had commissioned. We concluded, from the scale and extent of the rot, that it was unlikely to have been caused by a single leak, four years earlier. It appeared to have developed and spread over a number of years.

So we said that the insurer was justified in rejecting the claim.

ISSUE 69: APRIL/MAY 2008

69/1 damp-proofing treatment covered by extended warranty—whether insurer can decline claim when policyholder unable to produce original versions of relevant documents

When Mr M discovered that his house was affected by damp, he arranged treatment to overcome the existing problem and prevent any recurrence. The company that carried out the work for him provided a guarantee. It also offered him a certificate of insurance, described as a 'backup guarantee'. He was told he would be able to rely on the backup guarantee if the building company failed to carry out its obligations to make good any faults in the damp-proofing work.

Some nine years later, Mr M put his property on the market after deciding to move abroad. A survey commissioned by a prospective buyer revealed that his house suffered from recurring damp.

Mr M tried to contact the company that had carried out the damp-proofing work. However, it had long since gone out of business. He therefore put in a claim to the insurer that provided the backup guarantee.

The insurer refused to pay the claim. It said it was a condition of the policy that certain documents were submitted with a claim. These included the original of the building company's initial report on the work required, its quotation for the work and the guarantee it had offered. Mr M had only supplied copies of these documents—not the originals.

After complaining unsuccessfully to the insurer about its refusal to pay his claim, Mr M referred the matter to us. He said he had never been given the original versions of the documents in question and had submitted the only versions he had. He noted that the paperwork the insurer sent him referred to its requirement that policyholders should submit the documents in question and said, 'If you do not have them, obtain copies from your contractor now, (they may make a small charge to cover administration)'.

In Mr M's view, this reference to obtaining copies indicated that the insurer was not able to insist on his providing originals. However, the insurer said it would only accept copies if they were authenticated by the original builder.

Complaint upheld

We found that the actual policy document contained no information about the procedure for making a claim or the need to supply original documents. This information was in a separate 'registration form' sent to policyholders after they had taken out the policy.

We agreed with Mr M that if the insurer intended to insist on policyholders supplying originals or authenticated copies of the documents in question, then it should have made this very much clearer. But in any event, we considered it would be unfair of the insurer to demand that Mr M should produce original or authenticated copies of the documents, when there was no real doubt that Mr M was entitled to the benefit of the policy.

We required the insurer to pay the cost of putting right the damage caused by the failure of the damp-proofing work. We said it should also reimburse Mr M for the administrative fee it had charged him when dealing with, and declining, his claim.

69/2 leather sofa covered by extended warranty—whether insurer can refuse claim for damage caused by policyholder's children

When Mrs D bought a new leather sofa she took out a five-year warranty that covered it against accidental damage. Just under two years later she made a claim under the warranty, because a hole had developed in the leather upholstery.

The insurer sent a technician to inspect the sofa. In his report, the technician noted that Mrs D told him the hole had appeared after her teenage sons had been picking at a weak spot in the upholstery. The technician identified this spot as a scar in the leather and he recommended that repair work should be carried out under the policy.

However, the insurer rejected the claim on the basis of the following exclusion in the policy: 'The insurer will not pay for costs attributable to or arising from ... any damage, soiling or staining caused ... deliberately by any person, including children'.

Mrs D then brought her complaint to us. She admitted that she had caught her teenage sons picking at the hole in the sofa. However, she said that she had tried to stop them. In her view, the damage was accidental and the insurer should repair it.

Complaint not upheld

We noted that the technician's report suggested that the nature and extent of the damage was consistent with 'interference of a nature scar by fingers'. We then considered whether the apparently deliberate acts of Mrs D's teenage children should be treated as accidents, or whether they fell within the policy exclusion that the insurer had cited in rejecting the claim.

We concluded that the policy wording and layout gave such prominence to the relevant exclusion that Mrs D could not reasonably have been unaware of it when she bought the policy. In light of this, the technician's report, and Mrs D's own admission that her sons had caused the damage, we agreed with the insurer that the claim should not be upheld.

69/3   insurer declines to pay claim on car covered by extended warranty

When Mr J bought a new car he took out a policy offering a motor vehicle breakdown warranty. This came into effect when the manufacturer's guarantee expired—12 months after the purchase date. It provided cover for four years.

Around 18 months after the start of the warranty, Mr J's car broke down. He put in a claim, which the insurer paid. A few months later he put in a further claim, totalling £4,000, for repairs and replacement parts. However, the insurer refused to pay up. It said Mr J had 'failed to satisfy a policy requirement to ensure the vehicle was serviced by a manufacturer-approved repairer, in accordance with the manufacturer's recommendations'.

Under the terms of the policy, a service was required every 24 months or every 12,000 miles. Mr J had arranged his car's second service just 17 months after the first service. However—by the time of the second service, the car had covered an additional 13,377 miles.

The insurer also noted that the manufacturer had accepted responsibility for replacing one of the parts. In the insurer's view, this indicated that the replacement had become necessary because of a 'latent manufacturing failure'. The policy specifically excluded claims made as a result of such problems. Unhappy with the situation, Mr J brought his complaint to us.

We looked into the details of the repairs that had been carried out, and why they had become necessary. We accepted that the car's second service had been carried out later than the manufacturer's recommendation. However, we were unable to see any connection between the nature of the repairs and the timing of the service. We also noted that the insurer had been aware of the timing of the second service when Mr J had made the first claim, some months earlier.

The insurer accepted our point that there was no connection between the timing of the second service and the nature of the repairs. We asked why it had not objected to the timing of the second service when the first claim was submitted. The insurer said that at the time of the first claim, the policy had been administered on its behalf by a different company, and that company had not checked the service details.

Complaint upheld

We said that by accepting the first of Mr J's claims, the insurer had waived its right to reject the claims solely because of his failure to have his car serviced within a certain timescale. And in any event, we did not consider that there had been a significant delay in getting the car serviced. Mr J had exceeded the permitted mileage by something over 10%, but had remained within the 24 months timescale.

We noted that the manufacturer had contributed towards the cost of one of the items that required repair. However, we did not believe that this amounted to confirmation that there had been a 'latent manufacturing defect', so it did not entitle the insurer to refuse to pay the balance of the cost of this item.

In all the circumstances of the case, we decided it was appropriate for the insurer to reimburse Mr J for the cost of all the repairs that had been carried out.

69/4   insurer declines claim made under extended warranty for damaged leather sofa

When Mr and Mrs C bought a new leather three-piece suite, they took out an extended warranty. The suite was covered by the manufacturer's warranty for the first 12 months. After that time, the extended warranty provided cover for four years for any accidental damage to the leather upholstery caused by 'rips, tears, burns, punctures and pets' as well as for 'structural damage' caused by a number of features including 'broken zips'.

Less than a year after they had bought the suite, Mr and Mrs C discovered that the leather upholstery on the sofa had been damaged where a metal component of the recliner mechanism had rubbed against it. The manufacturer repaired this free of charge under its own warranty.

Unfortunately, eight months later Mr and Mrs C had further problems with the sofa. By then, it was no longer covered by the manufacturer's warranty, so the couple made a claim under the extended warranty. They reported that further damage had occurred since the initial repairs had been carried out. They noted that the frame of the sofa needed repair, the leather was badly marked and the zips on the arm pads were damaged.

The insurer rejected the claim. It said the damage had come about because of the poor standard of the repairs carried out by the manufacturer. The extended warranty did not cover the manufacturer's 'negligent failure'. Mr and Mrs C then referred their complaint to us.

Complaint upheld

After looking closely at the terms of the policy for the extended warranty, we concluded that the wording was very poor. There was considerable uncertainty about exactly what the insurer intended to cover and about how it could invoke various exclusions.

Applying the normal legal test in such situations, we said that since the insurer's policy wording was ambiguous and unclear, it should be interpreted in the manner most favourable to the policyholders, and with their reasonable expectations in mind.

We examined the detailed report prepared by the insurer's technician. This said there was no evidence of any structural damage to the frame of the sofa. The report suggested that some of the decline in the quality of the leather had arisen 'as a result of a gradual process through use of the furniture over time' and was therefore not covered by the policy. However, the technician thought that the more serious tears and markings were covered by the policy.

We concluded that the insurer should pay the cost of repairing all of the accidental damage to the leather suite, including rips, punctures, broken zips and everything arising from the manufacturer's failure to carry out previous repair works properly.

69/5 whether trade federation warranty covered faulty guttering installed with new conservatory

When Mr and Mrs B had a conservatory fitted to the side of their house, the company that installed it offered them a trade federation warranty. This supplemented the supplier's warranty, which only covered the first year.The trade federation warranty provided cover for faulty workmanship by the conservatory installation company and any 'failure of PVC-U windows, doorframes or conservatory roof sections to operate in accordance with the manufacturer's specification'.

Around eighteen months after the conservatory had been fitted, Mr and Mrs B discovered some damage to the side of their house. This had been caused by overflows from the gutter that had been installed with the conservatory—and that ran between the conservatory and the main wall of the house. The couple put in a claim under the trade federation warranty.

The insurer rejected the claim on the basis that the damage had arisen because of a fault in the way the gutter had been assembled. The insurer said the policy excluded any loss or damage due to defective design of any part of the conservatory other than the 'conservatory roof sections'.

Complaint upheld

We reviewed the terms of the policy, together with the details of the problem with the guttering and the resulting damage. The gutter was clearly failing to operate in accordance with the manufacturer's specification. We concluded that this was partly because of a miscalculation of the volume of water the gutter would have to cope with. However, the problem had occurred mainly because the gutter had not been installed correctly.

We decided that the insurer should pay the claim, on the basis both that the gutter assembly was itself a 'conservatory roof section' and also that its malfunction had resulted, at least in part, because it had not been installed properly.

So we said the insurer should pay all reasonable costs for putting right the problems with the gutter and the resulting damage to the property. We said the insurer should also pay Mr and Mrs B £100 to compensate them for the distress and inconvenience they had been caused.

ISSUE 71: AUGUST 2008

71/1 customer says he was never told that a payment protection policy was optional when he took out a credit card

A trainee chef, Mr A, complained about the way in which he was sold a payment protection policy when he applied for a credit card. He said he had understood he was being insured, but had not been told that the policy was optional.

He said he was not given any information about the cost or benefits of the policy. And he stated that a representative of the credit card company had simply filled in the application form for him, written a small 'x' at the bottom of the form, and then asked him to sign his name next to the 'x'.

The credit card company rejected his complaint. It said it was clear from the application form that the insurance policy was optional and that Mr A had chosen to take it. The company also said that the insurance premiums were itemised on Mr A's credit card statement each month, so he must have been aware that he was paying for an additional—optional—product.

Complaint upheld

We asked the credit card company to send us Mr A's application form. We noted that on the final page, close to the space for the customer's signature, there was a 'tick box' next to a statement that the customer wanted payment protection insurance. This had been ticked.

The tick in the box, the written details entered on the form, and the small 'x' placed next to the signature all appeared to have been written in the same handwriting, using a ballpoint pen. However, the signature itself looked markedly different and had been written with a thick, felt-tipped pen. This tended to support Mr A's account of events.

We also noted that Mr A had been 19 years of age at the time of the sale. This was the first time he had applied for any financial product or service other than a basic bank account.

We did not agree with the credit card company that it was clear from the application form that the insurance cover was optional. Nor did we agree that, by signing the form, Mr A had clearly indicated his wish to buy the policy. There was no evidence that he had been told anything about the cover at the time of the sale. And the fact that Mr A's statement showed that the premium was collected monthly did not mean he must have been aware the insurance was optional.

We upheld the complaint and told the company to return to Mr A all the premiums he had paid to date, plus interest.

71/2 couple in financial difficulties take out a succession of loans and are sold a new single-premium payment protection policy each time, adding to their outstanding debt

Mr and Mrs J had been experiencing financial difficulties for some while and their situation worsened in early 2005, after Mrs J gave up work to look after their children. Finding it difficult to meet the monthly repayments on their loan, they approached a different lender to see if it could help.

The lender offered them a new loan of £18,000. This allowed them not only to settle their existing loan (for around £11,000) but also to clear the overdraft on their current account and settle several credit card debts and sizeable bills. In order to keep their monthly repayments as low as possible, the couple chose to take the new loan over 10 years.

Unfortunately, Mr and Mrs J's financial problems did not resolve themselves and within 18 months they again approached the lender for help. It agreed a new and higher loan. This was spread over 15 years and was secured by a second mortgage on the couple's home.

Some time later, a friend pointed out to them that each time they had obtained a new loan they had also been sold a new payment protection policy. So they asked the lender if it would refund their insurance premiums, as part of a wider settlement of their continuing debt problems. The lender said it would arrange a small, partial refund if the couple cancelled their policy. Unhappy with this, the couple referred their dispute to us.

Complaint upheld

We noted that each time Mr and Mrs J had taken out a loan they had been asked to pay for the insurance by means of a single premium. This was added to the underlying loan and repaid (plus interest) over the entire length of the loan, even though—in each case—the policy itself only provided cover for 5 years.

There was nothing to suggest that the lender had explained to Mr and Mrs J the significance of this arrangement—particularly the fact that that they would still be paying for the policy for some time after the cover had ended.

Although the lender told us it did not offer advice, it was clear that it had actively encouraged the couple to buy the policies. In view of the couple's financial circumstances, we did not consider the sale of these policies to have been appropriate.

Flexibility was an important consideration, as it seemed likely the couple would need to restructure the loan at a later date. They would not wish to incur significant costs in doing this.

However, the policies they were sold lacked flexibility and, because of the limitations on the refund of premiums, were particularly costly if they were cancelled after a relatively short period.

In our view, the lender should not have encouraged the couple to buy these policies, and the couple would not have wanted the policies if the business had explained matters more fully.

We said the lender should re-calculate the amount outstanding on the couple's loan account, putting them in the position they would have been in if they had not bought the policies. We said the business should also pay the couple back the amount they had paid for the policies, plus interest on these amounts.

We had some concerns about the way in which the lender had dealt with Mr and Mrs J, given their overall financial difficulties. We therefore suggested it should look at ways of assisting them with a wider settlement of the debt, including waiving the fees it had levied in recent months in connection with several overdue loan repayments.

71/3 consumer says he was not told his payment protection policy offered only limited benefits to the self-employed

Mr D had a small shop specialising in interior design. His complaint concerned the single-premium payment protection policy he had been sold when he took out a personal loan. He thought the business concerned should have realised the policy was unsuitable for him, as he was self-employed and therefore entitled to only a limited number of benefits under the policy.

When the business refused to refund all the premiums he had paid, plus interest, Mr D brought his complaint to us.

Complaint upheld

We noted that the benefits available to self-employed policyholders were more limited than those available to employees. In particular, the redundancy benefit was only available to policyholders if their employer had ceased trading or had been declared insolvent. We accepted Mr D's view that these terms were likely to make the policy less attractive to someone who was self-employed.

In this particular case, although the business clearly knew that Mr D was self-employed, it had not mentioned that this would limit the benefits he could get under the policy. The business had given him a written summary of the policy benefits. However, we did not consider that this leaflet adequately highlighted the limited cover he would get from the policy.

We concluded that the business had not given Mr D sufficient information to enable him to make an informed choice.

We upheld the complaint. We told the business to put the loan back where it would have been if he had not taken the policy, and to refund all of his payments for the policy, with interest.

71/4 consumer in financial difficulties complains about sale of a payment protection policy that she considered unsuitable for her needs and too expensive

Miss A did not earn a great deal from her job in a local bookshop and as well as having a large overdraft, she was close to her spending limit on several credit cards. Despite this, she felt she had been managing her finances reasonably well.

After she split up with her partner, however, she realised that she had become increasingly reliant on his help to meet the household bills and other expenses.

Alarmed by the extent of her financial difficulties, she applied to the business for a loan. It agreed a sum of £20,000, to be repaid over 15 years and secured by a second mortgage on Miss A's flat. The business also sold her a payment protection policy.

Some time later, Miss A complained about the sale of this policy, saying it was too expensive and she had never been told that it was optional.

Complaint upheld

We had significant doubts about the sales practices of the business concerned. However, we accepted that the business might reasonably have believed Miss A had a need for a payment protection policy. And we thought Miss A should have been aware, from the written information she was given, that the policy was optional. However, the business only offered its loan customers one type of payment protection policy—and we did not think that particular policy was suitable in this case.

Moreover, despite being well aware that Miss A needed to reduce her outgoings, the business had effectively understated the true cost of the policy. It had not explained exactly how much she would pay for it, but had simply told her that the premiums would 'increase the monthly payments by only £47 a month'. The policy offered cover for five years and had a single premium of over £5,000.

This sum was added to the loan and spread over the loan's 15-year lifetime, plus interest. Miss A was therefore paying a total of nearly £8,500 for the policy.

We looked at the restrictions placed on the sickness and unemployment benefits available under the policy. If a policyholder made a successful claim, their loan payments would be covered for up to 12 months. But the policyholder would then need to have returned to work for a minimum of three months before they could make any subsequent claim.

We calculated that in order to recoup the total amount she was paying for the policy, Miss A would need to make three separate claims, each for 12 months' worth of benefits, during the five years that the policy was in operation.

The business disputed our calculations, pointing out that there was no limit on the number of claims that could be made. It also noted that we had not taken account of the death benefit, which would pay off the loan in full if Miss A died while the policy was in force.

However, we said the policy was expensive and inflexible and we remained unconvinced that it had been suitable for Miss A. If she had needed life cover, she could have obtained it at a very modest cost.

We thought it unlikely that, in practice, the value of any benefit payments she received from the policy would exceed the amount she was paying. We told the business to put Miss A's loan back as it would have been without the payment protection policy. We said it should refund all the payments she had made for the borrowing on the policy premiums—and pay her a modest sum for distress and inconvenience.

71/5   consumer complains about sale of payment protection policy after he repays his loan early and gets only a partial refund of the amount he paid for the policy

Mr K applied to the business for a loan so that he could buy a car for his daughter, who had just started at university. His finances were under some pressure at the time. Not only was he committed to paying part of his daughter's course fees, but the firm he worked for had recently made significant cut-backs in its bonus payments. For some while, Mr K had relied on these payments as a very welcome supplement to his income.

The business arranged to lend him the sum he needed, over 30 months. It also offered him a payment protection policy, covering the same period as the loan. Mr K paid for the policy with a single premium and the cost was added to the loan.

Unfortunately, Mr K's daughter found it difficult to settle at university and after six months she gave up her course and took a temporary job abroad. So Mr K asked the business if he could settle his loan early and cancel the policy.

Surprised to learn that only a very small proportion of the premium he had paid would be refunded to him, Mr K complained to the business. He said it should not have sold him an expensive policy that he did not need—and that represented very poor value for money.

Complaint not upheld

The evidence suggested that Mr K had been given adequate opportunity at the time of the sale to consider the details of the policy. The literature set out the policy's key features—and its costs—very clearly.

We did not think the literature explained the conditions regarding the refund of premiums as well as it should have done. But in view of his circumstances at the time of the sale, we thought that however clearly these conditions had been stated, Mr K would still have bought the policy. He had a clear need for insurance to cover his loan repayments. The loan was for a modest amount and for a relatively short period. And Mr K had no particular need at the time to ensure the loan arrangement was flexible. We did not uphold the complaint.

71/6   insurer suspends payment of unemployment benefit under payment protection policy, saying there was insufficient proof he was looking for work

Mr B was made redundant from his engineering job at a local factory. He took some comfort from the fact that a year earlier, when he had taken a loan to buy a car, he had also taken a payment protection policy.

For five months Mr B received unemployment benefit under the policy, to cover his loan repayments. But the insurer then suspended his benefit. It expressed some surprise that he had not yet obtained employment, and said it needed proof that he was still actively looking for work before it could reinstate his payments.

Mr B complained to the insurer, saying that he attended the jobcentre every week and had also registered his details with an internet employment agency. He thought it unreasonable of the insurer to expect him to send written evidence of every job application he had made. It was rare for companies to acknowledge receipt of an application or to write to tell him if he was thought unsuitable.

The insurer then said it would be prepared to accept instead a letter from Mr B's jobcentre, confirming that he was actively seeking work. But when he provided this, the insurer wrote to tell him it was unable to pay him any further unemployment benefit, as there was insufficient proof that he was looking for work. Mr B then referred his complaint to us.

Complaint upheld

We were not surprised that Mr B had been unable to obtain a new job immediately. His job had been fairly specialised and his skills were not readily transferable to other areas of work.

Neither were we surprised that Mr B had been unable to produce many letters acknowledging—or rejecting—his applications for particular jobs. It is relatively common these days for companies to contact only those job applicants who are shortlisted for an interview.

The insurer did not dispute that it had originally agreed to reinstate Mr B's benefit payments if he provided a letter from his jobcentre confirming that he was still looking for work. It was unable to explain why it had then gone back on its word. And we could see nothing in the terms and conditions of the policy that might justify its refusal to pay the unemployment benefit in this case.

We looked at the dates on the few letters of acknowledgment or rejection that Mr B had been able to supply—and checked these against the information provided by the jobcentre. We concluded that Mr B had been looking for work for a period of eight months from the date when the insurer had stopped paying him any benefits.

We said it should pay him the amount he had been entitled to under his policy during that period. We said it should also make a small additional payment in recognition of the inconvenience and distress it had caused.

ISSUE 72: SEPTEMBER/OCTOBER 2008

72/1   motor insurer declines claim for theft of car—on grounds that car could not have been taken without the use of the programmed key

Mrs D's teenage son arrived home one afternoon and said her car was missing from the spot where she always left it, just outside her house. Not long afterwards the car was discovered just a short distance away. It was badly damaged and appeared to have been driven off the road and to have caught fire.

The insurer turned down Mrs D's claim. It said its loss adjusters had noted that the car could only have been operated by someone using an 'intelligent' (programmed) key. The key had not been left in the car and Mrs D had not reported that either of her two keys had been lost or stolen. When asked to produce the keys, she had at first been able to find only one of them, although she later found the other key.

Mrs D challenged the insurer's insistence that the car could only have been taken by someone who had the programmed key. In response, the insurer cited a report from motor vehicle security experts, which it said supported its view.

The insurer also suggested that the only other way in which the car could have been moved was by means of a transporter or tow-truck. Either of these would have caused the car's alarm to sound, alerting Mrs D to the theft. But in any case, as far as the insurer was concerned, the fact that the car had been driven off the road immediately before the fire indicated that a key must have been used.

Complaint not upheld

Mrs D then referred her complaint to us. She said she had been extremely distressed by the firm's stance and by its implication that she—or someone in her family—had taken the car and caused the accident.

She produced evidence from the original dealer to support her argument that the car's security could be by-passed, and that the car could be operated without the use of the programmed key.

It was clear that the incident had caused Mrs D much distress and we did not doubt her honesty. However, we did not uphold the complaint. We noted that the technical evidence Mrs D produced, supplied by the original dealer, was of a very general nature. It did not make any specific reference to the make and model of Mrs D's car. By contrast, the technical evidence produced by the insurer referred very specifically to the exact make and model that Mrs D had owned.

We also took account of the particular circumstances of the case and the possible alternative explanations for what had happened. We concluded, on a balance of probabilities, that the firm had sufficient reasons to refuse to pay the claim.

72/2 motor insurance—theft claim turned down because policyholder failed to disclose relevant information

Mr G referred his complaint to us after his claim for the theft of his car was turned down. The insurer said Mr G failed to disclose relevant information when he applied for his policy. He had not mentioned a claim he made three years earlier for car theft. He had also failed to disclose an earlier accident claim, made the year before he took out this particular policy.

The insurer said that if he had provided all relevant information, the premium would have been approximately £1,000 higher than the amount he had been charged.

Complaint upheld in part

Mr G did not dispute that he had failed to provide the information in question. He said the earlier theft had simply slipped his mind when he was filling in the application form, and he had 'not particularly concentrated on the issue of past claims' when he was seeking a quote.

He argued that his claim should be paid in full, as he did not consider he had done anything wrong. He said he would have been happy to pay the additional £1,000 if he had been asked to do so, and he suggested the firm should deduct this sum from his current claim.

After seeking clarification from both parties, we concluded that Mr G's failure to disclose relevant information was unlikely to have been an 'accidental' or 'casual' oversight, which might in some circumstances have meant that the insurer should still meet the claim.

Equally, we could find no evidence to suggest that Mr G had been dishonest in failing to provide the required information. But he did appear to have been very careless and we said the insurer was entitled to turn down the claim, even though there was no reason to doubt the car had been stolen.

However, we did not agree that the insurer had acted correctly when, after deciding not to meet the claim, it retained Mr G's insurance premium. We said it should return this sum to him, together with interest.

72/3 motor insurer declines claim for theft of car—saying car could not have been driven away without use of its programmed key

As he left the house on his way to work one morning, Mr F discovered that his car was missing from the spot where he always parked it overnight. He immediately reported the theft to his insurer and to the police.

The insurer subsequently refused to pay his claim. It said the car could only have been driven away by someone using one of the car's programmed keys. And it provided expert evidence illustrating just how difficult it was to start the ignition on that particular make and model of car without one of the original keys.

Mr F had only been able to produce one of his two keys when it had asked him to hand them over. In the insurer's view, this cast serious doubts over his story.

Complaint upheld

Mr F referred the dispute to us. He said he had not had a working second key for some time. He had intended to buy a new one. However, the age of his car meant it was no longer serviced by the main dealer and he had not got round to finding an alternative supplier. As he was the only driver, he had not felt there was any urgency about the matter.

Mr F stressed that he had reported the loss of his car very promptly. He had also provided evidence that he had been at home the evening before he had found the car missing.

After reviewing all the evidence, we found nothing to indicate that it would have been impossible to start the car without one of the programmed keys, even though the firm's technical evidence indicated that this would clearly have been difficult.

More importantly, however, we noted that Mr F had very recently had some remedial work done on the car at a local garage. He had previously had the car serviced at several other garages in the area. All of these garages had access to the key—which could be replicated with the appropriate technology.

We noted that Mr F provided strong evidence that he had not left his house at all on the evening immediately before he had reported the car missing. And the insurer accepted that the police report did not indicate anything untoward. On the balance of probabilities, we decided the evidence pointed towards the car having been stolen. We said the insurer should pay Mr F's claim, reimbursing him for the value of the car.

72/4   several months after repair of accidental damage to his car, policyholder notifies insurer of damage apparently overlooked during the repair

After Mr B's car was damaged in a road traffic accident, his insurer accepted his claim under his comprehensive motor insurance policy. One of the insurer's approved repairers carried out the necessary remedial work and Mr B signed off the work as having been satisfactorily completed.

Four months later, Mr B was involved in another road traffic accident. He later said that as there was only minor damage to his car, he had not contacted his insurer but had simply gone ahead and arranged the repairs.

Mr B said that, while repairing the car, the garage had spotted some damage to the boot that did not seem to have been caused by the most recent accident. So he told the insurer the original repairers must have failed to complete the job properly.

The insurer arranged for a different garage to inspect the reported damage. It also asked the engineer who had inspected the car after the first accident to review his report and the photographs taken at the time.

As a result of its findings, the insurer refused Mr B's request that it should pay for the repair of the boot as part of the original claim. It said there was nothing to connect this damage to the original accident. Mr B then brought his complaint to us.

Complaint not upheld

After looking at all the evidence, we found nothing to support Mr B's view that his car's boot had been damaged in the original accident. And we did not agree that there had been any 'negligent act or omission' on the part of the repairers who had carried out the remedial work after the first accident.

The insurer had not been required to disprove Mr B's allegations. However, by instructing independent experts and seeking clarification from the original inspecting engineer, it had gone to some lengths to try to establish whether it was liable for the damaged boot.

Although it had declined to consider the damaged boot as an outstanding issue from the original claim, the insurer had offered to deal with it as a new claim, subject to a new policy excess. We said we thought this was a fair and reasonable offer and we did not uphold the complaint.

ISSUE 73: OCTOBER/NOVEMBER 2008

73/6   household contents insurer refuses claim for theft of 'minimoto' from policyholder's garage

Mr W was very surprised when his insurer said it would only pay part of his claim, after several items were stolen from his house and garage. The insurer refused to pay for the replacement of his young son's 'minimoto' (a very small powered bike), that had been kept in the garage. The reason given was that Mr W's contents and personal belongings policy excluded 'Motor vehicles, electrically, mechanically or power-assisted vehicles (other than domestic gardening equipment)'.

Mr W argued that the minimoto was not a 'motor vehicle' as described in the policy but a child's toy. He said its engine was tiny, it had a top speed of less than 20 mph and it was incapable of being used to transport people from A to B. It could not be used on roads and no motor or motorbike insurance was available for it.

The insurer disagreed. It said the powered bike did fall within the policy definition. It was a power-assisted vehicle and even with the limited engine in the model in question, could reach speeds of up to 35 mph. The insurer added that if minimotos were toys, they would be readily available from toyshops. However, this was not the case and they could usually only be obtained from specialist dealers.

Unhappy with the insurer's stance, Mr W brought his complaint to us.

Complaint not upheld

We took account of evidence provided by Mr W that some minimotos were sold as toys and were available from toy shops and toy websites.

However, Mr W acknowledged that his son's minimoto could travel at speeds of over 20 mph. It was therefore difficult to accept his claim that it should be classed as a child's toy. No adult could effectively supervise a child using it. And while we accepted Mr W's point that it was not a means of transport, it was capable of being used for sporting purposes. It was also considerably faster than other powered toys used by children, such as mini cars and go-karts intended for domestic use.

We concluded that in the particular circumstances of this case, the insurer had acted correctly in declining the claim for the theft of the minimoto.

73/7 insurer tells policyholder that 'accidental damage' cover does not apply to his damaged lawnmower

Mr M was very annoyed when his insurer refused to pay for the expensive repair work his lawnmower needed, after it was damaged in an accident. He had been confident that his claim would be met, as he had paid an additional premium for 'accidental damage' cover when he took out his household contents insurance policy.

The insurer turned down the claim, saying the lawnmower was covered only for specified events, including fire, flood and theft.

Mr M then referred the complaint to us, saying he thought the insurer was attempting to 'hide behind the small print' so that it would not have to pay out on what he considered a 'perfectly straightforward and valid claim'.

Complaint not upheld

We examined the policy documents that Mr M had been given when he took out the insurance. Like most household policies, it provided cover against certain specified events including fire, flood and theft.

The terms of the accidental damage cover that Mr M had selected as an 'add-on' to his policy were set out very clearly and referred specifically to:

- 'Accidental damage to TV, video, hifi, computer or telecommunications equipment; and
- accidental breakage of glass and furniture and fixed kitchen appliances.'

We found nothing to indicate that the accidental damage cover had been described to Mr M in an inaccurate or misleading way. So while we sympathised with his honest misunderstanding about the nature of the cover he had bought, we did not uphold his complaint.

73/8 insurer rejects claim for collapse of garden wall and resulting damage

The retaining wall at the end of Mrs K's garden collapsed after a short period of exceptionally heavy rainfall, causing extensive damage to her garden, garden shed and garden furniture.

However, her insurer turned down her claim. It said that the wall (which was over 140 years old) had collapsed because of its poor construction and its age. Mrs K's policy only provided for specific perils and events, such as storm or flooding. The insurer said there was no evidence of storm conditions or flooding in the period leading up to the collapse of the wall, so there were no grounds on which Mrs K could claim under her policy.

Extremely unhappy with this response, Mrs K instructed a surveyor to inspect the collapsed wall and produce a report about it, which she then sent to the insurer.

The surveyor said the wall had been in a good state of repair. Its collapse had not come about because of its poor construction or its age, but because a substantial amount of water had built up behind it. In the surveyor's view, the wall's age was relevant only in so far as it meant the wall lacked features such as 'weep holes' that a more recently-constructed wall would have had—and that might have helped it to withstand the water pressure.

The surveyor's report included weather records showing that in each of the three months before the wall collapsed, the rainfall in that part of the country had been considerably above the regional average. In the month immediately before the wall collapsed, the rainfall was the highest ever recorded in that area for a single month.

The insurer did not respond to Mrs K for some considerable time after receiving this report. When it did eventually contact her, it simply confirmed that its position had not altered and it did not consider there were any grounds for paying her claim. Mrs K then came to us.

Complaint upheld

We had little sympathy with the insurer's argument that the faulty construction of the wall was to blame for its collapse. Modern construction methods are not the same as those in use 140 years ago, and insurance cannot be offered on the basis that old structures must conform to more recent building standards.

The more difficult issue to decide was whether the damage to the wall had been caused by 'flood'. The insurer had been correct in saying no flooding had taken place in the area. However, the problem had not arisen as a result of rising surface water but because of the very rapid build-up of water behind the wall. We concluded that this could, in itself, constitute a 'flood'. We said the incident was therefore covered under the terms of the policy and that the insurer should pay Mrs K's claim.

We said it should also pay her £750 in recognition of the distress and inconvenience she had suffered as a result of its excessive delay in progressing her complaint and dealing with her queries about it.

73/9   insurer rejects claim for quantity of metal stolen from policyholder's garden

Mr T put in a claim under his household contents policy after thieves removed a large quantity of copper, brass, lead and aluminium from his back garden. The insurer rejected the claim on the grounds that the policy did not cover 'scrap metal'.

Mr T then complained to us, saying the insurer had acted unfairly and that the claim should be met. He said he had only been keeping the metal in his garden temporarily, until he had time to use it. He had bought some of it in order to repair his front porch and he intended to use the rest to make garden furniture.

Complaint not upheld

We examined the terms of the policy and noted that cover was provided for 'household goods, valuables, personal money, deeds and documents, business equipment and personal belongings'.

The insurer said that this clearly did not include scrap metal or raw materials used in the course of construction work.

We accepted Mr T's evidence that he had been keeping the lead in his garden with the specific intention of repairing the roof of his front porch, and that he had indeed made garden furniture out of the remaining materials in the past. After discussing the complaint with us, the insurer said it was prepared to cover the loss of the lead that Mr T had intended to use for the repair of the front porch. However, it would not pay the remainder of the claim.

We told Mr T that the insurer's offer was a fair one in the circumstances and we advised him to accept it. We did not believe he had been misled about what the policy covered. The lead was intended for household repairs, so it was reasonable for it to be covered under the terms of the household contents policy. However we retained some doubt as to the intended use of the remaining materials. Mr T told us he would accept the insurer's offer.

ISSUE 74: DECEMBER 2008/JANUARY 2009

74/7   annual travel insurance—retired couple cancel holiday at their own expense after disclosing an illness that occurred after they booked the trip

In September 2007, Mr and Mrs K booked a trip to the Seychelles for early in the New Year, to celebrate Mr K's retirement. Unfortunately, Mr K suffered a stroke a few weeks after making the booking. This appeared to be relatively minor and the couple had every expectation that he would be well enough to travel by the time of their trip.

At the beginning of November, the couple received the renewal notice for their annual travel insurance policy. This asked for details of any changes in their health since the policy was last renewed. Mr K provided information about his recent stroke. The insurer then said it would add an exclusion clause to the new policy, stating that he would not be covered for any claims arising 'directly or indirectly from that stroke'.

Mr and Mrs K told the insurer this was unfair. They said they felt uneasy about travelling without cover for any health problems related to the stroke. And they said the insurer was punishing them for being honest.

In its response, the insurer stressed that it was important for all policyholders to provide accurate information in answer to its questions about their health. Failure to do this could lead to claims being refused. It said it had been entitled to add the exclusion clause to Mr and Mrs K's policy, and that it would only continue to provide them with cover on that basis.

Mr and Mrs K were unhappy about the situation they found themselves in. And they felt they had no option but to cancel their trip, at their own expense, when their doctor said that in view of Mr K's stroke, this might not be the best time to travel. The couple then complained to us. They said the insurer had acted unreasonably in adding the exclusion clause to the policy and forcing them into the position where they felt obliged to cancel their holiday.

Complaint upheld in part

We said the insurer had made a legitimate commercial decision in excluding cover for Mr K, in relation to his change in health. But in the circumstances of this case, we thought it should have given the couple the opportunity to cancel the trip and claim under their existing policy, which did not include the exclusion. We therefore said that the insurer should reimburse Mr and Mrs K for the costs of cancelling their holiday.

74/8 owner of small business disputes insurer's rejection of his claim for business interruption and damage to shop contents

Mr L had a small business selling office supplies. Within the space of 14 days he made two claims on the insurance policy that covered his shop for 'trade contents and business interruption'.

The first claim related to a leak of water through his ceiling from the flat above, as a result of a faulty washing machine. This damaged some of his stock and other contents.

The incident that led to the second claim happened after a couple of days of severe weather and localised flooding. A large amount of rainwater fell through the flat felt roof that covered part of his premises. The water damaged contents in a part of the shop that had not been affected by the first incident.

Mr L claimed for these contents and also for 16 days' loss of trade. He said he had been advised to close his premises for health and safety reasons after the second incident.

The insurer agreed to meet Mr L's first claim, but not the second one. It argued that there had been a problem with the flat roof for some years—certainly since before Mr L had taken out the policy.

In its view, it was a defect in the roof—rather than the bad weather—that had caused the rainwater to come through into Mr L's shop. The insurer also told Mr L that it did not consider the water damage would have been serious enough to necessitate his closing the premises. Unhappy with this outcome, Mr L brought his complaint to us.

Complaint upheld

The insurer had cited a policy exclusion that enabled it to turn down claims where the insured premises were suffering from 'inherent vice' or 'latent defect'. In other words, where the damage had come about because the premises had a structural weakness.

Our investigation revealed that there had been some structural problems with the roof before the date when Mr L took out his policy. However, there was evidence that repairs had been carried out well before the period of severe weather that had led to the claim. There was no evidence that those repairs had been faulty in any way, and there was insufficient evidence to back up the insurer's opinion that the roof had an inherent flaw.

We concluded that it was the severe weather that caused the incident leading to the claim for damaged contents. The policy exclusion did not apply in these circumstances, so we said the insurer should meet this part of Mr L's second claim.

We then looked at the part of the claim relating to Mr L's loss of business. He supplied detailed evidence about the work that had been carried out after the rainwater came in through the flat roof. This showed that the electricity had been turned off at the mains for several days. Several large industrial dehumidifiers had then been required to help dry out the premises before the cleaning up and remedial work could begin.

We concluded, from the evidence, that Mr L had no alternative but to close his premises during that period. We therefore told the insurer that it should meet his claim for business interruption.

74/9 insurer rejects claim for theft and damage after thieves break into premises of a small business

Mrs A ran a small graphic design business from premises above a retail unit. One evening, after locking up the premises and going home, she realised she had left some important paperwork behind. She decided to have a meal and then return to pick up the paperwork, as she needed it early the next morning for a meeting with a client.

When she arrived back at her business premises at around 10.00pm, Mrs A discovered that thieves had broken in, stealing computer equipment and causing significant damage in the process.

In due course she put in a claim to her insurer. To her great surprise, this was turned down. Mrs A's policy contained a 'condition precedent', stipulating that claims of this nature would only be paid if specific security devices were installed and in use, and all the doors of the insured premises were made of solid wood.

The insurer acknowledged that the correct security devices had been in place. However, it said it was unable to meet the claim because some of the doors (including the one used by the intruders to gain entry to the premises) were not 'of the correct construction'.

Mrs A did not agree that the doors of her business premises failed to meet the criteria set out in her policy, and when the insurer refused to reconsider the matter she brought her complaint to us.

Complaint upheld

It is generally accepted within the insurance industry that claims brought by some smaller businesses should be handled in the same way as if they had been brought by a consumer.

We take the view that it is fair and reasonable to judge complaints from large businesses—and from those with a more sophisticated knowledge of insurance—by legal standards. However, if we think it should have been clear to the insurer or intermediary that the business was an unsophisticated buyer of insurance, we are likely to judge the complaint as if it had been made by a consumer.

Mrs A's business turnover was modest and she had only two part-time employees. So we thought the insurer should have treated her claim as if it had been made by a consumer—not a business.

In such circumstances, if a claim would otherwise be unsuccessful only because of the policyholder's failure to meet a 'condition precedent', the insurer can consider whether this failure was actually connected to the loss. Where it is not, the claim should be paid.

In this case, we noted that the thieves gained entry to Mrs A's premises by forcing the front door off its hinges. So we concluded that they would have got in to the premises regardless of the precise construction of the door. We therefore told the insurer to meet the claim.

74/10 insurer cites policy exclusion when owner of a small groundworks business makes a claim on his commercial insurance policy

Mr G, who ran his own small groundworks business, was sub-contracted to carry out some work at an RAF base. While he was drilling on a runway at the base he struck a fuel-line. As well as resulting in a loss of fuel, this caused substantial damage to the surrounding area, including contamination of a local watercourse.

Later that same day Mr G learned from the main contractor that he would be held liable for any damage. He therefore contacted his insurer to say he would be claiming on his commercial policy.

The insurer told Mr G that it would not meet any claim in relation to this incident. It considered the RAF base to be an airport, and his policy specifically excluded cover for any works carried out 'on or at airports'.

Dismayed by this news, Mr G contacted the insurer again a few days later. He said he had studied the wording of his policy very carefully and did not agree that the exclusion applied in this case. In his view, the RAF base was not an 'airport'. He said that dictionary definitions of the word all related to civil aircraft and the large-scale transportation of the public—not to the specialised functions of an RAF base.

However, the insurer refused to reconsider its position. It said that the statutory definition of an airport would include the RAF base. But regardless of the exact definition, the policy exclusion was intended to cover high-risk locations and the work Mr G had carried out at the RAF base clearly fell into that category.

Mr G then referred the dispute to us.

Complaint upheld

When considering disputes involving the precise wording of a policy, we look at whether the insurer has provided a clear definition. If it has not, then we apply the ordinary, everyday meaning to the word in question, rather than a statutory definition.

Following this general approach, we concluded in this case that a reasonable person would be unlikely to think of an RAF base as an airport.

We noted that in the section of the policy that listed exclusions, the insurer had listed the word 'airport' next to 'railway'. We thought this significant, as it suggested these exclusions had a common theme of public transport, rather than of high-risk locations, as the insurer had suggested.

We concluded that the ordinary meaning of 'airport' was a narrow one that did not include an RAF base. So we said the insurer could not reasonably decline Mr G's claim by using an exclusion that applied to airports.

We had already established, at an early stage of our investigation, that any claim would be likely to exceed £100,000, which is the statutory limit on any award we are able to make. So before we had finished investigating the complaint, we contacted both Mr G and the insurer. We explained that if we upheld the complaint, we had no power to require the insurer to pay any sum over that £100,000 limit, although we could recommend that it should do so. The insurer confirmed that it would pay any claim in full, and it did that when we subsequently upheld Mr G's complaint.

ISSUE 75: JANUARY/FEBRUARY 2009

75/6   when part of a matching bathroom suite is damaged—policyholder asks insurer to contribute to cost of an entire new suite

The basin in Mrs N's bathroom was accidentally damaged, so she rang her insurer to check she was covered for the cost of replacing it. The basin was part of a matching suite and she was worried she might not find a new basin that looked the same as the rest of the suite.

The insurer later told us it outlined what its normal approach would be where a matching item could not be obtained. It said it explained to Mrs N that it would meet the full cost of replacing the damaged item. It would probably also make a contribution towards the cost of replacing the undamaged items in the bathroom suite. Its contribution was likely to be about 50% of the cost. This approach is the one we would usually expect an insurer to take in such circumstances.

Mrs N said the insurer had told her it was 'highly unlikely' an exact replacement could be obtained for her basin. She should therefore get a quotation for a new bathroom suite.

A few days after phoning the insurer, Mrs N visited a bathroom supplier and obtained a quotation. Meanwhile, the insurer's representative arranged to inspect the damaged basin. He told Mrs N he would establish whether or not an identical replacement could be sourced, and he would then report back to the insurer.

Before the representative had submitted his report, and without contacting the insurer again, Mrs N went ahead and bought a new bathroom suite. She then put in a claim for the full cost of the new basin and for half the cost of the rest of the suite.

The insurer told her it would only meet the part of her claim that related to the basin. It said its representative had managed to find an identical replacement for the damaged basin. There had therefore been no need for her to replace the whole suite.

Mrs N complained that the insurer was being unreasonable, and in due course she referred the matter to us.

Complaint not upheld

Mrs N was adamant that the insurer had said it was 'highly unlikely' that an exact replacement could be found. She said it was only because the insurer was so certain about this that she had bought the new bathroom suite.

We listened to the insurer's tape recording of its conversations with Mrs N. The insurer had said it was unlikely that a new basin could be found that matched the remaining items in the suite. However, the insurer had also stressed that its representative would look into this for her. The insurer made it very clear that she should wait for the representative to report back. She should then contact the insurer again before taking things any further.

We looked at the length of time the insurer and its representative had taken to progress matters. We did not think this was at all unreasonable. And there was nothing to suggest that the insurer had misled Mrs M in any way, either about what the policy covered or about how it would deal with her claim.

We said the insurer had not acted unreasonably, in the circumstances, and we did not uphold the complaint.

75/7 policyholder replaces entire bathroom suite when insurer fails to let her know if a matching replacement can be obtained for her damaged bath

Miss A contacted her insurer after her bath was badly damaged. The insurer said its representative would inspect the bath. He would then find out if it was possible to replace it with a new bath that matched the rest of her bathroom suite.

The insurer's representative failed to turn up on the day he had agreed to visit Miss A at home. The insurer apologised and arranged a new appointment for a couple of weeks later. Unfortunately, the representative again failed to turn up.

By this time, Miss A was getting very annoyed at the insurer's apparent lack of progress with her claim. She visited a number of suppliers to try and find a suitable bath herself. However, she concluded that nothing was available that was even an approximate match to the rest of her bathroom suite. She therefore ordered and paid for an entirely new suite and put in a claim for the total cost.

The insurer told her that, under the terms of her policy, she was only entitled to the cost of replacing her bath. It refused to pay for more than that and it dismissed her complaint that she had been unfairly treated. Miss A then came to us.

Complaint upheld

The insurer maintained that it had made a fair offer in the circumstances. It said that Miss A had not given it the opportunity to establish whether it could obtain a new bath that matched the rest of her bathroom suite. If that was possible, then there would be no need for her to replace the entire suite.

We noted that the insurer's representative had twice failed to keep an appointment to inspect the damaged bath. And on neither of these occasions had anyone contacted Miss A to let her know the appointment was cancelled.

We listened to the insurer's tape recordings of its conversations with Miss A. These showed it had discussed very little with her other than the arrangements for the representative to visit her. She was certainly not given any clear explanation of how her claim would be progressed.

We said the insurer should pay Miss A an amount equal to the full value of the replacement bath. It should also pay 50% of the value of the other items in the new bathroom suite. We explained that this was in line with what is generally regarded as good practice in such cases, and Miss A was happy to accept.

75/8 insurer refuses claim for a lost designer watch because policyholder cannot provide any proof of ownership

Mr B made a claim under his contents policy for the cost of replacing his designer watch. He said he lost the watch while on a mountain-walking trip one weekend. As soon as he got home he reported the loss to the police and obtained a crime reference number.

His policy covered personal belongings in and away from his home. He told the insurer that the watch had been worth over £1,800. However, he was aware that his policy had a limit of £1,500 for single items. He had therefore managed to find and buy a replacement that was similar in style to the watch he had lost, but that only cost £1,450.

The insurer said it needed to establish his ownership of the lost watch before it could consider the claim. It asked to see the original receipt. Mr B said he did not have a receipt because the watch had been a gift. He thought it highly unlikely that the friend who gave him the watch would still have the receipt. In any event, he did not feel he could ask her about it.

When the insurer said it was unable to take matters further without the receipt, Mr B complained to us.

We looked in detail at the contents policy. Like many such policies, it included a section about the need for policyholders to provide proof of ownership when making a claim.

We reminded the insurer that possession of a receipt was not the only means of establishing ownership. If Mr B was unable to ask his friend for the receipt—or for a copy of her credit card statement showing the purchase of the watch—he might be able to produce the guarantee or the box the watch had come in. Or he might have a photograph that clearly showed him wearing the watch.

We contacted Mr B and asked if he could provide any such evidence. A few days later he wrote to tell us he was withdrawing his complaint and no longer wished to pursue the matter.

75/9 after claiming for a damaged carpet, policyholder questions insurer's assessment of its replacement value and the offer of a reduced cash settlement

Mr and Mrs K's living room carpet was badly damaged after a substantial amount of water came through the ceiling from the flat above. After contacting the firm that had supplied the carpet and obtaining a quotation for replacing it, they rang their contents insurer.

The insurer arranged for a loss assessor to inspect the damaged carpet. The loss assessor agreed that the carpet would have to be replaced. However, he said the quotation the couple had obtained was too high.

Under the terms of the policy, the insurer could decide whether to make a cash payment to the policyholder or to source the replacement item itself. In this case, the insurer decided to source the replacement itself. It sent Mr and Mrs K a letter authorising them to visit a specific supplier and select a new carpet. The insurer would then settle the bill direct with the supplier.

The couple visited the supplier in question and looked at the carpets that were available. They were concerned that the insurer had set them an overall price limit that was much lower than they thought it should have been. But in any event, the supplier had no carpets of a similar colour to the one that had been damaged.

Mr and Mrs K then contacted the insurer. They said the supplier they had visited had nothing suitable for them. The retailer who supplied their original carpet had assured them it was of a particularly good quality because of the density of the pile. They therefore said the insurer should increase the amount it was prepared to pay for a replacement. They asked the insurer to pay this amount direct to them, as a cash settlement. They would then find a suitable replacement themselves, from their own choice of supplier.

The insurer said the replacement value of the carpet was based on what the loss assessor considered appropriate. He had examined the damaged carpet carefully and had not found it to be of an especially high quality. The insurer was therefore not prepared to offer more than the amount it had already stated. And it said that any cash settlement would be 25% less than that amount. This was because it would have been able to obtain the carpet at a reduced cost if the couple had used its preferred supplier.

Unable to reach agreement with the insurer, Mr and Mrs K brought their complaint to us.

Complaint upheld

When we looked into the case in detail, we found that the quality of Mr and Mrs K's carpet was not as high as their supplier had led them to believe. They were naturally very disappointed to learn this, as it suggested they had received a poor deal when they bought it. However, we considered that the replacement value they were offered was reasonable.

Taking into account all the circumstances of this dispute, including the couple's increasingly difficult relations with the insurer, we said the insurer should make a cash settlement. The amount should be sufficient for Mr and Mrs K to obtain, from a supplier of their own choice, a new carpet of the same quality as the one that was damaged. The insurer could not deduct the 25% reduction it would have got from its own supplier.

75/10   **policyholder told by insurer to replace stolen antique jewellery by selecting new items from a limited list of high-street retailers**

Mrs W returned home from work one evening to find that someone had broken in and stolen some of her possessions, including several small items of antique jewellery.

When she rang her insurer, it confirmed that it would meet her claim. She told the insurer that she was particularly distressed over the loss of the antique jewellery. She was aware that the individual items were not especially valuable in themselves. However, they were unusual pieces that had been passed down in her family over four or five generations.

A few days later the insurer wrote to Mrs W about her claim. She was very upset when she read the letter, which listed a couple of well-known high-street jewellers and a department store. The insurer told her to obtain replacements for the stolen jewellery at any of the shops on the list.

Mrs W told the insurer that its response to her claim was unacceptable. She said it was 'ludicrous' to suggest that the retailers it had listed could supply suitable replacements for her antique jewellery.

Initially, the insurer refused to change its stance. Mrs W said she wanted a cash settlement, so that she could choose where to shop. She said this was the only way she would have any chance of finding jewellery of a similar style and quality to the stolen items.

Eventually, the insurer agreed to her request. However, it said the amount would be 20% less than the amount it had already agreed her claim was worth. This was because its initial offer reflected the preferential terms it could obtain from the suppliers on its list. Mrs W then referred her complaint to us.

Complaint upheld

We told the insurer we were surprised to learn of the approach it had taken in this case. Our views on what is reasonable—where an insurer has to decide whether to repair or replace an item, or offer a cash settlement—are well-established. Indeed this topic featured in an *Ombudsman News* article as long ago as October 2001 (issue 10).

We upheld Mrs W's complaint. We told the insurer to pay her a cash settlement equal to the full cost of replacing the jewellery. We said it should not deduct the 20% discount that it could get from its preferred suppliers. We said it should also pay Mrs W a modest sum to reflect the distress and inconvenience she had been caused by its poor handling of her claim.

ISSUE 76: MARCH/APRIL 2009

76/8   **travel insurer refused to pay cancellation claim on grounds that consumer had not been eligible for cover under the policy**

To celebrate her retirement, Mrs G booked a holiday cruise to the Baltic States and asked her friend, Mrs M, to accompany her. The two women had worked together for many years until Mrs M had moved away from the UK some eighteen months earlier to live with her family in Spain.

Sadly, two weeks before the start of the cruise, Mrs G received a phone call from Mrs M's son, telling her his mother had suffered a fatal heart attack. Mrs G then cancelled the holiday.

When she booked the cruise at the travel agent she had also arranged travel insurance for herself and Mrs M. So in due course she put in a claim to cover the costs she incurred in cancelling the trip. She also passed on the policy details to Mrs M's son, Mr M, so he could claim on behalf of his late mother.

However, the insurer refused to meet Mr M's claim. It said Mrs M had not been eligible for cover as she had been living outside the UK for more than 12 months at the time the policy was taken out.

The insurer said it did not provide cover for people who lived outside the UK, as they might use the travel policy as a cheap means of obtaining medical insurance, rather than as cover for any emergencies that might arise in relation to a holiday.

When the insurer rejected Mr M's complaint about its refusal to meet the claim, he referred it to us.

Complaint upheld

At the time the policy was sold, travel agents did not fall within the scope of statutory financial services regulation. However, it was generally accepted as good industry practice that when travel agents acted on behalf of an insurer, the insurer was responsible for the way in which travel agents marketed and sold insurance policies.

In this instance, when the travel agent completed the application form for Mrs G, he entered her name as 'the lead passenger'—and gave her address. The only information entered on the form about Mrs M was her name. We found no evidence that either the travel agent or the insurer had asked for her address or checked whether she was eligible for cover under the policy.

We were satisfied that Mrs M had genuinely been seeking insurance to cover a holiday. There was nothing to suggest she had been intending to use the policy to obtain medical cover more cheaply than she would have been able to get it (as a Spanish resident) if she had applied for a medical insurance policy. We upheld the complaint and said that—in the circumstances—the fair and reasonable outcome was for the insurer to pay the claim.

76/9   travel insurer turns down claim for cost of cancellation as policy did not come into force before the holiday began

In mid-October Miss W booked a holiday to Tenerife, due to depart a month later on 17 November. She was planning several other foreign trips over the following 12 months, so she told the travel agent she would not take the single-trip insurance policy it offered.

Instead, she contacted an insurer direct and bought an annual travel policy. This was set up to come into effect from 17 November—the date of her departure to Tenerife. Like most travel policies, the benefits it provided included cover against cancellation.

On 1 November, Miss W visited her doctor as she was feeling very unwell. The doctor diagnosed a 'cardiac arrhythmia'. When Miss W mentioned her forthcoming holiday, the doctor told her that, in the circumstances, it might not be wise to travel abroad. Miss W therefore cancelled the holiday and put in a claim under her travel policy.

The insurer told her it could not meet the claim, as her policy had not yet come into force. Miss W was very upset to learn this and she complained that it was on the advice of the insurer itself that she had agreed the start date for the policy.

She said that the insurer knew the date of her forthcoming holiday, so it should have explained that there was a risk in having a policy that did not come into force until the day that holiday began. If it had done so, she would have insisted on an earlier start date.

The insurer would not discuss the matter further with her but simply repeated that it would not pay the claim. Miss W then referred the matter to us.

Complaint upheld

In order to decide this case we had to establish whether the insurer had made Miss W sufficiently aware that, by buying a policy that did not start until the actual day of her holiday, she would not be covered if she had to cancel her trip.

We obtained a tape recording of Miss W's initial phone conversation with the insurer, when the policy had been arranged. It was clear from this that she had told the insurer she was going to Tenerife on 17 November—and that the representative had suggested that would be a suitable start date for the policy.

While it could not be said that the representative had actually 'advised' Miss W to have a policy that started on that date, he had not made any attempt to explain the implications of not having insurance in place before then.

When we raised this with the insurer, it said the policy documents made it clear that the policyholder would not be covered if the holiday was cancelled before the policy came into force.

However, in our view the insurer had not done enough to highlight to Miss W the risk that she was taking. We thought it unlikely that she would have agreed to the start date suggested by the insurer if she had understood this risk.

We told the insurer to treat the claim as if the policy had been in force on the date when Miss W cancelled her holiday. We said it should add interest to any payment due under the policy.

76/10   **travel insurer refuses to pay claim for cancellation of holiday on ill-health grounds**

On 10 September, three weeks before he was due to go on holiday to Greece, Mr C phoned an insurer to arrange some travel insurance.

During that call, the insurer read out a list of medical conditions and asked Mr C if he had ever suffered from any of them. It also asked if he was aware of 'any condition that could reasonably be expected to affect your health during the period of the policy?' Mr C answered 'no' to both questions and the insurer issued him with a travel policy.

Unfortunately, a week before his holiday was due to begin, Mr C had to cancel it. He did this on the advice of his GP—as he had developed a severe chest infection.

However, the insurer rejected Mr C's claim. It said he must have been aware he had the illness that led to the cancellation at the time he applied for the policy—but he had failed to disclose it.

Mr C thought the insurer was being unreasonable. At the time he bought the policy, he had a mild cough. This was not one of the medical conditions in the list that the insurer had read out to him over the phone. And he did not agree that he should have known—at the time of his call—that it might develop into a more serious condition that would affect his holiday.

When the insurer refused to reconsider its position, Mr C came to us.

Complaint upheld

We established that Mr C's cough began a day or two before he phoned the insurer to arrange his travel policy. However, it had not at that time seemed to him to be anything worth worrying about.

It was only around a week later—on 17 September—that Mr C decided to see his GP, as his cough was not getting any better. The GP prescribed medication and said he expected Mr C's condition would start to improve within a few days.

However, on 26 September Mr C went back to his doctor and reported that he was still feeling far from well. The doctor prescribed stronger antibiotics and arranged for Mr C to have a chest x-ray. He also suggested that it might not be a good idea for Mr C to travel. Mr C cancelled his trip later that day.

In our view, there was no reason why—at the time he applied for the policy—Mr C should have told the insurer about his cough. He would only have needed to mention it if he knew there was a realistic possibility that the cough would develop into something serious enough to threaten his holiday plans. The evidence did not suggest that this was the case.

We also questioned whether it would have made any difference to the cover the insurer provided if Mr C had mentioned his cough when he applied for the policy. We thought this unlikely, as there had been nothing at that stage to indicate that Mr C was suffering from anything more than a minor seasonal ailment.

We therefore upheld the complaint and told the insurer to deal with Mr C's claim—adding interest to any payment it made.

76/11   **travel insurer accepted premium intended to provide cover for pre-existing conditions but failed to ensure the policy was properly in force**

Mr and Mrs K were given a 'free' annual travel insurance policy as one of the benefits of their bank account. However, when they checked through the policy's terms and conditions before booking a holiday, they found that they were not covered for their 'pre-existing' medical conditions.

Anxious to ensure that they had adequate insurance in place before their trip, Mrs K contacted a different insurer. She was quoted just over £200 to cover their pre-existing conditions and she paid this amount over the phone, using her debit card.

Unfortunately, while the couple were on holiday, Mrs K was taken seriously ill and had to spend several days in hospital. When she returned home she put in a claim to the insurer, backed up by a medical certificate that showed her illness had been connected to one of the pre-existing conditions for which she had sought cover.

However, the insurer turned down the claim. It said the cover for pre-existing conditions did not operate as an independent policy but was only available as an 'add-on' for customers who also bought the insurer's 'base' travel insurance. As the couple had not bought the 'base' cover, they did not have a valid policy under which they could make a claim.

Mrs K complained that the insurer had failed to make it clear that she needed to buy the 'base' cover. She pointed out that she would hardly have spent 'so much money' to cover the pre-existing conditions if she had realised this cover was 'worthless' on its own. The insurer then offered to refund the premium she had paid. However, it still refused to meet the claim, so Mrs K came to us.

Complaint upheld

We asked the insurer to let us have its tape recording of the phone conversation during which Mrs K arranged the cover for pre-existing medical conditions. We noted from this that the insurer's representative had mentioned the 'base' cover. However, he had not made it clear that the cover for pre-existing conditions only operated in conjunction with that 'base' cover.

The insurer maintained that it had explained this point over the phone. It also said that it had sent Mr and Mrs K a letter which 'clearly explained' that they needed to buy the 'base' cover. We asked for a copy of the letter in question, but did not agree that it was clear. Overall, we were not at all surprised that Mr and Mrs K had thought they had adequate cover in place.

We told the insurer that we did not consider it had done enough to make Mr and Mrs K aware that the cover for pre-existing conditions only came into force if they also bought the 'base' policy. We said that, in any event, the insurer should not have put itself in a position where it might be accepting premiums without providing any valid cover.

We said the insurer should accept and pay Mr and Mrs K's claim—subject to the policy terms and conditions and taking account of the premium the couple would have paid for the 'base' policy, if they had realised they had to do this.

76/12   consumer obtains a 'free' travel policy when she applies for a credit card—and later complains that extent of the insurance cover was not clearly explained

When Mrs J applied successfully to her bank for a credit card, she was also given a 'free' annual travel insurance policy. The policy provided cover for Mrs J and—as a concession—it also covered 'a spouse or partner' when that person was travelling with her.

Eighteen months later, while travelling in South Africa on his own, Mrs J's husband suffered a heart attack and incurred substantial medical expenses. He subsequently made a claim on his wife's annual travel policy. This was turned down on the grounds that he was only covered when he and his wife were travelling together.

Mrs J then complained to her bank. She said that when she had obtained the credit card, she had been led to believe that her husband would benefit from the 'free' travel insurance, even when he was travelling on his own.

The bank rejected this complaint. It insisted that it had not misinformed her in any way her about the nature of the travel policy and the cover it provided. Mrs J then referred her complaint to us.

Complaint not upheld

When we discussed the complaint with her, Mrs J admitted that neither she nor her husband had been entirely sure if he was covered by the policy when travelling by himself. However, she insisted that the bank should have explained the position more clearly when it offered her the policy.

In our view, the policy documents and all the accompanying literature made it perfectly clear that the card-holder's spouse or partner was covered only when travelling with the card-holder.

It was not at all unusual for a policy of this type to extend limited cover to a spouse or partner, so this was not a feature that needed to be specially highlighted. We concluded that the bank had not misled Mrs J about the extent of the cover and we did not uphold the complaint.

ISSUE 77: MAY/JUNE 2009

77/5   private medical insurer refuses to pay claim for treatment undertaken while policyholder was abroad

While she was working temporarily in Portugal, Mrs J was referred to a medical consultant as she had been suffering from a persistent sore throat. Concerned that she might have a form of cancer, the consultant recommended that she should undergo a biopsy *'as soon as possible'*.

This procedure was carried out ten days later, in Portugal, and Mrs J put in a claim to her medical insurer. However, the insurer refused to pay out. It said she was only covered for medical treatment outside the UK if it was required as a result of a '*medical emergency*'. The insurer did not consider this case to have been a medical emergency.

Mrs J thought this was unfair. She complained to the insurer, saying it had failed to take into account the consultant's '*expert opinion that immediate action was required*'.

In response, the insurer pointed to the fact that the biopsy had not taken place until ten days after she had seen the consultant. The insurer added that, in its view, it would not have been particularly difficult for Mrs J to have returned home, so that the biopsy could be carried out in the UK. Flights could be arranged at short notice and at a relatively low cost.

Mrs J then referred her complaint to us.

Complaint upheld in part

We noted that the policy terms and conditions clearly excluded medical treatment that was undertaken outside the UK, except in an emergency. The exact meaning of '*emergency*' was not defined, but (as is normal in such circumstances) could be taken to have its ordinary, everyday meaning.

We noted the Portuguese consultant's opinion that Mrs J needed a biopsy in order to establish whether or not she had cancer. There was clearly some urgency about carrying out the procedure. However, we noted that the consultant had said that action was required '*as soon as possible*', not immediately.

The biopsy had taken place ten days after Mrs J had first consulted him. Given the timescale involved, we concluded on balance that the situation had not been a '*medical emergency*'.

However, we noted that if Mrs J had returned to the UK to have the biopsy, the insurer would have been obliged to pay for it, under the terms of the policy.

We said that the fair and reasonable outcome in this case was for the insurer to pay Mrs J the amount she would have been charged for the biopsy in the UK. This was, in fact, considerably less than the amount she had actually paid.

77/6 private medical insurer refuses to pay the full cost of a consultation with a specialist who is not on its approved list

Mrs C, who was in her 60s, was experiencing increasing problems with mobility. She had private medical insurance and her GP decided to refer her to Mr Q, a consultant at the local hospital.

Before confirming the date of her appointment, Mrs C contacted her insurer to get authorisation. She was taken aback when the insurer said it would not pay for her to see Mr Q. The insurer explained that although her policy covered the costs of a consultation with a specialist, that specialist would have to be chosen from those on its approved list.

The insurer sent her its list of approved consultants and suggested she should ask her GP to refer her to one of them. However, Mrs C discovered that none of these consultants were based in her home town—or even within what she felt was reasonable travelling distance. She therefore contacted the insurer again.

Mrs C explained that visiting any of the consultants on its list would entail a lengthy journey for her. She said she would find this difficult—not only because of her mobility problems but also because she suffered from incontinence.

The insurer told Mrs C that it appreciated the particular problems she faced. However, it said that Mr Q's fees were higher than those of the consultants on its list.

The insurer offered to pay her an additional amount, in recognition of any distress or inconvenience caused by its handling of the matter. However, it insisted that it was unable to meet the cost of a consultation with Mr Q. Mrs C then referred her complaint to us.

Complaint upheld

We noted that over that past year or so, the insurer had been gradually reducing its list of approved consultants. In our view, this left Mrs C in a position where she was unable to receive the full benefit of her policy. Her medical condition was covered, but none of the consultants on the insurer's list were within reasonable travelling distance for her.

Our enquiries suggested that Mr Q's fees were not particularly high, when compared to the fees charged by other consultants in the area. So we said that in these particular circumstances, the insurer should pay her the amount it would cost to see one of its approved consultants. She could then use that sum to see Mr Q at her local hospital.

77/7   private medical insurer refuses to authorise the ongoing use of a drug it considers to be 'experimental'

After being diagnosed with cancer in 2004, Mr J successfully underwent a course of chemotherapy. Within a year he was in remission and able to return full-time to his job as a draftsman for a large construction firm.

Unfortunately, in April 2008 he suffered a relapse. His specialist recommended a further course of chemotherapy, using a different drug, and Mr J's private medical insurer agreed to meet the cost of this treatment.

By August of that year, Mr J was again in remission. However, his consultant recommended that '*in order to achieve complete remission . . . to remove residual disease . . .* ' he should continue receiving infusions of the same drug, at three-monthly intervals, for an initial period of 12 months.

Before undertaking this treatment, Mr J contacted his insurer. It had not crossed his mind that there would be any difficulty in obtaining the insurer's authorisation. However, the insurer said it was unable to pay for the proposed treatment. It told him it did not think the use of this particular drug would have any impact on his underlying condition, which had now become '*chronic*'.

It also said that it considered the use of the drug in question for treatment after remission was '*experimental*'. And it reminded him that it had written to all its policyholders in May 2005, saying it was withdrawing funding for '*experimental*' treatment.

Mr J told the insurer he thought its attitude was '*unreasonable*'. He pointed out that his consultant had told him the proposed treatment was '*effective, recognised and authorised for use*' in treating his particular condition. However, the insurer still insisted that it was unable to fund the treatment. Mr J then brought his complaint to us.

Complaint upheld

We noted that the policy explicitly covered treatment, '*intended to stabilise and bring under control a chronic condition*'. However, there was also an exclusion that clearly stated the insurer would not pay for '*the use of a drug or treatment which has not been established as being effective or which is experimental*'.

The insurer was committed to reimburse the cost of medical treatment covered by the policy and it was for the policyholder's consultant, not the insurer, to decide the appropriate treatment. What we needed to do was to determine whether the insurer had applied the policy exclusion fairly and reasonably, in all the circumstances of this particular case.

We noted that the drug in question was one that the insurer mentioned in its letter to policyholders of May 2005, when it said it was withdrawing funding for treatment using certain types of drug. However, the insurer had authorised and paid for Mr J's treatment using that same drug in April 2008.

We looked at medical evidence, provided by both the insurer and by Mr J's consultant, concerning the use of the drug in question. We found the drug was widely considered to be a well-established and effective treatment for patients in a similar situation to Mr J. The evidence suggested that the chance of complete remission after treatment was up to 10%, while there was a 60% chance of partial remission.

We took the view that, on the balance of the evidence, the insurer should authorise the use of the drug in this case. The evidence on its use and potential effectiveness indicated that it was no longer experimental—and that it could improve, or at least stabilise, Mr J's condition.

We told the insurer that it should pay for the proposed course of treatment, if Mr J decided to proceed with it. We also said the insurer could exclude the cost of any treatment, medical attention or surgery that might arise in any future claims from Mr J, if they came about as a consequence of his undergoing treatment with this drug.

77/8   private medical insurer refuses to authorise payment for surgical procedure it says is 'unproven'

After being referred to a consultant surgeon, Mr E was told he needed prostate surgery. He rang his insurer to obtain authorisation and was told the procedure was covered by his policy. A few days later, Mr E received a letter confirming the insurer's authorisation.

The exact procedure that Mr E's surgeon planned to carry out was to be undertaken as a robot-assisted operation. The surgeon was aware that some insurers had declined to cover this particular procedure in the past. So even though he knew Mr E had already obtained authorisation, the surgeon told him he would contact the insurer. He wanted to be certain it was fully aware of what was proposed.

Mr E then decided he ought to phone the insurer again himself, just to check the position. Initially, he was told that the exact procedure he was having was covered by his policy. Later the same day, however, the insurer rang Mr E to say it would not be able to pay the full cost of the procedure.

The insurer told Mr E that the proposed treatment was considered to be *'experimental or unproven'*, so it was not covered by the policy. The insurer was prepared to pay an amount *'equivalent to the cost of the procedure based on conventional treatment'*. But it pointed out that there would probably still be a shortfall, which would be Mr E's responsibility.

Very unhappy with this outcome, Mr E complained to the insurer that it had *'reneged'* on its agreement. He disagreed with the insurer's view that the robot-assisted procedure was *'experimental'*, and he said he understood the procedure was widely used in many NHS hospitals.

In its response, the insurer said it accepted it *'could have been more clear about exactly what costs were covered'*. It said it would therefore increase the sum it had already agreed to pay towards the cost of his surgery. However, it still insisted that it was unable to cover the full cost of a robot-assisted procedure.

Mr E thought it unacceptable that he would still have to pay a certain amount towards a procedure that—in his view—should be fully covered by his policy. He therefore brought his complaint to us.

Complaint not upheld

To decide the complaint, we needed to determine whether the robot-assisted procedure was *'experimental and/or unproven'*, and whether the insurer had acted fairly and reasonably by offering to pay no more than the cost of an equivalent conventional procedure.

We noted that the policy wording clearly set out that it would not pay for *'treatment which has not been established as being effective or which is experimental'*.

In assessing the claim, the insurer had referred to guidance issued by NICE (The National Institute for Health and Clinical Excellence). This suggested it was not yet clear whether a robot-assisted procedure offered any advantage over a conventional procedure.

NICE is an independent organisation providing national guidance on areas such as public health, treatment regimes, procedures within the NHS, and clinical practice.

Given the status of NICE, we thought it reasonable for the insurer to take its findings into account.

The insurer had offered to pay Mr E an amount equivalent to the cost of undergoing a conventional procedure, together with an additional sum in recognition of the confusion it had caused by its poor handling of the claim. We told him we thought this was fair and reasonable, in all the circumstances of the case.

ISSUE 79: SEPTEMBER/OCTOBER 2009

79/6   motor insurer rejects claim for repair on grounds that damage resulted from 'normal wear and tear'

Mr K's insurer arranged for one of its approved repairers to carry out some remedial work on his car, after it was involved in an accident. When the car was returned to him, Mr K was concerned to find it had developed a strange creaking noise.

At the insurer's request, the repairer took the car back for inspection but was unable to establish what was causing the problem. The insurer then asked an independent motor engineer to inspect the car. He, too, was unable to say what was causing the creaking noise. Finally, the insurer suggested that Mr K should ask his local car dealer to try to pinpoint the cause of the problem.

The dealer told Mr K the noise was related to damage sustained in the accident, so he agreed it should carry out additional repairs to resolve the matter. The bill for this work came to £1,616.58. Mr K settled up with the garage and then put in a claim.

He was very surprised when the insurer refused to reimburse him. It told him he should have obtained its approval before having the work done. And it said that, in the view of the independent motor engineer, the damage his dealer had rectified was not caused by the accident but had come about through '*normal wear and tear*'. It was therefore not covered by the policy.

Mr K strongly disputed this and the insurer eventually offered him £400 as '*a gesture of goodwill*'. However, it refused to pay him more than this, so Mr K brought his complaint to us.

Complaint upheld

We agreed with the insurer that Mr K should have obtained its approval before asking his dealer to carry out the additional work. However, the main issue here was whether the damage put right by the dealer had been caused by the accident, or through normal wear and tear.

The report prepared for the insurer by the independent engineer did not seem to us to be particularly conclusive. However, it appeared to indicate that it was more likely than not that the creaking arose because of the accident. We therefore upheld the complaint and said the fair and reasonable outcome was for the insurer to reimburse Mr K for the cost of the additional work.

79/7 consumer complains of poor workmanship by motor insurer's approved repairer

Mrs G asked her insurer if she could get her car repaired by her local dealer, after the car's offside rear body panel and door were badly damaged in an accident. However, the insurer said it would arrange for one of its approved repairers to carry out the necessary work. She later told us she had been assured that the quality of the workmanship would be '*as good*' as that provided by her local dealer—and the parts and materials used would be '*of the same high standard*'.

Unfortunately, Mrs G was not at all happy with the quality of the repair work. And she complained to her insurer that additional damage had appeared, in the form of scratch marks that had not been present before the car went in for repair.

Although the insurer arranged for its approved repairer to carry out further remedial work, the scratch marks were still evident when the car was returned to Mrs G. And she established that the paint used for the re-spray was not '*dealership-approved*', as it was required to be under the terms of the paintwork warranty she held with the dealer.

The insurer was at first reluctant to accept that Mrs G still had any grounds for complaint. Eventually, it agreed that the paint had not been of the required standard and it offered Mrs G £100 compensation. She thought this inadequate, as she had asked the insurer to pay for the whole car to be re-sprayed. She therefore referred the complaint to us.

Complaint upheld

We found the standard of the work carried out by the insurer's repairer was very poor—and we did not think the insurer had treated Mrs G fairly when dealing with her claim.

We said the insurer should pay for the repair work to be rectified at a car-body shop approved by Mrs G's dealer. The work would be inspected when completed and would include removing the paintwork from the affected areas and re-spraying those areas using dealer-approved paint. The rest of the car would be machine-buffed and polished with a paint-protection lacquer to seal the paint and provide a high-gloss finish.

In view of the distress and inconvenience caused by the insurer's poor handling of the claim, we said it should also pay Mrs G £200.

79/8 consumer complains of poor standard of work by motor insurer's repairer after her car was involved in an accident

Mrs J had an accident while driving home from work one evening. Her car was badly damaged and the necessary repair work was carried out by a repairer approved by her insurer. However, when the car was returned to her, Mrs J complained that the brakes and clutch appeared to be faulty.

She told the insurer this must have been the result of damage caused while the car was being repaired. She was unable to produce any evidence of this, but the insurer agreed to cover the cost of additional repair work, as a gesture of goodwill.

Soon after this work was completed, Mrs J asked her local garage to carry out repairs to the car's braking system, suspension and tyres—at a total cost of £1,778.

She then put in a claim for this amount to her insurer. She said that problems had persisted even after the car had gone back to the insurer's repairer for a second time. She said she had lost faith in the repairer's ability to do the work to an acceptable standard, so had asked her local garage to '*get the car back to the condition it had been in before the accident*'.

Mrs J said her garage had '*confirmed*' that all the work it had carried out on the car was related to the accident—and that the cost would be covered by her policy. However, the insurer refused to meet the claim. Mrs J then came to us.

Complaint not upheld

Mrs J told us the insurer's repairer had '*not made a proper assessment of the structural and mechanical damage*' and had '*failed to restore the car to its pre-accident condition*'. She said the extent of the work her own garage had subsequently carried out '*proved*' that the initial repair job had not been done properly.

We looked at the details of Mrs J's claim for the additional repairs. We also examined the report prepared after the accident by an engineer appointed by the insurer. We found nothing to back up Mrs J's assertion that the damage had not been properly assessed at the outset. And there was nothing to suggest that the work subsequently carried out by Mrs J's garage was related to damage sustained in the accident.

As Mrs J had insisted that her garage '*confirmed*' its work was related to the accident, we asked her to obtain a report from the garage. She told us this was not possible. In the absence of any evidence to support her claim, we did not uphold her complaint.

79/9 consumer dissatisfied with quality of work provided by insurer's repairer after car accident

Mr A was very dissatisfied with the standard of the repairs carried out on his car after it was damaged in an accident. The insurer said it would arrange for its approved repairer to take the car in again and carry out further work. However, Mr A said he had no confidence that the repairer would complete the work successfully.

So after arranging an inspection of the car and agreeing details of the work still outstanding, the insurer said it would pay for Mr A's local garage to carry out these remaining repairs.

Once the work was completed, Mr A settled the bill and put in a claim to the insurer. However, it refused to reimburse him for the full amount. It pointed out that one of the items on the invoice related to repairs to the car bonnet—and this was not on the list of outstanding repairs that it had agreed.

Mr A argued that the insurer was liable to meet the cost of *all* the repairs, as they all related to the accident. The insurer did not agree, so Mr A brought the dispute to us.

Complaint not upheld

The insurer had agreed with Mr A that the original repairs were not completed to an acceptable standard. And it had responded to his concerns by agreeing to pay for an alternative repairer—of his choosing—to put matters right.

Before the additional work was undertaken, the insurer had asked one of its technicians and a representative of Mr A's local garage to inspect the car together and produce a detailed list of the outstanding work. We thought it unlikely that any damage to the car's bonnet would have been overlooked—either during this inspection or when Mr A checked through the list before agreeing it with the insurer.

But in any event, we found no evidence to suggest that the bonnet of the car had been damaged in the accident. We therefore agreed that the insurer should not reimburse Mr A for this part of his claim.

79/10 insurer refuses to pay claim for theft of car because consumer had not disclosed the modifications made to his vehicle

Mr T's car was stolen from the street where he parked it while he was visiting his local gym. He put in a claim under his motor policy and later told us he was '*totally shocked*' when his insurer refused to pay out.

The insurer said it was clear from the information Mr T provided in his claim that the car had been modified. However, he had never notified the insurer of any modifications and he had answered '*no*', when asked on the proposal form if he had modified or altered the car.

The insurer had therefore '*voided*' his policy (in effect treating it as though it had never existed) and it told Mr T he was not covered for the theft. Mr T complained that he was being treated unfairly, but the insurer would not alter its view, so he came to us.

Complaint upheld

Mr T confirmed that he had added '*a satnav unit, Bluetooth kit, Playstation and CD changer*'. However, he said he regarded these as '*simple additions, not modifications*'.

We looked at the proposal form that Mr T had completed when applying for his policy. This included a question headed '*Modifications*', asking if there had been '*any changes to the engine, plus any cosmetic changes to the bodywork, suspension, wheels or brakes*'. Mr T had answered '*no*'.

We accepted the insurer's point that the changes Mr T had made could well have made his car more attractive to thieves. However, there was nothing on the proposal form to indicate that it considered changes of this type to be '*modifications*'. We did not see that Mr T could reasonably have been expected to know, from the examples given by the insurer, that he should have answered '*yes*' to the question about modifications.

We upheld the complaint and said the insurer should settle the claim in line with the usual terms and conditions of the policy. We said it should also add interest, from the date when the car was stolen to the date when the claim was settled.

79/11 insurer refuses to pay claim for theft of car because consumer had not disclosed the modifications made to his vehicle

Mr C returned from a short business trip to find his car had been stolen from the side-road where he usually parked it, close to his house. He rang the insurer to report the theft and, while confirming the details, he mentioned that several modifications had been made to the car.

The insurer was not aware that the car had been modified in any way. It told Mr C it would never have offered him insurance if it had known about the modifications. It declared his policy '*void*' and rejected his claim. Very unhappy with this outcome, Mr C brought his complaint to us.

Complaint upheld

Mr C accepted that he had made a number of changes to his car—but he disputed the insurer's view that these changes amounted to '*modifications*'.

We looked at what the insurer had said about modifications when Mr C applied for his policy. He had completed his application online and we noted that there was a clearly-worded section asking for details of any modifications. Applicants were told to phone the insurer if they were at all unsure about the type of information they were required to provide in this section.

We then checked what Mr C had told the insurer when he reported the theft of his car. The insurer's recording of the call showed that Mr C had not had any difficulty understanding the question when asked if his car had '*any modifications*'. He had responded by detailing all the changes that had been made to his car. We therefore concluded that he had been aware these changes amounted to modifications and that he had failed to disclose them when he applied for his policy.

The insurer argued that Mr C's failure to disclose the modifications was a '*material fact*'—in other words, something that would influence an underwriter when deciding whether to offer insurance in a particular case, and the terms and conditions that should apply.

In cases where a consumer '*deliberately*' or '*recklessly*' fails to disclose a material fact, the insurer is able to '*void*' the policy (treat it as if it never existed). But if the non-disclosure was '*innocent*' or '*inadvertent*', then the insurer should re-write the insurance on the terms it would have offered—if it had known all the facts.

When we asked the insurer to provide evidence of the approach it would have adopted, if it had known the full facts in this case, it sent us a copy of its underwriting manual. This indicated that if the insurer had known about the modifications, it would still have offered to cover Mr C, but it would have increased the premium by 75%.

We had found no evidence to suggest that Mr C had acted '*deliberately*' or '*recklessly*' in failing to disclose the modifications—and we concluded that his non-disclosure was '*inadvertent*'. The premium he had paid was only a proportion of the full amount he would have paid—if the insurer had known all the facts. So we said the insurer should pay part of Mr C's claim to reflect the proportion of the (correct) premium that he had actually paid.

ISSUE 80: OCTOBER/NOVEMBER 2009

80/1   insurer rejects claim for unemployment benefit when policyholder loses her job through redundancy

When Miss J, who worked for a large high street retailer, obtained a credit card she also took out payment protection insurance (PPI). This covered her monthly repayments, should she become unemployed because of sickness, disability or redundancy.

Around the time she applied for the credit card and insurance, there was some comment in the media about her employer facing a difficult period. The retailer had recently published very disappointing financial results and there was much speculation among her colleagues about its future prospects. Miss J had therefore thought the redundancy cover offered by the policy might prove useful. However, at that stage she had no particular reason to think she would lose her job.

A few weeks after she had obtained her credit card and policy, Miss J's employer announced that it would be consulting staff about possible job losses throughout the company. Three months later, Miss J was told that her own job was one of those at risk of redundancy. And ten weeks after that, Miss J was selected for redundancy and left the company.

Shortly afterwards, Miss J submitted a claim under her payment protection policy for unemployment benefit. This was turned down, on the grounds that the policy terms excluded unemployment claims if the policyholder became '*aware of any increase in the risk of unemployment*' within 90 days of the policy's start date.

After complaining unsuccessfully to the insurer about what she thought was '*a very unfair decision*', Miss J referred her complaint to us.

Complaint upheld

We accepted that the insurer needed to limit the scope of its policy, as a safeguard against people applying for cover at a stage when they already knew they were very likely to lose their jobs. However, we took the view in this case that the exclusion was so broad that it was unfair.

On a strict reading of the exclusion, if, for example, there was any deterioration in the UK's economic environment during the first three months of the policy, then this might result in policyholders losing all unemployment cover under the policy.

If the insurer wished to exclude cover because a policyholder's knowledge or circumstances changed within the first three months of a policy, then it needed to word its exclusion very clearly—setting out what change or changes had to take place for the exclusion to apply. This had not happened in this case. The insurer also needed to ensure that consumers were made aware of the exclusion, at the time they bought the policy. Again, this had not happened here.

We considered that Miss J had acted honestly and in good faith. At the time she took out the policy, she had no particular reason to believe she was at risk of redundancy. So we said it was neither fair nor reasonable for the insurer to reject the claim.

80/2   insurer stops payment of sickness benefit on grounds that policyholder is well enough to return to work

Mr C, who was in his early 40s, worked full-time as a messenger at a large transport company. After being diagnosed with anxiety and stress-related conditions, he put in a claim for sickness benefit under his income protection policy. The insurer accepted his claim and—as his condition did not improve sufficiently for him to return to work—it continued paying him benefit over the next four years.

In line with the policy terms, at the end of that period the insurer carried out a detailed review of Mr C's situation. The assessment that his consultant provided, as part of this review, suggested there was some doubt about whether Mr C was '*truly fit to return to work*'. However, this opinion did not appear to be based on any clear medical grounds. The insurer therefore asked Mr C to undergo an independent medical examination.

The specialist who conducted this examination concluded that Mr C was fit enough to return to work—and that returning to work would be beneficial for him. So the insurer told Mr C there was '*insufficient medical evidence*' to support his '*continued inability to work as a result of a medical condition*'.

Mr C complained that it was '*unfair and unreasonable*' to stop his benefits. He said that as well as suffering from '*ongoing mental illness*', he now had '*a number of physical disorders*' that prevented him from working. Mr C was unable to provide any evidence of these *'disorders'*, so the insurer said it was unable to reconsider the matter. Mr C then brought his complaint to us.

Complaint not upheld

The issue for us to determine was whether the insurer had adequately established that Mr C's condition no longer fell within the policy's definition of *'incapacity for employment'*.

We found that the medical evidence tended to support the insurer's stance. Mr C's symptoms were not consistent with a disabling mental illness. And we noted that the independent consultant had said Mr C would benefit from returning to work.

We considered what Mr C had said about his *'physical disorders'*, but we found that the medical evidence did not suggest he had any physical symptoms that would result in his meeting the policy definition of *'incapacity for employment'*.

We concluded that the insurer had been entitled to terminate the claim, so we did not uphold the complaint.

80/3 insurer refuses to pay sickness benefits on grounds that policyholder's illness was a 'pre-existing condition'

Mr G, who was in his early 50s, was diagnosed with a serious respiratory condition. As this prevented him from working, he made a claim for sickness benefit under his payment protection insurance policy (PPI).

The insurer turned down the claim. It told Mr G he was not eligible for benefit as he had been diagnosed with respiratory problems before the policy's start date. It said he therefore *'would have been aware, or should reasonably have been aware'*, that he already had this condition when he took out the policy.

The insurer said Mr G's medical records showed that, before the policy's start date, his GP had referred him to a consultant because of a problem that would have caused the shortness of breath. This problem was known to be linked to his now more serious condition. The insurer added that the medical records showed that Mr G might already have acquired the more serious respiratory condition before he took out the policy.

Mr G disputed the insurer's conclusion. He said his GP had confirmed there were references in his medical records to the more serious condition—and these dated from *before* Mr G applied for the policy. However, the GP had not told him that he had—or might have—the more serious condition. The GP had simply noted, for his own reference, some possible causes for the problems Mr G was experiencing. Mr G had only known he had the more serious condition when the actual diagnosis was made—after the policy had started.

When the insurer said it was unable to reconsider the matter, Mr G complained to us.

Complaint upheld

After examining the evidence in this case, we were satisfied that—at the time he took out the policy—Mr G had not known he was suffering from a serious respiratory condition. We were also satisfied that he had not known that the seemingly minor symptoms he was experiencing suggested he had an illness of this nature. No definite diagnosis had been made before the policy was taken out.

And the notes made by the GP—which included speculation about several possible causes for Mr G's symptoms—had not been shown to Mr G or discussed with him.

We told the insurer that it was not appropriate in this case for it to cite the exclusion relating to *'pre-existing medical conditions'* in order to reject the claim. We said it should pay the claim, in accordance with the terms of the policy.

80/4 insurer turns down claim because consultant's description of policyholder's illness does not fall within the policy definition for that particular condition

After his GP referred him to a consultant neurologist, Mr B was diagnosed with multiple sclerosis. He put in a claim under his critical illness policy, which was designed to pay out a lump sum if he was diagnosed with one of the serious illnesses listed in the policy—and met the qualifying circumstances.

The insurer told Mr B that his condition did not fall within the definition of 'multiple sclerosis', as set out in the policy, as no definite diagnosis had yet been made. In a letter sent to Mr B's GP, the consultant had referred only to 'probable' multiple sclerosis.

A few months later the consultant saw Mr B again and gave him a definite diagnosis. The insurer had said it would review the claim if this happened, and on the basis of the medical evidence it received at this stage, it agreed to meet the claim.

The insurer said it would pay the claim from the date of the definite diagnosis. Mr B said payment should be back-dated to when he first saw the consultant. He said that if the insurer had investigated his original claim more thoroughly—and had contacted the consultant direct—then the diagnosis would have been confirmed at that point.

Unable to reach agreement with the insurer, Mr B referred his complaint to us.

Complaint not upheld

Generally speaking, the descriptions and definitions of the illnesses covered in policies of this type have been standardised across the insurance industry. We did not, therefore, need to look into this aspect of the case. The issue for us to determine was whether the insurer had acted reasonably in turning down Mr B's initial claim.

At the time he made his first claim for multiple sclerosis, there was a widely-accepted diagnostic approach within the medical profession for establishing if a patient had this condition.

The diagnostic test the consultant carried out, in accordance with this approach, showed that Mr B's multiple sclerosis was only '*probable*' at that stage. It was not until some time later that the diagnostic test confirmed the disease as '*definite*'.

We did not uphold Mr B's complaint and we explained to him why, in the circumstances, we did not think the insurer had acted unfairly in refusing to meet his initial claim.

In situations involving illnesses where such a widely-accepted diagnostic approach does not exist, we would expect insurers to use the best available medical evidence in order to establish whether a condition meets the criteria set out in the policy.

80/5 insurer refuses to pay benefits to policyholder who becomes too ill to work

Miss M, who worked full-time in a garden centre, took out a payment protection policy (PPI) when she got a loan from her bank. The policy was designed to ensure her monthly loan repayments would still be paid if she lost her job through redundancy—or developed a serious illness or disability that prevented her from working.

Some time after taking out the policy, Miss M became unwell. It was soon evident that hers was a chronic condition and she became very anxious about the effect it would have on her ability to continue in her job.

She tried to book an appointment with her GP to discuss the situation but was told she would be unable to see him for some while. He was shortly going on holiday and had no free appointments before he went.

Feeling desperate about her worsening state of health, Miss M then contacted her employer. She said she was resigning, as she saw no prospect of being well enough to return to work. Two weeks later, Miss M was able to see her GP, who gave her a medical certificate confirming her inability to work. She then put in a claim under her payment protection policy.

The insurer refused to pay the claim. It did not doubt the state of her health but it pointed out that the policy was designed to cover people who were in employment. At the time she put in her claim she had already resigned from her job, so she was not eligible for cover.

Complaint upheld

We were satisfied from the evidence that—at the point at which she resigned from her job—Miss M's state of health met the policy definition of '*disability*'. She would therefore have qualified for benefit under the policy if she had been able to get an appointment with her GP within a reasonable time.

We did not think it appropriate for the insurer to take advantage of the fact that she was unable to do this. We said that the fair and reasonable outcome in this case was for it to meet her claim.

82/8 insurer refuses to pay for theft of van when keys were left in the ignition and the van doors were locked

Mr B, who ran a local delivery business, complained about his motor insurer's refusal to pay out after his van was stolen. He had left the van in the road nearby while he delivered goods from a hardware store to a customer's home. He admitted that he had left the keys in the ignition and the engine running (apparently to avoid running down the battery while he was on his delivery round). However, he said he had taken care to lock all the van doors, with a spare key, before he had left the vehicle.

He said he returned to the road just a few minutes later to find that his van had gone. The police later told him that the thief had broken into the van by smashing a window—and had then driven away. The insurer declined Mr B's claim, citing a '*keys in car*' policy clause that excluded cover for theft in certain circumstances.

Complaint upheld

We noted that the '*keys in car*' exclusion in Mr B's policy was worded in an unusual way. It said the insurer would not provide cover for theft where the ignition keys were left in or on the vehicle and the vehicle was left '*unlocked and unattended*'.

Although Mr B did not dispute that he had left one set of keys in the ignition, he insisted that he had used his spare keys to lock the van before leaving it. And it seemed to us unlikely that the thief would have smashed the window unless he had found the doors locked.

We were satisfied that Mr B had not recognised the risk of theft as a result of leaving his keys in the ignition, and he had not acted recklessly.

We told the insurer that as Mr B had not left his van '*unlocked*', it could not apply the exclusion. We therefore upheld the complaint and told the insurer to pay the claim.

82/9 motor insurer turns down claim for theft of a car when it was stolen from outside a fast-food restaurant

Mr G's car was stolen while he was having a meal in a fast-food restaurant. He said that after parking the car outside the restaurant he had removed the keys from the ignition and checked that all the doors were locked. He had then put his car keys in his coat pocket and gone in to the restaurant.

The restaurant was fairly quiet and Mr G left his coat and a newspaper on a table close to the food counter before going up to get his food. He admitted that he did not look over to the table to check his belongings, even though he stood waiting for several minutes before he was served. It was only after Mr G had eaten his meal and was getting ready to leave that he discovered the keys were missing from his coat pocket. He went outside and found that someone had taken his car.

The insurer refused to pay Mr G's claim. It said he had breached a policy condition that required him to '*take reasonable care*' of his car—and it considered he had been '*reckless*' in leaving his keys '*unattended*'.

Complaint upheld

In 1993, the Court of Appeal considered '*reasonable care*' conditions in the case of *Sofi* v *Prudential Assurance*. It decided that in determining whether or not someone had taken '*reasonable care*' of their property, the test was whether they had deliberately courted a risk or taken measures that they knew were inadequate to protect the property. In either case, this lack of care was tantamount to '*recklessness*', and meant that the person in question did not care what happened to their property.

In the light of this judgment, in order to determine whether the insurer had been entitled to reject Mr G's claim, we had to be satisfied that Mr G had acted recklessly in leaving his keys unattended.

It was clear from the evidence provided by Mr G that the restaurant was relatively quiet; he had expected to be served right away; and he had left the keys just a couple of metres behind him. We were therefore satisfied that Mr G had not recognised the risk of theft and had not acted recklessly when leaving his coat—with the car keys in the pocket—on the table. Since we did not think Mr G had '*deliberately courted*' the risk of theft, we told the insurer to pay the claim.

82/10 **motor insurer turns down claim for the theft of a van while the owner was working nearby**

A construction worker, Mr K, complained about the way in which his motor insurer dealt with his claim for theft. His van was stolen one afternoon, while he was working on a building site. He said that an urgent problem had arisen with the mechanical digger he was operating, and he had gone to fetch some tools from the back of his van, in order to fix the problem.

He had quickly gone back to the digger, which was just a few metres away from the van, and had left the back doors of his van open and the keys on top of his jacket, which was on the ground next to the van.

The theft took place while Mr K was mending the digger. He said the mechanical problem had not taken very long to fix—but it had been more complicated and had required more concentration than he had expected. He accepted that this must have diverted his attention briefly from the van, providing someone with the opportunity to steal it. However, he thought that his insurer had acted unfairly in telling him it was unable to pay out because he had left the van *'unattended'*.

Complaint upheld

We noted that although Mr K had left the rear doors of the van open—with the keys nearby—he had never been more than a few metres away from the van. He had been working on private property that was sufficiently well secluded to prevent access by casual passers-by. And we accepted his view that, while mending the digger, he had been close enough to the van to be able to intervene if he saw anyone attempting to steal it.

So we were satisfied that Mr K could not be said to have left the van *'unattended'*—nor had he acted recklessly, as he had not appreciated that the vehicle was at risk of theft. We therefore told the insurer to meet Mr K's claim.

82/11 **insurer refuses claim for theft of a car left 'unattended' in the driveway of the owner's house**

Mrs D's insurer turned down the claim she made on her motor policy after her car was stolen from the driveway of her house. She said the car had been taken one morning, while she was preparing to leave for work. Several minor domestic problems had needed sorting out before she set out. Immediately before leaving the house she had therefore rung her manager to warn him she might be a little late.

She said she had already got into the car and started it up when she realised she still had the house phone with her. She left the car on the driveway, with the engine still running and the driver's door open, while she took the phone back to the house. Very shortly afterwards, she came out to find that the car had gone.

The insurer refused to pay out, as it said she had left the vehicle *'unattended'*. Mrs D disputed this and eventually referred her complaint to us. She said she had left the car where it was clearly visible to her husband. At the time he had been in the living room, which faced the driveway at the front of the house.

Complaint not upheld

In this case there was no question that the keys had been left in the car and the doors unlocked—Mrs D admitted as much when making her claim. She maintained that the car could not have been out of her sight for more than 10 seconds. She said she had not seen anyone *'hanging around'* near the driveway, and she had neither seen nor heard the car being driven away.

After looking carefully at photographs showing the driveway and exterior of Mrs D's house, we concluded that her recollection of events surrounding the theft might not have been wholly accurate. We thought it unlikely that within so short a period of time anyone could have been in a position to have seen Mrs D leave the car—and to then have made their way to the vehicle, got in it and driven away—all without being seen or heard.

We also noted that although the car might have been left in a spot where it was visible from Mrs D's house, neither she nor her husband could have been watching it while she returned the phone—otherwise one or both of them would have seen the theft taking place.

In the circumstances, we were satisfied that the vehicle had been left unattended and that the risk of theft would have been apparent to Mrs D. We said it was reasonable for the insurer to have turned down the claim, citing the *'keys in car'* exclusion. We did not uphold the complaint

82/12   insurer refuses claim for theft of car left with door unlocked and key in ignition

Mrs J complained about her insurer's refusal to pay for the theft of her car. Her husband, who was included as a *'named driver'* on the car's insurance policy, had gone out in the car to the local supermarket. He had stopped off on his way home in order to post a letter. He said he had parked the car and crossed a busy road to reach the post box. As he turned round to make his way back to the car, he saw it being driven away.

The insurer cited the *'keys in car'* exclusion in order to turn down the claim. He admitted having left his keys in the ignition and the car door unlocked when he got out of the car to post the letter. Mr J acknowledged that he had been *'silly to take a chance'*. However, he said it was unfair of the insurer to rely on such an *'unreasonable'* exclusion, which he had not been told about and which meant he and his wife would lose the entire value of the car. Unable to reach agreement with the insurer, Mr and Mrs J brought their complaint to us.

Complaint not upheld

The insurer sent us a recording of the phone call during which Mrs J had bought the policy. In the course of this call, the insurer had explained the *'keys in car'* exclusion to Mrs J. We noted that the exclusion was also clearly and prominently set out in the policy document.

We did not accept Mr J's view that the insurer was at fault for not telling him about the exclusion. Mrs J was the main driver and the insurer had properly drawn the exclusion to her attention. We thought it reasonable of the insurer to have expected her to pass on the information to her husband.

We concluded that, in view of the circumstances in which the theft took place, the insurer had not acted unfairly in applying the policy exclusion. We did not uphold the complaint.

ISSUE 83: FEBRUARY/MARCH 2010

83/6   consumer complains about the handling of her claim under her *gas boiler breakdown* insurance policy

Mrs G complained to her insurer about the way in which it had dealt with her claim after her gas central heating boiler stopped working properly. She said that delays and poor service had caused an *'unacceptable level of inconvenience'*.

She had first contacted the insurer after having to shut down the central heating because of *'loud and unusual'* noises coming from the boiler. The engineer sent by the insurer to inspect the boiler was unable to find the cause of the problem. Two subsequent inspections by different engineers also failed to resolve matters. The insurer then told Mrs G that she needed to have a power flush carried out on the boiler—and that her breakdown cover would be suspended until that work had been done.

So Mrs G arranged for an engineer to carry out the power flush. When he had done this, he told Mrs G to call the insurer and order a replacement valve, as he said a new valve was needed before the heating could be turned on again.

Although Mrs G called her insurer that same day, it was over a week before an engineer came to fit the new valve. Once the heating was working again, she complained to the insurer.

She said she doubted that the power flush had been necessary. She thought the insurer had told her to arrange it simply because the engineers had been unable to find the real cause of the problem. And she asked for compensation for the period when she and her elderly mother had been left without any heating or hot water.

The insurer strongly refuted Mrs G's suggestion that the power flush had not been necessary. However, it acknowledged that there had been some delays and it offered £75 to Mrs G as a *'goodwill gesture'*.

Mrs G said she remained *'unconvinced'* that the power flush had been necessary. She also said that the offer of compensation was *'far from adequate'* and that she thought £2,000 would be a more appropriate sum. Unable to reach agreement with the insurer, Mrs G referred the complaint to us.

Complaint upheld in part

In the light of the available evidence, we concluded that the power flush had indeed been necessary. So we did not uphold this part of Mrs G's complaint.

We looked at what Mrs G had said about the amount of inconvenience that she and her mother had suffered during the period when their boiler was out of action. We agreed that they had been inconvenienced and understandably annoyed by the delay—and we did not think the insurer's offer of £75 had been sufficient. However, we could not see that Mrs G was justified in asking for £2,000. We said that, in the circumstances of this case, £350 was appropriate, and the insurer agreed to pay this amount.

83/7   consumer complains about insufficient offer of compensation from insurer after his boiler broke down over Christmas

Three days before Christmas, Mr and Mrs M's boiler broke down. It was covered by *breakdown protection* insurance, and the insurer sent an engineer out the following day to repair it. All appeared to be well until the afternoon of Christmas day, when the boiler broke down again.

The engineer sent out by the insurer two days later was unable to repair the boiler. He told Mr M that it needed a new pump. Unfortunately, the exact model required was not in stock and would have to be specially ordered. He did not know how long this would take and he said that some delay was inevitable because of office and warehouse closures over the holiday period.

Mr and Mrs M were very upset to learn this. They said they could not manage without hot water and central heating. Several members of their family were staying with them over the Christmas and New Year break, including two young children and Mr M's elderly father.

With the agreement of the insurer, Mr M rang round a few independent contractors and found someone local who said he could supply and fit the exact model of pump required. The insurer agreed to reimburse Mr M for the cost of getting the work done independently—and in due course, Mr M put in a claim to the insurer.

The insurer offered him £250, which was the full cost of supplying and fitting the new pump. Mr M was also offered £120 for the distress and inconvenience he had been caused.

Mr M did not think this was enough. He asked for £825, to compensate him for the disruption to his family's Christmas and to cover the cost of the portable heaters he had been obliged to hire. When the insurer refused to increase its original offer, Mr M referred the complaint to us.

Complaint upheld

The claim for the cost of the repair was not in dispute, as the insurer had already offered full reimbursement of the £250 paid to the independent contractor. But we agreed with Mr M that £120 was insufficient compensation, in the circumstances.

We noted that, under his policy, Mr M could have claimed for alternative accommodation while he was waiting for the insurer to obtain the pump and repair his boiler. However, he had not done this and the insurer had not suggested it.

We said that the insurer should reimburse Mr M for the full cost of hiring the heaters. It should also pay him £250 for the distress and inconvenience it had caused.

83/8   insurer refuses to reimburse consumer for cost of work carried out on advice of its contractor

When Mr T's boiler broke down he contacted the insurer, under his *home emergency* insurance policy. A few days later, a contractor employed by the insurer inspected the boiler and said it had a faulty valve. Mr T later said he had been under the impression that the contractor would order a replacement and return in due course to fit it.

However, the following morning the contractor left a phone message for Mr T, telling him that the problem had been caused by '*sludge on the valve*' and that Mr T would need to arrange a power flush to release it. The contractor said Mr T would have to get the work done at his own expense, as it was not covered by the policy.

So Mr T went ahead and had the power flush carried out, at a cost of £400. The heating engineer who did the work expressed the view that it had not been necessary, as there had been no debris in the system and the fault with the boiler remained unresolved.

Mr T then contacted the insurer. He asked it to reimburse him for the cost of the power flush, on the grounds that it had only been carried out on the advice of the contractor, and it had proved unnecessary.

The insurer refused to pay up. It said Mr T's contractor should not have continued with the power flush if he thought it unnecessary. Unable to reach agreement, Mr T referred the complaint to us.

Complaint upheld

The insurer accepted that Mr T had arranged the power flush on the basis of advice from the insurer's contractor. We said that the contractor was acting on the insurer's behalf when he inspected the boiler and advised Mr T on the cause of the fault, and whether it was covered by the policy.

It was clear from the evidence supplied by Mr T's heating engineer that the power flush had *not* been necessary and had not resolved the problem with the boiler. So we said that the insurer should reimburse Mr T for the cost of the power flush, together with interest—backdated to when Mr T had put in his claim.

83/9   consumer complains about insurer's handling of claim for damage resulting from a leaking toilet

At the beginning of August an elderly widow, Mrs D, contacted her insurer as she thought there was a leak in her bathroom.

The contractor sent by the insurer said the problem was coming from the outlet pipe of the toilet. He confirmed that the cost of repair was covered under Mrs D's *complete utilities* cover insurance policy. However, he said he thought the toilet itself might be cracked—so there was a risk that it could be damaged further if any work was done on the outlet pipe. He advised Mrs D to buy a new toilet before having any repairs done.

Mrs D was concerned about the cost that this would entail. She told the contractor she did not think she could raise the money right away to pay for a new toilet. She later said she '*got the impression there was no urgency*' about arranging the repairs.

Mrs D did not see any further signs of a leak over the next few weeks. But she then noticed that water marks had started to appear on her bathroom floor and that the toilet had become backed-up, which meant there was a risk of it overflowing when flushed.

She contacted the insurer, who sent out the same contractor. Mrs D warned him not to flush the toilet, but he did so and it overflowed. The contractor did not offer any help in clearing up the mess, nor did he attempt any repair. Instead, he told Mrs D to '*keep an eye on the situation*' and he said he would '*call in again in a day or so*'.

By that time, however, Mrs D had moved in temporarily with a neighbour. Waste water had leaked through the bathroom floor to the sitting-room below—and the smell was so unpleasant that she had been unable to stay in the house. On her neighbour's advice, she rang the insurer again to explain what had happened.

Two days later, the insurer sent a different contractor to Mrs D's house. He repaired the leak—and told her the toilet itself was not damaged and there was no need to replace it.

With her neighbour's help, Mrs D subsequently claimed for the costs she incurred in putting right the damage caused by the leak. She also complained about the insurer's poor handling of the matter—and for the distress and inconvenience the incident had caused her. When the insurer rejected her claim, Mrs D brought her complaint to us.

Complaint upheld

We considered the information provided by both the insurer and Mrs D. The insurer's notes confirmed that the first contractor had flushed the toilet, despite the warning from Mrs D that he should not do this. We thought it likely that his actions had caused some damage. The insurer's notes also confirmed that the second contractor had completed a satisfactory repair without needing to replace the toilet.

If the repair had been carried out promptly when Mrs D first contacted the insurer, we thought it more likely than not that there would have been no damage to the bathroom floor or to the ceiling of the room below.

We told the insurer to reimburse Mrs D for the costs she had incurred in repairing the damage caused by the leak. We said it should add interest, backdated to when she first made her claim for the damage. We also said it should pay her £450 for the distress and inconvenience she had been caused.

83/10   consumer complains about the handling of his claim under his boiler care insurance policy

Mr A's boiler was covered by a *boiler care* insurance policy. He contacted the insurer under this policy after his boiler broke down in early June.

It took four visits from a gas engineer before the boiler was finally repaired—nearly a month later. The boiler stopped working again in the first week of November. This time, after inspecting the boiler, the insurer's engineer told him it was *'uneconomical'* to carry out a repair. When Mr A disputed this, the engineer said it was best to take up the matter direct with the insurer.

Mr A rang the insurer as soon as the engineer left. And although he was told that someone would call him back the same day, it was nearly a fortnight before the insurer contacted him.

The insurer then confirmed that the boiler was *'beyond economic repair'*. Mr A was offered a *'discretionary payment'* of £100 towards the cost of a replacement. Mr A was very unhappy about this and made a formal complaint about the poor service he had received.

The insurer offered Mr A £150 to compensate him for its delay in confirming that it would not repair the boiler, after he had reported the breakdown in November. However, it was not prepared to reconsider its decision not to carry out further repairs.

Mr A then complained to us. He said he thought the insurer should either repair the boiler or pay for a replacement.

Complaint not upheld

We looked at the terms and conditions of Mr A's insurance policy. These stated clearly that the insurer could refuse to repair the boiler in circumstances where it decided it was not economical to do so. In such circumstances, the insurer was not required to replace the boiler.

We accepted that Mr A had been put to some inconvenience during the period when he was waiting for the insurer to confirm whether or not it would repair the boiler. But we thought the offer of £150 compensation for this, together with £100 towards the cost of a new boiler, was fair and reasonable in the circumstances. We did not uphold the complaint.

ISSUE 85: APRIL/MAY 2010

85/1   equine insurance—insurer refuses to pay claim because policyholder did not disclose earlier illness suffered by her horse

Mrs C's horse, Acorn, died after suffering a serious bout of colic. Mrs C put in a claim under her equine insurance policy for related veterinary fees but her insurer refused to pay out.

The insurer said Mrs C had failed to comply with the terms and conditions of the policy. This was because Acorn had suffered an earlier episode of colic, during the first year he was covered by the policy. Mrs C had not mentioned this when she renewed her policy. The insurer said that if she had *'made a proper disclosure of all relevant facts'* then it would have renewed her policy but excluded any future claims for colic.

Mrs C did not think this was reasonable. She said that Acorn's previous bout of colic had been very minor and she had not needed to make any claim. She had therefore not thought it worth mentioning when she came to renew the policy.

Complaint upheld

The terms and conditions stated that the policy did not cover the insured animal for any illnesses suffered *before* the policy was taken out, unless the insurer had specifically agreed otherwise, in writing. And similarly, the policy would not cover any illnesses that occurred more than once after the insurance had begun, unless the insurer agreed otherwise, in writing.

In our view, this put a significant restriction on the policy. The restriction should have been clearly brought to the policyholder's attention, in accordance with good industry practice. However, we saw no evidence that the insurer had highlighted the significance of this restriction, either before Mrs C took out the policy or when she later renewed it.

We thought it highly likely that if Mrs C had known the insurer would not cover future bouts of colic, she would have sought insurance elsewhere.

Given that Acorn's earlier episode of colic had not been at all serious, we did not think another insurer would have refused to cover him for this condition. So we were satisfied that if Mrs C had changed insurers she could have recovered the veterinary fees she eventually claimed for. We upheld the complaint and told the insurer to pay the claim.

85/2   farmer disputes amount paid by insurer under a 'total loss' claim, after his horse trailer was stolen

After Mr B's horse trailer was stolen he put in a claim to his insurer. He complained that the amount the insurer offered to pay him was '*by no means a fair representation*' of the trailer's value.

The insurer insisted that the amount it was offering was fair. It told Mr B that its estimate of the trailer's value was based on recent advertisements in the press for similar trailers. Mr B pointed out that the advertisements in question were for trailers that were far older than his own. When the insurer refused to reconsider its offer, Mr B brought his complaint to us.

Complaint upheld

We looked at the details of Mr B's policy and, in particular, at the section relating to claims such as this one, for '*total loss*'. We thought the wording of this section was so unclear that it would have been difficult for any policyholder to know how their claim would be settled.

Mr B produced convincing evidence to support his view that the insurer's offer did not reflect the value of his stolen trailer. We said the insurer should not have based its offer on newspaper advertisements. It should instead have obtained accurate information from a specialist trailer manufacturer or dealer.

We upheld the complaint and told the insurer to pay Mr B a sum equivalent to the market value of his trailer, at the date when it was stolen.

85/3   health insurer tells policyholder in rural area to travel to nearest city for treatment as local clinic not on 'approved list'

Mrs K, who was in her late 70s, was unhappy with the way in which her private health insurer dealt with her claim for a cataract operation.

Several years earlier her husband had undergone the same operation. He had been very pleased with the care he received at a small clinic, conveniently situated near their home in a rural part of Scotland. So Mrs K told her insurer she would like to have her operation at that same clinic.

She was very disappointed when her insurer said the clinic was not on its '*approved list*'. The insurer suggested that Mrs K should instead be treated at a hospital over 80 miles from her home.

Mrs K was anxious about the awkward journey she would have to undertake, travelling to and from the recommended hospital. She was also concerned that a large hospital might not provide the same standard of care that her husband had experienced in the local clinic. So after much thought, she decided to go ahead and have the operation at the clinic, at her own expense.

Several weeks after her operation her son, who was based abroad with the army, came home on leave. He advised Mrs K to contact the insurer again, as he thought it should have made at least some contribution towards the cost of her operation. However, the insurer was adamant that it could not reimburse any of Mrs K's expenses. She then brought her complaint to us.

Complaint upheld

It is not unusual for insurers to state that they can only meet claims when medical treatment is carried out at a hospital on an '*approved*' list. However, it is not always the case that a listed hospital is the closest, or most convenient for the policyholder.

Under some policies, the insurer offers to provide treatment at specific hospitals, and will arrange payment direct with the hospital and consultant concerned. In this case, however, the terms and conditions said that the insurer would reimburse policyholders for the costs incurred in obtaining treatment at an approved hospital.

So it was clear that if Mrs K's operation had been carried out at an approved hospital, her costs would have been reimbursed in full. We upheld the complaint. We said that in the particular circumstances of this case, the insurer should pay Mrs K the amount it *would have* paid, if her operation had been carried out at the city hospital. This was slightly less than the total amount she had paid for treatment at the local clinic.

85/4   commercial insurer refuses to pay claim from hay merchant after fire destroys season's crop

A hay merchant, Mr M, supplied a number of farms in the surrounding area with horse hay. When a serious fire in one of his barns destroyed most of the season's crop, he claimed under his commercial insurance policy for '*restoration costs*' and '*business interruption*' losses.

The insurer turned down his claim. It said it had concluded he was the '*only person with the means, motive and opportunity to have started the fire*'. It also said it would invoke the '*fraudulent claim*' clause and '*avoid*' his policy (treat it as if it had never existed).

Mr M then complained to us.

Complaint not upheld

We noted that the terms and conditions of the policy said that a policy could be '*avoided*' if '*a claim made by you or anyone acting on your behalf to obtain a policy benefit is fraudulent or intentionally exaggerated, whether ultimately material or not*'.

The insurer sent us details of the information it had obtained before concluding that Mr M had started the fire himself. It had commissioned forensic experts to investigate the claim. Their report stated, among other things, that the fire had been started deliberately; there were at least three separate '*seats of ignition*'; and '*an accelerant*' had been used to encourage the spread of the fire.

After receiving this report, the insurer had interviewed Mr M and his employees. It had also looked into Mr M's financial situation. And it had obtained further evidence that called into question Mr M's credibility and integrity.

Mr M told us he objected strongly to the insurer's view that he had started the fire himself. But he refused to comment on the evidence that had led the insurer to that view, other than to confirm that he was in very serious financial difficulties.

We noted that the '*fraudulent claim*' clause in Mr M's policy reinforced the common law position that an insured person is unable to benefit from their policy if they have intentionally brought about the loss for which they have claimed.

The insurer had carried out a careful and thorough investigation and produced convincing evidence to support its actions in this case. We did not uphold the complaint.

FOS STATISTICS AND COMPLAINT TRENDS
2005–2010

FOS STATISTICS AND COMPLAINT TRENDS 2005–2010[1]

No of complaints	2005/6	2006/7	2007/8	2008/9	2009/10
Front line enquiries and complaints	672,973	627,814[2]	794,648	789,877[3]	925,095
Of which total cases referred to adjudicators	112,923[4]	94,392	123,089	127,471	163,012[5]
Of which total were insurance related	14,270	15,730	27,286[6]	50,168[7]	69,034[8]
Cases reaching the Ombudsman	1 in 10	6%	1 in 10	8%	1 in 6
Complaints resolved by the companies themselves (excluding mortgage endowment)	95–98%	N/A	N/A	N/A	N/A
Technical advice desk	20,595	18,213	18,354	15,650	16,319
No of cases worth more than £100,000	3%				

1. The data below has been collated from FOS Annual Reviews.
2. Decrease due to trend in getting information from the website.
3. Although as expected the mortgage endowment complaints reduced sharply, there was an unexpected increase in overall number of claims due to the financial market turmoil, and a wave of claims relating to payment protection insurance, unauthorised overdraft charges and credit card default charges.
4. This represented a peak up to 2005/6 in the number of total complaints referred to an adjudicator as a result of 69,000 new mortgage endowment complaints referred to an adjudicator. The figures for mortgage endowment complaints reduced thereafter to 46,000 in 2006/7, 13,800 in 2007/8, 5,800 in 2008/9 and 5,400 in 2009/10.
5. This is the highest number in the FOS ten-year history.
6. Increase due mainly to increased payment protection insurance ("PPI") claims towards the end of the year, fuelled by the media. In 2007/8, these made up 39% of the new insurance claims referred to adjudicators.
7. Of which PPI complaints accounted for 31,066 (compared to 10,652 in 2007/8 and 1,832 in 2006/7) and car/motor complaints accounted for 6,267.
8. This represents an increase of 38% on 2008/9, largely due to PPI complaints which accounted for 49,196 or 71% of the insurance claims, and 5,451 car/motor complaints. Three out of every ten new cases referred to an adjudicator were PPI complaints.

	2005/6	2006/7	2007/8	2008/9	2009/10
Resolution time (excl mortgage endowment complaints in 2005/6, 2006/7 and 2007/8)					
within 6 months	74%	81%	83%	56%[9]	67%
within 1 year	89%	92%	96%	88%[10]	89%
Resolution					
Total	119,432[11]	111,673	99,699	113,949	166,321
Of which resolved by adjudicator	110,229	104,831	91,739	105,275	155,591
And of which resolved by an ombudsman	9,203	6,842	7,960	8,674	10,730
Ombudsman decisions resolved in favour of insured wholly or partly	$\frac{1}{3}$ to $\frac{1}{2}$	40%	41% of insurance claims	89% of PPI claims, but 41% of other insurance claims	89% of PPI claims, but 40% of other insurance claims
Case fees[12]					
Standard fee	£360 after the first 2	£360 after the first 2	£450 after the first 2	£450 after the first 3	£500 after the first 3

9. The unexpected increase in cases led to delays in case resolution, and some work was out-sourced and new staff were recruited and trained.
10. Excluding the 15,000 unauthorised overdraft charges cases on hold pending a high court decision.
11. This was the highest on record since the FOS began.
12. Case fees represent 75% of FOS total income.

	2005/6	2006/7	2007/8	2008/9	2009/10
How many firms covered by the FOS paid a case fee	7%	6.5%	3.5%[13]	895 firms = <1%	1,064 firms = about 1%
How many financial services groups accounted for about half the total number of complaints received during the year	12	10	6	6	4
How many firms had no complaint referred to the FOS	81.5%	82%	>95%	>95%	>95%
Satisfaction					
Customers who won and were satisfied with FOS handling	96%	88%	86%	83%	87%
Customers who lost and were satisfied with FOS handling	64%	48%	47%	42%	46%
Firms responding, who thought that the FOS provides a good independent dispute resolution service	75%	62%	67%	66%	63%
Independent Assessor					
Who	Michael Barnes CBE	Michael Barnes CBE	Michael Barnes CBE	Michael Barnes CBE	Michael Barnes CBE
No of referrals	322	326	281	265	262
of which investigated	186 (including 13 from firms)	206 (including a small no from firms, of which 6 were upheld)	170 (including 13 from firms)	185 (including 24 from firms)	165 (including 20 from firms)
of which upheld wholly or in part	76	88	80	83	67
of which D&I awarded in how many cases	68 (average award was £200–£400)	82 (half awarded £250–£500; most of the rest < £200)	77 (most awarded £250–£450)	78 (most awarded £200–£450)	60 (40% awarded £50–£250; 48% £250–£500)

13. From April 2007 the FOS remit was extended to cover some 80,000 businesses with a standard consumer credit licence.

	2005/6	2006/7	2007/8	2008/9	2009/10
Income	£52.0m	£53.1m	£55.5m	£65.8m	£98.4m
Operating costs	£52.6m	£55.0m	£52.9m	£58.0m	£92.4m
Unit cost[14]	£433	£484	£529[15]	£508[16]	£555[17]
Staff	1,015	956	825	1,083	1,015[18]

14. Unit cost is calculated by dividing total FOS costs (before financing charges and any bad debt charge) by the number of cases the FOS completes.
15. The FOS lost the significant economies of scale it had achieved in handling large volumes of mortgage endowment work, because there were significantly fewer of these complaints, and because out of those there were, more went to the ombudsman, which involves more cost and time.
16. In 2001/2 the unit cost was £684, and that would be £900 in 2008/9 if that figure had increased in line with inflation.
17. This figure is higher than the FOS wants it to be, as about 300 adjudicators were recruited and trained during the year and were only reaching their operating potential towards the end of the year.
18. This is an average figure for the year, and does not include more than 400 staff out-sourced as a result of the huge increase in caseload.

ICOBS (RELEVANT EXTRACTS)*

ICOBS 2.1 CLIENT CATEGORISATION

Introduction

ICOBS 2.1.1 Guidance

Different provisions in this sourcebook may apply depending on the type of person with whom a firm is dealing:

(1) A policyholder includes anyone who, upon the occurrence of the contingency insured against, is entitled to make a claim directly to the insurance undertaking.

(2) Only a policyholder or a prospective policyholder who makes the arrangements preparatory to him concluding a contract of insurance (directly or through an agent) is a customer. In this sourcebook, customers are either consumers or commercial customers.

(3) A consumer is any natural person who is acting for purposes which are outside his trade or profession.

(4) A commercial customer is a customer who is not a consumer.

Customer to be treated as consumer when status uncertain

ICOBS 2.1.2 Rule

If it is not clear in a particular case whether a customer is a consumer or a commercial customer, a firm must treat the customer as a consumer.

Customer covered in both a private and business capacity

ICOBS 2.1.3 Guidance

If a customer is acting in the capacity of both a consumer and a commercial customer in relation to a particular contract of insurance, the customer is a commercial customer.

Customer classification examples

ICOBS 2.1.4 Guidance

In practice, private individuals may act in a number of capacities. The following table sets out a number of examples of how an individual acting in certain capacities should, in the FSA's view, be categorised.

CUSTOMER CLASSIFICATION EXAMPLES

CAPACITY	CLASSIFICATION
Personal representatives, including executors, unless they are acting in a professional capacity, for example, a solicitor acting as executor.	Consumer
Private individuals acting in personal or other family circumstances, for example, as trustee of a family trust.	Consumer

CAPACITY	CLASSIFICATION
Trustee of a trust such as a housing or NHS trust.	Commercial customer
Member of the governing body of a club or other unincorporated association such as a trade body and a student union.	Commercial customer
Pension trustee.	Commercial customer
Person taking out a policy covering property bought under a buy-to-let mortgage.	Commercial customer
Partner in a partnership when taking out insurance for purposes related to his profession.	Commercial customer

ICOBS 6.1 GENERAL

Responsibilities of insurers and insurance intermediaries

ICOBS 6.1.1 Rule

An insurer is responsible for producing, and an insurance intermediary for providing to a customer, the information required by this chapter and by the distance communication rules (see ICOBS 3.1). However, an insurer is responsible for providing information required on mid-term changes, and an insurance intermediary is responsible for producing price information if it agrees this with an insurer.

ICOBS 6.1.2 Rule

If there is no insurance intermediary, the insurer is responsible for producing and providing the information.

ICOBS 6.1.3 Rule

An insurer must produce information in good time to enable the insurance intermediary to comply with the rules in this chapter, or promptly on an insurance intermediary's request.

ICOBS 6.1.4 Rule

These general rules on the responsibilities of insurers and insurance intermediaries are modified by ICOBS 6 Annex 1 R if one of the firms is not based in the United Kingdom, and in certain other situations.

Ensuring customers can make an informed decision

ICOBS 6.1.5 Rule

A firm must take reasonable steps to ensure a customer is given appropriate information about a policy in good time and in a comprehensible form so that the customer can make an informed decision about the arrangements proposed.

ICOBS 6.1.6 Guidance

The appropriate information rule applies pre-conclusion and post-conclusion, and so includes matters such as mid-term changes and renewals. It also applies to the price of the policy.

ICOBS 6.1.7 Guidance

The level of information required will vary according to matters such as:

    (1) the knowledge, experience and ability of a typical customer for the policy;
    (2) the policy terms, including its main benefits, exclusions, limitations, conditions and its duration;

(3) the policy's overall complexity;

(4) whether the policy is bought in connection with other goods and services;

(5) distance communication information requirements (for example, under the distance communication rules less information can be given during certain telephone sales than in a sale made purely by written correspondence (see ICOBS 3.1.14 R)); and

(6) whether the same information has been provided to the customer previously and, if so, when.

ICOBS 6.1.8 Guidance

In determining what is "in good time", a firm should consider the importance of the information to the customer's decision-making process and the point at which the information may be most useful. Distance communication timing requirements are also relevant (for example, the distance communication rules enable certain information to be provided post-conclusion in telephone and certain other sales (see ICOBS 3.1.14 R and ICOBS 3.1.15 R)).

ICOBS 6.1.9 Guidance

Cancellation rights do not affect what information it is appropriate to give to a customer in order to enable him to make an informed purchasing decision.

ICOBS 6.1.10 Guidance

A firm dealing with a consumer may wish to provide information in a policy summary or as a key features document (see ICOBS 6 Annex 2).

Providing evidence of cover

ICOBS 6.1.11 Guidance

Under Principle 7 a firm should provide evidence of cover promptly after inception of a policy. Firms will need to take into account the type of customer and the effect of other information requirements, for example those under the distance communication rules (ICOBS 3.1).

Group policies

ICOBS 6.1.12 Guidance

Under Principle 7, a firm that sells a group policy should provide appropriate information to the customer to pass on to other policyholders. It should tell the customer that he should give the information to each policyholder.

Price disclosure: connected goods or services

ICOBS 6.1.13 Rule

(1) If a policy is bought by a consumer in connection with other goods or services a firm must, before conclusion of the contract, disclose its premium separately from any other prices and whether buying the policy is compulsory.

(2) In the case of a distance contract, disclosure of whether buying the policy is compulsory may be made in accordance with the timing requirements under the distance communication rules (see ICOBS 3.1.8 R, ICOBS 3.1.14 R and ICOBS 3.1.15 R).

Exception to the timing rules: distance contracts and voice telephony communications

ICOBS 6.1.14 Rule

Where a rule in this chapter requires information to be provided in writing or another durable medium before conclusion of a contract, a firm may instead provide that information in accordance with the distance communication timing requirements (see ICOBS 3.1.14 R and ICOBS 3.1.15 R).

ICOBS 8.1 INSURERS: GENERAL

ICOBS 8.1.1 Rule

An insurer must:

(1) handle claims promptly and fairly;
(2) provide reasonable guidance to help a policyholder make a claim and appropriate information on its progress;
(3) not unreasonably reject a claim (including by terminating or avoiding a policy); and
(4) settle claims promptly once settlement terms are agreed.

ICOBS 8.1.2 Rule

A rejection of a consumer policyholder's claim is unreasonable, except where there is evidence of fraud, if it is for:

(1) non-disclosure of a fact material to the risk which the policyholder could not reasonably be expected to have disclosed; or
(2) non-negligent misrepresentation of a fact material to the risk; or
(3) breach of warranty or condition unless the circumstances of the claim are connected to the breach and unless (for a pure protection contract):
   (a) under a 'life of another' contract, the warranty relates to a statement of fact concerning the life to be assured and, if the statement had been made by the life to be assured under an 'own life' contract, the insurer could have rejected the claim under this rule; or
   (b) the warranty is material to the risk and was drawn to the customer's attention before the conclusion of the contract.

DISP AS UPDATED (RELEVANT EXTRACTS)*

DISP 1.2 CONSUMER AWARENESS RULES

DISP 1.2.1 Rule

To aid consumer awareness of the protections offered by the provisions in this chapter, respondents must:

(1) publish appropriate summary details of their internal process for dealing with complaints promptly and fairly;

(2) refer eligible complainants in writing, to the availability of these summary details:

    (a) in relation to a payment service in the information on out-of-court complaint and redress procedures required to be provided or made available under regulations 36(2)(e) (Information required prior to the conclusion of a single payment service contract) or 40 (Prior general information for framework contracts) of the Payment Services Regulations; or

    (b) otherwise, in writing at, or immediately after, the point of sale; and

(3) provide such summary details in writing to eligible complainants:

    (a) on request; and

    (b) when acknowledging a complaint.

DISP 1.2.2 Rule

Where the activity does not involve a sale, the obligation in DISP 1.2.1 R (2)(b) shall apply at, or immediately after, the point when contact is first made with an eligible complainant.

DISP 1.2.3 Guidance

These summary details should cover at least:

(1) how the respondent fulfils its obligation to handle and seek to resolve relevant complaints; and

(2) that, if the complaint is not resolved, the complainant may be entitled to refer it to the Financial Ombudsman Service.

DISP 1.2.4 Guidance

The summary details may be set out in a leaflet, and their availability may be referred to in contractual documentation.

DISP 1.2.5 Guidance

Respondents may also display or reproduce the Financial Ombudsman Service logo (under licence) in:

(1) branches and sales offices to which eligible complainants have access; or

(2) marketing literature or correspondence directed at eligible complainants;

provided it is done in a way which is not misleading.

DISP 1.4 COMPLAINTS RESOLUTION RULES

DISP 1.4.1 Rule

Once a complaint has been received by a respondent, it must:

(1) investigate the complaint competently, diligently and impartially;
(2) assess fairly, consistently and promptly:
    (a) the subject matter of the complaint;
    (b) whether the complaint should be upheld;
    (c) what remedial action or redress (or both) may be appropriate;
    (d) if appropriate, whether it has reasonable grounds to be satisfied that another respondent may be solely or jointly responsible for the matter alleged in the complaint;
    taking into account all relevant factors;
(3) offer redress or remedial action when it decides this is appropriate;
(4) explain to the complainant promptly and, in a way that is fair, clear and not misleading, its assessment of the complaint, its decision on it, and any offer of remedial action or redress; and
(5) comply promptly with any offer of remedial action or redress accepted by the complainant.

DISP 1.4.2 Guidance

Factors that may be relevant in the assessment of a complaint under DISP 1.4.1 R (2), include the following:

(1) all the evidence available and the particular circumstances of the complaint;
(2) similarities with other complaints received by the respondent;
(3) relevant guidance published by the FSA, other relevant regulators, the Financial Ombudsman Service or former schemes; and
(4) appropriate analysis of decisions by the Financial Ombudsman Service concerning similar complaints received by the respondent.

DISP 1.4.3 Guidance

The respondent should aim to resolve complaints at the earliest possible opportunity, minimising the number of unresolved complaints which need to be referred to the Financial Ombudsman Service.

DISP 1.4.4 Rule

Where a complaint against a respondent is referred to the Financial Ombudsman Service, the respondent must cooperate fully with the Financial Ombudsman Service and comply promptly with any settlements or awards made by it.

DISP 1.4.5 Guidance

DISP App 1 contains guidance to respondents on the approach to assessing financial loss and appropriate redress where a respondent upholds a complaint concerning the sale of an endowment policy for the purposes of repaying a mortgage.

DISP 1.6 COMPLAINTS TIME LIMIT RULES

Keeping the complainant informed

DISP 1.6.1 Rule

On receipt of a complaint, a respondent must:

(1) send the complainant a prompt written acknowledgement providing early reassurance that it has received the complaint and is dealing with it; and

(2) ensure the complainant is kept informed thereafter of the progress of the measures being taken for the complaint's resolution.

Final or other response within eight weeks

DISP 1.6.2 Rule

The respondent must, by the end of eight weeks after its receipt of the complaint, send the complainant:

    (1) a final response[1]; or

    (2) a written response which:

        (a) explains why it is not in a position to make a final response and indicates when it expects to be able to provide one;

        (b) informs the complainant that he may now refer the complaint to the Financial Ombudsman Service; and

        (c) encloses a copy of the Financial Ombudsman Service standard explanatory leaflet.

DISP 1.6.3 Guidance

Respondents are not obliged to comply with the requirements in DISP 1.6.2 R where they are able to rely on any of the following rules:

    (1) the complainant's written acceptance rule (DISP 1.6.4 R);

    (2) the rules for respondents with two-stage complaints procedures (DISP 1.6.5 R); or

    (3) the complaints forwarding rules (DISP 1.7).

Complainant's written acceptance

DISP 1.6.4 Rule

DISP 1.6.2 R does not apply if the complainant has already indicated in writing acceptance of a response by the respondent, provided that the response:

    (1) informed the complainant how to pursue his complaint with the respondent if he remains dissatisfied; and

    (2) referred to the ultimate availability of the Financial Ombudsman Service if he remains dissatisfied with the respondent's response.

Respondents with two-stage complaints procedures

DISP 1.6.5 Rule

If, within eight weeks of receiving a complaint, the respondent sends the complainant a written response which:

    (1) offers redress or remedial action (whether or not it accepts the complaint) or rejects the complaint and gives reasons for doing so;

    (2) informs the complainant how to pursue his complaint with the respondent if he remains dissatisfied;

    (3) refers to the ultimate availability of the Financial Ombudsman Service if he remains dissatisfied with the respondent's response; and

---

1. "Final Response" is defined in the Glossary of the FSA Handbook in respect of DISP as follows: a written response from a respondent which:

    (a) accepts the complaint and, where appropriate, offers redress or remedial action; or

    (b) offers redress or remedial action without accepting the complaint; or

    (c) rejects the complaint and gives reasons for doing so;

and which:

    (d) encloses a copy of the Financial Ombudsman Service's standard explanatory leaflet; and

    (e) informs the complainant that if he remains dissatisfied with the respondent's response, he may now refer his complaint to the Financial Ombudsman Service and must do so within six months.

(4) indicates it will regard the complaint as closed if it does not receive a reply within eight weeks;

the respondent is not obliged to continue to comply with DISP 1.6.2 R unless the complainant indicates that he remains dissatisfied, in which case, the obligation to comply with DISP 1.6.2 R resumes.

DISP 1.6.6 Rule

If the complainant takes more than a week to reply to a written response of the kind described in DISP 1.6.5 R, the additional time in excess of a week will not count for the purposes of the time limits in DISP 1.6.2 R or the complaints reporting rules.

DISP 1.6.6A Guidance

The information regarding the Financial Ombudsman Service required to be provided in responses sent under the complaints time limit rules (DISP 1.6.2 R, DISP 1.6.4 R and DISP 1.6.5 R) should be set out prominently within the text of those responses.

Speed and quality of response

DISP 1.6.7 Guidance

It is expected that within eight weeks of their receipt, almost all complaints to a respondent will have been substantively addressed by it through a final response or response as described in DISP 1.6.4 R or DISP 1.6.5 R.

DISP 1.6.8 Guidance

When assessing a respondent's response to a complaint, the FSA may have regard to a number of factors, including, the quality of response, as against the complaints resolution rules, as well as the speed with which it was made.

DISP 1.8 COMPLAINTS TIME BARRING RULE

DISP 1.8.1 Rule

If a respondent receives a complaint which is outside the time limits for referral to the Financial Ombudsman Service (see DISP 2.8) it may reject the complaint without considering the merits, but must explain this to the complainant in a final response in accordance with DISP 1.6.2 R and indicate that the Ombudsman may waive the time limits in exceptional circumstances.

DISP 2.2 WHICH COMPLAINTS CAN BE DEALT WITH UNDER THE FINANCIAL OMBUDSMAN SERVICE?

DISP 2.2.1 Guidance

The scope of the Financial Ombudsman Service's three jurisdictions depends on:

(1) the type of activity to which the complaint relates (see DISP 2.3, DISP 2.4 and DISP 2.5);
(2) the place where the activity to which the complaint relates was carried on (see DISP 2.6);
(3) whether the complainant is eligible (see DISP 2.7); and
(4) whether the complaint was referred to the Financial Ombudsman Service in time (see DISP 2.8).

DISP 2.6 WHAT IS THE TERRITORIAL SCOPE OF THE RELEVANT JURISDICTION?

Compulsory Jurisdiction

DISP 2.6.1 Rule

The Compulsory Jurisdiction covers only complaints about the activities of a firm (including its appointed representatives) or of a payment service provider (including agents of a payment institution) carried on from an establishment in the United Kingdom.

DISP 2.6.2 Guidance

This:

    (1) includes incoming EEA firms, incoming EEA authorised payment institutions and incoming Treaty firms; but

    (2) excludes complaints about business conducted in the United Kingdom on a services basis from an establishment outside the United Kingdom.

Consumer Credit Jurisdiction

DISP 2.6.3 Rule

The Consumer Credit Jurisdiction covers only complaints about the activities of a licensee carried on from an establishment in the United Kingdom.

Voluntary Jurisdiction

DISP 2.6.4 Rule

The Voluntary Jurisdiction covers only complaints about the activities of a VJ participant carried on from an establishment:

    (1) in the United Kingdom; or

    (2) elsewhere in the EEA if the following conditions are met:

        (a) the activity is directed wholly or partly at the United Kingdom (or part of it);

        (b) contracts governing the activity are (or, in the case of a potential customer, would have been) made under the law of England and Wales, Scotland or Northern Ireland; and

        (c) the VJ participant has notified appropriate regulators in its Home State of its intention to participate in the Voluntary Jurisdiction.

Location of the complainant

DISP 2.6.5 Guidance

A complaint can be dealt with under the Financial Ombudsman Service whether or not the complainant lives or is based in the United Kingdom.

DISP 2.7 IS THE COMPLAINANT ELIGIBLE?

DISP 2.7.1 Rule

A complaint may only be dealt with under the Financial Ombudsman Service if it is brought by or on behalf of an eligible complainant.

DISP 2.7.2 Rule

A complaint may be brought on behalf of an eligible complainant (or a deceased person who would have been an eligible complainant) by a person authorised by the eligible complainant or authorised by law. It is immaterial whether the person authorised to act on behalf of an eligible complainant is himself an eligible complainant.

Eligible complainants

DISP 2.7.3 Rule

An eligible complainant must be a person that is:

    (1) a consumer[2];

    (2) a micro-enterprise[3]:

        (a) in relation to a complaint relating wholly or partly to payment services, either at the time of the conclusion of the payment service contract or at the time the complainant refers the complaint to the respondent; or

        (b) otherwise, at the time the complainant refers the complaint to the respondent;

    (3) a charity which has an annual income of less than £1 million at the time the complainant refers the complaint to the respondent; or

    (4) a trustee of a trust which has a net asset value of less than £1 million at the time the complainant refers the complaint to the respondent.

DISP 2.7.4 Guidance

In determining whether an enterprise meets the tests for being a micro-enterprise, account should be taken of the enterprise's 'partner enterprises' or 'linked enterprises' (as those terms are defined in the Micro-enterprise Recommendation). For example, where a parent company holds a majority share-holding in a complainant, if the parent company does not meet the tests for being a micro-enterprise then neither will the complainant.

DISP 2.7.5 Guidance

If a respondent is in doubt about the eligibility of a business, charity or trust, it should treat the complainant as if it were eligible. If the complaint is referred to the Financial Ombudsman Service, the Ombudsman will determine eligibility by reference to appropriate evidence, such as audited accounts or VAT returns.

DISP 2.7.6 Rule

To be an eligible complainant a person must also have a complaint which arises from matters relevant to one or more of the following relationships with the respondent:

    (1) the complainant is (or was) a customer or payment service user of the respondent;

    (2) the complainant is (or was) a potential customer or payment service user of the respondent;

    (3) the complainant is the holder, or the beneficial owner, of units in a collective investment scheme and the respondent is the operator or depositary of the scheme;

    (4) the complainant is a beneficiary of, or has a beneficial interest in, a personal pension scheme or stakeholder pension scheme;

    (5) the complainant is a person for whose benefit a contract of insurance was taken out or was intended to be taken out with or through the respondent;

    (6) the complainant is a person on whom the legal right to benefit from a claim against the respondent under a contract of insurance has been devolved by contract, assignment, sub-rogation or legislation (save the European Community (Rights against Insurers) Regulations 2002);

    (7) the complainant relied in the course of his business on a cheque guarantee card issued by the respondent;

---

2. "Consumer" is defined in the Glossary to the FSA's Handbook as "any natural person acting for purposes outside his trade, business or profession.

3. "Micro-enterprise" is defined in the Glossary to the FSA's Handbook as follows: "an enterprise which:

    (a) employs fewer than 10 persons; and

    (b) has a turnover or annual balance sheet that does not exceed €2 million.

In this definition, 'enterprise' means any person engaged in an economic activity, irrespective of legal form and includes, in particular, self-employed persons and family businesses engaged in craft or other activities, and partnerships or associations regularly engaged in an economic activity."

(8) the complainant is the true owner or the person entitled to immediate possession of a cheque or other bill of exchange, or of the funds it represents, collected by the respondent for someone else's account;

(9) the complainant is the recipient of a banker's reference given by the respondent;

(10) the complainant gave the respondent a guarantee or security for:
   (a) a mortgage;
   (b) a loan;
   (c) an actual or prospective regulated consumer credit agreement;
   (d) an actual or prospective regulated consumer hire agreement; or
   (e) any linked transaction as defined in the Consumer Credit Act 1974 (as amended);

(11) the complainant is a person about whom information relevant to his financial standing is or was held by the respondent in operating a credit reference agency as defined by section 145(8) of the Consumer Credit Act 1974 (as amended);

(12) the complainant is a person:
   (a) from whom the respondent has sought to recover payment under a regulated consumer credit agreement or regulated consumer hire agreement in carrying on debt-collecting as defined by section 145(7) of the Consumer Credit Act (1974) (as amended); or
   (b) in relation to whom the respondent has sought to perform duties, or exercise or enforce rights, on behalf of the creditor or owner, under a regulated consumer credit agreement or regulated consumer hire agreement in carrying on debt administration as defined by section 145(7A) of the Consumer Credit Act (1974) (as amended);

(13) the complainant is a beneficiary under a trust or estate of which the respondent is trustee or personal representative.

(14) (where the respondent is a dormant account fund operator) the complainant is (or was) a customer of a bank or building society which transferred any balance from a dormant account to the respondent.

DISP 2.7.7 Guidance

DISP 2.7.6 R (5) and DISP 2.7.6R (6) include, for example, employees covered by a group permanent health policy taken out by an employer, which provides in the insurance contract that the policy was taken out for the benefit of the employee.

DISP 2.7.8 Guidance

In the Compulsory Jurisdiction, under the Ombudsman Transitional Order and the Mortgages and General Insurance Complaints Transitional Order, where a complainant:

(1) wishes to have a relevant new complaint or a relevant transitional complaint dealt with by the Ombudsman; and

(2) is not otherwise eligible; but

(3) would have been entitled to refer an equivalent complaint to the former scheme in question immediately before the relevant transitional order came into effect;

if the Ombudsman considers it appropriate, he may treat the complainant as an eligible complainant.

Exceptions

DISP 2.7.9 Rule

The following are not eligible complainants:

(1) (in all jurisdictions) a firm, payment service provider, licensee or VJ participant whose complaint relates in any way to an activity which:
   (a) the firm itself has permission to carry on; or
   (ab) the firm or payment service provider itself is entitled to carry on under the Payment Services Regulations; or
   (b) the licensee or VJ participant itself conducts;
   and which is subject to the Compulsory Jurisdiction, the Consumer Credit Jurisdiction or the Voluntary Jurisdiction;

(2) (in the Compulsory Jurisdiction) a complainant, other than a trustee of a pension scheme trust, who was:
    (a) a professional client; or
    (b) an eligible counterparty;
    in relation to the firm and activity in question at the time of the act or omission which is the subject of the complaint; and
(3) (in the Consumer Credit Jurisdiction):
    (a) a body corporate;
    (b) a partnership consisting of more than three persons;
    (c) a partnership all of whose members are bodies corporate; or
    (d) an unincorporated body which consists entirely of bodies corporate.

DISP 2.7.10 Guidance

In the Compulsory Jurisdiction, in relation to relevant new complaints under the Ombudsman Transitional Order and relevant transitional complaints under the Mortgages and General Insurance Complaints Transitional Order:

(1) where the former scheme in question is the Insurance Ombudsman Scheme, a complainant is not to be treated as an eligible complainant unless:
    (a) he is an individual; and
    (b) the relevant new complaint does not concern aspects of a policy relating to a business or trade carried on by him;
(2) where the former scheme in question is the GISC facility, a complainant is not to be treated as an eligible complainant unless:
    (a) he is an individual; and
    (b) he is acting otherwise than solely for the purposes of his business; and
(3) where the former scheme in question is the MCAS scheme, a complainant is not to be treated as an eligible complainant if:
    (a) the relevant transitional complaint does not relate to a breach of the Mortgage Code published by the Council of Mortgage Lenders;
    (b) the complaint concerns physical injury, illness, nervous shock or their consequences; or
    (c) the complainant is claiming a sum of money that exceeds £100,000.

DISP 2.8 WAS THE COMPLAINT REFERRED TO THE FINANCIAL OMBUDSMAN SERVICE IN TIME?

DISP 2.8.1 Rule

The Ombudsman can only consider a complaint if:

(1) the respondent has already sent the complainant its final response; or
(2) eight weeks have elapsed since the respondent received the complaint.

DISP 2.8.2 Rule

The Ombudsman cannot consider a complaint if the complainant refers it to the Financial Ombudsman Service:

(1) more than six months after the date on which the respondent sent the complainant its final response; or
(2) more than:
    (a) six years after the event complained of; or (if later)
    (b) three years from the date on which the complainant became aware (or ought reasonably to have become aware) that he had cause for complaint;
    unless the complainant referred the complaint to the respondent or to the Ombudsman within that period and has a written acknowledgement or some other record of the complaint having been received; unless:

(3) in the view of the Ombudsman, the failure to comply with the time limits in DISP 2.8.2R or DISP 2.8.7 R was as a result of exceptional circumstances; or

(4) the Ombudsman is required to do so by the Ombudsman Transitional Order; or

(5) the respondent has not objected, on the grounds that the time limits in DISP 2.8.2 R or DISP 2.8.7 R have been exceeded, to the Ombudsman considering the complaint.

DISP 2.8.3 Guidance

The six-month time limit is only triggered by a response which is a final response. A final response must tell the complainant about the six-month time limit that the complainant has to refer a complaint to the Financial Ombudsman Service.

DISP 2.8.4 Guidance

An example of exceptional circumstances might be where the complainant has been or is incapacitated.

Reviews of past business

DISP 2.8.5 Rule

The six-year and the three-year time limits do not apply where:

(1) the time limit has been extended under a scheme for review of past business approved by the Treasury under section 404 of the Act (Schemes for reviewing past business); or

(2) the complaint concerns a contract or policy which is the subject of a review directly or indirectly under:

    (a) the terms of the Statement of Policy on "Pension transfers and Opt-outs" issued by the FSA on 25 October 1994; or

    (b) the terms of the policy statement for the review of specific categories of FSAVC business issued by the FSA on 28 February 2000.

Mortgage endowment complaints

DISP 2.8.6 Guidance

If a complaint relates to the sale of an endowment policy for the purpose of achieving capital repayment of a mortgage, the receipt by the complainant of a letter which states that there is a risk (rather than a high risk) that the policy would not, at maturity, produce a sum large enough to repay the target amount is not, itself, sufficient to cause the three year time period in DISP 2.8.2 R (2) to start to run.

DISP 2.8.7 Rule

(1) If a complaint relates to the sale of an endowment policy for the purpose of achieving capital repayment of a mortgage and the complainant receives a letter from a firm or a VJ participant warning that there is a high risk that the policy will not, at maturity, produce a sum large enough to repay the target amount then, subject to (2), (3), (4) and (5):

    (a) time for referring a complaint to the Financial Ombudsman Service starts to run from the date the complainant receives the letter; and

    (b) ends three years from that date ("the final date").

(2) Paragraph (1)(b) applies only if the complainant also receives within the three year period mentioned in (1)(b) and at least six months before the final date an explanation that the complainant's time to refer such a complaint would expire at the final date.

(3) If an explanation is given but is sent outside the period referred to in (2), time for referring a complaint will run until a date specified in such an explanation which must not be less than six months after the date on which the notice is sent.

(4) A complainant will be taken to have complied with the time limits in (1) to (3) above if in any case he refers the complaint to the firm or VJ participant within those limits and has a written acknowledgement or some other record of the complaint having been received.

(5) Paragraph (1) does not apply if the Ombudsman is of the opinion that, in the circumstances of the case, it is appropriate for DISP 2.8.2 R (2) to apply.

DISP 3.2 JURISDICTION

DISP 3.2.1 Rule

The Ombudsman will have regard to whether a complaint is out of jurisdiction.

DISP 3.2.2 Rule

Unless the respondent has already had eight weeks to consider the complaint or issued a final response, the Ombudsman will refer the complaint to the respondent.

DISP 3.2.3 Rule

Where the respondent alleges that the complaint is out of jurisdiction, the Ombudsman will give both parties an opportunity to make representations before he decides.

DISP 3.2.4 Rule

Where the Ombudsman considers that the complaint may be out of jurisdiction, he will give the complainant an opportunity to make representations before he decides.

DISP 3.2.5 Rule

Where the Ombudsman then decides that the complaint is out of jurisdiction, he will give reasons for that decision to the complainant and inform the respondent.

DISP 3.2.6 Rule

Where the Ombudsman then decides that the complaint is not out of jurisdiction, he will inform the complainant and give reasons for that decision to the respondent.

DISP 3.3 DISMISSAL WITHOUT CONSIDERATION OF THE MERITS AND TEST CASES

DISP 3.3.1 Rule

Where the Ombudsman considers that the complaint may be one which should be dismissed without consideration of the merits, he will give the complainant an opportunity to make representations before he decides.

DISP 3.3.2 Rule

Where the Ombudsman then decides that the complaint should be dismissed without consideration of the merits, he will give reasons to the complainant for that decision and inform the respondent.

DISP 3.3.3 Guidance

Under the Ombudsman Transitional Order and the Mortgage and General Insurance Complaints Transitional Order, where the Ombudsman is dealing with a relevant complaint, he must take into account whether an equivalent complaint would have been dismissed without consideration of its merits under the former scheme in question, as it had effect immediately before the relevant transitional order came into effect.

Grounds for dismissal

DISP 3.3.4 Rule

The Ombudsman may dismiss a complaint without considering its merits if he considers that:

    (1)   the complainant has not suffered (or is unlikely to suffer) financial loss, material distress or material inconvenience; or

    (2)   the complaint is frivolous or vexatious; or

(3)   the complaint clearly does not have any reasonable prospect of success; or

(4)   the respondent has already made an offer of compensation (or a goodwill payment) which is:

    (a) fair and reasonable in relation to the circumstances alleged by the complainant; and

    (b) still open for acceptance; or

(5)   the respondent has reviewed the subject matter of the complaint in accordance with:

    (a) the regulatory standards for the review of such transactions prevailing at the time of the review; or

    (b) the terms of a scheme order under section 404 of the Act (Schemes for reviewing past business); or

    (c) any formal regulatory requirement, standard or guidance published by the FSA or other regulator in respect of that type of complaint;

    (including, if appropriate, making an offer of redress to the complainant), unless he considers that they did not address the particular circumstances of the case; or

(6)   the subject matter of the complaint has previously been considered or excluded under the Financial Ombudsman Service, or a former scheme (unless material new evidence which the Ombudsman considers likely to affect the outcome has subsequently become available to the complainant); or

(7)   the subject matter of the complaint has been dealt with, or is being dealt with, by a comparable independent complaints scheme or dispute-resolution process; or

(8)   the subject matter of the complaint has been the subject of court proceedings where there has been a decision on the merits; or

(9)   the subject matter of the complaint is the subject of current court proceedings, unless proceedings are stayed or sisted (by agreement of all parties, or order of the court) in order that the matter may be considered under the Financial Ombudsman Service; or

(10)   it would be more suitable for the subject matter of the complaint to be dealt with by a court, arbitration or another complaints scheme; or

(11)   it is a complaint about the legitimate exercise of a respondent's commercial judgment; or

(12)   it is a complaint about employment matters from an employee or employees of a respondent; or

(13)   it is a complaint about investment performance; or

(14)   it is a complaint about a respondent's decision when exercising a discretion under a will or private trust; or

(15)   it is a complaint about a respondent's failure to consult beneficiaries before exercising a discretion under a will or private trust, where there is no legal obligation to consult; or

(16)   it is a complaint which:

    (a) involves (or might involve) more than one eligible complainant; and

    (b) has been referred without the consent of the other complainant or complainants;

    and the Ombudsman considers that it would be inappropriate to deal with the complaint without that consent; or

(16A)   it is a complaint about a pure landlord and tenant issue arising out of a regulated sale and rent back agreement; or

(17)   there are other compelling reasons why it is inappropriate for the complaint to be dealt with under the Financial Ombudsman Service.

Test cases

DISP 3.3.5 Rule

The Ombudsman may dismiss a complaint without considering its merits, so that a court may consider it as a test case, if:

    (1) before he has made a determination, he has received in writing from the respondent:

        (a) a detailed statement of how and why, in the respondent's opinion, the complaint raises an important or novel point of law with significant consequences; and

        (b) an undertaking in favour of the complainant that, if the complainant or the respondent commences court proceedings against the other in respect of the complaint in any court in the United Kingdom within six months of the complaint being dismissed, the respondent will: pay the complainant's reasonable costs and disbursements (to be assessed if not agreed on an indemnity basis) in connection with the proceedings at first instance and any subsequent appeal proceedings brought by the respondent; and make interim payments on account of such costs if and to the extent that it appears reasonable to do so; and

(2) the Ombudsman considers that the complaint:

    (a)   raises an important or novel point of law, which has important consequences; and

    (b)   would more suitably be dealt with by a court as a test case.

DISP 3.3.6 Guidance

Factors the Ombudsman may take into account in considering whether to dismiss a complaint so that it may be the subject of a test case in court include (but are not limited to):

(1) whether the point of law is central to the outcome of the dispute;

(2) how important or novel the point of law is in the context of the dispute;

(3) the significance of the consequences of the dispute for the business of the respondent (or respondents in that sector) or for its (or their) customers;

(4) the amount at stake in the dispute;

(5) the remedies that a court could impose;

(6) any representations made by the respondent or the complainant; and

(7) the stage already reached in consideration of the dispute.

DISP 3.5 RESOLUTION OF COMPLAINTS BY THE OMBUDSMAN

DISP 3.5.1 Rule

The Ombudsman will attempt to resolve complaints at the earliest possible stage and by whatever means appear to him to be most appropriate, including mediation or investigation.

DISP 3.5.2 Guidance

The Ombudsman may inform the complainant that it might be appropriate to complain against some other respondent.

DISP 3.5.3 Guidance

Where two or more complaints from one complainant relate to connected circumstances, the Ombudsman may investigate them together, but will issue separate provisional assessments and determinations in respect of each respondent.

DISP 3.5.4 Rule

If the Ombudsman decides that an investigation is necessary, he will then:

(1) ensure both parties have been given an opportunity of making representations;

(2) send both parties a provisional assessment, setting out his reasons and a time limit within which either party must respond; and

(3) if either party indicates disagreement with the provisional assessment within that time limit, proceed to determination.

Hearings

DISP 3.5.5 Rule

If the Ombudsman considers that the complaint can be fairly determined without convening a hearing, he will determine the complaint. If not, he will invite the parties to take part in a hearing. A hearing may be held by any means which the Ombudsman considers appropriate in the circumstances, including by telephone. No hearing will be held after the Ombudsman has determined the complaint.

DISP 3.5.6 Rule

A party who wishes to request a hearing must do so in writing, setting out:

    (1) the issues he wishes to raise; and

    (2) (if appropriate) any reasons why he considers the hearing should be in private; so that the Ombudsman may consider whether:

    (3) the issues are material;

    (4) a hearing should take place; and

    (5) any hearing should be held in public or private.

DISP 3.5.7 Guidance

In deciding whether there should be a hearing and, if so, whether it should be in public or private, the Ombudsman will have regard to the provisions of the European Convention on Human Rights.

Evidence

DISP 3.5.8 Rule

The Ombudsman may give directions as to:

    (1) the issues on which evidence is required;

    (2) the extent to which evidence should be oral or written; and

    (3) the way in which evidence should be presented.

DISP 3.5.9 Rule

The Ombudsman may:

    (1) exclude evidence that would otherwise be admissible in a court or include evidence that would not be admissible in a court;

    (2) accept information in confidence (so that only an edited version, summary or description is disclosed to the other party) where he considers it appropriate;

    (3) reach a decision on the basis of what has been supplied and take account of the failure by a party to provide information requested; and

    (4) dismiss a complaint if a complainant fails to supply requested information.

DISP 3.5.10 Guidance

Evidence which the Ombudsman may accept in confidence includes confidential evidence about third parties and security information.

DISP 3.5.11 Guidance

The Ombudsman has the power to require a party to provide evidence. Failure to comply with the request can be dealt with by the court.

DISP 3.5.12 Guidance

The Ombudsman may take into account evidence from third parties, including (but not limited to) the FSA, other regulators, experts in industry matters and experts in consumer matters.

Procedural time limits

DISP 3.5.13 Rule

The Ombudsman may fix (and extend) time limits for any aspect of the consideration of a complaint by the Financial Ombudsman Service.

DISP 3.5.14 Rule

If a respondent fails to comply with a time limit, the Ombudsman may:

    (1) proceed with consideration of the complaint; and

(2) include provision for any material distress or material inconvenience caused by that failure in any award which he decides to make.

DISP 3.5.15 Rule

If a complainant fails to comply with a time limit, the Ombudsman may:

(1) proceed with consideration of the complaint; or
(2) dismiss the complaint.

DISP 3.6 DETERMINATION BY THE OMBUDSMAN

Fair and reasonable

DISP 3.6.1 Rule

The Ombudsman will determine a complaint by reference to what is, in his opinion, fair and reasonable in all the circumstances of the case.

DISP 3.6.2 Guidance

Section 228 of the Act sets the "fair and reasonable" test for the Compulsory Jurisdiction and the Consumer Credit Jurisdiction and DISP 3.6.1 R extends it to the Voluntary Jurisdiction.

DISP 3.6.3 Guidance

Where a complainant makes complaints against more than one respondent in respect of connected circumstances, the Ombudsman may determine that the respondents must contribute towards the overall award in the proportion that the Ombudsman considers appropriate.

DISP 3.6.4 Rule

In considering what is fair and reasonable in all the circumstances of the case, the Ombudsman will take into account:

(1) relevant:
    (a) law and regulations;
    (b) regulators' rules, guidance and standards;
    (c) codes of practice; and
(2) (where appropriate) what he considers to have been good industry practice at the relevant time.

DISP 3.6.5 Guidance

Where the Ombudsman is determining what is fair and reasonable in all the circumstances of a relevant new complaint or a relevant transitional complaint, the Ombudsman Transitional Order and the Mortgage and General Insurance Complaints Transitional Order require him to take into account what determination the former Ombudsman might have been expected to reach in relation to an equivalent complaint dealt with under the former scheme in question immediately before the relevant transitional order came into effect.

The Ombudsman's determination

DISP 3.6.6 Rule

When the Ombudsman has determined a complaint:

(1) the Ombudsman will give both parties a signed written statement of the determination, giving the reasons for it;
(2) the statement will require the complainant to notify the Ombudsman in writing, before the date specified in the statement, whether he accepts or rejects the determination;
(3) if the complainant notifies the Ombudsman that he accepts the determination within that time limit, it is final and binding on both parties;

(4) if the complainant does not notify the Ombudsman that he accepts the determination within that time limit, the complainant will be treated as having rejected the determination, and neither party will be bound by it; and

(5) the Ombudsman will notify the respondent of the outcome.

DISP 3.7 AWARDS BY THE OMBUDSMAN

DISP 3.7.1 Rule

Where a complaint is determined in favour of the complainant, the Ombudsman's determination may include one or more of the following:

(1) a money award against the respondent; or

(2) an interest award against the respondent; or

(3) a costs award against the respondent; or

(4) a direction to the respondent.

Money awards

DISP 3.7.2 Rule

A money award may be such amount as the Ombudsman considers to be fair compensation for one or more of the following:

(1) financial loss (including consequential or prospective loss); or

(2) pain and suffering; or

(3) damage to reputation; or

(4) distress or inconvenience;

whether or not a court would award compensation.

DISP 3.7.3 Guidance

Where the Ombudsman is determining what amount (if any) constitutes fair compensation as a money award in relation to a relevant new complaint or a relevant transitional complaint, the Ombudsman Transitional Order and the Mortgages and General Insurance Complaints Transitional Order require him to take into account what amount (if any) might have been expected to be awarded by way of compensation in relation to an equivalent complaint dealt with under the former scheme in question immediately before the relevant transitional order came into effect.

DISP 3.7.4 Rule

The maximum money award which the Ombudsman may make is £100,000.

DISP 3.7.5 Guidance

For the purpose of calculating the maximum money award, the following are excluded:

(1) any interest awarded on the amount payable under a money award;

(2) any costs awarded; and

(3) any interest awarded on costs.

DISP 3.7.6 Guidance

If the Ombudsman considers that fair compensation requires payment of a larger amount, he may recommend that the respondent pays the complainant the balance.

DISP 3.7.7 Rule

The Ombudsman will maintain a register of each money award.

Interest awards

DISP 3.7.8 Rule

An interest award may provide for the amount payable under the money award to bear interest at a rate and as from a date specified in the award.

Costs awards

DISP 3.7.9 Rule

A costs award may:

  (1) be such amount as the Ombudsman considers to be fair, to cover some or all of the costs which were reasonably incurred by the complainant in respect of the complaint; and
  (2) include interest on that amount at a rate and as from a date specified in the award.

DISP 3.7.10 Guidance

In most cases complainants should not need to have professional advisers to bring complaints to the Financial Ombudsman Service, so awards of costs are unlikely to be common.

Directions

DISP 3.7.11 Rule

A direction may require the respondent to take such steps in relation to the complainant as the Ombudsman considers just and appropriate (whether or not a court could order those steps to be taken).

Complying with awards and settlements

DISP 3.7.12 Rule

A respondent must comply promptly with:

  (1) any award or direction made by the Ombudsman; and
  (2) any settlement which it agrees at an earlier stage of the procedures.

DISP 3.7.13 Guidance

Under the Act, a complainant can enforce through the courts a money award registered by the Ombudsman or a direction made by the Ombudsman.

DISP 3.8 DEALING WITH INFORMATION

DISP 3.8.1 Rule

In dealing with information received in relation to the consideration of a complaint, the Financial Ombudsman Service will have regard to the parties' rights of privacy.

DISP 3.8.2B Rule

This does not prevent the Ombudsman disclosing information:

  (1) to the extent that he is required or authorised to do so by law; or
  (2) to the parties to the complaint; or
  (3) in his determination; or
  (4) at a hearing in connection with the complaint.

DISP 3.8.3 Rule

So long as he has regard to the parties' rights of privacy, the Ombudsman may disclose information to the FSA or any other body exercising regulatory or statutory functions for the purpose of assisting that body or the Financial Ombudsman Service to discharge its functions.

FINANCIAL SERVICES AND MARKETS ACT 2000 (RELEVANT EXTRACTS)

Section 66—Disciplinary powers

(1) The Authority may take action against a person under this section if—
    (a) it appears to the Authority that he is guilty of misconduct; and
    (b) the Authority is satisfied that it is appropriate in all the circumstances to take action against him.

(2) A person is guilty of misconduct if, while an approved person—
    (a) he has failed to comply with a statement of principle issued under section 64; or
    (b) he has been knowingly concerned in a contravention by the relevant authorised person of a requirement imposed on that authorised person by or under this Act [or by any directly applicable Community regulation made under the markets in financial instruments directive].

(3) If the Authority is entitled to take action under this section against a person, it may—
    (a) impose a penalty on him of such amount as it considers appropriate; or
    (b) publish a statement of his misconduct.

(4) The Authority may not take action under this section after the end of the period of two years beginning with the first day on which the Authority knew of the misconduct, unless proceedings in respect of it against the person concerned were begun before the end of that period.

(5) For the purposes of subsection (4)—
    (a) the Authority is to be treated as knowing of misconduct if it has information from which the misconduct can reasonably be inferred; and
    (b) proceedings against a person in respect of misconduct are to be treated as begun when a warning notice is given to him under section 67(1).

(6) "Approved person" has the same meaning as in section 64.

(7) "Relevant authorised person", in relation to an approved person, means the person on whose application approval under section 59 was given.

[AMENDMENT

Sub-s. (2): in para. (b) words from "or by any" to "financial instruments directive" in square brackets inserted by SI 2007/126, reg. 3(5), Sch. 5, paras. 1, 5.
    Date in force (for certain purposes): 1 April 2007: see SI 2007/126, reg. 1(2).
    Date in force (for remaining purposes): 1 November 2007: see SI 2007/126, reg. 1(2).

SEE FURTHER

See further, in relation to the application of this section, with modifications, in respect of the Authority's functions under the Payment Services Regulations 2009, SI 2009/209: the Payment Services Regulations 2009, SI 2009/209, reg. 95, Sch. 5, Pt 1, para. 1.]

Section 150—Actions for damages

(1) A contravention by an authorised person of a rule is actionable at the suit of a private person who suffers loss as a result of the contravention, subject to the defences and other incidents applying to actions for breach of statutory duty.

(2) If rules so provide, subsection (1) does not apply to contravention of a specified provision of those rules.

(3) In prescribed cases, a contravention of a rule which would be actionable at the suit of a private person is actionable at the suit of a person who is not a private person, subject to the defences and other incidents applying to actions for breach of statutory duty.

(4) In subsections (1) and (3) "rule" does not include—

(a) [Part 6 rules]; or

(b) a rule requiring an authorised person to have or maintain financial resources.

(5) "Private person" has such meaning as may be prescribed.

[AMENDMENT

Sub-s. (4): in para. (a) words "Part 6 rules" in square brackets substituted by SI 2005/381, reg. 6.

Date in force: 1 July 2005: see SI 2005/381, reg. 1(2).]

Section 225—The scheme and the scheme operator

(1) This Part provides for a scheme under which certain disputes may be resolved quickly and with minimum formality by an independent person.

(2) The scheme is to be administered by a body corporate ("the scheme operator").

(3) The scheme is to be operated under a name chosen by the scheme operator but is referred to in this Act as "the ombudsman scheme".

(4) Schedule 17 makes provision in connection with the ombudsman scheme and the scheme operator.

Section 228—Determination under the compulsory jurisdiction

(1) This section applies only in relation to the compulsory jurisdiction [and to the consumer credit jurisdiction].

(2) A complaint is to be determined by reference to what is, in the opinion of the ombudsman, fair and reasonable in all the circumstances of the case.

(3) When the ombudsman has determined a complaint he must give a written statement of his determination to the respondent and to the complainant.

(4) The statement must—

(a) give the ombudsman's reasons for his determination;

(b) be signed by him; and

(c) require the complainant to notify him in writing, before a date specified in the statement, whether he accepts or rejects the determination.

(5) If the complainant notifies the ombudsman that he accepts the determination, it is binding on the respondent and the complainant and final.

(6) If, by the specified date, the complainant has not notified the ombudsman of his acceptance or rejection of the determination he is to be treated as having rejected it.

(7) The ombudsman must notify the respondent of the outcome.

(8) A copy of the determination on which appears a certificate signed by an ombudsman is evidence (or in Scotland sufficient evidence) that the determination was made under the scheme.

(9) Such a certificate purporting to be signed by an ombudsman is to be taken to have been duly signed unless the contrary is shown.

[AMENDMENT

Sub-s. (1): words "and to the consumer credit jurisdiction" in square brackets inserted by the Consumer Credit Act 2006, s. 61(3).

Date in force: 16 June 2006: see SI 2006/1508, art. 3(1), Sch. 1.]

Section 229—Awards

(1) This section applies only in relation to the compulsory jurisdiction [and to the consumer credit jurisdiction].

(2) If a complaint which has been dealt with under the scheme is determined in favour of the complainant, the determination may include—

(a) an award against the respondent of such amount as the ombudsman considers fair compensation for loss or damage (of a kind falling within subsection (3)) suffered by the complainant ("a money award");

(b) a direction that the respondent take such steps in relation to the complainant as the ombudsman considers just and appropriate (whether or not a court could order those steps to be taken).

(3) A money award may compensate for—

(a) financial loss; or

(b) any other loss, or any damage, of a specified kind.

(4) The Authority may specify [for the purposes of the compulsory jurisdiction] the maximum amount which may be regarded as fair compensation for a particular kind of loss or damage specified under subsection (3)(b).

[(4A) The scheme operator may specify for the purposes of the consumer credit jurisdiction the maximum amount which may be regarded as fair compensation for a particular kind of loss or damage specified under subsection (3)(b).]

(5) A money award may not exceed the monetary limit; but the ombudsman may, if he considers that fair compensation requires payment of a larger amount, recommend that the respondent pay the complainant the balance.

(6) The monetary limit is such amount as may be specified.

(7) Different amounts may be specified in relation to different kinds of complaint.

(8) A money award—

(a) may provide for the amount payable under the award to bear interest at a rate and as from a date specified in the award; and

(b) is enforceable by the complainant in accordance with Part III of Schedule 17 [or (as the case may be) Part 3A of that Schedule].

(9) Compliance with a direction under subsection (2)(b)—

(a) is enforceable by an injunction; or

(b) in Scotland, is enforceable by an order under section 45 of the Court of Session Act 1988.

(10) Only the complainant may bring proceedings for an injunction or proceedings for an order.

[(11) "Specified" means—

(a) for the purposes of the compulsory jurisdiction, specified in compulsory jurisdiction rules;

(b) for the purposes of the consumer credit jurisdiction, specified in consumer credit rules.

(12) Consumer credit rules under this section may make different provision for different cases.]

[AMENDMENTS

Sub-s. (1): words "and to the consumer credit jurisdiction" in square brackets inserted by the Consumer Credit Act 2006, s. 61(3).

Date in force: 16 June 2006: see SI 2006/1508, art. 3(1), Sch. 1.

Sub-s. (4): words "for the purposes of the compulsory jurisdiction" in square brackets inserted by the Consumer Credit Act 2006, s. 61(4).

Date in force: 16 June 2006: see SI 2006/1508, art. 3(1), Sch. 1.

Sub-s. (4A): inserted by the Consumer Credit Act 2006, s. 61(5).

Date in force: 16 June 2006: see SI 2006/1508, art. 3(1), Sch. 1.

Sub-s. (8): in para. (b) words "or (as the case may be) Part 3A of that Schedule" in square brackets inserted by the Consumer Credit Act 2006, s. 61(6).

Date in force: 16 June 2006: see SI 2006/1508, art. 3(1), Sch. 1.

Sub-ss. (11), (12): substituted, for sub-s. (11) as originally enacted, by the Consumer Credit Act 2006, s. 61(7).

Date in force: 16 June 2006: see SI 2006/1508, art. 3(1), Sch. 1.]

Section 230—Costs

(1) The scheme operator may by rules ("costs rules") provide for an ombudsman to have power, on determining a complaint under the compulsory jurisdiction [or the consumer credit jurisdiction], to award costs in accordance with the provisions of the rules.

(2) Costs rules require the approval of the Authority.

(3) Costs rules may not provide for the making of an award against the complainant in respect of the respondent's costs.

(4) But they may provide for the making of an award against the complainant in favour of the scheme operator, for the purpose of providing a contribution to resources deployed in dealing with the complaint, if in the opinion of the ombudsman—

(a) the complainant's conduct was improper or unreasonable; or

(b) the complainant was responsible for an unreasonable delay.

(5) Costs rules may authorise an ombudsman making an award in accordance with the rules to order that the amount payable under the award bears interest at a rate and as from a date specified in the order.

(6) An amount due under an award made in favour of the scheme operator is recoverable as a debt due to the scheme operator.

(7) Any other award made against the respondent is to be treated as a money award for the purposes of paragraph 16 of Schedule 17 [or (as the case may be) paragraph 16D of that Schedule].

[AMENDMENTS

Sub-s. (1): words "or the consumer credit jurisdiction" in square brackets inserted by the Consumer Credit Act 2006, s. 61(8)(a).

Date in force: 16 June 2006: see SI 2006/1508, art. 3(1), Sch. 1.

Sub-s. (7): words "or (as the case may be) paragraph 16D of that Schedule" in square brackets inserted by the Consumer Credit Act 2006, s. 61(8)(b).

Date in force: 16 June 2006: see SI 2006/1508, art. 3(1), Sch. 1.]

Section 231—Ombudsman's power to require information

(1) An ombudsman may, by notice in writing given to a party to a complaint, require that party—
  (a) to provide specified information or information of a specified description; or
  (b) to produce specified documents or documents of a specified description.
(2) The information or documents must be provided or produced—
  (a) before the end of such reasonable period as may be specified; and
  (b) in the case of information, in such manner or form as may be specified.
(3) This section applies only to information and documents the production of which the ombudsman considers necessary for the determination of the complaint.
(4) If a document is produced in response to a requirement imposed under this section, the ombudsman may—
  (a) take copies or extracts from the document; or
  (b) require the person producing the document to provide an explanation of the document.
(5) If a person who is required under this section to produce a document fails to do so, the ombudsman may require him to state, to the best of his knowledge and belief, where the document is.
(6) If a person claims a lien on a document, its production under this Part does not affect the lien.
(7) "Specified" means specified in the notice given under subsection (1).

Section 232—Powers of court where information required

(1) If a person ("the defaulter") fails to comply with a requirement imposed under section 231, the ombudsman may certify that fact in writing to the court and the court may enquire into the case.
(2) If the court is satisfied that the defaulter failed without reasonable excuse to comply with the requirement, it may deal with the defaulter (and, in the case of a body corporate, any director or officer) as if he were in contempt [; and "officer", in relation to a limited liability partnership, means a member of the limited liability partnership].
(3) "Court" means—
  (a) the High Court;
  (b) in Scotland, the Court of Session.

[AMENDMENT

Sub-s. (2): words "; and "officer", in relation to a limited liability partnership, means a member of the limited liability partnership" in square brackets inserted by SI 2001/1090, reg. 9(1), Sch. 5, para. 21.

Date in force: 6 April 2001: see SI 2001/1090, reg. 1.

MODIFICATION

The Limited Liability Partnerships Act 2000 provides for the creation of Limited Liability Partnerships (LLPs). The Limited Liability Partnerships Regulations 2001, SI 2001/1090, regulate LLPs by applying to them, with appropriate modifications, the appropriate provisions of this Act: see SI 2001/1090, regs 6, 10.]

Section 404—Schemes for reviewing past business

(1) Subsection (2) applies if the Treasury are satisfied that there is evidence suggesting—

(a) that there has been a widespread or regular failure on the part of authorised persons to comply with rules relating to a particular kind of activity; and

(b) that, as a result, private persons have suffered (or will suffer) loss in respect of which authorised persons are (or will be) liable to make payments ("compensation payments").

(2) The Treasury may by order ("a scheme order") authorise the Authority to establish and operate a scheme for—

(a) determining the nature and extent of the failure;

(b) establishing the liability of authorised persons to make compensation payments; and

(c) determining the amounts payable by way of compensation payments.

(3) An authorised scheme must be made so as to comply with specified requirements.

(4) A scheme order may be made only if—

(a) the Authority has given the Treasury a report about the alleged failure and asked them to make a scheme order;

(b) the report contains details of the scheme which the Authority propose to make; and

(c) the Treasury are satisfied that the proposed scheme is an appropriate way of dealing with the failure.

(5) A scheme order may provide for specified provisions of or made under this Act to apply in relation to any provision of, or determination made under, the resulting authorised scheme subject to such modifications (if any) as may be specified.

(6) For the purposes of this Act, failure on the part of an authorised person to comply with any provision of an authorised scheme is to be treated (subject to any provision made by the scheme order concerned) as a failure on his part to comply with rules.

(7) The Treasury may prescribe circumstances in which loss suffered by a person ("A") acting in a fiduciary or other prescribed capacity is to be treated, for the purposes of an authorised scheme, as suffered by a private person in relation to whom A was acting in that capacity.

(8) This section applies whenever the failure in question occurred.

(9) "Authorised scheme" means a scheme authorised by a scheme order.

(10) "Private person" has such meaning as may be prescribed.

(11) "Specified" means specified in a scheme order.

Schedule 17—Part III—The Compulsory Jurisdiction

Introduction

12 This Part of this Schedule applies only in relation to the compulsory jurisdiction.

Authority's procedural rules

13—(1) The Authority must make rules providing that a complaint is not to be entertained unless the complainant has referred it under the ombudsman scheme before the applicable time limit (determined in accordance with the rules) has expired.

(2) The rules may provide that an ombudsman may extend that time limit in specified circumstances.

(3) The Authority may make rules providing that a complaint is not to be entertained (except in specified circumstances) if the complainant has not previously communicated its substance to the respondent and given him a reasonable opportunity to deal with it.

(4) The Authority may make rules requiring an authorised person [, or a payment service provider within the meaning of the Payment Services Regulations 2009,] who may become subject to the compulsory jurisdiction as a respondent to establish such procedures as the Authority considers appropriate for the resolution of complaints which—

(a) may be referred to the scheme; and

(b) arise out of activity to which the Authority's powers under Part X do not apply.

The scheme operator's rules

14—(1) The scheme operator must make rules, to be known as "scheme rules", which are to set out the procedure for reference of complaints and for their investigation, consideration and determination by an ombudsman.

(2) Scheme rules may, among other things—

    (a) specify matters which are to be taken into account in determining whether an act or omission was fair and reasonable;

    (b) provide that a complaint may, in specified circumstances, be dismissed without consideration of its merits;

    (c) provide for the reference of a complaint, in specified circumstances and with the consent of the complainant, to another body with a view to its being determined by that body instead of by an ombudsman;

    (d) make provision as to the evidence which may be required or admitted, the extent to which it should be oral or written and the consequences of a person's failure to produce any information or document which he has been required (under section 231 or otherwise) to produce;

    (e) allow an ombudsman to fix time limits for any aspect of the proceedings and to extend a time limit;

    (f) provide for certain things in relation to the reference, investigation or consideration (but not determination) of a complaint to be done by a member of the scheme operator's staff instead of by an ombudsman;

    (g) make different provision in relation to different kinds of complaint.

(3) The circumstances specified under sub-paragraph (2)(b) may include the following—

    (a) the ombudsman considers the complaint frivolous or vexatious;

    (b) legal proceedings have been brought concerning the subject-matter of the complaint and the ombudsman considers that the complaint is best dealt with in those proceedings; or

    (c) the ombudsman is satisfied that there are other compelling reasons why it is inappropriate for the complaint to be dealt with under the ombudsman scheme.

(4) If the scheme operator proposes to make any scheme rules it must publish a draft of the proposed rules in the way appearing to it to be best calculated to bring them to the attention of persons appearing to it to be likely to be affected.

(5) The draft must be accompanied by a statement that representations about the proposals may be made to the scheme operator within a time specified in the statement.

(6) Before making the proposed scheme rules, the scheme operator must have regard to any representations made to it under sub-paragraph (5).

(7) The consent of the Authority is required before any scheme rules may be made.

Fees

15—(1) Scheme rules may require a respondent to pay to the scheme operator such fees as may be specified in the rules.

(2) The rules may, among other things—

    (a) provide for the scheme operator to reduce or waive a fee in a particular case;

    (b) set different fees for different stages of the proceedings on a complaint;

    (c) provide for fees to be refunded in specified circumstances;

    (d) make different provision for different kinds of complaint.

Enforcement of money awards

16 A money award, including interest, which has been registered in accordance with scheme rules may—

    (a) if a county court so orders in England and Wales, be recovered by execution issued from the county court [under section 85 of the County Courts Act 1984] (or otherwise) as if it were payable under an order of that court;

    (b) be enforced in Northern Ireland as a money judgment under the Judgments Enforcement (Northern Ireland) Order 1981;

    (c) be enforced in Scotland by the sheriff, as if it were a judgment or order of the sheriff and whether or not the sheriff could himself have granted such judgment or order.

[AMENDMENTS

Para. 13: in sub-para. (4) words ", or a payment service provider within the meaning of the Payment Services Regulations 2009," in square brackets inserted by SI 2009/209, reg. 126, Sch. 6, Pt 1, para. 1(2).

    Date in force: 2 March 2009: see SI 2009/209, reg. 1(2)(a).

Para. 16: in sub-para. (a) words "by execution issued from the county court" in italics repealed and subsequent words in square brackets substituted by the Tribunals, Courts and Enforcement Act 2007, s. 62(3), Sch. 13, para. 134.

Date in force: to be appointed: see the Tribunals, Courts and Enforcement Act 2007, s. 148(5).]

UNFAIR TERMS IN CONSUMER CONTRACTS REGULATIONS 1999 (SI 1999 NO 2083)

Whereas the Secretary of State is a Minister designated for the purposes of section 2(2) of the European Communities Act 1972 in relation to measures relating to consumer protection:

Now, the Secretary of State, in exercise of the powers conferred upon him by section 2(2) of that Act, hereby makes the following Regulations—

1 Citation and commencement

These Regulations may be cited as the Unfair Terms in Consumer Contracts Regulations 1999 and shall come into force on 1 October 1999.

2 Revocation

The Unfair Terms in Consumer Contracts Regulations 1994 are hereby revoked.

3 Interpretation

(1) In these Regulations—

"the Community" means the European Community;

"consumer" means any natural person who, in contracts covered by these Regulations, is acting for purposes which are outside his trade, business or profession;

"court" in relation to England and Wales and Northern Ireland means a county court or the High Court, and in relation to Scotland, the Sheriff or the Court of Session;

"[OFT]" means [the Office of Fair Trading];

"EEA Agreement" means the Agreement on the European Economic Area signed at Oporto on 2nd May 1992 as adjusted by the protocol signed at Brussels on 17th March 1993;

"Member State" means a State which is a contracting party to the EEA Agreement;

"notified" means notified in writing;

"qualifying body" means a person specified in Schedule 1;

"seller or supplier" means any natural or legal person who, in contracts covered by these Regulations, is acting for purposes relating to his trade, business or profession, whether publicly owned or privately owned;

"unfair terms" means the contractual terms referred to in regulation 5.

[(1A) The references—

    (a) in regulation 4(1) to a seller or a supplier, and

    (b) in regulation 8(1) to a seller or supplier,

include references to a distance supplier and to an intermediary.

(1B) In paragraph (1A) and regulation 5(6)—

"distance supplier" means—

    (a) a supplier under a distance contract within the meaning of the Financial Services (Distance Marketing) Regulations 2004, or

    (b) a supplier of unsolicited financial services within regulation 15 of those Regulations; and

        "intermediary" has the same meaning as in those Regulations.]

(2) In the application of these Regulations to Scotland for references to an "injunction" or an "interim injunction" there shall be substituted references to an "interdict" or "interim interdict" respectively.

[AMENDMENTS

Para (1): in definition "OFT" reference to "OFT" in square brackets substituted, for word "Director" as originally enacted, by virtue of the Enterprise Act 2002, s. 2.
    Date in force: 1 April 2003: see SI 2003/766, art. 2, Schedule; for transitional and transitory provisions and savings see the Enterprise Act 2002, s. 276, Sch. 24, paras. 2–6.
    Para. (1): in definition "OFT" (definition "Director" as originally enacted) words "the Office of Fair Trading" in square brackets substituted by virtue of the Enterprise Act 2002, s. 2.
    Date in force: 1 April 2003: see SI 2003/766, art. 2, Schedule; for transitional and transitory provisions and savings see the Enterprise Act 2002, s. 276, Sch. 24, paras. 2–6.
    Paras. (1A), (1B): inserted by SI 2004/2095, reg. 24(1), (2).
    Date in force: 31 October 2004: see SI 2004/2095, reg. 1.]

4 Terms to which these Regulations apply

(1) These Regulations apply in relation to unfair terms in contracts concluded between a seller or a supplier and a consumer.
(2) These Regulations do not apply to contractual terms which reflect—
  (a) mandatory statutory or regulatory provisions (including such provisions under the law of any Member State or in Community legislation having effect in the United Kingdom without further enactment);
  (b) the provisions or principles of international conventions to which the Member States or the Community are party.

5 Unfair terms

(1) A contractual term which has not been individually negotiated shall be regarded as unfair if, contrary to the requirement of good faith, it causes a significant imbalance in the parties' rights and obligations arising under the contract, to the detriment of the consumer.
(2) A term shall always be regarded as not having been individually negotiated where it has been drafted in advance and the consumer has therefore not been able to influence the substance of the term.
(3) Notwithstanding that a specific term or certain aspects of it in a contract has been individually negotiated, these Regulations shall apply to the rest of a contract if an overall assessment of it indicates that it is a pre-formulated standard contract.
(4) It shall be for any seller or supplier who claims that a term was individually negotiated to show that it was.
(5) Schedule 2 to these Regulations contains an indicative and non-exhaustive list of the terms which may be regarded as unfair.
[(6) Any contractual term providing that a consumer bears the burden of proof in respect of showing whether a distance supplier or an intermediary complied with any or all of the obligations placed upon him resulting from the Directive and any rule or enactment implementing it shall always be regarded as unfair.
(7) In paragraph (6)—
"the Directive" means Directive 2002/65/EC of the European Parliament and of the Council of 23 September 2002 concerning the distance marketing of consumer financial services and amending Council Directive 90/619/EEC and Directives 97/7/EC and 98/27/EC; and
"rule" means a rule made by the Financial Services Authority under the Financial Services and Markets Act 2000 or by a designated professional body within the meaning of section 326(2) of that Act.]

[AMENDMENT

Paras. (6), (7): inserted by SI 2004/2095, reg. 24(1), (3).
    Date in force: 31 October 2004: see SI 2004/2095, reg. 1.]

6 Assessment of unfair terms

(1) Without prejudice to regulation 12, the unfairness of a contractual term shall be assessed, taking into account the nature of the goods or services for which the contract was concluded and by referring, at the time of conclusion of the contract, to all the circumstances attending the conclusion of the contract and to all the other terms of the contract or of another contract on which it is dependent.

(2) In so far as it is in plain intelligible language, the assessment of fairness of a term shall not relate—

    (a) to the definition of the main subject matter of the contract, or

    (b) to the adequacy of the price or remuneration, as against the goods or services supplied in exchange.

7 Written contracts

(1) A seller or supplier shall ensure that any written term of a contract is expressed in plain, intelligible language.

(2) If there is doubt about the meaning of a written term, the interpretation which is most favourable to the consumer shall prevail but this rule shall not apply in proceedings brought under regulation 12.

8 Effect of unfair term

(1) An unfair term in a contract concluded with a consumer by a seller or supplier shall not be binding on the consumer.

(2) The contract shall continue to bind the parties if it is capable of continuing in existence without the unfair term.

9 Choice of law clauses

These Regulations shall apply notwithstanding any contract term which applies or purports to apply the law of a non-Member State, if the contract has a close connection with the territory of the Member States.

10 Complaints—consideration by [OFT]

(1) It shall be the duty of the [OFT] to consider any complaint made to [it] that any contract term drawn up for general use is unfair, unless—

    (a) the complaint appears to the [OFT] to be frivolous or vexatious; or

    (b) a qualifying body has notified the [OFT] that it agrees to consider the complaint.

(2) The [OFT] shall give reasons for [its] decision to apply or not to apply, as the case may be, for an injunction under regulation 12 in relation to any complaint which these Regulations require [it] to consider.

(3) In deciding whether or not to apply for an injunction in respect of a term which the [OFT] considers to be unfair, [it] may, if [it] considers it appropriate to do so, have regard to any undertakings given to [it] by or on behalf of any person as to the continued use of such a term in contracts concluded with consumers.

[AMENDMENTS

Provision heading: reference to "OFT" in square brackets substituted by virtue of the Enterprise Act 2002, s. 2.
    Date in force: 1 April 2003: see SI 2003/766, art. 2, Schedule; for transitional and transitory provisions and savings see the Enterprise Act 2002, s. 276, Sch. 24, paras. 2–6.
    Para. (1): reference to "OFT" in square brackets in each place it occurs substituted by virtue of the Enterprise Act 2002, s. 2.
    Date in force: 1 April 2003: see SI 2003/766, art. 2, Schedule; for transitional and transitory provisions and savings see the Enterprise Act 2002, s. 276, Sch. 24, paras. 2–6.
    Para. (1): word "it" in square brackets substituted by virtue of the Enterprise Act 2002, s. 2.
    Date in force: 1 April 2003: see SI 2003/766, art. 2, Schedule; for transitional and transitory provisions and savings see the Enterprise Act 2002, s. 276, Sch. 24, paras. 2–6.
    Para. (2): reference to "OFT" in square brackets substituted by virtue of the Enterprise Act 2002, s. 2.
    Date in force: 1 April 2003: see SI 2003/766, art. 2, Schedule; for transitional and transitory provisions and savings see the Enterprise Act 2002, s. 276, Sch. 24, paras. 2–6.
    Para. (2): word "its" in square brackets substituted by virtue of the Enterprise Act 2002, s. 2.
    Date in force: 1 April 2003: see SI 2003/766, art. 2, Schedule; for transitional and transitory provisions and savings see the Enterprise Act 2002, s. 276, Sch. 24, paras. 2–6.
    Para. (2): word "it" in square brackets substituted by virtue of the Enterprise Act 2002, s. 2.
    Date in force: 1 April 2003: see SI 2003/766, art. 2, Schedule; for transitional and transitory provisions and savings see the Enterprise Act 2002, s. 276, Sch. 24, paras. 2–6.

Para. (3): reference to "OFT" in square brackets substituted by virtue of the Enterprise Act 2002, s. 2.

Date in force: 1 April 2003: see SI 2003/766, art. 2, Schedule; for transitional and transitory provisions and savings see the Enterprise Act 2002, s. 276, Sch. 24, paras. 2–6.

Para. (3): word "it" in square brackets in the first and second places it occurs substituted by virtue of the Enterprise Act 2002, s. 2.

Date in force: 1 April 2003: see SI 2003/766, art. 2, Schedule; for transitional and transitory provisions and savings see the Enterprise Act 2002, s. 276, Sch. 24, paras. 2–6.

Para. (3): word "it" in square brackets in the final place it occurs substituted by virtue of the Enterprise Act 2002, s. 2.

Date in force: 1 April 2003: see SI 2003/766, art. 2, Schedule; for transitional and transitory provisions and savings see the Enterprise Act 2002, s. 276, Sch. 24, paras. 2–6.]

11 Complaints—consideration by qualifying bodies

(1) If a qualifying body specified in Part One of Schedule 1 notifies the [OFT] that it agrees to consider a complaint that any contract term drawn up for general use is unfair, it shall be under a duty to consider that complaint.

(2) Regulation 10(2) and (3) shall apply to a qualifying body which is under a duty to consider a complaint as they apply to the [OFT].

[AMENDMENTS

Para. (1): reference to "OFT" in square brackets substituted by virtue of the Enterprise Act 2002, s. 2.

Date in force: 1 April 2003: see SI 2003/766, art. 2, Schedule; for transitional and transitory provisions and savings see the Enterprise Act 2002, s. 276, Sch. 24, paras. 2–6.

Para. (2): reference to "OFT" in square brackets substituted by virtue of the Enterprise Act 2002, s. 2.

Date in force: 1 April 2003: see SI 2003/766, art. 2, Schedule; for transitional and transitory provisions and savings see the Enterprise Act 2002, s. 276, Sch. 24, paras. 2–6.]

12 Injunctions to prevent continued use of unfair terms

(1) The [OFT] or, subject to paragraph (2), any qualifying body may apply for an injunction (including an interim injunction) against any person appearing to the [OFT] or that body to be using, or recommending use of, an unfair term drawn up for general use in contracts concluded with consumers.

(2) A qualifying body may apply for an injunction only where—
    (a) it has notified the [OFT] of its intention to apply at least fourteen days before the date on which the application is made, beginning with the date on which the notification was given; or
    (b) the [OFT] consents to the application being made within a shorter period.

(3) The court on an application under this regulation may grant an injunction on such terms as it thinks fit.

(4) An injunction may relate not only to use of a particular contract term drawn up for general use but to any similar term, or a term having like effect, used or recommended for use by any person.

[AMENDMENTS

Para. (1): reference to "OFT" in square brackets in both places it occurs substituted by virtue of the Enterprise Act 2002, s. 2.

Date in force: 1 April 2003: see SI 2003/766, art. 2, Schedule; for transitional and transitory provisions and savings see the Enterprise Act 2002, s. 276, Sch. 24, paras. 2–6.

Para. (2): reference to "OFT" in square brackets in both places it occurs substituted by virtue of the Enterprise Act 2002, s. 2.

Date in force: 1 April 2003: see SI 2003/766, art. 2, Schedule; for transitional and transitory provisions and savings see the Enterprise Act 2002, s. 276, Sch. 24, paras. 2–6.]

13 Powers of the [OFT] and qualifying bodies to obtain documents and information

(1) The [OFT] may exercise the power conferred by this regulation for the purpose of—
    (a) facilitating [its] consideration of a complaint that a contract term drawn up for general use is unfair; or

  (b) ascertaining whether a person has complied with an undertaking or court order as to the continued use, or recommendation for use, of a term in contracts concluded with consumers.

(2) A qualifying body specified in Part One of Schedule 1 may exercise the power conferred by this regulation for the purpose of—

  (a) facilitating its consideration of a complaint that a contract term drawn up for general use is unfair; or

  (b) ascertaining whether a person has complied with—

    (i) an undertaking given to it or to the court following an application by that body, or

    (ii) a court order made on an application by that body,

as to the continued use, or recommendation for use, of a term in contracts concluded with consumers.

(3) The [OFT] may require any person to supply to [it], and a qualifying body specified in Part One of Schedule 1 may require any person to supply to it—

  (a) a copy of any document which that person has used or recommended for use, at the time the notice referred to in paragraph (4) below is given, as a pre-formulated standard contract in dealings with consumers;

  (b) information about the use, or recommendation for use, by that person of that document or any other such document in dealings with consumers.

(4) The power conferred by this regulation is to be exercised by a notice in writing which may—

  (a) specify the way in which and the time within which it is to be complied with; and

  (b) be varied or revoked by a subsequent notice.

(5) Nothing in this regulation compels a person to supply any document or information which he would be entitled to refuse to produce or give in civil proceedings before the court.

(6) If a person makes default in complying with a notice under this regulation, the court may, on the application of the [OFT] or of the qualifying body, make such order as the court thinks fit for requiring the default to be made good, and any such order may provide that all the costs or expenses of and incidental to the application shall be borne by the person in default or by any officers of a company or other association who are responsible for its default.

[AMENDMENTS

Provision heading: reference to "OFT" in square brackets substituted by virtue of the Enterprise Act 2002, s. 2.
  Date in force: 1 April 2003: see SI 2003/766, art. 2, Schedule; for transitional and transitory provisions and savings see the Enterprise Act 2002, s. 276, Sch. 24, paras. 2–6.
  Para. (1): reference to "OFT" in square brackets substituted by virtue of the Enterprise Act 2002, s. 2.
  Date in force: 1 April 2003: see SI 2003/766, art. 2, Schedule; for transitional and transitory provisions and savings see the Enterprise Act 2002, s. 276, Sch. 24, paras. 2–6.
  Para. (1): in sub-para. (a) word "its" in square brackets substituted by virtue of the Enterprise Act 2002, s. 2.
  Date in force: 1 April 2003: see SI 2003/766, art. 2, Schedule; for transitional and transitory provisions and savings see the Enterprise Act 2002, s. 276, Sch. 24, paras. 2–6.
  Para. (3): reference to "OFT" in square brackets substituted by virtue of the Enterprise Act 2002, s. 2.
  Date in force: 1 April 2003: see SI 2003/766, art. 2, Schedule; for transitional and transitory provisions and savings see the Enterprise Act 2002, s. 276, Sch. 24, paras. 2–6.
  Para. (3): word "it" in square brackets substituted by virtue of the Enterprise Act 2002, s. 2.
  Date in force: 1 April 2003: see SI 2003/766, art. 2, Schedule; for transitional and transitory provisions and savings see the Enterprise Act 2002, s. 276, Sch. 24, paras. 2–6.
  Para. (6): reference to "OFT" in square brackets substituted by virtue of the Enterprise Act 2002, s. 2.
  Date in force: 1 April 2003: see SI 2003/766, art. 2, Schedule; for transitional and transitory provisions and savings see the Enterprise Act 2002, s. 276, Sch. 24, paras. 2–6.]

14 Notification of undertakings and orders to [OFT]

A qualifying body shall notify the [OFT]—

  (a) of any undertaking given to it by or on behalf of any person as to the continued use of a term which that body considers to be unfair in contracts concluded with consumers;

  (b) of the outcome of any application made by it under regulation 12, and of the terms of any undertaking given to, or order made by, the court;

  (c) of the outcome of any application made by it to enforce a previous order of the court.

Provision heading: reference to "OFT" in square brackets substituted by virtue of the Enterprise Act 2002, s. 2.

Date in force: 1 April 2003: see SI 2003/766, art. 2, Schedule; for transitional and transitory provisions and savings see the Enterprise Act 2002, s. 276, Sch. 24, paras. 2–6.

Reference to "OFT" in square brackets substituted by virtue of the Enterprise Act 2002, s. 2.

Date in force: 1 April 2003: see SI 2003/766, art. 2, Schedule; for transitional and transitory provisions and savings see the Enterprise Act 2002, s. 276, Sch. 24, paras. 2–6.]

15 Publication, information and advice

(1) The [OFT] shall arrange for the publication in such form and manner as [it] considers appropriate, of—

    (a) details of any undertaking or order notified to [it] under regulation 14;

    (b) details of any undertaking given to [it] by or on behalf of any person as to the continued use of a term which the [OFT] considers to be unfair in contracts concluded with consumers;

    (c) details of any application made by [it] under regulation 12, and of the terms of any undertaking given to, or order made by, the court;

    (d) details of any application made by the [OFT] to enforce a previous order of the court.

(2) The [OFT] shall inform any person on request whether a particular term to which these Regulations apply has been—

    (a) the subject of an undertaking given to the [OFT] or notified to [it] by a qualifying body; or

    (b) the subject of an order of the court made upon application by [it] or notified to [it] by a qualifying body;

and shall give that person details of the undertaking or a copy of the order, as the case may be, together with a copy of any amendments which the person giving the undertaking has agreed to make to the term in question.

(3) The [OFT] may arrange for the dissemination in such form and manner as [it] considers appropriate of such information and advice concerning the operation of these Regulations as may appear to [it] to be expedient to give to the public and to all persons likely to be affected by these Regulations.

Para. (1): reference to "OFT" in square brackets in each place it occurs substituted by virtue of the Enterprise Act 2002, s. 2.

Date in force: 1 April 2003: see SI 2003/766, art. 2, Schedule; for transitional and transitory provisions and savings see the Enterprise Act 2002, s. 276, Sch. 24, paras. 2–6.

Para. (1): word "it" in square brackets in the first place it occurs substituted by virtue of the Enterprise Act 2002, s. 2.

Date in force: 1 April 2003: see SI 2003/766, art. 2, Schedule; for transitional and transitory provisions and savings see the Enterprise Act 2002, s. 276, Sch. 24, paras. 2–6.

Para. (1): word "it" in square brackets in the second, third and final places it occurs substituted by virtue of the Enterprise Act 2002, s. 2.

Date in force: 1 April 2003: see SI 2003/766, art. 2, Schedule; for transitional and transitory provisions and savings see the Enterprise Act 2002, s. 276, Sch. 24, paras. 2–6.

Para. (2): reference to "OFT" in square brackets in both places it occurs substituted by virtue of the Enterprise Act 2002, s. 2.

Date in force: 1 April 2003: see SI 2003/766, art. 2, Schedule; for transitional and transitory provisions and savings see the Enterprise Act 2002, s. 276, Sch. 24, paras. 2–6.

Para. (2): word "it" in square brackets in each place it occurs substituted by virtue of the Enterprise Act 2002, s. 2.

Date in force: 1 April 2003: see SI 2003/766, art. 2, Schedule; for transitional and transitory provisions and savings see the Enterprise Act 2002, s. 276, Sch. 24, paras. 2–6.

Para. (3): reference to "OFT" in square brackets substituted by virtue of the Enterprise Act 2002, s. 2.

Date in force: 1 April 2003: see SI 2003/766, art. 2, Schedule; for transitional and transitory provisions and savings see the Enterprise Act 2002, s. 276, Sch. 24, paras. 2–6.

Para. (3): word "it" in square brackets in the first place it occurs substituted by virtue of the Enterprise Act 2002, s. 2.

Date in force: 1 April 2003: see SI 2003/766, art. 2, Schedule; for transitional and transitory provisions and savings see the Enterprise Act 2002, s. 276, Sch. 24, paras. 2–6.

Para. (3): word "it" in square brackets in the final place it occurs substituted by virtue of the Enterprise Act 2002, s. 2.

Date in force: 1 April 2003: see SI 2003/766, art. 2, Schedule; for transitional and transitory provisions and savings see the Enterprise Act 2002, s. 276, Sch. 24, paras. 2–6.]

[16 The functions of the Financial Services Authority]

[The functions of the Financial Services Authority under these Regulations shall be treated as functions of the Financial Services Authority under the [Financial Services and Markets Act 2000].]

[AMENDMENTS

Inserted by SI 2001/1186, reg. 2(a).
    Date in force: 1 May 2001: see SI 2001/1186, reg. 1.
    Words "Financial Services and Markets Act 2000" in square brackets substituted by SI 2001/3649, art. 583.
    Date in force: 1 December 2001: see SI 2001/3649, art. 1.]

Schedule 1 (Regulation 3)—Qualifying Bodies

Part One

[1 The Information Commissioner.
2 The Gas and Electricity Markets Authority.
3 The Director General of Electricity Supply for Northern Ireland.
4 The Director General of Gas for Northern Ireland.
5 [The Office of Communications].
6 [The Water Services Regulation Authority].
7 [The Office of Rail Regulation].
8 Every weights and measures authority in Great Britain.
9 The Department of Enterprise, Trade and Investment in Northern Ireland.
10 The Financial Services Authority.]

[AMENDMENTS

Substituted by SI 2001/1186, reg. 2(b).
    Date in force: 1 May 2001: see SI 2001/1186, reg. 1.
    Entry 5: words "The Office of Communications" in square brackets substituted by SI 2003/3182, art. 2.
    Date in force: 29 December 2003: see SI 2003/3182, art. 1.
    Entry 6: words "The Water Services Regulation Authority" in square brackets substituted by SI 2006/523, reg. 2.
    Date in force: 1 April 2006: see SI 2006/523, reg. 1(2); for transitional provisions see reg. 3 thereof.
    Entry 7: words "The Office of Rail Regulation" in square brackets substituted by virtue of the Railways and Transport Safety Act 2003, s. 16(4), (5), Sch. 3, para. 4.
    Date in force: 5 July 2004: see SI 2004/827, art. 4(b), (h); for savings see the Railways and Transport Safety Act 2003, s. 16, Sch. 3.

SEE FURTHER

Reference to the "Director General of Water Services" and other related expressions revoked by virtue of the Water Act 2003, s. 34(3).]

Part Two

11 Consumers' Association

SCHEDULE 2 (Regulation 5(5))—Indicative and Non-Exhaustive List of Terms which may be Regarded as Unfair

1 Terms which have the object or effect of—
    (a) excluding or limiting the legal liability of a seller or supplier in the event of the death of a consumer or personal injury to the latter resulting from an act or omission of that seller or supplier;
    (b) inappropriately excluding or limiting the legal rights of the consumer vis-à-vis the seller or supplier or another party in the event of total or partial non-performance or inadequate

performance by the seller or supplier of any of the contractual obligations, including the option of offsetting a debt owed to the seller or supplier against any claim which the consumer may have against him;

(c) making an agreement binding on the consumer whereas provision of services by the seller or supplier is subject to a condition whose realisation depends on his own will alone;

(d) permitting the seller or supplier to retain sums paid by the consumer where the latter decides not to conclude or perform the contract, without providing for the consumer to receive compensation of an equivalent amount from the seller or supplier where the latter is the party cancelling the contract;

(e) requiring any consumer who fails to fulfil his obligation to pay a disproportionately high sum in compensation;

(f) authorising the seller or supplier to dissolve the contract on a discretionary basis where the same facility is not granted to the consumer, or permitting the seller or supplier to retain the sums paid for services not yet supplied by him where it is the seller or supplier himself who dissolves the contract;

(g) enabling the seller or supplier to terminate a contract of indeterminate duration without reasonable notice except where there are serious grounds for doing so;

(h) automatically extending a contract of fixed duration where the consumer does not indicate otherwise, when the deadline fixed for the consumer to express his desire not to extend the contract is unreasonably early;

(i) irrevocably binding the consumer to terms with which he had no real opportunity of becoming acquainted before the conclusion of the contract;

(j) enabling the seller or supplier to alter the terms of the contract unilaterally without a valid reason which is specified in the contract;

(k) enabling the seller or supplier to alter unilaterally without a valid reason any characteristics of the product or service to be provided;

(l) providing for the price of goods to be determined at the time of delivery or allowing a seller of goods or supplier of services to increase their price without in both cases giving the consumer the corresponding right to cancel the contract if the final price is too high in relation to the price agreed when the contract was concluded;

(m) giving the seller or supplier the right to determine whether the goods or services supplied are in conformity with the contract, or giving him the exclusive right to interpret any term of the contract;

(n) limiting the seller's or supplier's obligation to respect commitments undertaken by his agents or making his commitments subject to compliance with a particular formality;

(o) obliging the consumer to fulfil all his obligations where the seller or supplier does not perform his;

(p) giving the seller or supplier the possibility of transferring his rights and obligations under the contract, where this may serve to reduce the guarantees for the consumer, without the latter's agreement;

(q) excluding or hindering the consumer's right to take legal action or exercise any other legal remedy, particularly by requiring the consumer to take disputes exclusively to arbitration not covered by legal provisions, unduly restricting the evidence available to him or imposing on him a burden of proof which, according to the applicable law, should lie with another party to the contract.

2 Scope of paragraphs 1(g), (j) and (l)

(a) Paragraph 1(g) is without hindrance to terms by which a supplier of financial services reserves the right to terminate unilaterally a contract of indeterminate duration without notice where there is a valid reason, provided that the supplier is required to inform the other contracting party or parties thereof immediately.

(b) Paragraph 1(j) is without hindrance to terms under which a supplier of financial services reserves the right to alter the rate of interest payable by the consumer or due to the latter, or the amount of other charges for financial services without notice where there is a valid reason, provided that the supplier is required to inform the other contracting party or parties thereof at the earliest opportunity and that the latter are free to dissolve the contract immediately.

Paragraph 1(j) is also without hindrance to terms under which a seller or supplier reserves the right to alter unilaterally the conditions of a contract of indeterminate duration, provided that he is required to inform the consumer with reasonable notice and that the consumer is free to dissolve the contract.

(c) Paragraphs 1(g), (j) and (l) do not apply to:
— transactions in transferable securities, financial instruments and other products or services where the price is linked to fluctuations in a stock exchange quotation or index or a financial market rate that the seller or supplier does not control;
— contracts for the purchase or sale of foreign currency, traveller's cheques or international money orders denominated in foreign currency.

(d) Paragraph 1(1) is without hindrance to price indexation clauses, where lawful, provided that the method by which prices vary is explicitly described.

MARINE INSURANCE ACT 1906 (RELEVANT EXTRACTS)

Section 17 Insurance is uberrimae fidei

A contract of marine insurance is a contract based upon the utmost good faith, and, if the utmost good faith be not observed by either party, the contract may be avoided by the other party.

Section 18 Disclosure by assured

(1) Subject to the provisions of this section, the assured must disclose to the insurer, before the contract is concluded, every material circumstance which is known to the assured, and the assured is deemed to know every circumstance which, in the ordinary course of business, ought to be known by him. If the assured fails to make such disclosure, the insurer may avoid the contract.

(2) Every circumstance is material which would influence the judgment of a prudent insurer in fixing the premium, or determining whether he will take the risk.

(3) In the absence of inquiry the following circumstances need not be disclosed, namely:—

(a) Any circumstance which diminishes the risk;

(b) Any circumstance which is known or presumed to be known to the insurer. The insurer is presumed to know matters of common notoriety or knowledge, and matters which an insurer in the ordinary course of his business, as such, ought to know;

(c) Any circumstance as to which information is waived by the insurer;

(d) Any circumstance which it is superfluous to disclose by reason of any express or implied warranty.

(4) Whether any particular circumstance, which is not disclosed, be material or not is, in each case, a question of fact.

(5) The term "circumstance" includes any communication made to, or information received by, the assured.

Section 19 Disclosure by agent effecting insurance

Subject to the provisions of the preceding section as to circumstances which need not be disclosed, where an insurance is effected for the assured by an agent, the agent must disclose to the insurer:—

(a) Every material circumstance which is known to himself, and an agent to insure is deemed to know every circumstance which in the ordinary course of business ought to be known by, or to have been communicated to, him; and

(b) Every material circumstance which the assured is bound to disclose, unless it come to his knowledge too late to communicate it to the agent.

Section 20 Representations pending negotiation of contract

(1) Every material representation made by the assured or his agent to the insurer during the negotiations for the contract, and before the contract is concluded, must be true. If it be untrue the insurer may avoid the contract.

(2) A representation is material which would influence the judgment of a prudent insurer in fixing the premium, or determining whether he will take the risk.

(3) A representation may be either a representation as to a matter of fact, or as to a matter of expectation or belief.

(4) A representation as to matter of fact is true, if it be substantially correct, that is to say, if the difference between what is represented and what is actually correct would not be considered material by a prudent insurer.

(5) A representation as to a matter of expectation or belief is true if it be made in good faith.

(6) A representation may be withdrawn or corrected before the contract is concluded.

(7) Whether a particular representation be material or not is, in each case, a question of fact.

Section 32 Double insurance

(1) Where two or more policies are effected by or on behalf of the assured on the same adventure and interest or any part thereof, and the sums insured exceed the indemnity allowed by this Act, the assured is said to be over-insured by double insurance.

(2) Where the assured is over-insured by double insurance—

    (a) The assured, unless the policy otherwise provides, may claim payment from the insurers in such order as he may think fit, provided that he is not entitled to receive any sum in excess of the indemnity allowed by this Act;

    (b) Where the policy under which the assured claims is a valued policy, the assured must give credit as against the valuation for any sum received by him under any other policy without regard to the actual value of the subject-matter insured;

    (c) Where the policy under which the assured claims is an unvalued policy he must give credit, as against the full insurable value, for any sum received by him under any other policy;

    (d) Where the assured receives any sum in excess of the indemnity allowed by this Act, he is deemed to hold such sum in trust for the insurers, according to their right of contribution among themselves.

Section 33 Nature of warranty

(1) A warranty, in the following sections relating to warranties, means a promissory warranty, that is to say, a warranty by which the assured undertakes that some particular thing shall or shall not be done, or that some condition shall be fulfilled, or whereby he affirms or negatives the existence of a particular state of facts.

(2) A warranty may be express or implied.

(3) A warranty, as above defined, is a condition which must be exactly complied with, whether it be material to the risk or not. If it be not so complied with, then, subject to any express provision in the policy, the insurer is discharged from liability as from the date of the breach of warranty, but without prejudice to any liability incurred by him before that date.

Section 34 When breach of warranty excused

(1) Non-compliance with a warranty is excused when, by reason of a change of circumstances, the warranty ceases to be applicable to the circumstances of the contract, or when compliance with the warranty is rendered unlawful by any subsequent law.

(2) Where a warranty is broken, the assured cannot avail himself of the defence that the breach has been remedied, and the warranty complied with, before loss.

(3) A breach of warranty may be waived by the insurer.

Section 55 Included and excluded losses

(1) Subject to the provisions of this Act, and unless the policy otherwise provides, the insurer is liable for any loss proximately caused by a peril insured against, but, subject as aforesaid, he is not liable for any loss which is not proximately caused by a peril insured against.

(2) In particular,—

    (a) The insurer is not liable for any loss attributable to the wilful misconduct of the assured, but, unless the policy otherwise provides, he is liable for any loss proximately caused by a peril insured against, even though the loss would not have happened but for the misconduct or negligence of the master or crew;

    (b) Unless the policy otherwise provides, the insurer on ship or goods is not liable for any loss proximately caused by delay, although the delay be caused by a peril insured against;

    (c) Unless the policy otherwise provides, the insurer is not liable for ordinary wear and tear, ordinary leakage and breakage, inherent vice or nature of the subject-matter insured, or for any loss proximately caused by rats or vermin, or for any injury to machinery not proximately caused by maritime perils.

Section 67 Extent of liability of insurer for loss

(1) The sum which the assured can recover in respect of a loss on a policy by which he is insured, in the case of an unvalued policy to the full extent of the insurable value, or, in the case of a valued policy to the full extent of the value fixed by the policy, is called the measure of indemnity.

(2) Where there is a loss recoverable under the policy, the insurer, or each insurer if there be more than one, is liable for such proportion of the measure of indemnity as the amount of his subscription bears to the value fixed by the policy in the case of a valued policy, or to the insurable value in the case of an unvalued policy.

Section 84 Return for failure of consideration

(1) Where the consideration for the payment of the premium totally fails, and there has been no fraud or illegality on the part of the assured or his agents, the premium is thereupon returnable to the assured.

(2) Where the consideration for the payment of the premium is apportionable and there is a total failure of any apportionable part of the consideration, a proportionate part of the premium is, under the like conditions, thereupon returnable to the assured.

(3) In particular—

    (a) Where the policy is void, or is avoided by the insurer as from the commencement of the risk, the premium is returnable, provided that there has been no fraud or illegality on the part of the assured; but if the risk is not apportionable, and has once attached, the premium is not returnable;

    (b) Where the subject-matter insured, or part thereof, has never been imperilled, the premium, or, as the case may be, a proportionate part thereof, is returnable:
Provided that where the subject-matter has been insured "lost or not lost" and has arrived in safety at the time when the contract is concluded, the premium is not returnable unless, at such time, the insurer knew of the safe arrival.

    (c) Where the assured has no insurable interest throughout the currency of the risk, the premium is returnable, provided that this rule does not apply to a policy effected by way of gaming or wagering;

    (d) Where the assured has a defeasible interest which is terminated during the currency of the risk, the premium is not returnable;

    (e) Where the assured has over-insured under an unvalued policy, a proportionate part of the premium is returnable;

    (f) Subject to the foregoing provisions, where the assured has over-insured by double insurance, a proportionate part of the several premiums is returnable:
Provided that, if the policies are effected at different times, and any earlier policy has at any time borne the entire risk, or if a claim has been paid on the policy in respect of the full sum insured thereby, no premium is returnable in respect of that policy, and when the double insurance is effected knowingly by the assured no premium is returnable.

LAW COMMISSIONS' DRAFT CONSUMER INSURANCE (DISCLOSURE AND REPRESENTATIONS) BILL 15/12/09

CONTENTS

DRAFT OF A BILL TO make provision about disclosure and representations in connection with consumer insurance contracts.

BE IT ENACTED by the Queen's most Excellent Majesty, by and with the advice and consent of the Lords Spiritual and Temporal, and Commons, in this present Parliament assembled, and by the authority of the same, as follows—

Main definitions

1 Main definitions

In this Act—
  "consumer insurance contract" means a contract of insurance entered into by an individual wholly or mainly for purposes unrelated to the individual's trade, business or profession;

"consumer" means the individual who enters into a consumer insurance contract, or proposes to do so;

"insurer" means the person who is, or would become, the other party to a consumer insurance contract.

Pre-contract and pre-variation information

2 Disclosure and representations before contract or variation

(1) This section makes provision about disclosure and representations by a consumer to an insurer before a consumer insurance contract is entered into or varied.

(2) It is the duty of the consumer to take reasonable care not to make a misrepresentation to the insurer.

(3) A failure by the consumer to comply with the insurer's request to confirm or amend particulars previously given is capable of being a misrepresentation for the purposes of this Act (whether or not it could be apart from this subsection).

(4) The duty set out in subsection (2) replaces any duty relating to disclosure or representations by a consumer to an insurer which existed in the same circumstances before this Act applied.

(5) Accordingly—
- (a) any rule of law to the effect that a consumer insurance contract is one of the utmost good faith is modified to the extent required by the provisions of this Act, and
- (b) the application of section 17 of the Marine Insurance Act 1906 (contracts of marine insurance are of utmost good faith), in relation to a contract of marine insurance which is a consumer insurance contract, is subject to the provisions of this Act.

3 Reasonable care

(1) Whether or not a consumer has taken reasonable care not to make a misrepresentation is to be determined in the light of all the relevant circumstances.

(2) The following are examples of things which may need to be taken into account in making a determination under subsection (1)—
- (a) the type of consumer insurance policy in question, and its target market,
- (b) any relevant explanatory material or publicity produced or authorised by the insurer,
- (c) how clear, and how specific, the insurer's questions were,
- (d) whether or not an agent was acting for the consumer.

(3) The standard of care required is that of a reasonable consumer: but this is subject to subsections (4) and (5).

(4) If the insurer was, or ought to have been, aware of any particular characteristics or circumstances of the actual consumer, those are to be taken into account.

(5) A misrepresentation made dishonestly is always to be taken as showing lack of reasonable care.

Qualifying misrepresentations

4 Qualifying misrepresentations: definition and remedies

(1) An insurer has a remedy against a consumer for a misrepresentation made by the consumer before a consumer insurance contract was entered into or varied only if—
- (a) the consumer made the misrepresentation in breach of the duty set out in section 2(2), and
- (b) the insurer shows that without the misrepresentation, that insurer would not have entered into the contract (or agreed to the variation) at all, or would have done so only on different terms.

(2) A misrepresentation for which the insurer has a remedy against the consumer is referred to in this Act as a "qualifying misrepresentation".

(3) The only such remedies available are set out in Schedule 1.

5 Qualifying misrepresentations: classification and presumptions

(1) For the purposes of this Act, a qualifying misrepresentation (see section 4(2)) is either—
- (a) deliberate or reckless, or
- (b) careless.

(2) A qualifying misrepresentation is deliberate or reckless if the consumer—
    (a) knew that it was untrue or misleading, or did not care whether or not it was untrue or misleading, and
    (b) knew that the matter to which the misrepresentation related was relevant to the insurer, or did not care whether or not it was relevant to the insurer.

(3) A qualifying misrepresentation is careless if it is not deliberate or reckless.

(4) It is for the insurer to show that a qualifying misrepresentation was deliberate or reckless.

(5) But it is to be presumed, unless the contrary is shown—
    (a) that the consumer had the knowledge of a reasonable consumer, and
    (b) that the consumer knew that a matter about which the insurer asked a clear and specific question was relevant to the insurer.

Specific issues

6 Warranties and representations

(1) This section applies to representations made by a consumer—
    (a) in connection with a proposed consumer insurance contract, or
    (b) in connection with a proposed variation to a consumer insurance contract.

(2) Such a representation is not capable of being converted into a warranty by means of any provision of the consumer insurance contract (or of the terms of the variation), or of any other contract (and whether by declaring the representation to form the basis of the contract or otherwise).

7 Group insurance

(1) This section applies where—
    (a) a contract of insurance is entered into by a person ("A") in order to provide cover for another person ("C"), or is varied or extended so as to do so,
    (b) C is not a party to the contract,
    (c) so far as the cover for C is concerned, the contract would have been a consumer insurance contract if entered into by C rather than by A, and
    (d) C provided information directly or indirectly to the insurer before the contract was entered into, or before it was varied or extended to provide cover for C.

(2) So far as the cover for C is concerned—
    (a) sections 2 and 3 apply in relation to disclosure and representations by C to the insurer as if C were proposing to enter into a consumer insurance contract for the relevant cover with the insurer, and
    (b) subject to subsections (3) to (5) and the modifications in relation to the insurer's remedies set out in Part 3 of Schedule 1, the remainder of this Act applies in relation to the cover for C as if C had entered into a consumer insurance contract for that cover with the insurer.

(3) Section 4(1)(b) applies as if it read as follows—
"(b) the insurer shows that without the misrepresentation, that insurer would not have agreed to provide cover for C at all, or would have done so only on different terms."

(4) If there is more than one C, a breach on the part of one of them of the duty imposed (by virtue of subsection (2)(a)) by section 2(2) does not affect the contract so far as it relates to the others.

(5) Nothing in this section affects any duty owed by A to the insurer, or any remedy which the insurer may have against A for breach of such a duty.

8 Insurance on life of another

(1) This section applies in relation to a consumer insurance contract for life insurance on the life of an individual ("L") who is not a party to the contract.

(2) If this section applies—
    (a) information provided to the insurer by L is to be treated for the purposes of this Act as if it were provided by the person who is the party to the contract, but
    (b) in relation to such information, if anything turns on the state of mind, knowledge, circumstances or characteristics of the individual providing the information, it is to be determined by reference to L and not the party to the contract.

9 Agents

Schedule 2 applies for determining, for the purposes of this Act only, whether an agent through whom a consumer insurance contract is effected is the agent of the consumer or of the insurer.

10 Contracting out

(1) A term of a consumer insurance contract, or of any other contract, which would put the consumer in a worse position as respects the matters mentioned in subsection (3) than the consumer would be in by virtue of the provisions of this Act is to that extent of no effect.

(2) That includes a term about the law applicable to the contract, if in the absence of such a term the law applicable to the contract would be the law of England and Wales or the law of Scotland.

(3) The matters are—
   (a) disclosure and representations by the consumer to the insurer before the contract is entered into or varied, and
   (b) any remedies for qualifying misrepresentations (see section 4(2)).

(4) This section does not apply in relation to a contract for the settlement of a claim arising under a consumer insurance contract.

Final provision

11 Consequential provision

(1) Any rule of law to the same effect as the following is abolished in relation to consumer insurance contracts—
   (a) section 18 of the Marine Insurance Act 1906 (disclosure by assured),
   (b) section 19 of that Act (disclosure by agent effecting insurance),
   (c) section 20 of that Act (representations pending negotiation of contract).

(2) The Marine Insurance Act 1906 is amended as follows—
   (a) in section 18, at the end add—
      "(6) This section does not apply in relation to a contract of marine insurance if it is a consumer insurance contract within the meaning of the Consumer Insurance (Disclosure and Representations) Act 2009.";
   (b) in section 19, the existing text becomes subsection (1), and after that add—
      "(2) This section does not apply in relation to a contract of marine insurance if it is a consumer insurance contract within the meaning of the Consumer Insurance (Disclosure and Representations) Act 2009.";
   (c) in section 20, at the end add—
      "(8) This section does not apply in relation to a contract of marine insurance if it is a consumer insurance contract within the meaning of the Consumer Insurance (Disclosure and Representations) Act 2009.".

(3) In section 152 of the Road Traffic Act 1988 (exceptions to duty of insurers to satisfy judgment against persons insured against third-party risks), in subsection (2)—
   (a) in paragraph (a), after "avoid it" insert "either under the Consumer Insurance (Disclosure and Representations) Act 2009 or, if that Act does not apply,";
   (b) in paragraph (b), after "policy or security" insert "under that Act or", and for "it" substitute "the policy or security".

12 Short title, commencement, application and extent

(1) This Act may be cited as the Consumer Insurance (Disclosure and Representations) Act 2009.

(2) This Act comes into force at the end of the period of 1 year beginning with the day on which it is passed.

(3) This Act applies only in relation to consumer insurance contracts entered into, and variations to consumer insurance contracts agreed, after the Act comes into force.

(4) Nothing in this Act affects the circumstances in which a person is bound by the acts or omissions of that person's agent.

(5) This Act extends to England and Wales and to Scotland (but not to Northern Ireland).

SCHEDULES

SCHEDULE 1: INSURERS' REMEDIES FOR QUALIFYING MISREPRESENTATIONS

PART 1: CONTRACTS

General

1 This Part of this Schedule applies in relation to qualifying misrepresentations made in connection with consumer insurance contracts (for variations to them, see Part 2).

Deliberate or reckless misrepresentations

2 If a qualifying misrepresentation was deliberate or reckless, the insurer—
  (a) may avoid the contract and refuse all claims, and
  (b) need not return any of the premiums paid, except to the extent (if any) that it would be unfair to the consumer to retain them.

Careless misrepresentations—claims

3 If the qualifying misrepresentation was careless, paragraphs 4 to 8 apply in relation to any claim.

4 The insurer's remedies are based on what it would have done if the consumer had complied with the duty set out in section 2(2), and paragraphs 5 to 8 are to be read accordingly.

5 If the insurer would not have entered into the consumer insurance contract on any terms, the insurer may avoid the contract and refuse all claims, but must return the premiums paid.

6 If the insurer would have entered into the consumer insurance contract, but on different terms (excluding terms relating to the premium), the contract is to be treated as if it had been entered into on those different terms if the insurer so requires.

7 In addition, if the insurer would have entered into the consumer insurance contract (whether the terms relating to matters other than the premium would have been the same or different), but would have charged a higher premium, the insurer may reduce proportionately the amount to be paid on a claim.

8 "Reduce proportionately" means that the insurer need pay on the claim only X% of what it would otherwise have been under an obligation to pay under the terms of the contract (or, if applicable, under the different terms provided for by virtue of paragraph 6), where—

$$X = \frac{\text{Premium actually charged}}{\text{Higher premium}} \times 100$$

Careless misrepresentations—treatment of contract for the future

9—(1) This paragraph—
  (a) applies if the qualifying misrepresentation was careless, but
  (b) does not relate to any outstanding claim.
(2) Paragraphs 5 and 6 (as read with paragraph 4) apply as they apply where a claim has been made.
(3) Paragraph 7 (as read with paragraph 4) applies in relation to a claim yet to be made as it applies in relation to a claim which has been made.
(4) If by virtue of sub-paragraph (2) or (3), the insurer would have either (or both) of the rights conferred by paragraph 6 or 7, the insurer may—
  (a) give notice to that effect to the consumer, or
  (b) terminate the contract by giving reasonable notice to the consumer.
(5) But the insurer may not terminate a contract under sub-paragraph (4)(b) if it is wholly or mainly one of life insurance.
(6) If the insurer gives notice to the consumer under sub-paragraph (4)(a), the consumer may terminate the contract by giving reasonable notice to the insurer.
(7) If either party terminates the contract under this paragraph, the insurer must refund any premiums paid for the terminated cover in respect of the balance of the contract term.
(8) Termination of the contract under this paragraph does not affect the treatment of any claim arising under the contract in the period before termination.
(9) Nothing in this paragraph affects any contractual right to terminate the contract.

10 This Part of this Schedule applies in relation to qualifying misrepresentations made in connection with variations to consumer insurance contracts.

11 If the subject-matter of a variation can reasonably be treated separately from the subject-matter of the rest of the contract, Part 1 of this Schedule applies (with any necessary modifications) in relation to the variation as it applies in relation to a contract.

12 Otherwise, Part 1 applies (with any necessary modifications) as if the qualifying misrepresentation had been made in relation to the whole contract (for this purpose treated as including the variation) rather than merely in relation to the variation.

PART 3: MODIFICATIONS FOR GROUP INSURANCE

13 Part 1 is to be read subject to the following modifications in relation to cover provided for C under a group insurance contract as mentioned in section 7 (and in this Part "A" and "C" mean the same as in that section).

14 References to the consumer insurance contract (however described) are to that part of the contract which provides for cover for C.

15 References to claims and premiums are to claims and premiums in relation to that cover.

16 The reference to the consumer is to be read—

    (a) in paragraph 2(b), as a reference to whoever paid the premiums, or the part of them that related to the cover for C,

    (b) in paragraph 9(4) and (6), as a reference to A.

PART 4: SUPPLEMENTARY

17 Section 84 of the Marine Insurance Act 1906 (return of premium for failure of consideration) is to be read subject to the provisions of this Schedule in relation to contracts of marine insurance which are consumer insurance contracts.

SCHEDULE 2: RULES FOR DETERMINING STATUS OF AGENTS

1 This Schedule sets out rules for determining, for the purposes of this Act only, whether an agent through whom a consumer insurance contract is effected is acting as the agent of the consumer or of the insurer.

2 The agent is to be taken as the insurer's agent in each of the following cases—

    (a) when the agent does something in the agent's capacity as the appointed representative of the insurer for the purposes of the Financial Services and Markets Act 2000 (see section 39 of that Act),

    (b) when the agent collects information from the consumer, if the insurer had given the agent express authority to do so as the insurer's agent,

    (c) when the agent enters into the contract as the insurer's agent, if the insurer had given the agent express authority to do so.

3—(1) In any other case, it is to be presumed that the agent is acting as the consumer's agent unless, in the light of all the relevant circumstances, it appears that the agent is acting as the insurer's agent.

(2) Some factors which may be relevant are set out below.

(3) Examples of factors which may tend to confirm that the agent is acting for the consumer are—

    (a) the agent undertakes to give impartial advice to the consumer,

    (b) the agent undertakes to conduct a fair analysis of the market,

    (c) the consumer pays the agent a fee.

(4) Examples of factors which may tend to show that the agent is acting for the insurer are—

    (a) the agent places insurance with only a small proportion of the insurers who provide insurance of the type in question,

    (b) the insurer provides the relevant insurance through only a limited number of agents,

    (c) the insurer permits the agent to use the insurer's name in providing the agent's services,

    (d) the insurance in question is marketed under the name of the agent,

    (e) the insurer asks the agent to solicit the consumer's custom.

INDEX

[All references are to paragraph number.]

415